(914) 633-2422

(914) 633-2422

Promotion Management
and
Marketing Communications

Terence A. Shimp
University of South Carolina

M. Wayne DeLozier
University of South Carolina

The Dryden Press

Chicago New York Philadelphia San Francisco Montreal Toronto
London Sydney Tokyo Mexico City Rio de Janeiro Madrid

Acquisitions Editor: Mary Glacken
Developmental Editor: Judy Sarwark
Field Staff Representative: Ken Crabb
Project Editor: Cate Rzasa
Managing Editor: Jane Perkins
Design Director: Alan Wendt
Design Supervisor: Jeanne Calabrese
Production Manager: Mary Jarvis
Permissions Editor: Doris Milligan

Text and Cover Designer: Russ Peterson
Copy Editor: Karen Hill
Compositor: The Clarinda Company
Text Type: 10/12 ITC Garamond Book

Library of Congress Cataloging in Publication Data
Shimp, Terence A.
    Promotion management and marketing
    communications.

    Includes bibliographies and indexes.
    1. Communication in marketing.   2. Sales
    promotion.   3. Advertising. 4. Direct
    marketing.   I. DeLozier, M. Wayne.
    II. Title.
HF5415.123.S54   1986   658.8′2   85-4463
ISBN 0-03-069414-0

Printed in the United States of America
678-016-987654321

Address orders:
383 Madison Avenue
New York, NY 10017

Address editorial correspondence:
One Salt Creek Lane
Hinsdale, IL   60521

CBS COLLEGE PUBLISHING
The Dryden Press
Holt, Rinehart and Winston
Saunders College Publishing

To Judy, John, Julie, my mother and brothers, and in memory of my father (TAS)

and

To Hannelore (MWD)

The Dryden Press Series in Marketing

Barry
Marketing: An Integrated Approach

Blackwell, Engel, and Talarzyk
Contemporary Cases in Consumer Behavior,
Revised Edition

Blackwell, Johnston, and Talarzyk
**Cases in Marketing Management and
Strategy**

Block and Roering
Essentials of Consumer Behavior,
Second Edition

Boone and Kurtz
Contemporary Marketing, *Fifth Edition*

Churchill
**Marketing Research: Methodological
Foundations,** *Third Edition*

Dunn and Barban
Advertising: Its Role in Modern Marketing,
Sixth Edition

Engel, Blackwell, and Miniard
Consumer Behavior, *Fifth Edition*

Futrell
Contemporary Cases in Sales Management

Futrell
**Sales Management: Behavior, Practice,
and Cases**

Green
Analyzing Multivariate Data

Hutt and Speh
**Industrial Marketing Management: A
Strategic View of Business Markets,**
Second Edition

Kurtz and Boone
Marketing, *Second Edition*

Marquardt, Makens, and Roe
**Retail Management: Satisfaction of
Consumer Needs,** *Third Edition*

Rachman
Marketing Today

Rosenbloom
Marketing Channels: A Management View,
Second Edition

Schary
Logistic Decisions: Text and Cases

Schnaars
MICROSIM
*A marketing simulation available for IBM PC®
and Apple®*

Sciglimpaglia
Applied Marketing Research

Shimp and DeLozier
**Promotion Management and Marketing
Communications**

Talarzyk
Cases for Analysis in Marketing, *Third Edition*

Talarzyk
Contemporary Cases in Marketing,
Third Edition

Terpstra
International Marketing, *Third Edition*

Young and Mondy
**Personal Selling: Function, Theory, and
Practice,** *Second Edition*

Zikmund
Exploring Marketing Research,
Second Edition

Zikmund, Lundstrom, and Sciglimpaglia
Cases in Marketing Research

Preface

Most texts dealing with promotion management and marketing communications treat the topics separately. We find this disjunctive approach both limiting and unnecessary. *Promotion Management and Marketing Communications,* as the title implies, takes the approach that promotion and communications cannot be fully understood when discussed in an isolated manner.

The practice of marketing communications is more general than promotion management. As a matter of academic convention, if not of business practice, the term *promotion* has been restricted to elements of the marketing mix regarded as promotional tools—primarily advertising, personal selling, and sales promotion. The effectiveness of these promotional tools, however, depends on coordinating them with all aspects of the marketing mix that communicate with customers—namely, packaging, product cues, brand name, price, store design, and so on. This text relates marketing communications theory, concepts, and research to the standard promotion elements that are key to sound management.

The text is designed primarily for advanced undergraduate and graduate students. We have attempted to present a text that is accessible to undergraduates without being simplistic. Although the text contains many contemporary theoretical concepts and discussions of relevant academic research, the format is easy to follow.

Organization

The text progresses from an overview of the nature of marketing communications and promotion management (Part I), to a review of the foundations of marketing communications (Part II), to a detailed discussion of promotion management tools (Parts III and IV), to an explanation of nonpromotional tools (Part V), to an integration of all aspects of the promotion planning process (Part VI). Much of the coverage is standard, but special emphasis has been given to topics that ordinarily are not treated in much detail. This unique coverage includes two chapters on sales promotion and separate chapters on direct marketing and point-of-purchase communications. The topic of nonpromotional tools (product/package/brand symbolism and price and place communications) is also discussed in more detail than typically found in other texts.

Special Features

Current Articles   We have made an attempt to bridge the gap between academe and practice. For every academic article referenced, at least two or more relevant citations are presented to practical publications such as *Advertising Age* and *Marketing Communications.*

Contemporary Examples   Real-world examples are used to enhance students' understanding of key promotional and marketing communications concepts. In addition, magazine advertisements are used throughout the text to illustrate concepts and to heighten reading interest and comprehension.

Full-Color Insert   Classic advertisements, presented in an eight-page, full-color insert, provide students with a number of award-winning advertising examples, which tie theory to common practice.

Cases   Fourteen cases are included in Part VII, allowing for in-depth evaluation of issues discussed in the chapters. Discussion questions accompany the cases, which are all real-world situations.

Instructor's Manual   The *Instructor's Manual*, which contains a test bank and transparency masters, parallels the text and includes the following items: lecture notes and outlines; answers to end-of-chapter questions and exercises; classroom projects; and suggested answers to questions that accompany the cases.

Acknowledgments

We are grateful to a number of people for their assistance in this project. We sincerely appreciate the thoughtful and constructive comments that were provided to us by the following reviewers: Robert Dyer, George Washington University; Denise Essman, Drake University; Robert Harmon, Portland State University; Ronald

Preface

Hill, American University; Geoffrey Lantos, Bentley College; John McDonald, Market Opinion Research; John Mowen, Oklahoma State University; Kent Nakamoto, University of California, Los Angeles; Edward Riordan, Wayne State University; Alan Sawyer, University of Florida; and Linda Swayne, University of North Carolina, Charlotte.

We wish to thank several students for their invaluable assistance. The efforts of Richard Easley, Jane Hassell, and Elnora Stuart are particularly noteworthy. We also appreciate the assistance of Craig Andrews of Marquette University.

Several other individuals deserve special thanks. Don Frederick, our program director, has provided a congenial and supportive work atmosphere that has made our task more pleasant than it might otherwise have been. A very special word of thanks to editors Mary Glacken, Judy Sarwark, and Cate Rzasa at The Dryden Press for their understanding, cooperation, and expertise throughout this project.

Terence A. Shimp
M. Wayne DeLozier

November 1985

About the Authors

Terence A. Shimp, D.B.A. (University of Maryland), is professor of marketing in the College of Business Administration, University of South Carolina. Professor Shimp has published widely in the areas of marketing, advertising, and consumer behavior. His articles have appeared in the *Journal of Consumer Research, Journal of Marketing Research, Journal of Marketing, Journal of Advertising Research, Journal of Advertising,* among others. Professor Shimp teaches undergraduate and graduate courses in promotion management and marketing communications, consumer behavior, and marketing research.

M. Wayne DeLozier, Ph.D. (University of North Carolina), is associate professor of marketing in the College of Business Administration, University of South Carolina. Professor DeLozier has authored or edited several college textbooks in the areas of marketing communications, consumer behavior, marketing management, experiential learning, and retailing. Professor DeLozier has written several articles and papers for leading journals and conference proceedings. He is the former editor-in-chief of the *Journal of Experiential Learning and Simulations* and is currently vice-president of publicity and public relations for the Academy of Marketing Science (AMS). He has also served on the board of governors for AMS and is a reviewer for the same organization. Professor DeLozier has been a visiting associate professor at the Amos Tuck School, Dartmouth College; the University of Hawaii; and the Catholic University of Santano Domingo, Dominican Republic.

Contents

PART I **Overview** 1

    CHAPTER 1 **Marketing Communications and Promotion Management: An Overview** 3

An Overview of Marketing Communications and Promotion Management 3
Marketing Communications 4
Promotion Management 4

A Conceptual Framework: The Three Modes of Marketing 8
Mode 1: The Basic Offer 9
Mode 2: Persuasive Communications 10
Mode 3: Promotional Inducements 10
Each Mode Reinforces the Other Modes 13

The Promotion Management Process 16
Step 1: Performing a Situation Analysis 18
Step 2: Establishing Marketing Objectives 19
Step 3: Setting the Promotion Budget 19
Step 4: Integrating and Coordinating Promotion Elements 19
Step 5: Implementing the Promotion Management Program 20
Step 6: Evaluating and Controlling Promotional Programs 21

Organization of Text 22
Summary 23
Discussion Questions 24
Exercises 24

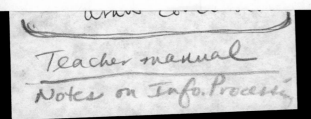

CHAPTER 2   Fundamentals of Communications   25

What is Communications?   25
The Communications Process   26
Interpersonal versus Mass Communications   28

Sharing Thought   29
Signs Must Be Shared   30
Two Basic Sign Systems   31

The Meaning of Meaning   32
How Meaning Is Learned   32
The Dimensions of Meaning   35

Summary   37
Discussion Questions   37
Exercises   38

PART II   Marketing Communications Theory and Research   39

CHAPTER 3   Behavioral Foundations of Marketing Communications   41

The CIP Perspective of Consumer Choice   42
Information Processing Stages   43
Exposure to Information   43
Attention to Information   44
Comprehension of What Is Attended   48
Agreement with What Is Comprehended   51
Retention of What Is Accepted and Search and Re   51
Deciding among Alternatives
Acting on the Basis of the Decision

An Integrated CIP Model
Processing Capacity
Motivation
Other Elements in Bettman's CIP Theory
Implications for Marketing Communications

A Hedonic Perspective on Choice Behavio
Summary
Discussion Questions
Exercises

CHAPTER 4   Attitudes and Persuasion in Marketing Communications

The Nature and Role of Attitudes
What Is an Attitude?
Why Have Attitudes?
How Well Do Attitudes Predict Behavior?

persuasive comm.
p. 41.
'active attempt to
change a person's
mind
e.g. Honda - no.

Comparing
interpersonal
versus
mass comm.
Adv. + disalv.
(have students
generate.)

Persuasion in Marketing Communications 81
Fundamentals of Persuasion 81
The Elaboration Likelihood Model: An Integrated Persuasion Theory 83

Additional Perspectives on Persuasion 87
The Theory of Reasoned Action 87
Attitude-toward-the-Ad Model 90

Changing Preferences 91
The Nature and Formation of Preferences 91
Changing Preferences 92

Summary 93
Discussion Questions 93
Exercises 94

CHAPTER 5   Message Factors in Marketing Communications 95

Message Structure 96
Message-Sidedness 96
Comparative Advertising 100
Order of Presentation 103
Drawing a Conclusion 104

Message Appeals 106
Fear Appeals 106
Humor 108
Distraction 109

Message Codes 110
Verbal Codes 110
Nonverbal Codes 112

Summary 117
Discussion Questions 117
Exercises 118

CHAPTER 6   Source Factors in Marketing Communications 119

Source Attributes 120
Source Power: The Process of Compliance 120
Source Attractiveness: The Process of Identification 121
Source Credibility: The Process of Internalization 128

Marketing Communications Sources 137
Company Image 138
Sales Representatives 138
The Media 139
Hired Promoters 139
Other Sources 140
Combined Source Effects 141

Summary 141
Discussion Questions 142
Exercises 143

CONTENTS

CHAPTER 7 Group Influences on Consumer Choice Behavior   145

Kinds of Groups   145
Cultural Groups   146
The Role of Values   148
The Role of Culture in International Business   152

Subcultural Groups   154
Religious Groups   155
The Black Subculture   155
The Hispanic Subculture   158

Social Groups   159
Reference Groups   159
The Family   168

Summary   174
Discussion Questions   175
Exercises   176

CHAPTER 8 Adoption and Diffusion Processes: The Role of Marketing Communications and Promotion Management   179

New Products and Innovativeness   179
Success Does Not Come Easy   179
The Degree of Innovativeness   181
The Role of Marketing Communications and Promotion Management   182

The Adoption and Diffusion Processes   183
The Adoption Process   184
The Diffusion Process   192

Opinion Leadership and Word-of-Mouth Influence   197
The Flow of Influence   197
Characteristics of Opinion Leaders   199
Stimulating Word-of-Mouth Influence   201

Summary   202
Discussion Questions   203
Exercises   203

PART III   **Promotion Management: Sales and Advertising**   205

CHAPTER 9 Environmental Influences on Promotion Management   207

Environmental Management and Promotion   208
The Technological Environment   208
Advances Related to Personal Selling   210
Advances Related to Advertising   211

*see Engel et al —
the extensive Problem
Solving —
(High involvement)*

CONTENTS

Advances Related to Direct Mail 212
Technological Developments Related to Other Marketing Communications Instruments 214

The Demographic Environment 214
Population Growth and Regional Geographic Developments 217
The Changing Age Structure 219
The Changing American Household 225
Changing Roles of Women 226
Income Dynamics 227
Minority Population Developments 228

The Regulatory Environment 228
Governmental Regulation of Promotion 230
Advertising Self-Regulation 236
The NAD/NARB Process 238

Summary 240
Discussion Questions 241
Exercises 242

CHAPTER 10   Sales Management 243

Sales Management Functions 245
Planning the Sales Function 245
Organizing the Sales Function 253
Staffing the Sales Function 256
Directing the Sales Force 261

Determinants of Salesperson's Performance 266
Role Perceptions 266
Aptitude 266
Skill Levels 266
Motivational Level 267

Performance Evaluation and Control 267
Summary 268
Discussion Questions 268
Exercises 269

CHAPTER 11   Personal Selling 271

Personal Selling: An Overview 271
Opportunities in Personal Selling 272
Salesperson Categories 273
Duties and Responsibilities of Salespeople 274

Traditional Approaches to Personal Selling 275
The Basic Steps in Personal Selling 277
Characteristics of the Super Salesperson 279
Other Characteristics of Successful Salespeople 281
The Dyadic Approach to Personal Selling 283
Similarity 285
Credibility 286

check stuff from Janet

A Neurolinguistic Approach   287
The Relational Communications Approach   289
A Contingency Approach to Personal Selling   292
Selling Behavior   293
Customer's Buying Task   294
The Salesperson's Resources   294
The Customer-Salesperson Relationship   294

Summary   295
Discussion Questions   296
Exercises   296

CHAPTER 12   An Overview of Advertising   297

Economic and Social Aspects of Advertising   297
Functions Performed by Advertising   298
Advertising's Economic Role   302
Advertising's Social Role   304

Advertising Management Overview   306
The Advertising Management Process   307

Setting Advertising Objectives   310
The Integrated Information Response Model   311
Different Sets of Advertising Objectives   313
Requirements for Setting Advertising Objectives   313

Budgeting for Advertising   317
Advertising Budgeting in Theory   317
Practical Advertising Budgeting   318
Budgeting Practices   318

Summary   322
Discussion Questions   323
Exercises   324

CHAPTER 13   Advertising Messages and Creative Strategy   325

The Image of Advertising   325
Advertising Effectiveness   326
Qualities of an Effective Ad   327
Making an Impression   328
Examples of Outstanding Commercials   329

Advertising Message Determinants and Creative Platform   331
Message Determinants   331
The Creative Platform   335

Creative Strategy Alternatives   336
Generic Strategy   336
Preemptive Strategy   336
Unique Selling Proposition Strategy   338
Brand Image Strategy   338
Positioning Strategy   340
Resonance Strategy   342
Affective Strategy   343

Specific Advertising Message Issues   344
Humor in Advertising   344
Sex in Advertising   346
Subliminal Advertising   349
Corporate Image and Issue Advertising   351

Summary   355
Discussion Questions   357
Exercises   357

CHAPTER 14   Media Selection in Advertising   359

The Media Planning Process   360
Target Audience Selection   361
Media Objectives   361
Media and Vehicle Selection   365
Media Scheduling   368
Media Plan for General Mills's Fruit and Blueberry Muffins   368

Television   371
Television Programming Segments   371
Network, Spot, Local, and Cable Advertising   372
Television Advertising: Strengths and Problems   374

Radio   377
Radio Is Red Hot   377
Radio Advertising: Strengths and Problems   377
A Note on Buying Radio Time   380

Magazines   381
Buying Magazine Space   381
Magazine Advertising: Strengths and Problems   383

Newspapers   384
Buying Newspaper Space   384
Newspaper Advertising: Strengths and Problems   385
Cooperative Advertising   386

Outdoor Advertising   388
Buying Outdoor Advertising   389
Outdoor Advertising: Strengths and Problems   389
Developments in Outdoor Advertising   390

Media Impact   390
Saturation   391
Omnipresence   391
Matching Media to Message   391
Unexpected Media Placement   391
Extreme Continuity   392
Use of Facilities of a Medium   392
Short-Term Blitzes   392
Shifting Media   392

Agency-Client Relations   393
Advertising Agency Role   393
Agency Compensation   394

Summary   396
Discussion Questions   396
Exercises   397

CHAPTER 15   Assessing Advertising Effectiveness   399

Advertising Effectiveness Measurement   399
The Ideal   399
The Reality   400

Positioning Advertising Copy Testing (PACT)   400
Copy Testing Techniques   403
An Overview of the Association Model   403
Advertising Research Techniques   406

Summary   418
Discussion Questions   419
Exercises   420

PART IV   Promotion Management: Direct Marketing,
           Sales Promotion, and Other Promotion
           Management Tools   421

✓ CHAPTER 16   Direct Marketing Communications   423

Direct Marketing   423
The Growth of Direct Marketing   426
Direct Response Advertising Media   427
Summary   435

Telemarketing   435
Outbound Telemarketing   436
Inbound Telemarketing   438

Summary   441
Discussion Questions   442
Exercises   442

CHAPTER 17   An Overview of Sales Promotion   445

The Nature of Sales Promotion   445
Sales Promotion's Rapid Growth   447
Reasons for Sales Promotion's Growth   447

The Role of Sales Promotion in the Marketing Mix   449
Specific Tasks of Sales Promotion   449
Determinants of Promotional Strategy   450

Sales Promotion Planning   452

CONTENTS

Sales Promotion Techniques   454
Sales-Force Motivation   454
Trade-Oriented Techniques   455

Summary   458
Discussion Questions   458
Exercises   459

CHAPTER 18   Consumer-Oriented Sales Promotion   461

Immediate Reward/Trial Impact Techniques   462
Sampling   462
Instant Coupons   467

Delayed Reward/Trial Impact Techniques   467
Media- and Mail-Delivered Coupons   468
The Advent of In-Store Coupons   477
Free-in-the-Mail Premiums   478

Immediate Reward/Franchise-Holding Techniques   479
Price-offs   479
Bonus Packs   480
In-, On-, and Near-Pack Premiums   480

Delayed Reward/Franchise-Holding Techniques   481
In- and On-Pack Coupons   481
Refunds and Rebates   481

Image Reinforcement Techniques   483
Self-Liquidating Premiums   483
Contests and Sweepstakes   484

Overlays and Group Promotions   485
Purpose of Overlay Programs   487
Successful Group Promotions   487
An Unsuccessful Group Promotion   488

Testing and Evaluating Sales Promotions   489
The Sales Promotion Research Process   489
Specific Research Methods   490

Summary   491
Discussion Questions   491
Exercises   492

**CHAPTER 19   Public Relations, Publicity, and
Specialty Advertising**   493

Public Relations and Publicity   493
Managing Public Relations   494
Public Relations Activities and Functions   495
Marketing Public Relations   496
Publicity   499

Specialty Advertising   503
Structure of the Specialty Advertising Industry   504

Summary   505
Discussion Questions   505
Exercises   506

CHAPTER 20   Point-of-Purchase Communication and
              Merchandising   507

Point of Purchase's Marketing Communication Role   508
POP in Action   510

Research on Point of Purchase   514
The POPAI/DuPont Consumer Buying Habits Study   514
The Role of Motion in Point-of-Purchase Displays   518

Point-of-Purchase Trends   519
Major Trends   520

Summary   521
Discussion Questions   521
Exercises   522

PART V   Nonpromotional Tools in Marketing
              Communications   523

CHAPTER 21   Product, Package, and Brand Symbolism   525

The Package   526
Package Symbolism   527
Packaging's Communication Components   528
Fitting Packaging into the Consumption System   536
Evaluating the Package: The VIEW Model   538

Physical Characteristics of the Product   539
Summary   540
Discussion Questions   541
Exercises   542

CHAPTER 22   Price and Place Communications   543

The Role of Price in Marketing Communications   543
Economic View of Price   544
Noneconomic View of Price   546
Psychological Effects in Pricing   550
Desensitizing the Consumer to Price   552
A Summary of Noneconomic Factors in Pricing   552

The Role of Place in Marketing Communications   553
Dimensions of Store Image   554

Summary   564
Discussion Questions   565
Exercises   565

PART VI   **Conclusion**   567

      CHAPTER 23   **Integrated Marketing Communications and Promotion Programs**   569

      Teaching Mothers Oral Rehydration Therapy   571
      The Situation Analysis   571
      Objectives   573
      The Budget   573
      Integration and Coordination   574
      Implementation and Program Management   575
      Evaluation and Control   576
      A Wrap-up   577

      Preparing a Marketing Communications Plan   578
      The Input Phase   578
      The Rough Draft   579
      The Final Draft   579
      The Approval Phase   580
      The Follow-up   580

      Summary   580
      Discussion Questions   581
      Exercises   581

PART VII   **Cases**   583

      Stanton Chemical Company   585
      CDs: The New Wave in Audio Technology   590
      BIC Disposable Razor Case   591
      Universal American Insurance Company, Inc.   596
      National Business Machines   599
      Missing Children of Greater Washington: Fund-Raising Strategy   602
      The Hydrosander Company   606
      Richtex Brick   609
      Pantera's Pizza   611
      Foster Care For Teens Program   613
      Roy Rogers Case   617
      Pan Am Airlines   622
      Mead Products: The Trapper Keeper®   626
      Pepsi. The Choice of a New Generation   630

      Glossary   635

      Name Index   646

      Subject Index   650

PART I

Overview

Part I introduces the student to the fundamentals of marketing communications and promotion management. Chapter 1 presents the three modes of marketing as a conceptual framework for understanding the various forms of marketing communications and the interrelationships among them. The promotion management process is also discussed in Chapter 1. The reader should study both of these frameworks thoroughly because they provide an overview for the entire text.

Chapter 2 helps the student to understand the fundamental and underlying concepts of communications. The chapter discusses the basic elements of the communications process, the definition and dimensions of meaning, and how meaning is learned. Each of these topics is related to marketing communications and promotion through illustrations and examples.

CHAPTER 1

Marketing Communications and Promotion Management

An Overview

The practice of marketing communications is universal. Business enterprises as well as not-for-profit organizations continuously promote themselves to customers and clients. A variety of marketing communications mechanisms are used to accomplish the following purposes: (1) *informing* prospective customers about the marketer's products and services, (2) *persuading* people to prefer particular products and brands, to shop in certain stores, to attend particular entertainment events, and to perform a variety of other behaviors, and (3) *inducing* action from customers such that buying behavior is directed toward the marketer's offering and is undertaken immediately rather than delayed. Examples of mechanisms of marketing communications include advertisements, salespeople, store signs, point-of-purchase displays, product packages, direct mail literature, free samples, coupons, publicity releases, and much more.

An Overview of Marketing Communications and Promotion Management

The topics of marketing communications and promotion management are closely related, yet they are also slightly different. It is important at this point to explain each and to clarify their differences.

Marketing Communications

Marketing communications can be understood best by examining the nature of its two constituent elements, marketing and communications. **Marketing** is the process whereby businesses and other organizations facilitate exchanges (i.e., transfers of value) between themselves and their customers and clients. **Communications** is the process whereby individuals share meaning and establish a commonness of thought.[1] Taken together, then, **marketing communications** represents the collection of all elements in an organization's marketing mix[2] that facilitate exchanges by accomplishing shared meaning with the organization's customers or clients.

Central to the definition of marketing communications is the notion that all marketing mix variables, not just the promotional variable alone, communicate with customers. The definition also permits the possibility that marketing communications can be either intentional, as in the case of advertising or personal selling, or unintentional (though effective nonetheless), as when a product feature, package cue, or price symbolizes something to customers that the marketer did not intend.

The definition further recognizes that a marketing organization is both a sender and a receiver of messages. In its role as sender, a marketing communicator attempts to inform, persuade, and induce the marketplace to take a course of action that is compatible with the communicator's interests. As receiver, the marketing communicator attunes itself to the marketplace in order to realign its messages to its present market targets, to adapt messages to changing market conditions, and to spot new communications opportunities.

Promotion Management

Promotion in its broadest sense means "to move forward."[3] In business, promotion has a similar meaning, namely, to motivate (or move, in a sense) customers to action. Promotion management employs a variety of tools for this purpose: advertising, personal selling, sales promotion, publicity, and point-of-purchase communication. Some brief definitions will clarify the distinctions among these promotional elements.

Advertising is a form of either mass communication or direct-to-consumer communication (i.e., direct mail) that is nonpersonal and paid for by an identified sponsor. **Personal selling** is a form of person-to-person communication in which a seller attempts to persuade prospective buyers to purchase the company's product or service. **Sales promotion** includes those marketing activities which act as incentives to stimulate quick buyer action; such activities include coupons, pre-

---

[1]Chapter 2 explains the communication process in detail.

[2]The marketing mix consists of an organization's total marketing offering and is conventionally delineated into four components: the product, price, place, and promotion.

[3]Promotion is derived from the Latin word *promovere; pro* meaning "forward" and *movere* meaning "to move."

miums, free samples, sweepstakes, and the like. **Publicity,** like advertising, is non-personal communication to a mass audience, but unlike advertising, publicity is *not* paid for by the company; publicity usually comes in the form of news items or editorial comments about a company's products or services. **Point-of-purchase communications** include displays, posters, signs, and a variety of other in-store materials that are designed to influence choice at the point of purchase.

The blend of the promotional elements just described is referred to as the **promotional mix. Promotion management** is, then, the practice of coordinating the various promotional mix elements, of setting objectives for what the elements are intended to accomplish, of establishing budgets that are sufficient to support the objectives, of designing specific programs (e.g., advertising campaigns) to accomplish objectives, of evaluating performance, and of taking corrective action when results are not in accord with objectives.

Thus, *marketing communications* and *promotion management* both contain the notion of communicating with customers. However, marketing communications is a general concept that encompasses communication via *all of the marketing mix variables;* promotion management is restricted to communications undertaken by the subset of mechanisms (advertising, personal selling, etc.) that are cataloged under the promotion variable in the marketing mix.

Some companies and not-for-profit organizations erroneously view the promotional mix as the sole communications link with customers. This kind of provincialism often leads to suboptimization of an organization's total communications effort. If viewed in isolation, promotion and other elements in the marketing communications mix may actually work against one another. Promotion mix elements must be coordinated with all other company actions that customers may perceive as communicating something about a company and its products.

A *product itself* communicates much to customers via its size, shape, brand name, package design, package color, and other features. These product cues provide the customer with subtle communications about the total product offering. Consider, for example, the package design for Sterling cigarettes (Figure 1.1). The package is obviously designed to portray this brand of cigarette as elegant, high in quality, and special.

Automobile design is another illustration of the importance of the physical product in communication. The Ford Motor Company's line of aerodynamically designed automobiles (the Thunderbird, Ford Tempo, and Mercury Topaz) represents just one of many examples of a product performing as a communication device. The Ford design (see Thunderbird advertisement in Figure 1.2) serves, in addition to providing aerodynamic efficiency, to communicate an impression of technological advancement, speed, and perhaps economy.

Price is another important communication mechanism. Price is often used by sellers to connote quality. Consider the following experience of a jewelry store merchant in Arizona. The merchant was having trouble selling some turquoise jewelry during the peak of the tourist season. She attempted a variety of merchandising and selling tricks, but none worked. Finally, with a sense of desperation as she was preparing to depart on an out-of-town buying trip, she scribbled the following note to one of her salesclerks: "Everything in this display case, price × ½."

FIGURE 1.1   **Use of Packaging to Communicate Prestige**

FIGURE 1.2   **Use of Product Design to Communicate Advanced Technology**

Upon returning several days later, she was delighted to learn that every turquoise item had sold. Her delight turned to surprise when she learned that the salesclerk had actually misread the scribbled note to read *double the price rather than cut it in half!* It appears that when the turquoise was merchandised at double its original price, tourists perceived it as more valuable and therefore more worthy for personal ownership or as a gift.[4]

Retail stores also have significant communications value for consumers. Stores, like people, possess personalities that consumers perceive readily and tend to associate with the merchandise located in the stores. Two stores selling similar products can project entirely different product images to prospective customers. A camera sold exclusively through specialty camera shops may project a higher quality image than an identical camera sold in a discount department store. Similarly, certain items may be perceived less favorably when sold through catalogs than when merchandised in exclusive boutiques. A case in point is the decision by the makers of Halston's women apparel to market their garments in JC Penney's catalogs in addition to their tradional distribution in fine department stores and boutiques. One can only wonder what effect this might have on consumers' perceptions of the Halston line.

A Conceptual Framework: The Three Modes of Marketing

Beem & Shaffer

The chapter up to this point has presented a general introduction to the nature of marketing communications and promotion management. It is now appropriate to tie the concepts discussed previously into a more thorough framework. Beem and Shaffer's "Three Modes of Marketing" provides a particularly useful conceptual framework.[5]

According to Beem and Shaffer, the overall marketing function consists of three overlapping sets of activities (or modes) whereby marketers seek to manage the demand for their offerings. Figure 1.3 displays the three modes: the basic offer (Mode 1), persuasive communications (Mode 2), and promotional inducements (Mode 3).

Also shown in Figure 1.3 is a connection between the traditional marketing concept and what Beem and Shaffer call the "promotion concept." The **marketing concept** embodies the notion that the marketer *adapts itself to the customer's needs and wants.* The basic offer is the mode that is primarily responsible for fulfilling the marketing concept. By comparision, the **promotion concept** attempts to *adapt the customer to the marketer's needs and wants.* This is accom-

---

[4]This illustration is presented in Robert B. Cialdini, *Influence: How and Why People Agree to Things* (New York: William Morrow and Company, 1984), pp. 15, 16.

[5]Eugene R. Beem and H. Jay Shaffer, *Triggers to Customer Action—Some Elements in a Theory of Promotional Inducement* (Cambridge, MA: Marketing Science Institute, December 1981, Report No. 81–106).

FIGURE 1.3   **The Three Modes of Marketing**

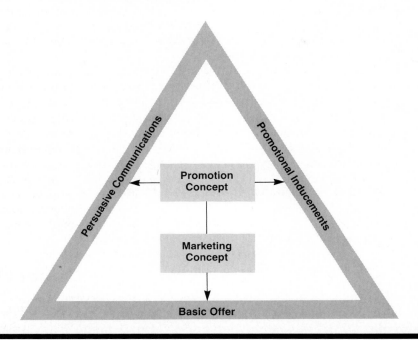

Source: Adapted from Eugene R. Beem and H. Jay Shaffer, *Triggers to Customer Action—Some Elements in a Theory of Promotional Inducement.* (Cambridge, MA: Marketing Science Institute, December 1981), p. 8.

plished by the other two modes, persuasive communications and promotional inducements.

There must be a meaningful coordination of efforts to satisfy both the marketing and promotion concepts. Excessive emphasis on customer fulfillment (the marketing concept) may lead to unnecessary expenditures and lost profits. Similarly, excessive emphasis on marketer fulfillment (the promotion concept) can lead to disgruntled customers and lost business.

Mode 1: The Basic Offer

The basic offer is "the regular or standard substantive benefits which the marketer offers to his targets as a possible solution to some problem."[6] The basic offer has two components: (1) the *product itself* and (2) the associated *terms of sale,* i.e., price, credit terms, warranties, and availability and delivery promises.

[6]Ibid., p. 4.

By way of illustration, consider a company that manufactures a line of hand-held microcomputers. The product itself is a calculatorlike device that is programmed with special function programs to simplify the routine calculation requirements of different occupational groups—architects, laboratory chemists, graphic artists, and others. The company's terms of sale include a price of $125, a one-year limited guarantee, a one-month return privilege for dissatisfied users, 2/10 net 30 credit terms, and speedy delivery.

The role of the basic offer is *to satisfy customers' needs and to move customers to action by offering superior value in comparison to substitute offerings.* For example, the hand-held microcomputer is superior to alternative calculation methods (e.g., conventional calculators) by virtue of requiring less calculation time and simplifying calculations. In general, superior value results from providing customers with more wanted gains or fewer unwanted costs.

Mode 2: Persuasive Communications

Mode 2, persuasive communications, consists of "messages directed to potential customers and designed to enhance their impressions of the basic offer."[7] Persuasive communications consist of *impersonal verbal messages* (advertising and publicity), *personal verbal messages* (personal selling and word-of-mouth support), and *nonverbal messages* (packaging cues, retailer imagery, etc.).

Whereas the basic offer is designed to meet customer needs, persuasive communications *are intended to stimulate wants by encouraging customers to imagine the benefits of the basic offer.* Marketers attempt to stimulate wants by supplying *facts* or by appealing to the customer's *fancy.*[8] An advertisement for the Canon Typestar personal electronic typewriter illustrates the use of fact in persuasive communications (see Figure 1.4). The advertising copy presents one product benefit after another. By comparison, Figure 1.5 illustrates the use of pure fancy (love, romance) to persuade consumers to desire to own real gold and, perhaps, to want someone else to purchase it for them.

Mode 3: Promotional Inducements

Promotional inducements comprise "extra substantive benefits, beyond the benefits of the basic offer, intended to motivate particular customer actions."[9] "Promotional inducements" is a new, yet descriptive, way of referring to what is more commonly called **sales promotion.** Marketing practitioners use three forms of promotional inducements: those representing the *character of the basic offer*

---

[7]Ibid., p. 6.

[8]Beem and Shaffer, *Triggers to Customer Action,* p. 9, use the fact versus fancy terminology. Similar distinctions in the marketing literature are factual versus evaluative and objective versus subjective. For more discussion, see Morris B. Holbrook, "Beyond Attitude Structure: Toward the Informational Determinants of Attitude," *Journal of Marketing Research,* Vol. 15, November 1978, pp. 545–556.

[9]Beem and Shaffer, *Triggers to Customer Action,* p. 7.

FIGURE 1.4   **Use of Fact to Persuade**

FIGURE 1.5   **Use of Pure Fancy to Persuade**

Source: Courtesy of International Gold Corporation Ltd.

(free samples, trial usage, extra goods at the same price, etc.), *price-related inducements* (discounts, money-off coupons, trade allowances for dealers, etc.), and inducements that are *external to the basic offer* (premiums, contests, trading stamps, etc.).

The role of promotional inducements is *to induce retailers and consumers to adopt the marketer's plan of action*. This means, in the case of retailers, to stock more of the marketer's product, to provide better display space, and to promote the marketer's product more aggressively. In the case of consumers, this means buying more of the marketer's product, buying it sooner than originally planned, and buying it more frequently. Marketers induce these actions by providing retailers and consumers with some form of reward (price savings, free merchandise, etc.).

Figures 1.6 and 1.7 illustrate the use of promotional inducements. The makers of Mounds and Almond Joy candy bars offer consumers an opportunity to win a luxury cruise to the South Seas by participating in the "Find Paradise" game. This promotion (Figure 1.6) illustrates an inducement that is external to the basic offer. Figure 1.7 illustrates a price-related inducement in the form of a $10 coupon offer on the rental of either a U-Haul truck or the U-Haul packing and loading service.

Table 1.1 provides a convenient summary of the three modes of marketing and the specific components of each mode.

Each Mode Reinforces the Other Modes

It should be apparent by now that the three modes of marketing overlap and reinforce each other.[10] The basic offer provides the *distinctiveness* that persuasive communications can feature. For example, the advertisement for the Canon electronic typewriter (Figure 1.4) is possible in this form only because the product itself possesses some unique product features and competitive advantages.

The basic offer also provides the foundation for effective promotional inducements. However, inducements cannot by themselves create product acceptance. The promotional inducement for the Mound and Almond Joy candy bars (Figure 1.6) is designed to encourage consumers to purchase these brands repeatedly, but this would not happen on a large scale unless consumers are fundamentally satisfied with the taste, price, size, and freshness of Mounds and Almond Joys.

Persuasive communications and promotional inducements both reinforce the basic offer. The advertisement for Sterling cigarettes (Figure 1.1) may serve, by associating the product with a luxury symbol (the Porsche automobile), to enhance the basic offer by giving cigarette smokers the impression that Sterling cigarettes are luxurious and of high quality. Promotional inducements reinforce the basic offer by adding substantive customer gains or subtracting costs, as in the case of the U-Haul coupon offer (Figure 1.7).

---

[10]Beem and Shaffer, *Triggers to Customer Action,* p. 14.

FIGURE 1.6   **An Inducement External to the Basic Offer**

CHAPTER 1   *Marketing Communications and Promotion Management*

FIGURE 1.7   **A Price-Related Inducement**

TABLE 1.1   **Examples of Three Modes of Marketing**

Basic Offer
- Product Itself
- Terms of Sale
  Availability and delivery
  Price
  Credit terms
  Guarantees or warranties

Persuasive Communications
- Impersonal Verbal Messages
  Publicity
  Measured advertising—radio, TV, newspaper, magazine
  Unmeasured advertising—direct mail, catalog, trade shows, point of purchase
- Personal Verbal Messages
  Personal selling messages
  Word-of-mouth support
- Nonverbal Messages
  Packaging of product
  Inherent in delivery of verbal message
  Symbolism derived from resellers, customers, pricing, etc.

Promotional Inducements
- Character of Basic Offer
  Free sample
  Free trial use
  Extra goods at same price
  Special terms of sale (other than price)
- Price Related
  Introductory discounts
  Money-off coupons
  Price specials
  Buy-back allowances to dealers
- External to Basic Offer
  Premium promotions—trading stamps, contests, sweepstakes, games, free gift in pack, continuity coupons
  "Free" offers to customers
  "Right to buy" other products—"self-liquidator," "commodity continuities"
  Cash awards—sales contests, "spiffs" to dealers

Source: Eugene R. Beem and H. Jay Shaffer, *Triggers to Customer Action—Some Elements in a Theory of Promotional Inducement* (Cambridge, MA: Marketing Science Institute, December 1981), p. 5.

Finally, promotional inducements and persuasive communications are mutually reinforcing. The strategic use of a promotional inducement (such as an exciting contest or sweepstakes offer) can, when placed in an advertisement, draw attention to other aspects of the persuasive communications.

The Promotion Management Process

Previous discussion pointed out that the promotion management component of the total marketing communications mix consists of six major tools: personal selling, mass media advertising, direct mail advertising, sales promotion, point-of-purchase communications, and public relations/publicity. These tools operate in concert with one another (at least in theory if not in practice) to help accomplish various marketing objectives.

The overall promotion management process consists of a logical sequence of decisions that have to be made in order to implement effective promotional programs and achieve marketing objectives. Figure 1.8 represents the promotion management process in terms of six major steps: situation analysis, marketing

FIGURE 1.8   **The Promotion Management Process**

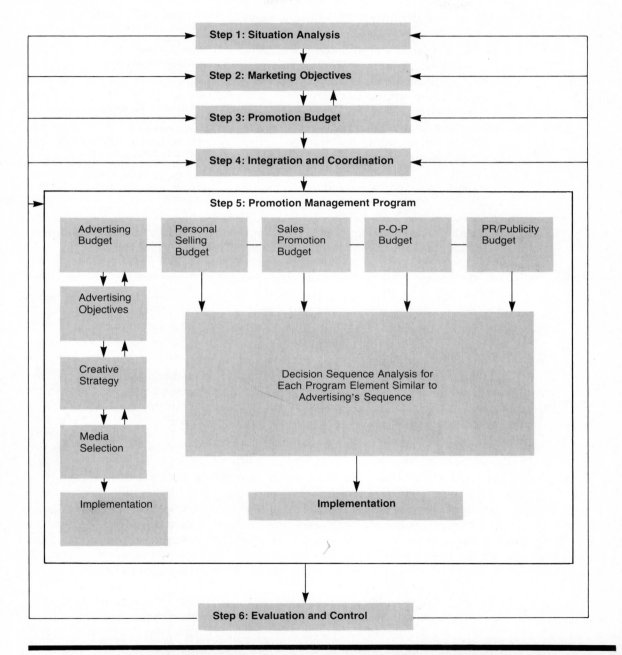

Source: Adapted from Michael L. Ray, "A Decision Sequence Analysis of Developments in Marketing Communication," *Journal of Marketing,* Vol. 37, January 1973, p. 31; and James F. Engel, Martin R. Warshaw, and Thomas C. Kinnear, *Promotional Strategy,* Fifth Edition, (Homewood, IL: Richard D. Irwin, 1983), p. 34.

objectives, promotion budget, integration and coordination, promotion management program, and evaluation and control.[11]

Step 1: Performing a Situation Analysis

The initial step in the promotion management process is to perform a thorough analysis of the situation confronting the particular product, brand, or service that is under consideration. Two types of analyses are needed. First is an **internal analysis** of an organization's strengths and weaknesses. Financial considerations and personnel matters are the primary issues in an internal analysis. A company with strong financial reserves and a talented team of promotion specialists has numerous opportunities for developing creative and perhaps expensive promotional programs, whereas an impoverished firm is limited in what it can hope to accomplish.

An **external analysis** is the second type of situation analysis. This involves a thorough review of environmental factors that are likely to influence promotional effectiveness and product success. The economic situation, competitive activity, sociocultural developments, the legal climate, and the channel of distribution considerations are typical factors involved in an external situation analysis.

An Illustration   Recall the earlier discussion of the company that manufactures hand-held microcomputers. This company, Applied Technology, Inc. (ATI), is a fledgling enterprise that has pioneered special function, calculatorlike microcomputers for use by several occupational groups (architects, laboratory chemists, metal distributors, etc.). A situation analysis of one product designed for architects reveals the following: (1) ATI's fund limitations place severe restrictions on the amount of promotional activity it can undertake; (2) direct competition is virtually nonexistent, although ATI's product faces indirect competition in the form of conventional calculators; (3) the economic climate has recently been conducive to product success because inflation has abated and customers are now making purchases they previously postponed; (4) architects are willing to try innovative products that promise meaningful time savings; (5) the only legal restrictions are standard requirements regulating product safety and promotional practices; and (6) office supply houses are available for distributing ATI's product, but most are unwilling to stock large inventories or to promote ATI's product.

An analysis such as this is invaluable in determining the scope and direction of a promotion program. In ATI's case, the situation analysis suggested the use of a direct mail advertising campaign that would enable the company to avoid distribu-

---

[11]The promotion management process as conceptualized here is an adaptation of two related works: Michael L. Ray, "A Decision Sequence Analysis of Developments in Marketing Communication," *Journal of Marketing,* Vol. 37, January 1973, pp. 29–38; and James F. Engel, Martin R. Warshaw, and Thomas C. Kinnear, *Promotional Strategy: Managing the Marketing Communications Process,* Fifth Edition (Homewood, IL: Richard D. Irwin, 1983), p. 34.

ting its product through inefficient distributors and allow it to reach prospective purchasers directly with relatively inexpensive yet effective advertising.

Step 2: Establishing Marketing Objectives

Establishing meaningful and realistic marketing objectives is the next step following the situation analysis. (Note that this discussion is about general marketing objectives and not marketing communications objectives per se.) Marketing objectives involve such matters as overall sales levels, marketing cost considerations, and sales performance with respect to specific market segments and geographical locales or in terms of time schedules.

Step 3: Setting the Promotion Budget

The promotion budget establishes the overall amount of funds that can be allocated to the various promotion mix elements. As shown in Figure 1.8 (by the two-way arrows), marketing objectives and the promotion budget are interactive decisions. That is, the initial statement of marketing objectives provides the basis for determining the size of the promotion budget; however, objectives often have to be revised because of insufficient funds.

Step 4: Integrating and Coordinating Promotion Elements

The promotion mix elements must work together in order to accomplish overall marketing objectives. To achieve optimal effectiveness, advertising campaigns, sales promotion deals, point-of-purchase programs, and publicity releases must be integrated with one another and coordinated with personal selling efforts. Many promotional programs have been unsuccessful due to coordination failures such as the following:

- An industrial sales force was unable to obtain sufficient trade support for a new product because the anticipated advertising campaign that was intended to presell the product was behind schedule by two months.
- New point-of-purchase displays for a supermarket product were less effective than marketers had anticipated because the displays were not coordinated with the advertising theme that was used to stimulate consumer buying interest.
- Retailers had insufficient inventories to cover consumer demand for an item for which a large number of coupons were distributed because the sales force was unaware of the coupon campaign and did not encourage retailers to stock up.

The preceding examples illustrate problems that occur when the promotion mix elements operate independently of one another rather than work in concert. Coordination is not something that occurs automatically; it has to be planned and managed. Many companies have created organizational positions in which one individual is responsible for assuring that proper coordination is achieved. Organization titles differ, but in some companies the label for this position is Marketing Communications Director. Coordination is handled in other companies by having individual vice-presidents of the promotion elements (e.g., Vice-President of Sales, Vice-President of Advertising and Sales Promotions) report directly to the Vice-President of Marketing. Such an arrangement is often found in both *functional* and *product* forms of organizational structure.

Step 5: Implementing the Promotion Management Program

The fifth step in Figure 1.8 presents a decision sequence analysis for the advertising component of the promotion mix and suggests that similar sequences apply to the remaining promotional elements. It is important to recognize that every stage in the decision sequence is interrelated with every other stage. This is indicated in Figure 1.8 by showing two-way arrows between a particular stage (e.g., advertising budget) and its subsequent stage (e.g., advertising objectives). Actually, were it not so cumbersome, a more realistic representation would show arrows between all the stages (e.g., from the advertising budget to media selection) because, in reality, decisions with respect to any one stage are influenced by decisions made for every other stage.

Advertising Budget   The decision sequence for advertising, as well as for every other promotional element, begins by setting an initial budget, which, as in the case of the overall promotion budget (Step 3), is subject to revision in light of proposed advertising objectives. Budgets for advertising are often set as a fixed percentage of the anticipated sales during the next fiscal period. The budget may have to be revised upward if the advertising objectives are particularly ambitious or revised downward in view of financial exigencies.

Advertising Objectives   As described previously, marketing objectives (Step 2) are typically stated in terms of sales or cost considerations. Advertising objectives are, by comparison, more often stated in terms of **communication goals.** The following are illustrative goals: (1) to create customer awareness of the marketer's product; (2) to facilitate customer understanding of the product, its attributes, benefits, and advantages; (3) to enhance the customer's attitude toward the marketer's offering; (4) to generate trial purchase behavior; and (5) to facilitate favorable word-of-mouth communication about the marketer's product.

The other promotion mix elements have their own specific objectives. For example, personal selling objectives are frequently stated in terms of desired sales levels or specified numbers of new accounts. Sales promotion objectives include generating trial purchase behavior, increasing the level of repeat purchasing, and getting more and better display space from retailers. Point-of-purchase objectives are directed at achieving superior display space and generating greater levels of in-store decision making.

Regardless of the specific nature of the objectives, it is critical that clearly defined, realistic, measurable, and consistent objectives be set for each promotional mix element. Such objectives direct the remainder of the promotional program (e.g., establishing advertising creative strategy and formulating media selection) as well as provide a quantitative basis for assessing program effectiveness and taking corrective action when necessary.

Creative Strategy   Creative advertising strategy, which deals with message content and presentation, follows from the statement of objectives. For example, if the objective is to facilitate prospective customers' understanding of product attributes and benefits, then a message format such as the one for Canon's personal electronic typewriter (Figure 1.4) is appropriate. If, however, the objective is merely to attract attention, then a different creative strategy is called for, such as in the case of the advertisement for Mounds and Almond Joy candy bars (Figure 1.6).

Media Selection   The choice of advertising media (TV, magazines, direct mail, etc.) is influenced by all of the preceding considerations: the available budget, objectives, and creative strategy. The previously mentioned manufacturer of hand-held microcomputers, Applied Technology, Inc., chose to depend on direct mail due to budgetary limitations and because direct mail was compatible with the company's advertising objectives and strategy. On the other hand, many packaged-goods companies (e.g., Procter & Gamble) depend heavily on television advertising because of that medium's ability to reach mass audiences, to demonstrate product features, and to facilitate vicarious learning.[12]

Implementation   Implementation deals with putting promotion programs into action. In the case of advertising, this means producing commercials and advertisements, selecting media and specific vehicles within media, buying broadcast time and print space, and ultimately printing or airing advertisements.

Step 6: Evaluating and Controlling Promotional Programs

The promotion management process does not end with implementation of advertising campaigns, sales promotion programs, or other promotional efforts. Rather, sophisticated promotion management requires that all programs be measured for effectiveness and that corrective action be taken where necessary. Effectiveness is evaluated by comparing actual performance against objectives. For example, if a sales force has as its objective to increase the number of accounts by 10 percent and accomplishes only a 3 percent growth, the reason for the deficit must be evaluated, and corrective action must be taken. This does not mean, however, that the sales force is necessarily responsible for the failure. The objective may have been set too high, or unforeseen developments may have prevented the accomplishment of the objective. Formal evaluation is necessary to cull out which reason(s) is (are) most plausible.

---

[12]The notion of vicarious learning deals with acquiring product knowledge by observing the behaviors of other people. The concept is described more completely in Chapter 3.

The value of a formal evaluation program is that it suggests possible revisions in the promotion management process for subsequent planning periods. This is shown in Figure 1.8 by the feedback flows from Step 6 to all five preceding steps. An evaluation may reveal that (1) the situation analysis was incomplete and needs to be expanded, (2) the marketing objectives are unreasonable and need to be revised, (3) the promotion budget is insufficient to accomplish the desired objectives, or (4) the various program elements are not being coordinated sufficiently.

In sum, a formal promotion management process that consists of six major steps has been described. Actual decision making does not proceed in the orderly fashion suggested by the straightforward presentation and the simplified model in Figure 1.8. The various steps do, however, capture the fundamentals of sophisticated promotion management programs and provide a set of working terminology that will be referred to throughout the text.

Organization of Text

The text is organized to first cover the fundamentals of marketing communications and then to treat in detail the various promotion mix elements. Chapter 2 reviews the fundamentals of communication that apply to all forms of marketing communications and promotion management.

Part II provides the foundation for the remainder of the text—marketing communications theory and research. Chapter 3 provides an overview of various aspects of buyer behavior theory and research that are pertinent to marketing communications and promotion management decision making. Subsequent chapters discuss the role of attitudes and persuasion in marketing communications, group influences on consumer choice behavior, adoption and diffusion processes, and message and source factors in marketing communications.

Part III focuses on the sales and advertising components of the promotion mix. Chapter 9 analyzes the influence that environmental factors such as socioeconomic developments have on promotion management decision making. Following chapters in Part III review the sales management process, personal selling, advertising budgeting and objective setting, advertising creative strategy, media selection, and evaluating advertising effectiveness.

Part IV examines the remaining promotion management tools. Chapter 16 is devoted specifically to the growing practices of direct marketing and telemarketing. Chapters 17 and 18 explore the role of sales promotion. Chapter 19 looks at public relations, publicity, and specialty advertising. The final chapter in Part IV, Chapter 20, studies the role of point-of-purchase communications and merchandising.

Part V contains two chapters that elaborate upon the marketing communications functions performed by the nonpromotional elements of the marketing mix. Chapter 21 looks at the communication roles of product symbols, packages, and brand names. Chapter 22 describes the communication functions of price and place variables.

The final chapter, Chapter 23 in Part VI, shows how the various marketing communication and promotion elements are integrated to achieve overall marketing objectives. This is illustrated with a review of a creative and successful program that was undertaken by the Agency for International Development (AID). The AID program consisted of a variety of communication efforts in The Gambia and Honduras that were designed to reduce the high levels of infant deaths from diarrheal dehydration. The case offers a fascinating illustration of how marketing communication methods are not restricted only to business applications but can also be applied to combatting a variety of difficult social problems. Part VII includes 14 cases that represent practical applications of a variety of promotion management and marketing communication practices.

Summary

This chapter introduces the fundamentals of marketing communications and promotion management. *Marketing communications* represents the collection of all elements in an organization's marketing mix that facilitate exchanges by accomplishing shared meaning with the organization's customers or clients. This description emphasizes that all marketing mix variables, and not just the promotional variable alone, communicate with customers. Product features, package cues, store image, and price are just some of the nonpromotional variables that perform important marketing communication functions.

Promotion, in its broadest sense, means "to move forward." Its general meaning in marketing is confined, however, to those communications activities which include advertising, personal selling, sales promotion, publicity, and point-of-purchase communication. The blend of these promotional activities is referred to as the *promotional mix. Promotion management* is the practice of coordinating the various promotional mix elements, setting objectives, establishing budgets, designing specific programs to accomplish objectives, and taking corrective actions when results are not in accord with objectives.

The "Three Modes of Marketing" serves as a useful conceptual framework to tie together the various marketing communications and promotion mix elements. There are, according to this framework, three overlapping sets of activities or modes whereby marketers seek to manage the demand for their offerings: (1) the *basic offer,* which is the product itself and its associated terms of sale; (2) *persuasive communications,* which consist of personal and impersonal messages that are designed to enhance customers' impressions of the basic offer; and (3) *promotional inducements,* which are extra substantive benefits (e.g., free samples, coupons, bonus packs) that are used to motivate particular customer actions. All three modes overlap and reinforce each other.

The overall *promotion management process* is also reviewed in this introductory chapter. Promotion management consists of a sequence of decisions that must be made in order to implement effective promotional programs and achieve marketing objectives. The six major steps of this process are as follows: performing a situation analysis, establishing marketing objectives, setting the promotion budget, integrating and coordinating promotion elements, implementing the promotion management program, and evaluating and controlling promotional programs. Each step is described, and relations between the various steps are discussed.

Discussion Questions

1. Discuss the following statement: "Promotion management is to marketing communications what personal selling is to marketing."
2. Marketing communication elements may communicate with customers in either an intentional or unintentional fashion. Explain what this means, and use several examples to back up your response.
3. In what sense does a retail outlet represent a communication vehicle for a manufacturer's product?
4. Compare and contrast the marketing concept and the promotion concept. What "modes" of marketing are used to actualize each of these concepts?
5. Finding a proper balance between the marketing and promotion concepts is essential for effective marketing. How can this be accomplished?
6. A manufacturer of sporting goods introduced a new line of fishing equipment (rods, reels, etc.). The items are sold at a premium price, but product quality is only average for the industry. The manufacturer's strategy is to advertise the merchandise very heavily and offer various inducements (e.g., price rebates) to move merchandise through retail outlets. Use Figure 1.3 to explain the manufacturer's strategy in terms of the three modes and the marketing and promotion concepts.
7. What is the "basic offer" that your college or university offers undergraduate students? What "persuasive communications" does it use to recruit students? Does it use any "promotional inducements"?
8. What is the difference between an "internal" and "external" situation analysis?
9. Figure 1.8 portrays a number of feedback flows from Step 6, evaluating and controlling promotional programs, to the preceding steps. Explain the underlying dynamic, or process, that each feedback flow is attempting to capture.

Exercises

1. Select a specific brand of a product of your choice and describe in detail, with illustrations, its most important marketing communications and promotion mix elements.
2. Select two brands from a product category different than the one used in the first exercise and perform a detailed analysis of their similarities and differences from a "three modes of marketing" perspective.
3. Identify three or four illustrations of product features which are, in your opinion, probably used by manufacturers to perform marketing communication functions in addition to their more basic product performance roles.

CHAPTER 2

Fundamentals of Communications

All the topics covered in this text—advertising, personal selling, sales promotion, public relations, package design, and so on—share one major commonality: they involve *communicating* with a company's prospective or current customers. For this reason, the present chapter, which deals with communication, is needed. The chapter reviews the fundamentals of the communications process, a process that is applicable to all forms of marketing communications and promotion.

What is Communications?

The word **communications** is derived from the Latin word *communis,* which translated means "common." Communications then can be thought of as the *process of establishing a commonness or oneness of thought between a sender and a receiver.*[1] This definition sets forth two important ideas. First, communications is a *process* and, as such, has elements and interrelationships that can be modeled and examined in a structured manner. Second, there must be a commonness of thought developed between sender and receiver if communication is to occur.

[1]Wilbur Schramm, *The Process and Effects of Mass Communications* (Urbana, IL: University of Illinois Press, 1955), p. 3.

Commonness of thought implies that a *sharing* relationship must exist between sender (an advertiser, for instance) and receiver (a consumer, for example).

Consider, for example, a situation in which a salesperson is delivering a sales presentation to a purchasing agent who appears to be listening to what the salesperson is saying but who actually is thinking about a personal problem at home. From an observer's point of view, it might appear that communication is taking place; however, thought is not being shared. Thus, no communication is occurring. The reason for the lack of communication in this instance is, of course, the passivity of the *intended receiver.* Though sound waves are bouncing against his eardrums, he is not actively receiving and thinking about what the salesperson is saying.

An analogy can be drawn between a human receiver and a television set. A television set is continuously bombarded by television (electromagnetic) waves from several or many different stations; yet, it will only receive the station to which the channel selector is tuned. Human receivers are also bombarded with stimuli from many sources simultaneously, and like the television set, people are selective in what information they choose to process. Both sender and receiver must be *active* participants in the same communicative relationship in order for thought to be shared. Communications is something one does *with* another person, not something one does *to* another person.

The Communications Process

In the simplest form, the communications process can be modeled as shown in Figure 2.1. The **sender** (or source) is a person or group of people who has a thought to share with some other person or group of people. The second element in this model is the **message.** A message is a symbolic expression of a sender's thoughts. The message may, for example, take the form of the printed or spoken word. In marketing, a magazine advertisement and a television commercial are examples. The third element, the **receiver** (or destination), is the person or group of people with whom the sender shares thoughts. In marketing, the receivers are the prospective and present customers of an organization's product or service.

Figure 2.2 depicts a slightly more complex model of the communications process. The model introduces several new elements: encoding, channel, decoding, noise, and feedback.

Encoding is the process of putting thought into symbolic form. This process is controlled by the source, who selects specific signs from a nearly infinite variety of words, sentence structures, symbols, and nonverbal elements to encode a message that will communicate effectively with the target audience. Similarly, **decoding** is the process of transforming message symbols back into thought. This process is controlled by the receiver. Both encoding and decoding are mental processes. The message itself is the manifestation of the encoding process and is the instrument used in sharing thought with a receiver.

The **channel** is the path through which the message moves from sender to receiver. Companies use the broadcast and print media to channel their messages to current and potential customers. Channel members (such as television networks

FIGURE 2.1   A Simple Communications Model

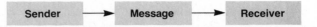

Source: M. Wayne DeLozier, *The Marketing Communications Process* (New York: McGraw-Hill, 1976), p. 2.

and magazines) are **transceivers,** that is, intermediaries who receive and then retransmit a company's message to the intended audience.

A message moving through a channel is subject to the influence of extraneous and distracting stimuli. These stimuli interfere with reception of the message in its pure and original form. Such interference and distortion is called **noise.** For example, a recent newspaper advertisement had the headline "SIN FOR FUN." It was a religious advertisement and should have read "SING FOR FUN." The absence of a single letter distorted the intended message (and probably created more than a slight amount of embarrassment for the newspaper personnel).

Noise occurs at all stages in the communications process (see Figure 2.2). For example, at the point of message encoding, the sender may be unclear what the message is intended to accomplish. A likely result is a poorly focused and perhaps

FIGURE 2.2   A Slightly More Complex Model of the Communications Process

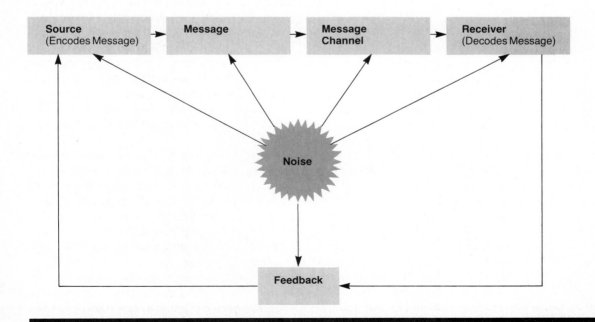

even contradictory message, rather than one that is clear-cut and integrated. Noise also occurs in the message channel — a fuzzy television signal, a crowded magazine page where an advertisement is surrounded by competitive clutter, and a personal sales interaction that is interrupted repeatedly by telephone calls are illustrations of channel noise. Noise is also present at the receiver/decoding stage of the process. An infant might cry during a television commercial and block out critical points in the sales message. A radio commercial may not be attended to because passengers in an automobile are talking.

The **feedback** element recognizes the two-way nature of the communications process. It points up that in reality individuals are both senders and receivers and interact with each other continually. Figure 2.3 illustrates this point. The feedback element affords the sender a way of monitoring how accurately the intended message is being received. Feedback enables the source to determine whether the original message hit the target accurately or whether it needs to be altered to evoke a clearer picture in the receiver's mind. Thus, the feedback mechanism offers the source some measure of control in the communications process. Advertisers frequently discover that their target markets do not receive (i.e., interpret) their campaign themes as management had intended. Based on research-based feedback from their markets, management can reexamine and often correct ineffective or misdirected advertising messages.

Interpersonal versus Mass Communications

The communications process that has been explained is fundamental and relevant to both interpersonal and mass communications. Both forms of communications share the same basic elements. Both share the same basic purpose. However, several unique characteristics of the mass communications process distinguish it from face-to-face (i.e., interpersonal) communications. First, mass communications is *indirect;* that is, it uses some technical vehicle (e.g., a television network) to connect the message source with receivers who are removed from the source in time, space, or both. Second, mass communications is *impersonal,* because the source directs a message to many people, instead of to a specific person. Third, mass

---

FIGURE 2.3   **A Simple Two-Way Communications Model**

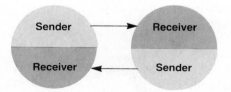

Source: M. Wayne DeLozier, *The Marketing Communications Process* (New York: McGraw-Hill, 1976), p. 4.

∴ hard to effectiveness assess media for of these promotion.

communications lacks a means of *immediate feedback.* Consequently, this form of communications is one-way, at least in the short run, and does not afford the communicator the opportunity to alter messages as might be dictated by the situation. In a sense, then, mass communications is a more complicated and less controllable form of communications. It is little wonder that many advertising campaigns and other mass marketing communication efforts are not as successful as the communicator would hope.

Sharing Thought

An individual's contact with other people occurs through sensory receptors (e.g., eyes, ears). A person's thought, as a mental phenomenon, cannot be detected by another person's sensory system. Thought itself cannot simply be picked up and placed in another person's head. Some vehicle that both sender and receiver can understand must be used to exchange thoughts.   *genie*

One way of sharing thought is with an *object-oriented* system. For example, a person can share thoughts with you about a vintage French wine by simply showing you a bottle of the wine. You can see the wine, touch it, smell it, and taste it. There are many obvious problems with an object-oriented method of sharing thought. For one, it would be necessary for us to carry around thousands, perhaps millions, of objects in order to communicate with others. Moreover, what objects would be used for sharing thoughts about freedom, love, and other abstract concepts?

Fortunately, another system of communication is available. This system developed early in the history of the human race, when people began to paint pictures on cave walls. They also uttered sounds when they saw animals or other people. These pictorial representations and sounds became associated with objects. People in families and tribes eventually developed signs (i.e., words and symbols) with which to share common meaning about objects in their environments. A **sign** is merely a stimulus that represents an object or idea. It is, in a sense, a label that is associated with the real object it represents. A sign has meaning only insofar as its association with the real-world object or idea is shared by other people. Figure 2.4 depicts the thought-sharing process.

The model in Figure 2.4 shows that a sender has stored within his or her mind a set of signs that can be used to represent his or her thoughts. The encoded thoughts can be placed into the receiver's environment by use of a transmitting system, in this case the voice box. The receiver detects the sound waves that have passed through the air by using his or her sensory system, in this example, his or her ears. The signs are decoded by using his or her mental sign system, thus sharing thought with the sender.

Needless to say, the model oversimplifies the process; however, it serves to illustrate the advantages of the sign system over the object system: First, the sign system is portable. We can store a vast number of mental signs in our brains and transmit them at any moment. Further, signs can be placed in combinations to represent a wide array of thoughts. Objects, on the other hand, cannot be combined so easily.

FIGURE 2.4   A Model of the Thought-Sharing Process

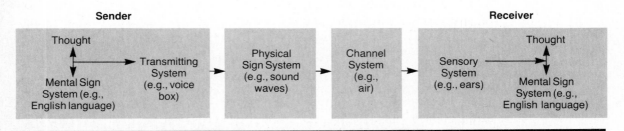

Source: M. Wayne DeLozier, *The Marketing Communications Process* (New York: McGraw-Hill, 1976), p. 5.

Signs Must Be Shared

A sign system of communicating can be effective only if the sender uses signs that the receiver can decode. That is, the sender must encode thoughts using signs that are common to both the sender's and the receiver's fields of experience. Figure 2.5 illustrates this point.

A field of experience, also called the perceptual field, is the sum total of all experiences a person has had during his/her lifetime. Signs contained in the perceptual field are numerous and include a person's language, such as English; gestures, such as waving good-bye; mathematical symbols, such as the summation sign (Σ); and even smiles and other emotional displays.

The larger the overlap or commonness in their perceptual fields, the greater the likelihood that signs used by the sender will be decoded by the receiver in the manner intended by the sender. To illustrate, consider a sender who transmits a message in Morse code. If you have never learned the code (i.e., if it is not in your

FIGURE 2.5   Overlapping Fields of Experience

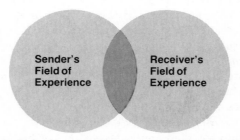

Source: M. Wayne DeLozier, *The Marketing Communications Process* (New York: McGraw-Hill, 1976), p. 6.

perceptual field), you will not be able to share thought with the sender. In similar fashion, advertisers, salespersons, and other marketing communicators sometimes employ symbols that are not part of their target audience's perceptual field. Effective communication is severely compromised when this occurs.

Two Basic Sign Systems

A sign system can take two basic forms. The most common is verbal; the other nonverbal. The verbal form is a formalized system that has evolved over the ages. The nonverbal form is generally less formalized and usually quite subtle.

Verbal   The verbal system, known as language, has a formal set of rules and methods. The verbal system employs a basic set of *cues,* such as letters in the alphabet, to form a large number of words. A specific ordering of cues is necessary to convey thought. Take, for example, the following cues:

$$i \quad e \quad l \quad v$$

These cues can be ordered in different ways to form various signs. There are, in fact, 24 distinct permutations of these particular letters. However, only four of these permutations are commonly used in the English language — *evil, live, veil,* and *vile.* These words contain the same four letters, but each word evokes an entirely different experience within a person's perceptual field.

Just as cues must have a specific order to form words, words must follow a certain order to form sentences. **Syntax** is the set of rules that provides for the orderly presentation of words. Syntax is the result of common usage among people using the same word-signs. Without syntax we might end up with any number of permutations of word-signs. For example, an advertising claim might read

"finger lickin' good is Kentucky Fried Chicken"
or
"Kentucky is good chicken lickin' fried finger"

instead of "Kentucky Fried Chicken is finger lickin' good."

Nonverbal   Nonverbal communication can either enhance or detract from much of a person's verbal efforts. The general role of nonverbal communications is to convey feelings and likings and either to support or contradict (as in the use of sarcasm) verbal expressions. People use numerous nonverbal signs to express emotion and thought. Smiles, tears, gestures, body movements, posture, speech rate, and intonation are examples. Marketing communicators are often adroit at using nonverbal signs to evoke certain feelings in receivers. For example, a magazine advertisement may capture the special look that conveys, without words, a feeling of warmth, love, happiness, or some other pleasant emotion. More will be said about the role of nonverbal communications in Chapter 5, which focuses specifically on the message component of marketing communications.

The Meaning of Meaning

Although we use signs to share meaning with others, the two terms (signs and meanings) should not be construed as synonomous.[2] Signs are simply stimuli, such as the ink configurations on this page, which are used to evoke an intended meaning within another person's head. The words we use do not have meanings; instead, people have meanings for words. Meanings are internal responses people hold for external stimuli. Many times people have different meanings for the same words. There is a simple proof of this. Ask five of your friends who have never taken a marketing course to define what "marketing" means to them. You will probably receive five decidedly different responses.

If signs have no meaning, it follows that meaning cannot be transmitted. "Only messages are transmittable, and meanings are not in the message, they are in the message-users."[3] Good communicators are people who select verbal and nonverbal signs that they feel will elicit the intended meaning. Marketing communicators must be especially careful to communicate their products and services using signs that will evoke the intended meaning in prospective buyers. All too often a company communicates its product offering in terms familiar to itself and not in terms familiar to its potential customers.

So far, this chapter has attempted to address the meaning of *meaning*. At best, it is a difficult concept to define. In any case, the authors prefer to think of meaning as the *set of internal responses and resulting predispositions evoked within a person when presented with a sign or stimulus-object.*[4]

Package designs, colors, and brand names evoke a set of responses that may become associated with the product itself. Consider, for example, the brand name and packaging of L'eggs (Figure 2.6). What do they bring to mind?

It should be clear at this point that meaning is internal, rather than external, to an individual. Meaning is found within an individual's perceptual field and is learned through the socialization process.

How Meaning Is Learned

One of the better explanations of how meaning is learned is provided by Charles Osgood's version of the Hull learning theory.[5] According to this theory, newborn babies are devoid of a set of meanings because they have no field of experience.

---

[2]Much of the subsequent discussion is based on David K. Berlo, *The Process of Communication* (San Francisco: Holt, Rinehart & Winston, 1960), pp. 168–216.

[3]Ibid., p. 175.

[4]Ibid., p. 184.

[5]Much of the subsequent discussion is based on Charles Osgood's expanded version of Hull's general learning theory. See Charles E. Osgood, *Method and Theory in Experimental Psychology* (New York: Oxford University Press, 1953), pp. 393–412.

FIGURE 2.6   **Illustration of How Package Design and Brand Name Evoke a Response to a Product**

Source: Courtesy of Hanes Group. L'EGGS is a registered trademark of L'EGGS Products, Inc.

Early reactions to stimuli (such as light or sound) are purely reflexive, i.e., involuntary. As time passes, infants begin to build associations between reflexive responses and the stimuli that evoke those responses.

To illustrate the process, consider a hungry baby who wants to be fed. Mother gives her a bottle. She makes several responses to the nipple on the bottle. She sucks (reflexive), feels full, burps, etc. The sucking and subsequent burping responses can be observed, but the internal responses cannot be observed. The bottle in the baby's mouth is called a **proximal stimulus,** that is, a stimulus that is in contact with the individual. When the bottle is in contact with the baby's mouth, it produces the responses mentioned. None of these responses are made, however, when the bottle is not in contact with the child.

As the baby develops, she becomes aware of distant stimuli. She sees the bottle setting on the table and begins making some of the same responses she makes when the bottle is in her mouth. The bottle setting on the table is a **distal stimulus,** that is, a stimulus not in contact with the child. The child at this point has made an association between the bottle at a distance and the bottle in her mouth. At this stage, the child has developed a higher level of meaning for the bottle.

Figure 2.7 shows that some of the responses made to the proximal stimulus are "detached" and are now made to the distal stimulus. These detached responses act to stimulate (S_M) the child to make specific overt responses (R_a, R_b, etc.) such as grabbing and crying for the bottle. The detached responses and the stimulation

FIGURE 2.7   Proximal–Distal Stimulus–Response Relationship

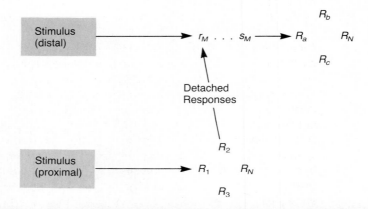

Source: After David K. Berlo, *The Process of Communication* (San Francisco: Holt, Rinehart & Winston, 1960), p. 181.

that they produce are part of what is called the "mediation process." Osgood describes the process as follows:

> *Of the total behavior elicited by a stimulus-object, some portion is relatively "object-tied" (probability of occurrence highly dependent on presence of the object) and another portion is relatively "detachable" (probability of occurrence largely independent of presence of the object). Signs tend to become conditioned to both types of reactions, but, when presented alone, are more likely to elicit "detachable" reactions.*[6]

Thus, a sign elicits a response set that is something less (certainly different) than what the physical object elicits. This phenomenon helps to explain why the sign system for sharing thought is far less than a perfect form of communication. The sign system simply does not enable a sender to transmit to receivers the full meaning of his or her thought. Nor does it allow the sender to encode his or her thought in a precise way.

Before leaving this topic, it will be useful to examine how the mediation process applies to marketing communications. Consider the situation in which you use a new brand of bathroom soap for the first time. When washing with the soap, you experience it as a proximal stimulus. The soap has a very pleasant scent, lathers generously, and washes away easily, leaving the skin feeling soothed and refreshed.

[6]Ibid., p. 397.

These responses to the physical object (the soap) correspond to the lower part of Figure 2.7. Over time, parts of these responses become "detached" and are made to the brand name itself (a distal stimulus). That is, just hearing or seeing the brand name of soap can evoke thoughts in your mind of how pleasant the soap smells, how nicely it lathers, and so forth. In other words, the distal stimulus (brand name) becomes conditioned to the total pattern of reactions elicited by the object itself. These conditioned or detached responses are not as intense as the responses evoked from actually using the product, but they are real and vivid nonetheless.

One role of advertising is to provide the right types of cues that will trigger in consumers pleasant thoughts about products they have tried previously but are not presently using. The right triggers can increase the odds that consumers will again select the advertiser's brand at some time in the future.

Some important ideas about meaning, then, are the following: First, meaning is in people, not in messages. Second, meanings are learned through a complex, mediational process. Third, no two people have exactly the same meaning for the same sign; each sign elicits a meaning peculiar to each individual's field of experience. Fourth, meanings for signs change as an individual's field of experience changes.

The Dimensions of Meaning

Although people learn meaning for individual signs, words (signs) are seldom used independently of each other. Normally, they are placed in a series according to prescribed rules of grammar. Because of this, individual signs may elicit different meanings depending upon their context and their syntactical relationships to other signs. Furthermore, some signs are more "object tied" than others. This section deals with four dimensions of meaning — denotative, connotative, structural, and contextual meaning.

Denotative Meaning   During childhood, people learn to associate words with physical objects. The sign *ball* becomes associated with the stimulus-object "ball." The child learns that a ball has several characteristics: it is round, it bounces, it rolls, etc. The sign *ball* evokes similar meanings within a large number of people because there is general agreement among these people about this particular word-object relationship. Denotative meaning, then, is a sign-object relationship. Words high in denotative meaning are words that are most strongly object tied.

Connotative Meaning   Some meanings are more complex than the simple sign-object, or denotative, relationship. Some words evoke meanings that are highly personal. These are called connotative meanings. A connotative meaning is the relationship between a sign, an object, and a person. Words such as *good, attractive, dependable,* and *quality* elicit different responses from different people.

Examples of connotative meaning are found in the way people describe restaurants, movies, people, and other subjective experiences. How often have the following situations (or something similar to these) happened to you?

- A friend tells you that a new restaurant is "good," but when trying it for the first time, you are very disappointed and find the dining experience to be anything but "good."
- You attend a movie with a friend. You think the movie was "excellent," but your friend thinks it was "mediocre."
- Someone tells you that another person, a mutual acquaintance, is "OK looking." In your opinion, however, this other person is "fantastic."

Words that elicit responses that are highly individualized (highly connotative) should be avoided when accurate reporting is required. Accuracy in communication decreases as connotation increases, and vice versa. However, audience interest level may be greater when words high in connotation are employed. This probably explains why advertisers and salespersons sometimes use exaggerated claims, e.g., "It's the 'best' product you can find"; "We'll give you an 'unbeatable' deal." Though lacking accuracy, such statements generate high levels of audience attention and interest.

Structural Meaning   It is usually necessary to put words together in a sequence in order to communicate clearly. Syntax and grammar provide procedures for sequencing words into patterns that are meaningful for the users of the language. These procedures guide the formation of sentences.

The structure of a sentence evokes a response from the receiver in much the same way a single word does. For example, if you are told that "a budgerigar has penna," you may not know what a "budgerigar" is nor what "penna" are. You *do* know from the structure of the sentence that a "budgerigar" has the property of "penna." Likewise, when the makers of "Scope" mouthwash claim that "Scope" has T_25^*, probably none of us knows what T_25^* is. We do know, however, that "Scope" mouthwash possesses the property T_25^*, whatever T_25^* might be.

From the foregoing examples, we see that the structure imposed on signs can help us to understand what another individual means. We can infer meaning because of the relationship one sign has with other signs. Thus, structural meaning is the understanding we get from a *sign-sign relationship*.

Contextual Meaning   The last dimension of meaning, contextual meaning, will be explained by expanding upon a previous example. Consider the following statement: "A budgerigar has penna. The budgerigar uses his penna to fly. His penna are beautiful shades of green, yellow, white, and black. The budgerigar is a popular cage pet and is often taught to talk."

Now we *have* shared our thought with you. We shared thought even though the words *budgerigar* and *penna* are not within your perceptual field. Undoubtedly you associated the other signs in the paragraph that evoked meaning in your mind with those two signs that evoked no meaning. You also used the sentence structure and sequence to aid in your associative process.

As consumers, we regularly use context (that is, surrounding signs) to interpret messages we receive from a variety of marketing communication sources. For example, let us assume a magazine advertisement neglects to say anything about the price of an advertised product. However, the ad is very stylish, and the magazine is itself prestigious. These clues lead us to infer that the advertised product is probably "high priced." We use context even when all the words used by the message source *are* familiar to us.

Summary

This chapter provides an overview of the fundamental aspects of communications. Communications is defined as the process of establishing a commonness, or oneness, of thought between a sender and a receiver. The process consists of the following elements: a source who encodes a message; a channel that transmits the message; a receiver who decodes the message; noise, which interferes with or disrupts effective communications at any of the previous stages; and a feedback mechanism that affords the source a way of monitoring how accurately the intended message is being received.

The concept of *signs* is introduced to explain how thought is shared between senders and receivers. The larger the overlap, or commonness, in their perceptual fields, the greater the likelihood that signs used by the sender will be decoded by the receiver in the manner intended by the sender. Signs have two basic forms— verbal and nonverbal — and include words, gestures, symbols, smiles, and body movements.

Signs are used to share meaning, but signs and meaning are not synonymous. Meanings are internal responses people hold for signs. Meaning is found within an individual's perceptual field. No two people have exactly the same meaning for the same sign; each sign elicits a meaning peculiar to each individual's field of experience.

Meaning is acquired through a complex mediational process whereby distal stimuli (i.e., signs in the form of words, symbols, etc.) become associated with physical objects (proximal stimuli) and evoke within individuals responses that are similar to those evoked by the physical objects themselves. Meaning has four basic dimensions: denotative, connotative, structural, and contextual.

Discussion Questions

1. Discuss the nature and importance of feedback. In what ways do marketing communicators get feedback from present and prospective customers?
2. Contrast verbal and nonverbal communications. How do marketers employ nonverbal communications in communicating with prospective buyers?
3. Why does the same sign evoke different meanings within people?
4. Under what circumstances should advertisers use highly denotative words in their messages? Highly connotative words?
5. How does the mediation theory help to explain the way consumers develop some of their meanings for products and brands? Use two examples of products to illustrate those responses which are likely to be "detachable" and

those that are not. Which responses do the signs (brand name, package, etc.) evoke?

6. How can a marketing communicator (such as an advertiser or salesperson) reduce noise when communicating a product message to customers?

Exercises

1. Some magazine advertisements show a picture of a product and mention the brand name but are virtually free of any verbal content except, perhaps, a single statement about the brand. Locate two or three ads of this type and explain what you think the advertiser is attempting to convey in each instance. Ask two friends to offer their interpretations of the same ads, and compare responses to determine the differences in meaning that these ads have for you and your friends.

2. Locate two or three additional magazine advertisements, but this time choose ones that are filled with verbal content. Analyze the verbal *and* nonverbal content, and identify specific instances of denotative, connotative, structural, and contextual meaning.

3. Arrange an interview with a salesperson, preferably one who calls on business accounts rather than a retail clerk. Ask this individual to explain how he or she acquires feedback during the course of a sales presentation. Also, ask him/her to explain the various forms of noise that occur most often during sales presentations and how he or she deals with the noise.

PART II

Marketing Communications Theory and Research

Part II builds a foundation for better understanding the nature and functioning of marketing communications and promotion management by examining theory and research dealing with buyer behavior, message and source factors, group influences, and adoption and diffusion processes. Chapter 3 examines two sides of consumer behavior: the logical, thinking person and the pleasure-seeking, feeling person. Chapter 4 continues the overview of buyer behavior by discussing the central concepts of attitudes and persuasion. These topics are important because marketing communications and promotion represent organized efforts to influence and persuade customers to make choices that are compatible with the marketing communicator's interests while simultaneously satisfying the customer's needs.

Chapters 5 and 6 explore message and source factors in marketing communications. Verbal and nonverbal messages, message appeals, source credibility, and endorser effectiveness are some of the topics covered. Chapter 7 broadens the perspective by examining group influences on individual consumer behavior. Culture, subculture, reference groups, and family forces are discussed in terms of their relevance to marketing communications and promotion. Chapter 8 looks at the adoption and diffusion processes. These topics are important because of their relevance to the acceptance of new products and ideas.

CHAPTER 3

Behavioral Foundations of Marketing Communications

Marketing communicators and promotion managers use a variety of practices that are designed to influence and to direct *consumer choice behavior*. As examples, salespersons, advertisers, package designers, merchandisers, and other marketing communicators coordinate their efforts to (1) attract additional consumers to purchase *their* brands, (2) influence consumers to shop more frequently at *their* stores, (3) persuade people to donate more funds to *their* nonprofit organizations (such as United Way), and (4) buy *their* products now rather than later. Influencing consumer choice behavior is the marketing communicator's job. To accomplish this goal, the marketing communicator must select appropriate stimuli (advertising symbols, packaging cues, brand names, and so forth), which, acting synergistically, can stimulate the intended market segment to action.

This chapter examines the first of two parts of consumer choice behavior. Whereas Chapter 4 offers a detailed treatment of the persuasion process in marketing communications, the present chapter examines two models of consumer choice behavior. The first uses a **consumer information processing (CIP) perspective**. In the CIP perspective, marketers view the consumer as a logical, highly cognitive, and systematic decision maker. For example, a consumer selects a particular home computer because he or she perceives that it offers superior performance characteristics and satisfies desired end benefits better than other models. An alternative perspective is the **hedonistic, or experiential, approach to consumption**,[1] which views the consumer as driven, *not* by rational and purely logi-

---

[1] Elizabeth C. Hirschman and Morris B. Holbrook, "Hedonic Consumption: Emerging Concepts, Methods, and Propositions," *Journal of Marketing,* Vol. 46, Summer 1982, pp. 92–101.

cal considerations, but rather by emotions in pursuit of "fun, fantasies, and feelings."[2]

To illustrate the differences between these two perspectives, let us examine the automobile-purchasing decisions of two consumers, both of whom are early middle-aged professional men. Jack, who has always owned American-made automobiles, became extremely dissatisfied with his last purchase, a 1981 Chevrolet Chevette. The car did not perform to his expectations (such as anticipated gas mileage). Jack's dissatisfaction reached a point at which he had to do something. He and his wife began actively searching for another automobile. They reviewed articles in *Consumer Reports,* visited dealerships, paid close attention to automobile advertisements, and talked with friends and acquaintances. They knew exactly what they wanted in a new car—durability, good gas mileage, suitable passenger and luggage space, good resale value, and an automatic transmission that shifted smoothly. They ultimately narrowed their choice to three possibilities: a Toyota Camry, a Ford Tempo, and a Honda Accord. After test driving all three and engaging in intense negotiations with the three respective dealers, Jack selected the Honda Accord. We see from this brief description that Jack was deliberate, logical, and systematic in his purchase—clearly a decision embraced by the consumer information processing (CIP) perspective of choice behavior.

Consider, by comparison, the automobile choice made by Doug, a man in his forties whom some might characterize as suffering from the middle-age "crazies." Doug, who has owned a variety of American- and foreign-made automobiles, currently drives a diesel-driven European car. Doug has been generally satisfied with this automobile and has informed his friends that he intends to keep it for at least another 50,000 miles. However, to the surprise of his associates, Doug arrived at work one morning with a new, top-of-the-line Toyota Camry. Doug, with virtually no prior thought about buying a new car, stopped at a Toyota dealership one day on his way home from work, fell in love with the new Camry, and decided on the spot to purchase it. Though he had voiced some minor complaints with his previous car, Doug's friends suspected that all along he had been fantasizing about owning a car more compatible with his style-conscious and status-oriented self-image.

The CIP Perspective of Consumer Choice

In this section of the chapter, several views of consumer information processing are presented. Special attention is devoted to Bettman's information processing theory of consumer choice[3] and to McGuire's descriptive framework.[4] Because a

---

[2]Morris B. Holbrook and Elizabeth C. Hirschman, "The Experiential Aspects of Consumption: Consumer Fantasies, Feelings, and Fun," *Journal of Consumer Research*, Vol. 9, September 1982, pp. 132–140.

[3]James B. Bettman, *An Information Processing Theory of Consumer Choice* (Reading, MA: Addison-Wesley, 1979).

[4]William J. McGuire, "Some Internal Psychological Factors Influencing Consumer Choice," *Journal of Consumer Research*, Vol. 4, March 1976, pp. 302–319.

fundamental understanding of consumer behavior is essential to a full appreciation of the intricacies and complexities of marketing communications and promotion management, the ideas presented here lay an important foundation to subsequent topical chapters.

Successful marketing practitioners *do* understand what makes consumers tick and reflect this understanding by constructing communication stimuli (such as advertisements, personal sales messages, and sales promotions) that consumers attend to, understand, remember, and ultimately use in making consumption choices. Bettman summarizes these points as follows:

> *The consumer is constantly being bombarded with information which is potentially relevant for making choices. The consumer's reactions to that information, how that information is interpreted, and how it is combined or integrated with other information may have crucial impacts on choice. Hence, decisions on* what *information to provide to consumers,* how much *to provide, and* how *to provide that information require knowledge of how consumers process, interpret, and integrate that information in making choices.*[5]

Information Processing Stages

Consumer information processing consists of various interrelated stages. This discussion focuses on the following eight stages:[6]

1. *Exposure* to information
2. *Selective attention and perception* of information
3. *Comprehension* of attended information   *(more selective w/ routinized response behavior)*
4. *Degree of agreement* with comprehended information
5. *Retention in memory* of accepted information
6. *Ability to retrieve* information from memory
7. Consumer *decision making* from available options
8. *Action* taken on the basis of the decision.

Exposure to Information

The marketing communicator's fundamental task is to get information to consumers, who, it is hoped, will process the information and be persuaded to undertake the course of action advocated by the marketer. Thus, exposure is an essential, preliminary step to subsequent stages of information processing. Beyond this, some researchers believe that the mere act of exposure performs an important role, which is known formally as the **mere exposure hypothesis**. This hypothesis asserts that a person's (or consumer's) repeated exposure to a stimulus may generate

[5]Bettman, *An Information Processing Theory of Consumer Choice*, p. 1.

[6]Based on McGuire, "Psychological Factors Influencing Consumer Choice."

positive affect toward the object (or advertised brand) through enhanced familiarity.[7] Although this finding has been demonstrated in research involving simplistic stimuli (e.g., nonsense syllables), some researchers do not agree that mere exposure to marketing stimuli can influence consumers' preferences.[8] At this point the mere exposure hypothesis is just that, an interesting hypothesis; however, some marketing communicators' apparent belief in this concept is reflected by their frequent use of extremely heavy advertising schedules with repetitive advertising content.

Attention to Information

Consumers attend to and process only a small fraction of marketing communication stimuli because attention is highly *selective*. Selectivity is necessary because information-processing capacity is limited, and effective utilization of this capacity requires the consumer to allocate mental energy (i.e., processing capacity) to only that information which is *relevant and of interest to current goals*.[9]

There are three kinds of attention: involuntary, nonvoluntary, and voluntary. **Involuntary attention** requires little or no effort on the part of a receiver. A stimulus intrudes upon a person's consciousness even though he does not want it to. In this case, attention is gained on the basis of the intensity of the stimulus—a loud sound, a bright light, etc. **Nonvoluntary attention,** sometimes called spontaneous attention, occurs when a person is attracted to a stimulus and continues to pay attention to the stimulus because it holds interest for him or her. A person in this situation neither resists the stimulus nor willfully attends to it initially. However, once his or her attention is attracted, the individual continues to give attention because the stimulus has some benefit or relevance. Generally, advertisers create messages to gain the nonvoluntary attention of an audience, since consumers do not in most situations willfully search out advertising messages. Therefore, advertisements must attract and maintain attention by being interesting and often entertaining. Finally, **voluntary attention** occurs when a person *willfully* notices a stimulus. Consumers who are considering the purchase of, say, a new automobile will consciously direct their attention to automobile advertising. Also, people who have recently purchased a product such as an automobile will voluntarily attend to messages about their make of car to reassure themselves of the correctness of their decision.

Discussion of the types of attention is not complete without mentioning the opposite of attention, **nonattention.** Nonattention (or inattention) occurs when a person (1) willfully selects a competing stimulus or (2) is distracted by an intruding stimulus of greater strength. The likelihood that a potential receiver will attend

[7]Robert B. Zajonc, "The Attitudinal Effects of Mere Exposure," *Journal of Personality and Social Psychology*, Vol. 9, 1968, pp. 1–27.

[8]George E. Belch, "The Effects of Television Commercial Repetition on Cognitive Response and Message Acceptance," *Journal of Consumer Research*, Vol. 9, June 1982, pp. 56–65.

[9]Bettman, *An Information Processing Theory of Consumer Choice,* p. 77.

to a message is high when the receiver *perceives a high net benefit* in relation to the perceived *expenditure of effort* required in attending a message. Thus, increasing individuals' perceived net reward and/or reducing their perceived effort will increase the probability that an audience will attend a message.[10]

It should be apparent that attention is highly selective. A number of factors account for this selectivity.[11] The following discussion reviews six sets of factors; the first two represent stimulus-based considerations (i.e., message properties) and the remaining four reflect consumer-based factors.

Stimulus Intensity   Intense stimuli (those that are louder, more colorful, bigger, etc.) are more likely to attract attention than less intense stimuli. The reason for this phenomenon is that intense stimuli are difficult to avoid, thus leading to involuntary or nonvoluntary attention. One need only walk through a supermarket and observe the various packages, displays, and shelf talkers to appreciate the special efforts marketers take to attract consumers' attention.

Advertisements, too, utilize *intensity* to attract attention. The magazine ad for Bright cigarettes (Figure 3.1) almost bursts out at the reader with its use of vivid colors.

Novel Stimuli   Marketing communications that are distinctive, unpredictable, or, in general, novel are effective attention-attracting stimuli. Unusual stimuli tend to produce greater attention than those that are familiar to a receiver. This phenomenon is based on the behavioral concept of *human adaptation.* People tend to adapt to the conditions around them. As a stimulus becomes more familiar, people become desensitized to it. For example, on the way to school or work each day you have probably driven past a billboard, noticing it less and less on each occasion. If the billboard were removed, you probably would notice it was no longer there. We *notice by exception!*

The advertisement for BIRDS EYE® COOL WHIP® Whipped Topping (Figure 3.2) illustrates the use of novelty. This ad attracts attention by its eye-catching portrayal of a piece of cheesecake suspended upside down. The unique portrayal is supported by the catchy headline: One taste and you will look at cheesecake a whole new way!

Past Reinforcement   A third determinant of selective attention is past reinforcement. This, specifically, involves the idea that people are more likely to attend those stimuli which have become associated with rewards. For example, attractive members of the opposite sex, babies, enchanting locations, appetizing food items, and gala events are some of the commonly used stimuli in advertisements, apparently because these symbols are inherently appealing to most people and because they are firmly associated in memory with good times and past enjoyment.

---

[10]Wilbur Schramm and Donald F. Roberts (eds.), *The Process and Effects of Mass Communication* (Urbana, IL.: The University of Illinois Press, 1971), p. 32.

[11]See McGuire, "Psychological Factors Influencing Consumer Choice," p. 308.

FIGURE 3.1   **Use of Intensity to Attract Attention**

FIGURE 3.2   **Use of Novelty to Attract Attention**

Source: Courtesy of General Foods Corporation.

Need States   Transient need states represent a fourth determinant of selective attention. Consumers are most likely to attend those stimuli which are congruent with current goals. A person who is looking for a new car, for example, will be particularly vigilant to information pertaining to automobiles. Automobile ads and overheard conversations involving cars will be attended even when the consumer is not actively seeking information. Advertisements for food products are especially likely to be attended to when an individual is hungry. You may recall, for example, the late-night television commercials for Burger King restaurants that asked rhetorically, "Aren't You Hungry?" and then proceeded to announce the expanded, late-night operating hours of many Burger King outlets.

Persisting Values   People are most likely to notice stimuli that relate to those aspects of life they value highly. Advertisers and salespeople frequently use references to family, to love, to belongingness, to caring, to sharing, to charity, and to other persisting values to attract attention and to influence consumer attitudes.

Expectations   Attention is guided by present expectations. One tends to notice what one's mind set has prepared one to look for. You may recall as a child having played the game of staring at a sky filled with cumulonimbus clouds and of attempting to locate certain figures and formations — animals, people's faces, or whatever. The sought-after figure was invariably found, provided sufficient patience. In similar fashion, a consumer who is interested in purchasing clothing will notice ads for new styles and fashions when perusing a magazine, yet avoid or almost entirely neglect advertisements for other products.

   In sum, attention involves allocating limited processing capacity in a selective fashion. Effective marketing communication demands that stimuli be designed to activate consumer interest and to draw attention away from competitive stimuli. This is no easy task, because marketing communication environments (stores and advertising media) are inherently *cluttered*. Recent research by Webb and Ray shows that clutter in television advertising reduces the effectiveness of individual commercials. Commercials appearing later in a stream of multiple commercials and those for low involvement products are particularly susceptible to the debilitating effects of clutter.[12]

Comprehension of What Is Attended

To comprehend is to understand and to make meaning out of complex stimuli and symbols. The term *comprehension* often is used interchangeably with *perception;* both terms refer to *interpretation*. Because people respond to their perceptions of the world and not to the world as it actually is, the topic of comprehension or perception is one of the most important subjects in marketing communications.

---

[12]Peter H. Webb, "Consumer Initial Processing in a Difficult Media Environment," *Journal of Consumer Research,* Vol. 6, December 1979, pp. 225–236; Peter H. Webb and Michael L. Ray, "Effects of TV Clutter," *Journal of Advertising Research,* Vol. 19, June 1979, pp. 7–12.

The perceptual process of interpreting stimuli is called **perceptual encoding.** Two main stages are involved.[13] **Feature analysis** is the initial stage whereby a receiver examines the basic features of a stimulus (brightness, depth, angles, etc.) and from this makes a preliminary classification. For example, a consumer is able to distinguish a motorcycle from a bicycle by examining such features as size, shape, number of controls, and so on.

The second stage of perceptual encoding, **active-synthesis,** goes beyond merely examining physical features. It involves a more refined perception. The context or situation in which information is received plays a major role in determining what is perceived and interpreted. In other words, consumers have stored in their memories expectations of the stimuli (products, brands, people, and so on) that are likely to be associated with certain contexts; interpretation results from combining or synthesizing stimulus features with expectations of what should be present in the context in which a stimulus is perceived. For example, a simulated fur coat placed in the window of a discount clothing store (the context) is likely to be perceived as a cheap imitation by the discerning dresser; however, the same coat, when attractively merchandised in an expensive boutique (a different context), might now be looked upon as a high-quality and stylish garment.

The important point in the preceding discussion is that consumers' comprehension of marketing stimuli is determined by stimulus characteristics and features and by characteristics of consumers themselves. Expectations play a particularly important role, but needs, moods, attitudes, and personality traits also influence consumer perceptions. A classic study conducted by McClelland and Atkinson demonstrates the relationship between a physiological need, hunger, and perception. A group of sailors at a submarine base were asked to identify "barely perceptible" objects on a screen. Though the screen actually was blank, the hungry sailors reported that they saw eating utensils.[14]

An individual's *mood* also can influence his or her perception of stimulus objects. In an imaginative study by Leuba and Lucas, subjects were placed in one of three different moods—a happy mood, a critical mood, and an anxious mood— through the use of hypnotic suggestions. They found that people in a happy mood paid little attention to detail; those in the critical mood focused on specific detail; and anxious subjects paid more attention to facial expressions in the pictures they were observing. Different moods seemed to affect not only what was observed but the meaning of what was observed.[15]

Recent research by social psychologists has found that when people are in a good mood they are more likely to retrieve positive than negative material from memory; are more likely to perceive the positive side of things; and, in turn, are

[13]Bettman, *An Information Processing Theory of Consumer Choice,* p. 79.

[14]David C. McClelland and J. W. Atkinson, "The Projective Expression of Needs: I. The Effect of Different Intensities of the Hunger Drive on Perception," *Journal of Psychology,* Vol. 25, April 14, 1948, pp. 205–222.

[15]C. Leuba and C. Lucas, "The Effects of Attitudes on Descriptions of Pictures," *Journal of Experimental Psychology,* Vol. 35, December 15, 1945, pp. 517–524.

likely to respond positively to a variety of stimuli.[16] These findings have potentially important implications for both advertising strategy and for personal selling activity. Both forms of marketing communications are potentially capable of placing consumers in positive moods and accordingly may enhance consumer perceptions and attitudes toward marketers' offerings.

People also tend to interpret stimuli in a manner consistent with their attitudes and values. In a study that verifies what every football fan already knows, Hastorf and Cantril describe how students from Dartmouth and Princeton attending a game between these two Ivy League schools saw two entirely different games. Early in the game a prospective All-American from Princeton was knocked out of the game with an injury. Shortly afterwards, a Dartmouth player left with a broken leg. After the hotly contested game, students and alumni from both schools accused the other team of dirty tactics. In effect, the fans witnessed two games—the one seen by Dartmouth fans and the other by Princeton supporters.[17] Consumers operate in similar fashion in how they perceive sales messages, advertisements, and other marketing stimuli. We tend, in other words, to extract content from messages with which we agree, while rejecting parts that are inconsistent with our position.

People select and distort messages according to their individual needs, moods, attitudes, and physiological nature. People do indeed choose messages and parts of messages that best fit into their cognitive structures, and if necessary, people will *misinterpret* messages to make them consistent with their perceptual fields.

Distorted perception and miscomprehension are a way of life. This point is illustrated rather dramatically in a major study by Jacoby and Hoyer,[18] who examined viewer miscomprehension of three forms of televised communication: programming content, advertisements, and public service announcements (PSAs). A total of 2,700 people from 12 test sites throughout the United States were exposed to 2 communication units from a pool of 60 units (i.e., 25 commercials, 13 PSAs, and 22 program excerpts). Respondents answered six true-false questions immediately after viewing the communication units. Two of the six statements were always true, and the remainder always false; half related to objective facts, and half were inferences. A high rate of miscomprehension was uncovered across all three forms of communications, with an average miscomprehension of nearly 30 percent! Surprisingly, advertisements were *not* miscomprehended any more than the other communication forms. Age and education were the only variables that were statistically related to miscomprehension, but the relationships were so weak as to have little practical significance. Thus, the general conclusion to be drawn from this

---

[16]Alice M. Isen, Margaret Clark, Thomas E. Shalker, and Lynn Karp, "Affect, Accessibility of Material in Memory, and Behavior: A Cognitive Loop," *Journal of Personality and Social Psychology,* Vol. 36, January 1978, pp. 1–12.

[17]A. Hastorf and H. Cantril, "They Saw a Game: A Case Study," *Journal of Abnormal and Social Psychology,* Vol. 49, January 17, 1954, pp. 129–134.

[18]Jacob Jacoby and Wayne D. Hoyer, "Viewer Miscomprehension of Televised Communication: Selected Findings," *Journal of Marketing,* Vol. 46, Fall 1982, pp. 12–26.

research is that miscomprehension of televised communications is a nearly universal phenomenon.[19]

Agreement with What Is Comprehended

A fourth information-processing stage involves the manner by which individuals yield to or agree with what they have comprehended in a message. Comprehension by itself does not assure that a persuasive message will change consumers' attitudes or influence their behaviors. Achieving impact requires that consumers agree with information they have comprehended. The quality of message arguments and source credibility are important mediators of the extent of agreement with persuasive communications. These points will not be elaborated on at this time, however, because they are treated in detail in Chapters 5 and 6.

Retention of What Is Accepted and Search and Retrieval of Stored Information

Retention and search/retrieval are discussed together because both involve *memory* factors relevant to consumer choice. The subject of memory is a complex topic that has been studied extensively by cognitive psychologists and others. Theories abound, and research findings are often contradictory. Research problems need not greatly concern us here, however, because our interest in the subject is considerably less technical and more practical. Fortunately, we are aided in our efforts to demonstrate the relevance of memory factors to marketing communications by the excellent review works by Bettman,[20] Mitchell,[21] and Olson.[22]

From a practical perspective, memory involves the related issues of what consumers remember (i.e., recognize and recall) about marketing stimuli and of how they access and retrieve information for purposes of making consumption choices. The subject of memory is inseparable from the process of learning, so the following paragraphs first discuss the basics of memory, then examine learning fundamentals, and, finally, place special emphasis on the practical application of memory

[19]It is relevant to note that the Jacoby and Hoyer research has stimulated considerable controversy. See Gary T. Ford and Richard Yalch, "Viewer Miscomprehension of Televised Communications—A Comment," *Journal of Marketing,* Vol. 46, Fall 1982, pp. 27–31; Richard W. Mizerski, "Viewer Miscomprehension Findings Are Measurement Bound," *Journal of Marketing,* Vol. 46, Fall 1982, pp. 32–34; and Jacob Jacoby and Wayne D. Hoyer, "On Miscomprehending Televised Communication—A Rejoinder," *Journal of Marketing,* Vol. 46, Fall 1982, pp. 35–43.

[20]Bettman, *An Information Processing Theory of Consumer Choice,* Chap. 6; and James B. Bettman, "Memory Factors in Consumer Choice: A Review," *Journal of Marketing,* Vol. 43, Spring 1979, pp. 37–53. For the following discussion the authors are particularly indebted to Bettman's writings.

[21]Andrew A. Mitchell, "Cognitive Processes Initiated by Advertising," in R. J. Harris (ed.), *Information Processing Research in Advertising* (Hillsdale, NJ: Lawrence Erlbaum Associates, 1983), pp. 13–42.

[22]Jerry C. Olson, "Theories of Information Encoding and Storage: Implications for Consumer Research," in A. A. Mitchell (ed.), *The Effect of Information on Consumer and Market Behavior,* (Chicago: American Marketing Association, 1978), pp. 49–60.

and learning principles of marketing communications. Particular attention is placed in the practical application's section on the role of *imagery.*

A current conceptualization of memory is that it consists of long-term memory (LTM), short-term memory (STM), and a set of sensory stores (SS). Information is received by one or more sensory receptors (sight, smell, touch, and so on) and passed to an appropriate SS, where it is rapidly lost (within fractions of a second) unless attention is allocated to the stimulus. Attended information is then transferred to STM, which serves as the center for current processing activity by bringing together information from the sense organs and from LTM. Limited processing capacity is the most outstanding characteristic of STM; individuals can process only a limited amount of information at any one time. An excessive amount of information will result in reduced recognition and recallability. Furthermore, information in STM that is not elaborated upon (i.e., thought about or rehearsed) will be lost from STM in about 30 seconds or less.[23] (This is what happens when you get a phone number from a telephone directory but then are distracted before you have an opportunity to dial the number: you must refer to the directory a second time, this time repeating the number to yourself, i.e., rehearsing it, so that you will not forget it again.) Telephone companies have recognized this problem and have placed a redial feature on many newer telephone models.

Suitably processed information in STM will be transferred to LTM, which cognitive psychologists consider to be a storehouse of virtually unlimited information. Information in LTM is organized into coherent and associated cognitive units, which are variously called *schemata, frames, scripts,* and *memory organization packets.* Though differing conceptually, all of these terms reflect the idea that LTM consists of associative links among related information, knowledge, and beliefs.[24] Consumers have packets of information about products and specific brands stored in LTM. Figure 3.3 presents one hypothetical consumer's information packet for a Ford Fiesta automobile.

The marketing practitioner's job is to provide positively valued information, which consumers will store in long-term memory and which will enhance the probability that their consumption choices are congruent with the marketer's interests. Stated differently, the marketing communicator's task is to facilitate consumer *learning,* where learning represents changes in the content or organization of information in consumers' long-term memories.[25] For example, if business air travelers consider it important to have seating assignments made at one time for all departing, connecting, and return flights (rather than waiting in line at each connection for a seating assignment), then the advertiser's job is to get business-people to learn that its airline provides this service.

---

[23]Richard M. Shiffrin and R. C. Atkinson, "Storage and Retrieval Processes in Long-Term Memory," *Psychological Review,* Vol. 76, March 23, 1969, pp. 179–193.

[24]See Mitchell, "Cognitive Processes Initiated by Advertising."

[25]Ibid., p. 21.

FIGURE 3.3   **A Hypothetical Consumer's Information Packet for a Ford Fiesta Automobile**

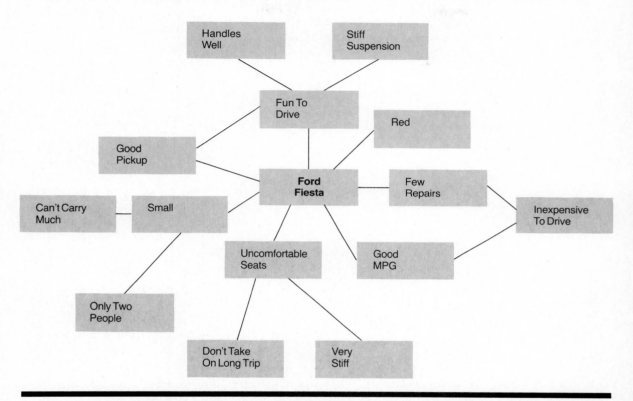

Source: Andrew A. Mitchell, "Cognitive Processes Initiated by Advertising," in Richard J. Harris (ed.), *Information Processing Research in Advertising* (Hillsdale, NJ: Lawrence Erlbaum Associates, 1983), p. 21. Adapted with permission.

At least three types of learning are relevant to marketing communication activity.[26] One type is the *strengthening of linkages among specific memory concepts.* The Ford Motor Company, for example, has invested heavily in promoting the theme "At Ford, Quality is Job 1." The purpose is to affix in consumer's memories a linkage between these two concepts, Ford cars and quality. A second form of learning is to *facilitate the formation of entirely new linkages.* Consider, by way of illustration, Arm & Hammer baking soda, a product that is used primarily for baking but which over the years has received a number of interesting and innovative secondary uses. The makers of Arm & Hammer capitalized on what some

[26]Ibid.

consumers had already known by aggressively promoting the product's secondary uses, e.g., as an odor absorber, for brushing teeth, and so on. In other words, advertising and package information were designed to facilitate consumers' learning to link Arm & Hammer with a variety of secondary uses, which represented entirely new linkages for many consumers.

A third form of learning, but one which is more a result of consumer experience than of marketer influence, occurs when *new schemata or scripts are formed when the consumer generalizes from previous experience.* For example, an American college student, who during his freshman and sophomore years takes mathematic and scientific courses from three non-American professors, may generalize that non-American professors are more oriented to quantitative subjects than American professors. In similar fashion, many consumers develop generalizations such as "you only get what you pay for," "airline food is mediocre," "store brands are good values," and so forth. Generalizations vary in their degree of generality and range from *nonspecific* generalizations (e.g., "you only get what you pay for") to *product-specific* generalizations (e.g., "American beers are bland in comparison with European beers) and *brand-specific* generalizations (e.g., "Campbell soups are good"). All levels of generalization influence consumer choice behavior, but the third level is probably of greatest relevance to marketers. However, many brand-specific generalizations are a function of a company's decisions concerning product quality rather than of advertising or other promotional activities.

Information that is learned and stored in memory has an impact on consumer choice behavior only when it is searched and retrieved. Precisely how retrieval occurs is beyond the scope of this chapter. Suffice it to say that retrieval is facilitated when a new piece of information is linked, or associated, with another concept that is itself well known and easily accessed. For example, IBM's microcomputer, the PC-jr., was easily remembered when introduced in late 1983 because it was associated with the already well-known predecessor model, the IBM-PC.

Concretizing is another means by which new information is both learned readily and accessed easily. That is, it is easier to remember and to retrieve concrete rather than abstract information. By way of illustration, consider the hypothetical name "Home-Aid" for a home computer; this would be a descriptive name for a personal computer, but it would suffer terribly from abstractness (just try to visualize anything meaningful from the name Home-Aid). By comparison, think about the name "Apple" and the associated rainbow-shaded logo used by one actual computer company. Though not at all descriptive of a home computer, "Apple" is a superb brand name. It is concrete (everyone can visualize an apple, even a rainbow-shaded one) and therefore is easily remembered and retrieved.

Television advertisers are particularly fond of concretizing their claims. Consider the following illustrations, which you may recall viewing. Delta Airlines, just prior to the 1984 Summer Olympics, employed shots of a discus thrower to highlight a rather abstract theme—that Delta uses teamwork. This was concretized by intermingling shots of Delta employees in action and a discus thrower in the process of releasing a discus. At the point of release, a Delta aircraft was shown lifting off. The discus thrower was embraced and congratulated by teammates as the commercial closed—thus a graphic juxtaposition of Delta's theme, "it takes teamwork to get an airline in flight." Schlitz Malt Liquor has for years used a rampaging bull to emphasize the product's strength and "punch." Rolaids antacid commercials use a sponge to demonstrate Rolaids' acid-absorption properties. Kellogg's Product 19 cereal, to convey the notion that it has more vitamins than other cereals, shows a vitamin capsule opening with Product 19 flakes pouring out in place of what normally would be vitamin pellets. Finally, a particularly fascinating commercial for Jeep vehicles portrays a young man riding a buffalo over rough terrain and then accompanied by a young lady while a background singer declares, "There's a feeling you can get, only in a Jeep."

Imagery   The preceding advertising examples highlight the important role of *imagery* in marketing communications. *Imagery*, by definition, represents a mental event involving visualization of a concept or relationship.[27] To better understand the notion of imagery, think of the following words: *pencil, tennis racket, dancing, duck-billed platypus, satisfaction,* and *standard deviation*. The first two, *pencil* and *tennis racket,* no doubt evoke distinct images in your mind; *dancing* also probably elicits a visualization, and some of you might even possess a visual concept for *platypus*. It is doubtful, however, that you have an image for *satisfaction* or *standard deviation,* both of which are inherently abstract concepts.

Mental imagery plays an important role in various aspects of consumer information processing (comprehension, recall, retrieval). The issue for practical purposes is, What can marketing communicators do to elicit imagery? Three different strategies are possible:[28] (1) use visual or pictorial stimuli, (2) present concrete verbal stimuli, and (3) provide imagery instructions. Only the first two of these will be discussed, since the third is not used extensively in marketing communications, although advertisers occasionally instruct listeners or readers to imagine themselves engaged in some behavior (e.g., "Think what it would be like to be vacationing in Hawaii at this moment").

Pictures and visuals are best remembered (compared with abstract or concrete verbalizations) because pictures are best able to elicit imagery. A more formal explanation is provided by the **dual-coding theory,** which holds that pictures are represented in memory in verbal as well as visual form, whereas words are less likely to have visual representations.[29] It would be expected, therefore, that visual imagery would play an important role in advertising, point-of-purchase stimuli, and

[27]Kathy A. Lutz and Richard J. Lutz, "Imagery-Eliciting Strategies: Review and Implications of Research," in H. Keith Hunt (ed.), *Advances in Consumer Research,* Vol. 5 (Ann Arbor, MI: Association for Consumer Research, 1978), pp. 611–620.

[28]Ibid.

[29]Allan Paivio, "Mental Imagery in Associative Learning and Memory," *Psychological Review,* Vol. 76, May 1969, pp. 241–263; and John R. Rossiter and Larry Percy, "Visual Imaging Ability as a Mediator of Advertising Response," in H. Keith Hunt (ed.), *Advances in Consumer Research,* Vol. 5 (Ann Arbor, MI: Association for Consumer Research, 1978), pp. 621–629.

TABLE 3.1   **Visual Imagery "Principles"**

General Advertising Principles

G–1: Visual content warrants relatively more advertiser attention than verbal content.
G–2: Use high imagery (more concrete) visuals rather than abstract visuals.
G–3: Use color in visuals for emotional motivation but black & white is sufficient for "information" provision.
G–4: "Interact" or juxtapose the product with the user or usage context in visuals.
G–5: High imagery visuals work far better than "instructions to image."

Print Advertising Principles

P–1: The larger the illustration, the better—except for direct-response ads of the informational variety.
P–2: Seek attention-holding illustrations (2 seconds or more) not just attention-getting illustrations.
P–3: Place the illustration where it will be seen before the headline and copy are read.
P–4: Attitudinal "wearout" should not be a problem with illustrations, but they may lose attention, suggesting use of variations on a theme for print advertising.

TV Advertising Principles

T–1: Hold key scenes for at least 2 seconds and alternate key and redundant scenes.
T–2: Put key scenes before related audio with audio in the "pauses."
T–3: Use atypical variations on a typical script.
T–4: For visual-word "supers" use high imagery words in positive sentences except, perhaps, for disclaimers.

Source: John R. Rossiter, "Visual Imagery: Applications to Advertising," in A. A. Mitchell (ed.), *Advances in Consumer Research,* Vol. 9 (Ann Arbor, MI: The Association for Consumer Research, 1982), pp. 101–106. Reprinted with permission.

other marketing communications. If nothing else, visual stimuli should enhance recall and recognition of company and brand names.

Lutz and Lutz found that people remembered significantly greater numbers of company names when these names were paired with meaningful pictorials. The name "Jack's Camera Shop," for example, was better remembered when the store name was presented along with a playing card jack shown holding a movie camera to its eye.[30] Many marketing communicators use similar pictorials, proven by perusing the Yellow Pages of any city telephone directory.

Visual imagery has a number of potential applications to advertising and to other aspects of marketing communications. Some of these applications have been discussed by Lutz and Lutz,[31] and Rossiter has proposed an extensive list of visual imagery "principles."[32] Thirteen principles are summarized in Table 3.1, which,

[30]Kathy A. Lutz and Richard J. Lutz, "The Effects of Interactive Imagery on Learning: Application to Advertising," *Journal of Applied Psychology,* Vol. 62, August 1977, pp. 493–498.

[31]Lutz and Lutz, "Image-Eliciting Strategies."

[32]John R. Rossiter, "Visual Imagery: Applications to Advertising," in A. A. Mitchell (ed.), *Advances in Consumer Research,* Vol. 9 (Ann Arbor, MI: The Association for Consumer Research, 1982), pp. 101–106.

pursuant to Rossiter, delineates five general advertising, four print advertising, and four TV advertising principles. This chapter will discuss the first four general advertising principles; the reader is referred to the original source to examine the others.

Rossiter's first hypothesis (G-1) restates the previously discussed point that visual stimuli are better remembered and are potentially more effective than verbalizations. The second point (G-2) is that concrete visuals (those representing objects, persons, or places that can be experienced by one or more of the senses) are learned more readily and better remembered than abstract visuals (those that cannot be experienced by the senses). Figure 3.4 illustrates the notion of visual concreteness with two vacation ads. One (Callaway Gardens) is a very concrete ad, with golf course, tennis court, and pleasant dining scenes; the other (for Holiday Inn) is less concrete, with its wash drawing of a seagull, palm trees, and other ocean scenery. The four-color ad for Callaway Gardens, though more costly than the black and white Holiday Inn ad, would appear to have a greater potential for impacting memory and generating positive affect.

The third general advertising principle (G-3) makes the important point that black and white visuals are sufficient for merely providing information, but color visuals are essential for generating emotional impact. Returning to Figure 3.4, it would appear that the black and white Holiday Inn advertisement might suffice if its purpose is simply to inform readers about special discount rates during the off season at the two resort areas mentioned; the four-color Callaway Gardens ad certainly is more emotionally appealing with its depiction of attractive scenes and desirable activities.

The fourth hypothesis (G-4) emphasizes the value of showing the user actually using (interacting with) the advertised product. Psychological research has dem-

FIGURE 3.4   Visual Concreteness in Advertising: Comparative Illustrations

onstrated that verbal learning is greater for interactive visuals compared with visuals that present pictures and words separately. The previously mentioned Lutz and Lutz research has demonstrated this point in an advertising context.[33] The Callaway Gardens ad in Figure 3.4 offers a vivid illustration of interactive visualization—actual tennis players, people dining, and (if you look closely) golfers on and surrounding a sand-trapped green.

So far, the present discussion of imagery in marketing communications has examined only the use of pictorials to evoke visual imagery. Discussion turns now to the role of verbal stimuli as a means of eliciting visual imagery. *Concreteness* is the single most important determinant of the imagery-producing power of words and more complex linguistic stimuli.[34] Concrete linguistic elements (words, phrases, and sentences) refer to objects, persons, or places that can be experienced by one's senses. For example, the word *shark* is highly concrete in comparison with the activity *debating*.

Psychological research has shown that using concrete verbal stimuli facilitates memory.[35] It would be inappropriate to make broad generalizations to advertising and other marketing communications, however, because the role of verbal concreteness in these areas has barely been investigated. A notable exception is research by Rossiter and Percy, who performed an experiment that manipulated both the degree of visual emphasis and verbal explicitness (concreteness) in advertisements for hypothetical German beers.

Figure 3.5 presents two experimental advertisements from the Rossiter and Percy research, one containing explicit (relatively concrete) verbal content, and the other implicit content (relatively abstract). Respondents' attitudes toward the beer and their purchase intentions were influenced significantly more by the concrete than by the abstract claims.[36]

Deciding among Alternatives

The six preceding stages have examined how consumers receive, encode, and store information that is pertinent to making consumption choices. Stored in consumers' memories are numerous information packets for different consumption alternatives. This information is in the form of bits and pieces of *knowledge* (e.g., "Members Only" is a brand of wearing apparel), specific *beliefs* (e.g., "the Honda Civic CRX" provides excellent gas mileage), and *evaluations* of purchase conse-

---

[33]Lutz and Lutz, "The Effects of Interactive Imagery."

[34]John R. Rossiter and Larry Percy, "Visual Communication in Advertising," in R. J. Harris (ed.), *Information Processing Research in Advertising* (Hillsdale, NJ: Lawrence Erlbaum Associates, 1983), pp. 83–125. Larry Percy, "Psycholinguistic Guidelines for Advertising Copy," in A. A. Mitchell (ed.), *Advances in Consumer Research*, Vol. 9 (Ann Arbor, MI: The Association for Consumer Research, 1982), pp. 107–111.

[35]For review, see Lutz and Lutz, "Imagery-Eliciting Strategies."

[36]John R. Rossiter and Larry Percy, "Attitude Change through Visual Imagery in Advertising," *Journal of Advertising,* Vol. 9, 1980, pp. 10–16.

(handwritten margin note: Abstract visual (no picture, ie. all verbal))

FIGURE 3.5 Illustrations of Relatively Concrete and Abstract Advertising Claims

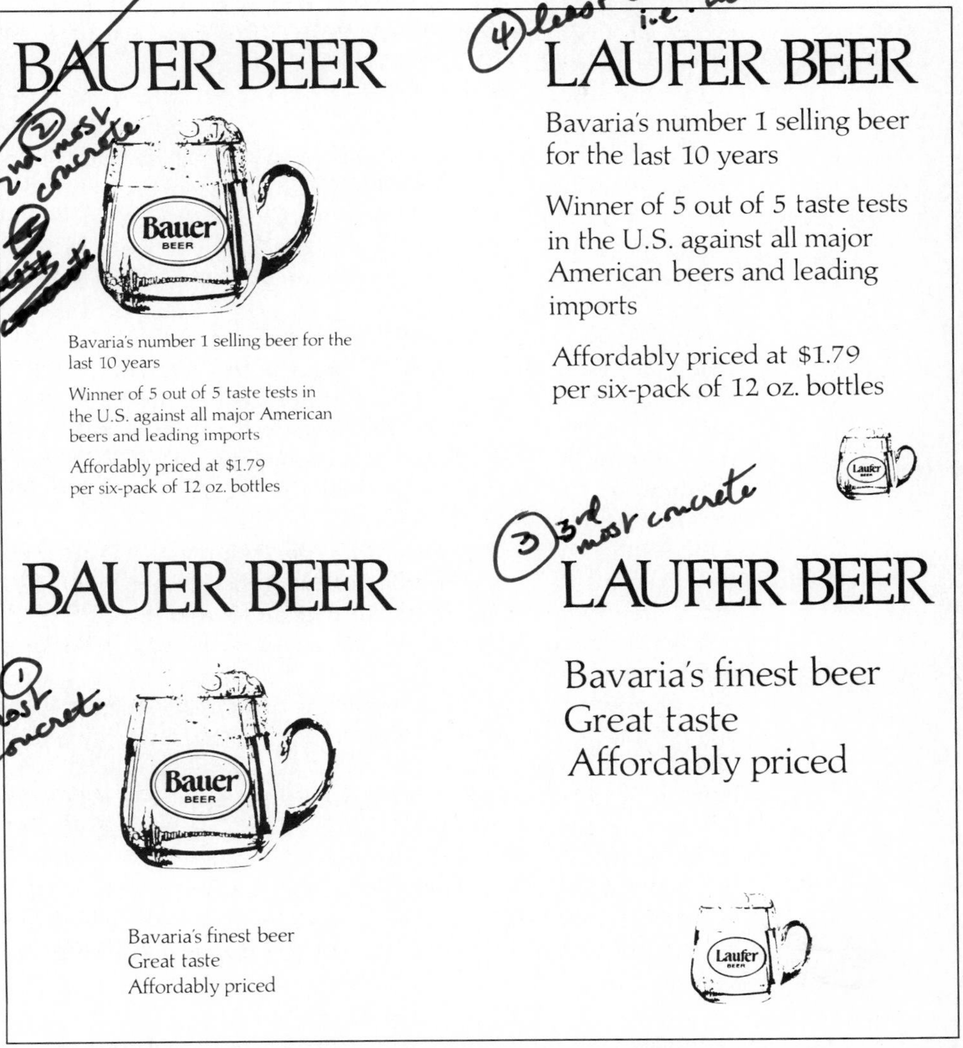

(handwritten margin note: Think of abstract - concrete visuals as a continuum.)

(handwritten margin note: Concrete visual (no verbal))

BAUER BEER

(handwritten note: 2nd most concrete)

Bavaria's number 1 selling beer for the last 10 years

Winner of 5 out of 5 taste tests in the U.S. against all major American beers and leading imports

Affordably priced at $1.79 per six-pack of 12 oz. bottles

BAUER BEER

(handwritten note: ① most concrete)

Bavaria's finest beer
Great taste
Affordably priced

(handwritten note: ④ least concrete - i.e. most abstract)

LAUFER BEER

Bavaria's number 1 selling beer for the last 10 years

Winner of 5 out of 5 taste tests in the U.S. against all major American beers and leading imports

Affordably priced at $1.79 per six-pack of 12 oz. bottles

(handwritten note: ③ 3rd most concrete)

LAUFER BEER

Bavaria's finest beer
Great taste
Affordably priced

Source: John R. Rossiter and Larry Percy, "Attitude Change through Visual Imagery in Advertising," *Journal of Advertising,* Vol. 9, No. 2, 1980, p. 13. Reprinted with permission.

quences (e.g., manufacturer reputability is more important, to some consumers, than price when purchasing automobile tires).

The issue for present discussion is, When making a purchase decision, how do consumers integrate and weigh information to decide whether to make a purchase, which product to purchase, which brand to choose, and at which retail outlet to actualize their choice?

Because *information processing capacity is limited,* consumers use simplifying strategies, or *heuristics* (rules), to make consumption choices. First, however, before describing specific heuristics, it should be instructive to review a decision that all of us have made and which, in many respects, is one of the most important we will ever make, namely, the choice of which college or university to attend. For some of you, there really was no choice—you went to a school you had always planned on attending, or perhaps your parents insisted on a particular institution. Others, especially those of you who work full- or part-time, may have selected a school purely as a matter of convenience or affordability; in other words, you really did not seriously consider other institutions. But some of you actively evaluated several or many colleges and universities before making a final choice. The process was probably done somewhat in the following manner: you *received information* from a variety of schools and formed preliminary impressions of these institutions; you *established criteria* for evaluating schools (academic reputation, distance from home, cost, curricula, availability of financial assistance, quality of athletic programs, etc.); you *formed weights* regarding the relative importance of these various criteria; and you eventually *integrated this information* to arrive at the all-important choice of which college to attend.

What heuristics do consumers use and what are the implications for marketing communications? Perhaps the simplest of all heuristics is **affect referral**.[37] With this strategy the consumer simply calls from memory his or her attitude (i.e., affect) toward relevant alternatives and picks that alternative in which affect is most positive. This type of choice strategy would be expected for frequently purchased items where risk is minimal (i.e., *low involvement* items). For example, a smoker routinely picks her favorite brand of cigarettes and a beer drinker regularly chooses any of two or three different brands.

By comparison, consider the situation in which a decision involves considerable financial, performance, or psychological risk. A **compensatory heuristic** is likely to be used when making a choice under such risky (or *high involvement*) circumstances. To understand how and why compensation operates, it is important to realize that rarely is a particular consumption alternative completely superior or dominant over other relevant alternatives. Although one brand may be preferable to others with respect to one, two, or several benefits, it is unlikely that it is superior in terms of all attributes or benefits that consumers are seeking. In making choices under such circumstances, consumers must give something up in order to

[37]Peter L. Wright, "Consumer Choice Strategies: Simplifying vs. Optimizing," *Journal of Marketing Research,* Vol. 11, February 1975, 60–67.

get something else. High involvement decision making requires that *trade-offs* be made. If you want more of a particular benefit, you typically have to pay a higher price; if you want to pay less, you often give something up in terms of performance, dependability, or durability. Returning to the university choice decision, a frequent trade-off is between the quality of academic and athletic programs.[38]

The *compensatory heuristic* requires that the consumer (1) establish importance weightings for each salient choice criterion, (2) form perceptions (beliefs) of how well each alternative satisfies each criterion, (3) then somehow integrate this information, and (4) arrive at a total "score" for each relevant alternative. Theoretically, then, choice is made by selecting the alternative with the highest overall score. The chosen alternative probably is not the best in terms of all criteria, but its superiority on some criteria offsets, or *compensates for,* its lesser performance on other criteria.[39]

In addition to compensatory choice behavior, consumers use a variety of so-called **noncompensatory heuristics.** Three in particular are the conjunctive, disjunctive, and lexicographic heuristics. According to the **conjunctive heuristic,** the consumer establishes cutoffs, or minima, on all pertinent choice criteria and an alternative is retained for further consideration only if it meets or exceeds all minima. As seen in the hypothetical university choice, for example, a particular consumer may establish these cutoffs: a viable school must have a major in building construction management, be no farther than 500 miles from home, and cost no more than $5,000 per year. All schools meeting these criteria receive further consideration, perhaps involving the application of a compensatory heuristic to arrive at a choice from the remaining options.

The *disjunctive heuristic* is a second noncompensatory heuristic. Whereas the conjunctive heuristic requires that an acceptable alternative must meet or exceed the minimum on choice criterion 1, *and* choice criterion 2, *and* choice criterion n, the disjunctive heuristic accepts an alternative if it meets any of the minimum standards, i.e., an alternative is acceptable if it meets or exceeds choice criterion 1, *or* choice criterion 2, *or* choice criterion n. It should be apparent that a disjunctive heuristic is basically one of "nearly anything is acceptable," which would represent the choice behavior of only the most indiscriminate of consumers under the rarest of circumstances.

A third noncompensatory heuristic carries a dictionary-sounding name, **lexicographic**. This heuristic operates in a fashion analogous to the way in which a

---

[38]For example, the president of the University of Alabama told a national TV audience in 1983 that his institution knows what it is like to be number one in football, and it now is working to achieve similar prominence for its academic programs. By comparison, we suspect that the president, alumni, and students of Northwestern University, which has an established academic reputation, would be happier if the football team won a few more games.

[39]The best known illustration of compensation in consumer behavior is the Fishbein attitude model, which states that one's attitude toward performing an act is the sum of one's beliefs regarding the consequences of the act weighed by one's evaluations of these consequences. Further discussion of this model will be delayed until Chapter 4, which describes attitude formation and change in context of the general topic of persuasion.

lexicon (dictionary) is compiled and the way users search to locate a word. To find a word, say *communicate,* one searches for words beginning with *c,* then *co, com,* and so on until the desired word, *communicate,* is located. There is, in other words, a strict alphabetical ordering of words in a dictionary. The lexicographic heuristic embodies the same notion, namely, for a particular purchase decision, consumers' choice criteria are ranked according to relative importance. Choice alternatives are then evaluated on each criterion, starting with the most important one. An alternative is selected if it is judged superior on the most important criterion. If, however, as often is the case, two or more alternatives are judged equal on the most important criterion (i.e., there is a tie), then the consumer examines these alternatives on the next most important criterion, then on the next most important, and so on until a tie is broken.

The foregoing discussion should not be misinterpreted to mean that consumers invariably use one and only one choice heuristic. On the contrary, a more likely possibility, especially in high involvement decisions, is that **phased strategies** are used, that is, consumers use a combination of heuristics in sequence or in phase with one another.[40] Consider a personal computer purchase decision that Susan Allender, a self-employed person who operates a small direct mail company that specializes in home crafts, plans to make. Susan needs a computer to maintain a mailing list, to control inventory, to use for accounting purposes, and to use for word processing. After considerable search and research, she concludes she needs a computer manufactured by a reputable firm that has two disc drives, at least 64K RAM, a letter-quality printer, and a total price not exceeding $4,000.

Susan's initial phase (using a conjunctive heuristic) is to eliminate all models that fail to satisfy all of her minimal requirements. Remaining options are then evaluated attribute by attribute (using a compensatory heuristic) until only two models, the Apple IIe and the IBM-PC, remain as viable alternatives. Susan regards these models as best for her needs but is undecided which is better. After considerable additional deliberation, she reorders the relative weighting of choice criteria such that manufacturer reputability takes on added significance. Her choice, ultimately, is the IBM-PC, because she personally would rather pay a higher price to obtain assurance that her new acquisition will always be backed by a large, dependable firm.

Acting on the Basis of the Decision

It might seem that consumer choice behavior operates in a simple, lockstep fashion. This, however, is not necessarily the case. People do not always behave in a manner consistent with their preferences.[41] A major reason is the presence of events that disrupt, inhibit, or otherwise prevent a person from following through

---

[40]Bettman, *Information Processing Theory,* p. 184

[41]Martin Fishbein and Icek Ajzen, *Beliefs, Attitude, Intention, and Behavior: An Introduction to Theory and Research* (Reading, MA: Addison-Wesley, 1975).

on his or her intentions.[42] Take the case of the hypothetical computer purchaser described previously. She decided to purchase an IBM-PC; however, when she goes to a preferred retail outlet to make the purchase, she might find that it is out of stock, that it is higher priced than she had originally thought, or that the salespersons are not as knowledgeable as she had hoped. Any of these factors could result in her purchasing the Apple IIe, her second choice, or even some other computer.

Situational factors are even more prevalent in the case of low involvement consumer behavior. Stock-outs, price-offs, in-store promotions, and shopping at a store other than where one regularly shops are just some of the factors that lead to the purchase of brands that are not necessarily the most preferred and which would not be the predicted choice based on some heuristic, such as affect referral.

What all this ultimately means for marketing communications and promotional management is that the three modes of marketing (refer to Chapter 1) must be coordinated and integrated to achieve the desired consumer behavior, which is trial and repeat purchasing of the marketer's offering. To accomplish this goal, marketing communicators design a *basic offer* that is congruent with consumer wants, employ *persuasive communications* that consumers will process, and devise *promotional inducements* that will influence consumers to choose the marketer's offering at the point of purchase.

An Integrated CIP Model

The explanation of consumer information processing has, to this point, been limited to examining individual stages. It will be helpful now to look at CIP in its true form, i.e., as a process of interrelated and dynamic stages. Figure 3.6 presents the basic structure of a well-known and respected theory of consumer information processing.[43] The theory has the following seven elements:

1. Processing capacity
2. Motivation
3. Attention and perception
4. Information acquisition and evaluation
5. Use of memory
6. Decision processes
7. Consumption and learning

Processing Capacity

Processing capacity is inherently limited, and these limitations have important implications for all aspects of information processing. As depicted in Figure 3.6 (by the arrows flowing into and out of each construct or box), processing capacity

---

[42]For further reading on the role of situational variables, see Russell W. Belk, "Situational Variables and Consumer Behavior," *Journal of Consumer Research*, Vol. 2, December 1975, pp. 157–164.

[43]Bettman, *Information Processing Theory.* The following discussion borrows heavily from this source.

FIGURE 3.6 **An Integrated Theory of Consumer Information Processing**

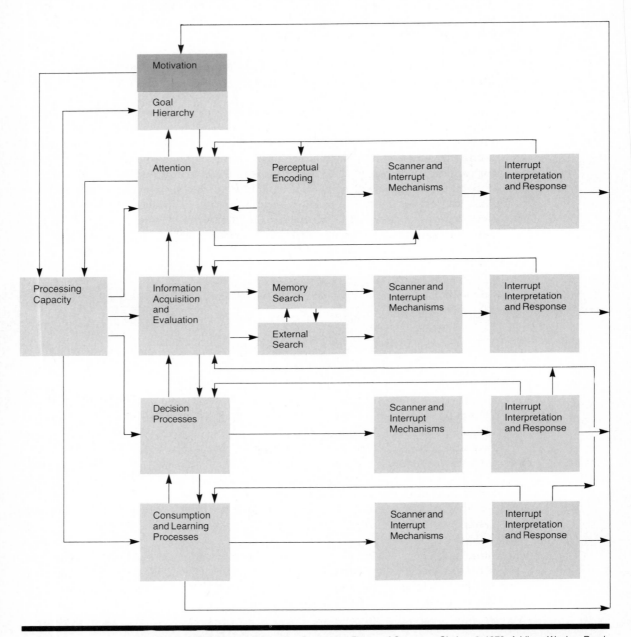

Source: James Bettman, *An Information Processing Theory of Consumer Choice,* © 1979, Addison-Wesley, Reading, Massachusetts. Page 17, Figure 3.7.

influences attention, information acquisition, decision processes, and so on. To return to the computer-purchasing example, because Susan Allender's capacity to process computer information is limited (due to job-related time pressures, limited knowledge of technical jargon, etc.), her information search will necessarily be restricted, her attention will be selective, and she will employ heuristics in making a decision.

Motivation

Motivation is a key component in any theory of human behavior. It naturally also plays a key role in the CIP model. Motivation is the catalyst that affects both the intensity and direction of behavior. Susan, in the example, is a highly motivated consumer who badly needs a computer for business purposes. Motivation, in a formal sense, controls a consumer's movement from some initial state toward some desired state. Susan's initial state is one of frustration. She dislikes having to conduct her mail-order business in an inefficient and unmechanized fashion. Her desired state is owning a computerized system that will improve her effectiveness and efficiency in conducting her small, but growing business.

To more fully understand the functioning of consumer motivation, two so-called control mechanisms need to be examined. They are a **hierarchy of goals** and an **interrupt mechanism and scanner.** A *goal* is "a specific state which, when attained, is instrumental in reaching the desired end state. This desired end state will be called the goal object. . . . Goals thus specify purposive behaviors whose enactment is necessary to progress toward the goal object."[44] A consumer's behavior, therefore, is guided by the hierarchy of goals existing at any time. In the computer illustration, the goal object, or desired end state, for Susan is the purchase and use of a personal computer. Susan, to accomplish this end state, must undertake various purposive behaviors (i.e., goals) that will enable her to make a satisfactory purchase decision. Because she is a newcomer to computers, an initial goal will be to determine which product properties should be evaluated. These, for example, might include memory capacity, unit portability, availability and cost of software packages, and purchase terms. Other purposive behaviors might be locating knowledgeable computer owners, identifying reputable dealers, evaluating alternative sources of finance, and perhaps even searching for ancillary items, such as appropriate furniture for the to-be-purchased computer.

Thus, consumers can use (undertake) a variety of purposive behaviors to achieve their desired goal states. This, however, does not mean that consumers, such as Susan, form a hierarchy of goals and then work methodically, in the fashion of an automaton, toward accomplishing every goal. On the contrary! Goals are subject to continual consumer evaluation and change. This concept is shown in Figure 3.6 as *scanning* and *interrupt* mechanisms. These mechanisms account for the consumer's adaptation to changing conditions by altering existing goals and

[44]Ibid., p. 19.

structuring new ones. Susan, for example, may have felt initially that any printer would suffice. But, after talking with salespersons and knowledgeable computer users, she realized that a letter-quality printer would be necessary.

Other Elements in Bettman's CIP Theory

The remaining elements of Bettman's theory are attention, information acquisition and evaluation, use of memory, decision processes, and consumption and learning. All of these elements were described in the previous discussion of individual information-processing stages. Using Susan Allender's computer purchase decision to illustrate the dynamic character and interrelations among these various stages, we trace her steps through Figure 3.6 from the attention stage on.

Susan, because she is highly motivated to make a wise computer choice, is receptive to information pertaining to microcomputers. She actively seeks information and carefully attends any items relevant to her decision. She encodes (interprets) information, possibly leading to the revision of extant goals, and this, perhaps, heightens her attention to subsequent information. The information Susan attends is evaluated against the knowledge and beliefs she already has stored in memory. For instance, learning from a business acquaintance about another computer model she has not previously considered would possibly activate search (external search in Figure 3.6) for additional information.

Susan will no doubt acquire a variety of information about different computer models and their properties and benefits. She eventually will possess a complete set of *beliefs* representing her perceptions of each computer model's suitability on each salient choice criterion. Her task, now, is to integrate her storehouse of knowledge and beliefs to arrive at a decision as to which of the various computer models to purchase, when to purchase, and where to purchase. Due to information-processing limitations, she will likely employ some simplifying heuristics involving a phased strategy using lexiocographic rules to eliminate some alternatives, followed by a compensatory rule to choose one specific computer model from the remaining set. The process does not end with purchase, however. As Susan uses her chosen computer and learns from this experience, she is likely to alter her goal hierarchy in subsequent decisions involving computers, computer ancillaries, and even unrelated products. Quite simply, the actual product usage is an important learning experience that has a major role in future purchase decisions.

Implications for Marketing Communications

This chapter has traced the fundamental elements of a detailed theory of consumer information processing. An understanding of these fundamentals is essential in formulating intelligent marketing communications. The following are four major implications for marketing:

1.   Because goal hierarchies direct information processing, it is crucial that marketing communicators understand the prototypical hierarchies of relevant market segments and then design communication programs compatible with

these hierarchies. Thus, companies should continuously monitor markets to stay on top of changes in consumer information needs and preferences.

2. Because there are inherent limitations in consumer processing capacity and because attention is selective, marketing communicators must carefully select media to reach the right consumers (i.e., those who are motivated or who can be motivated) and create innovative messages that attract consumers' attention—messages that otherwise may simply be lost among the competitive clutter.

3. Because memory plays an instrumental role in determining the specific meaning that consumers acquire from information processing, marketing communicators must use consumer beliefs and opinions toward the marketer's brand and toward competitive brands to develop the foundation for designing intelligent communications.

4. Because consumers use heuristics in making choice decisions, marketing communicators must design messages in concert with these heuristics. If, for example, consumers use a conjunctive decision rule in the first phase of evaluating alternatives, then marketing communicators must determine the relevant choice criteria to use in creating communication programs that inform consumers that the marketer's brand does indeed satisfy these criteria. The Adam Family Computer System provides an interesting example (Figure 3.7). Through comparison advertising, this ad attempts to convey the impression that the Adam computer meets or exceeds the minima for important product features (memory, word processing capability, printer, and so on) and that these features are part of Adam's standard package.

The preceding discussion has focused on consumers' information processing for an expensive, inherently risky, and high-involvement product. It is important to realize, however, that most consumer decisions involve routine, inexpensive, and low-involvement purchases. In such instances, motivation is restricted, processing capacity is limited (due to low motivation levels), and consumers, therefore, are less attentive to marketing communications and are more selective in what they comprehend and retain. The marketing communicator's task differs between high- and low-involvement products. In the former case, special emphasis is placed on providing the "right" information, whereas in the latter, much greater attention must be devoted to getting attention and creating brand awareness.

A Hedonic Perspective on Choice Behavior

A hedonic perspective is, as noted at the beginning of the chapter, an alternative view to the CIP framework, though the two are not necessarily mutually exclusive. Hirschman and Holbrook describe **hedonic consumption** as the consumer's multisensory images, fantasies, and emotional arousal elicited in using products.[45]

---

[45]Hirschman and Holbrook, "Hedonic Consumption," and Holbrook and Hirschman, "Experiential Aspects of Consumption."

FIGURE 3.7   **Matching Advertising Information with Consumers' Choice Criteria**

WHEN YOU COMPARE FEATURES AND PRICE THERE'S NO COMPARISON.

COMPARE*

The retail price for ADAM™ the COLECOVISION™ Family Computer System is the **total price** for the whole system.

With all other computer companies the base price is just the beginning.

ADAM COLECOVISION FAMILY COMPUTER SYSTEM	TEXAS INSTRUMENTS 99/4A	COMMODORE 64	ATARI® 800	APPLE® IIe	IBM® PERSONAL COMPUTER
Console with 80K RAM	Console with 16K RAM	Console with 64K RAM	Console with 48K RAM	Console with 64K RAM	Console with 64K RAM
INCLUDED: Mass memory storage drive with FASTRANSFER™ circuitry **INCLUDED:** SMARTWRITER™ word processing built in **INCLUDED:** "Letter-quality" daisy-wheel printer **INCLUDED:** 2 joystick game cursor controllers with built-in numeric keypads **INCLUDED:** Coleco's SMARTBASIC™ program **INCLUDED:** The Official BUCK ROGERS™ PLANET OF ZOOM™ arcade-quality video game	**EXTRA:** Expansion/interface box **EXTRA:** Extra Ram **EXTRA:** Printer interface **EXTRA:** Printer cable **EXTRA:** Daisy-wheel printer **EXTRA:** Mass memory drive **EXTRA:** Joysticks (pair) **EXTRA:** Mfg's. word processing software **EXTRA:** Hit arcade game	**EXTRA:** Printer interface **EXTRA:** Printer cable **EXTRA:** Daisy-wheel printer **EXTRA:** Mass memory drive **EXTRA:** Joysticks (pair) **EXTRA:** Mfg's. word processing software **EXTRA:** Hit arcade game	**EXTRA:** Letter quality printer **EXTRA:** Mass memory drive **EXTRA:** Joysticks (pair) **EXTRA:** Mfg's. word processing software **EXTRA:** Hit arcade game	**EXTRA:** Printer interface **EXTRA:** Printer cable **EXTRA:** Daisy-wheel printer **EXTRA:** Mass memory drive **EXTRA:** Joysticks (pair) **EXTRA:** Mfg's. word processing software **EXTRA:** Hit arcade game	**EXTRA:** Printer interface **EXTRA:** Printer cable **EXTRA:** Daisy-wheel printer **EXTRA:** Mass memory drive **EXTRA:** Joysticks (pair) **EXTRA:** Mfg's. word processing software **EXTRA:** Hit arcade game **EXTRA:** BASIC programming language

*Comparison information obtained by survey taken August 29, 1983.

For what most companies charge for a daisy wheel printer alone, Adam gives you an 80K computer, a word processor, a printer, a memory drive, a detachable professional quality keyboard, and a super game system. All in one package. Ready to use. The most incredible price/value package ever. Use the chart above when you go to buy Adam to compare what you'd have to spend for this package with any ordinary home computer.

And discover that now you can afford to command the powers of a *complete computer system* for the whole family: Adam.

THE COLECOVISION® FAMILY COMPUTER SYSTEM.

Source: Courtesy of Coleco Industries, Inc.

Products viewed from this perspective are more than mere objective entities (perfume, cars, sofas, etc.) and are, instead, *subjective symbols* representing love, pride, status, achievement, pleasure, and so forth.

People consume hedonic products based on the pursuit of fun, amusement, fantasy, arousal, sensory stimulation, and enjoyment.[46] Products most compatible with the hedonic perspective include the performing arts (opera, modern dance, etc.), the so-called plastic arts (photography, crafts), popular forms of entertainment (movies, rock concerts), fashion apparel, sporting events, leisure activities, and recreational pursuits (wind surfing, hang gliding, golf, tennis).[47]

From a marketing communications viewpoint, how does the hedonic consumption model differ from the CIP perspective? This question is best addressed by comparing these two views of consumer behavior. Holbrook and Hirschman performed such a comparison (see Figure 3.8).[48] Note that this framework links six major elements in the consumer behavior process: (1) *environmental inputs* (products, stimulus properties, and communication content) and (2) *consumer inputs* (resources, involvement, search, etc.) determine consumers' (3) *choice criteria,* which, through a (4) *learning process,* are incorporated into (5) an *intervening response system* consisting of cognition, affect, and behavior; the (6) *output consequences* of a present behavior are stored in memory (as cognition and affect) and play a role in future choice behavior. The model uses slash marks to distinguish between the CIP and hedonic perspectives. At each stage the CIP view is always on the left side of the slash mark, and the hedonic view is always on the right side. For example, the pertinent cognitive elements from a CIP perspective are memory, knowledge structure, and beliefs; whereas the subconscious, fantasies, and imagery are the relevant cognitions in the hedonic view.

The marketing communication differences between these two general views of consumer behavior should now be somewhat apparent. Whereas the communication of CIP-relevant products tends to emphasize verbal stimuli, which are designed to be processed analytically (left brain activity) and to affect consumers' beliefs and attitudes, the communication of hedonic-relevant products emphasizes nonverbal content and is intended to generate images, fantasies, and positive emotions and feelings. Thus, product consumption from the hedonic perspective results from the *anticipation* of having fun, fulfilling fantasies, receiving enjoyment, or having pleasurable feelings. Comparatively, product choice behavior from the CIP perspective is based on the thoughtful evaluation that the chosen alternative will be more functional and provide better results than will other alternatives.

A vivid contrast between the CIP and hedonic orientations is illustrated in the differences in the advertisements for the Adam computer (Figure 3.7) and the Parker Brothers' Monopoly game (Figure 3.9). The former ad uses verbal content in describing objective product features, with the apparent intent of convincing

[46]Hirschman and Holbrook, Ibid.

[47]Ibid., p. 91.

[48]Holbrook and Hirschman, "Hedonic Consumption," p. 133.

FIGURE 3.8   A Hedonic/Experiential Perspective of Consumer Choice Behavior

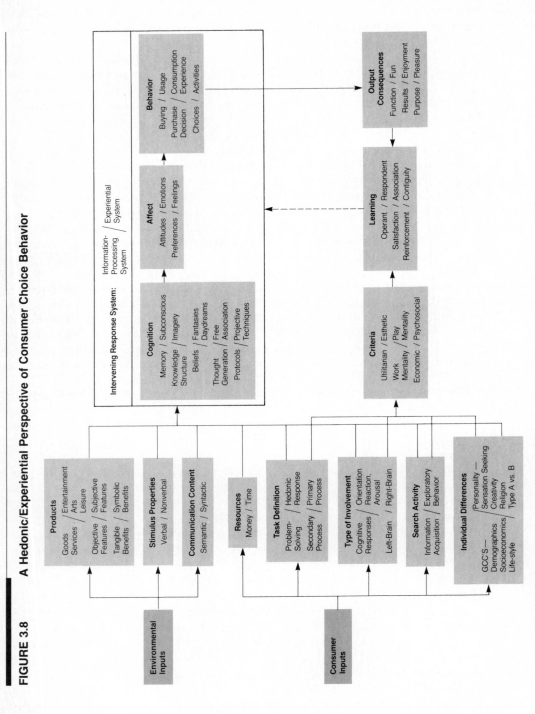

Note: The slash marks indicate a comparison between the information-processing view (left side) and the experiential perspective (right side).

*Source: Morris B. Holbrook and Elizabeth C. Hirschman, "The Experiential Aspects of Consumption: Consumer Fantasies, Feelings, and Fun," *Journal of Consumer Research*, Vol. 9, September 1982, p. 133. Reprinted with permission.*

FIGURE 3.9   **Example of Concrete Visualization in Advertising**

Source: Used with permission. Parker Brothers, Beverly, MA 01915.

consumers that Colecovision's Adam computer is a better buy than the Apple IIe, the IBM-PC, and other competitive models. The Monopoly ad shown in Figure 3.9 is actually the second page of a two-page magazine ad; the lead-in page (not shown in the figure) simply presents a montage of Parker Brothers' parlor games along with a single statement: "Parker Brothers' kind of fun brings families together." The accompanying pictorial (Figure 3.9) concretizes this theme by portraying a cast of rather old-fashioned, Norman Rockwell characters enjoying themselves playing Monopoly. This concrete visualization apparently intends to leave consumers with the impression that their families, too, will be brought together and have fun if they buy Monopoly or other Parker Brothers' games.

It is important to emphasize that the hedonic approach to marketing communications is *not* restricted to only the arts, entertainment, and leisure activities. Although the special character of these products is especially amenable to communications by a nonverbal, fantasy-feeling-fun orientation, this does not mean that more traditional, CIP-oriented products cannot also use an hedonic approach. For example, at present (circa 1984) there are signs that the advertising of home computers is becoming more hedonic in view of the inevitable trend toward interbrand homogeneity. Some home computer advertisers are emphasizing the role of the home computer as a vehicle for family entertainment; others are capitalizing on some parents' fantasies that a personal computer will transform their sons and daughters into outstanding students.

The prior discussion has emphasized advertising, but it should be apparent that the differences between CIP and hedonic views of consumer behavior apply as well to other forms of marketing communications, especially to personal selling. A salesperson may emphasize product features and tangible benefits in attempting to sell a product, or he or she may also attempt to convey the fun, fantasies, and pleasures that prospective customers can enjoy with product ownership. Successful salespersons employ both approaches and orient the dominant approach to the consumer's specific "hot buttons." That is, successful salespersons know how to *adapt* their presentations to different customers.

Finally, no one marketing communication approach, whether CIP or hedonically oriented, is effective in all instances. What works best depends upon the specific character and needs of the targeted market segment and upon the form of communication and marketing effort competitors undertake.

Summary

This chapter provides an introduction to the fundamentals of consumer choice behavior. Two relatively distinct perspectives of choice behavior are the consumer information processing (CIP) perspective and the hedonic, or experiential, approach. Proponents of the CIP approach view the consumer as an analytical, systematic, and logical decision maker. According to this perspective, consumers are motivated to achieve desired goal states. The CIP process involves attending, encoding, retaining, retrieving, and integrating information so that a person can achieve a suitable choice among consumption alternatives.

The hedonic, or experiential, perspective is an alternative to the CIP view. Supporters of this approach believe that consumer choice for many products results from the mere pursuit of fun, fantasy, and feeling. Therefore, some consumer behavior (such as in the consumption of the arts, popular forms of entertainment, and leisure activities) is based on emotional considerations rather than upon objective, functional, and economic factors.

The distinction between the CIP and hedonic views of consumer choice is an important one for marketing communications and promotion management. The techniques and creative strategies for affecting consumer choice behavior clearly are a function of the prevailing consumer orientation. Specific implications and appropriate strategies are emphasized throughout the chapter.

Discussion Questions

1. Describe the eight information processing stages.
2. Explain the mere exposure hypothesis.
3. Distinguish among involuntary, nonvoluntary, and voluntary attention.
4. Attention is said to be highly selective. What does this mean?

5. Describe four or five general factors that account for the selectivity of attention.

6. In what sense are marketing communication environments cluttered?

7. Explain each of the following related concepts: perceptual encoding, feature analysis, and active-synthesis.

8. Why do consumers selectively perceive, distort, and miscomprehend messages?

9. Distinguish among the three types of learning described in the chapter.

10. What is meant by "concretizing"?

11. What is "imagery"?

12. Explain the dual-coding theory.

13. What is a heuristic? Distinguish between compensatory and noncompensatory heuristics.

14. Distinguish between conjunctive and disjunctive choice heuristics.

15. What is a "phased" choice strategy?

16. What is a "goal hierarchy"?

17. What is the role of "scanner" and "interrupt" mechanisms in Bettman's integrated CIP theory?

18. What is the meaning of hedonic- or experiential-based choice behavior?

19. Is hedonic choice restricted to the arts and recreational and leisure pursuits?

Exercises

1. Review advertisements and provide three examples of ads that attempt to attract consumer attention via the use of intense and novel stimuli.

2. Provide specific illustrations of advertisements that attempt to facilitate consumer learning by establishing linkages between specific memory concepts or by attempting to establish entirely new linkages.

3. Interview a small sample of consumers and attempt to discover some of the generalizations that people have about products, stores, and other consumption objects.

4. Give examples of advertisements that attempt to promote mental imagery.

5. Provide several examples of both concrete and abstract visual advertisements.

6. Provide examples of how package designers use concrete visuals.

7. Describe a recent (within the past year) purchase decision you have made, and characterize it in terms of the decision heuristics you might have used.

8. Provide examples of advertisements that appear to be directed at CIP consumers and examples of ads directed at hedonic consumers.

CHAPTER 4

Attitudes and Persuasion in Marketing Communications

The previous chapter introduced the fundamentals of consumer behavior by examining two general models, consumer information processing and hedonic consumption, that provide a general overview of the forces which motivate and direct the consumer behavior process. The present chapter builds on these general frameworks and looks at two specific topics, attitudes and persuasion, that are fundamental to understanding the workings and intricacies of marketing communications and promotion management.

Attitudes and persuasion are closely related topics. To understand one requires an understanding of the other. Each topic is described in detail throughout the chapter, but making a basic distinction between the two should be helpful at this point. **Attitude** is a mental property of the consumer, whereas **persuasion** is an effort by a marketing communicator to influence the consumer's attitude and behavior in some manner.

The Nature and Role of Attitudes

Attitudes is one of the most extensively examined topics in the study of human behavior. The reason is simple: Understanding how people feel toward different objects (such as brands within a product category) makes it possible to predict and to influence behavior so that it is compatible with the communicator's interests.[1]

What Is an Attitude?

Psychologists and other students of human behavior refer to attitudes as hypothetical constructs. This means that scholars hypothesize the presence of a mental property, in this case attitude, which is presumed to exist but which has no readily observable physical presence. Attitudes cannot be seen, touched, heard, or smelled. Because attitudes cannot be observed, a variety of perspectives have developed over the years in attempting to describe what they are.[2] Fortunately, there is now widespread agreement that the term *attitude* should be used to refer *to a general and enduring positive or negative feeling about some person, object, or issue*.[3] "I like Yoplait yogurt," "I despise designer jeans," and "I love shopping at Marshall Field's in Chicago" are examples of consumer attitudes that express feelings toward different objects.

The preceding description of attitude focuses on feelings and evaluations or what is commonly referred to as the **affective** component of an attitude. Attitude theorists recognize two additional components, cognitive and behavioral.[4] The **cognitive** component refers to a person's knowledge and thoughts about an object or issue. The **behavioral** component (or what sometimes is also referred to as the **conative** component) represents one's behavioral tendency toward an object. In consumer behavior terms, the conative component represents a consumer's intention to purchase a specific item. Allport integrated these two components when formulating his classic definition: "Attitudes are learned predispositions to respond to an object or class of objects in a consistently favorable or unfavorable way."[5]

The cognitive, affective, and behavioral model is a tripartite model of attitudes. A clear progression is implied in this model. An individual becomes aware of an object, such as a new product, then acquires information and forms beliefs about the product's ability to satisfy consumption needs and desires (cognitive compo-

---

[1]Not all agree that the concept of attitudes is necessary. In fact, the so-called radical behaviorists regard attitudes and other purely hypothetical mental constructs to be of no value in predicting and controlling human behavior.

[2]A number of major theories of attitudes and attitude change processes have developed over the last half century. Seven particularly significant theories are reviewed in Richard E. Petty and John T. Cacioppo, *Attitudes and Persuasion: Classic and Contemporary Approaches* (Dubuque, Iowa: Wm. C. Brown Company, 1981).

[3]Ibid., p. 7.

[4]See, for example, Richard P. Bagozzi, Alice M. Tybout, C. Samuel Craig, and Brian Sternthal, "The Construct Validity of the Tripartite Classification of Attitudes," *Journal of Marketing Research,* Vol. 16, February 1979, pp. 88–95; Richard J. Lutz, "An Experimental Investigation of Causal Relations among Cognitions, Affect, and Behavioral Intention," *Journal of Consumer Research,* Vol. 3, March 1977, pp. 197–208.

[5]Gordon W. Allport, "Attitudes," in C. A. Murchinson (ed.), *A Handbook of Social Psychology,* (Worcester, Mass.: Clark University Press, 1935), pp. 798–844.

nent). Beliefs are integrated and evaluated, and feelings toward the product are developed (affective component). On the basis of these feelings, an *intention* is formed to purchase or not to purchase the new product (behavioral component). An attitude, then, is characterized by progression from "thinking," to "feeling," to "behaving."[6]

An illustration will help clarify the notion of progression in attitudes. Consider Jack's purchase of a Honda Accord that was described in the previous chapter. Jack and his wife knew precisely what they wanted in a new automobile: economy, reasonable passenger and luggage space, good resale value, and a smooth-shifting automatic transmission. They acquired a variety of information about the Honda Accord and other models from friends and acquaintances, from advertisements, and from their own shopping experiences. They formed beliefs about product features and about specific automobile models as a result of this information search and processing activity. These beliefs (representing the cognitive attitude component) led Jack and his wife to form specific feelings (affective component) about various automobile models. They liked the Toyota Camry but considered it a bit too expensive for their budget. They also liked the Ford Tempo, except for what they considered to be a rather jerky-shifting automatic transmission. Overall, their most positive affect was toward the Honda Accord, and their intention to purchase this model (behavioral component) finally materialized when they drove their new automobile from the Honda dealership.

Why Have Attitudes?

Why do people form attitudes? What role or functions do attitudes serve?[7] The preceding discussion intimated one fundamental function performed by attitudes, namely, *to serve as convenient summaries of consumers' beliefs* about different products, brands, stores, and other objects for consumption. Beyond this, attitudes perform a variety of other functions. Four are particularly well recognized: utilitarian, value-expressive, ego-defensive, and knowledge functions.[8]

Utilitarian Function   An attitude has utility for consumers by facilitating and simplifying decision making. Jack's belief that the Ford Tempo does not shift smoothly enables him to eliminate this model from further serious consideration.

---

[6]The view that this strict progression applies to all behavior and that cognition must necessarily precede affect is not uncontested. Various alternative "hierarchies of effect" have been postulated. For further discussion, see Michael L. Ray, "Marketing Communication and the Hierarchy of Effects," in P. Clarke (ed.), *New Models for Mass Communication Research* (Beverly Hills, Calif.: Sage Publications, 1973), pp. 147–175.

[7]Parts of the following discussion extend from similar treatments by Petty and Cacioppo, *Attitudes and Persuasion*, pp. 7–8, and by Henry Assael, *Consumer Behavior and Marketing Action* (Boston, Mass.: Kent Publishing Company, 1984), pp. 170–172.

[8]Daniel Katz, "The Functional Approach to the Study of Attitudes," *Public Opinion Quarterly,* Vol. 24, Summer 1960, pp. 163–204.

Marketing communicators direct many of their efforts at the utility function. For example, advertisers claim that only their brand has a certain desirable product feature; industrial sales representatives attempt to convince customers to purchase now before prices go up; and commercial banks advertise that consumers are entitled to a gift when opening a new account.

Value-Expressive Function

When holding a certain attitude allows a person to express an important value to others, the value-expressive function is served. For example, stating one's pleasure from attending symphonies and operas tells others that one has sophistication. Telling friends that you support Mothers Against Drunk Driving (MADD) might label you as a concerned and responsible person. Similarly, in a consumer context, shopping at certain stores may serve to identify a person as a discriminating dresser.

Appeals to the value-expressive function are common in marketing communications. Such appeals are often made in a subtle, oblique fashion rather than directly, as is more typical with appeals to the utilitarian function. For example, advertisers during the 1970s often portrayed female users of their products as superwomen—successful career women who also were shown to be caring mothers, loving wives, and charismatic entertainers. Automobile advertisers and salespeople routinely appeal to value expressiveness by emphasizing the prestige one will enjoy by buying their models.

Ego-Defensive Function

Attitudes that are held because they help protect people from unflattering truths about themselves serve the ego-defensive function. The heavy drinker protects himself by holding the view that "I'm just a social drinker." "I'm not overweight, I just have a large frame" is another illustration of the ego-defensive function.

Advertisers of self-help and personal care products are especially likely to appeal to ego defense. For example, one advertiser probably had this in mind when introducing the catchy theme "You're not getting older, you're getting better."

Knowledge Function

A final function that attitudes perform is to assist people in organizing knowledge and in understanding events and people around them better. For example, people who dislike the Soviet Union and its leaders probably had little difficulty understanding why the Korean airliner 007 was shot down over Russian territory in 1983. They might have reasoned that despicable leaders do despicable things. Consumers tend to follow thought patterns similar to that of the example, which partially explains why many consumers readily accept new products from respected companies. They reason that "they've always made good products, so this new one must also be good."

In summary, attitudes perform various useful functions for consumers. Attitudes also serve marketing communicators, who by diagnosing attitudes can understand why consumers behave as they do and can predict how consumers might behave in the future.

How Well Do Attitudes Predict Behavior?

The usefulness of the concept of attitude depends in large part on the ability to predict behavior from attitudes. Marketing communicators research consumers' attitudes with expectations of being able to predict accurately which brands consumers will purchase, in which stores they will shop, etc. Whether attitudes do in fact predict behavior accurately has been controversial in studying consumer behavior, as well as in the more general study of psychology.

In a major review of the psychology literature on attitude-behavior consistency, Wicker concluded that it is *unlikely* that attitudes are closely related to overt behavior.[9] Day and Deutscher, in a marketing context, examined the relationship between consumers' attitudes toward brands of major appliances and their actual brand choices and found that attitudes were *not* strongly predictive of which brands consumers chose.[10]

Do Wicker's conclusion and Day and Deutscher's findings mean that attitudes do not predict behavior? The answer is emphatically, "No!" Attitudes can and do offer reasonably accurate predictions of behavior under the right conditions. The real issue is, not *whether*, but *when* do attitudes predict behavior.[11] Accurate prediction depends on two major factors: appropriate measurement and choice of the proper behavior to study.

Measurement Considerations A fundamental problem in much attitude research has been invalid data resulting from measuring attitudes and behavior *at different levels of specificity.* Four important components of any overt behavior must be considered in order to obtain accurate measures: a target, an action, a context, and a time.[12] For example, when a college senior buys a conservative, navy blue suit for the purpose of job interviewing, "buying" is the *action* (rather than borrowing, stealing, etc.); the *target* is "a navy blue suit"; the *context* is "for the purpose of job interviewing"; and the *time* is "during the senior year in college."

Attitude will not, however, predict behavior unless both are measured at the same level of specificity. If at the beginning of the semester someone asked,

---

[9]A. W. Wicker, "Attitudes Versus Actions: The Relationship of Verbal and Overt Behavioral Responses to Attitude Objects," *Journal of Social Issues,* Vol. 25, Autumn 1969, pp. 41–78.

[10]George S. Day and Terry Deutscher, "Attitudinal Predictions of Choices of Major Appliance Brands," *Journal of Marketing Research,* Vol. 19, May 1982, pp. 192–198.

[11]D. T. Regan and R. H. Fazio, "On the Consistency between Attitudes and Behavior: Look to the Method of Attitude Formation," *Journal of Experimental Psychology,* Vol. 13, 1977, pp. 28–45; see also Deborah L. Roedder, Brian Sternthal, and Bobby J. Calder, "Attitude-Behavior Consistency in Children's Responses to Television Advertising," *Journal of Marketing Research,* Vol. 20, November 1983, pp. 337–349.

[12]Martin Fishbein and Icek Ajzen, *Belief, Attitude, Intention, and Behavior: An Introduction to Theory and Research* (Reading, Mass.: Addison-Wesley, 1975).

"What's your opinion of navy blue suits?" your response might have been, "I don't like suits very much and navy blue suits are particularly boring." If, then, at a later date you actually purchased a navy blue suit, your behavior would be inconsistent with your earlier-announced attitude toward blue suits. This inconsistency would be because the measure of your attitude was too general and lacked specificity. Your expressed attitude would likely have been considerably different if the question had been, "What is your opinion of buying a navy blue suit for job interviewing this semester?" Because this question is specific with regard to the purpose and timing of purchasing a navy blue suit, your response would probably reflect a somewhat favorable attitude (because you know that navy blue suits are generally regarded as appropriate attire for job interviewing). This response would then be consistent with your subsequent act of purchasing a navy blue suit.

Thus, in order to predict a specific behavior accurately, the attitude measurement must also be specific with regard to action, target, context, and time. The strength of the attitude-behavior relationship is strengthened appreciably when these requirements are satisfied.

Type of Behavior   Another determinant of attitude-behavior consistency is the type of behavior to be predicted. Type of behavior refers to whether the behavior is based on direct or indirect experience with the attitude object. *Direct experience* is gained by the consumer when he or she has actually tried or used the attitude object, whereas *indirect experience* refers to any product knowledge or experience short of actual use. A series of psychological experiments by Fazio and colleagues have demonstrated that attitudes based on direct experience predict behavior better than do attitudes based on indirect experience.[13]

In one study Regan and Fazio tried to predict the proportion of time people would play with different puzzles based on their attitudes toward the puzzles. One group of subjects (the direct-experience group) played with sample puzzles prior to indicating their attitudes toward the puzzles. Another group (the indirect-experience group) received verbal descriptions of the various puzzles but did not actually play with them prior to revealing their attitudes. Both groups, after indicating their attitudes, then played with the various puzzles. The researchers recorded subjects' puzzle-playing behavior in terms of the proportion of time they devoted to each puzzle. The correlation between attitudes and behavior was predictably higher for the direct-experience group ($r = .53$) than for the indirect-experience group ($r = .21$).[14]

Smith and Swinyard tested these same notions in a more realistic marketing study. These researchers performed an experiment with undergraduate business

---

[13]R. H. Fazio, M. P. Zanna, and J. Cooper, "Direct Experience and Attitude-Behavior Consistency: An Information Processing Analysis," *Personality and Social Psychology Bulletin,* Vol. 4, Winter 1978, pp. 48–52; R. H. Fazio and M. P. Zanna, "On the Predictive Validity of Attitudes: The Roles of Direct Experience and Confidence," *Journal of Personality,* Vol. 46, June 1977, pp. 228–243.

[14]Regan and Fazio, "On the Consistency between Attitudes and Behavior."

students by studying a new (to the study region) snack food item (a cheese-filled pretzel) as the experimental product. The researchers divided students into two groups: a direct-experience group, which actually sampled the pretzels, and an indirect-experience group, which simply read an advertisement about the pretzels. In concert with the results from Regan and Fazio's research, Smith and Swinyard also found considerably higher levels of attitude-behavior consistency for the direct-experience subjects than for the indirect-experience subjects.[15]

In sum, the most notable conclusion from the research findings cited and from the prior discussion on measurement issues is that attitudes can and do predict behavior reasonably accurately *under the appropriate conditions:* Measurements of attitudes must be as specific as the behavior being predicted, and consumers must have direct rather than indirect behavioral experience with the attitude object.

Persuasion in Marketing Communications

Persuasion is the essence of marketing communications. Salespeople attempt to convince customers to purchase one product rather than another; advertisers appeal to consumers' fantasies and feelings and attempt to create desired images for their brands; manufacturers use coupons, samples, rebates, and other devices to induce consumers to try their products and to purchase now rather than later. All these persuasive efforts are directed at influencing attitudes—with particular emphasis targeted at the cognitive attitude component in some instances (such as with new product introductions), at the affective component on other occasions (such as in the case of image-oriented advertising), and at the behavioral component at other times (such as when using samples and other sales promotion devices).

Fundamentals of Persuasion

Five sets of factors are fundamental in the persuasion process: message arguments, peripheral cues, communication modality, receiver involvement, and receiver's initial position.

Message Arguments The *strength or quality of message arguments* is often the major determinant of whether and to what extent persuasion occurs. Consumers are much more likely to be persuaded by convincing and believable messages than by weak arguments. It may seem strange, then, that much advertising fails to present substantive information or compelling arguments. The reason this is so is that the majority of advertising, particularly television commercials, is for product

---

[15]Robert E. Smith and William R. Swinyard, "Attitude-Behavior Consistency: The Impact of Product Trial Versus Advertising," *Journal of Marketing Research,* Vol. 20, August 1983, pp. 257–267.

categories (e.g., soft drinks, detergents) in which interbrand differences are modest or virtually nonexistent.[16]

Peripheral Cues   The second major determinant of persuasion is message cues that are peripheral to the primary message arguments. These include such elements as the message source (e.g., a celebrity endorser), background music, scenery, and graphics. As will be explained in a later section, these cues, under certain conditions, play a more important role than message arguments in determining the outcome of a persuasive effort.

Communication Modality   The third important mediator of persuasion is the mode of communication, whether television, radio, or magazines. Research by Chaiken and Eagly is particularly impressive in highlighting the role of communication modality. Their experiments have shown that a likable communicator is more persuasive when presenting a message via broadcast media, whereas an unlikable source is more persuasive when the communication is written.[17] The reason for this phenomenon is that people pay closer attention to the quality of message arguments when processing written rather than broadcast messages.

Receiver Involvement   The personal relevance that a communication has for a receiver is a critical determinant of the extent and form of persuasion. Highly involved consumers (e.g., people who are in the market for an expensive, risky product) are motivated to process message arguments when exposed to marketing communications, whereas uninvolved consumers are likely to exert minimal attention to message arguments and to focus instead on peripheral cues. The upshot is that involved and uninvolved consumers are persuaded in entirely different ways. This will be detailed fully in the section in this chapter titled "Elaboration Likelihood Model."

Receiver's Initial Position   Scholars now agree that persuasion results not from external communication per se but from the self-generated thoughts, or **cognitive responses,** that consumers produce in response to persuasive efforts. Persuasion, in other words, is self-persuasion, or, stated poetically, "thinking makes it so."[18]

What are cognitive responses and why do they occur? People in response to persuasive attempts will, if involved in the communication issue, think about and

---

[16]L. Bogart, "Is All This Advertising Necessary?" *Journal of Advertising Research,* Vol. 18, October 1978, pp. 17–26.

[17]Shelly Chaiken and Alice H. Eagly, "Communication Modality as a Determinant of Persuasion: The Role of Communicator Salience," *Journal of Personality and Social Psychology,* Vol. 45, August 1983, pp. 241–256.

[18]Richard M. Perloff and Timothy C. Brock, " 'And Thinking Makes It So': Cognitive Responses to Persuasion," in M. E. Rioloff and G. R. Miller (eds.), *Persuasion: New Directions in Theory and Research* (Beverly Hills, Calif.: Sage Publications, 1980), pp. 67–99.

evaluate message claims and react mentally or subvocally. There are three general forms of reactions (cognitive responses): supportive arguments, counter arguments, and source derogations.[19] **Supportive arguments** occur when a receiver agrees with a message's arguments. **Counter arguments** and **source derogation** occur when the receiver challenges message claims (i.e., counterargues) and when the receiver disputes the source's ability to make such claims (i.e., derogates the source).

Whether a persuasive communication accomplishes its objectives depends on the balance of cognitive responses. If the combination of counter arguments and source derogations exceeds supportive arguments, it is unlikely that many consumers will be convinced to undertake the course of action advocated. Marketing communications may effectively persuade consumers, however, if more supportive than negative arguments are registered.

The Elaboration Likelihood Model: An Integrated Persuasion Theory

The various factors that play a role in the persuasion process have been presented. Now, thanks to the work of two social psychologists, how these factors combine into a coordinated explanation or theory of persuasion can be described. Petty and Cacioppo, in their Elaboration Likelihood Model (ELM), have postulated two different mechanisms by which persuasion occurs.[20] They refer to these as the "central" and "peripheral" routes to persuasion. Figure 4.1 displays the ELM and the two persuasion routes.

The *central route,* which is the left side of Figure 4.1, postulates that when a receiver is involved in a message topic and considers it to be personally relevant, he or she will be *motivated* to attend to and comprehend message arguments. If the receiver is then *able* to process the arguments (i.e., he or she has the intellectual capacity, is not distracted, etc.), *cognitive response mediation* will occur. The nature of the cognitive responses—whether predominantly favorable (support arguments), predominantly unfavorable (counterarguments and source derogations), or neutral—will lead to *cognitive structure changes,* which take the form of *enduring positive attitude change* or *enduring negative attitude change.* In the former case, the message accomplishes what the communicator intends, that is, *persuasion,* whereas in the latter it *boomerangs.*

In the event that some or all of the foregoing antecedents fail to occur (the receiver is unmotivated or unable to process information, does not engage in cognitive processing, etc.), the ELM provides for an alternative, *peripheral route* to persuasion, which is shown on the right side of Figure 4.1. In the peripheral route, persuasion occurs not as a result of a consumer's processing salient message argu-

---

[19]Peter L. Wright, "The Cognitive Processes Mediating the Acceptance of Advertising," *Journal of Marketing Research,* Vol. 10, February 1973, pp. 53–62.

[20]Petty and Cacioppo, *Attitudes and Persuasion.*

FIGURE 4.1   The Elaboration Likelihood Model of Persuasion

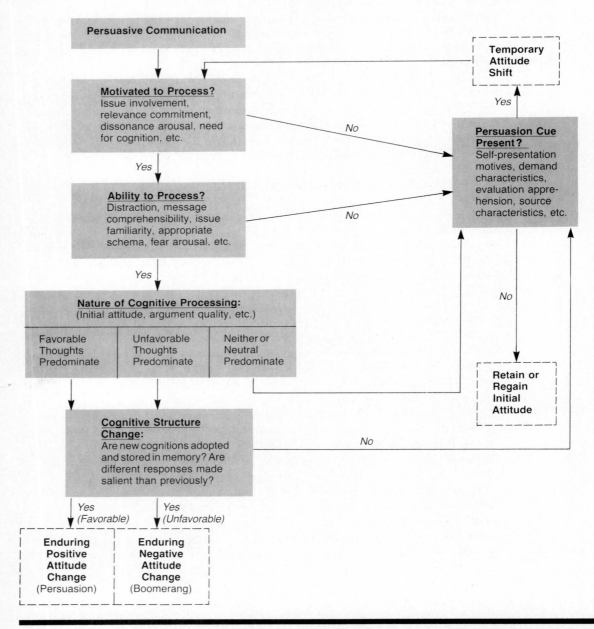

Source: Richard E. Petty and John T. Cacioppo, "Central and Peripheral Routes to Persuasion: Application to Advertising," in L. Percy and A. G. Woodside (eds.), *Advertising and Consumer Psychology* (Lexington, MA: Lexington Books), pp. 3–24.

ments but by virtue of his or her attending to relevant (though peripheral to the main message argument) persuasion cues. However, according to the ELM theory, people experience only *temporary* attitude change when persuaded via the peripheral route in comparison with the *enduring* change experienced under the central route.

Thus, in circumstances in which receivers think about and process message arguments (i.e., when the "elaboration likelihood" is high), persuasion may occur (if the message does not boomerang) and, if so, attitudes that are formed will be relatively enduring and somewhat resistant to change. Comparatively, when the elaboration likelihood is low (because the communication topic is not particularly relevant to the message recipient), attitude change may nevertheless occur (by virtue of receivers' processing peripheral cues) but will only be temporary unless consumers are exposed continuously to the peripheral cues.

Considerable empirical evidence has been marshalled in support of this two-route ELM theory of persuasion. A study by Petty, Cacioppo, and Schumann is illustrative.[21] These researchers performed an experiment by influencing subjects either to want to process message arguments (high involvement subjects) or not to want to (low involvement subjects). Four different advertisements were created for "Edge," a fictitious brand of disposable razor, by varying advertising messages in terms of argument quality (strong or weak) and type of endorsement (message endorsed either by celebrity athletes or by noncelebrity, average citizens). Example mock ads for Edge appear in Figure 4.2.

According to the ELM theory, the high involvement subjects should be motivated to process message arguments (i.e., claims made about Edge razor) and be persuaded by the quality of message arguments, that is, positive attitude change would be expected in the group presented with strong, believable arguments, and negative attitude change would be expected in the group exposed to weak, specious arguments. Low involvement subjects, by comparison, would be expected not to process message arguments but rather concentrate on the message source and be more persuaded by the celebrity than by the noncelebrity endorsers.

Experimental results (summarized in Table 4.1) were generally in accord with the ELM predictions. Specifically, the nature of the product endorser had a significant impact on product attitudes *only* under low involvement information-processing conditions. Argument quality had an impact on product attitudes under both low and high involvement, but the impact of argument quality on attitudes was significantly greater under high, rather than low, involvement. Thus, this study and others[22] support the proposition that different features of a marketing communication effort may be more or less effective, depending on receivers' information-processing involvement.

---

[21]Richard E. Petty, John T. Cacioppo, and David Schumann, "Central and Peripheral Routes to Advertising Effectiveness: The Moderating Role of Involvement," *Journal of Consumer Research,* Vol. 10, September 1983, pp. 135–146.

[22]See Petty, Cacioppo, and Schumann, "Central and Peripheral Routes," for discussion of other studies.

FIGURE 4.2   **Mock Advertisements from the Edge Razor Experiment**

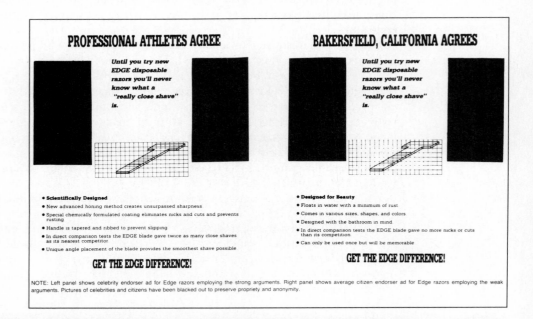

Source: Richard E. Petty, John T. Cacioppo, and David Schumann, "Central and Peripheral Routes to Advertising Effectiveness: The Moderating Role of Involvement," *Journal of Consumer Research,* Vol. 10, September 1983, p. 140. Reprinted by permission.

TABLE 4.1   **Summary of Results from Edge Razor Experiment: Means and Standard Deviations for Each Experimental Cell on the Attitude Index**

	Low Involvement		High Involvement	
	Weak Arguments	Strong Arguments	Weak Arguments	Strong Arguments
Citizen Endorser	−.12 (1.81)	.98 (1.52)	−1.10 (1.66)	1.98 (1.25)
Celebrity Endorser	1.21 (2.28)	1.85 (1.59)	−1.36 (1.65)	1.80 (1.07)

Note: Attitude scores represent the average rating of the product on three nine-point semantic differential scales anchored at -4 and $+4$ (bad–good, unsatisfactory–satisfactory, and unfavorable–favorable). Standard deviations are in parentheses.
Source: R. E. Petty, J. T. Cacioppo, and D. Schumann, "Central and Peripheral Routes to Advertising Effectiveness: The Moderating Role of Involvement," *Journal of Consumer Research,* Vol. 10, September 1983, p. 141.

Additional Perspectives on Persuasion

The Elaboration Likelihood Model is a general persuasion theory. However, various special-purpose theories have also captured the attention of consumer behavior researchers and marketing communication researchers. The theory of reasoned action and the attitude-toward-the-ad model are particularly prominent perspectives.

The Theory of Reasoned Action

Fishbein and Ajzen's theory of reasoned action proposes that much human behavior is planned, systematic, reasoned, and under conscious control.[23] *Personal attitudes* and *normative influences* constitute the theory's two primary determinants of behavior. Three central equations conveniently summarize the theory:

$$B \sim B1 = Aact + SN \tag{4.1}$$

$$Aact = \sum_{n} b_i e_i \tag{4.2}$$

$$SN = \sum_{k} NB_j MC_j \tag{4.3}$$

where:

$\quad$ B = overt behavior
$\quad$ BI = behavioral intention
Aact = attitude toward performing a specific behavior
$\quad$ SN = subjective norm (i.e., internalization of what others think one should do)
$\quad$ b_i = the expectation or belief that the performance of behavior B will lead to desired outcome i
$\quad$ e_i = the positive or negative evaluation of the ith outcome
$\quad$ NB_j = the expectation that performance of behavior B is desired or expected by an important person or referent group j.
$\quad$ MC_j = the motivation to comply with the jth person or group
$\quad$ n,k = the number of salient outcomes and groups, respectively

An illustration should help in understanding the preceding equations and their constituent elements. Consider the decision facing Julie, a senior marketing major, who is in the process of deciding where to attend graduate school for her MBA degree. She has narrowed the choice to two universities: the major university in her home state and a prestigious private university located nearly 1,000 miles from her home. Thus, the behavior in question—B—is the choice between two universities.

---

[23]Fishbein and Ajzen, *Belief, Attitude, Intention, and Behavior.*

To predict her choice, it is necessary to first know what she considers to be the salient outcomes or consequences of her decision and whose opinions she considers important. Table 4.2 presents a hypothetical set of salient outcomes and referents along with Julie's personal beliefs (b_i) and evaluations (e_i) pertaining to the n outcomes and her normative beliefs (NB_j) and motivations to comply (MC_j) with the k salient referents.

As shown in Table 4.2, the outcomes that Julie considers most salient in choosing an MBA program are, in descending order of importance, quality of education, job opportunities upon completion of her degree, cost, distance from home, and recreational/cultural opportunities during the period of her education. Her expectations and evaluations of each of these are shown in Table 4.2, along with her normative beliefs and motivations to comply with three salient referents: parents, potential employers, and friends.

Julie's total scores for Aact, SN, and their sum are displayed at the bottom of Table 4.2. By making the simplifying assumption that Aact and SN are equally im-

---

TABLE 4.2   **Application of the Theory of Reasoned Action: Hypothetical University Choice Process**

Salient Choice Outcomes	Evaluation (e_i)[a]	Beliefs (b_i)[b] State U.	Private U.
High quality of education	+5	+1	+3
Favorable job opportunities	+5	0	+3
Low cost	+3	+2	−2
Close to home	+2	+3	−2
Ample recreational/cultural opportunities	+2	+1	+3
$\sum_{i=1}^{n} b_i e_i =$		+19	+26

Salient Choice Referents	Motivations to Comply (MC_j)[c]	Normative Beliefs (NB_j)[d] State U.	Private U.
Parents	+4	+3	−1
Potential employers	+5	0	+3
Friends	+3	+2	+1
$\sum_{j=1}^{k} NB_j MC_j =$		+18	+14
$\sum_{i=1}^{n} b_i e_i + \sum_{j=1}^{k} NB_j MC_j =$		+37	+40

[a]Higher scores indicate more favorable evaluations. For example, quality of education (+5) is more important to Julie in choosing a university than is distance from home (+2).

[b]Positive scores indicate Julie's belief that a university will deliver a salient outcome, whereas negative scores indicate her belief that a university is undesirable with respect to some outcome. For example, Julie perceives Private U. to be more costly.

[c]Higher scores indicate stronger motivations to comply with a referent. Julie is, for example, more strongly motivated to comply with her parents' beliefs than with those of her friends.

[d]Positive scores indicate Julie's normative belief that a referent thinks she should attend a particular university, whereas negative scores evidence her belief that a referent opposes her attending a university.

portant, it can be surmised from the data that Julie will choose to attend the prestigious private university rather than her state institution. Although she had solid reasons for wanting to stay closer to home (because of parental pressure, friendships, and cost considerations), the overriding importance of educational quality and future job opportunities dictated that she travel away from home and attend the private university.

Attitude Change Strategies   The theory of reasoned action offers marketing communicators various suggestions for influencing and persuading consumers. Three strategies for changing the attitude component, Aact, are suggested:[24]

Change an Existing Belief   Marketing communicators continually attempt to alter consumer perceptions about their brands on one or more product attributes. In terms of the model elements in the theory of reasoned action, this amounts to changing consumers' *beliefs.* Consider, for example, the advertising campaign by one soft drink marketer, Seven-Up, which promotes the claim that Seven-Up contains no caffeine. The intent is to influence consumers to perceive Seven-Up favorably and to perceive other soft drinks unfavorably because they, unlike Seven-Up, *do* contain caffeine.

Change an Existing Evaluation   This strategy attempts to influence consumers to reassess the value of a particular attribute and to alter their *evaluations* of the attribute's value. Seven-Up, for example, wants consumers to evaluate the presence of caffeine in cola drinks negatively and value its absence in Seven-Up positively.

Add a New Attribute   A third strategy is to get consumers to add an entirely new product attribute into their cognitive structures. This attribute, of course, would be one on which the marketer's product fares especially well. The Seven-Up campaign also typifies this strategy because the first task, before attempting to influence consumer beliefs or evaluations, is to encourage consumers to think first about caffeine as a relevant consideration when selecting a soft drink.

Marketing communicators, in addition to influencing consumer behavior by strategies directed at changing consumers' attitudes, also appeal to normative influences, the other major determinant of behavior. Changes in consumers' normative structure elements (i.e., normative beliefs and motivations to comply) may lead to changes in their behavior. Marketers have limited ability, in most instances, to influence consumers' subjective norms, but this does not discourage marketing communicators from attempting to do so. Advertising campaigns directed at deleterious behaviors (e.g., smoking) often appeal to an individual's sense of concern for what impact his or her behavior may have on others. Advertisers also make

[24]Richard J. Lutz, "Changing Brand Attitudes through Modification of Cognitive Structure," *Journal of Consumer Research,* Vol. 1, March 1975, pp. 49–59.

frequent attempts to show how their products will enhance the consumer's status in the eyes of important referents.

A prime example is an advertising campaign during the mid-1970s for a moderately luxurious American automobile. The central advertising theme was beautiful in its simplicity, "If your friends could only see you now." This campaign evidently was targeted at socially and geographically mobile achievers who had achieved some success in life and who were being reminded by the advertiser to demonstrate their success to old friends (those who apparently could not "see you now") by purchasing the advertised automobile.

Attitude-toward-the-Ad Model

Implicit in the foregoing discussion is the idea that marketing communicators persuade consumers by effecting changes in their cognitive elements, i.e., beliefs and evaluations. Emotional conditioning is, however, another persuasion mechanism, according to the attitude-toward-the-ad model of communications. Emotional conditioning is a special case of classical conditioning, which repeatedly pairs an unconditioned stimulus with a to-be conditioned stimulus until the latter evokes nearly the same response as the former. In an advertising context, emotional conditioning involves associating the advertised brand with an emotionally arousing situation, a joyous family gathering, an innocent romantic encounter, an exciting and enjoyable recreational activity, etc., with expectations that the advertised brand may eventually evoke some of the same positive emotions that are elicited by the emotionally arousing ad.[25]

Advertisers, by virtue of their frequent use of emotional conditioning, consider attitude-toward-the-ad advertising to be an effective form of persuasion. Researchers have provided evidence that supports the role of emotional conditioning in advertising. Mitchell and Olson paired advertisements for fictional brands of facial tissues with either positively evaluated visual stimuli (e.g., a kitten) or a neutrally evaluated visual stimulus (an abstract painting). Results revealed that the brands associated with the positively evaluated visual stimuli generated significantly more positive brand attitudes than did the brands associated with the neutral visual stimulus.[26]

Research by Gorn provides additional support for the role of classical conditioning.[27] Experimental subjects were informed that an advertising agency was trying to select music (the unconditioned stimulus) for use in a commercial for a ballpoint pen (the to-be conditioned stimulus). Subjects then listened to music while they viewed slides of the pen. The positive unconditioned stimulus for half the

---

[25]For more discussion of classical conditioning in advertising, see John R. Rossiter and Larry Percy, "Attitude Change through Visual Imagery in Advertising," *Journal of Advertising,* Vol. 9, No. 2, 1980, pp. 10–17.

[26]Andrew A. Mitchell and Jerry C. Olson, "Are Product Attribute Beliefs the Only Mediator of Advertising Effects on Brand Attitude?" *Journal of Marketing Research,* Vol. 18, August 1981, pp. 318–332.

[27]Gerald J. Gorn, "The Effects of Music in Advertising on Choice Behavior: A Classical Conditioning Approach," *Journal of Marketing,* Vol. 46, Winter 1982, pp. 94–101.

subjects was music from the movie *Grease,* and the negative unconditioned stimulus for the other subjects was classical Indian music. The simple association between music (the unconditioned stimulus) and the advertised pen (conditioned stimulus) affected product preference—nearly 80 percent of the experimental subjects exposed to the positively valenced *Grease* music chose the advertised pen, whereas only 30 percent of the subjects exposed to the negatively valenced Indian music chose the advertised pen.[28]

Changing Preferences

Marketing communicators, as discussed throughout this chapter, engage in persuasive efforts with hopes of effecting changes in consumers' attitudes. The ultimate objective is to influence consumers to prefer the marketer's offering over competitive alternatives, but what exactly is a preference, how are preferences formed, and how can they be changed?

The Nature and Formation of Preferences

Preference is a notion used routinely by all of us in casual, day-to-day conversations. "I prefer Wendy's hamburgers," "I prefer jazz," and "I prefer the Washington Redskins to win the Superbowl" are some typical preferences used in daily language. Behavioral scientists have a meaning for *preference* that is similar to its common usage. According to one authority, "A preference is a behavioral tendency that exhibits itself not so much in what the individual thinks or says about the object, but how s/he acts toward it. Does s/he take it, does s/he approach it, does s/he buy it, does s/he marry it?"[29] Preferences are, in the final analysis, behavioral phenomena.[30] Proof of preferences is in an act rather than a thought.

Scholars and marketing practitioners have been intrigued for years with the question, How are preferences formed? Various explanations have been offered, but currently preferences are thought to have basis *both in cognition and in affect.* **Cognitive-based preference** means that a consumer prefers a particular consumption object because he or she believes that that object is best able to satisfy his or her consumption needs. The theory of reasoned action, presented previously, presumes a cognitive basis for preferences. Julie, in an earlier example, chose the prestigious private university over her state university because she per-

[28]A caveat is in order. Although Mitchell and Olson's experiment and Gorn's experiment both appear to support a classical conditioning explanation, other theories may also explain the results or the results may be biased by the experimental methods. For more discussion on these points, see the discussions by Chris T. Allen and Thomas J. Madden, "Examining the Link between Attitude towards an Ad and Brand Attitude: A Classical Conditioning Approach," unpublished working paper, University of Massachusetts, September 1983; and Julie A. Edell and Marian C. Burke, "The Moderating Effect of Attitude toward an Ad on Ad Effectiveness under Different Processing Conditions," in Thomas Kinnear (ed.), *Advances in Consumer Research,* Vol. 11 (Provo, Utah: Association for Consumer Research, 1984).

[29]Robert B. Zajonc and Hazel Markus, "Affective and Cognitive Factors in Preferences," *Journal of Consumer Research,* Vol. 9, September 1982, pp. 123–131.

[30]Ibid.

ceived the private university as better able to satisfy her salient needs. Her preference was cognitively based.

Consumers also form preferences in the absence of true cognition. To appreciate this possibility, it is necessary to understand what is meant by **true cognition.** True cognition can be said to exist when a person is able and motivated to discriminate an object (e.g., microcomputers) in terms of meaningful dimensions or features and to form perceptions or beliefs about specific items (e.g., microcomputer brands) within the object category. However, people often form preferences for food items and other objects in the absence of true cognition.[31] Young children, for example, develop preferences for specific products before they are able to discriminate cognitively. Thus, consumer preferences are often **affectively based.**

Consider your own preferences for different products, brands, and stores. How many of these preferences were formed during years of early childhood socialization? Do you really prefer Brand X because its attributes have greater utility than Brand Y's (a cognitive-based rationale for your preference), or do you prefer Brand X because your parents may have preferred it (an affect-based rationale)?

Changing Preferences

Marketing communicators' efforts to change preferences by appealing to cognitions may meet with utter failure if the preferences have an affective basis. Furthermore, even when preference is primarily cognitive based, affect may become independent of the cognitive elements that were originally its basis.[32] The upshot is that the only way to influence some strongly held preferences may be by using methods that have direct emotional impact.[33] Many marketing practitioners evidently agree with this, because appeals to emotion are widespread, particularly in the case of television advertising.[34]

In addition to emotional conditioning, marketers use a variety of other methods to change consumer preferences that do not first require changing cognitions. These methods and procedures fall under the general heading **behavioral modification** and include various forms of classical and operant conditioning, modeling, and ecological modification.[35] **Shaping,** for example, is one application of behavior modification by which marketers attempt to shape certain behaviors through a process "of arranging conditions which change the probabilities of certain behav-

---

[31]Ibid.

[32]Ibid.

[33]Ibid.

[34]Terence A. Shimp, "Attitude toward the Brand as a Mediator of Consumer Brand Choice," *Journal of Advertising,* Vol. 10, No. 2, 1981, pp. 9–15.

[35]Walter R. Nord and J. Paul Peter, "A Behavior Modification Perspective on Marketing," *Journal of Marketing,* Vol. 44, Spring 1980, pp. 36–47; J. Paul Peter and Walter R. Nord, "A Clarification and Extension of Operant Conditioning Principles in Marketing," *Journal of Marketing,* Vol. 46, Summer 1982, pp. 102–107; Michael L. Rothschild and William C. Gaidis, "Behavioral Learning Theory: Its Relevance to Marketing and Promotions," *Journal of Marketing,* Vol. 45, Spring 1981, pp. 70–78.

iors not as ends in themselves, but to increase the probabilities of other behaviors."[36] Loss leaders, other special deals, and free trial periods are just some of the practices that marketers use to shape consumer behavior.[37]

Vicarious learning, or modeling, is another behavior modification principle that has widespread application in marketing. Vicarious learning attempts to change preferences and behavior "by having an individual observe the actions of others (i.e., models) and the consequences of those behaviors."[38] Television commercials frequently apply modeling techniques. An advertiser of automobile oil filters uses the theme, "You can pay me now or pay me later," and backs up the theme with visual scenes of the undesirable consequences of failing to change filters frequently enough. Producers of weight-loss products use modeling techniques to influence preferences by showing individuals receiving approbation from family and friends as a result of losing weight.

Summary

Marketing communication in its various forms (advertising, personal selling, and so on) involves efforts to persuade consumers by influencing their attitudes and ultimately their behavior. This chapter describes the role and nature of attitudes, the functions they serve, and the ways they can be changed.

The nature of persuasion is discussed with particular emphasis on the Elaboration Likelihood Model (ELM). Two alternative persuasion mechanisms are presented: A *central route,* which explains persuasion under conditions where the receiver is involved in the communication topic, and a *peripheral route,* which accounts for persuasion when receivers are not highly involved. The theory of reasoned action and the attitude-toward-the-ad model are presented as two specialized attitude theories, the former being more compatible with the central persuasion route and the latter more compatible with the peripheral persuasion route.

Marketing communicators strive to change consumer preferences, but changing preferences is difficult. Appeals to cognitions will often be unsuccessful in attempting to alter consumers' preferences because preferences often are affectively rather than cognitively based. For this reason, many marketing communicators use various principles of behavioral modification, such as emotional conditioning, shaping, and modeling to influence consumers' preferences and behavior.

Discussion Questions

1. What does it mean to say that an attitude is a hypothetical construct?
2. Distinguish among the cognitive, affective, and behavioral components of an attitude and provide examples of each using your attitude toward a personal career in selling and sales management.

[36]Nord and Peter, "A Behavior Modification Perspective," p. 39.
[37]Ibid.
[38]Ibid., p. 40.

3. Explain how your attitude toward a personal career in selling and sales management might serve utilitarian, value-expressive, ego-defensive, and knowledge functions.

4. Explain the roles of measurement considerations and type of behavior as determinants of the degree of attitude-behavior consistency.

5. Accurate attitude measurement requires specificity with regard to action, target, context, and time. Using a campus blood drive as the illustration, explain how each of these criteria applies.

6. Attitudes can accurately predict behavior when people have direct experience with the attitude object but not when the experience is indirect. Explain.

7. Distinguish between message arguments and peripheral cues as fundamental determinants of persuasion.

8. Receiver involvement is the fundamental determinant of whether people may be persuaded via a central route or via a peripheral route. Explain.

9. The theory of reasoned action contains two major determinants: personal attitudes and normative influences. What is the distinction between these two concepts?

10. There are three general strategies for changing attitudes. Explain each using a hotel chain as your illustration.

11. Explain the role of emotional conditioning in the attitude-toward-the-ad model.

12. What is the distinction between affective- and cognitive-based preferences?

13. Why are appeals to cognitions potentially ineffective when attempting to alter consumer preferences?

14. Explain what shaping and modeling mean.

Exercises

1. Review five magazine advertisements for food items and explain how each attempts to persuade consumers.

2. Construct a series of questions for measuring attitudes toward a product of your choosing which satisfy the "specificity requirements" described in the text.

3. Provide illustrations based on your personal observations of two marketing practices that apparently are intended to shape consumer behavior. Be specific.

4. Provide illustrations of three specific advertisements that employ vicarious learning (modeling) principles.

CHAPTER 5

Message Factors in Marketing Communications

This chapter examines three broad categories of message factors that play important roles in marketing communications: **message structure, message appeals,** and **message codes.** Where possible, the chapter identifies some generalizations about messages that may be applied to all forms of marketing communications, e.g., advertisements, sales messages, or publicity releases.

It is important to realize that generalizations are not the same as true principles (i.e., laws or axioms), which do not exist in marketing communications. Two factors account for this. First, because marketing communications and the buyer behavior that the communications are designed to influence are both exceedingly complex phenomena, it is difficult to arrive at straightforward explanations of how the phenomena operate. Second, because the scientific knowledge of marketing communications is based on experiments that have necessarily been conducted under somewhat artificial conditions, it is impossible to draw clear-cut inferences to applied marketing settings. Thus, the generalizations presented should be considered suggestive rather than definitive. It is well that we heed the advice of a philosopher, who said, "Seek simplicity and distrust it."[1]

---

[1]Abraham Kaplan, *The Conduct of Inquiry: Methodology for Behavioral Science* (New York: Intext Educational Publishers, Chandler Publishing Co., 1964).

Message Structure

Message structure refers to the organization of elements in a message. Three structural issues have particular relevance to marketing communicators: (1) message-sidedness, (2) order of presentation, and (3) conclusion drawing.

Message-Sidedness

All persuasive messages can be viewed in terms of whether message arguments are presented in a one-sided or two-sided fashion. A one-sided message is one in which the entire orientation is toward the communicator's position. The weaknesses in the communicator's position or the strengths of opposing views are never mentioned. A two-sided message, also called a **refutational argument,** is a message in which the communicator advocates one position but at the same time admits either (1) to some weaknesses in his or her stand or (2) to the strengths of an opposing view. Although a two-sided message presents both sides of an issue, the communicator's position prevails.

Is a message more persuasive when it presents one side or both sides of an issue? Although this question has been the subject of much investigation, the answer is not simple. Which approach is more effective depends upon three conditions that are related to the audience of the persuasive message: (1) the audience's initial opinion on the issue, (2) the audience's likelihood of exposure to subsequent counterarguments, and (3) the audience's educational level.

Initial Opinion   A one-sided argument is generally preferable if an audience already agrees with the communicator's position. If, however, the audience initially disagrees with the communicator's viewpoint, a two-sided argument will generally be more effective. A one-sided argument serves to strengthen or reinforce the prior beliefs of an audience who already *agrees* with the communicator's position; a two-sided message may place some doubts in their minds. For the audience who initially *disagrees* with the communicator, a two-sided message is more effective because it serves to enhance the communicator's credibility, that is, the communicator is perceived to be more objective and honest. The one-sided approach is more likely to be disregarded by the audience because it runs counter to what they already believe.

The research in support of the preceding generalizations is abundant. A classic study by Hovland, Lumsdaine, and Sheffield is illustrative.[2] These researchers asked three groups of World War II soldiers to estimate how long the fighting against Japan would continue after the defeat of Germany. After measuring the soldiers' initial opinions, the researchers exposed one group to a one-sided argument that

---

[2] C. I. Hovland, A. A. Lumsdaine, and F. D. Sheffield, "Studies in Social Psychology in World War II," *Experiments on Mass Communication*, Vol. 3, (Princeton, NJ: Princeton University Press, 1949), pp. 201–227.

claimed the fighting would continue for a long time due to Japan's military strengths. A second group was presented with a two-sided argument that took the same position but which noted some of Japan's weaknesses. The results supported the hypotheses that (1) soldiers who already believed that the war with Japan would be long were influenced more by the one-sided argument than the two-sided argument and (2) soldiers who held the belief that the war would be short were influenced more by the two-sided than the one-sided argument.

Exposure to Subsequent Counterarguments
If a communicator knows (or anticipates) that the audience will be exposed to subsequent counterclaims (i.e., persuasive arguments running counter to the communicator's position), a two-sided message is generally preferable.

By presenting a two-sided argument to an audience and then refuting the opposing arguments (i.e., product weaknesses or competitive strengths), a communicator can prepare receivers to discount subsequent counterarguments when they are made by competing communicators. A two-sided message, when combined with refutations of opposing arguments, makes it possible for a marketing communicator to *inoculate* an audience against a competitor's subsequent counterclaims.

Research by Szybillo and Heslin affords support for the inoculation role of two-sided refutational messages in a marketing context.[3] These researchers tested inoculation theory by examining the belief that "inflatable air bags should be installed as passive safety devices in all new cars." The objective was to determine how resistant to change subjects' beliefs would be when they were exposed to either a supportive advertisement or a refutational advertisement prior to being exposed to an attack advertisement that challenged the belief that air bags should be installed.

The supportive ad stated that the belief in question was obviously valid and then presented three arguments to support the belief. The refutational ad also stated that the belief in question was valid but, in addition, mentioned three counterarguments that might be used to attack air bags. The refutational advertisement then proceeded to refute the counterarguments. These counterarguments were identical to the ones that subsequently appeared in the attack advertisement.

The major study finding was that subjects exposed to the refutational ad were more resistant to persuasion than were subjects exposed to the supportive ad. That is, the beliefs of refutational subjects were *more resistant to change* from the attack advertisement than were the beliefs of the supportive subjects.

Research by Sawyer offers additional support for the role of refutational appeals in marketing communications.[4] He presented a series of slides of print ads to adult

---

[3]George J. Szybillo and Richard Heslin, "Resistance to Persuasion: Inoculation Theory in a Marketing Context," *Journal of Marketing Research,* Vol. 10, November 1973, pp. 396–403.

[4]Alan G. Sawyer, "The Effects of Repetition of Refutational and Supportive Advertising Appeals," *Journal of Marketing Research,* Vol. 10, February 1973, pp. 23–33.

female shoppers. The slides included either refutational or supportive advertisements for five products. Table 5.1 summarizes the experimental brands and the
various advertising claims.

Sawyer found that two-sided refutational ads were more effective (in terms of
influencing purchase intentions) than were one-sided supportive ads for those subjects who were users of the competitive brand, not users of the advertised brand.
The two-sided ads apparently served to enhance credibility, whereas the one-sided
appeals were viewed with suspicion. The results did not, however, find refutational
ads to be superior when the advertising recipients were users of only the advertised brand, nonusers of both the advertised and the competitive brand, or users
of both brands.

Thus, this study supports the notion that two-sided refutational ads are superior
to one-sided ads only when the audience is composed of users of competitive
brands. Of course, advertisers would be most likely to use two-sided appeals in
these instances, such as when introducing a new brand that is trying to attract
users from competitive brands.

**TABLE 5.1   Repeated Supportive and Refutational Advertisements
and Competitive Advertisements**

Repeated Ad	Supportive Appeal	Refutational Appeal	Competitive Ad
Bayer aspirin	"Bayer works wonders. Relax with Bayer . . . Bayer is 100% aspirin."	"Buffer it, square it, squeeze it, fizz it, . . . Nothing has ever improved aspirin. Bayer is 100% aspirin."	Bufferin. "Take aspirin. I did but I still have a headache. Next time take Bufferin."
Lava soap	"For real dirty hands, reach for Lava—the soap that can really clean . . ."	"Lava—world's worst bath soap! Lava users have revolted. They argue that Lava is not only a good soap for hands but for anything else too . . ."	Phase III. "Both a deodorant and a cream soap . . ."
Parker pen	"Just one could be all you ever need. At $1.98 it's the best pen value in the world. Up to 80,000 words . . ."	"Why pay $1.98 for a ballpoint pen? You can get them for 49¢, 69¢, or for free. The kind that skip, stutter, etc. and run out of ink. You pay $1.98 for a Parker, but you never have to buy another."	Scripto. "Only 49¢."
Renault automobiles	"Sales are climbing. Renault's new features and fine construction are paying off . . ."	"Sure, they save money but I wouldn't want to take a long trip in one. Foreign cars are easy on the wallet but hard on everything else. Renault is changing all that."	Volvo. "The car that won't self-destruct in two years."
Slender diet drink	"The same appetite that made you fat can make you thin. Slender is a bona fide meal."	"A 225-calorie meal is easy. A good-tasting 225-calorie meal is hard . . ."	Sego. "For the joy of a slender figure . . . Sego has more tasty flavors."

Source: Alan G. Sawyer, "The Effects of Repetition of Refutational and Supportive Advertising Appeals," *Journal of
Marketing Research,* Vol. 10, February 1973, p. 25.

Educational Level   A two-sided argument is more effective in changing opinions of better-educated people, whereas one-sided arguments are more effective for less-educated people. One explanation for this generalization is that better-educated individuals are capable of seeing both sides of an argument. By admitting to some weaknesses in an argument or by recognizing some of the strengths in the competing side, a communicator is perceived by the educated audience as more objective and reliable. Lesser-educated people, on the other hand, are more likely to accept what they are told and fail to see another side of an issue. They may even become a bit confused by two-sided arguments, wondering what it is the communicator wants them to believe.

Some Marketing Communications Implications   The question arises, Are the findings on message-sidedness transferrable from experimental settings to the marketplace? Faison addressed this question in an experiment involving nearly 500 vocational school, high school, and university students. Half of his subjects listened to one-sided radio commercials for an automobile, a gas range, and a floor wax. These commercials were conventional in the sense that they presented only positive product features. The remaining subjects listened to comparable two-sided commercials that presented some negative product features in addition to describing positive features. The following are some of the major conclusions from Faison's research:[5]

1.   In general, the two-sided advertising message was significantly more effective than the one-sided message for all three products.
2.   The two-sided advertisement was more effective for higher-educated subjects, whereas the one-sided advertisement was more effective for less-educated subjects.
3.   For subjects who used competing brands, the two-sided commercial was more effective. The one-sided argument was more effective, however, for those using the brand advertised in the commercial. The subject's brand use is similar to an audience's initial position on a topic.

Given the evidence on the conditions favoring either one-sided or two-sided messages, several marketing inferences can be drawn. First, where it is possible to segment consumers into loyal and nonloyal categories, a good strategy may be to direct one-sided ads toward the loyal group and two-sided ads toward the nonloyal group. Accessibility to each market segment may, however, pose a problem, particularly through the use of mass advertising. In some instances, however, this problem might be overcome by designing two versions of the sales message and mailing brochures to each segment.

In introducing a new brand, companies should seriously consider using two-sided ad campaigns because the new brand will eventually undergo retaliation from the counterarguments of competitive brands. A two-sided campaign could,

---

[5]Edmund W. J. Faison, "Effectiveness of One-Sided and Two-Sided Mass Communications in Advertising," *The Public Opinion Quarterly,* Vol. 25, Fall 1961, pp. 468–469.

thus, inoculate consumers against such counteradvertising. In a similar vein, sales representatives can also use the inoculation effects of a two-sided sales presentation by admitting to any minor weaknesses in their products.

In sum, there are legitimate reasons for using two-sided messages *under certain marketing communication conditions;* nevertheless, advertising agencies and their clients generally refuse to use two-sided ads. There seems to be an inherent fear in admitting to product weaknesses or competitor's strengths.

Comparative Advertising

Comparative advertising refers to the practice in which advertisers directly compare their products or brands with competitive offerings, typically claiming that the advertised item is superior in one or several important purchase considerations. Most comparative advertising is one-sided in the sense that the advertised brand is compared with one or more competitive brands in terms of product attributes for which the advertised brand is superior. Comparative advertising could, however, provide a convenient format for presenting a two-sided message. Figure 5.1 provides an illustration of a comparative advertisement.

Making comparative claims has always been practiced in the print advertising media, but it was not until the early 1970s that the television networks—at the urging of the Federal Trade Commission—revised their policies and permitted comparative advertising on television. Since then, all media have experienced a notable increase in the use of comparative advertising.

Advertisers face a number of difficult questions when deciding whether to use comparative advertising. The following quotation is a useful summary of the issues:

> *Is comparative advertising more effective than non-comparative advertising? How do comparative and non-comparative advertisements compare in terms of differential impact on awareness, believability, credibility, comprehension and advertiser identification? Do they differ with regard to effects on purchase intentions, brand preferences, purchase behavior? What are the effects of copy claim variation and substantiation on the performance of competitive advertisements? Is effectiveness influenced by factors such as prior brand loyalty or competitive position? Should companies use comparative advertisements and, if so, under what conditions?*[6]

Researchers have performed a number of comparative advertising studies since the mid-1970s. As usual, study findings are frequently inconclusive, and even contradictory at times. Lack of definitive results is to be expected, however, because advertising is a complex phenonmenon that varies greatly from situation to situa-

[6]Stephen B. Ash and Chow-Hou Wee, "Comparative Advertising: A Review with Implications for Further Research," in R. P. Bagozzi and A. M. Tybout (eds.), *Advances in Consumer Research,* Vol. 10 (Ann Arbor, MI: Association for Consumer Research, 1983), p. 374.

FIGURE 5.1   Illustration of a Comparative Advertisement

Ford Escort
spends less time in the air than these Japanese imports.

Ford Escort has been carefully engineered to help lower your cost of ownership by reducing required scheduled maintenance operations.

Number of Scheduled Maintenance Operations Required*	
Honda Accord	58
Nissan Sentra	54
Toyota Tercel	37
Ford Escort	20

The chart above shows just how well it stacks up against the leading Japanese imports.

Escort's efficient CVH engine will also do its part to help keep your operating costs way down. 37 EPA Est. MPG, 56 Est. HWY.**

So enjoy Ford Escort's economy and front-wheel drive. The smooth ride of its four-wheel independent suspension. The surprising room of its comfortable interior. And spend more time on the road, and less time up on the hoist.

The Best-Built American Cars.

Based on a consumer survey, Ford makes the best-built American cars. The survey measured owner-reported problems during the first three months of ownership of 1983 cars designed and built in the U.S.

Plus a Lifetime Service Guarantee.

Participating Ford Dealers stand behind their work in writing with a free Lifetime Service Guarantee. No other car companies' dealers, foreign or domestic, offer this kind of security. Nobody. See your participating Ford Dealer for details.

*For five years or 50,000 miles. Scheduled maintenance performed at regular intervals is, of course, essential. But don't forget that other vehicle checks (fluid levels, tire pressure, headlight alignment, etc.) also should be performed periodically by you or a qualified technician. Vehicles in severe use require additional maintenance.

**For comparison. Your mileage may vary depending on speed, trip length, weather. Actual highway mileage lower. Escort mileage applicable to sedans with FS engine and without power steering and A/C. Not available in California.

Have you driven a Ford... lately?   *Ford*

Get it together — Buckle up.

Source: Courtesy of Ford Motor Company; Agency: J. Walter Thompson.

tion in terms of executional elements, audience characteristics, media characteristics, and other factors. To repeat a theme presented at the beginning of this chapter, simple answers should not be expected, and in fact, they are rarely found. The research does, however, permit the following general observations:[7]

1. *Situational factors* (i.e., characteristics of audience, media, message, company, and product) play an important role in determining whether comparative advertising is more effective than noncomparative advertising. For example, Prasad found that perceived credibility ratings of claims of product superiority made in a comparative advertisement were significantly lower for subjects who had a prior preference for the comparison brand (i.e., the brand that the advertised brand was compared with) than for subjects who did not have a prior preference for the comparison brand.[8]

2. Comparative advertising may be more suitable for *low-involvement products* (e.g., convenience goods) than for durable goods, certain services, and other high-involvement products. This observation is speculative because the research support is limited, but it is not without logical support. Specifically, advertisements for low-involvement products have difficulty attracting the consumer's attention; therefore, comparative advertisements may be more effective for these products because the novelty of comparative advertising provides a means of attracting viewer attention. High-involvement products are, on the other hand, more concerned with conveying information and influencing purchase intentions than with merely attracting attention.

3. Comparative advertising may be particularly effective for promoting *new brands that possess distinct advantages relative to competitive brands.* One study found that comparative advertising is more effective for a new market entrant, whereas noncomparative advertising appears to be more effective for established brands.[9] When a new brand has a distinct advantage over competitive brands, comparative advertising provides a powerful method to convey this advantage. The only drawback is that users of the comparison brand may discount the new brand's claim of superiority.

4. Comparative advertising is likely to be more effective if its claims are *made to appear more credible.* There are various ways to accomplish this: (1) have an independent research organization support the superiority claims, (2) present impressive test results to back up the claims, (3) use a credible source as spokesperson, and (4) use a two-sided message presentation.

   A study by Etgar and Goodwin supports the use of a two-sided message. Etgar and Goodwin designed hypothetical experimental advertisements by

[7]The following comments are adapted from Ash and Chow-Hou, "Comparative Advertising," primarily p. 374.

[8]V. Kanti Prasad, "Communications Effectiveness of Comparative Advertising: A Laboratory Analysis," *Journal of Marketing Research,* Vol. 13, May 1976, pp. 128–137.

[9]Terence A. Shimp and David C. Dyer, "The Effects of Comparative Advertising Mediated by Market Position of Sponsoring Brand," *Journal of Advertising,* Vol. 7, No. 3, 1978, pp. 13–19.

manipulating both message-sidedness (one- or two-sided) and comparative format (comparison or noncomparison). One version claimed that the advertised brand was superior to three named competitors on all attributes, whereas the other version acknowledged that the advertised brand was less appealing on one or more attributes. The two-sided comparative ad generated a significantly more favorable attitude toward the new brand.[10]

5.   Because it is generally perceived by consumers to be more *interesting* than noncomparative advertising, comparative advertising may also be appropriate for established brands in which sales are static and noncomparative advertising has been ineffective.

6.   *Print media* appear to be better vehicles for comparative advertisements than broadcast media. Print lends itself to more thorough comparisons, and consumers have control over the time needed to process the large amount of information that is usually found in comparative ads.

Order of Presentation

Another important structural message issue is the order of presentation. The fundamental issue is the following: In presenting a one-sided message, which is the typical marketing communications message form, should the communicator present the most important points at the beginning, in the middle, or at the end of the message? To address this question, it is necessary to establish the working vocabulary for various order structures. First, a **climax order** is used when a communicator presents the strongest arguments at the end of the message. An **anticlimax order** exists when the most important points are presented at the beginning. A **pyramidal order** is used when the most important materials appear in the middle.

No one order of presentation stands out as best for every situation. Useful generalizations do emerge, however, when the level of audience interest in the communication topic is taken into account.

When an audience has a *low level of interest* in the material being presented, the *anticlimax order* tends to be the most effective order of presentation. When audience interest is low, the anticlimax order is superior because of the attention-gaining potential of presenting the stronger, more interesting material first. However, the communicator runs the risk of audience letdown by finishing with weak points.

When an audience has *a high level of interest* in the material being presented, the *climax order* tends to be most effective. Under conditions of high audience involvement, the message's emphasis can be directed at affecting attitudes rather than merely gaining attention. The climax order is therefore favored because the later points exceed "the expectations created by those presented initially"[11] and

---

[10]Michael Etgar and Stephen A. Goodwin, "One-Sided Versus Two-Sided Comparative Message Appeals for New Brand Introductions," *Journal of Consumer Research*, Vol. 8, March 1982, pp. 460–465.

[11]C. I. Hovland, I. L. Janis, and H. H. Kelley, *Communication and Persuasion* (New Haven: Yale University Press, 1953), p. 119.

the audience is likely to be left with a favorable opinion toward both the communicator and the communications topic.

The *pyramidal order* is the least effective order of presentation, regardless of the level of audience interest.

From the marketing communicator's perspective, for low-involvement products (i.e., those products that are typically inexpensive and involve little purchase risk) the strongest message arguments should typically be presented early in the message. For high-involvement products, the strongest arguments should be delayed until later in the message. It is unwise in any case to place strong arguments in the middle (pyramidal order) of a message. Material in the middle is attended to least, is the least well learned, and the least persuasive.

Drawing a Conclusion

Another question regarding the effective structural arrangement of a message is whether the communicator should draw an explicit conclusion for the audience or let the audience draw its own conclusion. Again, the answer is not a simple one and depends upon various factors. Experimental evidence suggests the following:[12]

1. In general, a communicator is more effective in changing opinions in the desired direction by drawing a conclusion for the audience.
2. For less-intelligent people, the communicator achieves greater opinion change in the desired direction by drawing a conclusion.
3. If an audience perceives that the communicator intends to manipulate them or has something to gain by stating a conclusion, or if the audience might feel that their intelligence is being questioned by having a conclusion drawn for them, the communicator would be more effective to leave the conclusion to the audience.
4. In a communication dealing with highly personal or ego-involving issues, the communicator may be more effective by allowing the audience to draw a conclusion themselves; for impersonal topics, stating a conclusion is generally more effective.
5. For highly complex issues, the communicator is more effective in stating a conclusion for the audience; for simple issues, the approach makes little difference.

The preceding statements are somewhat oversimplified, especially when several conditions may be present for one audience. Thus, the generalization made in number 1 provides the communicator with some guidance when he or she is unsure of audience characteristics.

---

[12]For examples see Hovland, Janis, and Kelley, *Communication and Persuasion,* pp. 103–105; C. I. Hovland and W. Mandell, "An Experimental Comparison of Conclusion-Drawing by the Communicator and by the Audience," *Journal of Abnormal and Social Psychology,* Vol. 47, July 1952, pp. 581–588; and D. L. Thistlethwaite, H. de Haan, and J. Kamenetzky, "The Effects of 'Directive' and 'Nondirective' Communication Procedures on Attitudes," *Journal of Abnormal and Social Psychology,* Vol. 51, July 1955, pp. 107–113.

In regard to the second generalization, the less-intelligent audience needs to have a conclusion stated because they will either draw no conclusion and wonder at the purpose of the message or make incorrect inferences.

The generalization presented in number 3 is composed of two ideas. First, if the audience perceives that the communicator has something to gain by arriving at a conclusion, their opinion may not change in the direction advocated by the communicator. If, on the other hand, the communicator leaves the conclusion to the audience, he or she may appear to have less manipulative intent and seem more credible.[13] If, by stating a conclusion, the communicator may insult the intelligence of the audience, the obvious action is to leave the conclusion to the audience. The communicator usually risks insulting an audience's intelligence when the intelligence level of the audience is high and when the issues and arguments are simple.

The fourth generalization concerns the kind of issues the communicator presents. Ego-involving issues or ones that are personal are likely to be closely examined by the audience, who will want to make up their own minds on the issue and not feel they are being directed to accept the communicator's opinion. When the topic is impersonal and the audience has low personal involvement, the audience is more likely to rely upon the communicator's stated conclusions.[14]

The last generalization also deals with the kind of issue involved in the communication. For complex issues the audience may require help in seeing what the implications are for a set of arguments. This is especially true for the less-intelligent audience, but in some instances it may also hold for the highly intelligent audience. A highly intelligent audience may need to have conclusions drawn for them on complex issues when their knowlege level is insufficient for the topic discussed. For example, a computer expert who talks to plant engineers about the superior technical attributes of a particular computer system over other available systems may find it advantageous to draw specific conclusions, even though he or she is addressing a highly intelligent group.

These generalizations must be applied cautiously by the marketer. Although drawing a conclusion is generally recognized as superior to leaving the conclusion to the audience, some writers believe that ambiguity in an advertisement permits the consumer to interpret the message and the product's benefits in a way that is personally most meaningful, thereby allowing the market to define itself. However, this approach runs the danger of consumers' inferring product benefits that the product cannot deliver, leading ultimately to consumer dissatisfaction.[15]

If a promotional message or the product itself is technically complex, it may be advisable to draw a conclusion for the consumer. Conclusion drawing would be warranted under these circumstances to help the consumer comprehend what the

---

[13]J. C. Freedman, J. M. Carlsmith, and D. O. Sears, *Social Psychology* (Englewood Cliffs, NJ: Prentice-Hall, Inc., 1970), p. 314.

[14]Hovland et al., *Communication and Persuasion,* pp. 103–105.

[15]Thomas S. Robertson, *Innovative Behavior and Communication* (New York: Holt, Rinehart, and Winston, Inc., 1971), p. 150.

product can do.[16] However, drawing conclusions may be counterproductive when the market is highly knowledgeable about a product and when the product or message is uncomplicated.

Message Appeals

Message appeal deals with what is said in a message. More specifically, it concerns the communicator's request for a favorable response toward the subject of the message. Several approaches that may be used to gain audience acceptance of the message request are described.

Fear Appeals

All of us have noticed companies that appeal to fear in their advertising. Mouthwashes, soaps, deodorants, toothpastes, and other products make us aware of the *social disapproval* we may suffer if our breath is not fresh, if our underarms are not dry, or if our teeth are not white. Also, some ads use appeals that are based on *physical danger.* Smoke detectors, smoking cigarettes, and driving under the influence of alcohol and other drugs are products and themes that advertisers use to induce fear in consumers. The logic of fear appeals is that fear will stimulate audience involvement in the message and promote message acceptance. Aside from the basic ethical issue of whether fear should be used at all, the fundamental issue for marketing communicators is determining how intense the fear presentation should be. A number of studies provide insight into this issue.

The earliest study on the use of fear appeals in persuasive communications was conducted by Janis and Feshbach in the early 1950s.[17] In their experiment three groups of high-school freshmen were exposed to messages on the subject of dental hygiene. Each group received a variation of the basic message concerning the consequences of poor dental hygiene. One group was subjected to a "strong fear appeal," a second group to a "moderate fear appeal," and a third group to a "minimal fear appeal."

The strong fear appeal made 71 references to unfavorable consequences that could result from improper dental hygiene. The strongest references were made to the possibility of cancer, blindness, and various mouth infections. The moderate appeal made 49 references to unfavorable consequences, and the minimal appeal included 18 references. The minimal appeal referred mainly to weaker consequences such as a "few cavities." In the strong and moderate appeals the verbal

---

[16]John Howard and Jagdish Sheth, *The Theory of Buyer Behavior* (New York: John Wiley and Sons, Inc., 1969), p. 383.

[17]I. Janis and S. Feshbach, "Effects of Fear-Arousing Communications," *Journal of Abnormal and Social Psychology,* Vol. 48, January 1953, pp. 78–92.

material was supplemented with highly vivid slides of tooth decay and mouth infection.

Janis and Feshbach found that the *minimal fear appeal* was the most effective approach in gaining conformity to the recommended actions. The generalization emerging from this study was that minimal fear appeals are more effective in persuading audiences than either strong or moderate fear appeals. By the 1960s, however, a number of additional studies were conducted, and many obtained findings that contradicted Janis and Feshbach's results.[18]

Ray and Wilkie performed an extensive review of the fear appeal literature with the objective of reconciling the apparently contradictory findings. They concluded that the differences in findings among the various studies was probably due to the use of varying degrees of fear appeals. Specifically, Ray and Wilkie suggested that the Janis and Feshbach study actually used three different degrees of strong fear appeals (although Janis and Feshbach claimed that they used one strong appeal, one moderate appeal, and one weak appeal) and that other studies used varying degrees of weaker fear appeals. Thus, the difference in research findings is probably attributable to the different definitions of high, moderate, and low fear appeals.[19]

Ray and Wilkie summarized the fear appeal literature by concluding:

> *Neither extremely strong nor very weak fear appeals are maximally effective. It seems that appeals at a somewhat moderate level of fear are best. A simple explanation for this might be that if an appeal is too weak, it just does not attract enough attention. If it is too strong, on the other hand, it may lead people to avoid the message or ignore the message's recommendations as being inadequate to the task of eliminating the feared event.*[20]

This conclusion is supported by additional research. For example, viewers tended to ignore a message by the Highway Traffic and Safety Commission that threatened people who did not wear seat belts with the possibility of severe safety consequences. However, viewer recall increased substantially when a milder seat belt campaign appealed to a person's family consciousness by claiming, "If you love me, you'll show me [by wearing your seat belt]."

Another example of modification of a fear appeal is that of Allstate Life Insurance, which sponsored a commercial in which a young man was shown playing ball with

---

[18]See L. Berkowitz and D. R. Cottingham, "The Interest Value and Relevance of Fear-Arousing Communication," *Journal of Abnormal and Social Psychology,* Vol. 60, No. 1, 1960, pp. 37–43; A. S. De Wolf and C. N. Governale, "Fear and Attitude Change," *Journal of Abnormal and Social Psychology,* Vol. 69, July 1964, pp. 119–123; H. Leventhal, R. P. Singer, and S. Jones, "Effects of Fear and Specificity of Recommendations upon Attitudes and Behavior," *Journal of Personality and Social Psychology,* Vol. 2, No. 1, 1965, pp. 20–29.

[19]Michael L. Ray and William L. Wilkie, "Fear: The Potential of an Appeal Neglected by Marketing," *Journal of Marketing,* Vol. 34, January 1970, pp. 54–62.

[20]Ibid., p. 55.

his son. The father's face was suddenly erased and a life insurance message given. This commercial received low levels of audience recall and was replaced by a milder version.[21]

Wright suggests that the optimum level of fear appeal depends on the *degree of relevance* a topic has for an audience—the greater the relevance, the lower the optimal level of fear. In other words, people who are highly involved in a topic can be motivated by a relatively small amount of fear, whereas a more intense level of fear is required to motivate uninvolved people. Wright also contends that the message content in fear-appeal advertisements should provide concrete recommendations that are timely, feasible, and understandable to the consumer. That is, the consumer must be able to take some action based on the appeal in order for the appeal to be effective.[22]

Additional research indicates that advertisers can be more effective in using fear appeals for converting nonusers of a product to its use than convincing consumers to switch brands.[23] Thus, for instance, fear appeals should be more useful in converting blade users to electric shavers than in changing a consumer's mind from Norelco to Remington.

Humor

Advertisers, politicians, actors and actresses, after-dinner speakers, professors, and indeed all members of the human race at one time or another use humor to gain a reaction from their audiences. Yet, researchers know very little, in a scientific sense, about how humor in marketing communications affects consumer behavior.

In advertising research, Sternthal and Craig have identified several tentative generalizations on the use of humor.[24] First, regarding the positive effects of humor, they conclude that humorous messages (1) attract attention, (2) can produce an increase in persuasion, (3) tend to enhance source credibility, and (4) evoke a positive mood in the audience. Humor can, however, inhibit consumers' comprehension of the intended meaning of a message. Because humorous appeals seem to inhibit audience comprehension of message points, Sternthal and Craig suggest that humor should be used only when the audience is familiar with product and brand

---

[21]Douglas W. Mellott, Jr., *Fundamentals of Consumer Behavior* (Tulsa, OK: Penn Well Publishing Co., 1983), p. 624; see also John J. Burnett and Richard L. Oliver, "Fear Appeal Effects in the Field: A Segmentation Approach," *Journal of Marketing Research,* Vol. 16, May 1979, pp. 181–190.

[22]Peter Wright, "Concrete Action Plans in TV Messages to Increase Reading of Drug Warnings," *Journal of Consumer Research,* Vol. 6, December 1979, pp. 256–269.

[23]John J. Wheatley, "Marketing and the Use of Fear-Anxiety Appeals," *Journal of Marketing,* Vol. 35, April 1971, pp. 62–64.

[24]Brian Sternthal and C. Samuel Craig, "Humor in Advertising," *Journal of Marketing,* Vol. 37, October 1973, pp. 12–18.

attributes and not when the product is substantially new or when there are a large number of facts for consumers to understand.[25]

There are some additional reasons why advertisers must be careful in their use of humor: (1) The effects of humor can differ due to differences in audience characteristics (e.g., an audience low in intelligence may misinterpret the humorous message), (2) the definition of what is funny in one country or region of a country is not necessarily the same in another country or region, and (3) a humorous message may be so distracting to an audience that receivers ignore the message content.

In more recent research, Brooker found that mild forms of humor are more persuasive than mild forms of fear, particularly among people with an education above the high-school level.[26] Madden and Weinberger examined humorous magazine advertisements and compared the level of reader recognition generated by humorous ads with that generated by nonhumorous ads. Their results indicated that humorous magazine ads tend to outperform other ads in gaining attention. They further found that men had higher attention scores than women for humorous ads and that predominantly white magazine readers had higher attention scores for humorous ads than did predominantly black readers.[27]

Whatever the effects advertisers are trying to achieve, they should proceed cautiously because consumers display a variety of tastes in humor. Companies should carefully research audiences nationwide and internationally before venturing into humorous advertising campaigns for national or international use.

Distraction

As was discussed in Chapter 2, all communication contexts are susceptible to outside interference, or noise, which can reduce communication effectiveness. However, under certain circumstances a persuasive communication may be made more effective by *intentionally* introducing something distracting into the message.

Pleasant forms of distraction (e.g., attractive models, enjoyable background music, or scenery) may enhance the effectiveness of a persuasive appeal in two ways. First, because persuasive messages are often met with counterarguments (i.e., receivers challenge message claims and deny their validity), distraction can be effective in diverting the receiver's attention from the primary message arguments and thereby reduce the chances that receivers will counterargue with the message arguments. Second, the pleasantness of the distraction may present a rewarding

---

[25]Brian Sternthal and C. Samuel Craig, *Consumer Behavior: An Information Processing Perspective* (Englewood Cliffs, NJ: Prentice-Hall, Inc., 1982), p. 272.

[26]George W. Brooker, "A Comparison of the Persuasive Effects of Mild Humor and Mild Fear Appeals," *Journal of Advertising,* Vol. 10, No. 4, 1981, p. 35.

[27]Thomas J. Madden and Marc G. Weinberger, "The Effects of Humor on Attention in Magazine Advertising," *Journal of Advertising,* Vol. 11, No. 3, 1982, pp. 8–14.

experience that is ultimately associated via conditioning with the advertised brand. On the other hand, *too much* distraction may render a persuasive message ineffective. The receiver may become so engrossed in the distraction that he or she fails to attend to the primary message.

Thus, the possibility of intentionally using distraction in marketing contexts is interesting but potentially dangerous. In fact, the research evidence is decidedly mixed.[28] A word of caution from two respected consumer behavior scholars is helpful.

> *Frankly it seems to be stretching matters a bit to try [to use distraction] in a real world setting. First of all, it is pretty hard to do in practice, especially in a television or print ad. It may be more feasible in a personal selling situation where staged interruptions, background music, and such can be manipulated. More crucial, however, is the fine line between reduction of counterargumentation and interference with comprehension. From what we [know about] information processing, people tend to screen out much of what we say anyway, so why make it easier for them? Perhaps this type of strategy is best left to the academic laboratory.[29]*

Message Codes

The notion of message code refers to the system used for encoding thoughts into coherent and effective messages. A thought can be expressed in a variety of ways depending upon the code or combination of codes used. Furthermore, a marketing communicator can choose from among several elements in both *verbal* and *nonverbal* code systems to accomplish communication objectives.

Verbal Codes

The verbal code refers to the system of word symbols that are combined according to a given set of rules. Many marketing communication practitioners believe that emotionally charged messages are effective in developing or changing customers' attitudes. In the English language, adjectives and adverbs are particularly effective verbal codes for enhancing the emotional impact of a message. An advertiser could,

---

[28]Stewart W. Bither, "Effects of Distraction and Commitment on the Persuasiveness of Television Advertising," *Journal of Marketing Research,* Vol. 9, February 1972, pp. 1–5; David Gardner, "The Distraction Hypothesis in Marketing," *Journal of Advertising Research,* Vol. 10, December 1970, pp. 25–31; and M. Venkatesan and Gordon A. Haaland, "Divided Attention and Television Commercials: An Experimental Study," *Journal of Marketing Research,* Vol. 5, May 1968, pp. 203–205.

[29]James F. Engel and Roger D. Blackwell, *Consumer Behavior,* 4th Ed. (Hinsdale, IL: The Dryden Press, 1982), p. 479.

for example, convey the same information about a product by using either of the following two statements:

1.   *The new plastic product resembling leather will soon be available to shoe manufacturers.*

or

2.   *The fabulous new plastic product which out-leathers leather will soon replace all other products used in the manufacture of superior-quality shoes.*[30]

The advertiser is more likely to use the second statement because the idea has been enhanced through the use of adjectives.

It is not enough simply to use adjectives for greater emotional impact. The selection of the right adjective is important if the communicator expects to elicit highly affective responses. Generally, a communicator can select among several words to express the same thought. However, synonyms that evoke approximately the same denotative meaning may evoke substantially different reactions emotionally. For example, you may refer to a thin woman as *skinny,* as *svelte,* or as *sylph-like.* All three words refer to physical thinness; however, only the latter two evoke positive thoughts.

Words with about the same denotative meaning often differ considerably in emotional intensity. A few examples are *trusting* (moderate) versus *gullible* (intense); *unattractive* (moderate) versus *revolting* (intense); and *marijuana user* (moderate) versus *pothead* (intense).[31] In deciding whether to use moderate or intense words, the communicator should be aware of the initial opinions of the audience. *Using highly emotional language is more effective on audiences who already agree with the communicator* because it reinforces their present attitudes. However, marketing communicators should exercise caution in the choice of emotional language, since receivers tend to respond negatively to extremely intense language.

Marketing communicators are particularly aware of the importance of *word combinations.* The specific words that are used in conjunction with a brand name can affect the brand image consumers form. Through careful selection of adjectives, adverbs, and modifying phrases, advertisers are able to imbue new brands with specific meanings. Such words as *quality, strong, dependable,* and *bright,* along with phrases such as "stronger than dirt," "whiter than white," and "best taste in America" all become part of a brand's meaning to consumers after continual repetition.[32]

---

[30]Both quotes are from E. P. Bettinghaus, *Persuasive Communication* (New York: Holt, Rinehart, and Winston, Inc., 1973), p. 135.

[31]Ibid., p. 134.

[32]Ibid., pp. 136–137.

Some additional useful suggestions about word choice follow:[33]

1. In general, advertising copywriters should use *high-frequency words* (i.e., familiar words) rather than obscure and difficult words because consumers can more easily decode and remember familiar words.

2. Advertisers should use *concrete words* (those that refer to objects, persons, places, etc.) instead of abstract words because consumers tend to remember concrete words better.

3. Advertisers should use *positive words,* sentences, and phrases rather than negative ones because consumers tend to process positive information more easily than negative information.

Nonverbal Codes

Nonverbal codes, like verbal codes, have symbols that can be combined according to a set of rules. The major difference between verbal and nonverbal codes is the kind of information that a person transmits and receives. Verbal codes are "better suited to the expression of cognitive things, such as the expression of an idea,"[34] whereas the nonverbal code elicits *feelings* and *emotions* within receivers and tells them about the communicator. Examples of nonverbal behaviors are facial expressions, gestures, posture, music, and color.

Functions of Nonverbal Behavior　Nonverbal behaviors perform five basic functions: pre-articulation, information processing, persuasion, deception, and subtlety.[35]

1. *Pre-articulation.* Pre-articulation indicates a communicator's emotions. Postural shifts, body movements, and speech disruptions are examples of pre-articulation behaviors.

2. *Information processing.* Information processing helps the receiver interpret and predict the sender's intentions. Examples are filled and unfilled pauses, sudden changes in muscle movements, pupil dilation, and eye blink. Astute salespersons are able to read these signs in customers. For example, certain body movements may signal that it is time to hasten the presentation, and a customer's dilated pupils might indicate growing excitement about the product.

3. *Persuasion.* A sender's nonverbal behaviors may serve also to change a receiver's beliefs and attitudes. A salesperson's enthusiasm (conveyed by changes in the level of activity in facial and vocal behavior) may be infectious and may enhance a customer's interest in the product or service under discussion.

---

[33]Larry Percy, "Psycholinguistic Guidelines for Advertising Copy," in A. Mitchell (ed.), *Advances in Consumer Research,* Vol. 9 (Ann Arbor, MI: Association for Consumer Research, 1982), pp. 107–111.

[34]Bettinghaus, *Persuasive Communication,* p. 119.

[35]Daniel Druckman, Richard M. Rozelle, and James C. Baxter, *Nonverbal Communications: Survey, Theory, and Research* (Beverly Hills, CA: Sage Publications, 1982), pp. 30–31.

4.   *Deception.* A sender practices deception when the intent is to mislead the receiver. Nonverbal manifestations of deceptive intent include shifts in eye contact and postural reorientation. For example, a used-car salesman may tell a customer one thing about a particular automobile but his eyes and body may say something entirely different.

5.   *Subtlety.* Some forms of nonverbal behavior are the artful and crafty use of communications to convey messages with fine distinctions in meaning. Subtlety can be achieved through facial expressions, voice qualities, and vocalizations. Voice qualities and vocalizations are called "paralinguistics"—a code that lies between verbal and nonverbal communications.

Voice qualities refer to such speech characteristics as "speech rate, rhythm pattern, pitch of voice, precision of articulation, and control of utterances by the lips, tongue, and other articulators."[36] Voice qualities communicate meanings such as urgency, boredom, friendliness, sarcasm, and various emotional conditions. You may recall, for example, John Houseman's precise articulation and other distinct voice qualities as he delivered an endorsement for Smith, Barney, the investment firm that, according to Houseman, does it the "old-fasioned way—they *earn* it."

Vocalizations refer to sounds that have no particular meanings in themselves but which do reflect certain emotions. Vocalizations such as yawning, sighing, "um," "uh-huh," as well as various voice intensities evoke a variety of responses depending upon the verbal messages they accompany.[37] Advertisers are keenly aware of the importance of selecting actors whose tonal qualities are appropriate to the product message. In advertising a facial cream that is soft and gentle on the skin, the advertiser utilizes an actor or actress who speaks softly and slowly and who uses the appropriate gestures consistent with the product message. A detergent that has strong, powerful ingredients to get the dirt out of work clothes is more appropriately advertised by someone who has a strong voice.

Visual Imagery   Visual imagery refers to the pictorial representations that appear in all visual forms of advertising. Advertising audiences process pictures and form images about advertised products and about the situations to which they relate. The use of visualizations in advertisements is potentially effective in influencing the consumer to imagine doing what is visually portrayed.

The use of visualizations makes it possible for advertisers to influence receivers' attitudes while using very little, if any, verbal content. In classical conditioning terms,[38] visual imagery serves as an unconditioned stimulus that may be associated with and transferred to the advertised product.[39] For example, a magazine ad (Figure 5.2) shows a brand of cigarettes (the to-be-conditioned stimulus) being used

---

[36]Bettinghaus, *Persuasive Communication,* p. 121.

[37]Ibid., pp. 121–122.

[38]Frances K. McSweeney and Calvin Bierley, "Recent Developments in Classical Conditioning," *Journal of Consumer Research,* Vol. 11, September 1984, pp. 619–631.

[39]John R. Rossiter and Larry Percy, "Attitude Change through Visual Imagery in Advertising," *Journal of Advertising,* Vol. 9, No. 2, 1980, pp. 10–16.

FIGURE 5.2   **Use of Visualization in Advertising**

by people who are apparently enjoying themselves in a congenial setting (the un-conditioned stimulus). The ad apparently intends for readers to imagine them-selves "going places" (in reference to the claim "Players Go Places") and enjoying themselves while smoking Players. The advertiser's hope is that any pleasant asso-ciations that the receiver may make with the advertised setting will be associated with the product.

Pictures in ads also facilitate an audience's recall of advertising content. In an early study, Shepard asked subjects to examine a set of illustrated magazine adver-tisements to determine whether they could later distinguish ads from the original set from a set of new but similar ads. The test consisted of 68 pairs of ads—one original ad matched with one new ad. An immediate recognition test produced a 98.5 percent correct recognition figure while a delayed test (one week later) yielded 90 percent accuracy. Not until four months later did subjects' recognition accuracy fall to 50 percent.[40] This study provides strong evidence that consumers are capable of storing and recalling visual images in advertisements. More recently, Lutz and Lutz found that when logos in Yellow Page ads combined both a pictorial and written element, recall for the brand name was improved substantially.[41]

Pictures in print advertisements have also been shown to influence how con-sumers process information. Edell and Staelin found that in pictorial advertise-ments where the verbal message does not relate the picture to the brand (so-called unframed pictures, e.g., a motor oil advertisement picturing a sunset), receivers seem to be distracted from evaluating the brand presented in the ad.[42] With ref-erence to the previous discussion on distraction effects, this suggests that un-framed pictures may tend to circumvent receivers' normal tendency to challenge advertising claims. Receivers, then, may be influenced without knowing it and per-haps may even be deceived.

Visual imagery also reinforces the verbal content of an advertisement to create a favorable brand attitude and a desire to buy. The verbal message may stimulate short-run sales with price-off statements, but the nonverbal message sets the stage for long-term brand attitudes and sales.[43] Thus, a retailer may use more highly verbalized messages for immediate sales, whereas the manufacturer would be more likely to opt for the visual imagery (nonverbal), long-term sales approach.[44]

Finally, effective visual imagery in advertising can vicariously place the audience member behind the wheel of a powerful sports car, in a fur coat attending an

[40]R. N. Shepard, "Recognition Memory for Words, Sentences, and Pictures," *Journal of Verbal Learning and Verbal Pictures,* February 1967, pp. 156–163.

[41]Kathy A. Lutz and Richard J. Lutz, "Effects of Interactive Imagery on Learning: Application to Adver-tising," *Journal of Applied Psychology,* Vol. 62, August 1977, pp. 493–498.

[42]Julie A. Edell and Richard Staelin, "The Information Processing of Pictures in Print Advertisements," *Journal of Consumer Research,* Vol. 10, June 1983, pp. 45–61.

[43]John R. Rossiter and Larry Percy, "Visual Imaging Ability as a Mediator of Advertising Response," in H. K. Hunt (ed.), *Advances in Consumer Research,* Vol. 5 (Ann Arbor, MI: Association for Consumer Research, 1978), pp. 621–629.

[44]Ibid.

important social event, on an ocean liner cruising toward the Caribbean, in a new suit heading to an important meeting, or in the situation of delivering packages of food and toys to needy people on Christmas eve. Much of what we feel and visualize internally is what we see. Perhaps as much as 70 to 80 percent of what we learn is visual.[45]

Music   Music provides yet another exciting area for nonverbal marketing communications. Although there are no definitive scientific conclusions, many marketing communication practitioners think that music helps to attract attention, influence brand image, increase comprehension, affect attitudes, and even influence brand choice. A few studies have been performed recently that show music can have positive effects.

Gorn's research, reviewed in Chapter 4, shows that attractive background music in an advertisement is capable of producing positive emotions toward the brand through classical conditioning and of influencing brand choice.[46]

In addition to the positive effects for advertising, background music appears to affect in-store shopping behavior. Milliman conducted an experiment on background store music by studying three experimental versions: (1) no music, (2) slow tempo music, and (3) fast tempo music. He concluded the following:

1. Higher sales volume is achieved with slow tempo music because customers move slowly through the store.
2. Lower sales volume results from fast tempo music because customers move quickly through the store.
3. The tempo of the music should be determined by the retailer's objectives (e.g., supermarkets may decide to use slow tempo music to slow customer movement and increase sales, whereas some restaurants may use fast tempo music to speed up customer turnover of seats, especially during the lunch hour).[47]

In the final analysis, music appears to be effective in creating customer moods, affecting sales, and stimulating buying preferences and choices. Of course, more research should be done to understand the actual (i.e., scientific) role of music in accomplishing various marketing communication functions. Yet, marketplace wisdom, as manifested by marketing communicators' nearly universal use of background music, would clearly suggest that music is an effective form of nonverbal communication.

[45]R. N. Shepard, "The Mental Image," *American Psychologist,* Vol. 33, February 1978, pp. 125–137.

[46]Gerald J. Gorn, "The Effects of Music in Advertising on Choice Behavior: A Classical Conditioning Approach," *Journal of Marketing,* Vol. 46, Winter 1982, pp. 94–101.

[47]Ronald E. Milliman, "Using Background Music to Affect the Behavior of Supermarket Shoppers," *Journal of Marketing,* Vol. 46, Summer 1982, pp. 86–91.

Summary

Three broad categories of message factors are examined in this chapter: message structure, message appeals, and message codes. *Message structure* refers to the organization of elements in marketing communication messages. Three structural issues that have particular relevance to marketing communicators are message-sidedness (one-sided versus two-sided messages), order of presentation (climax order, anticlimax order, and pyramidal order), and conclusion drawing.

Message appeals deals with what is said in a message. Several appeals that are widely used by marketing communicators are fear appeals, humor, and distraction.

Message codes refers to the system used for encoding thoughts into coherent and effective messages. Message codes include verbal, nonverbal, and paralinguistic codes. Voice qualities, vocalizations, visual imagery, and music are some of the nonverbal codes discussed.

Discussion Questions

1. A company markets a line of household laundry products and cleaning items. The channel of distribution is direct to consumers. Consumers of the company's products are highly heterogeneous in terms of socioeconomic and demographic characteristics, but most of them are highly brand loyal. This company is in the process of developing a national advertising campaign to generate greater product usage from its existing customer base. Comment on the advisability of developing a two-sided message.

2. Develop a list of products for which you feel fear appeals might be a viable approach to persuading consumer acceptance of a brand. What kinds of products do not lend themselves to fear appeals? Explain why you feel these products are not appropriate for fear appeals.

3. A sales representative calls upon customers who are very knowledgeable about the saleman's products. In fact, their knowledge of technical product features is greater than his. Yet there are occasions when, after making a sales presentation, it seems that customers did not get the primary point that the salesman attempts to make. Comment on the advisability of conclusion drawing in this situation.

4. Television commercials for inexpensive, low-risk consumer packaged goods (low-involvement products) are often received by consumers in an unenthusiastic and passive information-processing mode. In view of this, comment on the relative merits of climax versus anticlimax orders of presentation.

5. Consumers occasionally find television commercials to be humorous and enjoy viewing them. Some advertising pundits claim that such commercials may capture attention but are frequently ineffective in selling products. Do you agree with this position? Justify your position.

6. Explain why nonverbal codes in a message are often more important in communicating an idea than the verbal codes they accompany. Provide specific examples to support your answer.

7. Advertisers and agencies seem reluctant to use two-sided messages. From their perspective, present an argument that looks at both sides of the issue.

8. The advertising agency for an automobile tire manufacturer is considering using a fear appeal message to promote its client's tires. What would you suggest to the advertising agency in terms of fear appeal strength?

9. An internationally known manufacturer of high-quality stereo equipment has learned from a pretest of several advertisements that its top-of-the-line stereo receiver was evaluated more highly when the message admitted to a weakness in the receiver. It is well known throughout the industry and among avid audiophiles that the receiver's amplifiers burn out much sooner than comparable competitors' models. However, the receiver is far superior to its rivals in terms of total harmonic distortion, channel separation, intermodulation distortion, and other specifications. Should the firm use a two-sided message in its advertising? Why or why not?

10. It appears that the use of distraction in marketing communications, especially advertising, may represent a double-edged sword. Explain.

11. Industrial advertisers sometimes use magazine advertisements with decorative models—i.e., scantily clad females who are there to adorn the ad but who serve no function in terms of the sales message. Why do you think industrial advertisers use decorative models? Present arguments explaining why you think such advertising may be effective *and* why it may be ineffective.

Exercises

1. Provide two or three examples of music in advertisements that you think is particularly effective. Explain for each example why you think the music is effective for this particular advertisement.

2. Examine used magazines, and clip several examples of comparative advertisements. Analyze each ad in terms of why you think the advertiser used a comparative advertising format and whether you think the advertisement is effective. Justify your position.

3. Identify three or four examples of television commercials that you regard as humorous ads. Interview five people (preferably nonstudents) and ask their opinions of these commercials. Summarize the responses for each commercial.

4. With reference to the Edell and Staelin study mentioned in the chapter, provide three examples of magazine advertisements that are framed and three that are unframed. For the unframed ads, explain what you think the manufacturer's rationale was in choosing the particular unframed pictures. For all six ads, be sure to justify why you regard each ad as framed or unframed.

5. Interview three seasoned salespersons (retail salespersons, manufacturer representatives, or whomever you can interview) and ask them to describe the types of sales approaches they have found to be most effective for them personally. Summarize the responses and show explicitly how the information you have acquired relates to the text. Be sure in your interviews to press for detailed responses.

CHAPTER 6

Source Factors in Marketing Communications

The source as a component in the communications process often has tremendous persuasive influence on receivers' attitudes and behavior. Some communicators are more persuasive than others. Two people can deliver the same message to an audience, yet one communicator may have far more influence on the audience's attitudes and opinions (that is, be more persuasive) than the other communicator. What are some of the characteristics that make one communicator more persuasive than another? This chapter attempts to answer that question. First, though, the chapter will specify who and what a marketing communications source is.

In simple, face-to-face communication, the communication source is obviously the person who is talking or gesturing at a particular time. Who is the source, however, when a celebrity endorser is citing the merits of a particular brand of beer in a TV commercial aired during "Monday Night Football"?

Communication scholars view the term **source** very broadly to include a person, a group, an organization, or even a label.[1] In marketing communications, consumers might view any one or a combination of the following as communication sources: (1) a hired spokesperson (such as Bill Cosby), (2) a company (such as IBM), (3) a company sales representative, (4) a media vehicle (such as *Business*

[1]Richard E. Petty, Thomas M. Ostrom, and Timothy C. Brock (eds.), *Cognitive Responses in Persuasion* (Hillsdale, NJ: Laurence Erlbaum Associates, 1981), p. 142.

Week), (5) a trade association (such as the American Dairy Association), (6) a reference group (such as fellow yuppies), among others. Clearly, the notion of source is a multifaceted concept.

Source Attributes

Most marketing communication scholars agree that three basic source attributes contribute to a source's effectiveness: (1) *power,* (2) *attractiveness,* and (3) *credibility.* Each attribute involves a different mechanism or process by which the source effects attitudinal or behavioral changes in receivers. Specifically, power operates through a *compliance* mechanism, attractiveness through *identification,* and credibility via *internalization.*[2] (See Table 6.1.)

The three categories of source attributes and the psychological processes through which they operate are conceptually different, yet they also interact, that is, the three attributes may be mixed in one source, and attitudes that initially result from an identification process or compliance may eventually become internalized. The following sections elaborate on source attributes—source power, attractiveness, and credibility—and the associated processes through which each operates.

Source Power: The Process of Compliance

Compliance results through a power relationship between the participants in the communications process. That is, a receiver complies with the persuasive efforts of the source because the source has the power, legitimate or otherwise, to administer rewards or punishments. General illustrations of compliance are parent-child

TABLE 6.1	Kelman's Source Attributes and Receiver Processing Modes

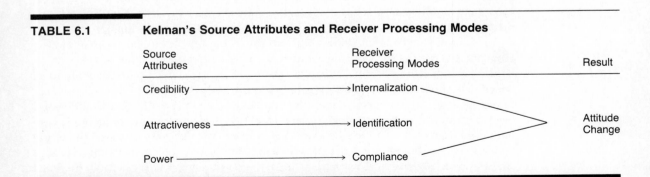

[2]This classification scheme is generally identified with the work of Kelman. See Herbert C. Kelman, "Processes of Opinion Change," *Public Opinion Quarterly,* Vol. 25, Spring 1961, pp. 57–78.

and employer-employee relations. For the most part, however, this form of persuasive influence is not used extensively in marketing communications.

Because the source can control rewards and punishments, he or she can often induce compliance to his or her advocated position. Receiver acceptance occurs, not because the receiver privately accepts the source's position, but because the receiver obtains external incentives, i.e., receives rewards or avoids punishment. The receiver's attitude change is therefore somewhat superficial; it is manifested in overt behavior rather than being internalized into the receiver's personal position.

In education, students often comply with what a teacher says although they may not agree with the teacher. The student anticipates that rewards will be forthcoming or punishment will be avoided as a result of exhibiting compliant behavior. Likewise, in business, industrial sales representatives sometimes possess a degree of power over buyers. The buyer may anticipate special favors by complying with the sales representative. Sales representatives who are in a seller's market (i.e., a situation where demand exceeds supply) are in a position of power because buyers are dependent on them for supplies of raw materials, parts, or merchandise. Purchasing personnel may feel that if they do not comply with a sales representative's requests their orders may be delayed (in favor of competitors' requests) or cut off completely.

Although in the short run a receiver may only comply (outwardly, not privately) with a source of perceived power, in the long run the receiver may internalize the new attitude. The reason for this long-term effect is that the receiver realizes that his or her privately held attitude is inconsistent with his or her overt behavior. Humans strive for internal consistency; thus, there is pressure for resolution. Furthermore, as external pressures exerted on the receiver become more powerful, the receiver will (up to a point) express greater agreement with the source. Over time the receiver may internalize the source's attitude. However, where external pressures are too great, compliance may remain high or even increase, but internalization of the attitude becomes less likely. Weak positive incentives or mild threats for compliance therefore increase the chance for attitude change.

Source Attractiveness: The Process of Identification

Source attractiveness is not a unidimensional concept but rather consists of three interrelated subcomponents: similarity, familiarity, and liking.[3] A source is considered attractive to receivers if they like and/or feel a sense of similarity or familiarity with the source. Persuasion occurs via an identification process when receivers find something in the source that is considered attractive. This does not mean simply physical attractiveness but includes any number of virtuous characteristics that receivers may perceive in a source, such as intellectual skills, personality properties, life-style characteristics, or athletic prowess. When receivers perceive a

[3]H. C. Triandis, *Attitudes and Attitude Change* (New York: John Wiley & Sons, 1971).

source to be attractive, they will very likely adopt the attitudes, behaviors, interests, or preferences of the source. This process is called **identification.**

Marketing communicators recognize that people have a natural tendency to seek relationships with other people whom they like and with whom they feel a sense of similarity and familiarity. An audience can perceive a communicator as similar to themselves in a number of ways: in personality, race, religion, political philosophy, interests, self-image, or group affiliation. That people tend to be more influenced by others similar to themselves is, in part, due to the tendency for people to like others similar to themselves. People also assume that others who are similar to themselves probably form their opinions and make their judgments using the same criteria that they would use.

Various experiments have been conducted that demonstrate and support these generalizations. In one study, two groups of college students were given the same speech, arguing for a broad, general education for college students. One group, composed of music majors, was told that a musician had written the speech, whereas the other group of engineering students was told the speech was prepared by an engineer. The findings revealed that students sharing similar professional interests with the communicator underwent greater opinion change than students having interests different from the communicator. That is, engineering students were persuaded more by the engineer than by the musician, and the music students were persuaded more by the musician than the engineer.[4]

Sales managers capitalize on this principle and select salespersons who are reasonably matched (intellectually, socially, educationally) with their customers. A sales representative who can establish a common interest with a customer increases the chances that his or her customer will view him or her positively. A good sales representative learns early what the interests, opinions, and background of a prospect are. Once the representative discovers a commonality, he or she attempts to develop the relationship around their similar interests. This means discussing basketball with Harry, the stock market with Jane, and politics with Juan.

Similarly, advertisers employ spokespersons who are liked, and perhaps even admired, by advertising audiences. Celebrities from athletic and entertainment fields are in great demand as product spokespersons. In fact, it is estimated that one-third of all television commercials use endorsements, most often involving athletic or entertainment celebrities.[5] Advertising agencies are willing to pay huge salaries to those celebrities who are liked and respected by target audiences and who will, it is hoped, favorably influence consumers' attitudes and behavior toward the endorsed products. This is probably justified in view of research, which shows

[4]J. Mills and J. Jellison, "Effect on Opinion Change of Similarity between the Communicator and the Audience He Addressed," *Journal of Personality and Social Psychology,* Vol. 9, No. 2, 1969, pp. 153–156.

[5]H. M. Spielman, "Pick Product Presenter Prudently," *Marketing News,* September 8, 1978, p. 5.

that consumers' attitudes and perceptions of quality are enhanced when celebrities endorse products.[6]

Communication researchers have not studied attractiveness extensively, and the research that has been conducted has focused on only one dimension of attractiveness—physical attractiveness. The research has generally shown the following:[7]

1. Attractive models increase a communicator's effectiveness in a limited way.
2. Attractive models produce more favorable evaluations of ads and advertised products than do less attractive models.
3. Physically attractive communicators are more liked than unattractive communicators.
4. Although attractive communicators are perceived as more dynamic by receivers than unattractive communicators, the attractive communicators are not generally considered to be more credible.

Source-Object Inconsistencies   What happens when a receiver's attitude toward a source is inconsistent with his or her attitude toward a product or brand that the source endorses? That is, if a consumer likes a particular brand that is endorsed by a spokesperson whom the consumer dislikes or if the consumer dislikes the brand but likes the source, what effect will this inconsistency have on the consumer's attitude toward both the brand and the source? Answers to these questions are found in theories that deal with the **principle of cognitive consistency.**

The basic premise of the principle of cognitive consistency is that the human mind has a persistent need to maintain harmony, congruency, balance, or consistency among the various cognitions, feelings, and behaviors recorded in the brain. When there are inconsistencies of these elements and structures, the human mind is compelled to adapt or make changes. In relation to marketing, attitude change toward the source, the product, or both is one way to reduce inconsistency. This section of the chapter examines two theoretical applications of the consistency principle—the *balance* and *congruity* models.

The Balance Model   Balance theory was the first theoretical analysis of the principle of cognitive consistency. It deals with a person's perception of social relationships.[8] Essentially, the model has three elements: (1) a perceiver (P), (2) another person (O), and (3) an object (X). The relationship between each pair of

[6]See, for example, R. B. Fireworker and H. H. Friedman, "The Effects of Endorsements on Product Evaluation," *Decision Sciences,* Vol. 8, July 1977, pp. 576–83; and H. H. Friedman, Salvatore Termini, and R. Washington, "The Effectiveness of Advertisements Utilizing Four Types of Endorsers," *Journal of Advertising,* Vol. 5, Summer 1976, pp. 22–24.

[7]W. Benoy Joseph, "The Credibility of Physically Attractive Communicators: A Review," *Journal of Advertising,* Vol. 11, No. 3, 1982, pp. 15–24.

[8]The father of balance theory is Heider. See Fritz Heider, "Social Perception and Phenomenal Causality," *Psychological Review,* Vol. 51, November 1944, pp. 358–374; and Fritz Heider, *The Psychology of Interpersonal Relations* (New York: John Wiley & Sons, 1958).

these elements may be positive (+) or negative (−), positive signifying a liking bond and negative signifying disliking. Depending on the configuration among these three elements, the model is either *balanced* or *unbalanced.* Balanced structures—those for which the arithmetic product of all three signs is positive—are stable and therefore create no dynamics for change. Unbalanced structures—those for which the arithmetic product is negative—are unstable and can effect change to restore balance. Figure 6.1 shows the eight possible combinations of triadic configurations.

As an example, assume that a perceiver (P) likes another person (O) and also likes an object (X). If the other person (O) dislikes the object (X), then the structure is not in balance. The perceiver likes someone (+) who does not like an object (−) that the perceiver does like (+). This condition is unbalanced, and the perceiver feels tension to alter the structural relationship toward balance. He or she can either dislike the other person or dislike the object. Such attitudinal change will bring the system into balance (see Figure 6.1 e and then b and c).

FIGURE 6.1   The Eight Possible Combinations of Balanced and Unbalanced States in Balance Theory

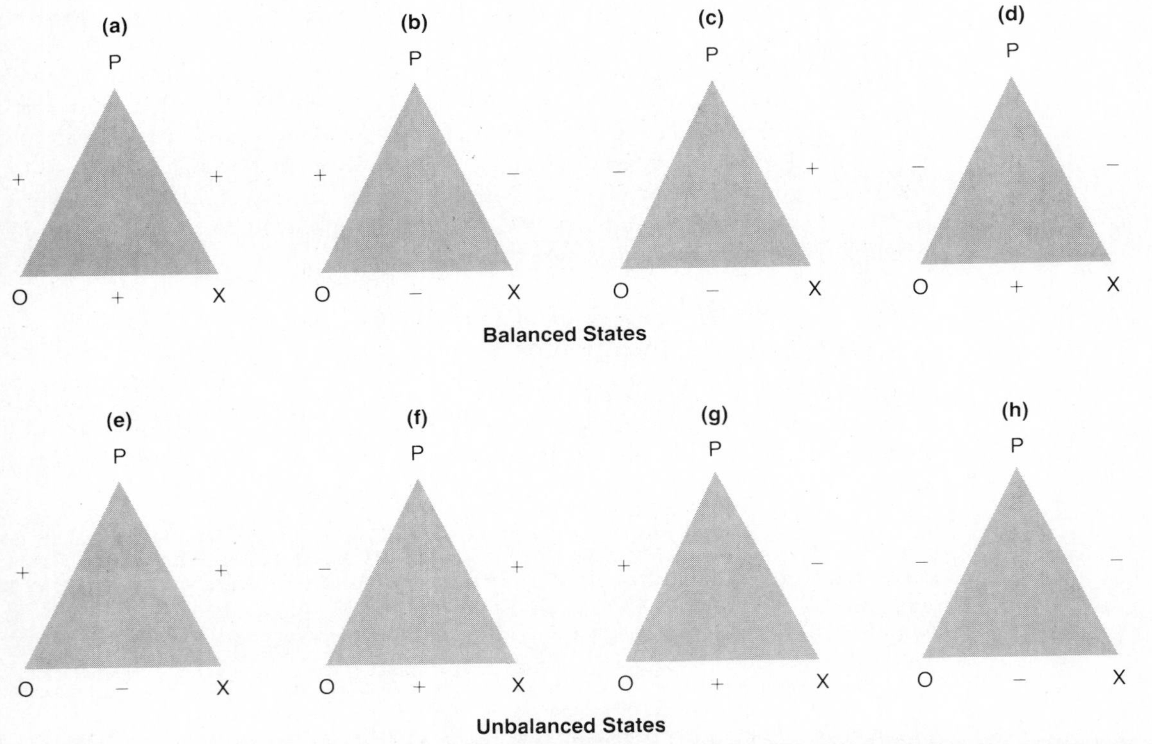

Balanced States

Unbalanced States

An advertiser could develop a commercial message using a hired spokesperson whom consumers like (+) to create an unbalanced condition for attitude change. For example, if the advertiser's goal was to increase orange juice consumption among current users who only drink orange juice at breakfast, an attempt could be made to encourage consumers to drink orange juice at other times and occasions—at lunch, at supper, after a tennis match, etc. If we assume that consumers like orange juice at breakfast but not at other times of the day, then the advertiser faces the condition shown in Figure 6.1.[9] That is, the consumer (P) likes (+) the hired spokesperson who likes (+) to drink orange juice at night, after an athletic event, etc. However, the consumer (P) does not like (−) to drink orange juice at these times.

In this situation, the consumer is faced with an unbalanced state and must either change his or her attitude toward the spokesperson or toward the times of day he or she drinks orange juice. If we assume the consumer's attitude toward the hired spokesperson is stronger than the consumer's attitude toward the times and occasions to drink orange juice, then we could predict that the consumer would balance the triadic relationship by becoming positive toward drinking orange juice at times and events other than breakfast. However, balance theory does not permit us to assume this because it deals only with the direction of relationships (positive or negative) but not their intensity. Fortunately, a more sophisticated model—congruity theory—takes the degree of strength into account.

The Congruity Model   According to congruity theory, if a receiver holds a certain attitude toward a source and a different attitude toward an object, idea, event, or person, then an *incongruent* relationship is said to exist. An **associative bond** results when the source makes positive statements about the object, and a **dissociative bond** occurs when the source makes negative statements about the object.[9] The following examples, first using an associative bond and then a dissociative bond, will clarify these points.

To illustrate attitude change from an associative bond, assume that a consumer has a positive attitude toward Bob Hope (let's say a + 2 on a seven-point, − 3 to + 3, scale) but a negative attitude toward Texaco petroleum products (say, − 1). Further assume that Bob Hope appears in advertising for Texaco extolling the greatness of Texaco products. In this situation, Bob Hope (+ 2) makes favorable comments about Texaco products, which the consumer views unfavorably (− 1). Incongruency exists in the consumer's mind, and tension to develop equilibrium results.

How will congruency be restored? Will the consumer change his or her attitude toward Bob Hope, Texaco, or both, and if so, how much attitude change will be necessary to restore congruency? At first, one might assume that the hypothetical consumer will achieve congruency by simply averaging his or her separate atti-

---

[9]Charles E. Osgood and Percy H. Tannebaum, "The Principle of Congruity in the Prediction of Attitude Change," *Psychological Review,* Vol. 62, January 1955, pp. 42–55.

tudes toward Bob Hope ($+2$) and Texaco (-1), resulting in a new congruent attitude of $+0.5$ toward both Bob Hope and Texaco. However, this ignores the fact that the consumer's two attitudes differ in strength. That is, the $+2$ position Bob Hope occupies in the consumer's mind is stronger than the -1 position of Texaco. This brings us to a basic principle of congruity theory: *extreme attitudes are less easily changed than milder attitudes.* People resist changing strongly held attitudes but are much less resistant to changing weakly held attitudes.

Figure 6.2 portrays in two parts (a and b) the consumer's original attitudes and the new equilibrium. Note that at the new equilibrium (i.e., attitude congruency) the consumer's attitude toward both Bob Hope and Texaco are $+1$. He or she feels somewhat less positive about Bob Hope because he endorsed a disliked product but more positive toward Texaco because Bob Hope, a person he or she likes, said positive things about Texaco. A simple mathematical explanation underlying the psychological process by which incongruency is resolved will be delayed momentarily until an illustration of a dissociative bond is presented.

Assume now, that the consumer's attitudes toward Bob Hope and Texaco remain as before—$+2$ and -1, respectively—but that Bob Hope makes statements about Texaco that the consumer perceives as unfavorable toward Texaco, perhaps in a comparative advertising format. This situation represents attitude incongruency resulting from a dissociative bond. Figure 6.3 shows that in this situation, attitude incongruency is resolved at the point where the consumer's attitude toward Bob Hope decreases (from $+2$ to $+1.67$) as does her attitude toward Texaco (from -1 to -1.67).

The formula for balancing an incongruous situation is the following:[10]

$$ R_o = \frac{|A_o|}{|A_o| + |A_s|} (A_o) + (d) \frac{|A_s|}{|A_o| + |A_s|} (A_s) $$

where

R_o = resolution for the object (Texaco in this illustration)
A_o = receiver's attitude toward the object
A_s = receiver's attitude toward the source (Bob Hope)
d = the direction of the assertion ($+1$ if favorable—an associative bond; -1 if unfavorable—a dissociative bond)

As you will note, the $| \; |$ signs represent the absolute values of the receiver's attitudes. Also note that the denominator for both fractions is the same, representing the distance between the receiver's attitudes towards object and source. The numerator of the fraction represents the strength, or pull, that each side (i.e., attitude toward object and toward source) has in this incongruency resolution tug-of-war.

[10]Ibid.

FIGURE 6.2   **The Effect of an Incongruous *Associative* Bond**

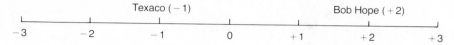

a. Original Positions

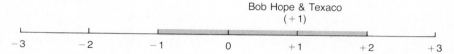

b. New Equilibrium

FIGURE 6.3   **The Effect of an Incongruous *Dissociative* Bond**

a. Original Positions

b. Equilibrium

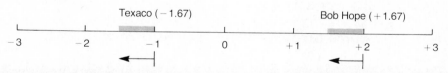

In the first instance, where Bob Hope (+ 2) makes a favorable statement (d = + 1) toward Texaco (− 1), the mathematics of the problem work out as follows:

$$R_o = \frac{|-1|}{|-1| + |+2|}(-1) + (+1)\frac{|+2|}{|-1| + |+2|}(+2)$$
$$= 1/3\,(-1) + 2/3\,(2)$$
$$= -1/3 + 4/3$$
$$= +1$$

The computed value is $+1$. According to the rule for associative bonds, equilibrium, or congruence, is restored when the receiver holds the same attitude toward both the source and the object. Thus, the hypothetical consumer's attitudes toward Bob Hope and Texaco are congruent when both are slightly positive, i.e., $+1$ (refer again to Figure 6.2).

In the second instance, where Bob Hope makes an unfavorable statement toward Texaco ($d = -1$), the mathematics are as follows:

$$R_o = \frac{|-1|}{|-1| + |+2|}(-1) + (-1)\frac{|+2|}{|-1| + |+2|}(+2)$$
$$= 1/3(-1) - 2/3(+2)$$
$$= (-1/3) + (-4/3)$$
$$= -1.67$$

The rule for dissociative bonds is that when the source expresses an unfavorable attitude toward the object, congruency occurs when the receiver perceives equal polarization between the source and object (i.e., a -1 and $+1$, a -2 and $+2$, etc.). In other words, the object and source are reflected in mirror-image positions. In this case, the consumer's attitude toward Bob Hope is $+1.67$ while his or her attitude toward Texaco is -1.67 (refer again to Figure 6.3).

In sum, the principle of congruity captures in simplified fashion the process that takes place when people hold conflicting attitudes toward objects and sources. Consistency is restored by altering one's attitude toward both the object and the source. The model, in its basic mathematics, demonstrates the psychological notion that the amount of attitude change is a function of the attitude extremity, that strongly held attitudes change less than weakly held attitudes.

A qualification is in order before leaving this subject. If a person perceives that the information received is not believable, he or she can simply choose to reject the information, and no attitude change will occur. Moreover, there may be some amount of belief, rather than total disbelief, in which case the receiver would modify his or her attitudes only slightly.[11]

Source Credibility: The Process of Internalization

In its most basic sense, credibility refers to the tendency to believe or trust someone or something, such as an organization or group. When a source of information is perceived as credible, the source can change attitudes through a psychological process called **internalization.** Internalization occurs when the receiver learns and adopts the source's position or attitude as his or her own. Once the receiver internalizes an attitude, the individual tends "to maintain that attitude even if the

[11]See, for example, Jonathan L. Freedman, J. Merrill Carlsmith, and David O. Sears, *Social Psychology* (Englewood Cliffs, NJ: Prentice-Hall, 1970), p. 263.

source of the message is forgotten and even if the source switches to a new position."[12]

A vast number of studies have been conducted to identify the characteristics of a credible source. Communication scholars have concluded that credibility is not a singular concept but rather an *entire set of perceptions* that receivers hold toward a source.[13] The audience's set of perceptions may include the source's prestige, expertise, power, trustworthiness, intentions to manipulate, age, skin color, voice qualities and articulations, and a host of other perceptual dimensions. It should be noted that some of these dimensions are somewhat similar. Furthermore, a receiver's total perception of a source's credibility may be a composite of the interactions among any combination of source traits.

Dimensions of Source Credibility   Source credibility dimensions include expertise, trustworthiness, status or prestige, and other characteristics of the message source.

Expertise   Expertise refers to the knowledge, experience, or skills possessed by a source as they relate to the communications topic. Expertise is a perceived, rather than absolute, phenomenon. Whether a communication source is indeed an expert is unimportant; all that matters is how he or she is perceived by the target audience. A source whom an audience perceives as an expert on a given subject is more persuasive in changing audience opinions pertaining to his or her area of expertise than a source whom an audience does not perceive as possessing the same characteristic.

Marketing communicators use a variety of techniques in attempting to convey source expertise. In the area of personal selling, salespersons often receive extensive training so that they are very knowledgeable of their company's product line. Many companies that market high-technology products frequently recruit sales representatives from university programs in engineering, computer science, and other scientific fields.

Efforts to achieve source credibility are widespread in advertising. For example, advertisements sometimes employ words and phrases to imply that the advertised product is technologically sophisticated. Advertisers frequently show products being used in situations that imply something positive about product quality and performance. Motor oil and automobile tires are frequently advertised in race-track settings; sporting goods are displayed in use on or alongside the playing field. Another technique that advertisers use to enhance credibility is the strategic selection of various props (lab coats, scientific paraphernalia, etc.) that when worn or used by a source give the impression of credibility. Moreover, athletic professionals are often used as brand spokespersons—Chris Evert-Lloyd, Jack Nicklaus, Dr. J, and John McEnroe are just a few of the well-known endorsers.

---

[12]Petty et al., *Cognitive Responses in Persuasion,* p. 143.

[13]Erwin P. Bettinghaus, *Persuasive Communication,* 2nd. Ed. (New York: John Wiley & Sons, 1969), p. 104.

Trustworthiness   Trustworthiness refers to the honesty, integrity, and believability of a source. While expertise and trustworthiness are not mutually exclusive, often a particular source is perceived as highly trustworthy but not particularly high in expertise. The degree of honesty or trustworthiness of a source depends primarily on the audience's perception of the source's intent. If the audience believes that the source has underlying motives, especially ones that will personally benefit the source, he or she will be less persuasive than someone the audience perceives as having nothing to gain or as entirely objective.

A study by Walston, Aronson, and Abrahams illustrates the point. These researchers used a convicted criminal as their source to argue against greater police powers. He created very little change in the audience's attitudes. However, when he argued *in favor* of stronger police powers before another audience, he generated a large amount of attitude change.[14] A similar effect results when the receiver believes he or she is hearing a message not intended for him or her. Such a message is called the overheard conversation. The receiver realizes that the communicator has no intent to affect change in him or her because the target of the message is someone else. Therefore, the source is more likely to be perceived as trustworthy. The effectiveness of the overheard conversation has been demonstrated in a number of studies.[15]

In advertising, the consumer is continually vigilant to the intentions of the advertiser. It is quite difficult to eliminate intent to persuade; however, some television advertisements have attempted to increase trustworthiness by using "candid" interviews with homemakers. In these commercials, the homemaker (typically a woman) is often asked to explain why she purchases the company's brand or asked if she would be willing to trade, for example, her detergent for two boxes of another leading detergent. This approach has also been used by asking homemakers to compare their brand of product with another, both in disguised form. The homemaker acts surprised when she learns that the sponsor's brand performs better than her regular brand. In all of these cases, the advertiser is attempting to show a degree of objectivity and thereby to establish greater trustworthiness for the message.

Advertisers also use the overheard conversation technique to enhance credibility. A television advertisement might show a middle-aged person overhearing one man explain to another why his brand of arthritis pain relief medicine is the best on the market. In this case, the commercial attempts to have audience members place themselves in the position of the person overhearing the conversation. E. F. Hutton, the investment firm, has perfected this technique in a continuing series of ads with the tag line, "When E. F. Hutton talks, everyone listens."

---

[14]E. Walston, E. Aronson, and D. Abrahams, "On Increasing the Persuasiveness of a Low Prestige Communicator," *Journal of Experimental Social Psychology,* Vol. 2, 1966, pp. 325–342.

[15]See, for example, E. Walster and L. Festinger, "The Effectiveness of 'Overheard' Persuasive Communication," *Journal of Abnormal and Social Psychology,* Vol. 65, No. 6, 1962, pp. 395–402.

A study by Hunt, Domzal, and Kernan provides further insight into the role of trustworthiness in enhancing a source's credibility. Their experiment tested whether a hidden camera spokesperson (i.e., one who is presumably extolling the virtues of a product without being aware of it) is more persuasive than a typical person spokesperson (i.e., one who is aware of his or her spokesperson role). They hypothesized that the hidden camera spokesperson should be considered more trustworthy because he or she is making favorable product claims without hidden motives. The hidden camera spokesperson was, in fact, shown to be less biased and more credible.[16]

In general, communicators must establish that they are not in any way attempting to manipulate the audience, that they have nothing to gain by their persuasive attempts, and that they are objective in their presentations. By doing so, they establish themselves as trustworthy and, therefore, credible.

Status-Prestige   All people have several roles they play each day. An individual may be a nuclear physicist, a mother, a wife, and P.T.A. chairperson. Each role carries with it a *status,* or level of prestige. When two or more roles are compared, people can ascribe a higher status to one role relative to another. A population as a whole can closely agree upon the relative ranking of statuses of many roles. For example, a United States senator is generally perceived to have higher status than a state senator, the chef of a restaurant more than the maître d', and an electrical engineer more than an electrician.

In general, a source who is perceived as having high prestige is more credible, and thus more persuasive, than one perceived as having low prestige. This is generally true for instances in which the source is communicating information on a topic related to his or her role. However, when a source occupying a status position in one role addresses an audience in another role position, he or she becomes less persuasive. For example, a nuclear physicist may be very persuasive in addressing the local P.T.A. on the safety of a nuclear power plant in the community but much less persuasive speaking as a mother to the P.T.A. on the topic of proper dress rules for students.

Other Dimensions of Source Credibility   Although other dimensions related to source credibility will not be dealt with in detail, some that are not obvious will be mentioned. For example, evidence suggests that age, sex, skin color, dress, mannerisms, and voice inflection affect source credibility.[17] Consider age, for example.

[16]James M. Hunt, Theresa J. Domzal, and Jerome B. Kernan, "Causal Attributions and Persuasion: The Case of Disconfirmed Expectancies," in A. Mitchell (ed.), *Advances in Consumer Research,* Vol. 9 (Pittsburgh: Association for Consumer Research, 1982), pp. 287–292.

[17]See, for example, E. Aronson and B. Golden, "The Effect of Relevant and Irrelevant Aspects of Communicator Credibility on Opinion Change," *Journal of Personality,* Vol. 30, June 1962, pp. 135–146; see also Peter Bennett and Harold Kassarjian, *Consumer Behavior* (Englewood Cliffs, NJ: Prentice-Hall, 1972), p. 89.

In some situations, older persons tend to be more influential than younger persons because older people may be expected to have greater experiences and more wisdom. Age and all of the other variables noted, however, perform a credibility-enhancing function only in certain communication situations. That is, an older person, by virtue of his or her age alone, may be perceived as credible with respect to certain communication topics but not credible in regard to other topics. This generalization applies to all other source characteristics.

Voice, accent, dress, and mannerisms also appear to relate to a source's credibility. A person who is dressed expensively, for example, may be more influential than a less well-dressed individual in describing financial investment programs. A person introduced as a scientist on automotive engineering might be more influential if he has a slight German accent than if he speaks with a Texas or New Jersey accent. Many times these and other subtle signs are extremely influential in determining the persuasive impact of a communicator's message.

The Low-Credibility Source   So far, the characteristics of a high credibility source have been discussed. What about the persuasive attributes of a low credibility source? Are there any circumstances in which he or she can be persuasive? Research says yes, at least under certain circumstances. Specifically, *the persuasion of a low credibility source is increased when he or she argues against his or her own self-interest.* By arguing against self-interest, the communicator establishes credibility by seeming not to intend to manipulate the audience or to gain anything. The low-credibility source under these conditions may be more persuasive than a high-prestige source presenting the same argument.[18]

Another way in which the low-credibility source can increase persuasiveness is when he or she is identified after, rather than before, presenting a message. When an audience knows in advance that they will be listening to a message presented by a low-credibility source, they will tune out the source's message. On the other hand, if they do not know the source's identity until after the message presentation, they are more inclined to be attentive to and persuaded by the source's arguments.

Greenberg and Miller offer support for this contention in a study in which two groups of subjects were exposed to a message on the dangers of frequent brushing of teeth. One group was introduced to a low-credibility source prior to the message; the other group was introduced to the low-credibility source after the message. Findings indicate that the group informed of the low credibility of the source after his or her message were more persuaded in the direction of the communicator's arguments than those informed prior to the message.[19] Sternthal, Dholakia, and Leavitt also manipulated source identification, whether before or after the mes-

---

[18]See E. Walston et al., "On Increasing the Persuasiveness."

[19]B. Greenberg and G. Miller, "The Effects of Low-Credible Sources on Message Acceptance," *Speech Monographs,* Vol. 33, June 1966, pp. 127–136.

sage was presented, and found that the high-credibility source was no better than the low-credibility source in generating opinion change in the audience.[20]

Perhaps the major determinant of whether a high-credibility source is more or less effective than a low-credibility source is the receiver's initial opinion toward the communication topic prior to receiving a persuasive message. To understand the discussion to follow, it is first necessary to examine the notion of *cognitive response theory,* a topic introduced in Chapter 4.

Cognitive response theory is a study of how receivers concurrently process incoming information with their existing knowledge and their present circumstances. Cognitive response scholars believe that message receivers tend to confront a communicator's persuasive attempts by critically analyzing incoming information. If the receiver is indeed an active information processor, he or she can be expected to compare the incoming information with his or her existing structure of beliefs and values. This comparison process generates critical thoughts, i.e., spontaneous cognitive responses, that represent the primary mediators of message acceptance.[21]

There are three forms of cognitive responses. *Counterargumentation* occurs when a message contradicts the receiver's current belief system. The receiver subvocally evaluates the source and message cues against his or her existing knowledge to neutralize the source's argument. For example, a customer may hear a claim that the seller's headache remedy is faster acting but internally counterargue that this brand is so strong that it creates or aggravates stomach ulcers. A second form of cognitive response, *source derogation,* occurs when the receiver internally expresses distrust or dislike for the message source. In effect, the receiver believes the source is biased and therefore does not perceive him or her as trustworthy. The third form of cognitive response, *supportive argumentation,* is a positive form of response. In this situation the receiver searches his or her knowledge bank and finds the source's message consistent with his or her own beliefs and values.

Using cognitive response theory as the theoretical basis, Dholakia and Sternthal made three predictions about the circumstances when a high-credibility source will be more, less, or equally effective with a low-credibility source:[22]

1. A high-credibility source should effect greater attitude change when receivers are initially *opposed* (i.e., have negative attitudes) to the communication topic. The basis for this prediction is that a high-credibility source under such circumstances should be able to inhibit the receiver's natural tendency to counterargue. Therefore, in the absence of these negative cognitive re-

---

[20]Brian Sternthal, Ruby Dholakia, and Clark Leavitt, "The Persuasive Effect of Source Credibility: Tests of Cognitive Response," *Journal of Consumer Research,* Vol. 14, March 1978, p. 259.

[21]Peter L. Wright, "The Cognitive Processes Mediating Acceptance of Advertising," *Journal of Marketing Research,* Vol. 10, February 1973, pp. 53–62.

[22]Ruby Roy Dholakia and Brian Sternthal, "Highly Credible Sources: Persuasive Facilitators or Persuasive Liabilities," *Journal of Consumer Research,* Vol. 3, March 1977, pp. 223–232.

sponses, positive attitude change should occur. In comparison, because a low-credibility source is unable to prevent counterargumentation, no positive attitude change should occur when a message is presented by a low-credibility source.

2. The opposite situation should prevail if receivers initially *favor* the topic of the persuasive communication. According to cognitive response theory, a low-credibility source should be more effective than a high-credibility source when attitudes are *already positive*. The rationale for this prediction is that receivers in response to an agreeable message from a low-credibility source should be inclined to perform the mental activity of bolstering their already positive thoughts (i.e., engage in supportive argumentation) because the low-credibility source does not provide external support for the receiver's already positive attitudes. Comparatively, receivers exposed to an agreeable message presented by a high-credibility source may be inclined simply to listen passively to what the source is saying rather than to expend the necessary cognitive effort to generate supportive arguments. In the absence of supportive argumentation, receivers' already positive attitudes cannot become more positive.

3. Finally, a high-credibility source should not be more or less effective than a low-credibility source when the receiver's attitudes are initially *neutral* toward the topic of the persuasive communications. Table 6.2 summarizes these cognitive response predictions.

Dholakia and Sternthal tested their predictions in an experiment in which arguments in favor of a consumer protection agency were delivered either by a high-credibility source (a Harvard lawyer) or a less credible source (a government spokesman).[23] Subjects (graduate students) gave their attitudes toward the pro-

---

TABLE 6.2   **Cognitive Response Theory Predictions Regarding Source Credibility Effectiveness**

Receiver's	Source Credibility	
Initial Attitude	Low	High
Negative	No positive attitude change	Positive attitude change
Positive	Positive attitude change	No positive attitude change
Neutral	No difference between low and high credibility sources in their ability to effect positive attitude change.	

Source: Adapted from Ruby Roy Dholakia and Brian Sternthal, "Highly Credible Sources: Persuasive Sources or Persuasive Liabilities?" *Journal of Consumer Research*, Vol. 3, March 1977, pp. 223–232.

---

[23]Ibid.

posed consumer protection agency and also were requested to sign a petition in its favor. With attitude as the dependent variable, there was no consistent evidence that the highly credible source was more effective than the less credible source; however, the petition was signed by a significantly greater number of subjects who had been assigned to the high-credibility condition.

Sternthal, Dholakia, and Leavitt performed two additional experiments to test Dholakia and Sternthal's predictions further.[24] Message recipients who were favorably predisposed to the consumer protection agency were found to generate a greater number of favorable cognitive responses (i.e., supportive arguments) to a moderately credible source. In comparison, when recipients were negatively predisposed toward the message topic, a highly credible source predictably induced more favorable cognitive responses.

Harmon and Coney extended this research orientation to a more applied setting by presenting businessmen with printed ads for microcomputers.[25] Their experimental design assigned respondents to a high or moderate credibility source condition and to a favorable or unfavorable initial disposition condition. The latter was operationalized by a "terms of purchase" condition, with a lease arrangement representing a more favorable form of purchase than buying the computer outright. In accord with the findings of Sternthal et al., Harmon and Coney's results showed that the moderately credible source was more effective under the lease condition when the businessmen's predispositions were already favorable, but the highly credible source was more effective in the buy condition when their attitudes were unfavorable.

In sum, the conclusion to be drawn from the cited research is that the decision of whether marketing communicators should employ high- or low-credibility sources depends largely on the target audience's existing opinion toward the topic of the persuasive communications. If the audience is known to have an unfavorable opinion, then a highly credible source is advisable. If, on the other hand, the audience's position is neutral or positive, a highly credible source may be no more persuasive than a less credible source. Since audiences (such as receivers of television commercials) are rarely homogeneous in their attitudes toward the communication's topic (such as their opinions toward Brand X), it would seem in general that the safest approach would be to use as highly credible sources as can possibly be justified economically.

Source Credibility Effects over Time

Suppose consumers are exposed to a sales message for a new product that is presented by a low-credibility source. It might be expected that consumers' immediate attitudes toward the product would not be very positive because the source lacks credibility. However, might there be a possibility that consumers would eventually forget about the message source, yet

---

[24]Sternthal et al., "The Persuasive Effect of Source Credibility."

[25]Robert P. Harmon and Kenneth A. Coney, "The Persuasive Effects of Source Credibility in Buy and Lease Situations," *Journal of Marketing Research*, Vol. 19, May 1982, pp. 255–260.

remember what the source said about the product, and consequently have a more favorable product attitude at some later date than they had initially?

The preceding question relates to a topic that has interested researchers for several decades. The first study involving the long-term effects of messages was performed by Hovland, Lumsdaine, and Sheffield, who exposed servicemen to a propaganda film and then measured their attitudes one week and nine weeks after exposure to the film. They found that the servicemen's agreement with what was communicated in the film was greater after nine weeks than after one week. They dubbed this increase in attitude over time the "sleeper effect." The soldiers presumably ruminated on, or "slept on," the propaganda idea, which became more persuasive over time.[26]

In general, the sleeper effect labels the phenomenon whereby the impact of a persuasive message increases over time. Hovland and colleagues explained this effect in terms of the "dissociative cue hypothesis."[27] "According to this hypothesis, the immediate persuasive impact of an otherwise compelling message is inhibited because of its association with a low credibility source or some other discounting cue [which lessens the persuasive impact of the message arguments]. With the passage of time, however, the message becomes dissociated from the discounting cue, resulting in increased message influence."[28] The theoretical sleeper effect is illustrated in Figure 6.4.

The sleeper effect has been challenged by several researchers who claim that (1) it does not exist,[29] (2) the methodology to demonstrate its existence has been inadequate,[30] and (3) it is time to lay the sleeper effect to rest.[31] More recent theorizing and research by Hannah and Sternthal has challenged the critics.[32] Hannah and Sternthal formulated a theoretical framework that explains the conditions under which a sleeper effect should and should not occur better than the dissociative cue hypothesis. The entire explanation is too technical to be described here. However, the basic conclusion from this important work is that a sleeper effect will materialize under the right set of message *and* consumer information-processing conditions.

Although a sleeper effect can be demonstrated under a set of well-controlled laboratory conditions, practicing marketing communicators would find little use in

---

[26]Carl Hovland, Arthur A. Lumsdaine, and Fred D. Sheffield, *Experiments on Mass Communication* (Princeton, NJ: Princeton University Press, 1949), pp. 188–189.

[27]Ibid.

[28]Darlene B. Hannah and Brian Sternthal, "Detecting and Explaining the Sleeper Effect," *Journal of Consumer Research,* Vol. 11, September 1984, p. 632.

[29]Noel Capon and James Hulbert, "The Sleeper Effect—An Awakening," *Public Opinion Quarterly,* Vol. 37, Fall 1973, pp. 333–358.

[30]C. Gruder, T. Cook, K. Hennigan, R. Flay, G. Alessis, and J. Halamaj, "Empirical Tests of the Absolute Sleeper Effect Predicted from the Discounting Cue Hypotheses," *Journal of Personality and Social Psychology,* Vol. 36, October 1978, pp. 1061–1074.

[31]Paulette M. Gillig and Anthony P. Greenwald, "Is It Time to Lay the Sleeper Effect to Rest?" *Journal of Personality and Social Psychology,* Vol. 29, January 1974, pp. 132–139.

[32]Hannah and Sternthal, "Detecting and Explaining the Sleeper Effect," p. 632.

FIGURE 6.4   **Theoretical Sleeper Effect**

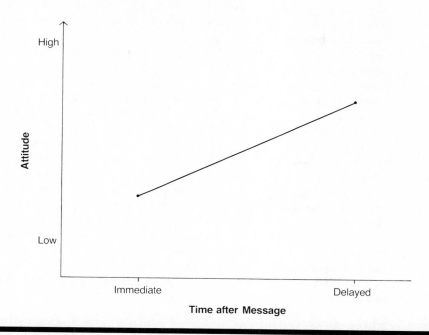

employing the conditions that are necessary to create a sleeper effect. Thus, marketing communicators should generally not use low-credibility sources but should instead use a highly credible source. Marketers should also repeatedly expose the target audience to the source so that the positive bond between the source and the message is firmly established and positive attitudes toward the marketer's product are maintained.

Marketing Communications Sources

Up to this point, the source of a message has been viewed as a rather vague entity possessing traits that are expected to influence a receiver's acceptance of a persuasive appeal. In marketing communications, the situation is more complex than this. Consumers may view several components within the marketing system as sources of marketing information. Moreover, these sources may have combined effects upon customer attitudes and the responses they make to a firm's marketing communications.

Sources of marketing communications include companies and their sales representatives, media, hired spokespersons, and retailers. Depending on the product and the situation, any one of these sources may play an important part in influencing consumer's attitudes.

Company Image

Although a company is a collection of people, materials, and machines, it is usually viewed by consumers as a single entity that possesses a distinct personality. People describe companies with such terms as "honest," "progressive," "undependable," "strong," and so on. The specific image a corporation has depends considerably upon its advertising and public relations campaigns. Some companies spend enormous sums of money in corporate image advertising, aside from money spent in advertising their brands. At other times, corporate advertising is integrated with brand advertising. For example, an advertisement for the Chevrolet Celebrity automobile ends with the theme "Chevrolet—taking charge," in reference to all Chevrolet models. Another example is the Textron company's advertising for a specific aerospace/electronics product that concludes with the phrase "Textron—where imagination becomes reality."

A corporation's image is a long-term investment and should be considered every time a decision is made at high or low levels of management. A company that is perceived as reputable, credible, progressive, and concerned for its customers and for the community has a valuable asset. Marketers should not underestimate the value of a firm's image and its effect upon customer behavior. For example, we can only wonder at the time of this writing what effect the tragic industrial accident in Bhopal, India, in December 1984 will have on Union Carbide's image and future.[33]

Sales Representatives

Sales representatives represent a critically important source of information, especially in business-to-business marketing. Company image and salesperson competence often complement one another. For example, a company's overall image will exert considerable influence on the effectiveness of sales representatives in their day-to-day contact with customers. Levitt demonstrated this in an industrial selling experiment.[34] Subjects were exposed to a ten-minute film in which a sales presentation was made on a new chemical ingredient used in making paint. One group saw a "good" presentation by a salesman representing a high-credibility company (Monsanto); another group observed a "poor" presentation by the same well-known firm. Two other groups saw "good" and "poor" sales presentations by sales representatives representing a relatively low-credibility firm. Levitt learned that there is an interaction effect between companies and sales representatives. That is, customers are more likely to favor the products of the poor sales representatives

---

[33]Over 2,500 people were killed when methyl isocyanate, a deadly chemical used to make pesticides, accidentally escaped into the air from a faulty valve. See "India's Night of Death," *Time,* December 17, 1984, pp. 22–31.

[34]Theodore Levitt, "Communications and Industrial Selling," *Journal of Marketing,* Vol. 31, April 1967, pp. 15–21.

from a well-known company than a good sales representative from an unknown company.

The effect demonstrated by Levitt gives the well-known company sales representative an advantage in the short run, even though customers perceive the sales representatives to be low in competence and trustworthiness. Reputable companies may, therefore, be more able to get by with less competent salespeople (at least in the short run), whereas less well known companies must carefully select and train their salespeople in order to compete with the more reputable firms. More will be said in Chapter 11 about how sales representatives can become more effective communicators.

The Media

Consumers sometimes view the media as sources of information. For example, *Good Housekeeping* and *Parents' Magazine* have established themselves as credible sources in many consumers' minds. Both have established standards that advertisers must meet in order to advertise in their magazines. Furthermore, they use seals of approval to endorse certain consumer products. Companies seek the approval of these media to gain a measure of prestige that is associated with these seals.

Hired Promoters

Hired promoters are often perceived as sources of advertising messages. Recent examples of successful hired promoters are Rodney Dangerfield, John Houseman, Bill Cosby, and George Burns. *Advertising Age* selected Dangerfield as the Star Presenter of the Year for 1983 "primarily for his significant contributions to the long-running Miller Lite campaign."[35] Dangerfield has also promoted rock stations, Pilot Pen, and Lo-Sal antacid tablets, among others. In the Lo-Sal campaign Dangerfield's personality was so dominant that he overshadowed the product—consumers remembered the comedian, but not the product. Perhaps the lesson from this experience is that a popular celebrity can overpower a brand in consumers' minds, particularly if (1) the brand is new and (2) the ad is not properly scripted and directed.

John Houseman is another person who has made a large impact on television viewers. His celebrated Smith, Barney advertisement significantly increased the public's awareness for a previously obscure brokerage company. Because of Houseman's age, speech pattern, and authoritarian and commanding demeanor, he comes across to viewers as a highly credible spokesman.

Bill Cosby is a very popular celebrity and has promoted a variety of products and services, among them Jello pudding, Coca Cola, Texas Instruments, and various health-related campaigns. Mr. Cosby received the most "mentions" from among

[35]James P. Forkan, "Dangerfield Is Star Presenter," *Advertising Age,* August 1, 1983, pp. 3, 32.

the many hired promoters who were represented in a consumer survey by *Advertising Age.*[36] Recall of celebrities in advertisements were relatively high for Bob Hope, Don Meredith, Jaclyn Smith, James Garner, Ed McMahon, Brooke Shields, Roger Staubach, and several others. However, consumers had a high degree of skepticism whether these endorsers use the products they tout. That is, most consumers believed that these endorsements were bought and were not honest testimonials.[37]

All hired celebrity promoters share the source characteristic of attractiveness. None really have any special expertise for the products they promote, nor the power characteristics to control rewards and punishments to persuade consumers. Therefore, we might surmise that celebrities are effective promoters primarily as a result of their *attractiveness* and perhaps also their *trustworthiness.*

Sometimes advertisers use unknown spokespersons dressed in lab coats to promote, for example, one cold capsule over other brands. Still another approach is to gain the endorsement of a well-respected association, such as the Council for Dental Therapeutics of the American Dental Association. This group has been used for years by Procter & Gamble to promote Crest toothpaste. Here the advertiser relies upon the perceived *prestige* and *expertise* of this highly respected council to promote their brand.

Testimonial advertising is perhaps the most frequently used approach in which hired promoters are used. The testimonial can be presented by either a well-known celebrity or someone who is unknown to the audience. As a perceived expert in golf, Jack Nicklaus may be quite persuasive as an endorser of MacGregor golf equipment. However, his motives may be questionable to some consumers. In an attempt to overcome this credibility problem, some advertisers have used testimonials from "average" homemakers to endorse products. Sometimes this takes the form of "candid" conversations with housewives. To the extent that consumers perceive these advertisements to be unrehearsed, unsolicited testimonials, the consumer is susceptible to the persuasiveness of the message.

Other Sources

Retailers often act as sources for product messages. "Take, for example, a message dealing with the sale of well-known national brands (which cannot be mentioned in the ad) at substantial savings by a given retailer. Clearly, the reader's perception of the source (the retailer) will have an important effect on the credibility of the message—especially with respect to what constitutes " 'well-known national brands' and 'substantial savings.' "[38] This ploy is often used in retail furniture store

---

[36]Scott Hume, "Stars Are Lacking Luster as Ad Presenters," *Advertising Age,* November 7, 1983, pp. 3, 92.

[37]Ibid.

[38]Harper W. Boyd, *Promotion: A Behavioral View* (Englewood Cliffs, NJ: Prentice-Hall, 1967), pp. 95–96.

advertising where "national" brands are relatively unknown to many customers. The retailer becomes the source of the message, and the extent to which local consumers are familiar with the retailer determines the effectiveness of the message.

Industries, trade associations, and organizations can also serve as sources of information. For example, the food industry, the United Auto Workers union, the federal government, and United Way may be perceived as potential sources of information. Further, current users of a particular brand or product may be perceived as influential sources of information, as in the case of tastemakers, trend setters, or opinion leaders, which are discussed in Chapter 8.

Combined Source Effects

To this point the chapter has treated each marketing source as a separate entity. In reality, the sources' effects combine to influence consumer evaluations of product messages. These combined effects can be illustrated by the following example: When a person reads an advertisement in *Tennis World* for Wilson rackets endorsed by Jimmy Connors, who is the source—the magazine, the company, or the famous tennis player? It is not necessary to define one source to the exclusion of the others. All three have a combined and, the advertiser hopes, synergistic impact on the reader.

In most situations, several sources interact to produce an impact on the customer. The marketing communicator must examine the extent to which one source may cancel the effectiveness of another source with which it is combined. In the short run, the prestigious company may carry the weight of ineffective sales representatives. Eventually, however, the company's reputation will suffer unless action is taken to improve the skills of the poor salesperson. The same holds true for retailers. A retailer who suffers from a poor image in the community may lower the prestige of the manufacturer's brands that it carries. Thus, careful selection of resellers is an important consideration for manufacturers in maintaining or enhancing their reputations. In similar fashion, advertisers must be careful to select spokespersons who enhance rather than detract from a brand's reputation.

Summary

This chapter reviews source factors in marketing communications. The notion of a source is a multifaceted concept that includes a person, a group, an organization, or even a label. Marketing communication sources influence receivers by possessing one or more of three necessary attributes: power, attractiveness, and credibility. Source power influences receivers via a compliance mechanism; attractiveness through identification; and credibility via the process of internalization.

An interesting situation occurs in marketing communications when the customer's attitude toward the source is either more or less favorable than his or her attitude toward the object of the persuasive message. In such instances, incongruency or inconsistency is said to exist. This creates mental pressure on the consumer to attempt to restore consistency by changing his or her attitude toward the source, the object, or both. The specific process by which this occurs is explained by balance and congruency theories. Congruency theory extends the balance theory by (1) explicitly considering the strength, as well as direction (positive or negative), of attitudes toward source and object and (2) considering whether the source says something favorable about the object (an associative bond) or something unfavorable (a dissociative bond).

Cognitive response theory is used to account for the conditions when a high-credibility source is likely to be more or less effective than a low-credibility source. This theory predicts that a high-credibility source should be more effective than a low-credibility source when the audience has a negative attitude toward the message topic, whereas a low-credibility source may be no less effective than a high-credibility source when the audience's initial attitude is positive.

The chapter concludes with a discussion of practical marketing communication sources: company reputation and image, sales representatives, the media, hired promoters, and retailers.

Discussion Questions

1.   Compare the processes of compliance, identification, and internalization.
2.   Explain why a marketing communicator would prefer to change consumer attitudes through an internalization process rather than through compliance or identification.
3.   What does it take to be an attractive source? Is Jimmy Connors more or less attractive than John McEnroe? Is Meryl Streep more or less attractive than Jaclyn Smith?
4.   A consumer (Elizabeth) likes Chanel #5 perfume, but she dislikes Catherine Deneuve, who endorses that product. In terms of balance theory, is this a balanced or unbalanced state? Which of the eight configurations in Figure 6.1 does this situation characterize? What might Elizabeth do to restore consistency?
5.   What is the difference between an associative and dissociative bond? Provide an example from an actual marketing communications situation of each of these bonds.
6.   The amount of attitude change is a function of attitude extremity. Explain.
7.   Distinguish between an attractive and a credible source. How can a source be both attractive and credible? Provide two or three examples of well-known product spokespersons who, in your opinion, are high in both attractiveness and credibility. Justify why you consider these individuals to possess both attributes.
8.   What are the requirements for a trustworthy source? Provide several examples of well-known product spokespersons who, in your opinion, are particularly trustworthy. In what sense are these individuals trustworthy?
9.   Distinguish among counterargumentation, supportive argumentation, and source derogation. Provide personal examples for each of these cognitive

responses as they may relate to you or some other consumer in response to the following hypothetical situation: Famous movie actor Robert Redford appears in a public service announcement and asserts that people should stop smoking cigarettes because smoking is dangerous to one's health, is unattractive, and invades the privacy of nonsmokers.

Exercises

1. Anheuser-Busch used the aged comedian George Burns in 1985 as a television spokesman to promote its low-alcohol beer, LA. With Figure 6.2 as the model, construct your own original position and new equilibrium for this situation.

2. Collect advertisements from used magazines, and locate two or three illustrations of each of the following: credible sources, attractive sources, trustworthy sources. Explain why you chose each example to illustrate a particular source characteristic.

3. Interview five fellow students who are not presently taking or have not previously taken this course. Ask them to describe what characteristics they think a successful sales representative for a computer manufacturer must possess. Then ask them the same question for an automobile salesperson. Summarize the responses separately for each type of salesperson in terms of attractiveness, credibility, trustworthiness, and any other characteristics that your respondents have used to describe these successful salespeople.

CHAPTER 7

Group Influences on Consumer Choice Behavior

Thus far this book has treated the receiver as though he or she were isolated from influence by people other than the sender. The approach facilitated discussion of the effects of important communications variables. Realistically, however, an individual does not transmit or receive messages in a vacuum. He or she moves through life influencing and being influenced by other people. A person's attention to and perception of marketing communications are influenced, and to a large extent altered, by the groups to which he or she belongs. A consumer's purchase decisions are likely to be influenced to varying degrees by group influences. The purpose of this chapter is to view the consumer (receiver) in the context of these groups.

Kinds of Groups

Each person belongs to many groups, and each group exerts different levels of influence upon people's lives. Groups influence the way we live and the way we communicate. In communications, groups shape the meanings we have for words and the way we use those words. In fact, the meanings we hold today for certain words and expressions may be dramatically different than the meanings previous generations held for these same words and expressions. Take, for example, the word *mean*. "That's a mean machine" does not suggest the machine is contemptible or despicable but rather that the machine (such as a motorcycle) possesses very strong, positive qualities. Though the meanings of some words change, most of our language remains relatively stable and is passed intact from generation to generation.

The sizes of what are considered to be groups can vary considerably. A group can be as large as an entire culture, encompassing millions of people, or as small as a two-person family. In general, a group is "a plurality of individuals who are in contact with one another, who take one another into account, and who are aware of some significant commonality."[1] Thus, the difference between a true group and a mere random assemblage of people is that group members interact with one another, share symbols and meanings, and in a sense have a common cause.

Groups vary greatly in terms of their sizes, forms, interaction patterns, degrees of formality, and so on. Sociologists and other students of group behavior have identified several different types of groups: (1) **formal groups** (those having specified membership requirements, bylaws, etc.) and **informal groups**; (2) **primary groups** (typically small, face-to-face groups) and **secondary groups**; (3) **membership groups** (ones in which a person actually "belongs") and **aspirational groups** (ones in which a person does not belong but wishes to); and (4) **dissociative groups** (those with which an individual identifies negatively and eschews associations with the group's members).[2]

Groups affect what a person elects to see or hear as well as what he or she comprehends or perceives from the stimuli. Furthermore, groups are influential in the diffusion of innovations. For example, members who belong to or associate with groups having modern norms tend to be more receptive to new ideas than members of groups holding more traditional norms. (Detailed coverage of product adoption and diffusion appears in Chapter 8.)

Groups obviously play an important role in the total marketing communications process. At this point several types of groups will be examined in some detail. The discussion extends from macro group influences—culture and subculture—to micro influences—reference groups and family. Figure 7.1 illustrates the nature of group influences on the individual from the most general form of cultural influence to the specific influence of reference groups and family.

Cultural Groups

The largest group that influences a person's behavior is the cultural group to which he or she belongs. The word *culture* has been defined in many different ways. This text will define **culture** as the "complex of values, ideas, attitudes, and other meaningful symbols created by man to shape human behavior and the artifacts of

---

[1]Michael S. Olmsted, *The Small Group* (New York: Random House, 1959), p. 21, as cited in Thomas S. Robertson, Joan Zielinski, and Scott Ward, *Consumer Behavior* (Glenview, IL: Scott, Foresman and Company, 1984), p. 420.

[2]For further discussion, see James F. Engel and Roger D. Blackwell, *Consumer Behavior,* 4th Ed. (Chicago: The Dryden Press, 1982), pp. 144–145.

FIGURE 7.1   **Group Effects on Individual Behavior**

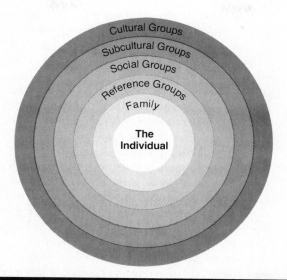

that behavior as they are transmitted from one generation to the next."[3] This definition is oriented to communications because it recognizes that people create meaningful symbols that shape human behavior. It also emphasizes that culture is learned behavior and not innate. Through language, people are able to preserve the values and ideas of their ancestors. Values, ideas, attitudes, and related artifacts are passed from generation to generation through the **socialization process,** i.e., the process of learning one's own cultural heritage. Socialization is a lifelong process, which commences in one's formative years with the influences of family, religion, and school and continues through life with the continuing influence of friends, work associates, mass media, and other sources.

Culture, because it is learned behavior, is subject to change. Although cultural change in most societies is typically slow and evolutionary, occurring over hundreds of years, cultural change in economically advanced societies is sometimes rather abrupt. Consider, for example, eating patterns in the United States. Our values and attitudes toward eating and the associated artifacts of eating (utensils, types of food, food preparation) are, of course, learned and transmitted from one generation to another. Past generations of Americans (up to at least the late 1950s in most parts of the United States) valued such ideas as eating three times a day, getting a balanced diet, eating at home with family members, consuming meat

[3]Ibid., p. 72.

and potatoes followed by a dessert, and so forth. Today, the attitudes toward eating have changed drastically: Many meals are eaten away from home, family members often eat alone rather than together, people eat on the run and sporadically rather than at fixed times (pop sociologists refer to this as "grazing"), a much greater variety of foods are consumed, and people are more health conscious in choosing what foods to eat.

These changes in America's eating culture have had and will continue to have implications for all aspects of marketing and marketing communications. For example, (1) restaurants and fast-food chains are open for extended hours to accommodate diner's eating whims; (2) food packages for in-home preparation now include smaller portions to enable individual family members to eat alone; (3) many food items are packaged to permit microwave cooking, the speed of which has much appeal for today's time-conscious consumers; (4) a variety of ethnic foods are now available for people who enjoy experimenting with food rather than eating the more standard American dishes; (5) more healthy foods, e.g., items lower in sodium and sugar, are available for society's health- and fitness-conscious consumers; and (6) low-calorie items (e.g., "Lean Cuisine" dinners) satisfy the needs of weight-conscious consumers.

The cultural changes associated with eating apply also to nearly all other aspects of American society. Successful companies and marketing communicators are those that know what changes are taking place in society and make the necessary changes in their products and marketing strategies to stay abreast of society's changing preferences and behavior patterns.

The Role of Values

The concept of **values** is basic to understanding the influence that culture has on marketing communications and promotion management. Although there is no universally accepted definition of what a value is, the writing of Milton Rokeach has been particularly influential in clarifying the meaning of values. Values, according to Rokeach, are enduring, culturally determined beliefs that a specific mode of behavior or end-state of existence is personally preferable to alternate modes of behavior or end-states.[4] Munson is perhaps a bit more specific when explaining that "values consist of beliefs about what the individual considers right, fair, just, or desirable. As such, values are used, for example, in comparison processes when people establish standards, judge issues, debate options, plan activities, reach decisions, resolve differences, change patterns, or exert influence."[5]

Researchers have distinguished between global or general cultural values and consumption-specific values.[6] Table 7.1 presents inventories of these two types of

---

[4]Milton Rokeach, *The Nature of Human Values* (New York: The Free Press, 1973).

[5]J. Michael Munson, "Personal Values: Considerations on Their Measurement and Application to Five Areas of Research Inquiry," in Robert E. Pitts, Jr., and Arch G. Woodside (eds.), *Personal Values and Consumer Psychology* (Lexington, MA: Lexington Books, 1984), p. 16.

[6]Donald E. Vinson, Jerome E. Scott, and Lawrence M. Lamont, "The Role of Personal Values in Marketing and Consumer Behavior," *Journal of Marketing,* Vol. 41, April 1977, pp. 44–50.

TABLE 7.1 **Cultural and Consumption-Specific Values in American Society**

Inventory of Cultural Values	Inventory of Consumption-Specific Values
A comfortable life	Prompt service
An exciting life	Reliable advertising claims
A world at peace	Responsiveness to consumer needs
Equality	Accurate information
Freedom	Elimination of pollution
Happiness	Free repair of defective products
National security	Convenient store locations
Pleasure	No deceptive advertising
Salvation	Courteous and helpful sales people
Social recognition	Low prices
True friendship	Solutions to urban decay and unemployment
A world of beauty	Legislation to protect the consumer
Family security	No product misrepresentation
Mature love	
Accomplishment	
Inner harmony	

Source: Henry Assael, *Consumer Behavior and Marketing Action* (Boston: Kent Publishing Company, 1984), p. 287. A compilation of data from the following sources: Cultural values from Milton J. Rokeach, "The Role of Values in Public Opinion Research," *Public Opinion Quarterly* 32 (Winter 1968): 554; Consumption-specific values from Donald E. Vinson, Jerome E. Scott, and Lawrence M. Lamont, "The Role of Personal Values in Marketing and Consumer Behavior," *Journal of Marketing* 41 (April 1977): 47. Reprinted with permission from the *Journal of Marketing.*

values. Both types play extremely important roles in influencing social behavior in general and consumer behavior specifically. Moreover, what is particularly important to promotion managers and other marketing communicators is that the priority of values changes from time to time. Value shifts have been especially pronounced in the United States during the past several decades. Traditional values, beliefs, and attitudes have been reappraised and challenged, and substantial changes have occurred. Daniel Yankelovich, a respected survey researcher and social commentator, described the United States as moving in a few short years "from an uptight culture set in a dynamic economy to a dynamic culture set in an uptight economy."[7] Many Americans have, in other words, challenged the traditional, Puritan ethic norm that social acceptability and personal success depend upon hard work, self-denial, and delayed gratification. These individuals (Yankelovich estimates that they represent as many as 80 percent of the American population[8]) have opted for a new norm that places highest priority on personal pleasure and self-fulfillment.

Manifestations of this "self-fulfillment culture" include a higher divorce rate, lower worker productivity, and increased drug consumption.[9] The self-fulfillment

[7]Daniel Yankelovich, "New Rules in American Life: Searching for Self-Fulfillment in a World Turned Upside Down," *Psychology Today,* April 1981, p. 43.

[8]Ibid., p. 39.

[9]Ibid.

trend has led to greater buy-now-and-pay-later purchasing and an increased willingness on the part of consumers to indulge and spoil themselves. Marketing communicators have altered their messages to reflect these underlying changes in consumer motivation and behavior. Many popular advertising themes (e.g., "You only go around once, so go for the gusto"; "You deserve a break today") have been created to reinforce the belief that being hedonistic is perfectly appropriate.

Various social commentators contend that the self-fulfillment period in the United States is simply a passing fancy and that more traditional values will return in due course. It is beyond the purpose of this text to evaluate this point. Rather, the more basic point is that social values are indeed subject to change, and marketing communicators must stay alert to these changes and incorporate them into promotional messages when appropriate.

Many marketing organizations are unable or unwilling to make the necessary investment to monitor changes in social values. For this reason various specialized research firms have evolved to perform such monitoring and to sell reports of their findings to interested companies. Prominent examples include *The Trend Report* published by futurist John Naisbitt, who has achieved notoriety with his publication of ten major megatrends that affect American society,[10] the Yankelovich *Monitor* published by Yankelovich, Skelly, and White, Inc., and the Stanford Research Institute's VALS (Values and Life-Styles) typology. This discussion will only deal with the VALS typology because it is probably the most influential of all social value monitoring services.

The VALS typology was created by Arnold Mitchell of the Stanford Research Institute.[11] The typology, which is based on a combination of values, attitudes, and demographic variables, consists of three main segments: (1) the Need Driven, (2) the Outer-Directed, and (3) the Inner-Directed. Each segment is, as we shall see, further subdivided into two or more subgroups.

The Need Driven   This VALS segment represents the physiologically needy and poor people in American society. It comprises approximately 11 percent of the adult population and consists of two distinguishable groups: survivors and sustainers. **Survivors** represent about 4 percent of the adult population and are the poorest group in American society with a median household income in 1979 of only $3,200. They are also the oldest of the VALS types, with a median age of 66. Many are separated or divorced. Survivors hold conventional attitudes toward morality.

The **sustainers** group, representing 7 percent of the population, consists predominantly of low-income families and minorities. Sustainers as a group are inclined to believe the system is against them and, accordingly, seek status and acceptance from among their peers rather than from the larger society.

---

[10]John Naisbitt, *Megatrends: Ten New Directions Transforming Our Lives* (New York: Warner Books, 1982).

[11]Arnold Mitchell, *Consumer Values: A Typology* (Menlo Park, CA: SRI International, 1978). For a more thorough review of Miller's work see Rebecca H. Holman, "A Values and Lifestyles Perspective on Human Behavior," in Pitts and Woodside, *Personal Values and Consumer Psychology,* pp. 35–54.

The Outer-Directed This VALS segment constitutes nearly two-thirds of the adult American population and consists of three subgroups—the belongers, emulators, and achievers. Outer-directed people are, in general, concerned with the expectations of others and adhere to the norms of society at large. This group represents what is commonly referred to as middle America.

Belongers, representing 35 percent of the population, is an older group, with a median age of 52. As the name suggests, the members of this group are deeply concerned with social acceptability and conformity. Belongers are mostly married, white, and live in small towns or rural areas. Attitudinally, they are satisfied with life, averse to taking risks, and trust others.

Emulators represent 10 percent of the population, are young (median age 28), live in urban areas, and tend to be somewhat dissatisfied with life because they perceive the system has somehow been unfair to them. They compensate for their felt inadequacies by emulating the behavior of higher status people. In fact, the emulators often spend beyond their means.

The last outer-directed group is the **achievers,** who constitute 22 percent of the adult American population. Achievers are, as the name suggests, the successful businesspeople, technocrats, and professionals in American society. Demographically, achievers are well-educated, middle-aged (median age of 42), relatively affluent (median income of $32,000 in 1979), and mostly white and married. Psychographically, achievers are highly self-confident, possess high need for achievement, and are very conservative.

The Inner-Directed People in this VALS group tend to "march to their own drummer" rather than concern themselves with meeting societal expectations and conforming; in a sense, they reject the intense material orientation that dominates the lives of the outer-directeds. Inner-directeds constitute only about 22 percent of the adult population, but this group has experienced the most rapid growth in the past decade. There are three major subgroups: the I-Am-Me's, the experientials, and the societally conscious.[12]

The **I-Am-Me's** represent the youngest group in the VALS typology, with over 90 percent being younger than 25. Many are college students who are the children of the achievers group. They tend to be somewhat flamboyant and exhibitionistic and experiment with the unconventional. The I-Am-Me stage tends to be short-lived because most I-Am-Meers become experientials as they age and mature.

Experientials as a group are young (median age 28), well educated, and reasonably well-off financially (median income of $22,300 in 1979). As suggested by the name, experientials are interested in experiencing life. They tend not to become committed to any long-term relationships and are, instead, relatively liberated and impulsive. From the perspective of the achievers group, experientials are

---

[12]A fourth group, called *integrateds,* has also been identified, but this group is much too small for practical marketing purposes.

unambitious. However, experientials obtain their primary gratification, not from work, but from other life experiences.

The **societally conscious** group is (1) the oldest of the inner-directeds (median age of 37), (2) the most educated of all the VALS groups, and (3) second only to the achievers in income level (median income of $25,500 in 1979). What most distinguishes this group is its concern for others and desire to improve life in general. Societally conscious individuals tend to support liberal causes and become involved in community affairs.

Implications for Marketing Communications   The VALS typology is a potentially valuable tool for consumer goods marketers and for advertising agencies. SRI performs customized studies for clients to determine how the users of a particular product category (the one marketed by the client) are distributed among the various VALS categories. Armed with this information, a company is then prepared to know how best to direct its marketing communication efforts and what appeals may be most effective in motivating the target group to action.

It is important to point out that VALS is no panacea. VALS data are generally insufficient as a sole basis for segmenting markets and formulating marketing mixes. It has been charged, in fact, that for segmentation purposes the VALS scheme is "too simple, too remote, too rigid, and too unreliable."[13] The fact remains, however, that many companies use VALS data as one of several inputs for purposes of identifying market segments, pinpointing appropriate media, and selecting effective advertising appeals. And, perhaps most important of all, the VALS typology offers a rich and meaningful working terminology for describing American consumers. The VALS typology has its limitations, but as George Burns said when asked how he felt about turning 80, "It's not bad, considering the alternative."

The Role of Culture in International Business

Understanding cultural values, attitudes, and artifacts is crucial to effective marketing communications activities in international business operations. Many companies have learned all too often that programs successful in domestic markets frequently fail in foreign markets. Ricks has compiled a number of illustrations of marketing communications blunders that businesses have committed when entering other cultural markets.[14] His interesting descriptions (see Figure 7.2 for illustrations) deserve careful attention. Note that in nearly every instance the blunder would probably not have been committed had someone taken the time to understand the culture where the blunder occurred.

---

[13]Sonia Yuspeh, "Syndicated Values/Lifestyles Segmentation Schemes: Use Them As Descriptive Tools, Not to Select Targets," *Marketing News,* May 25, 1984, pp. 2, 12 in Section 2.

[14]David A. Ricks, *Big Business Blunders* (Homewood, IL: Dow Jones-Irwin, 1983).

FIGURE 7.2   **Illustrative Big Business Blunders in Marketing Communications**

Product and Package Mistakes

Campbell Soup Company erred when they introduced their popular American *condensed* soups into the British soup market. Although competitively priced with existing British soups, the campaign initially failed since the British are accustomed to buying soups which are not condensed (i.e., don't require a liquid additive such as water) and therefore believed they would be buying half as much soup in the Campbell's can. (p. 24)

Mistakes with Brand Names

Automobile companies have had their share of cultural problems in naming (or, perhaps, misnaming) their cars. Examples are (a) Chevrolet's Nova, in Spanish, means "it doesn't go"; (b) AMC's "Matador" means "killer" in Puerto Rico; (c) Ford's low-cost truck, the "Fiera," means "ugly old woman" in Spanish; (d) Ford renamed their "Comet" automobile "Caliente" for the Mexican market, only to find the word is slang for streetwalker; (e) the Ford "Pinto" was marketed in Brazil under its American name, but was quickly changed when the company learned that pinto is Portuguese slang for "a small male appendage"; and (f) Rolls Royce learned that the English name "Silver Mist" would not appeal to the German market since the word "mist" means "dung" or "manure." (pp. 38–40)

Advertising Mistakes

When companies enter markets in other cultures, they should carefully consider local customs. What are "normal" displays of behavior in one culture may be offensive in other cultures. In promoting a mouthwash in Thailand, a firm used ads showing a young man and woman holding hands. The promotion failed since Thais, as well as other cultures, view physical contact between members of the opposite sex as unacceptable and offensive behavior. The company changed the ads to show two women discussing the product, and the Thais found them acceptable. At the other end of the continuum, however, the French and Germans do not find such ads offensive, and in fact, feature in many ads near or total nudity. (p. 63)
In Saudi Arabia an airline company nearly didn't get off the ground when Saudi officials viewed their proposed newspaper advertisements. The ads depicted beautiful hostesses serving champagne to happy male passengers. What was "normal" advertising in the home country and other countries was not acceptable to Saudi Arabians since alcohol is illegal, and unveiled women are not allowed to mingle with men. The Saudis perceived these pictorial ads as an intrusion upon their religious customs. (pp. 66–68)

Translation Mistakes

Careless interpretations of promotional messages are the most frequent mistakes companies make in translation. An American automobile company promoted its cars as "topped them all." However, when translated for the French Canadian market, it read "topped by them all." Another American company advertised its car battery as "highly rated." When introduced to Venezuela, the ad said the car battery was "highly overrated." Perhaps the most difficult language problems international companies have are in the use of *idioms*. Many *expressions* that a culture uses are idiosyncratic to a particular country or region of a country. These expressions cannot be translated literally to convey their intended meanings. When Pepsi used their "Come Alive with Pepsi" promotion campaign in Germany, the literal translation was "Come out of the grave." In Asia, the translation was "Bring your ancestors back from the grave." (p. 84)

Source: Adapted from *Big Business Blunders* by David A. Ricks. Copyright by Dow Jones-Irwin. Used with permission. Page numbers for each example are in parentheses above.

Marketing Communications Theory and Research

Subcultural Groups

The overall culture of a society, the global culture, so to speak, encompasses the set of values, attitudes, beliefs, and related artifacts that are transmitted from one generation to the next via the process of socialization. In reality, however, there is no such thing as a single culture in the United States, or in any other society that shares a rich diversity of racial, national, ethnic, and religious groups. Each subgroup possesses its own configuration of cultural elements, i.e., its own set of values or beliefs that are somewhat different from, though not necessarily incompatible with, the global culture's.

Anthropologists and sociologists use the label *subculture* in referring to these cultural subgroups. Strictly speaking, a **subculture** is a group that possesses a social heritage distinct from the global culture's heritage.[15] This perspective is too restrictive, however, for practical marketing purposes. Marketing and consumer behavior scholars consider subcultures to be definable segments within the global culture that have relatively unique values and norms[16] and manifest "distinguishing modes of behavior."[17] In this sense, then, it is meaningful to talk about ethnic, religious, national, and geographic subcultures. Of course, cultural diversity exists within subcultures just as it does within global cultures. All Hispanics do not share the same values, norms, and behaviors, nor do all blacks, Jews, or other subcultures. Jews, for example, vary greatly in socioeconomic status and religious orientation, ranging from orthodox Jews to "Jews for Jesus."

Intragroup diversity aside, people within subcultures share more commonalities than differences. The statistical concept of **cluster analysis** provides a useful analogy in this regard. Cluster analysis is a procedure for grouping objects (e.g., people) into sets of collectively exhaustive and mutally exclusive groups (clusters). Statistically determined clusters possess the property of having less within-cluster variability than between-cluster variability. That is, objects assigned to a particular cluster are more like one another than they are like objects in other clusters. In similar fashion, people within subcultures differ among themselves in terms of values, norms, etc., yet their differences are less than their similarities. Thus, there are clusters (subcultures) of Jews, blacks, Hispanics, and so forth.

Marketing communications with these subcultures must be customized to be effective. The following sections examine three subcultures that are important to marketing communicators because of their size and unique characteristics: religious groups, blacks, and Hispanics.

---

[15]Robertson, Zielinski, and Ward, *Consumer Behavior*, p. 528.

[16]The notion of unique values and norms is implicit in the description of subculture by Engel and Blackwell, *Consumer Behavior*, p. 79.

[17]Gerald Zaltman, *Marketing Contributions from the Behavioral Sciences* (New York: Harcourt, Brace, & World, 1965), p. 7.

Religious Groups

Religious groups, because of their different attitudes and behaviors toward products and services, can often have a profound effect upon a company's marketing communications program. Protestants, Catholics, Jews, Mormons, and born-again Christians are examples of the religious diversity within the United States. Each religion has its beliefs and norms regarding the consumption and symbolic significance of particular foods, alcoholic beverages, cosmetics, jewelry, and the like.

As an example of an important religious subculture in the United States, the Jewish community has characteristics that distinguish it from other religious groups. Besides the fact that they are generally born into a culture and religion at the same time, Jews in the United States (1) are predominantly found in higher socioeconomic strata, (2) are considered high achievers in society, (3) are high in innovativeness, (4) are instrumental in adopting and diffusing new products, and (5) are disproportionately high in opinion leadership.[18] Media that reach Jewish consumers are therefore ideal for generating new product adoption and stimulating product diffusion via word of mouth and opinion leadership.

Another religious group, born-again Christians, is a growing segment that has attracted attention from many marketers.[19] National surveys have identified over 50 million adults as born-again Christians; roughly one out of three adults falls into this subculture. Marketing communicators have recently begun to direct their attention to the born-again category. For example, Sterling Drugs sponsored a radio program, the "Pat Boone Show," to promote Bayer aspirin to a Christian audience via Christian radio. Several national advertisers (e.g., Dart & Kraft) now advertise on cable television (the Christian Broadcasting Network) to reach the 25 million households who receive the "700 Club" and other Christian programs.

One observer has recommended that companies observe three basic guidelines when communicating with the born-again Christian community: (1) advertise in secular media, (2) stress conservative attitudes and life-styles, and (3) recognize the duality of the Christian mindset (see Figure 7.3 for details).

The Black Subculture

The black subculture is characterized more by its common heritage than by its skin color. This heritage includes "a shared history of discrimination and suffering, confined housing opportunities, and denial of participation in many aspects of the majority culture."[20] Many, perhaps most, black Americans share a common culture

---

[18]Elizabeth C. Hirschman, "American Jewish Ethnicity: Its Relationship to Some Selected Aspects of Consumer Behavior," *Journal of Marketing,* Vol. 45, Summer 1981, pp. 102–110.

[19]George E. Barna, "Study Research before Targeting 'Born-Again' Segment," *Marketing News,* January 4, 1985, p. 35. The description is extracted from this article.

[20]Engel and Blackwell, *Consumer Behavior,* p. 85.

FIGURE 7.3   **Guidelines for Marketing to Born-Again Christians**

The most effective way to reach Christians is to advertise in secular media. Christian media, both electronic and print, reach less than 5% of the total born-again population. Christians have a relatively strong appetite for news and information programs on secular TV, and are least likely to watch movies. These consumers also prefer radio stations which feature news, talk shows, and contemporary music.

Stress conservative attitudes and life-styles. Advertising and promotions which imply new moral codes or breaks with traditional life-styles will be hard to sell to this group. Even when Christians accept new styles and values, it is usually some time after they've been embraced by the rest of society. Born-agains are neither trendsetters nor immediate trend followers.

Marketing campaigns should recognize the duality of the Christian mindset. Increasing numbers of Christians are becoming aware of the inconsistency between their dominant ways of thinking and behaving and the ways of life described in the Bible. This has produced a profound sense of confusion and guilt in the minds of many born-again adults.

Marketers would likely profit by recognizing this dilemma and avoiding communications that stimulate such concerns. Rather than capitalizing on the materialistic or hedonistic tastes of Christians, campaigns which seek to promote higher values within a competitive market environment would strike a pleasing note in the minds of many born-again people.

Thus, products which have the capacity for producing pleasure can be positioned as such, but within a context which corresponds with more traditional, nonexploitative values which would satisfy Biblical standards.

Source: George E. Barna, "Study Research before Targeting 'Born-Again' Segment," *Marketing News,* January 4, 1985, p. 36.

in that they have similar values, beliefs, and distinguishable behaviors. Yet, blacks do not represent a single culture any more than whites do.

Black Americans represent an attractive market for many companies. Several notable reasons account for this: (1) the aggregate income of black consumers exceeds $140 billion; (2) the average age of black Americans is 24.9 compared with 31.3 for whites; (3) blacks are geographically concentrated, 65 percent of all blacks live in the top 15 U.S. markets; (4) black consumption in some product categories is disproportionately greater than general population usage, e.g., blacks purchase 36 percent of hair-conditioning products, 23 percent of chewing gum, and 20 percent of rice; and (5) blacks tend to purchase prestige and name-brand products in greater proportion than do whites.[21]

These impressive figures notwithstanding, many companies make no special efforts to communicate with blacks. This is probably foolish because research indicates that blacks are responsive to advertisements placed in black-oriented media and advertisements that make personalized appeals by using black models and advertising contexts with which blacks can identify.[22] For example, the advertisement in Figure 7.4 would very likely have considerable appeal to black, as well as

[21]David Astor, "Black Spending Power: $140 Billion and Growing," *Marketing Communications,* July 1982, pp. 13, 14.

[22]Ibid.

FIGURE 7.4   **Use of Advertising to Appeal to Blacks and Whites**

It's exactly what it looks like.
Learning.

Speak & Spell, Speak & Read, Speak & Math from Texas Instruments.

Make learning fun and the world is your child's classroom. That's exactly what these sturdy, kid-size electronic learning aids from Texas Instruments are designed to do. They talk. Your child just touches the keyboard to enter an answer. "You are correct," these products say with praise when your child is right. And they offer encouragement if the answer is wrong.

Speak & Spell gives your child a head start in tackling troublesome areas in spelling such as homonyms, irregular verb endings and words with silent letters.

Speak & Read lets children hear words as well as see them used in

context so they can strengthen comprehension, draw conclusions and begin to see how words are made up by breaking them into sounds and syllables.

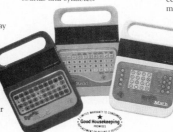

Speak & Math has 100,000 math problems and activities built into it to help children practice important mathematical operations and concepts. So even if you don't think of math as fun, your children can.

But best of all when these products work their magic, your children won't even think they're learning. They'll just think they're having fun.

TEXAS INSTRUMENTS
Creating useful products and services for you.

Source: Courtesy of Texas Instruments Incorporated.

white, parents who are concerned about enhancing their children's learning opportunities.

Several major corporations do, however, have effective programs for communicating with black consumers. Anheuser-Busch, for example, advertises in black-oriented media, uses black models and entertainers, and has a number of sales promotions that appeal to black consumers.[23] The Eastman-Kodak Company also recognizes the importance of black consumers and reflects this by advertising on network black radio, on Black Entertainment Television, and in black magazines such as *Ebony* and *Essence.*[24]

The black consumer market is not homogeneous, however. All black consumers are not alike, just as consumers in any country or culture are not alike. Blacks exhibit different purchasing behaviors according to their life-styles, values, and demographics. Companies must therefore use different advertising media, distribution channels, advertising themes, and pricing strategies in marketing to the several subsegments of the black subculture.

The Hispanic Subculture

Hispanics compose one of the fastest-growing segments of the American population. Experts predict that by the year 2020 Hispanics will surpass blacks as the largest minority in the United States—nearly 47 million Hispanics and 45 million blacks.[25] About 75 percent of U.S. Hispanics are concentrated in five states: California, Texas, New York, Florida, and Illinois.[26]

According to the U.S. Census Department, Hispanics in the United States have several outstanding characteristics in comparison with other members of the American population. They are younger, have larger families, tend to live in urban clusters, and are becoming increasingly mobile as they are beginning to fan out from the five states in which they are concentrated.[27] Over 50 percent of Hispanics are under age 35; Hispanic households average 3.7 persons compared with 2.8 for all U.S. households; and 88 percent of Hispanics concentrate in metropolitan areas, compared with 81 percent blacks and 75 percent whites.[28]

Marketing communicators need to be aware of several important points when attempting to reach Hispanic consumers:

1. Over 40 percent of Hispanic Americans speak only Spanish or just enough English to get by; consequently, many Hispanics can be reached only via Spanish-language media.[29]

---

[23]Ibid., p. 15.

[24]Ibid., p. 16.

[25]Renee Blakkan, "Reaching a Growing Market Where It Lives," *Advertising Age,* March 19, 1984, p. M–10.

[26]Ibid.

[27]Craig Endicott, "Marketing to Hispanics: Making the Most of Media," *Advertising Age,* March 19, 1984, p. M–10.

[28]Blakkan, "Reaching a Growing Market."

[29]"Hispanic Ethnic Market: 27,000,000 by 2000," *POPAI News,* Vol. 6, Number 2, 1982, p. 7.

2. A further reason for using Spanish-language media is that over one-half of Hispanics use Spanish media primarily, and 70 percent watch, listen to, or read Spanish media every week.[30]

3. Over 70 percent of Hispanics report resenting ads that appear to them as little more than perfunctory adaptations of English ads.[31]

4. Advertisers must be very careful in using the Spanish language. Humberto Valencia has identified a number of snafus committed by advertisers when translating their English campaigns to Spanish. For example, "Frank Perdue of Perdue Chickens had one of his slogans literally translated and the English phonics added so he could read it to Hispanics in Spanish. The slogan in English was something like, 'It takes a strong man to make a tender chicken.' It was quickly misinterpreted as something that back-translated[32] into, 'It takes a sexually excited man to make a tender chicken.' "[33]

Social Groups

A **social group** may be defined as a collection of people who interact on a regular basis, affecting each other psychologically, and who collectively have a distinct personality. All college students in the United States may be considered a group in a general sense, but not a social group because they do not interact with or affect each other in any particular way. On the other hand, a family, a sorority, a soccer team, and members of a collegiate chapter of the American Marketing Association are social groups because their members do interact with and influence one another. In general, social groups are collections of people who interact; who share values, needs, and attitudes; and who depend upon other members in the group for the achievement of common goals and satisfaction of common needs.

The following section focuses on two social groups of considerable importance to marketing communicators—reference groups and the family.

Reference Groups

A **reference group** can be thought of as "an actual or imaginary individual or group conceived of having significant relevance upon an individual's evaluations, aspirations, or behavior."[34] To appreciate the influence that reference groups exert

---

[30]Ibid.

[31]Ibid.

[32]Back-translation in advertising is the procedure whereby an advertisement in its original language is translated into a foreign language by one translator and then translated by another translator back into its original language. This is done to ensure that the translation captures the meaning intended in the original language.

[33]"Snafus Persist in Marketing to Hispanics," *Marketing News,* June 24, 1983, p. 3.

[34]V. Parker Lessig and C. Whan Park, "Promotional Perspectives of Reference Group Influence: Advertising Implications," *Journal of Advertising,* Vol. 7, 1978, p. 41; C. Whan Park and V. Parker Lessig, "Students and Housewives: Differences in Susceptibility to Reference Group Influence," *Journal of Consumer Research,* Vol. 4, September 1977, p. 102.

on individuals, it is necessary to realize that products are symbolic objects and that much consumer behavior is influenced more by a product's social meaning than its functional utility.[35] Because products have symbolic significance, people look to others for information and indeed approval when making product, store, and brand choice decisions.

It has been suggested that group influence is most likely for products that are high in visibility (i.e., can be seen by others), complexity, and perceived risk but low in testability (i.e., cannot be experienced prior to purchase).[36] A study of preferences for different brands of bread (a product low in visibility, complexity, and perceived risk but relatively high in testability) offered support for this hypothesis by showing that brand preferences were predictably *not* affected by group influence.[37]

A study in Great Britain found that interpersonal sources of information (peer groups, friends, spouse, etc.) represented the dominant source of information for men when buying a suit, which is a visible and important symbolic product. These men relied more upon what other people wear and what they say about suits than upon marketer-controlled information or other sources of impersonal information.[38]

Another study has shown that when people observe others evaluating a product favorably they, too, tend to perceive the product more favorably. Others' evaluations and opinions are often interpreted as if they were fact.[39] Nearly everyone takes others' opinions into account at one time or another. For example, we may be aware of a certain movie or play but have no opinion about it until someone whose opinion we trust tells us how good (or bad) it really is. We take their opinion as statement of fact.

Reference groups have different kinds of influence on their members. Park and Lessig suggest three types of reference group influence: informational, utilitarian, and value expressive.[40]

Informational Influence   Informational influence is strictly related to factual data rather than normative principles. That is, an informational reference group functions to provide an individual with facts, figures, and other forms of information

[35]Sidney J. Levy, "Symbols for Sale," *Harvard Business Review,* Vol. 37, July-August 1959, pp. 117–124; Elizabeth C. Hirschman and Morris B. Holbrook, "Hedonic Consumption: Emerging Concepts, Methods, and Propositions," *Journal of Marketing,* Vol. 46, Summer 1982, pp. 92–101; Michael R. Solomon, "The Role of Products as Social Stimuli: A Symbolic Interactionism Perspective," *Journal of Consumer Research,* Vol. 10, December 1983, pp. 319–329.

[36]Thomas S. Robertson, *Innovative Behavior and Communication* (New York: Holt, Rinehart, & Winston, 1971).

[37]Jeffrey D. Ford and Ellwood A. Ellis, "A Reexamination of Group Influence on Member Brand Preference," *Journal of Marketing Research,* Vol. 17, February 1980, pp. 125–132.

[38]David M. Midgley, "Patterns of Interpersonal Information Seeking for the Purchase of a Symbolic Product," *Journal of Marketing Research,* Vol. 20, February 1983, pp. 74–83.

[39]Robert E. Burnkrant and Alain Cousineau, "Informational and Normative Social Influence in Buyer Behavior," *Journal of Consumer Research,* Vol. 2, December 1975, pp. 206–215.

[40]Lessig and Park, "Promotional Perspectives," pp. 41–42; and Park and Lessig, "Students and Housewives," pp. 102–103.

rather than with rules of conduct. The receiver of such information is most likely to accept the influence when the reference group is perceived as credible and when the individual feels uncertain with a purchase or lacks necessary product information. Opinion leaders often perform an informational reference group function. Product endorsements from respected industry or scientific associations and from individual scientists and other influential people also often serve an informational function. One might, for example, consider taking vitamin C tablets after learning that Linus Pauling, a Nobel Prize winner, daily consumes 10 or more grams of vitamin C. The endorsement of the *Wall Street Journal* by William H. Gates III, a noted computer software genius, provides information reference group influence for those individuals who admire his intellect and creative talents (see Figure 7.5).

Utilitarian Influence   Utilitarian influence operates when an individual complies with a reference group that either possesses or is perceived to possess the ability to control important rewards or punishmments. For example, a new employee may adhere closely to a company's informal dress code for fear that deviation from this code will diminish his or her chances for job advancement. Likewise, many advertisements are directed at encouraging consumers to purchase a particular brand because only it, according to the ad's implicit urging, is the "correct" brand. The advertisement (Figure 7.6) for ArtCarved college rings illustrates this form of influence attempt. By wearing this brand of ring, the reader is promised special status and the feeling of being a discriminating purchaser.

Value-Expressive Influence   Value-expressive influence operates when an individual utilizes a reference group to express himself or herself or to bolster his or her self-concept and ego to an outside world. Thus, the value-expressive function relates to an individual's motivation to enhance his or her self-concept. An individual is influenced by a value-expressive reference group because of the favorable psychological image portrayed by the group and the appeal of the group (or an individual exemplar of the group). By identifying with a liked group and engaging in behavior that is believed to be compatible with what group members would support or do themselves, one can enhance one's self-image.

Advertisers appeal to the value-expressive need by showing people using products with whom target audiences identify. The "yuppies"[41] in the Michelob advertisement in Figure 7.7 are portrayed in a diversity of life-styles that fellow yuppies—the apparent intended market of Michelob's efforts—would find attractive and desirable. Rolex's use of Frederick Forsyth (see Figure 7.8) further illustrates the use of value-expressive influence in advertising. Salespersons also use value-expressive influence by telling prospective customers about desirable other individuals who have already purchased the product or service. Some products and brands are more subject to reference group influence than are others. Figure 7.9 illustrates the variability in reference group influence across

---

[41]Yuppies are discussed in Chapter 9.

FIGURE 7.5   Example of *Informational* Reference Group Influence

FIGURE 7.6   **Example of *Utilitarian* Reference Group Influence**

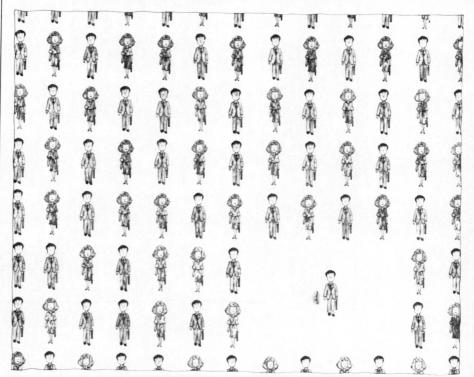

Distinguish yourself from the other 960,000 grads hitting the job market this year.

ArtCarved College Rings.

Set yourself apart. The hand that hands over the resume looks so much more impressive with an ArtCarved college ring.

That's because an ArtCarved college ring is no ordinary piece of jewelry. We've been fashioning the finest rings in America since 1850. And we were the very first company to make college rings stylish. Even though we're still the leader in new designs, we haven't forgotten our roots. We make beautiful traditional rings, too. Visit your campus bookstore to see the entire collection. Your ArtCarved college ring. It's as much a part of your business suit—as your briefcase.

ARTCARVED
CLASS RINGS

© 1984. ArtCarved Class Rings

Source: Courtesy of ArtCarved Class Rings.

FIGURE 7.7   Example of *Value-Expressive* Reference Group Influence

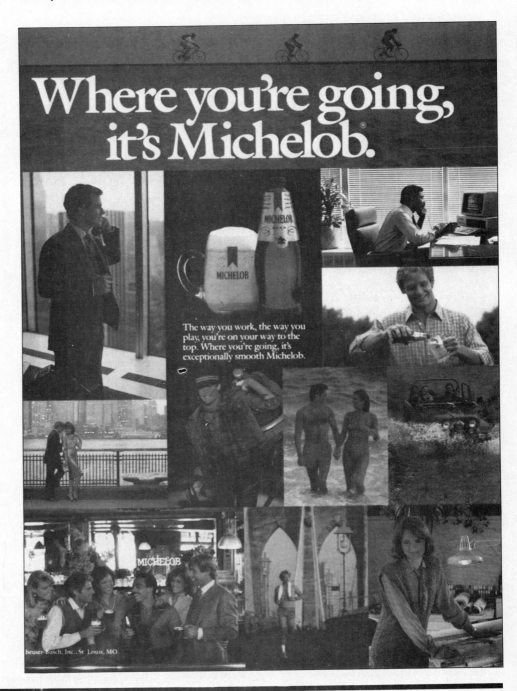

FIGURE 7.8 **Another Example of *Value-Expressive* Reference Group Influence**

Frederick Forsyth's Rolex is like his novels. Tough, accurate and very stylish.

Frederick Forsyth is not a prolific writer.

In fact, in the past twelve years he has completed just four full-length novels.

And yet *The Day of the Jackal, The Odessa File, The Dogs of War* and *The Devil's Alternative* have all become instant best-sellers around the world.

Already his first three books have been made into successful feature films.

Forsyth's writing is characterized by a blend of uncannily authentic detail and superb storytelling.

The facts are drawn from his own many experiences as a front-line war correspondent; the fiction, from something the craftsmen at Rolex appreciate only too well — a sense of style.

Frederick Forsyth wears a Rolex Oyster Day-Date in 18kt. gold, with matching President bracelet.

"It is very tough and well made," he says. And, it is also immensely practical.

"I can wear my Rolex all the time. I never have to take it off, even to use a chain saw. Nothing seems to bother it."

Apart from his Rolex, Frederick Forsyth is particularly pleased with the coat you see him wearing in the photograph.

He spotted it in a shop in London, and asked of what fur the collar was made.

The assistant told him.

"Jackal."

ROLEX

Pictured: The Rolex Day-Date Chronometer. Available in 18kt. gold, with matching President bracelet.

Write for brochure. Rolex Watch, U.S.A., Inc., Dept. 608, Rolex Building, 665 Fifth Avenue, New York, New York 10022-5383. World headquarters in Geneva. Other offices in Canada and major countries around the world.

Source: Courtesy of Rolex Watch U.S.A., Inc.

FIGURE 7.9   **Degree of Relative Influence of Reference Groups on Selected Consumer Products and Brands.**

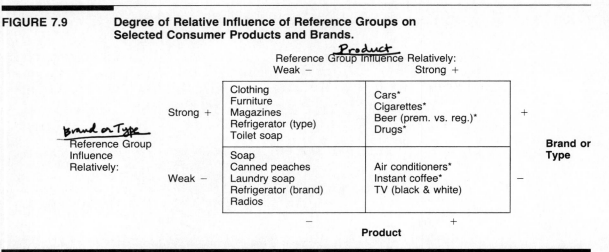

Product classifications marked with an asterisk (*) are based on experimental evidence. Other products are classi-
fied speculatively on the basis of judgment of research in this area. [*Source: Bureau of Applied Social Research,
Columbia University* (Charles Y. Glock, Director). *After Francis Bourne (ed.),* Group Influence in Marketing and
Public Relations *(Ann Arbor, Mich.: Foundation of Research on Human Behavior, 1956), p. 8.*]

products and brands. The figure shows that reference groups have (1) strong influence on the purchase of both product and brand of cars, cigarettes, beer, and
drugs; (2) strong influence on brand, but not product, for such items as clothing,
furniture, magazines, refrigerators, and toilet soap; (3) weak influence on brand
and product for radios, refrigerators, laundry soap, etc.; and (4) strong influence
on product, but weak influence on brands, in the case of items such as air condi-
tioners, instant coffee, and television sets.

The illustration in Figure 7.9 is a classic in the marketing literature. However,
the ideas contained in the figure should be regarded as merely suggestive rather
than definitive. That is, the scheme is based on limited empirical support that is
badly dated. Fortunately, more recent work by Bearden and Etzel provides us with
a contemporary perspective on reference group influence.[42] These researchers
studied the three forms of reference group influence described previously to determine how the influence varies across four general categories of products: (1)
publicly consumed luxuries, (2) publicly consumed necessities, (3) privately consumed luxuries, and (4) privately consumed necessities. By definition, **public
products** (e.g., an automobile) are ones that other people can observe the owner
using, and **private products** are not readily identifiable. **Luxury products** are
those that have a degree of exclusivity, whereas **necessities** are nonexclusive. Of
course, the labels *public/private* and *necessity/luxury* are intended as end points

[42]William O. Bearden and Michael J. Etzel, "Reference Group Influence on Product and Brand Purchase
Decisions," *Journal of Consumer Research,* Vol. 9, September 1982, pp. 183–194.

on a continuum rather than as absolutes, i.e., products vary in their degree of both publicness and luxuriousness.

Bearden and Etzel hypothesized that the strength of reference group influence on product and brand purchase decisions depends upon a product's status as a public or private item and as a necessity or luxury. Figure 7.10 presents their hypotheses.

Figure 7.10 shows that reference group influence is expected to be—

1. *strong* for both products and brands in the case of *public luxuries* (e.g., snow skis);
2. *weak* for brands but *strong* for products in the case of *private luxuries* (e.g., trash compactor);
3. *weak* for both products and brands for *private necessities* (e.g., refrigerator);
4. *strong* for brands but *weak* for products in the case of *public necessities* (e.g., automobile).

The researchers conducted two studies to test the hypotheses in Figure 7.10. As predicted, they found that reference group influence was greater for luxuries than necessities and also greater for publicly consumed items than for necessities. Moreover, they determined that reference group influence is more pronounced for brand decisions than for product decisions. The managerial implication of this finding is that reference group influence has a greater role to play in stimulating selective, rather than primary, demand.

Additional implications of reference group influence for marketing communicators were stated years ago by Bourne, but they apply equally well today.

1. Where neither product nor brand appear to be associated strongly with reference group influence—as in the case of private necessities—promotional

---

FIGURE 7.10   **Product and Brand Reference Group Influence Delineated by Public-Private and Luxury-Necessity Product Dimensions**

		Public	
	Product Brand	Weak Reference Group Influence (−)	Strong Reference Group Influence (+)

Necessity Strong reference
group influence
(+)
		Public necessities Influence:
		Weak product and strong brand
		Examples: Wristwatch, automobile,
		   man's suit
			Public luxuries Influence:
			Strong product and brand
			Examples: Golf clubs, snow skis,
			   sailboat

Weak reference
group influence
(−)
		Private necessities Influence:
		Weak product and brand
		Examples: Mattress, floor lamp,
		   refrigerator
			Private luxuries Influence:
			Strong product and weak brand
			Examples: TV game, trash
			   compactor, icemaker
				Luxury

		Private	

Source: William O. Bearden and Michael J. Etzel, "Reference Group Influence on Product and Brand Purchase Decisions," *Journal of Consumer Research*, Vol. 9, September 1982, p. 185. Reprinted by permission.

emphasis should be placed on the product's attributes, intrinsic qualities, price, and competitive advantages.

2. Where reference group influence is operative—for public luxuries, public necessities, and private luxuries—marketing communications should stress the kinds of people who buy the product or brand and reinforce or broaden the existing stereotypes of product/brand users. This involves learning what the stereotypes are and what specific reference groups are most influential so that appeals can be "tailored" to each major group.[43]

The Family

The American family has changed greatly over the past several decades because of major societal developments, including a rising divorce rate, falling fertility figures, the widespread use of contraceptives, and increases in the numbers of married women in the work force.[44] These developments have affected consumer behavior and, consequently, marketing behavior. For this reason the family unit and its relevance to marketing communications and promotion management will be examined. The following discussion describes the nature of family decision making, examines the concept of family life cycle, and discusses the implications both of these topics have for marketing communicators.

Family Decision Making A regular finding in consumer behavior research is that *joint decision making* plays an important role in the process by which most products and services are acquired.[45] However, within the family, certain purchase decisions are made predominantly by the husband, some predominantly by the wife, and others are made more or less equally. Children are also influential in many household purchase decisions. Thus, it is important to marketing communicators to understand the decision-making process for their products and to acquire knowledge of the relative roles of wives, husbands, and children. The following discussion is restricted to the traditional notion of a family (husband, wife, and possibly children), but the need to understand the joint decision-making process applies also to cohabitating couples and other nontraditional households.

Marketing and consumer behavior scholars study household decision making by using the sociological concept of *role structure*. A particularly influential application of this concept was a study by Davis and Rigaux who examined husband and wife decision making for 25 purchase decisons.[46] The researchers had both hus-

---

[43]Francis S. Bourne, "Group Influence in Marketing and Public Relations," report of a seminar conducted by the Foundation for Research on Human Behavior, March 26–27, 1956, Ardsley-on-Hudson, NY (Ann Arbor, MI: The Foundation for Research on Human Behavior, 1956), p. 10.

[44]Patrick E. Murphy and William A. Staples, "A Modernized Family Life Cycle," *Journal of Consumer Research,* Vol. 6, June 1979, p. 12.

[45]Lakshman Krishnamurthi, "The Salience of Relevant Others and Its Effect on Individual and Joint Preferences: An Experimental Investigation," *Journal of Consumer Research,* Vol. 10, June 1983, p. 62.

[46]Harry Davis and Benny P. Rigaux, "Perception of Marital Roles in Decision Processes," *Journal of Consumer Research,* Vol. 1, June 1974, pp. 51–62.

bands and wives indicate their individual influence for all 25 products. A score of 1 was assigned if the husband had the major influence, 2 if the decision was joint, and 3 if the wife had the major influence. The graphic illustration in Figure 7.11 summarizes the study results.

The triangular figure in Figure 7.11 contains four sections: wife dominant, autonomic, husband dominant, and syncratic. Brief discussion of how the figure was constructed is necessary before describing the specific results and implications. The vertical scale represents the relative influence of husbands and wives; the horizontal scale indicates the extent of role specialization. The 25 products in Figure 7.11 were positioned in terms of these two axes. Davis and Rigaux described the procedure as follows:

> *Given the coding that was used in this study, average relative influence for a decision when aggregated over families can range along a continuum from 1 (if all respondents report husband dominance) to 3 (if all respondents report wife dominance). The mean score of a decision along this axis does not, however, reflect the extent of role specialization in those families. For example, a mean of 2 could imply either a complete lack of specialization where all couples decide jointly, or a complete specialization where the decision is wife dominant in 50 percent of the families and husband dominant in the remaining 50 percent. Indeed, any percentage of families making the decision jointly combined with an even split between husband dominant and wife dominant cases would also yield a mean of 2. Notice that ambiguity about the extent of role specialization only arises when one wants to aggregate scores for two families or more. Thus, the second axis is a scale of the extent of role specialization as measured by the percentage of families reporting that a decision is jointly made.*[47]

Based on these scaling conventions, a **syncratic** decision is one where more than 50 percent of all husbands and wives participate in the decision jointly. Wife dominant, autonomic, and husband dominant decisions are, on the other hand, ones where fewer than 50 percent of the decisions involve joint influence. As the names suggest, **wife dominant** and **husband dominant** decisions are those that in the majority of households are made by wives or husbands alone. The important point about these one-spouse-dominant decisions is that the spousal dominance is essentially consistent across nearly all households. That is, the wife typically makes the decision or the husband typically makes the decision. In the Davis and Rigaux study, cleaning products were especially wife dominant, and insurance was especially husband dominant (see Figure 7.11). An interesting finding about autonomic decisions, on the other hand, is that spousal dominance still prevails—as with wife or husband dominant decisions—but in some households the wife dominates the decision and in others the husband dominates the decision. For example, husband's

---

[47]Ibid., p. 53.

FIGURE 7.11   Marital Roles in 25 Purchase Decisions

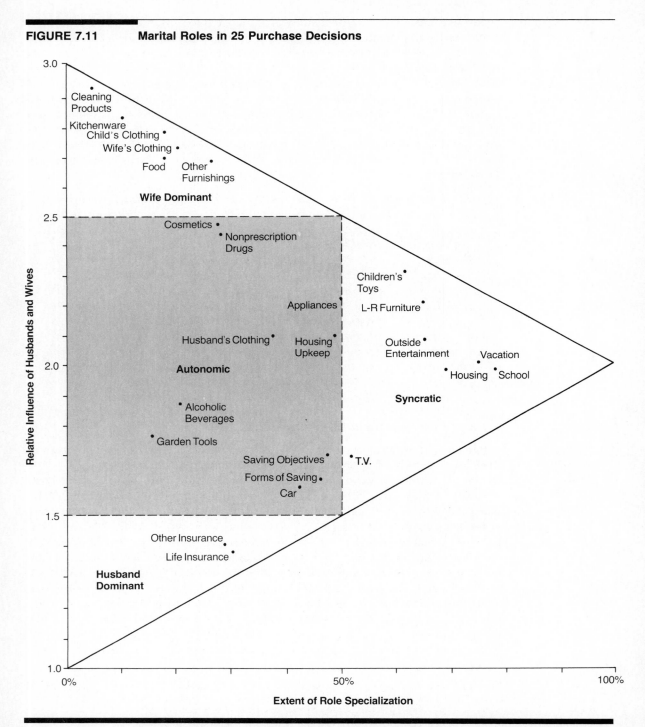

clothing, alcoholic beverages, and garden tools are all autonomic products according to the Davis and Rigaux findings.

The four types of household decisions have several implications for marketing communications. First, husband or wife dominant decisions call for communications strategies that are directed at one or the other spouse. Second, syncratic decisions require that communicators construct messages targeted to both spouses simultaneously, which treat the couple as one entity and show how the marketer's product can satisfy husbands' and wives' separate needs.

Television commercials by the publishers of *Time/Life* home repair books illustrate the proper approach when syncratic decision making is involved. Opening scenes depict husbands and wives experiencing household problems; later scenes then show couples working together (with, of course, a *Time/Life* repair book in hand) making home repairs and then enjoying the fruits of their labor.

Finally, for products that are subject to autonomic decision making, the communicator's task is complicated because separate communication programs may be needed in order to appeal to the unique needs and buying interests of husbands and wives. Distinct messages and media channels may be required to reach and motivate husbands in some households and wives in others.

Two caveats are in order before leaving the topic of family decision making. First, one should be careful not to overgeneralize from the results in Figure 7.11. The results are based on responses from a very small sample, only 73 Belgian couples. It is questionable whether the same results would be obtained today with a representative sample of American households. Moreover, the results in Figure 7.11 actually represent an aggregation of responses across three separate decision-making phases—problem recognition, search, and choice. The actual location of products varies somewhat from phase to phase. For example, appliances are classified as autonomic in the information search phase, but the actual choice involves a syncratic decision.[48]

A second note of caution is to avoid the tendency to stereotype the nature of household decision making. Many people, including some marketing communicators, hold the fallacious view that husbands make "important" product decisions (e.g., which model of automobile to purchase) and that wives make "simple" decisions such as the choice of color. It *is* done this way in some families, but this certainly is not the norm in most modern families. Decision making involves conflict, bargaining, cooperation, deference, and other processes whereby husbands and wives, along with their children, accommodate one another's interests, needs, and special consumption abilities. Wives often, contrary to myth, make important decisions involving what are typically considered male products. Likewise, husbands are often involved in decisions (e.g., the selection of curtains) that are regarded as feminine items. Undeniably, decision making for some products does

---

[48]Davis and Rigaux, "Perception of Marital Roles," present two figures in addition to the one shown in Figure 7.11. These additional figures illustrate the changes in decision influence from the problem-recognition phase to the search phase and from search to choice.

break down along stereotypical lines,[49] but this may be the exception rather than the rule. The implication for promotion management is obvious: research each product to determine the actual roles of the husbands, wives, and children who constitute the target audience.

The Family Life Cycle   The concept of family life cycle encompasses the different stages that a family moves through over time. One of the older modelings of the life cycle includes nine stages: (1) bachelor stage (young single people not living at home); (2) newly married couples with no children; (3) married couples with youngest child under six years old; (4) married couples with youngest child six or over; (5) older married couples with dependent children; (6) older married couples with no children living at home—household head in labor force; (7) older married couples with no children living at home—household head retired; (8) solitary survivor in labor force; and (9) solitary survivor retired.[50] Wells and Gubar found that for most products, life cycle is a better predictor of product purchases than is age.[51]

A more contemporary family life cycle was devised by Murphy and Staples, who took into account social developments (rising divorce rate, postponement of first marriages, etc.) that have led to changes in the family structure. Such changes imply more single parents with children at home, single parents without children at home, and older parents with children at home.[52] Murphy and Staples's modernized family life cycle (see Figure 7.12) shows the usual flow of life cycle development as well as a recycled flow. The traditional family flow is the route that most past generations followed but which today has been altered, perhaps permanently, as a result of the various social developments alluded to previously. Nevertheless, the two biggest life cycle categories (based on 1973 census data) are "young married with children" (17.1 percent) and "middle-aged married with children" (33 percent).[53] Murphy and Staples's modernized family life cycle typology excludes some important segments of society (e.g., cohabitative couples, people who are separated but not divorced), but it is, nonetheless, a useful conceptual improvement over the typology presented previously.[54]

---

[49]See Jack J. Kasulis and Marie Adele Hughes, "Husband-Wife Influence in Selecting a Family Professional," *Journal of the Academy of Marketing Science,* Vol. 12, Winter/Spring 1984, p. 125; and Dennis L. Rosen and Donald H. Granbois, "Determinants of Role Structure in Family Financial Management," *Journal of Consumer Research,* Vol. 10, September 1983, p. 256.

[50]William D. Wells and George Gubar, "Life Cycle Concept in Marketing Research," *Journal of Marketing Research,* Vol. 3, November 1966, pp. 355–363.

[51]Ibid.

[52]Murphy and Staples, "A Modernized Family Life Cycle," pp. 12–22.

[53]Ibid., p. 16, Table 2.

[54]The improvement may be little more than conceptual. One study found that the modernized family life cycle was no more effective than the traditional family life cycle in predicting clothing expenditures. Of course, research on other product categories may find the modernized family life cycle to be superior.

FIGURE 7.12   A Modernized Family Life Cycle

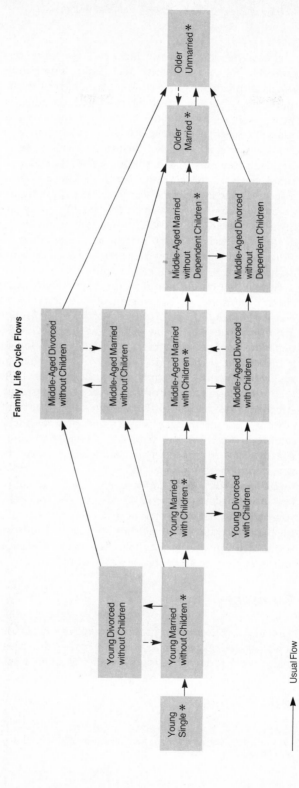

Family Life Cycle Flows

Usual Flow

Recycled Flow

* Traditional Family Flow

Source: Patrick E. Murphy and William A. Staples, "A Modernized Family Life Cycle," *Journal of Consumer Research,* Vol. 6, June 1979, p. 17. Reprinted by permission.

The value of the family life cycle for marketers stems from the fact that consumption needs and family decision-making processes change over the life cycle. For example, young married couples have a particular need for appliances, furniture, and other durables. Middle-aged couples without dependent children also have needs for replacement furniture and other durables; however, the type and quality of products demanded by middle-aged couples is often different (e.g., smaller appliances, better furniture) than those demanded by young couples. As families progress through the life cycle, they also devote larger proportions of their incomes to travel and other services. These differences in consumer behavior represent significant market segmentation opportunities for many companies.

Families at different stages of the life cycle also vary in the amount of joint decision making. Research shows that joint decision making is particularly great during the early years of marriage but declines over time.[55] As couples age, individuals develop their own special areas of consumption expertise, thereby reducing the need for joint decision making.

For marketing communications, this means that joint decision appeals are especially important when catering to younger couples but less important for older couples. Of course, this should *not* be interpreted to mean that all young couples make joint decisions and older couples make only separate decisions. Consumer behavior is never so straightforward. The point, instead, is that older couples are less likely to make joint decisions. The actual amount of joint decision making varies from family to family and from product to product.

Because advertisers communicate with mass markets, they must design message strategies that appeal to the average family within targeted market segments. Thus, ads directed to younger couples may portray husbands and wives making purchase decisions together (as with the *Time/Life* home repair commercials mentioned previously), and appeals to middle-aged couples may show husbands and wives acting separately.

Salespersons, unlike advertisers, have the luxury of being able to tailor sales presentations to each couple. Astute salespeople realize that each couple differs somewhat in decision-making dynamics; the wife is dominant in some families, the husband in others, and neither spouse is dominant in others. The astute salesperson is able quickly to identify the relative decision influence of husband and wife and design sales presentations accordingly.

Summary

This chapter examines group influences on consumer behavior. The coverage extends from macro group influences—culture and subculture—to micro influences—reference groups and family. Culture, which deals with the transmission of

[55]Robert Ferber and Lucy Chao Lee, "Husband-Wife Influence in Family Purchasing Behavior," *Journal of Consumer Research*, Vol. 1, June 1974, pp. 43–50; and Rosen and Granbois, "Determinants of Role Structure," pp. 253–258.

values, beliefs, attitudes, symbols, and material artifacts from one generation to the next, is the most general and pervasive influence on individual behavior. Value shifts in the United States have been particularly pronounced during the past several decades. There has been a trend toward a self-fulfillment culture, which has influenced all facets of society, including marketing communications. The diversity of value systems that are extant in American society are perhaps best captured in the Stanford Research Institute's VALS typology. The typology is based on a combination of values, attitudes, and demographic variables and consists of three main segments: the need driven, the outer-directed, and the inner-directed. Each general category is further subdivided into additional segments.

Subcultures are subgroups in society whose culture differs somewhat from the dominant culture. Marketing communications directed to subcultures must be customized to be effective. The chapter examines three subcultures: religious groups (Jews and born-again Christians), blacks, and Hispanics. All of these groups are large and influential in society and require specialized marketing communications. Especially important is the tremendous growth in the numbers of black and Hispanic consumers in the United States.

Reference groups represent any group with which an individual associates or disassociates and that influences the individual's evaluations, aspirations, and behavior. There are three interrelated forms of reference group influence: informational, utilitarian, and value expressive. All forms are used by advertisers, salespersons, and other marketing communicators.

The family plays an important role in marketing communications because much decision making involves joint family influence, and the family performs a strategic role in socializing children. Family decision making is discussed in terms of role dynamics and is categorized into its general forms: wife dominant, husband dominant, autonomic, and syncratic. Each form has distinct marketing communication implications. Finally, the family is also delineated into life cycle stages, and marketing communication implications are discussed.

Discussion Questions

1. Values play a central role in consumer behavior. They also are important to advertisers and other marketing communicators. Explain how.
2. The advertising director for a major manufacturer of washing machines, dryers, and other appliances has expressed some interest in using the VALS typology as a tool for advertising decisions. However, a skeptical colleague, who has a background in marketing research, contends that the typology is worthless. What is your opinion?
3. Many Americans have, according to Daniel Yankelovich, shifted their value orientations to emphasize self-fulfillment over everything else. Assuming Yankelovich's characterization accurately portrays America, what significance does this have for marketing communicators?
4. Make clear distinctions among the concepts of culture, subculture, and reference groups. Do not parrot the definitions in the text, but use instead your own language to explain these different concepts. Use one of your grandpar-

ents as an example to illustrate the concepts. Explain what his or her culture, subculture, and reference groups are.

5. It is claimed in the chapter that many companies make no special efforts to communicate with black consumers. Do your observations support this generalization? If yes, explain why you think many companies avoid special communications with blacks. If no, present evidence to support why you think many companies do make special efforts to communicate with black consumers.

6. It is claimed by some marketing observers that Hispanic consumers are generally less weight conscious than are non-Hispanics in the United States. Assuming this to be true, what is the cultural justification for this? What implications does this hold for advertisers? Be specific in responding to the latter question and identify particular product categories rather than talking in generalities.

7. Using your own language, not the text's, distinguish among informational, utilitarian, and value-expressive reference group influences. Provide one specific example of each as it applies to your personal behavior in the past six months or so.

8. Give two examples other than the ones presented in the chapter for products that characterize the four general categories of public luxuries, private luxuries, public necessities, and private necessities. Explain for which of these products reference group influence likely prevails and whether the influence affects consumers' product or brand decisions, both, or neither.

9. Assume you are the marketing manager of a line of plastic plumbing products for do-it-yourself home repairs. These products make faucet replacements and other plumbing repairs much easier than conventional metal fixtures. You have charged your marketing research staff with the task of determining the nature of family decision making for your products. What do you think the marketing research staff will learn? What implications will this finding have for your advertising efforts?

Exercises

1. Review magazine advertisements and select examples that appear to be targeted at each of these VALS groups: belongers, emulators, achievers, I-am-me's, experientials, and societally conscious. Describe the features in each ad that led you to the conclusion that the ad is directed at the particular VALS group that you designated.

2. Select examples from magazine ads of informational, utilitarian, and value-expressive reference group influence. Describe the features in each ad that led you to the conclusion the ad is directed at each particular reference group influence.

3. Interview three retail salespersons who have extensive interaction with married couples. Salespersons from product categories such as automobiles, major appliances, floor care products, home computers, and VCRs would be

appropriate. Ask each salesperson to describe the typical pattern of influence between husbands and wives when making decisions for that particular product. Then follow up to determine how decision-making influence might vary between different types of couples—young versus middle-aged couples, middle- versus lower-class couples, and black versus white couples. Summarize your results in terms of a general explanation of family decision-making influence.

4. Interview two married or cohabitating couples and have each couple explain the decision-making process for a major purchase decision they made within the past year or so. Determine which partner initially recognized the need for purchase (problem recognition), who searched for information, and who was primarily responsible for the final choice. Probe for detailed responses regarding specific aspects of the final choice, i.e., do not simply determine which partner was more influential in selecting, say, the brand of furniture, but ask also about other aspects of the choice—model type, color, quality, etc.

CHAPTER 8

Adoption and Diffusion Processes

The Role of Marketing Communications and Promotion Management

Commercial marketers introduce new products and services continuously. For most industries and companies, introducing a stream of new products is absolutely essential for success and long-term growth. Likewise, the continued viability of many nonbusiness organizations (charitable groups, trade associations, religious organizations, etc.) depends on their ability to develop and introduce new ideas to their constituencies. An illustration of this is the ambitious recent undertaking by an association of cotton producers and manufacturers of fibers, fabrics, and apparel (the "Crafted with Pride U.S.A. Council") that attempted to encourage consumers to look for the "Made in the USA" label when buying clothing and home fashion items (see Figure 8.1).

New Products and Innovativeness

Success Does Not Come Easy

Despite the huge investments and concerted efforts to introduce new products and ideas, many are never successful. It is impossible to pinpoint the percentage of new ideas and products that eventually fail because organizations vary in how they define a "success"; estimates range, however, from as high as 90 percent to

FIGURE 8.1   **The Promotion of a New Idea**

PHOTOGRAPH BY FRANCESCO SCAVULLO

She'll be looking for US in her blouse.

And in her dresses. And jackets. And suits.

Because as a result of Congressional legislation, consumers will have a choice. All apparel and home fashions manufactured in this country after December 24 will proudly carry a "Made in U.S.A." label.

Your customers are going to come looking for it. And we'll be telling them *why* they should look for it in a big, big way.

We're mounting a multi-million dollar campaign that will make consumers aware of the quality, the style, and the value of merchandise made in the U.S. It's clear that we mean business. Big business for you. You already know you get better delivery with US. And that you can reorder easily with US. And that you don't have to commit your money far up in front with US. So as you plan Fall '85, look at US before you leap overseas.

Take a good look at US.

Crafted With Pride U.S.A. Council, Inc.—a unified force of American cotton producers, labor, and manufacturers of fibers, fabric, apparel, and home fashions who are working to promote merchandise made in the U.S.

Source: Courtesy of Crafted With Pride U.S.A. Council, Inc.

as low as a 33 percent failure rate among new product introductions.[1] The rates of success and failure depend on several factors, of which two of the most important are (1) the type of industry and (2) the degree of innovativeness. For example, the failure rate is likely to be far higher for the consumer package goods market than in the electrical components field.[2] This is because the consumer marketplace is considerably more dynamic, volatile, and unpredictable than is the electrical components field. Whereas consumers are typically unable to tell marketers exactly what new products they want, buyers of electrical components are able to give detailed information to component manufacturers.

The Degree of Innovativeness

An **innovation** is an idea, practice, product, or service that an individual perceives to be new. How people view an object determines whether it is an innovation. For example, an electronics firm may introduce a stereo receiver, which, *objectively speaking,* significantly reduces outside interference in stereo-FM reception. However, if consumers view the stereo receiver as just another receiver, then the receiver *is* just another receiver. People who believe something is an innovation behave differently toward the object than people who do not perceive the object as new.

The degree of newness is an important dimension of innovation. Innovations can be classified along a continuum according to their degree of impact on established consumption patterns. Table 8.1 presents an innovativeness continuum and labels the end points "continuous" and "discontinuous" and provides examples of different degrees of innovativeness along the continuum.[3]

TABLE 8.1   The Innovation Continuum

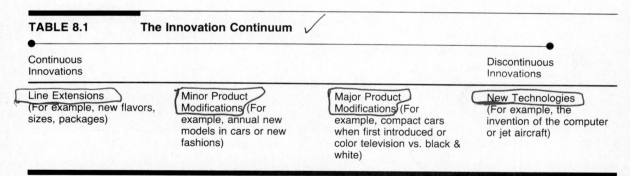

Source: Thomas S. Robertson, Joan Zielinski, and Scott Ward, *Consumer Behavior* (Glenview, IL: Scott, Foresman and Company, 1984), p. 369.

[1]"Survey Finds Sixty-Seven Percent of New Products Succeed," *Marketing News,* February 8, 1980, p. 1.

[2]This point and related discussion are adapted from William Zikmund and Michael D'Amico, *Marketing* (New York: John Wiley & Sons, 1984), p. 295.

[3]The innovation continuum notion is attributable to Thomas S. Robertson, *Innovation Behavior and Communication* (New York: Holt, Rinehart, and Winston, 1971), p. 7.

A **continuous innovation** is one that generally represents a minor change from existing products and which has limited impact on customers' consumption patterns. That is, the consumer can buy and use the new product in much the same way that he or she has used another product to satisfy the same need. Table 8.1 shows that new flavors, sizes, and packages represent typical continuous innovations. For example, some cigarette manufacturers have recently introduced 25 cigarettes to a pack in comparison with the standard 20-unit pack; toothpaste makers are using pump containers to replace the old squeeze package; soap companies regularly introduce new fragrances; and Diet Pepsi and Diet Coke have switched to 100 percent NutraSweet-sweetened colas from their NutraSweet/saccharin blend products.

In comparison, a **discontinuous innovation,** which anchors the other extreme of the innovation continuum, requires substantial relearning and fundamental alterations in basic consumption patterns. The automobile, computer, and television are probably the most significant mass-market discontinuous innovations of the twentieth century.

The bulk of new products, services, and ideas are certainly not discontinuous innovations, but rather they represent varying degrees of continuous innovations or **dynamically continuous innovations.** The latter term represents innovations that require some disruption in established behavioral patterns, rather than fundamental alterations. Word processing, microwave ovens, VCR equipment, and teleconferencing are some of the more notable dynamically continuous innovations.

The Role of Marketing Communications and Promotion Management

Regardless of the degree of innovativeness, an organization's marketing communications specialists and promotion management team have major roles to play in assuring new product success. This perhaps can best be appreciated by showing a relatively simple model of the new product adoption process.[4] This model, Figure 8.2, indicates with square blocks the three main stages through which an individual becomes a new brand consumer: awareness class, trier class, and repeater class.

The first step in adoption is to make the consumer aware of a new product's existence. Figure 8.2 shows that four marketing mix variables influence the **awareness class:** free samples, coupons, advertising, and distribution. The first three variables are distinctly promotion mix variables, and the fourth, distribution, is closely allied with promotion in that the sales force is responsible for gaining distribution, providing reseller support, and making point-of-purchase materials available to the trade.

Once a consumer becomes aware of a new product or brand, there is an increased probability that the consumer will actually try the new offering. Coupons,

[4]The following discussion is adapted from Chakravarthi Narasimham and Subrata K. Sen, "New Product Models for Test Market Data," *Journal of Marketing,* Vol. 47, Winter 1983, pp. 13, 14.

FIGURE 8.2   **Model of New Product Adoption Process**

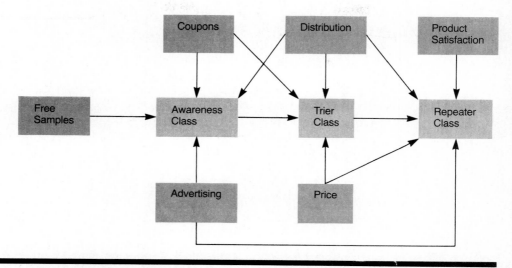

Source: Chakravarthi Narasimhan and Subrata K. Sen, "New Product Models for Test Market Data," *Journal of Marketing,* Vol. 47, Winter 1983, p. 13.

distribution, and price are the variables that affect the **trier class.** Only the first of these, coupons, is a promotional mix element, but as mentioned in Chapter 1 and elaborated upon in Chapter 22, price and distribution variables perform important communication functions in addition to their more basic economic and logistical roles.

Repeat purchasing, the **repeater class,** is a function of four primary forces: advertising, price, distribution, and product satisfaction. That is, consumers are more likely to continue to purchase a particular brand if advertising reminds them about the brand, if the price is considered agreeable, if the brand is accessible, and if product quality is considered satisfactory.

It is evident from this discussion that promotion management—indeed all aspects of marketing communications—is essential to new product success. The following sections will explain in greater detail the processes by which innovations are adopted by individual consumers and diffused throughout the marketplace.

The Adoption and Diffusion Processes

The distinction between adoption and diffusion is a matter of perspective. The **adoption process** views the mental stages an individual goes through in accepting and becoming a repeat purchaser of an innovation (a micro viewpoint). The **diffusion process** is concerned with the broader issue of how an innovation is communicated and adopted throughout the marketplace (a macro viewpoint). These topics have been studied extensively by researchers from many disciplines—sociology, anthropology, psychology, marketing, etc.

Marketing communicators are interested in adoption and diffusion because by understanding how the processes work it is possible to accelerate the rate of new product adoption and thereby increase the probability of product success. Marketers are, in fact, beginning to realize this goal. Olshavsky found corroboration for an earlier study by Young that the rate of adoption of innovations in consumer markets is increasing over time.[5] Qualls, Olshavsky, and Michaels determined that the rate of adoption of household appliances has increased rapidly throughout the latter half of the twentieth century. Three factors have apparently contributed to faster adoption/diffusion rates: (1) improved channels of communications, (2) increased marketing sophistication, and (3) increased consumer affluence.[6]

Although there is evidence that consumers are adopting new, successful products more rapidly, there still is the problem of a high percentage of failure in the introduction of new products. Therefore, the subject of adoption and diffusion processes is as critical to successful marketing as ever.

The Adoption Process

Much of what we know about the adoption and diffusion processes is due to the research and writings of Everett Rogers, a respected scholar in this area. This section will present Rogers's most recent conceptualization of the adoption process, which he refers to as the *innovation-decision process.* This process consists of five stages: (1) knowledge, (2) persuasion, (3) decision, (4) implementation, and (5) confirmation.[7]

Each of the five major stages is affected by a wide array of variables, each acting to increase or retard the innovation-decision process. Among the broad groups of variables are previous consumption experiences (what Rogers calls "previous practices"), felt needs and problems, social system norms, socioeconomic characteristics, personality variables, and perceived characteristics of the innovation (relative advantage, compatibility, and so on) (see Figure 8.3).

Knowledge Stage In the knowledge stage, which is similar to the "awareness class" that was mentioned in a previous section, the individual becomes aware of the innovation and learns something about how the innovation functions. For example, and individual learns that a video cassette recorder (VCR) costs from approximately $300 to over $1,000, that it can be used to record television programs

---

[5]Richard W. Olshavsky, "Time and Rate of Adoption of Innovations," *Journal of Consumer Research,* Vol. 6, March 1980, pp. 425–428. His reference to Young's study is Robert B. Young (1964), "Product Growth Cycles—A Key to Growth Planning," unpublished results, Stanford Research Institute, Menlo Park, California.

[6]William Qualls, Richard W. Olshavsky, and Ronald E. Michaels, "Shortening of the PLC—An Empirical Test," *Journal of Marketing,* vol. 45, Fall 1981, pp. 76–80.

[7]Everett M. Rogers, *Diffusion of Innovations,* 3rd Ed. (New York: The Free Press, 1983), p. 7.

FIGURE 8.3   **Model of the Innovation-Decision Process**

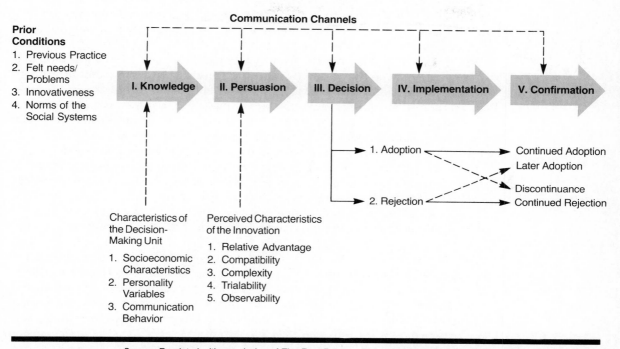

Source: Reprinted with permission of The Free Press, a Division of Macmillan, Inc., from *Diffusion of Innovations,* Third Edition, by Everett M. Rogers, p.165. Copyright © 1962, 1971, 1983, by The Free Press.

for delayed playback and to play prerecorded movies, that different brands vary in terms of their specific functions and ease of installation and use, and that there are two different format machines, Beta and VHS, which are incompatible. Beta programs cannot be played on VHS machines, and vice versa.

Studies have revealed that distinct differences exist between those who know about an innovation early and those who are late in recognizing it. Those who recognize an innovation early have a higher level of education, a higher social status, a greater exposure to mass media and interpersonal channels of communications, and greater social participation; they are also more cosmopolitan than those who are aware of it later.[8] VCR owners in the United States, for example, are better educated and better off financially than most Americans.[9]

---

[8]Ibid., pp. 168–169.

[9]"VCRs: Coming on Strong," *Time,* December 24, 1984, p. 45. By the end of 1984, there were 17 million VCRs in use in the United States—one for every five homes with a television.

Persuasion Stage   Though an individual may be aware of an innovation for a long period of time and may know how to use it, he or she may not have developed an attitude toward the innovation. The persuasion stage begins when the individual develops an attitude toward the innovation. The mental activity at the knowledge stage was mainly cognitive (or thinking), but at the persuasion stage it is mainly affective (or feeling).[10]

In forming an attitude toward the innovation, a consumer often goes through a vicarious trial of the product. This helps the consumer to reduce the uncertainty of using the new product or service. Although uncertainty is reduced and a positive attitude is possibly formed, this does not ensure that consumers will convert their positive attitudes into actual adoption. That is, a favorable attitude does not necessarily lead to immediate purchase. There is, however, strong evidence that positive attitudes toward innovations coincide with actual purchase behavior.

Promotion management can play a major role in determining consumer attitudes toward innovative products and services. This is done by influencing five innovation-related characteristics that research has shown to be predictive of consumers' attitudes toward new products and services. In particular, these characteristics are relative advantage, compatibility, complexity, trialability, and observability (see Figure 8.3).

Relative Advantage   The degree to which an innovation is *perceived* as better than an existing idea or object is termed **relative advantage.** Relative advantage is a function of whether a person perceives the new product to be better than competitive offerings, not a function of whether the product is objectively better. The experience of a large acoustical tile company illustrates this. The company developed an acoustical tile that reduced room noise level by 40 percent over the best existing tile on the market. Unfortunately, the tile failed to move in the marketplace. This was because the new tile was designed without holes in it—a design at odds with the standard product at that time—and consumers believed that the new tile had to be less effective than existing brands because their past experiences told them that holes are what give acoustical tile the ability to trap and absorb noise.

Relative advantage is positively correlated with an innovation's adoption rate. There are various determinants of the extent to which customers perceive a new brand or product to possess relative advantages over existing offerings. In general, relative advantages accrue to the product adopter to the extent that the new product offers (1) *increases in comfort,* (2) *savings in time and effort,* and (3) *immediacy of reward.* Each of these depends to some extent on the inherent characteristics of the product itself but can also be influenced by persuasive communications. For example, overnight delivery by air package companies (e.g., Federal Express) offers the real relative advantage of quicker delivery in comparison with conventional mailing; however, advertising must accentuate this real advan-

---

[10]Rogers, *Diffusion of Innovations,* p. 170.

tage in order for potential users to fully appreciate the advantages of using overnight delivery.

Compatibility   The degree to which an innovation is perceived to fit into a person's way of doing things is termed **compatibility.** In general, the more compatibile an innovation is with a person's need structure, personal values and beliefs, and past experiences, the more rapid its rate of adoption. Innovations that are compatible with a person's existing situation are less risky, are more meaningful, and require less effort to incorporate into a person's behavioral mode. The adoption of acupuncture by American physicians has been slow because the procedure does not fit into their accustomed methods of anesthetizing patients before an operation.

Establishing compatibility is partially a function of product design. Beyond this, however, marketing communicators are largely responsible for assuring compatibility in the minds of customers by selecting the right combination of packaging, brand, price, and other symbols that will convey compatibility with the target market's beliefs, past experiences, etc. For example, in India the word condom had a very negative meaning as a contraceptive method, because it was associated with venereal disease. However, when the Indian government used the word *Nirodh,* meaning "protection," their advertising campaign succeeded in producing increases in condom adoptions.[11]

Complexity   **Complexity** refers to the degree of perceived difficulty of an innovation. The more difficult an innovation is to understand or use, the slower the rate of adoption. Home computers have been adopted slowly because many homeowners perceive that they are too difficult to understand and use. Advertisers have confronted this by creating subtle (and not-so-subtle) television commercials that attempt to convey the notion that anybody can easily learn to use a computer, even little kids. Companies have also redesigned their products and introduced new products that *are* more easy to use. The Macintosh computer is an example (see Figure 8.4).

Trialability   **Trialability** is the extent to which an innovation can be used on a limited basis. Trialability is tied closely to the concept of perceived risk. Test drives of new automobiles, free samples of sausage given at local supermarkets, and small packages of new detergents all permit the consumer experimental use of the product, which, in turn, can serve to reduce the risk of a consumer's being dissatisfied with a product after having permanently committed to it through an outright purchase. The Macintosh advertisement (Figure 8.4) is a novel effort by this computer company to give people a chance to try the computer in the comfort of their homes for one full day. This opportunity to have already used the product should make it much easier (i.e., less risky) for people who have tried the

[11]Ibid., p. 228.

FIGURE 8.4   **Novel Effort to Promote Product Trialability**

Macintosh to decide to purchase the computer. The "Test Drive a Macintosh" promotion was indeed a success. Approximately 200,000 Macintoshes were, in fact, "test driven" during the promotional period, and dealers attributed 40 percent of their sales volume during the period to the promotion.[12] In general, products that lend themselves to trialability are adopted at a more rapid rate.

Observability **Observability** refers to visibility, or the degree to which other people can observe one's ownership and use of a new product. That is, the more a consumption behavior can be sensed by other people (i.e., seen, smelled, etc.), the more visible it is said to be. Thus, driving an automobile with a new type of engine is less visible than driving an automobile with a unique body design. Similarly, the adoption of a new perfume fragrance is less visible than adopting a hairstyle that is avant-garde. In general, innovations that are high in visibility lend themselves to rapid adoption.

In sum, the persuasion stage represents an important area of concern for marketing communicators. In this stage the potential adopter is making up his or her mind about the innovation. Many times an individual will mentally or vicariously "try" the innovation to see how it applies to his or her present situation. Advertisers facilitate this vicarious trial by showing the new product being used by people with whom the target audience identifies positively. Sales representatives do the same by informing prospective customers of other desirable individuals who have already purchased the product. Through the right choice of symbols and appeals, marketing communicators can assist product designers in expediting the rate of product adoption and in increasing the chances of product success.

Decision Stage   The decision stage represents the period during which a person chooses either to adopt or reject an innovation. However, similar options are open to the individual even after he or she has made one of these decisions. If the individual rejects the innovation, it may continue to be rejected or later adopted. If the individual initially accepts the innovation, he or she may later discontinue adoption. (Refer again to Figure 8.3.) Discontinuance may be based on the introduction of another innovation that the individual perceives to have relative advantage over the prior innovation, or the individual may simply become tired of or disenchanted with the innovation.

Implementation Stage   The implementation stage occurs when a person puts the new product or idea to use. In the previous stage (decision), the individual simply makes a mental commitment either to use the product or sample it on a trial basis. However, no full-scale commitment is made. In the implementation stage the individual wants the answers to questions such as, "How do I use this product?" and "How do I solve these operational problems?" In such instances the

---

[12]William A. Robinson and Kevin Brown, "Best Promotions of 1984: Back to Basics," *Advertising Age,* March 11, 1985, p. 42.

role of a salesperson is to provide technical assistance by giving the customer helpful suggestions and modes of operation.[13]

Confirmation Stage   A well-established characteristic of all human behavior is that people often seek additional information *after* an important adoption decision in an attempt to confirm the wisdom or appropriateness of their decision. The need to seek confirming information is explained by dissonance theory. It will be helpful to digress briefly to discuss **cognitive dissonance** and show why it is an important concept in the confirmation stage of the innovation-decision process.

Cognitive dissonance is a psychological state of tension or discomfort that results when two or more cognitions are perceived to be inconsistent with one another or with an individual's behavior. These cognitions consist of beliefs, feelings, and opinions a person holds about things in the environment. A dissonance relationship is said to exist when cognitions do not fit together or when they are inconsistent with a person's behavior. Dissonance produces tension, which acts to motivate a person to reduce the tension. Dissonance represents a psychological disequilibrium that must be brought into equilibrium (or consonance) if the tension is to be reduced.

Dissonance can arise in three basic ways. First, any *logical inconsistency* can produce dissonance. For example, it might be illogical for a consumer to invest in a high-priced product that she knows to be inferior in quality to some lower-priced competitive brand. Second, dissonance may result from *inconsistency between an attitude and a behavior or between two behaviors.* John depises Communism and the Russian way of life, yet he knowingly drinks imported Russian vodka. This is an example of inconsistency between an attitude and a behavior. Elizabeth, a product manager, has the company's marketing research department conduct a large-scale and expensive survey to assist in determining which new product idea—A, B, or C—should be pursued; yet, when the research findings are available to her, she disregards them in favor of the product idea she liked best in the first place. This is an example of two inconsistent behaviors. It should be noted here that the person performing the behavior must *perceive* the two acts or the attitude and act as inconsistent or illogical for dissonance to occur. Finally, when a *firmly held expectation is disconfirmed,* dissonance will likely occur.

There are three ways to reduce dissonance. One way is for the person to *rationalize* the situation. Another is for the person to *seek additional information* that is supportive of his or her cognitions and behavior. And third, the person can *eliminate or alter* some of the dissonant elements. This can be done by simply forgetting or suppressing the dissonant element, or more likely, a person can alter attitudes, opinions, or beliefs so that they are no longer in a dissonant relationship with his or her behavior or another cognitive element.

Consider, for example, the person who believes these two positions: (1)

---

[13]Rogers, *Diffusion of Innovations,* p. 174.

Mercedes are well-built cars; (2) I own a new Mercedes that squeaks, rattles, and fails to start on occasion. This person holds two cognitions, one about a make of automobile and one about his own automobile, which belongs to the same class. The two cognitions do not fit together well. This situation is most likely to create dissonance. To reduce the dissonance, he might tell himself that even the best cars develop squeaks and rattles and that pollution control devices make starting a car very difficult. This type of thinking represents *rationalization.* On the other hand, he might *search for information* that confirms his opinion that Mercedes are among the best built cars in the world. In this situation he might begin to amplify the importance of the steering and handling of the car, its comfortable ride, and its durability. Here he is adding and amplifying consonant elements, which in turn reduce the relative importance of the dissonant elements and the magnitude of his dissonance. Finally, he might *eliminate or change* the dissonant elements. He could either change his opinion about Mercedes because he is unable to tolerate the problems his car has, or he might trade his Mercedes in for another Mercedes, believing that he was unfortunate in buying a lemon.

This example represents one form of cognitive dissonance that is often found during the innovation-decision process. This special application is called **postdecisional dissonance.** As the name implies, it refers to dissonance that occurs after an individual makes an important decision. Postdecisional dissonance results from the decision to select one alternative from among several, all of which have both positive and negative characteristics. The decision maker recognizes that he or she selected an alternative that possesses some negative or undesirable aspects and that the unchosen alternatives have positive aspects that he or she has given up. Postdecisional dissonance is greatest when the alternatives are very similar to each other.

After making a decision, a person begins to reevaluate the wisdom of a selection. During the immediate postdecision period, the individual enters a regret phase. During this phase the individual amplifies the undesirable traits of the selected alternative and views more favorably the characteristics of the unselected alternatives. In fact, if given the chance, the person may rate the unchosen alternatives higher than his or her own selection, with a resulting change of viewpoint. However, the regret phase is often brief and is soon followed by a dissonance reduction period. During dissonance reduction the chosen alternative is frequently perceived as more favorable than at the time the decision was made. Ordinarily the individual changes evaluations toward both the selected and unselected alternatives by increasing his or her appraisal of the selection and decreasing his or her appraisal of the unchosen alternatives.

In the innovation-decision process, the confirmation stage represents the time period in which postdecisional dissonance, regret, and dissonance reduction occur. People usually seek out friends to tell them of the attractiveness of their adoption and printed sources to assure them of the value of their decisions. If a person cannot be adequately assured of the correctness of an adoption decision, he or she may discontinue the adoption. Sales representatives have a special role in this stage. Products must not only be sold but resold. An axiom in personal selling is, "You must continue to sell after the sale."

The Diffusion Process

Diffusion is, in simple terms, the process of "spreading out." In a marketing communications sense, this means that a product or idea is adopted by more and more customers as time passes. By analogy, consider a situation where gas is released into a small room. The fumes eventually spread throughout the entire room. Similarly, product innovations spread ideally to all parts of a potential market. The word *ideally* is used because, unlike the physical analogy, the communication of an innovation in the marketplace is often impeded by factors such as unsuitable communication channels, competitive maneuverings, and other imperfect conditions.

This section will deal with the aggregate behavior of groups of customers rather than individuals. Specifically, it will examine the communications network between groups and the characteristics that are typical of each group in the diffusion process.

Adopter Categories   Five groups of adopters are described: (1) innovators, (2) early adopters, (3) early majority, (4) late majority, and (5) laggards. As a matter of convention, these five categories are presumed to follow a normal statistical distribution with respect to the average time of adoption following the introduction of an innovation (see Figure 8.5). That is, in accordance with the properties of a normal distribution, 68 percent of all people who ultimately adopt an innovation fall within plus ("late majority") or minus ("early majority") one standard deviation of the mean time of adoption. The other adopter categories are inter-

---

FIGURE 8.5   **Classification of Adopter Groups Based on Innovativeness**

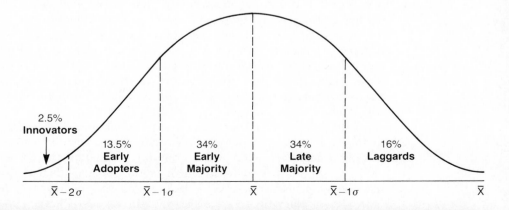

Source: Reprinted with permission of The Free Press, a Division of Macmillan, Inc., from *Diffusion of Innovations,* Third Edition, by Everett M. Rogers, p. 247. Copyright © 1962, 1971, 1983 by The Free Press.

preted in a similar manner. Though the categorization is arbitrary, it has been found meaningful in the study of the diffusion process.

Innovators   The first adopter group, innovators, lies two standard deviations to the left of the mean adoption time. They represent the first 2.5 percent of all potential adopters. In general, a number of sociological and marketing studies have produced similar results in profiling innovators. Rogers notes that innovators exhibit a high level of *venturesomeness*. They are bold and display a willingness to take risks. Furthermore, they seek social relationships outside their local peer group, that is, they are *cosmopolites*. Innovators tend to be *youngest* in age and highest in *social status*. They are typically wealthier and better educated than other groups.

Innovators' communications behavior is characterized by close contact with scientific information sources. They interact mostly with other innovators and rely heavily on impersonal sources, rather than upon other people, to satisfy their information needs. Innovators display a broader range of interests than non-innovators.[14] Innovators not only have interests in those areas in which they innovate but have interests in diverse areas.

The Early Adopter   Early adopters are the second group to adopt an innovation. The size of this group is defined statistically as 13.5 percent of all potential adopters.[15] Early adopters are *localites,* in contrast to innovators, whom we described as cosmopolites. The early adopter is well integrated within his or her community and is highly *respected* by his or her friends.[16] Because of this respect, the early adopter is often sought for advice and information about new things. The respect he or she commands among peers makes the early adopter a very important determinant of the success or failure of an innovation. Opinion leaders come primarily from the early adopter group. Their characteristics and role in the diffusion process are discussed later in the chapter.

The Early Majority   The early majority are a sizable group, composing about 34 percent of all potential adopters of an innovation. As shown in Figure 8.5, the early majority adopt the product prior to the average time of adoption. Members of this group are *deliberate* and *cautious* in their adoption of an innovation.[17] They spend more time in the innovation-decision process than the two earlier groups. They have considerable contact with local adopters and peers. Though the group displays some opinion leadership, it is well below that shown by early adopters. This

---

[14]Thomas S. Robertson and James N. Kennedy, "Prediction of Consumer Innovators: Application of Discriminant Analysis," *Journal of Marketing Research,* Vol. 5, February 1968, pp. 64–69, citing America's Tastemakers, Research Reports Nos. 1 and 2 (Princeton, NJ: Opinion Research Corporation, 1959).

[15]That is, the area under the normal curve between one and two standard deviations from the mean.

[16]Rogers, *Diffusion of Innovations,* pp. 248–249.

[17]Ibid.

group is slightly above average in education and social status but below that of the early adopter group.

The Late Majority   Again referring to Figure 8.5, the late majority is depicted as 34 percent of potential adopters just below the average time of adoption. The key word that characterizes the late majority is *skepticism.*[18] They require immense peer pressure before finally adopting an innovation. By the time they adopt the innovation, the majority of the market has already done so. Peers are the primary source of new ideas for the late majority; the late majority makes little use of mass media. Demographically, they are below average in education, income, and social status. Penetration of this group for adoption purposes is difficult.

The Laggards   The final group to adopt an innovation is laggards, and they represent the bottom 16 percent of potential adopters. These people are *bound in tradition.*[19] Laggards as a group focus on the past as their frame of reference. Their collective attitude may be summarized as, "If it was good enough for my parents, it's good enough for me." Laggards are tied closely to other laggards and to their local community and have limited contact with the mass media. This group, as might be expected, has the lowest social status and income of all adopter groups. If and when laggards adopt an innovation, it usually occurs after one or more innovations have replaced the earlier innovation.

A Summary of Research Findings on Adopters   Over 2,000 studies have examined various aspects of the adoption and diffusion processes. By integrating findings from these studies, it is possible to draw generalizations regarding fundamental differences between people who adopt innovations relatively early in the innovations' life cycles (earlier adopters) and people who are relatively late in adopting innovations (later adopters). These generalizations are summarized into three groups of considerations: (1) socioeconomic status, (2) personality variables, and (3) communication behavior (see Table 8.2).

Generally speaking, the earlier adopter is a person who has what most Western societies deem to be favorable or positive characteristics. For instance, the earlier adopter has more years of formal education, displays greater empathy, is less dogmatic, is more intelligent, has a higher achievement motivation, and overall has other more desirable characteristics than later adopters.

These profiles offer a number of suggestions for marketing communicators. For example, in the early stages of a new product when earlier adopters represent the primary market, advertising and personal selling appeals can be more sophisticated, somewhat more abstract, and appeal more to social reasons for adopting than when efforts are directed at later adopters (see Table 8.2 for other communication implications).

[18]Ibid.
[19]Ibid., p. 250.

TABLE 8.2   **A Profile of Earlier versus Later Adopters of Innovations***

Characteristics	Adopter Profile	
	Earlier Adopters	Later Adopters
Socioeconomic		
Age	No difference	
Education	More	Less
Literacy	Higher	Lower
Social status	Greater	Lower
Upward social mobility	Greater	Less
Attitude toward credit	More favorable	Less favorable
Personality Variables		
Empathy	Greater	Less
Dogmatism	Less	More
Ability to deal with abstractions	Greater	Less
Rationality	Greater	Less
Intelligence	Greater	Less
Attitude toward change	More favorable	Less favorable
Ability to cope with risk	Greater	Less
Attitude toward education	More favorable	Less favorable
Attitude toward science	More favorable	Less favorable
Fatalism	Less	More
Achievement motivation	Higher	Lower
Aspiration level	Higher	Lower
Communication Behavior		
Social participation	More	Less
Integration within social system	Higher	Lower
Cosmopoliteness	More	Less
Change agent contact	More	Less
Exposure to mass media	Greater	Less
Exposure to interpersonal communication channels	Greater	Less
Information seeking	More	Less
Knowledge of innovations	Greater	Less
Opinion leadership	Higher	Lower

*This table is a summary of general characteristics based on research findings compiled by Everett M. Rogers, *Diffusion of Innovations* (New York: The Free Press, 1983); see pp. 251–259.

Managing the Diffusion Process[20]   The actual course of diffusion for a new product is partly determined by a company's marketing actions (product quality, sales force efforts, advertising level, price strategy, etc.) and partly by external forces that are largely beyond a firm's control (competitive actions, shifts in consumers' buying moods and desires, the state of the economy, etc.). However, to the extent possible, firms generally hope to manage the diffusion process so that the new product or service accomplishes the following:

1.   Secures initial sales as quickly as possible (i.e., achieves a *rapid takeoff*)
2.   Achieves cumulative sales in a steep curve (i.e., achieves *rapid acceleration*)

[20]This section is adapted from Thomas S. Robertson, Joan Zielinski, and Scott Ward, *Consumer Behavior* (Glenview, IL: Scott, Foresman and Company, 1984), pp. 380–382.

3.   Secures the highest possible sales potential in the targeted market segment(s) (i.e., achieves *maximum penetration*)

4.   Maintains sales for as long as possible (i.e., achieves a *long-run franchise*).

Figure 8.6 displays the desired pattern that satisfies the preceding conditions and compares it against the typical pattern. The typical diffusion pattern involves a relatively slow takeoff, a slow rate of sales growth, maximum penetration below the full market potential, and sales decline sooner than what would be desired.

What can promotion management do to make the typical pattern more like the desired pattern? The answer to this all-important question is what this text is about in large part. Parts III and IV (Chapters 9 through 20) supply a number of potential promotion management strategies that can move a company toward achieving a desired diffusion pattern. For present purposes, however, several summary comments are in order.

First, *rapid takeoff* can be facilitated by having a promotion budget that is sufficiently large to permit (1) aggressive sales force efforts that are needed to secure trade support for new products, (2) intensive advertising to create high product awareness levels among the target market, and (3) sufficient sales promotion activity to generate desired levels of trial purchase behavior. Second, *rapid acceleration* may be accomplished (1) by assuring that product quality is suitable and will

FIGURE 8.6   "Desired" and "Typical" Diffusion Patterns

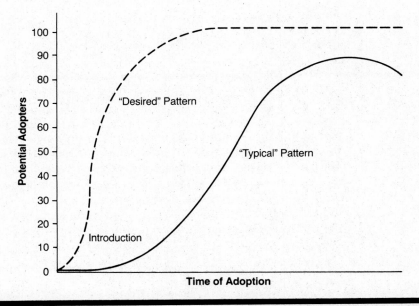

Source: Thomas S. Robertson, Joan Zielinski, and Scott Ward, *Consumer Behavior* (Glenview, IL: Scott, Foresman and Company, 1984), p. 381.

promote positive word-of-mouth communication, (2) by continuing to advertise heavily to reach later adopter groups, (3) by assuring that the sales force provides reseller support, and (4) by using sales promotion creatively so that incentives are provided for repeat purchase behavior. Third, *maximum penetration* can be approached (1) by continuing the same strategies that stimulated rapid acceleration and (2) by revising product design and advertising strategies in such a fashion that the product or service appeals to the needs of the later adopters. Finally, a *long-run franchise* can be maintained by assuring (1) that the "old" product continues to meet the market's needs, (2) that distribution is suitable to reach the market, and (3) that advertising continues to remind the market about the product.

Consider the following illustration to see what one venerable marketing giant, IBM, did to help achieve a desirable diffusion pattern for one of its products—the PCjr home computer.[21] IBM introduced the PCjr in November 1983. However, despite a marketing budget estimated at $40 million, the initial sales were sluggish (i.e., a very slow takeoff). IBM undertook a number of efforts to rescue the PCjr. A first step was to help dealers by allowing them to delay payments six months longer than normal. Second, a number of new PCjr features and options were added. IBM then combined dramatic price cuts with blitzkrieg advertising in a number of media, even direct mail. Then, dealers were offered a $250 rebate and encouraged to pass on the savings to consumers by selling the PCjr with heavily discounted software and peripheral equipment. The result of all this marketing effort? Sales increased from a few units in July 1984 to over 90,000 in November of the same year. Thus, IBM, through its aggressive actions, was able to transform a "dog" into a product with a relatively rapid acceleration. However, it will be some time before it will be possible to know whether these actions will help achieve a desired penetration level and a long-term franchise for the PCjr.

Opinion Leadership and Word-of-Mouth Influence

As noted earlier in the chapter, promotion management's goal is to shorten the length of the diffusion process. This section examines the flow of influence and a key element in the flow, the opinion leader, who can assist promotion management in facilitating more rapid product adoption and diffusion.

The Flow of Influence

How does information and influence flow from the marketers of a new product to members of the target market? What are the roles of the mass media (impersonal sources) and opinion leaders and other personal sources?

Early thinking on the flow of information and influence attributed great power to mass media in directly affecting audience behavior. The communication flow of

---

[21]The following discussion is adapted from "A Flop Becomes a Hit," *Time*, December 24, 1984, p. 60.

influence was conceived as a direct one-step process from the mass media to consumers. The model of this process has been referred to as the hypodermic needle model because of the postulated direct and immediate effect of the source on receivers.

To support the credence of this model, a research team conducted a study concerning the influence of mass media on voting behavior in the 1940 presidential election. To the research team's surprise, they found that a two-step flow, rather than their hypothesized one-step flow, of communications was present. The first step consisted of an information flow from mass media to opinion leaders, and the second step involved a flow of influence from opinion leaders to other people (followers) whom they influenced. From this study evolved a new model called the "two-step flow model."[22] The two-step flow model captures the idea that information flows from the mass media to opinion leaders and from opinion leaders to followers.

Both the one-step and two-step models are oversimplified pictures of reality. We know, for example, that opinion leaders both seek and are sought by followers. Furthermore, opinion leaders influence and are influenced by other opinion leaders. Also, the number of steps involved in the flow may be only one in some instances and several in other instances. Opinion leaders do not always rely on the mass media for their information. In some instances *change agents* (i.e., sales representatives, repairmen, and other individuals) serve as information sources for opinion leaders.

A model that comes a step closer to reflecting the reality of these multiple flows is shown in Figure 8.7. This multistep model depicts several possible communications flows. For example, information can flow *directly* from the mass media to people characterized as Followers (A), who in turn may also seek additional information and opinions from an Opinion Leader (1). In this case the followers actually *seek out* a person whom they respect for additional information. Another flow is one in which Opinion Leader (2) learns a new idea from the mass media and actively seeks out his or her Followers (B). Sometimes an Opinion Leader (4) seeks or receives information from another Opinion Leader (3) and in turn seeks out or is sought by Followers (C). On occasion, an opinion leader does not obtain his or her information from the mass media either directly or indirectly but gains knowledge from a change agent (e.g., a salesperson). This flow is shown where Opinion Leader (5) interacts with the change agent and then influences Followers (D). It is left to the reader to imagine how much more complicated the picture can become by combining these and other possibilities.

It should be noted here that the primary function of the mass media appears to be that of an information source, whereas personal sources function as influencers. Opinion leaders, therefore, are probably more important in the persuasion stage because of their perceived credibility and the opportunity for two-way communication.

[22]Paul F. Lazarsfeld, Bernard Berelson, and Hazel Gaudet, *The People's Choice,* 2nd Ed. (New York: Columbia University Press, 1948).

FIGURE 8.7 **Multi-Step Model of Communications Flows**

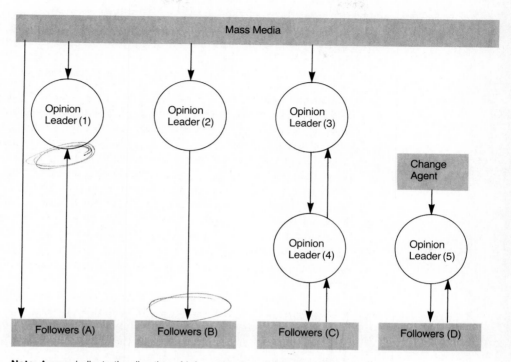

Note: Arrows indicate the direction of information flows between sources and receivers.

Characteristics of Opinion Leaders

An *opinion leader* is a person who "is able to influence informally other individuals' attitudes or overt behavior in a desired way with relative frequency."[23] Opinion leaders perform several important functions: they inform other people (followers) about new products and ideas, they provide advice and reduce the follower's *perceived risk* in purchasing a new product, and they provide positive feedback to support or confirm decisions that followers have already made. Thus, an opinion leader is an *informer,* a *persuader,* and a *confirmer.* It is important to note, however, that opinion leadership influence is typically restricted to one or several consumption topics rather than applying universally across many consumption domains. That is, a person who is an opinion leader with respect to issues and

[23]Rogers, *Diffusion of Innovations,* p. 271.

products in one consumption area (say, motorcycling or skiing or cooking) is *not* generally influential in other unrelated areas. It would be very unlikely, for example, that one person would be respected for his or her knowledge and opinions concerning all three of the listed consumption topics. Moreover, opinion leaders are found in every social class. In most instances, information moves horizontally through a social class instead of vertically from one class to another.

Opinion leaders have profiles that are distinctly different from their followers. Table 8.3 summarizes opinion leaders' most outstanding characteristics.

1. In general, opinion leaders are more *cosmopolitan* and have greater contact with the mass media and with change agents than do followers.

2. Opinion leaders are usually *more gregarious* than the general population and have more social contacts and thus more opportunity for discussing and passing information than followers. As an example of the latter point, women are more likely than men to be opinion leaders in clothing fashions because they have, in general, more interest in clothing fashions, shop more for clothing, and talk to others (such as salespeople) about clothing more than men. This leads us to the next point—opinion leaders must be *accessible*. They must have opportunity, as well as ability, to influence others.

3. Opinion leaders tend to have *higher socioeconomic status* than followers; however, their higher social status is usually only *slightly* above that of their followers. If they were much higher, this would reduce accessibility and, thus, the chance of social contact. Followers tend to seek information from people who are slightly higher in social status, innovativeness, and exposure to mass media than themselves. Followers perceive the opinion leader to have knowledge or competence that the followers do not possess. Thus, the advice of opinion leaders is valued.

4. Opinion leaders are generally *more innovative* than followers and especially so when change is favored by the social system. For example, the public educational system in the United States is currently in the throes of heated debate concerning whether teachers are adequately fulfilling their societal obligation. As such, the system is ripe for change, and opinion leadership

---

TABLE 8.3   **A Profile of the Opinion Leader***

External Communications	Greater exposure to mass media, more cosmopolite, and have greater change agent contact than followers.
Accessibility	Greater social participation than followers.
Socioeconomic Status	Higher socioeconomic status than followers.
Innovativeness	Very innovative when system favors change; not very innovative when system is traditional; also, generally more innovative than followers.

*Everett M. Rogers, *Diffusion of Innovations* (New York: The Free Press, 1983), pp. 282–288.

influence should be especially active. The same applies to computers and other high-tech areas that are undergoing rapid technological changes, thus making opinion leader influence prevalent.

Stimulating Word-of-Mouth Influence

What motivates opinion leaders to give information? It seems that opinion leaders are willing to participate in word-of-mouth (WOM) communications with others because they derive satisfaction from telling others what their opinions are and what they know about new products and services. To share what they know about innovations, and thus to gain satisfaction from telling others, the opinion leaders continually strive, and even feel obligated, to keep themselves informed. Ernest Dichter, a famous motivational researcher, claims that "prestige" is at the heart of WOM. "We like being the bearers of news. Being able to recommend gives us a feeling of prestige. It makes us instant experts."[24]

A vice-president of marketing for Paramount Pictures suggests that the key to generating good WOM is by finding "cheerleaders," i.e., consumers who will get the talk started. This usually is a carefully selected target group that is most likely to love a new movie.[25] In the book industry, cheerleading is stimulated by giving free copies of a new book to a select group of opinion leaders. For example, in the case of *Megatrends,* a leading seller by John Naisbitt, the book publisher sent more than 1,000 copies to chief executive officers of major corporations. Within one month of publication, it became a "must read" book by literally thousands of businesspeople.[26]

Thus, positive word-of-mouth communication is a critical element in a new product or service's success. However, unfavorable WOM can have devastating effects on adoption; consumers seem to place more weight on negative information in making evaluations than upon positive information.[27] Marketing communicators can, however, do several things to minimize the level of negative word-of-mouth:[28] (1) At minimum, companies need to show customers that they are responsive to legitimate complaints; (2) manufacturers can do this by providing detailed warranty and complaint procedure information on labels or in package inserts; (3) retailers can demonstrate their responsiveness to customer complaints

[24]Eileen Prescott, "Word-of-Mouth: Playing on the Prestige Factor," *Wall Street Journal,* February 7, 1984, p. 1.

[25]Ibid.

[26]Ibid.

[27]Richard J. Lutz, "Changing Brand Attitudes through Modification of Cognitive Structure," *Journal of Consumer Research,* Vol. 1, March 1975, pp. 49–59; Peter Wright, "The Harrassed Decision Maker: Time Pressures, Distractions, and the Use of Evidence," *Journal of Applied Psychology,* Vol. 59, October 1974, pp. 555–561.

[28]Marsha L. Richins, "Negative Word-of-Mouth by Dissatisfied Consumers: A Pilot Study," *Journal of Marketing,* Vol. 47, Winter 1983, p. 76.

by positive employee attitudes, store signs, and inserts in monthly billings to customers; (4) companies can offer toll-free numbers to provide customers with a easy and free way to voice their complaints and suggestions. By being responsive to customer complaints, companies can avert negative WOM and perhaps even create positive WOM.[29]

Summary

The continual introduction of new products and services is critical to the success of most business organizations. The likelihood of success depends in part on the degree of innovativeness. Innovations are classified along a continuum ranging from slightly new at one end *(continuous innovations)* to dramatically different at the other end *(discontinuous innovations).*

The concepts of adoption and diffusion explain the processes by which new products and services are accepted by more and more customers as time passes. The *adoption process* views the mental stages an individual goes through in accepting and becoming a repeat purchaser of an innovation. The process consists of five stages: knowledge, persuasion, decision, implementation, and confirmation. Each of these stages is affected by a wide array of variables, which act to expedite or retard the rate of product adoption. The *diffusion process* is concerned with the broader issue of how an innovation is communicated and adopted throughout the marketplace. *Diffusion,* in simple terms, is the process of "spreading out." Diffusion scholars have identified five relatively distinct groups of adopters. These groups, moving from the first to adopt an innovation to the last, are innovators, early adopters, early majority, late majority, and laggards. Research has shown these groups to differ considerably in terms of such variables as socioeconomic status, risk-taking tendencies, and peer relations.

Opinion leadership and word-of-mouth influence are important elements in facilitating more rapid product adoption and diffusion. *Opinion leaders* are individuals who are respected for their product knowledge and opinions. Opinion leaders inform other people (followers) about new products and services, they provide advice and reduce the follower's perceived risk in purchasing a new product, and they confirm decisions that followers have already made. In comparison to followers, opinion leaders are more cosmopolitan, more gregarious, have higher socioeconomic status, and are more innovative. Positive word-of-mouth influence is often critical to new product success. It appears that people talk about new products and services because they gain a feeling of prestige from being the bearer of news. Marketing communicators can take advantage of this prestige factor by stimulating cheerleaders, who will talk favorably about a new product or service.

[29]Ibid.

Discussion Questions

1. Classify the following products and services as continuous innovations, dynamically continuous, or discontinuous innovations: light beer, biogenetic engineering, low-alcohol beer, low-salt foods, the Jarvik artificial heart, Softsoap (i.e., liquid bathroom soap as an alternative to bar soap), three-wheel "dirt" bikes (i.e., machines resembling motorcycles with three balloon wheels), satellite dishes for homeowner use, skin-care products for men, and oversized tennis rackets.

2. Using facial skin-care products for men as the illustration, explain the process by which marketing variables can influence men to become part of the awareness, trier, and repeater classes (refer to Figure 8.2).

3. Explain the difference between the adoption and diffusion processes.

4. What determines whether a new product or service has relative advantages over competitive offerings? What are the relative advantages of low-alcohol beer (e.g., Anheuser-Busch's LA)?

5. What does it mean to say that a potential adopter of a product or service "vicariously tries" the product before adopting it? What do marketing communicators do to promote vicarious trial?

6. Provide a brief explanation of the role of cognitive dissonance during the confirmation stage of product adoption.

7. Compare and contrast innovators and early adopters.

8. Explain why one-step and two-step models of information flow are incomplete and need to be supplanted by a more complete multistep flow model.

Exercises

1. Pick a new product or service of your choice and describe in detail how this product or service satisfies the following success requirements: relative advantages, compatibility, communicability, trialability, and observability.

2. Interview three people who have recently attended a particular movie. Determine how they learned about this movie and why they decided to attend it. Probe for detailed responses, rather than superficial replies. Integrate their responses into a coherent explanation of movie attendance behavior.

3. Suppose you are manager of a new restaurant located in your college or university community. Your fledgling restaurant cannot yet afford media advertising, so the promotional burden rests upon stimulating positive word-of-mouth communication. Develop a strategy of how you would go about doing this.

PART III

Promotion Management: Sales and Advertising

Part III introduces the reader to two prevalent forms of promotions—sales and advertising. To set the stage for these and remaining topics, Chapter 9 looks at various environmental factors that affect promotion decision making. Discussion focuses on technological, demographic, and regulatory forces.

Chapters 10 and 11, on sales management and personal selling, go hand in hand. Chapter 10 provides an overview of the many facets involved in planning, organizing, staffing, directing, and controlling a sales force. The personal selling chapter, Chapter 11, offers both theoretical and practical ideas on how to improve the selling effectiveness of sales personnel.

Chapters 12 through 15 cover a variety of issues related to the process and management of advertising. Chapter 12 introduces the subject by highlighting advertising's economic and social importance and then focuses on the managerial activities of setting advertising objectives and formulating budgets. Creative strategies and approaches in preparing advertising messages are covered in Chapter 13. Chapter 14 examines the media-planning process and looks in detail at characteristics, strengths, and weaknesses of television, radio, magazine, newspaper, and outdoor media. Finally, Chapter 15 addresses the issue of measuring advertising effectiveness and describes a number of techniques that are used for this purpose.

CHAPTER 9

Environmental Influences on Promotion Management

Promotion management decisions are typically influenced by a variety of external forces. Marketing writers have traditionally referred to these as "uncontrollable factors." For example, McCarthy's widely used conceptual model views marketing as three concentric circles: the consumer in the inner circle is surrounded by the "controllable factors" (product, place, price, and promotion), which are surrounded in turn by an outer circle of "uncontrollables" (social and cultural factors, competitive forces, political and legal considerations, and so on).[1] Central to the discussion of environmental influences is the nature of the relationship between marketing organizations and their environments. Marketing theorists have traditionally viewed marketing management as a rather passive process of merely reacting and adapting to environmental forces. This view has changed in recent years, however, and some theorists now take the position that marketers *can* modify the environment in which their firms operate. This new perspective is appropriately termed *environmental management*.[2] Organizations implement a

---

[1]E. Jerome McCarthy and William D. Perreault, Jr., *Basic Marketing,* 8th Ed. (Homewood, IL: Richard D. Irwin, 1984).

[2]Carl P. Zeithaml and Valarie A. Zeithaml, "Environmental Management: Revising the Marketing Perspective," *Journal of Marketing,* Vol. 48, Spring 1984, pp. 46–53; "Kotler: Rethink the Marketing Concept," *Marketing News,* September 14, 1984, pp. 1ff.

variety of strategies that are designed to modify existing environmental conditions.[3] For example, legal action can modify the competitive environment, political action may create a more favorable business environment, and coalitions may be formed between businesses to enhance each firm's competitive position.

Environmental Management and Promotion

The environmental management perspective provides a useful framework for examining environmental influences as they relate to the promotion component of marketing management. Promotion decisions are subject to persistent environmental pressures. The task of promotion management is to adapt and respond appropriately to these pressures and, where possible, to manage (i.e., influence and alter) environmental circumstances so that the organization's interests are best served.

Organizations are not, of course, always able to manage their environments. It is critical, nevertheless, that they monitor their environments and be prepared to alter policies, strategies, or tactics to be compatible with environmental circumstances and developments. Successful companies anticipate environmental developments and are prepared in advance, rather than simply reacting to major changes after they have occurred.

The relationship between promotion management and the environment is illustrated in Figure 9.1. Environmental influences are shown to consist of five major elements: economic, competitive, technological, social-cultural/demographic, and regulatory. The figure further portrays, via double-headed arrows, the four categories of marketing decisions as both adapting to environmental influences as well as attempting to manage these influences. The promotion component of the marketing mix is delineated into its six major components, all of which are, of course, subject to environmental influences.

All of the environmental forces depicted in Figure 9.1 play major roles in promotion management. This chapter, however, will focus on only three major environmental forces: the technological, demographic, and regulatory environments. Detailed discussions of the economic and competitive environments are beyond the primary scope of the text and would, in fact, be redundant with comparable presentations found in any basic marketing text. The sociocultural environment was discussed previously (Chapter 7) in the context of the discussion of group influences on consumer behavior.

The Technological Environment

Technology involves the application of art, science, and engineering for purposes of developing material objects. Technological advances during the past several decades have been incredible, leading one marketing scholar to observe that tech-

---

[3]Zeithaml and Zeithaml, "Environmental Management," provide a typology of 16 different environmental management strategies.

FIGURE 9.1   **Environmental Influences and Promotion Management**

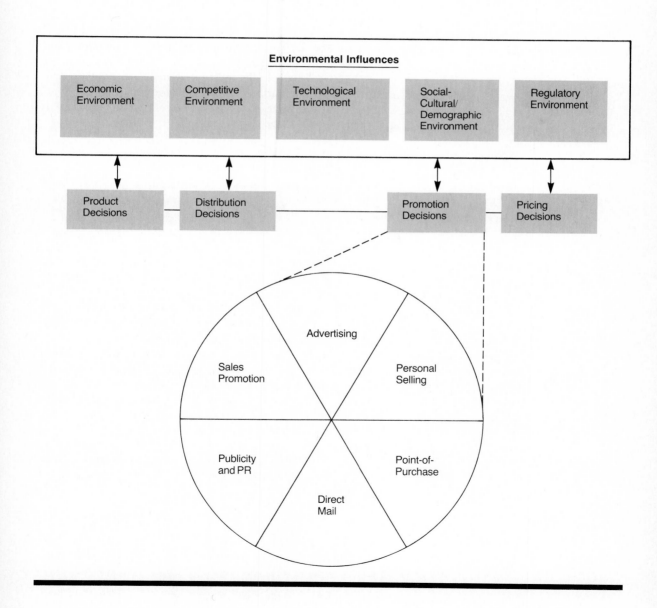

nology is the "most dramatic force shaping people's destiny."[4] Technological developments affect all aspects of our lives and, of course, also influence the behavior of promotion managers and other marketing communicators. This influence is felt both indirectly and directly.

Indirect influence refers to technological developments that do not affect marketing communication technology itself but which influence other aspects of social/economic and marketing behavior. For example, technological advances spur the development of new products, thereby presenting challenges and opportunities for advertisers, salespeople, and other marketing communicators. Other technological developments affect society in general, consumers more specifically, and thus marketing communicators. The advent of birth-control pills, for example, had profound effects on family size, women's rights, household incomes (due to more working wives); consequently, birth-control pills influenced various aspects of consumer behavior and marketing communications behavior indirectly.

Various technological developments that have had *direct effects* on promotion and marketing communications will now be discussed.

Advances Related to Personal Selling

Personal selling has been influenced by several major technological advances, most of which involve computer technology and improvements in communication transmission made possible by satellite transmission and glass optical fibers that transmit light pulses instead of electric signals.

One major communications development is *teleconferencing*. Satellite teleconferences permit individuals (such as sales managers) at one location to engage in audiovisual interaction with individuals in other geographical sites. The following examples illustrate how teleconferencing can be used:[5] (1) General Motors of Canada introduced its line of new 1983 cars and trucks to its dealers with a television type of teleconference. Over 6,000 people in six cities were included in the teleconference; (2) Tandem Computer Corporation uses teleconferences to telecast marketing updates to its sales force; (3) Avon Products Inc. flew 850 top sales representatives and managers to Hawaii for an expense-paid vacation and then telecast the awards ceremony to runners-up on the mainland.

The videocassette recorder (VCR) is not just a favorite household entertainment vehicle; it has also found its way into use by sales departments. For example, Avon purchased 20,000 VCRs for its sales force and provides each salesperson with a monthly cassette showing the company's new products and sales presentations.[6]

Other technological advances affecting personal selling include electronic order entry and cellular telephones. *Electronic order entry* involves the transmission of

---

[4]Philip Kotler, *Marketing Management: Analysis, Management, and Control,* 5th Ed. (Englewood Cliffs, NJ: Prentice-Hall, 1984), p. 99.

[5]Laurel Leff, "When Meetings Go on Camera," *Marketing Communications,* January 1983, pp. 25–27.

[6]"VCRs: Coming on Strong," *Time,* December 24, 1984, p. 47.

sales orders from remote sites (i.e., locations where salespersons work and live) directly to mainframe computers at sales branches and corporate headquarters. Several days were required in the past for orders to be transmitted via the mail. Now, route salespersons (for supermarket and drugstore products) can electronically transmit daily orders and thereby expedite both order processing and order fulfillment.

Cellular telephones are freestanding units that do not require electronic cables and other hardware required by conventional telephones. Rather, cellular telephones make transmissions via satellite linkages. The advantage of the cellular telephone is, of course, that it permits telephone contact from a salesperson's or manager's automobile, boat, or any other site where a conventional phone is unavailable. The technology for making cellular telephoning possible is widespread in Scandinavia and other parts of Europe and is just now entering the United States on a broader scale.

Advances Related to Advertising

Technological developments have affected advertising in three related ways: (1) how messages are transmitted, (2) how messages are produced, and (3) how messages are received by consumers (or perhaps, how messages are avoided).

Cable television is possibly the major technological development related to advertising. Cable TV has altered people's viewing habits and increased the media outlets available to advertisers. The A. C. Nielsen Company reported that over one-third (39.3%) of all U.S. households were wired for cable in 1983; over 2 million cable homes are located in the New York City market alone.[7] This "cabling of America" has created vast viewing opportunities for consumers but has complicated the advertiser's job. Audiences are now fragmented in comparison with pre-cable audiences, who were limited to the three major networks. (More discussion is devoted to this topic in Chapter 14.)

Videocassette recorders have affected advertising, as well as personal selling. By the end of 1984 there were nearly 17 million VCRs in use in American homes.[8] Advertising has been affected by VCRs in at least two ways. First, people are exposed to fewer television advertisements because they spend their time viewing movies and other nontelevision content. Second, even when viewing television programs, people are "zapping" commercials with the fast-scan button. A major advertising agency estimates that by 1987 the loss in commercial ownership will be almost 1 percent. This figure sounds small until the dollar amounts are considered—it amounts to a $200 million loss in ad revenue.[9] Advertising technicians are trying to develop new types of commercials that will enable commercial messages to get across even when played at fast-scan speeds.[10]

[7]*Advertising Age Yearbook 1984* (Chicago: Crain Communications, 1984), p. 146.

[8]"VCRs," p. 45.

[9]Ibid., p. 53.

[10]Ibid.

Methods of producing television commercials have changed as a result of computer developments and other technological advances. Computer-generated commercials are exemplary in this regard. The reader may recall seeing commercials from one company—TRW—which has produced some superb computer-generated commercials. The commercials were designed to dramatize the copy claim: "Just when you think you've seen the whole picture, the picture changes." A bird/fish interlocking pattern was generated by computer to provide a graphic juxtaposition of the verbal claim.

> *The commercial opens with a closeup of a bird's eye, which winks at the camera. As the camera pulls away from the bird, which is carrying a cherry in its beak, the screen displays more and more computer graphic birds, fully animated and flying in unison. Eventually, the birds are seen to be part of an interlocking pattern. When they finally lock together, a positive-negative illusion is created. Within the negative spaces of the birds, the cherries turn into the eyes of fish. As the birds begin to disappear, the computer graphic fish begin to swim in unison. The camera continues to pull away until the birds and fish become merely the dots in a half-tone pattern of a man's face. At this moment, the man winks.[11]*

Scenes from this fascinating and ingenious commercial are shown in Figure 9.2.

Improvements in printing processes have led to vast improvements in the quality of advertising reproductions in print media, particularly newspapers. For example, the quality of color reproduction in newspaper ads has improved considerably in recent years. The extensive use of color print in *USA Today* illustrates the state of printing technology. Another advancement in print media is the ability to reproduce chemically and to encapsulate the smell of cosmetics, soaps, and other items and imprint these on magazine advertisements. These scratch-and-sniff ads provide advertisers the opportunity to reach consumers through the sense of smell in addition to the visual sense.

Advances Related to Direct Mail

As is discussed later in Chapter 16, direct mail marketing has experienced a phenomenal increase in recent years. Part of this increase is due to fundamental developments in American society (e.g., the increase in the number of working wives), but technological factors are also instrumental. Three factors in particular stand out.[12] First, the computer has revolutionized direct mail marketing and has, in certain respects, made direct mail feasible on the scale that it is practiced today. Storage and retrieval of huge mailing lists depends on electronic processing to do

---

[11]Hooper White, "Computers & Commercials: The Production Revolution," *Advertising Age Yearbook 1984* (Chicago: Crain Communications, 1984), p. 24.

[12]Robert F. DeLay, "Direct Marketing: Healthy & Growing," *Advertising Age Yearbook 1984* (Chicago: Crain Communications, 1984), pp. 13, 14.

FIGURE 9.2   **Scenes from TRW's Computer-Generated Commercial**

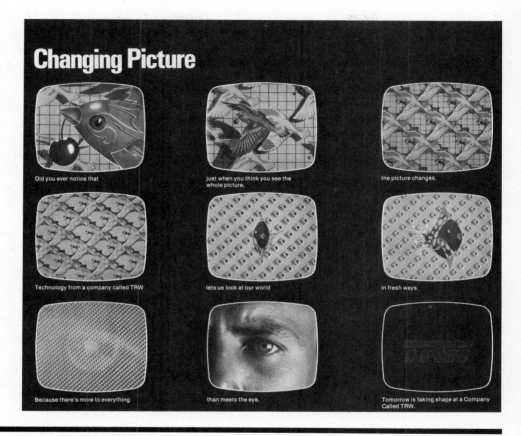

Source: Courtesy of TRW Inc.

what is manually impossible. Moreover, the power of computers to search through huge data files and generate tailor-made lists has facilitated sophisticated market segmentation in the direct mail industry. The computer also facilitates the analysis and evaluation of direct mail effectiveness.

A second technological factor responsible for the rapid growth is, simple as it may seem, the emergence and widespread adoption of credit cards. Credit cards facilitate consumer ordering and expedite credit checking by direct marketers.

A third technological development that has spurred direct marketing's growth is the availability of toll-free WATS numbers. The ability to place a purchase order immediately by phone after reading a direct mail advertisement or viewing a direct marketing television commercial increases the chances that consumers and industrial buyers will in fact order an advertised item rather than procrastinate.

Technological Developments Related to Other Marketing Communications Instruments

Sales promotion, point-of-purchase displays, packaging, and brand name selection have all benefitted from technological developments. In sales promotion, for example, improvements in printing have enhanced the quality of coupons, and packaging-design advances have facilitated more effective free-sample containers and packages for carrying premium devices.

Point-of-purchase displays have become much more aesthetically appealing, more functional, and more effective as a result of technological advances. It is now economically feasible to construct displays out of building materials (e.g., wood veneer) that are economical as well as attractive. The design of large, integrated or component displays (e.g., one display devoted entirely to hair-care products) has made it possible for manufacturers and retailers to increase sales, for retailers to conserve floor space, and for consumers to simplify their shopping. Chapter 20 describes these advances in more detail.

Packaging has also benefitted from technological advances. For example, hermetic packages make nonrefrigerated storage feasible for milk and other perishables. Motor oil can now be sold in convenient plastic containers, which replace messy cans. Packaging aesthetics have also improved immeasurably. Improvements were largely made possible, for example, by advances in glassware technology, which previously was uneconomical for commercial purposes. The new glass technology is illustrated by the outstanding package for Finlandia vodka (see Figure 9.3). This design is a superb communication device that sets Finlandia apart (at least on the shelf) from the profusion of other brands in this highly competitive product category.

Finally, one of the last areas in which technological impact has been felt is in naming brands. Selecting a brand name is an inherently subjective and human task, yet the selection process is facilitated with the computer. Take the case of the Exxon brand name, which was selected only after company officials spent millions of dollars and thousands of man-hours. A computer was used to generate 10,000 four- and five-letter words, the desired word length. A committee then narrowed this list down to a manageable number and ultimately selected the name *Exxon* because it is easy to remember and pronounce and because it can be used universally since it means nothing in any language.[13]

The Demographic Environment

Demographic variables are measurable characteristics of populations, including such characteristics as age distribution, household living patterns, income distribution, minority population patterns, and regional population statistics. By moni-

---

[13]An excellent review of the evolution of the Exxon brand name is presented by Ben M. Enis, "Exxon Marks the Spot," *Journal of Advertising Research,* Vol. 18, December 1978, pp. 7–14.

FIGURE 9.3   **Illustration of Packaging Technology**

Source: Courtesy of ALKO Ltd.

toring demographic shifts, marketers are better able to (1) identify and select market segments, (2) forecast product sales, and (3) select media for reaching target customers.[14]

The demographic structure of the United States is experiencing dramatic and profound changes. The importance to marketers of monitoring demographic trends has been stated very clearly by the editor of *American Demographics:* "You cannot understand the consumer marketplace today without an appreciation of demographic trends. . . . Demographic characteristics help shape preferences, determine attitudes, and mold values. So when these characteristics change rapidly, as they have in recent years, the marketplace changes too."[15] Some of the major forces underlying the reshaping of America are the following:

1.   *A maturing society.* There now are more people over 65 than there are teenagers. By 1990 the number of people who are 65 or older is expected to surpass 31 million while the teenage population shrinks to 23 million.[16]
2.   *Lure of the Sunbelt.* The immigration to the South and West will continue. Forecasters estimate that between 1984 and 1990 the populations of the ten Sunbelt states will increase by at least 20 percent.[17]
3.   *Women on the move.* In the early 1960s approximately 30 percent of married women worked outside the home. Now the percentage is approaching 60 percent. Moreover, the number of women on college campuses now is greater than men.[18]
4.   *Rise of minorities.* The combined population of Hispanics, blacks, and Asian Americans is growing at a disproportionately faster rate than the remainder of the population. These minorites will together constitute about 17 percent of the total U.S. population by the year 2000 in comparison with their 14.4 percent representation in 1983.[19]

The following sections will focus on six major demographic topics that are important to marketing communicators: (1) population growth and regional geographic developments, (2) the changing age structure, (3) household composition developments, (4) the changing roles of women, (5) income dynamics, and (6) minority population developments.

[14]Thomas S. Robertson, Joan Zielinski, and Scott Ward, *Consumer Behavior* (Glenview, IL: Scott, Foresman and Company, 1984), p. 340.

[15]"The Year 2000: A Demographic Profile of the Consumer Market," *Marketing News,* May 25, 1984, p. 8.

[16]For more details see Alex Kucherov, "10 Forces Reshaping America," *U.S. News and World Report,* March 19, 1984, pp. 40–52.

[17]Ibid.

[18]Ibid.

[19]"Prediction: Sunny Side Up," *Time,* September 19, 1983, p. 28.

Population Growth and Regional Geographic Developments

The world population is experiencing an incredible and alarming increase. In 1960 the population was barely over 3 billion people, in 1984 it approached 5 billion, and by the year 2025 it is projected to exceed 8 billion.[20] The most rapid growth is occurring in China, India, and parts of Africa and South America.[21]

The U.S. population in 1984 was approximately 236 million and is expected to grow to approximately 267 million by 2000[22] and to 286 million by 2025.[23] The projected population growth on a state-by-state basis is shown in Figure 9.4. Table 9.1 presents population statistics for the ten most populous states at three time periods. What makes the U.S. population most interesting is not its size or growth per se but rather the shifts that are taking place in its geographical distribution.

FIGURE 9.4   **Projected U.S. Population Growth (1980 to 2000)**

AMERICA IN THE YEAR 2000

Projected population growth or loss, by percent, 1980 to 2000

More than 100%   50-100%   25-50%   0-25%   Loss

TIME Map by Paul J. Pugliese

Source: "Prediction: Sunny Side Up," *Time,* September 19, 1983, p. 28. Copyright 1983 Time Inc. All rights reserved. Reprinted by permission from Time.

[20]"People, People, People," *Time,* August 6, 1984, pp. 24, 25.

[21]Ibid.

[22]"Prediction: Sunny Side Up."

[23]"People, People, People."

TABLE 9.1   **Top Ten U.S. States: Population Projections for 1980, 1990, and 2000**

Top Ten—1980

1.	California	23,668,600
2.	New York	17,557,300
3.	Texas	14,228,400
4.	Pennsylvania	11,866,700
5.	Illinois	11,418,500
6.	Ohio	10,797,400
7.	Florida	9,740,000
8.	Michigan	9,258,300
9.	New Jersey	7,364,200
10.	North Carolina	5,874,400

Top Ten—1990

1.	California	27,525,600
2.	Texas	17,498,200
3.	New York	16,456,700
4.	Florida	13,316,000
5.	Pennsylvania	11,720,400
6.	Illinois	11,502,500
7.	Ohio	10,753,100
8.	Michigan	9,394,300
9.	New Jersey	7,513,100
10.	North Carolina	6,473,400

Top Ten—2000

1.	California	30,613,100
2.	Texas	20,739,400
3.	Florida	17,438,000
4.	New York	14,990,200
5.	Pennsylvania	11,207,600
6.	Illinois	11,187,500
7.	Ohio	10,356,800
8.	Michigan	9,207,600
9.	New Jersey	7,427,600
10.	North Carolina	6,867,800

Source: U.S. Census Bureau. Reprinted in "Census Looks West for Fastest Growth," *Advertising Age,* September 12, 1983, p. 10.

Historically the population was concentrated in the industrial Northeast and Midwest, but by the year 2000 a solid majority of Americans will be southerners or Pacific coasters—"the turn-of-the-century teenager more likely than not will be a sun-drenched type who goes around chirping, 'Fer shure, y'all.' "[24]

The Nine Nations of North America   Marketers are vitally interested in regional differences in consumption behavior. These differences have implications for market segmentation, media selection, and other marketing decisions. Past efforts at

[24]"Prediction: Sunny Side Up."

geographical delineation have been rather simplistic, but a new approach by Joel Garreau, author of *The Nine Nations of North America*, holds considerable promise for practical marketing purposes.[25] Garreau's scheme divides North America into nine relatively distinct geographical regions, which he calls "nations." Capsule summaries of the nine nations are presented in Figure 9.5. These should be studied carefully to appreciate the degree of diversity that prevails in the United States and throughout North America.

The summaries reveal differences among the "nations" that go much beyond mere geography. Rather, the nations vary greatly in terms of economic structure, demographic characteristics, values, and life-styles. This is what makes the Nine Nations scheme potentially valuable to advertising managers and other marketing decision makers. In fact, one major advertising agency, Ogilvy & Mather, has applied the scheme by cross-classifying eight of Garreau's nations (minus Quebec) with a variety of demographic and psychographic variables and with the Values and Life Styles (VALS) typology (refer to discussion in Chapter 7) to form an informative profile of the "Eight Nations of the United States." Figure 9.6 presents a summary of Ogilvy & Mather's findings.[26]

Ogilvy & Mather's summaries reveal a rich profile of regional differences in terms of consumer demographics, self-perceptions, and VALS characteristics. These findings have obvious implications for identifying market opportunities that are congruent with a brand's image and for determining advertising strategy that is compatible with the market's attitudes and self-perceptions. Ogilvy & Mather has summed it up this way:

> *As our systematic regional analysis shows, we are many nations, each with a different personality, a different style, and a different set of values and need perceptions. We may buy many of the same brands, but we do so for different reasons, and we have to be advertised to and persuaded in ways that reflect our regional personae.*[27]

The Changing Age Structure

One of the most dramatic features of the American population is its relentless aging; the median age of Americans was 28 in 1970 and 30 in 1980, and it will rise to 33 by 1990 and 36 by the year 2000.[28] In 1983 there were more than 27 million Americans over the age of 65; there were, by comparison, fewer than 18 million under the age of five.[29]

---

[25]Joel Garreau, *The Nine Nations of North America* (New York: Avon Books, 1981).

[26]"Ogilvy & Mather's Eight Nations of the United States," *Listening Post,* December 1983, No. 57, pp. 2, 3, 6.

[27]Ibid., p. 1.

[28]"The Year 2000."

[29]"Matters of Note about Demographics," *American Demographics,* September 1984, p. 13.

FIGURE 9.5 **Summary Descriptions of the Nine Nations of North America**

Capsule summaries of the Nine Nations

(EDITOR'S NOTE: The information and opinions in the capsule summaries are taken from *The Nine Nations of North America* and interviews with Joel Garreau.)

The Foundry

NATION: Foundry
CAPITAL: Detroit
GEOGRAPHY: Ohio, Pennsylvania, New Jersey, northeastern Illinois, northern Indiana, Michigan (excluding northwest region), New York (excluding Manhattan), southwest Connecticut, northern Virginia, northern Maryland, eastern Wisconsin, northern Delaware, northern West Virginia, and southeastern Ontario.
DESCRIPTION: The industrialized northeast that is losing population, jobs, and investment to the other "nations" is marked by gritty "urban prison camps," decaying infrastructures, heavy trade unionism, obsolete technologies, and racial friction. "The whole point of living in the Foundry is work," Joel Garreau observes. "No one ever lived in Buffalo for its climate or Gary for its scenic vistas. Work is so central to the Foundry experience, that when people are thrown out of it they literally go crazy."
OUTLOOK: This is the only "nation" on decline, due to soft demand for autos, steel, rubber, and its other major products. It no longer represents "America" in a business or social sense, even though it is home to 90 million people. However, it will bounce back in a different form, probably in the early 21st century, according to Garreau. The Foundry's major asset is water, which gives it a competitive edge over most of the other "nations."

MexAmerica

NATION: MexAmerica
CAPITAL: Los Angeles
GEOGRAPHY: Southwest and south central California, southern Arizona, western New Mexico, southern Texas, southern Colorado, and Mexico.
DESCRIPTION: The southwest "nation" of North America has as its capital the second largest Mexican city in the world. Its language, culture, economics, food, politics, and lifestyle are under heavy Hispanic influence. "There are great numbers of Hispanics in the southwest who can't be told by Anglos to 'go back where you came from.' They *are* where they came from," Garreau said. Houston, which is starting to strongly resemble Los Angeles, is the world's new energy capital, bordering MexAmerica on the east. Phoenix is now the 11th largest city in the U.S. MexAmerica is a watershed of the future, but its No. 1 problem is water, most of which is "imported."
OUTLOOK: It is rapidly becoming the most influential of all the nations. If a circle were drawn around Southern California, it would be the 14th wealthiest country in the world. A strong entrepreneurial spirit and "unlimited growth" perspective attract hard-working Anglos and Hispanics. But "northern" influences are creeping in. The southwestern "sombrero, siesta"; the Los Angeles "hot tub, laid-back, flakiness"; and the Houston "all (oil) well, cowboy hat" stereotypes are no longer accurate.

The Islands

NATION: The Islands
CAPITAL: Miami
GEOGRAPHY: Florida south of the Jupiter Inlet, northern Venezuela, northern Columbia, Cuba, Jamaica, Puerto Rico, Bahamas, Virgin Islands, Dominican Republic, Haiti, and dozens of other smaller Caribbean islands.
DESCRIPTION: This "nation" consists of southern Florida, which looks south for its future, and the Caribbean, which sees Miami as its capital. The major industries are (1) the $55 billion illegal drug trade, (2) trade with the "Latin American Rim," and (3) non-Anglo tourism. The Latin American influence is strong and pervasive. The *Miami Herald* circulates editions in Central America. JC Penney stores in Miami stock fur coats in the summer—for tourists south of the equator who arrive during their own winter.
OUTLOOK: The "weirdest and hardest to track" civilization in North America," Garreau calls The Islands. Miami has become a world-class capital with a Caribbean influence, "although southern Florida doesn't want to admit it," he adds. The main point is that southern Florida has very little in common with the rest of the state, let alone Dixie.

Quebec

NATION: Quebec
CAPITAL: Quebec City
GEOGRAPHY: Province of Quebec
DESCRIPTION: The French-speaking area of Canada, steeped in history, tradition, ethnic pride, and a homogeneous culture. It is blessed with plentiful hydroelectric power, prosperous transportation industries, a diversified economy, and a perspective conducive to the acceptance of high technology.
OUTLOOK: Because they've had to struggle to maintain their identity since the first French settlers arrived, the Quebecois feel they've withstood the test of time. "They feel they're not only different from the rest of Canada, but different from the rest of the world," Garreau notes. Fiercely independent, the Quebecois make a habit of saying they want to be "mai tres chez nous," or "masters of our own house." While Quebec may never separate from the rest of Canada, the important point is that the people feel they can, and would succeed on their own.

Dixie

NATION: Dixie
CAPITAL: Atlanta
GEOGRAPHY: Georgia, Alabama, Mississippi, Louisiana, Arkansas, Kentucky, Tennessee, North Carolina, South Carolina, southern Virginia, southern Maryland, southern Illinois, southern Indiana, southern Missouri, north and central Florida, eastern Texas, southeastern Oklahoma, southern West Virginia, and southern Delaware.
DESCRIPTION: Dixie is that "forever-underdeveloped North American nation across which the social and economic machine of the late 20th century has most dramatically swept," Garreau notes. Dixie is an emotion, an idea, a way of life in small towns and cities, calling oneself a "Southerner," the Confederate flag, and waving to strangers. It is knowing where and who you are.
OUTLOOK: No longer predominantly backward, rural, poor, and racist, Dixie is undergoing the most rapid social and economic change on the continent. However, Dixie's growth is all "catch up," since most of its "impressive" growth statistics (per-capita income, for example) are still below the national average. Southern cities tend to annex surrounding towns with industries, thus creating "artificial" population growth. Yet, the people are among the most optimistic about the future. "Dixie isn't the 'sunbelt,'" Garreau warns. "There is no such place as the sunbelt."

New England

NATION: New England
CAPITAL: Boston
GEOGRAPHY: Massachusetts, Maine, New Hampshire, Vermont, Rhode Island, eastern Connecticut, Nova Scotia, Prince Edward Island, Labrador, Newfoundland, and New Brunswick.
DESCRIPTION: With virtually no energy or raw materials, little agriculture, few basic industries, high taxes, and expensive home fuel and auto gas, New England is the poorest of the nine "nations" (poverty is actually chic). The oldest and most civilized Anglo "nation" on the continent has people who are environmentally aware, tolerant, intelligent, political, fair, but somewhat elitist, Garreau notes. They feel "we're all in this together."
OUTLOOK: New England was the first "nation" to enter economic decline and a post-industrial society. It is rebounding thanks to an influx of high-tech industries, the proprietors and employees of which like New England's charm and quality of life. New England is once again a land of pioneers, only this time they're resurrecting a fully depreciated "nation."

Empty Quarter

NATION: Empty Quarter
CAPITAL: Denver
GEOGRAPHY: Wyoming, Nevada, Montana, Utah, Idaho, western Colorado, eastern California, northern Arizona, western Oregon, western Washington, northwestern New Mexico, northern Alaska, Yukon, Northwest Territories, eastern British Columbia, Alberta, northern Manitoba, north and southwest Saskatchewan, and northern Ontario.
DESCRIPTION: The Intermountain West boasts wide-open spaces, energy (oil, gas, tar sands, oil shale), and minerals (gold, silver, copper, zinc, iron, magnesium, uranium, and hundreds of others). While it is the largest "nation" in terms of land area, it has the smallest population, which makes it politically weak-voiced. With its pristine environment, it is the true "west." There's plenty of fresh air, but the land is high and dry, and largely government-owned. It's not uncommon for residents to drive 200 miles to see a movie.
OUTLOOK: The future of the Empty Quarter will largely be determined by outsiders: environmentalists who want to preserve its beauty, and the "rape-and-run boys," who want its energy, Garreau said. The people still believe in the "frontier ethic," but this "nation" will undergo radical change over the next 20 years. It's estimated that development of the Overthrust Belt alone could result in one million jobs and eight million additional population.

Ecotopia

NATION: Ecotopia
CAPITAL: San Francisco
GEOGRAPHY: Northwest California, western Oregon, western Washington, western British Columbia, and southeastern coastal Alaska.
DESCRIPTION: The only part of the west blessed with adequate water and renewable resources (and volcanoes). The home of "Silicon Valley," computer chips, aluminum, timber, hydroelectric power, fisheries, bioengineering, environmentalism, outdoor nature lovers, energy conservation, and recycling. "Quality of life" is a religion in the great Pacific Northwest, which considers the rest of North America "screwed up." Strongly antinuclear, with a penchant for seriously discussing "appropriate technology" and holistic medicine, Ecotopians have as their motto: "Leave. Me. Alone."
OUTLOOK: Ecotopia's economy is interest-rate-based, so it won't explode with opportunity until interest rates fall, Garreau said. Still, the residents will only want clean, high-tech industries, and will cling to the "small-is-beautiful" ideology. Ecotopia is best positioned to exploit the growing Pacific Rim nations. Unlike the eastern part of the U.S. and Canada, which is European-oriented, Ecotopia looks to Asia for its future.

Breadbasket

NATION: Breadbasket
CAPITAL: Kansas City
GEOGRAPHY: Minnesota, Iowa, Kansas, North Dakota, South Dakota, Nebraska, northern Missouri, western Wisconsin, northwest Michigan, western and central Oklahoma, eastern New Mexico, eastern Colorado, western and central Illinois, north and central Texas, southeastern Saskatchewan, southern Manitoba, and southwest Ontario.
DESCRIPTION: The Breadbasket is marked by agriculture and agriculture-related industries and economies. If there is a mainstream America, this is it—conservative, hard-working, religious residents. "People in the Breadbasket are the ratifiers of social change," Garreau explains. "Ideas still must *play* in Peoria before they become accepted. When the people in Kansas starting opposing the Vietnam War, you knew the war would soon be over."
OUTLOOK: This nation works best. It is stable and at peace with itself by virtue of its enviable, prosperous, renewable economy. The Great Plains also have acquired great political power because of the strategic world importance of food. But farmers are being hurt financially by their own productivity: they are 3% of the population yet feed North Americans and millions of others around the world.

Aberrations

EVERY RULE HAS EXCEPTIONS, including the "Nine Nations" theory. Some cities and states in the U.S. simply don't "fit in" with their regions; Joel Garreau calls them "aberrations."

WASHINGTON, D.C.: The atmosphere of this city is directed inward to government, bureaucracies, lobbyists, lawyers, consultants, the news media, and the military. While its interests are not those of average Americans (Washington, D.C. residents like to find out what's going on "out there"), this city refuses to admit it's different, isolated, and a parody of its own institutions. Excluding the poor blacks in the city, the Washington, D.C. area has the highest per-capita income in the U.S., and more psychiatrists per capita than any other U.S. city. After a few years in office, former President Jimmy Carter commented, "Washington is out of tune with America."

MANHATTAN: While residents of the Washington, D.C. area refuse to recognize their uniqueness, people in Manhattan are actually proud of being different—and the rest of America views Manhattan as different. As Garreau observes, "You just don't find transvestite discos in Oklahoma City." In the 1970s, Manhattan considered becoming the 51st state, and many residents still feel civilization ends at the Hudson River. The world, in their view, is divided into two parts: New York and Not New York. With Wall Street, Madison Avenue, Times Square, Broadway, the United Nations, and three-room apartments with $1,500 monthly rents, Manhattan surely must be considered an aberration.

HAWAII: Many Americans feel Hawaiians are on vacation every day of the year, thanks to a tropical climate, Aloha spirit, and easygoing lifestyle. Hawaii *is* beautifully different, but it also has its problems, among them no energy resources, sky-high prices, racial tensions, and feelings of being isolated—out of sync with the Mainland. It is the only state where whites of European stock (haoles) are a minority; two-thirds of the population is Asian. There are few Hispanics and even fewer blacks. And, while Hawaiians take pride in their cultural diversity, the locals resent the presence of military personnel. "Anglo kids fear the last day of the school year," Garreau notes. "The locals call it 'kill a haole day.' The Japanese and Filipinos encounter similar problems." Hawaii's major industry is tourism, followed by the military and agriculture (the No. 1 cash crop is marijuana).

ALASKA: While Garreau included parts of Alaska in Ecotopia and the Empty Quarter, he feels the state as a whole is an aberration. "Alaskans—whose judgments about anything must be measured against their decision to live in a place where tomatoes won't—think that theirs is a separate nation," he said. Alaskans refer to people from other states as "outsiders," and high-ranking Alaska politicians admit their state would like to secede from the U.S. Due to the influx of tax money from the Alaskan pipeline, the state income tax was eliminated. Alaskans are politically "schizophrenic," Garreau said, pointing out that possession of marijuana is legal there.

The earth is perpetually frozen; garbage is dumped in front yards because the items are too expensive to ship out and too difficult to bury. Despite the mountain snow, Alaska actually receives less rainfall than the Sahara Desert. It has great mineral wealth, but only 1% of the land is in public hands. Alaska has the lowest population age in the U.S., and Anglos are a distinct minority. The Eskimos, in fact, feel more allied with other residents of the Arctic Circle than they do with the U.S. "All you need are heavy boots, a hunting rifle, and a piece of earth-moving machinery and you'll fit right in," Garreau said.

Source: Adapted from *The Nine Nations of North America,* paperback edition, by Avon Books.

FIGURE 9.6   **The Eight Nations of the United States**

The Breadbasket is "the middle" of America—both geographically and attitudinally. People who live here are middle-aged, middle income, and politically middle-of-the-road. Average marital status, average education, and an average occupational profile complete the picture. Conformist Belongers are well represented in this nation. Except for their own sense of awkwardness, The Breadbasket populace has neither inflated nor deflated self-perceptions. The American Dream seems to work for this group, either because of or in spite of its middleness.

Dixie still seems to be on a "catch-up" curve. Its residents are older, downscale, and conservative. Their view of *themselves* is awkward and not terribly efficient, and seems to mirror Northerners' stereotypical views of a slow-moving South. Interestingly, Dixie folk do not consider themselves to be particularly amicable. Home of few Inner Directeds, Dixie includes more Need Drivens and Belongers than any other nation. Economy-mindedness and persuasibility are high among this group.

Ecotopia, where "small is beautiful," thrives on demographic attractiveness: young, educated, affluent, white collar. Only a high divorce rate mars the picture of healthy, successful, well adjusted folk. Politically liberal, Ecotopians describe themselves as affectionate, amicable and creative. This is hard-core Inner Directed territory, especially for outdoor, nature-loving Experimentals. But, in spite of other available information, it is interesting that they *do not see themselves* as particularly experimental.

The Empty Quarter is the only nation where men outnumber women. The "frontier ethic" seems to dominate residents of this nation, steeling them to the geographic and economic challenges of a vast population-poor and resource-rich area. Hardworking, conservative, middle income, blue collar residents are the norm. While the straightforward citizens of The Empty Quarter claim to be broadminded and creative, they also reveal the attributes of a nation with a mission: to tame the last U.S. wilderness. Personally, they are frank, stubborn, dominating and not particularly amicable. Brave and stern Inner Directeds live in this nation. They are *not* conformist, style conscious, persuasible or brand loyal.

The Foundry residents have a rich array of self-perceptions which sound complacently positive. These middle-aged, upscale liberals describe themselves as amicable, sociable, funny, intelligent, and refined. They also recognize that they are tense and egocentric—perhaps the result of a "nation-on-decline" defensiveness. Claiming to be both conformist and style conscious, Foundry residents are also ecology-minded. As a result, both Emulators and Inner Directeds (especially the I-Am-Me sons and daughters of Achievers) are well represented in The Foundry mix.

The Islands (Southern Florida) is different from the rest of the state, and different from the Dixie nation. Both young and old live here with modest or fixed incomes. Our scant data belies the importance of The Islands nation as a major U.S. link to Central and South American countries that are having an increasingly critical impact in our social, economic and political arenas. The business value of isolating this nation may involve corporate objectives that extend beyond domestic sales and marketing figures.

Mexamerica is an interesting mixture of highly educated and poorly educated. At the same time, overall employment and wealth are very high. Liberal political attitudes predominate and, not surprisingly, extend into the domestic arena where non-married alternatives seem to prevail. The relative youth of Mexamericans determines many of their self-perceptions. They do *not* see themselves as being cautious, conformist, efficient, or economy-minded. They claim *not* to be style conscious. Perhaps this is because they perceive themselves to be the style *innovators* for other nations to follow. Emulators and Achievers, as well as the Societally Conscious, live in Mexamerica—creating a nicely balanced population. This nation clearly has the potential to become the "most influential of all the nations."

New England is the "most civilized Anglo nation." New Englanders are older, upper-middle income professionals. Widowed people are a noteworthy segment, with a high part-time worker population.
Politically diverse, and self-described as amicable and sociable, New England's stalwart nature is revealed as cautious, *not* impulsive, brand loyal and ecology-minded. The second most Inner Directed nation (especially Societally Conscious), New England also plays host to Achievers—perhaps drawn to the newly developing hi-tech industries.

Source: Ogilvy & Mather *Listening Post Research Survey,* December 1983, p. 266. Reprinted by permission.

222

FIGURE 9.7   **The Legacy of the Baby Boom and Bust
(U.S. Population by Age: 1985 and 1995, in Millions)**

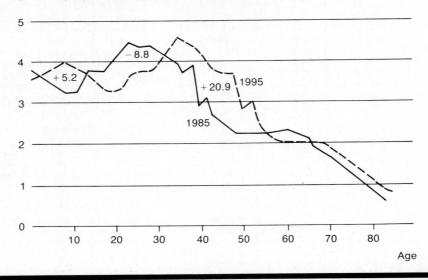

Source: U.S. Census Bureau. Reprinted in Bryant Robey and Cheryl Russell, "The Year of the Baby Boom," *American Demographics,* May 1984, p. 20.

The Baby-Boom Generation   The changing age structure is attributable in large part to what demographers term the "baby boom"—the 74 million Americans born between 1947 and 1964.[30] The effects of the baby boom (and subsequent bust) can be seen vividly in Figure 9.7, which portrays three major developments:[31]

1.   By 1995 there will be 5.2 million more Americans aged 2 to 13 than in 1985; the original "baby boomers" are creating a mini baby boom as they reach childbearing age.
2.   The number of teenagers and young adults is declining. "By 1995 there will be 8.8 million fewer Americans aged 14 to 30 than in 1985 because the baby-bust generation, born in the 1960s and 1970s, will be moving through those age groups."[32]
3.   As the baby-boom generation ages, the number of people aged 31 to 56 will grow by 20.9 million between 1985 and 1995.

[30]Bryant Robey and Cheryl Russell, "The Year of the Baby Boom," *American Demographics,* May 1984, p. 19.
[31]Ibid., p. 20.
[32]Ibid.

The baby-boom generation has had and will continue to have powerful effects on consumer goods markets. In addition to the changing age structure, the baby-boom generation is fundamentally different than previous generations in terms of *education* and *women's roles.* "The baby-boom generation is much better educated than previous generations. Only 15 percent of Americans aged 35 and older have completed college, while nearly 24 percent of those aged 25 to 34 have had at least four years of college."[33] The other major change resulting from the baby boom is that young women are much better educated and more likely, as a result, to participate in the labor force—fully 70 percent of all women aged 20 to 34 are working or looking for work.[34]

The preceding developments hold considerable promise for many marketers but problems for others. Considering the problems possibility first, marketers who appealed to the teenage and young adult markets during the 1970s have suffered as the size of these markets declined. The blue jeans industry is a case in point. Blue jean sales reached a tremendous peak in 1981, when an estimated 600 million pairs were sold in the United States alone.[35] Since then, sales have declined, due in large part to the baby-boom generation's changing tastes and preferences as they have matured and turned to other types of clothing.

On the positive side, the baby-boom generation offers tremendous potential for many marketers. Research shows that baby boomers are more interested than older people in such products as digital watches, 35mm cameras, home stereos, videotape recorders, TV videogames, and automobiles.[36] Also, because of this group's relatively high levels of education and affluence, they are also good prospects for such investments as life insurance, real estate, and savings accounts.[37]

Automobile marketers seem particularly attentive to the baby-boom market.[38] For example, General Motors designed three new lines of sports coupes (the Oldsmobile Calais, the Buick Somerset Regal, and the Pontiac Grand Am) specifically for the group of young professional baby boomers referred to as "yuppies." Yuppies represent the vanguard of the baby boom and have been characterized as affluent, influential, and extremely materialistic.[39] The marketing manager for GM's Pontiac Division pointed out that the Grand Am is the first mass-volume car that the Pontiac division had ever marketed to such a specifically targeted market seg-

[33]Ibid., p. 21.

[34]Ibid.

[35]"Beyond the Blue Horizon," *Time,* August 20, 1984, p. 106.

[36]"Marketers Should Scrutinize Needs and Preferences of the Class of '74," *Marketing News,* March 4, 1983, p. 3.

[37]Ibid.

[38]William Dunn, "Wheels for the Baby Boom: Detroit Discovers Demographics," *American Demographics,* May 1984, pp. 27–29.

[39]An excellent review of yuppies and the yuppie market is presented in various articles in the December 31, 1984, issue of *Newsweek,* which was devoted to "The Year of the Yuppie."

ment.[40] The Chrysler Corporation also aimed its efforts at young professionals from the baby-boom generation with its introduction of the LeBaron GTS and Dodge Lancer. The company dubbed these two cars their "Yuppiemobiles."

The Mature Market   The number of middle-aged households is increasing rapidly as members of the baby-boom generation grow older; in fact, as noted previously, the 31 to 56 age group will increase by nearly 21 million between 1985 and 1995. In terms of specific age groups, the 35 to 44 group will increase by 34 percent over this ten-year period, when the total U.S. population will grow barely 10 percent.[41] The 45 to 64 group is another substantial group. The numbers are rather astounding, in fact. There are twice as many people 45 to 64 years old in the United States as the total population of Canada; this age group is, moreover, bigger than the combined populations of all of Denmark, Finland, Sweden, Norway, Austria, and Belgium.[42] The 45 to 64 market accounts for about 40 percent of all spending power in the United States.[43] A number of products enjoy above-average consumption by mature people. These include travel, sewing machines, electric razors, hair-coloring products, and decaffeinated coffee.[44] It is estimated that 43 percent of all new cars sold in 1984 were bought by customers aged 50 and over.[45]

Many marketers have historically ignored the mature market, but the aging of the American population would urge against this in the future. A variety of implications accompany marketing communication efforts that are directed at the mature market. Some authorities contend that mature customers are less gullible because of their vast storehouse of accumulated knowledge and experience.[46] It would also be advisable in advertising directed at this group to portray them as active, vital, busy, forward looking, and concerned with looking attractive and being romantic.[47] Advertisers are beginning to appeal to the mature market in a flattering fashion as typified by the use of attractive, middle-age models to represent clothing, cosmetics, and other products, which had been the exclusive advertising domain of youthful models.

[40]James Risen, "GM Targeting Sports Coupes for the Baby-Boomers," *The State* (Columbia, SC: Ben R. Morris, September 16, 1984), p. 3–G.

[41]Peter Francese, "Middle-Years Growth Will Aid Travel, Finance," *Advertising Age,* August 23, 1984, p. 50.

[42]Stephen O. Frankfurt, "Middle Age: A Forgotten Market," *Advertising Age,* January 21, 1980, p. 56.

[43]Ibid.

[44]Ibid.

[45]"No. 1 Car Market? Grumpies," *Advertising Age,* September 10, 1984, p. 12.

[46]See Frankfurt, "Middle Age," p. 58.

[47]"Market Profile: The Graying of America's Consumer," *POPAI News,* Vol. 7, No. 1, 1983, p. 5.

The Changing American Household

The traditional American household, as portrayed stereotypically in television and other mass media, is a nuclear family, consisting of mother, father, and two or three children. Millions of such households do in fact exist in the United States, but the composition of households is changing dramatically. In 1950, families (i.e., a married couple with or without children) constituted 90 percent of all households; this percentage fell to 74 percent in 1980 and is projected to fall to 69 percent by 1995.[48] As of 1984, nuclear families (mother, father, and one or more children) comprised only 29 percent of all households, while people who live alone occupied 23 percent of households.[49] The number of people who live in families headed by a man or woman without a spouse soared from 21.7 million in 1970 to 35 million in 1983, this due in large part to the rising divorce rate and the increasing incidence of out-of-wedlock births.[50]

The publisher of *American Demographics,* a respected chronicle of demographic developments, contends that American households have been altered forever by the combined effects of changes in marriage patterns, widespread birth control, more working women, and rising divorce rates.[51] Households are growing in number, shrinking in size, and changing in character. "We now have about 85 million households and expect 95 million by 1990. During the past decade households grew twice as fast as the population, while household size declined rapidly in all of the 50 states."[52]

The changing composition of the American household has tremendous implications for marketing communicators, especially advertisers. Advertising will have to reflect the widening range of living situations that exist. This is particularly true in the case of the "singles market."[53] Singles represent a large and ever-growing group. There are, for example, over 9 million men in the United States who live without female partners and do their own shopping, cooking, and household chores.[54] The total singles market (not just men) accounts for roughly one-eighth of all consumer spending in the United States.[55]

The growth of the singles market is changing the way advertising is done. Many advertisers make special appeals to the buying interests and needs of singles, ap-

[48]"Demographic Forecasts," *American Demographics,* May 1984, p. 50.

[49]Peter Francese, "Baby Boom's Echo Keeps Economy Moving," *Advertising Age,* July 19, 1984, p. 12.

[50]"Death of the Family?" *Newsweek,* January 17, 1983, p. 26.

[51]Francese, "Baby Boom's Echo."

[52]Ibid.

[53]The singles label is certainly too crude to constitute a true market segment because a variety of different groups are included in the general category (people who have never been married, divorced people, widowed people, etc.).

[54]"Marketers Slighting Many Male 'Settlers,' " *Advertising Age,* July 25, 1983, p. 47.

[55]Gay Jervey, "Y & R Study: New Life to Singles," *Advertising Age,* October 4, 1982, p. 14.

pealing, for example, to such needs as ease of preparation, maintenance simplicity, small serving sizes, etc. Reaching singles requires special media selection efforts because they (1) tend not to be big prime-time TV viewers but are skewed instead toward the late-fringe hours (i.e., after 11 p.m.), (2) are disproportionately more likely than the rest of the population to view cable television, and (3) are heavy magazine readers.[56]

Changing Roles of Women

Marketing communicators have tended to view women in the stereotypical roles as wife, mother, homemaker, and hostess or as a single girl preparatory to these roles.[57] However, major changes in the roles of women over the past two decades have forced marketing communicators to portray women more realistically in advertising and to develop a wider range of appeals that reflect women's changing needs and status.

Some of the most notable changes in women's roles are the following: (1) the number of women in the nation's work force increased from under 25 million in 1960 to over 46 million in 1983; fully 67 percent of the women between the ages of 18 and 34 are in the labor force;[58] (2) today, women head almost one-third of all households compared with one in seven in 1950;[59] (3) a larger share of women are remaining single into their thirties; this trend results from more educational and occupational opportunities, as well as disenchantment with marriage because of the divorce rate.[60]

Although advertisers have made strides in appreciation of women's changing roles, it is probably fair to conclude that women are still being portrayed in a limited range of roles, which do not fully reflect the actual working position and status of women in today's society.[61] This, fortunately, is changing, albeit slowly, as advertisers are increasingly recognizing the importance of women as major decision makers. Kerin, Lundstrom, and Sciglimpaglia have summed it up rather nicely:

> *Advertising which remains locked into the traditional roles of mother/*
> *homemaker will play to a decreasing audience in the future. Although*
> *a woman may fulfill these roles in a partial capacity, the desire to shed*

[56]Ibid.

[57]Alladi Venkatesh, "Changing Roles of Women—A Lifestyle Analysis," *Journal of Consumer Research,* Vol. 7, November 1980, p. 189.

[58]"A Portrait of America," *Newsweek,* January 17, 1983, p. 30.

[59]Daphne Spain and Suzanne M. Bianchi, "How Women Have Changed," *American Demographics,* May 1983, pp. 18–25.

[60]Ibid.

[61]A number of studies have detected stereotypical role portrayal of women. For a review see Roger A. Kerin, William J. Lundstrom, and Donald Sciglimpaglia, "Women in Advertisements: Retrospect and Prospect," *Journal of Advertising,* Vol. 8, No. 3, 1979, pp. 37–42.

this image will lead to dual roles, role switching, and role blending. Thus, both women and men can be expected to be portrayed in roles which show a person in more than one capacity; a man doing "woman's" work, and men and women jointly deciding on a purchase decision. In short, the modern woman is not, and will not, accept a thrusting into traditional roles, and expect to be found in an expanding number of positions replacing her male counterpart.[62]

Income Dynamics

American society in the 1980s is characterized by increasing numbers of people at both extremes of the income distribution. At the low end, there are more than 30 million Americans living below the poverty level (defined as an annual income of $9,287 for a family of four).[63] The situation is particularly bleak for blacks and Hispanics, whose poverty rates far exceed that for whites.

At the other end of the distribution, a number of American households are enjoying continually rising incomes. Households making $40,000 or more a year jumped from 4 percent of the population in 1975 to 19 percent in 1982. In that same year approximately 8 percent of the adult population had incomes between $40,000 to $49,000; 6 percent made between $50,000 and $75,000, and another 6 percent made over $75,000.[64] These impressive figures are due in large part to increasing numbers of women entering the labor force. The median income in households where the wife does not work is $21,000; it rises to $28,000 in households where she works part-time and to $32,000 in households where both husband and wife work full-time.[65]

Many companies are interested in the affluent consumer because of his or her spending power. Aside from the spending power, there appears to be a subtle shift taking place in many consumers' attitudes toward consumption. The research firm of Yankelovich, Skelly and White characterizes this shift as a transition from a "disposable psychology" to an "investment psychology." Many affluent and relatively affluent Americans are showing much more enthusiasm for quality merchandise, things that will last, and values that will grow. There is taking place, according to Yankelovich, Skelly and White, a return to elegance away from flamboyance. This has been referred to as the "Europeanization of America."[66]

[62]Ibid., p. 41.

[63]"A Portrait of America," p. 31.

[64]"The Rich, the Very Rich, and the Super Rich," *Marketing Communications,* November/December 1982, p. 22.

[65]Bernie Whalen, "The 'Vanishing' Middle Class: A Passing Demographic Aberration," *Marketing News,* May 25, 1984, p. 6.

[66]"The Rich," p. 25.

Special marketing communication efforts are required to reach and motivate the affluent market. In terms of advertising claims, appeals to elegance, quality, and durability are especially effective. Media selection is critical because research shows that media behavior patterns change with increases in income—TV viewing and radio listening drop, and magazine readership increases (see Table 9.2).[67]

Minority Population Developments

America has always been a melting pot, and it became even more so in the 1970s, the decade of the immigrant. The numbers of immigrants admitted to the United States in the 1970s surpassed those for any year since 1924.[68] The largest number of immigrants were Asians and Pacific islanders, who together represented an increase of nearly 128 percent in 1980 over their U.S. population base in 1970. Other racial and ethnic groups also experienced large population increases in the United States between 1970 and 1980. The black population increased 17.3 percent (from 22.6 million to 26.5 million). The Spanish-origin population (primarily Mexicans, Puerto Ricans, and Cubans) increased 61 percent (from 9.1 million to 14.6 million). Comparatively, the white population increased only 5.8 percent (from 178.1 million to 188.3 million) between 1970 and 1980.

Specific characteristics of the black and Hispanic markets, as well as implications for promotion management, were discussed in Chapter 7 and will not be repeated here. The reader may wish to review this material before proceeding to the next topic.

The Regulatory Environment

Advertisers, sales managers, and other marketing communicators are faced with a variety of regulations and restrictions that influence their decision-making latitude. Although regulation is inherently antithetical to the philosophical premises of a free-enterprise society, the history of the past century has shown that regulation is required to protect consumers and competitors from fraudulent, deceptive, and unfair practices, which some businesses choose to perpetrate.

Regulation is most needed *when consumer decisions are based on false or limited information.*[69] Consumers under such circumstances are likely to make decisions they would not otherwise make and, as a result, to incur economic, physical, or psychological injury. Competitors are also harmed because they lose business that they might have otherwise enjoyed.

---

[67]For further reading on the affluent market, see "The Gold Plated Consumer," *Marketing Communications,* December 1984, pp. 23–27.

[68]"Lands of Our Fathers," *Newsweek,* January 17, 1983, p. 22.

[69]Michael B. Mazis, Richard Staelin, Howard Beales, and Steven Salop, "A Framework for Evaluating Consumer Information Regulation," *Journal of Marketing,* Vol. 45, Winter 1981, pp. 11–21.

TABLE 9.2   ### Relationship between Magazine Readership and Income

Readership/ Viewing	Magazine Readership (A)	Television Viewing (M)	Radio Listening (M)
$ 40,000–$49,999	5.1	25	16
$ 50,000–$59,999	5.8	24	15
$ 60,000–$74,999	6.3	22	16
$ 75,000–$99,999	7.0	22	15
$100,000–$149,999	7.6	22	15
$150,000 or more	9.0	20	13

Mag. Readership: per month
Viewing/Listening: Hrs. per week

(A): Average
(M): Median

Affluent Magazines**	Subscribers' Median Household Income*
Architectural Digest	$63,356
Atlantic	37,680
Barron's	50,800
Bon Appetit	30,276
Business Week	46,050[a]
Cuisine	33,880
Dun's Business Month	75,130
Food & Wine	41,571
Forbes	55,820
Fortune	46,500
Geo	67,500
Golf	31,371[b]
Golf Digest	40,630[a]
Gourmet	46,118
Home	38,700
Money	45,500
New York	42,040
New Yorker	41,548
New York Times Magazine	45,400
Runner's World	29,512
Ski	38,800[c]
Smithsonian	31,906
Tennis	39,410[a]
Town & Country	63,000
Travel & Leisure	36,475
W	66,242

Magazines' own subscriber study   **Folio: 400 1982
Source: "The Rich, the Very Rich, and the Super Rich," *Marketing Communications,* November/December 1982, p. 26.
[a]1982 Simmons Market Research Bureau Total Readership Study
[b]1982 Monroe Mendelsohn, Inc. Survey of Adults and Markets of Affluence
[c]1981 Simmons Market Research Bureau Total Readership Study

In theory, regulation is justified if the benefits therefrom exceed the costs. What are the benefits and costs of regulation?[70] Regulation offers three major *benefits:* First, *consumer choice* among alternatives is improved when consumers are better informed in the marketplace. Second, when consumers become better informed, *product quality* tends to improve in response to consumers' changing needs and preferences. For example, when consumers learned of the dangers of tar and nicotine in cigarettes, manufacturers began marketing lower tar and nicotine cigarettes. A third regulatory benefit is *reduced prices* resulting from a reduction in a seller's "informational market power." For example, prices of used cars would undoubtedly fall if dealers were required to inform prospective purchasers about a car's defects, since consumers would not be willing to pay as much for an automobile with known problems.

Regulation is not costless. One cost is the *cost of complying* with a regulatory remedy. For example, U.S. cigarette manufacturers are now required to rotate over the course of a year four different warning messages for three months each. This obviously is more costly than the single message that was required previously. *Enforcement costs* represent a second cost category. A third cost are the costs to buyers and sellers of *unintended side effects,* which might result from regulations. A regulation may unintentionally harm sellers if buyers switch to other products or reduce their level of consumption after regulation is imposed. The cost to buyers may increase if sellers pass along, in the form of higher prices, the costs of complying with a regulation.

In sum, then, regulation is theoretically justified only if the benefits exceed the costs. Many people in American society evidently believe that regulatory benefits *do* exceed costs, because the amount of regulation has increased significantly over the past several decades. The following sections examine the two forms of regulation that affect promotion decision making: governmental regulation and industry self-regulation.

Governmental Regulation of Promotion

The Federal Trade Commission (FTC) is the government agency that has primary responsibility for regulating American business. The FTC, created in 1914, was concerned during its early years with preventing *anticompetitive* practices, i.e., protecting businesses rather than consumers. Congress realized by 1938 that the FTC's mandate should be expanded to offer more assistance to consumers as well as businesses, especially in the area of false and misleading advertising. The *Wheeler-Lea Amendment of 1938* accomplished this objective by changing a principal section of the original FTC Act of 1914 from "unfair methods of competition" to "unfair methods of competition and unfair or deceptive acts or practices in commerce." This seemingly minor change enhanced the FTC's regulatory powers

---

[70]The following discussion is adapted from Mazis et al.

appreciably and provided a legal mandate for it to protect consumers against fraudulent business practices.

Over the years the FTC has acquired increased authority through a series of so-called FTC Improvement Acts. FTC powers were broadened especially during the late 1960s through mid-1970s, but the 1980s have been marked by a "strong backlash from the business community"[71] and a corresponding cutback in FTC powers.

The FTC's regulatory authority cuts across three broad areas that directly affect marketing communicators: deceptive advertising, unfair practices, and information regulation.

The Regulation of Deceptive Advertising
The legal standard of deceptiveness involves proof only that an advertisement has the capacity to deceive consumers, not that it has actually deceived.[72] Theoretically, however, **advertising deception** occurs when "an advertisement (or advertising campaign) leaves the consumer with an impression(s) and/or belief(s) different from what would normally be expected if the consumer had reasonable knowledge, and that impression(s) and/or belief(s) is factually untrue or potentially misleading."[73]

The preceding definition suggests that there are two requirements for deception to occur: (1) an advertising claim or an impression left by a claim must be *false,* i.e., there must be a claim-fact discrepancy, and (2) the false claim must be *believed* by consumers. The important point is that a false claim is not necessarily deceptive by itself. "What matters is what consumers believe. A false claim does not harm consumers unless it is believed, and a true claim can generate harm if it generates a false belief."[74]

It should be apparent from the foregoing explanations that the determination of deception is often difficult and even somewhat subjective. Although the FTC makes deception rulings case by case, it does employ some general guidelines in deciding whether a particular case is deceptive. A ruling of deception is likely to occur when any of the following practices are detected:

1.   An advertiser uses a misleading statement or unsubstantiated claim.
2.   An advertising claim creates a misleading impression.
3.   An advertiser uses a misleading testimonial.
4.   There is a misleading use of the term *free.*
5.   There is a misleading television demonstration.

(List continues on page 232.)

---

[71]William L. Wilkie, Dennis L. McNeill, and Michael B. Mazis, "Marketing's 'Scarlet Letter': The Theory and Practice of Corrective Advertising," *Journal of Marketing,* Vol. 48, Spring 1984, p. 11.

[72]Ivan L. Preston, "A Review of the Literature on Advertising Regulation," in James H. Leigh and Claude R. Martin (eds.), *Current Issues and Research in Advertising 1983* (Ann Arbor, MI: University of Michigan, 1983), p. 7.

[73]David M. Gardner, "Deception in Advertising: A Conceptual Approach," *Journal of Marketing,* Vol. 39, January 1975, p. 42.

[74]J. Edward Russo, Barbara L. Metcalf, and Debra Stephens, "Identifying Misleading Advertising," *Journal of Consumer Research,* Vol. 8, September 1981, p. 120.

6.   An advertiser uses a bait and switch tactic by advertising an item at one price and attempting to trade customers up to a higher-priced product when they come to the store by claiming that the advertised item is of inferior quality or out of stock.

In addition to these general guidelines, the FTC has prepared specific guidelines for over 175 industries. These guidelines were formulated by the FTC in consultation with spokespersons for the various industries and involve specific trade practice rules that identify illegal practices in each industry.[75]

Current Deception Policy   Deception policy at the Federal Trade Commission is not inscribed in granite but rather is subject to shifts, depending upon the regulatory philosophy of different FTC chairmen and the prevailing political climate. The FTC's present enforcement policy against deception reflects the conservative political mood and the corresponding opposition to business regulation.

The current deception policy declares that the FTC will find a business practice deceptive "if there is a representation, omission or practice that is likely to mislead the consumer acting reasonably in the circumstances, to the consumer's detriment."[76] Three elements undergird this policy:[77]

1.   *There must be a representation, omission, or practice that is likely to mislead the consumer.* A misrepresentation is defined by the FTC as an express or implied statement contrary to fact, whereas a misleading omission is said to occur when qualifying information necessary to prevent a practice, claim, representation, or reasonable expectation or belief from being misleading is not disclosed.

2.   *The act or practice must be considered from the perspective of the reasonable consumer.* The FTC's test of reasonableness is whether the consumer's interpretation or reaction to an advertisement is reasonable. That is, the commission determines the effect of the advertising practice on a reasonable member of the group to which the advertising is targeted. "For instance, if a company markets a cure to the terminally ill, the practice will be evaluated from the perspective of how it affects the ordinary member of that group. Thus, terminally ill consumers might be particularly susceptible to exaggerated cure claims. By the same token, a practice or representation directed to a well-educated group, such as a prescription drug advertisement to doctors, would be judged in light of the knowledge and sophistication of that group."[78]

[75]Otto Kleppner, *Advertising Procedure,* 7th Ed. (Englewood Cliffs, NJ: Prentice-Hall, 1979), p. 551.

[76]Public copy of letter dated October 14, 1983, from FTC Chairman James C. Miller III to Senator Bob Packwood, Chairman of Senate Committee on Commerce, Science, and Transportation.

[77]Ibid.

[78]Ibid.

The policy with regard to reasonableness further declares that the FTC is not likely to pursue advertising cases based on subjective claims (taste, feel, appearance, smell) or those involving exaggerated, or "puffed," claims because it believes that such claims are unlikely to deceive consumers acting reasonably.

3. *The representation, omission, or practice must be material.* A material representation involves information that is important to consumers and which is likely to influence their choice or conduct regarding a product. In general, the FTC considers information material when it pertains to the central characteristics of a product or service (performance features, size, price, etc.).

The new FTC deception policy is endorsed by the advertising industry but is opposed by critics in the Congress and even within the Federal Trade Commission. For example, FTC Commissioner Bailey contends that the new policy will weaken consumer protection law and introduce a new set of enforcement problems for the FTC.[79] What Commissioner Bailey and other critics most object to is that *proof of consumer detriment is required before deception can be established.* This is a rigorous requirement that goes considerably beyond prior policy, which simply required the FTC to establish that an act or practice has the capacity to mislead a substantial number of consumers in a material way and that the deception was likely to cause injury to consumers.[80]

The new deception policy also creates uncertainty for advertisers, who must wait for congressional hearings and possibly court tests to determine what is and is not permissible advertising practice.

The Regulation of Unfair Practices   As noted at the beginning of this section, the Wheeler-Lea Amendment of 1938 gave the Federal Trade Commission authority to regulate *unfair,* as well as *deceptive,* acts or practices in commerce. Unfairness is inherently a nebulous and elusive concept. For this reason the unfairness doctrine received limited use by the FTC until 1972, when in a famous judicial decision *(FTC v. Sperry & Hutchinson Co.)* the Supreme Court noted that consumers, as well as businesses, must be protected from unfair trade practices.[81] A finding of unfairness to consumers may, unlike deception, go beyond questions of fact and relate merely to public values.[82] The criteria used to evaluate whether a business act is unfair involve such considerations as whether the act (1) offends public policy as it has been established by statutes, (2) is immoral, unethical, oppressive,

---

[79]Patricia P. Bailey, "Does the New FTC Deception Policy Fill the Bill?" *Advertising Age,* February 13, 1984, p. M-27.

[80]Ibid., p. M-28.

[81]For further discussion see Dorothy Cohen, "Unfairness in Advertising Revisited," *Journal of Marketing,* Vol. 46, Winter 1982, p. 74.

[82]Dorothy Cohen, "The Concept of Unfairness as It Relates to Advertising Legislation," *Journal of Marketing,* Vol. 38, July 1974, p. 8.

or unscrupulous, and (3) causes substantial injury to consumers, competitors, or other businesses.[83]

The FTC has applied the unfairness doctrine in three major areas: (1) for the advertising substantiation program, (2) in cases involving promotional practices directed to children, and (3) when promulgating trade regulation rules.[84]

Advertising Substantiation   The ad substantiation program is based on a simple premise: it is unfair for advertisers to make claims about their products without having a reasonable basis for making the claims. Unfairness results, according to the FTC, from imposing on the consumer the unavoidable economic risk that the product may not perform as advertised if neither the consumer nor the manufacturer has a reasonable basis for belief in the product claim. Advertisers under the ad substantiation program are required to have documentation (i.e., test results or other data) indicating that they have a "reasonable basis" for making a claim *prior to the dissemination of advertisements.*[85]

Unfairness Involving Children   Because children are more credulous and less well equipped than adults to protect themselves, public policy officials are especially concerned with protecting youngsters against unscrupulous and misleading promotional practices. The unfairness doctrine is especially useful when applied to cases involving children because many advertising claims are not deceptive per se but are nonetheless potentially unethical, unscrupulous, or inherently dangerous to children. For example, the FTC considered unfair a company's use of Spider Man vitamin advertising because such advertising was judged capable of inducing children to take excessive and dangerous amounts of vitamins.[86]

Trade Regulation Rules   Whereas most Federal Trade Commission actions are taken on a case-by-case basis, the use of trade regulation rules (TRRs) enables the FTC to issue a regulation that restricts an entire industry from some objectional practice. For example, the FTC issued a TRR to vocational schools that required the schools to disclose enrollment and job placement statistics in their promotional materials. The rule was later rejected by a court of appeals on grounds that the FTC had failed to define the unfair practices that the rule was designed to remedy.[87]

---

[83]Cohen, "Unfairness in Advertising Revisited."

[84]Ibid., pp. 75–76.

[85]For further discussion see Dorothy Cohen, "The FTC's Advertising Substantiation Program," *Journal of Marketing,* Vol. 44, Winter 1980, pp. 26–35; and Debra L. Scammon and Richard J. Semenik, "The FTC's 'Reasonable Basis' for Substantiation of Advertising: Expanded Standards and Implications," *Journal of Advertising,* Vol. 12, No. 1, 1983, pp. 4–11.

[86]Cohen, "Unfairness in Advertising Revisited."

[87]Ibid., p. 75.

Information Regulation   Although the primary purpose of advertising regulation is the prohibition of deceptive and unfair practices, there was considerable emphasis during the 1970s directed at compelling or persuading businesses to provide consumers with information they might not otherwise receive.[88] The corrective advertising program is arguably the most important of the FTC's information provision programs.[89]

Corrective advertising is based on the premise that a firm which misleads consumers should have to use future advertisements to rectify any deceptive impressions it has created in consumers' minds. The purpose is, in other words, to prevent a firm from continuing to deceive consumers; the purpose is not to punish the firm. The texts of four early corrective advertisements are shown in Figure 9.8. In parentheses at the bottom of each corrective ad is the FTC's stipulation for how often the corrective ad was to be advertised. For example, the stipulation for Profile Bread required that the corrective statement be printed or aired in 25 percent of Profile's ads for one full year.

The most prominent corrective advertising order to date is the case of Warner-Lambert's Listerine mouthwash. According to the FTC, Warner-Lambert had been deceptive over a number of years in misleading consumers into thinking that Listerine was able to prevent colds and sore throats or lessen their severity. The FTC required Warner-Lambert to run the following corrective advertisement statement: "Listerine will not help prevent colds or sore throats or lessen their severity." The corrective campaign ran for 16 months (September 1978 to February 1980), and a total of $10.3 million was spent, mostly on television commercials.

A number of studies have been conducted to evaluate the effectiveness of the Listerine corrective advertising order.[90] For example, the FTC conducted a field study that consisted of seven waves of questionnaire mailings to over 10,000 households. The research results revealed only partial success for the Listerine corrective campaign. On the positive side, there was a reported 40 percent drop in the amount of mouthwash used for cold and sore throat prevention, but on the negative side, (1) 42 percent of Listerine users still believed at the end of the campaign that Listerine was still being promoted as effective for colds and sore throats, (2) 57 percent of Listerine users continued to rate cold and sore throat effectiveness as a key attribute in their purchasing (only 15 percent of Scope users reported a similar goal), and (3) 39 percent of Listerine users reported continued use of mouthwash to relieve or prevent a cold or sore throat.

The conclusion to be drawn from this and other corrective advertising research is that "corrective advertising has 'worked,' but not nearly well enough to even approach correcting the misimpression levels in the marketplace."[91] It appears that previous corrective advertising orders, including the one for Listerine, have not

[88]Preston, "Literature on Advertising Regulation," p. 14.

[89]The following discussion borrows heavily from the excellent review article by Wilkie, McNeill, and Mazis, "Marketing's 'Scarlet Letter.' "

[90]See Wilkie, McNeill, and Mazis, "Marketing's 'Scarlet Letter,' " for review.

[91]Ibid., p. 26.

FIGURE 9.8   **Texts of Four Early Corrective Ads**

Profile Bread

"Hi, (celebrity's name) for Profile Bread. Like all mothers, I'm concerned about nutrition and balanced meals. So, I'd like to clear up any misunderstanding you may have about Profile Bread from its advertising or even its name. "Does Profile have fewer calories than any other breads? No. Profile has about the same per ounce as other breads. To be exact, Profile has seven fewer calories per slice. That's because Profile is sliced thinner. But eating Profile will not cause you to lose weight. A reduction of seven calories is insignificant. It's total calories and balanced nutrition that count. And Profile can help you achieve a balanced meal because it provides protein and B vitamins as well as other nutrients. "How does my family feel about Profile? Well, my husband likes Profile toast, the children love Profile sandwiches, and I prefer Profile to any other bread. So you see, at our house, delicious taste makes Profile a family affair."
(To be run in 25% of brand's advertising, for one year.)

Amstar

"Do you recall some of our past messages saying that Domino Sugar gives you strength, energy, and stamina? Actually, Domino is not a special or unique source of strength, energy, and stamina. No sugar is, because what you need is a balanced diet and plenty of rest and exercise."
(To be run in one of every four ads for one year.)

Ocean Spray

"If you've wondered what some of our earlier advertising meant when we said Ocean Spray Cranberry Juice Cocktail has more food energy than orange juice or tomato juice, let us make it clear: we didn't mean vitamins and minerals. Food energy means calories. Nothing more. "Food energy is important at breakfast since many of us may not get enough calories, or food energy, to get off to a good start. Ocean Spray Cranberry Juice Cocktail helps because it contains more food energy than most other breakfast drinks. "And Ocean Spray Cranberry Juice Cocktail gives you and your family Vitamin C plus a great wake-up taste. It's . . . the other breakfast drink."
(To be run in one of every four ads for one year.)

Sugar Information, Inc.

"Do you recall the messages we brought you in the past about sugar? How something with sugar in it before meals could help you curb your appetite? We hope you didn't get the idea that our little diet tip was any magic formula for losing weight. Because there are no tricks or shortcuts; the whole diet subject is very complicated. Research hasn't established that consuming sugar before meals will contribute to weight reduction or even keep you from gaining weight."
(To be run for one insertion in each of seven magazines.)

Source: William L. Wilkie, Dennis L. McNeill, and Michael B. Mazis, "Marketing's 'Scarlet Letter': The Theory and Practice of Corrective Advertising," *Journal of Marketing,* Vol. 48, Spring 1984, p. 13.

been based on sufficient research to understand how consumers would respond to the corrective advertising statements. Past corrective advertising statements have been prepared by FTC staff personnel, rather than by copywriters guided by experts in consumer behavior. Thus, corrective advertising has probably not been as effective as it needs to be to remove the misimpressions that were created through years of deceptive advertising.

Advertising Self-Regulation

Self-regulation is, as suggested by the name, undertaken by advertisers themselves, rather than by governmental bodies. Advertising self-regulation was a response in the 1970s to heightened consumer criticism of advertising and stricter government controls.[92] Four major groups sponsor self-regulation programs: (1) advertising associations (e.g., American Association of Advertising Agencies, Association of National Advertisers), (2) special industry groups (such as the Council of Better Business Bureaus), (3) media associations (e.g., National Association of Broadcasters), and (4) trade associations.[93]

Self-regulation by the Council of Better Business Bureaus' National Advertising Division (NAD) and National Advertising Review Board (NARB) has been the most publicized and perhaps most effective form of self-regulation. The NAD and NARB were established in 1971 with the goal of sustaining "high standards of truth and accuracy in national advertising."[94] NARB is the umbrellalike term applied to the combined NAD/NARB self-regulatory mechanism; however, by strict definition, NARB is a court of appeals consisting of 50 representatives who are formed into five-member panels to hear appeals of NAD cases when one or more of the involved parties is dissatisfied with the initial verdict.[95] NAD is the investigative arm of NARB and is responsible for "receiving or initiating, evaluating, investigating, analyzing and holding initial negotiations with an advertiser on complaints or questions from any source involving truth or accuracy of national advertising."[96]

A review of several recent advertising cases will demonstrate the nature of NAD/NARB activities.

The Mobil Oil Case[97]   Television commercials for Mobile 1 oil showed labels of 24 competitive products in succession while claiming, "The best engine protection you can give your car. Do you know how many of these motor oils would love to make this claim? Well, one can. Mobil 1." A competitor questioned whether Mobile had proof of product superiority over virtually every domestic motor oil. The NAD, upon reviewing the case, concluded that Mobil had not demonstrated that Mobile 1 provided superior protection under *typical driving conditions*. In response to this challenge, Mobile changed its advertising to state, "Do you know which of these oils gives you the best engine protection under the toughest driving conditions—subzero cold or blazing heat? This one. Mobile 1."

The Wella Balsam Shampoo Case[98]   Advertising for Wella Balsam shampoo claimed that "only Wella Balsam takes care of split ends, flyaways and dryness." In response to a competitor's challenge, the NAD investigated Wella Balsam's claim

---

[92]Priscilla A. LaBarbera, "Analyzing and Advancing the State of the Art of Advertising Self-Regulation," *Journal of Advertising,* Vol. 9, No. 4, 1980, p. 27.

[93]Ibid., p. 28.

[94]*Statement of Organization and Procedures of the National Advertising Review Board* (Washington, DC: National Advertising Review Board, June 19, 1980).

[95]Erick J. Zanot, "A Review of Eight Years of NARB Casework: Guidelines and Parameters of Deceptive Advertising," *Journal of Advertising,* Vol. 9, No. 4, 1980, p. 20.

[96]*Statement of Organization and Procedures.*

[97]This discussion is adapted from "NAD Inquiry Gets Mobile to Change Claim," *Advertising Age,* August 16, 1984, p. 3.

[98]This discussion is adapted from "NAD, Wella Splitting Hairs on Ad Claim," *Advertising Age,* July 16, 1984, p. 10.

and challenged the laboratory evidence Wella had used as the basis for making its exclusivity claim. Wella Balsam ultimately terminated the advertising campaign and withdrew the comparative claims from further use.

The Sony TV Case[99]   The Sony case centers on two commercials that claimed superior product performance for Sony and which made reference to Sony's winning an Emmy award as evidence of its touted superior performance. "RCA questioned whether claims for superior performance in 1983–84 could be based on an Emmy awarded in 1972–73."[100] NAD agreed with RCA that future Sony ads should, to prevent further misunderstanding, disclose the date of the Emmy award. Sony, in response, proposed the addition of a superimposed statement, "Awarded 1972–73. Nobody else has even won one." NAD deemed this change insufficient. The case has, at the time of this writing, been referred to the NARB for a final ruling.

The NAD/NARB Process

The preceding cases illustrate some of the fundamentals of the NAD/NARB self-regulatory process. This section details the specific activities that are involved from the time a complaint is initiated until it is resolved.[101] The discussion centers around Figure 9.9.

Complaint Screening and Case Selection   The process begins with the NAD screening complaints against allegedly deceptive or misleading advertising. Complaints originate from four major sources: (1) competitors (as in all of the cited cases), (2) consumers and consumer groups, (3) Better Business Bureaus, and (4) NAD's own monitoring activities. The NAD pursues those complaints which it regards as having merit. Between 1971 and October 1981 it investigated 1,909 cases.

Initial NAD Evaluation   Some cases are administratively closed because they fall outside NAD's jurisdiction, but in most cases NAD contacts the advertiser and opens a dialogue. There are three possible outcomes from this dialogue: (1) the disputed advertisement is found acceptable; this outcome occurred in only 2 percent of all the opened cases reviewed by NAD through October 1981 (see percentages in parentheses in Figure 9.9); (2) the advertisement is considered questionable; or (3) it is deemed unacceptable because NAD feels it violates a precedent or may be misinterpreted by consumers.

---

[99]This discussion is adapted from "NAD Taking Sony TV Set Case to NARB," *Advertising Age*, April 16, 1984, p. 6.

[100]Ibid.

[101]The following discussion borrows heavily from the thorough presentation by Gary M. Armstrong and Julie L. Ozanne, "An Evaluation of NAD/NARB Purpose and Performance," *Journal of Advertising*, Vol. 12, No. 3, 1983, pp. 19–23.

FIGURE 9.9   The NAD/NARB Process

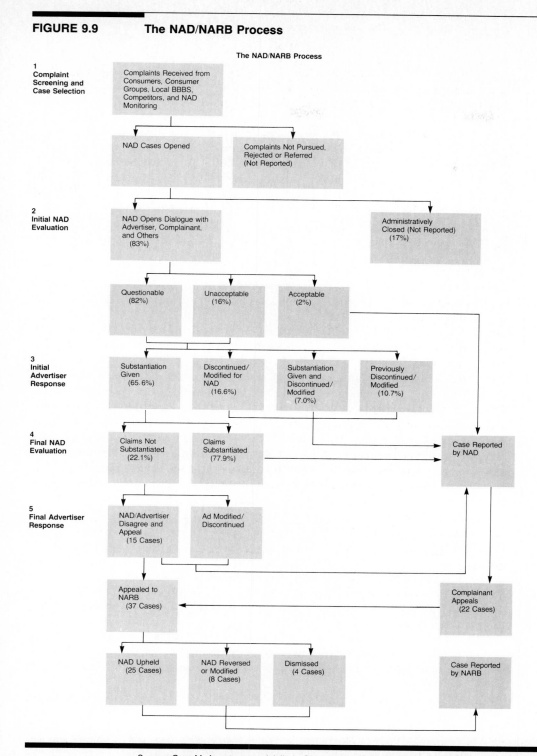

The NAD/NARB Process

1 Complaint Screening and Case Selection

Complaints Received from Consumers, Consumer Groups, Local BBBS, Competitors, and NAD Monitoring

NAD Cases Opened

Complaints Not Pursued, Rejected or Referred (Not Reported)

2 Initial NAD Evaluation

NAD Opens Dialogue with Advertiser, Complainant, and Others (83%)

Administratively Closed (Not Reported) (17%)

Questionable (82%)

Unacceptable (16%)

Acceptable (2%)

3 Initial Advertiser Response

Substantiation Given (65.6%)

Discontinued/ Modified for NAD (16.6%)

Substantiation Given and Discontinued/ Modified (7.0%)

Previously Discontinued/ Modified (10.7%)

4 Final NAD Evaluation

Claims Not Substantiated (22.1%)

Claims Substantiated (77.9%)

Case Reported by NAD

5 Final Advertiser Response

NAD/Advertiser Disagree and Appeal (15 Cases)

Ad Modified/ Discontinued

Appealed to NARB (37 Cases)

Complainant Appeals (22 Cases)

NAD Upheld (25 Cases)

NAD Reversed or Modified (8 Cases)

Dismissed (4 Cases)

Case Reported by NARB

Source: Gary M. Armstrong and Julie L. Ozanne, "An Evaluation of NAD/NARB Purpose and Performance," *Journal of Advertising,* Vol. 12, No. 3, 1984, p. 20.

Advertiser's Initial Response   Figure 9.9 shows that advertisers can respond to NAD by providing sufficient substantiation to show that the disputed advertising claim is justified or by discontinuing or modifying the claim.

NAD's Final Evaluation   All ads that have been discontinued or modified are publicly reported by NAD. For example, the three cases discussed previously were reported in various isues of *Advertising Age,* a publication that has wide distribution in the advertising community. Ads for which advertisers have provided substantiation are then reviewed by NAD to assess the adequacy of the evidence provided. In most instances NAD rules that the disputed claims have been adequately substantiated (Figure 9.9 shows the percentage to be 77.9 percent). Claims that NAD considers insufficiently substantiated are subject to appeal to NARB.

Advertiser's Final Response   Thirty-seven cases were appealed to NARB between 1971 and October 1981. These appeals were originated in some instances by advertisers and in other instances by NAD. The NAD's ruling may be upheld, reversed, or dismissed by NARB. However, because NAD/NARB is merely a self-regulatory body without legal jurisdiction or power, the ultimate resolution of disputed cases depends on voluntary cooperation between advertisers and NAD/NARB.

In conclusion, self-regulation has a variety of potential benefits to consumers and to businesses. It can strengthen effectiveness by "discouraging exaggerated or misleading promises which lower the believability and selling power of advertising."[102] Self-regulation may also reduce the demand for government regulation. Furthermore, because advertisers are strongly motivated to point out their competitors' deceptive advertising practices, they help, in their efforts to protect themselves, to maintain the general integrity of advertising and in so doing to protect consumers. The evidence would thus seem to indicate that consumers have benefitted substantially from NAD/NARB's self-regulatory efforts. [103]

Summary

This chapter examines the role of environmental influences on promotion management. The concept of *environmental management* is introduced to explain how promotion managers can influence their environments rather than simply reacting to environmental forces.

The chapter concentrates on three major environmental forces, namely, the technological, demographic, and regulatory environments. Technological developments are described as influencing promotion and marketing communications both

[102]LaBarbera, "Analyzing and Advancing Advertising Self-Regulation."

[103]Armstrong and Ozanne, "NAD/NARB Purpose and Performance," p. 25.

indirectly and directly. Primary discussion focuses on the direct effects that various technological advances have had on personal selling, advertising, direct marketing, and other marketing communications tools.

Six major demographic developments are reviewed: (1) population growth and regional geographic developments, (2) the changing age structure, (3) household composition developments, (4) the changing roles of women, (5) income dynamics, and (6) minority population developments. The presentation covers a variety of relevant topics for promotion managers, such as the "Nine Nations of North America" geocultural delineation, the "baby-boom" generation, and the growth of the "singles market."

The regulatory environment is described with respect to both government regulation and industry self-regulation. The Federal Trade Commission's role is explained in terms of its regulation of deception, unfair practices, and information regulation. Specific topics covered are the advertising substantiation program, trade regulation rules, and the corrective advertising program. Self-regulation by the Council of Better Business Bureaus' National Advertising Division (NAD) and National Advertising Review Board (NARB) are discussed, with emphasis placed on the process by which the NAD/NARB regulates national advertising.

Discussion Questions

1. Explain the meaning of *environmental management.*
2. Identify which of the nine nations of North America is yours, and then analyze how accurate the capsule summaries in Figures 9.5 and 9.6 are in characterizing "your nation's" people.
3. Explain why consumer goods marketers are so interested in the baby-boom generation.
4. Demographers tell us that households in the United States are growing in number, shrinking in size, and changing in character. What implications do these changes hold for marketing communicators?
5. One theoretical benefit of business regulation is an improvement in product quality. The text cited lower tar and nicotine cigarettes as one illustration of this. Identify two additional instances in which regulation improved product quality.
6. What is the distinction between a deceptive and an unfair business practice?
7. In your opinion, should a firm be required to have substantiating evidence (i.e., test results or other data) for an advertising claim prior to making the claim? Why or why not?
8. In theory, corrective advertising represents a potentially valuable device for regulating deceptive advertising. In practice, however, corrective advertising must perform a very delicate balancing act by being "strong enough without being too strong." Explain the nature of this strong-enough-without-being-too-strong dilemma.
9. What is the distinction between the self-regulatory roles of the NAD and NARB?

Exercises

1. Interview four or five people who originated from different parts of the United States and ask them to comment on the accuracy of their "nation's" description as it is summarized in Figure 9.5.

2. Identify three or four technological advances, other than the ones presented in the chapter, that have influenced marketing communications. Provide specific illustrations.

3. Identify three or four examples of advertising campaigns that appear to be directed at nontraditional households.

4. Identify two or three examples of deceptive or unfair marketing communication practices that you have experienced in the past year or so. Explain precisely why each practice is, in your opinion, deceptive or unfair.

5. Locate two recent issues of *Advertising Age* that carry reports of the NAD/NARB's monthly activities. (*Note:* These reports are typically published in *Advertising Age* around the middle of each month.) Compare each reported case in terms of the process presented in Figure 9.9.

CHAPTER 10

Sales Management

Sales management is the process of planning, organizing, staffing, directing, and controlling an organization's selling function within the context of environmental limitations and corporate and marketing constraints. The purpose of sales management is to acquire, direct, and stimulate competent salespeople to perform tasks that move the company or organization toward its objectives and mission. Therefore, sales management provides a significant link between an organization's corporate and marketing strategies and the salespeople who actuate the marketing transaction. The sales manager must be

> *the tactician who translates plans into action. He or she implements the various programs for market analysis, direction of sales effort, training, performance appraisal and compensation . . . [and] also has a longer-term responsibility for planning market development and account coverage in his/her area. He or she provides management with information on the organization's effectiveness and conditions in the marketplace as inputs to management's analysis, planning and control activities.*[1]

An overview of the sales management functions is shown in the model in Figure 10.1. Sales management activities do not operate within a vacuum. Therefore, sales

---

[1]John P. Steinbrink, "Field Sales Management," in Steuart Henderson Britt and Norman F. Guess (eds.), *Marketing Manager's Handbook* (Chicago: Dartnell Corporation, 1983), p. 984.

FIGURE 10.1 The Sales Management Process

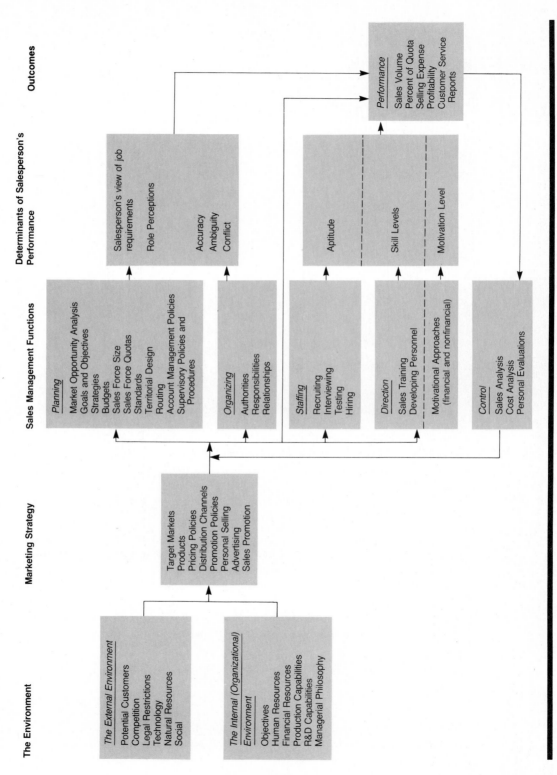

Source: Adapted from Gilbert A. Churchill, Jr., Neil M. Ford, and Orville C. Walker, Jr., *Sales Force Management* (Homewood, IL: Richard D. Irwin, 1981).

managers must take into account the external and internal environments of the organization. Additionally, they must consider their roles within the overall strategic plan of the firm.

The **external environment,** which affects sales management and sales performance, includes the behavior of potential customers, the competition, the legal restrictions, the speed of change in technology, the abundance or lack of natural resources, and the social/cultural changes, among others. The **internal (organizational) environment** also affects the operation of the sales management functions. In particular, sales managers are subject to the organization's objectives, the human and financial resources of the organization, its production capabilities and delivery schedules, its research and development capabilities, and its managerial philosophy. These environmental conditions pose both opportunities and constraints on sales management teams and their sales forces.

Another set of constraints within which sales management must work is the marketing strategy that upper-level management imposes on them. Marketing managers determine the company's target markets, which the sales people must approach. Marketing management also decides on product design, packaging, brand names, and pricing policies that sales management and sales people must work with. Furthermore, marketing management creates policies on advertising, sales promotion, distribution methods, and other promotions. Therefore, sales management objectives and strategies hinge on the competence of upper-level management. That is, they determine the parameters within which sales management and the sales force can operate. Thus, sales management must create and provide guidelines and operative directives to the sales force that fall within the overall plan of the organization and which optimize profitable sales within the constraints and opportunities available.

The next section details the sales management functions. Bear in mind, of course, that these functions must be in the context of and coordinated with the overall mission and plans of the organization.

Sales Management Functions

There are five basic management functions that sales managers must perform to be effective at their job. They are (1) *planning,* (2) *organizing,* (3) *staffing,* (4) *direction,* and (5) *control.* (Refer again to Figure 10.1.) Each of these functions is discussed in the following sections.

Planning the Sales Function

Planning is the process of establishing a broad set of policies, procedures, and goals to achieve organizational objectives. Planning occurs at all levels of the organization, and sales management is no exception. At the sales management level, the sales manager and his or her staff must perform several activities: (1) analyzing market opportunities, (2) setting sales goals and objectives, (3) developing sales strategies, (4) creating sales budgets, (5) establishing sales force size, (6) setting sales force quotas, (7) designing sales territories, (8) providing sales force routing direction, (9) creating account management policies, (10) and designing supervisory policies and procedures. Each of these planning activities is briefly discussed.

Analyzing Market Opportunities   A key element in the development of marketing and sales planning is management's analysis of marketing opportunities. This analysis encompasses both potential threats and emerging opportunities to the company, its territories, and its sales force. *Forecasting* is a major component and technique that management uses in developing plans, goals, and objectives in the sales management process. Forecasting is used at all levels of the organization, from the salesperson in the field to the top levels of management. At the intermediary level of sales management, the manager must consider the forecasts, goals, and objectives of top-level management and the forecasts, goals, and objectives of the field sales force. That is, he or she must look from the top down and the bottom up.

This analysis depends upon management's assessment of the following:

1. *Market potential.* The *expected* sales within a market or set of markets for a given product, product group, or service over a stated time period.
2. *Sales potential.* The company's *expected* share of the market potential.
3. *Sales forecast.* An *estimate* of either (or both) the company's monetary or unit sales for a product item, product line, or product mix over a specified period of time.
4. *Sales quota.* An objective measure of performance in terms of monetary or unit sales that management expects from a marketing unit.[2]

Setting Goals and Objectives   Goals are broad statements of what higher-level marketing management wants to achieve over some specific time period. Goals provide sales management, their staffs, and salespeople with *guidelines* of what the organization is trying to do. That is, they give the sales force fundamental statements about the company's *philosophies, direction, coordination,* and *control.*[3]

Objectives are derived from the goals of the company and the sales management team. In particular, objectives should be stated in specific and measurable terms. That is, they should be expressed in terms of a *specific level of activity* and a *specified time frame.* For example, a sales management objective might be "to achieve $1 million in sales (level of activity) by June 30, 198X (time frame)."

Developing Sales Strategies   After the company has analyzed its market opportunities, stated its goals, and set its objectives, it is ready to begin developing sales strategies. In devising sales strategies, the sales manager must define the prob-

[2]Gilbert A. Churchill, Jr., Neil M. Ford, and Orville C. Walker, Jr., *Sales Force Management* (Homewood, IL: Richard D. Irwin, 1981), p. 111.

[3]Danny Bellenger and Thomas N. Ingram, *Professional Selling* (New York: Macmillan Publishing Co., 1984), pp. 294–295.

lem(s) of the sales force, understand his or her customer buying process (refer to Chapter 3), analyze his or her resources, evaluate alternative approaches to reaching the stated objectives, and select the best alternative. Furthermore, the strategic sales plan should provide the specific tasks the sales force should perform and the methods for control and evaluation. The tasks within the sales force strategy include developing sales budgets, determining sales force size, assigning sales force quotas, designing territories and routes, establishing account management policies, formulating supervisory policies, and setting standards.

Developing Sales Budgets   "The sales force budget is the amount of money available or assigned for a definite period of time, usually a year. It is based on estimates of expenditures during that period of time . . . [and] depends on the sales forecast and the amount of revenue expected to be generated for the organization during that period."[4] The sales manager must then determine an allocation of these funds to lower-level management and the sales personnel. The purpose of the budget is to provide the sales manager with information regarding his or her planning, staffing, direction, and control activities. The sales manager must then decide how to allocate his or her limited financial resources to the sales force and capital necessary to achieve the company's goals and objectives. These decisions provide some of the criteria for the purposes of *control and evaluation* of sales personnel.

The budget periods are typically created on one of three bases—yearly, semiannually, and quarterly. Some companies prepare budgets for all three periods. The shorter the budgeting period, the more control management has over its operations because management's predictions are likely to be more accurate in the short run.

As mentioned earlier, the first step in developing a budget is to analyze market opportunity based upon several forecasts of market potential, sales potential, and sales forecasts. Then management must estimate the amount of money required to accomplish the tasks to achieve its forecasted sales. Two basic procedures for apportioning funds are (1) the *line-item budget* and (2) the *program budget* method. In **line-item budgeting,** management allocates funds in meticulous detail to each identifiable cost center. For example, the sales department may budget funds for such areas as office supplies, wages, research, travel, etc.[5] With this approach management would have to forecast and account for each item in great detail.

The second method, **program budgeting,** avoids many of the problems of line-item budgeting. With this approach, management provides each administrative unit with a lump sum of money that each administrative head can use as he or she sees fit to accomplish the stated objectives. This method provides considerable flexibility by allowing each administrative head to shift funds as he or she deems neces-

---

[4]Charles M. Futrell, *Fundamentals of Selling* (Homewood, IL: Richard D. Irwin, 1984), p. 465.

[5]William J. Stanton and Richard H. Buskirk, *Management of the Sales Force* (Homewood, IL: Richard D. Irwin, 1983), p. 431.

sary. For example, funds for travel and/or entertainment can be shifted to recruitment in the event that one or more salespersons change jobs, retire early, or die.

Designing Sales Territories   Designing sales territories requires both science and intuition. Mathematical formulae have been developed that use linear programming, dynamic programming, and various heuristic models to develop the ideal, or optimal, sales territory and routing schedule. However, these mathematical models fail to take into account behavioral and motivational aspects of territory design and routing solutions. Where a person decides to live and the life-style he or she chooses can make a difference in productivity. Therefore, the quantitative approach to this problem should be tempered with managerial intuition and experience.

> *A sales territory is a group of present and potential customers that are assigned to a salesperson, branch, dealer, or distributor for a given period of time. Territories are often specified by their geographic boundaries; however, geographic boundaries do not determine territories. Rather, the key word in the preceding definition is* customers. *"Good" sales territories are made up of customers who have money to spend and the willingness to spend it. . . . The design of sales territories affects sales force morale, the firm's ability to serve the market, and the firm's ability to control the selling effort financially.*[6]

The ideal situation is to create sales territories of equal potential and equal work load. In this way, the sales manager can more easily evaluate and control each sales person's performance. The concept of equal sales territories also implies equal work loads among the sales representatives, which therefore leads to greater sales force motivation and morale. This ideal situation is rare, if not impossible, to achieve; however, the sales manager should attempt to design an equitable situation.

The design of sales territories involves the following six steps: (1) select the basic control unit, (2) estimate the market potential in each control unit, (3) combine control units into tentative territories, (4) perform work load analysis, (5) adjust tentative territories to allow for differences in potential sales and work load across territories, and (6) assign salespeople to territories (see Figure 10.2).

Select the Basic Control Unit   Depending on the size of the company, the products the company sells, and the nature of the business, sales managers typically break down territories by states, trading areas, counties, cities, standard metropolitan statistical areas (SMSAs), and zip code areas.[7] That is, they use elemental geographic areas.

---

[6]Churchill, Ford, and Walker, *Sales Force Management,* p. 155.

[7]Ibid., pp. 168–173.

FIGURE 10.2 **Stages in Territory Design**

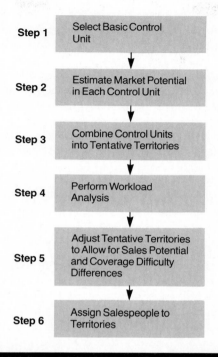

Step 1 Select Basic Control Unit

Step 2 Estimate Market Potential in Each Control Unit

Step 3 Combine Control Units into Tentative Territories

Step 4 Perform Workload Analysis

Step 5 Adjust Tentative Territories to Allow for Sales Potential and Coverage Difficulty Differences

Step 6 Assign Salespeople to Territories

Source: Gilbert A. Churchill, Jr., Neil M. Ford, and Orville C. Walker, Jr., *Sales Force Management*, (Homewood, IL: Richard D. Irwin, 1981), p. 168. Copyright 1981 by Richard D. Irwin, Inc.

Estimate Market Potential The second step is to estimate the market potential of each basic control unit. The sales manager should use data from sales forecasts described earlier in this chapter to make these delineations. Previous sales records, emerging sales opportunities, and competitive concentration help the sales manager in making these estimates.

Form Tentative Territories In step three, the sales manager combines "contiguous basic control units into larger geographic units."[8] Salespeople, therefore, do not have to cross each other's paths in reaching their customers. Again, the sales manager is attempting to develop sales territories of equal potential.

[8]Ibid., p. 175.

Perform Work Load Analysis In step four, the sales manager must consider the amount of work that is necessary to attain the market's potential. Although two salespeople may have equal sales potential in their respective territories, they could have unequal work loads to reach those potentials. For example, one salesperson may have to travel longer distances, endure more severe weather conditions, and have many small accounts to call on.

Adjust Tentative Territories In step five, the sales manager attempts to equalize sales potentials and work loads across all territories. In this stage the sales manager often must rely upon a combination of quantitative tools, subjectivity, and trial and error.

Assign Salespeople to Territories Finally, the sales manager must designate which salespeople are to be assigned to the various sales territories. If we assume that all territories have the same work load and have the same sales potential, and we further assume that all salespeople have the same selling skills, product knowledge, etc., then the territorial assignment task would be simple. However, all salespeople are not the same; the sales manager must devise a method that is fair to all and which optimizes the firm's profits.

> *One way of allowing for differences in general ability among salespeople is by converting each representative's ability to index form. The best salesperson might be rated 1.0, for example, and all other salespeople rated relative to them. One such relative scheme is to consider that a salesperson with a rating of 0.8 could secure 80 percent of the business in the territory that a representative with a rating of 1.0 could obtain. One can then systematically vary the assignments of salespeople to territories to determine which assignment maximizes the company's return.*[9]

Establishing Routes and Schedules Routing, scheduling, and managing time are interrelated activities. Sales representatives spend a lot of time on the road. Thus, the sales manager should determine how to minimize travel time and maximize call value. The most common routing patterns are the following:

1. *Straight line.* In this scheme the sales representative calls on customers from one end of the territory to the other, and perhaps makes calls along the way back to the home base, or follows a different straight line, making calls on the way to the home office.
2. *Circular patterns.* As the name implies, the sales representative leaves the home office in a circular pattern, covering the outer and inner parts of the territory, but always with the home office as the central point of the various adjacent circles.

[9]Ibid., p. 179.

3. *Cloverleaf pattern.* This pattern is a series of circles from the home office, which resemble a cloverleaf. These adjacent circles eventually cover the entire territory.

4. *Hopscotch.* In the hopscotch pattern, the sales representative starts at the point farthest from home base and makes his or her calls on the way back to the office.[10]

Sales call scheduling certainly depends on routing, but also must consider the necessary call frequency and time management for each of the sales representative's customers and potential customers. Among the criteria the sales manager must consider in determining schedules for his or her sales representatives are the following:

1. Estimated sales from an existing account
2. Potential sales from prospective customers
3. Customer service time required
4. Time needed for nonselling functions, such as display arrangements, customer participation in advertising, etc.
5. Required time to demonstrate new and related products
6. Time necessary to entertain current and prospective customers[11]

The adage that "time is money" is as true today as when it was coined years ago. Routing, scheduling, and time management are among the most important concerns for both the salesperson and the company.

Setting Sales Force Quotas   **Sales quotas** are specific performance goals that management sets for sales representatives, territories, organizational branches, middlemen, and/or other marketing units. Quotas perform several functions: (1) They indicate strengths and weaknesses in the selling structure by highlighting variances from management-established forecasts, (2) they provide the sales force with goals and incentives by establishing expectation levels, (3) they control sales representatives' activities by encouraging them to direct their efforts toward other endeavors, such as new customers, more customer service, etc., through various incentives, (4) they give management yardsticks by which to evaluate salespeople in their performances on the job, and thus provide a basis for job promotion and/ or salary raises, (5) they induce greater incentives to salespeople on straight salary, who receive additional money for meeting or exceeding quota, (6) they control selling expenses by tying such expenses to the sales generated by the sales representative (e.g., 6 percent of sales), and (7) they provide evaluation criteria for sales contest results.[12]

[10]Dan H. Robertson and Danny N. Bellenger, *Sales Management* (New York: Macmillan Publishing Co., 1980), pp. 307–308.

[11]Ibid., p. 308.

[12]Stanton and Buskirk, *Management of the Sales Force,* pp. 474–476.

Types of Quotas   Sales managers most frequently base their quotas on (1) sales volume, (2) gross margin or net profit, (3) expenses, (4) activities, and (5) a combination of the preceding four methods.[13]

The most typical method for developing quotas is by the use of **sales volume quotas.** These quotas can be based on geographical areas, product lines, individual customers, time periods, or a combination of these factors. The smaller the territorial areas and the shorter the time periods (such as monthly or quarterly), the more effective the quotas are. Sales volume objectives are used because they are easy to understand and simple to use. However, sales volume quotas do not measure or control expenses, profits, nonselling activities, etc.

Profit quotas provide sales managers with another means of controlling a sales representative's behavior in the marketplace. Since some sales representatives prefer to sell low-profit, fast-moving items rather than products that contribute greater amounts to company profits, profit quotas become a more attractive alternative for many companies than do sales quotas. Two weaknesses, however, of the profit quota approach are the clerical and administrative expenses involved and the lack of understanding that sales representatives have regarding how the method measures their progress.

Expense quotas relate the sales representative's expenses to his or her sales volume. That is, a salesperson should not spend more than, say, 5 percent in travel, entertainment, food, lodging, etc. of monetary sales volume. This quota system can be regressive because the sales representative is concentrating on reducing expenses instead of producing profitable sales.

Activity quotas are those which emphasize "such tasks as (1) daily calls, (2) new customers called on, (3) orders from new accounts, (4) product demonstrations made, and (5) displays built."[14] Although these types of quotas stimulate a balanced approach to sales representatives' jobs, they generally fail to show whether the activity was actually performed or whether it was done effectively.

Combination quotas are those which intergrate the strengths of the four systems previously discussed and minimize the weaknesses of those same systems. This method is complex and may be confusing for both management and the sales representatives. However, if properly communicated and utilized, a combination quota system can be close to an ideal approach.

In summary, to develop quota levels, the sales manager must examine previous sales, sales potentials, sales forecasts, sales representative's reports, characteristics of the industry and the territories, characteristics of the sales representative's selling skills and product-customer knowledge, and the financial data, sales budget, and profit objectives of the company.

Establishing Account Management Policies   Some accounts provide greater sales and profits than others. Thus, sales management must establish policies or guidelines that they and sales representatives should follow in developing their

---

[13]Ibid., pp. 476–479.
[14]Ibid., p. 478.

schedules and routes. Environmental changes are causing many firms to focus on large accounts instead of small accounts. Larger accounts provide a disproportionately greater share of the company's sales volume. The change from small to large accounts is true for both industrial and consumer products. Many firms are moving toward a dual sales force—those who call on small accounts and those who specialize in large accounts. Dual policies mean that sales managers must adjust their sales strategies (and therefore their sales force) to meet the profit objectives of the firm.

Establishing Supervisory Policies and Procedures   Supervision refers to the working relationship between a subordinate and a superior. In particular, this working relationship includes the training, sales assistance, control, morale, and field intelligence that a superior provides his or her subordinates. Thus, supervision is essentially a communications process in which facts, opinions, information, suggestions, concepts, and attitudes are presented by a sales manager to his or her sales representatives.[15]

The amount of supervision necessary depends on the abilities and knowledge of the sales force. A high-quality sales force would require less supervision than a sales force of lower quality. Additionally, geographic distribution of the sales force, the size of the sales force, the compensation plan used, and the nature of the product (such as a highly technical one versus a simple one) are factors that affect the supervisory policies and procedures sales management devises.

Organizing the Sales Function

In organizing the sales management function, management must define the authority, responsibilities, and relationships within the marketing unit framework. This structure provides all management, staff, and sales personnel with an understanding of what is expected of them, who they report to, and what their obligations are.

Types of Sales Organizations   There are various ways to create sales organizations. Most companies organize or specialize their sales departments in one of four ways: (1) geographical territories, (2) product types, (3) customer classes, or (4) a combination of these.[16]

Specialization by *geographical territories* is probably the most common form of sales management organization. Figure 10.3 provides a typical organizational chart using geographic specialization. Depending on the size of the business, the manager who runs a territory is called a regional, divisional, or district sales manager. In many cases this territorial manager, regardless of the title he or she is given, is

---

[15]Stanton and Buskirk, *Management of the Sales Force,* pp. 334–336.

[16]Ibid., p. 60.

FIGURE 10.3   **Sales Organization by Geographical Territories**

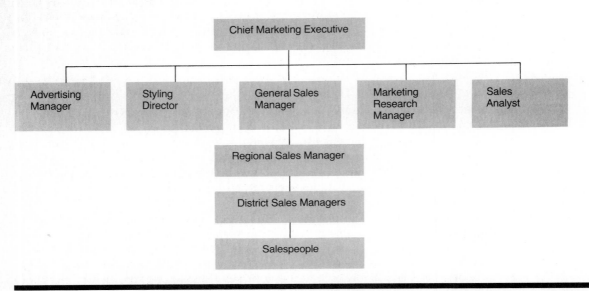

Source: William J. Stanton and Richard H. Buskirk, *Management of the Sales Force*, Sixth Edition (Homewood, IL: Richard D. Irwin, 1983), p. 61. Copyright 1983 by Richard D. Irwin, Inc.

basically running his or her own "business within a business." That is, he or she is like the president of his or her own firm.

Although a company's sales organization can be very effective for one product line, the same type of organizational structure may not be effective for a company that carries highly diverse product offerings. That is, a company that offers a set of unrelated or heterogeneous products should consider organizing or reorganizing by *product types or groups.* Figure 10.4 shows a basic example of a sales organizational structure used in product specialization.

Management's idea is that sales representatives should use their particular *knowledge* for specific products to increase company profits. That is, sales representatives may have a good understanding of, say, the company's electrical equipment but not the chemical operations. This organizational structure works well if the customers that the sales representatives call on do not overlap. For example, if a company sells both electrical and chemical products to the same customer, using different members of the sales force, then there is an inefficiency (because of overlap) in the system.

The last sales organizational structure that will be discussed is one that uses the marketing concept of *consumer orientation.* This structure, which has been growing in popularity among many major firms over the past decade, emphasizes customer groups rather than products. General Foods, General Electric, IBM, Xerox,

FIGURE 10.4   Sales Organization with Product-Operating Specialization

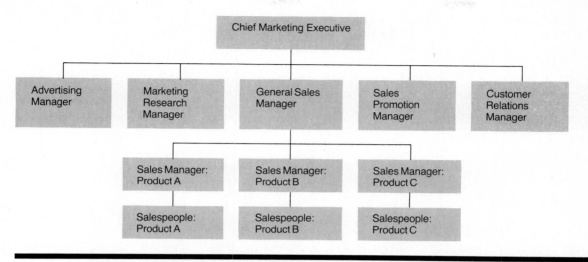

Source: William J. Stanton and Richard H. Buskirk, *Management of the Sales Force*, Sixth Edition (Homewood, IL: Richard D. Irwin, 1983), p. 63. Copyright 1983 by Richard D. Irwin, Inc.

Gulf Oil, and NCR, among many other major corporations, use this form of organizational sales structure.[17] Figure 10.5 illustrates an organization based on customer type.

Companies may find that specialization by customer type is to their advantage when their customer groups' needs are significantly different, when the customer groups are geographically concentrated, and/or when the company uses different channels of distribution and therefore wants to minimize friction among them.[18]

We can understand why an electric car manufacturer, for example, may want to have different sales forces (and in fact, a different marketing plan) selling to the government market (post office, military, etc.), to the industrial market, to the institutional market, and to the ultimate consumer (through dealers). Each market's buying behavior is different and therefore requires a different approach and a different sales organization for the company, which attempts to serve all customer groups effectively.

[17]See Mack Hanan, "Reorganize Your Company Around its Markets," *Harvard Business Review,* Vol. 52, November-December, 1974, pp. 63–74; "NCR's Radical Shift in Marketing Tactics," *Business Week,* December 8, 1973, p. 102; and "Specialist Selling Makes New Converts," *Business Week,* July 28, 1973, p. 44.

[18]Stanton and Buskirk, *Management of the Sales Force,* pp. 67–68.

FIGURE 10.5   **Sales Organization Specialized by Type of Customer**

Source: William J. Stanton and Richard H. Buskirk, *Management of the Sales Force*, Sixth Edition (Homewood, IL: Richard D. Irwin, Inc., 1983), p. 67. Copyright 1983 by Richard D. Irwin, Inc.

Staffing the Sales Function

To have a good football team, a good basketball team, a good baseball team, or any other athletic team, a coach must be able to recruit and select the best players who meet the team's needs. The same is true in staffing a sales force. To staff any organization properly, the manager must understand fundamental principles in the recruiting and selection process. The first step in creating or reorganizing a staff is to do the following:

1. *Perform a job analysis.* This includes determining what activities, duties, responsibilities, customer and product knowledge, selling skills, and personal attributes management believes sales representatives should have in filling the required positions.

2. *Write a job description.* This document is a written statement of management's job analysis. It includes a job title, the specific duties and responsibilities of the sales representative, the authoritative relationships with other immediate members of the organization, and the opportunities for advancement. Good job descriptions include the following:

    a. The general description of the product(s) or service(s) the sales representative must sell.

    b. The types of customers the sales representative must call on. This statement should include the frequency of sales calls on specific types of customers and the specific personnel the sales representative should contact.

c. The specific tasks and responsibilities the sales representative must carry out. These tasks and responsibilities include customer service, clerical work, reports, information collection, and promotional activities.

d. The authoritative relationships between the sales representative and other positions within the company. This statement provides information regarding who the sales representative reports to and who and under what circumstances he or she interacts with other departmental personnel.

e. The mental, physical, and social demands of the job. The sales representative must understand the product knowledge and skills he or she should have, the physically demanding travel involved, and the social obligations (such as cocktail parties) he or she must meet.

f. The environmental factors that affect job performance. These include market trends, competitive activities, the company's reputation among consumers, and resource and supply problems.[19] Table 10.1 provides a typical job description for a field sales representative.

Job descriptions can be developed for a wide array of sales personnel, including (1) *account representatives*—personnel who call mostly on established accounts but do very little new account development; (2) *detail salespeople*—those who perform promotional activities and introduce new products but do not ask for orders; (3) *sales engineers*—people who provide technical support for the product, such as in the computer field; (4) *industrial products salespersons, nontechnical*—people with no high degree of technical knowledge who sell to industrial and commercial accounts; (5) *service salespeople*—those who sell intangibles, such as insurance, business consulting advice, and legal services.[20]

3.   *Develop a statement of job qualifications.* Whereas the job description provides information on the salesperson's activities, responsibilities, assignments, and authorities, the job qualifications document describes the personal features, characteristics, and abilities that management wants so that a person may perform the job effectively and efficiently. These qualifications may include educational level attained, business experience, personality, perceived attitude toward the work ethic, ability to get along with others, dress, smile, and other subjective measures.

Developing a Recruiting System   After management has conducted a job analysis and written specific job descriptions and job specifications, they must devise a recruiting system. The purpose of a recruiting system is to match people who

---

[19]Churchill, Ford, and Walker, *Sales Force Management,* p. 300.

[20]Bellenger and Ingram, *Professional Selling,* p. 300.

TABLE 10.1	**Position Description for Sales Representative**

I. BASIC FUNCTION

The sales representative is charged with building profitable volume, broadening distribution, and maintaining a professional image with assigned accounts.

II. SPECIFIC DUTIES

A. Sells sufficient profitable products to customers to reach assigned objectives.

B. Calls on selected commercial consumers in order to convert them to the use of our products.

C. Organizes and plans territory coverage for the most effective use of time.

D. Gains commitment from assigned accounts for our promotions.

E. Conducts effective organized product knowledge and promotional sales meetings with assigned accounts.

F. Prospects for new business at the distributor and consumer levels.

G. Maintains an awareness of competitive activity and opportunities.

H. Submits concise and accurate reports on time; maintains records and responds to assignments.

I. Transmits marketing and sales intelligence relating to competition and changes in the marketplace.

J. Works within assigned expense budget.

III. RELATIONSHIPS

A. Reports to and is accountable solely to regional/district sales manager.

B. Has a close working relationship with other members of the region and district.

C. Develops effective relationships with decision makers in assigned accounts.

have the specific and desired qualifications (specifications) with management's written job descriptions in order to meet the sales, marketing, and company goals and objectives (see Figure 10.6).

To locate potentially qualified applicants for a sales job, recruiters can use advertising, employment agencies, employee referrals, internal training programs, educational institutions, internal transfers, unsolicited applications, competitors' employees, and those people with whom management deals—from suppliers of products or information (such as an account executive from an advertising agency) to customer salespeople (someone in a wholesale or retailing business, for example). In a study conducted for the Dartnell Corporation, Robert McMurry found that the most effective recruiting methods were direct ads, internal training programs, agencies, and employee referrals, in that order.[21]

[21]Robert N. McMurry, *How to Recruit-Select and Place Salesmen* (Chicago: Dartnell Corporation, 1978).

FIGURE 10.6   **Simple Model of the Recruiting System**

Interviewing, Testing, and Hiring   In the final stage of the staffing function, the manager must determine whether applicants match the company's job specifications and which person will do the best job. Several methods are available to the sales manager for accomplishing this objective, including "patterned interviews, telephone checks, home interviews, biographical summaries, physical records," and various types of intelligence, aptitude, and personality tests.[22]

In the selection process, the sales manager should first review the prospect's application form. Typically, the application form includes (1) *personal information* (name, address, citizenship, etc.), (2) *education* (high schools and colleges attended, degrees attained, grade point averages, etc.), (3) *military service* (length of service, rank attained, branch, duties, etc.), (4) *activities* (hobbies, membership in organizations, honors, awards, offices held, etc.), (5) *employment history* (previous employers, reasons for leaving former employer, sales experience, salary, etc.), (6) *references* (names and addresses of previous employers, educational institutions, etc.) regarding job performance, character, and other pertinent matters, and (7) *general information* about the prospect's desired position, expected starting salary, relatives currently employed by the company, etc.[23]

The *physical examination* is a second important aspect in the selection process. Because selling is strenuous work, on the road as well as at home, most companies schedule physical examinations for prospective employees. The sales manager can eliminate potential problems early in the selection process by determining the prospect's physical condition.

A third important input to the selection process is *the personal interview*. Sales management can use the personal interview to verify and alter the information they reviewed in the prospect's application form. Also, the interviewer has the opportunity to evaluate the prospect face to face. This form of experience means that the recruiter can evaluate the applicant's verbal skills—vocabulary, grammar, and general conversational ability—and also observe the prospect's mannerisms,

[22]Steinbrink, "Field Sales Management," p. 989.

[23]Charles A. Kirkpatrick and Frederick A. Russ, *Effective Selling* (Cincinnati: South-Western Publishing Co., 1981), p. 400.

physical appearance, voice quality, and eye contact to gain insights into the candidate's personal and persuasive skills.

All sales managers and recruiting staff must be informed of the laws and liabilities regarding interviewing and selection standards. A series of federal laws have been passed to monitor the personnel policies and practices of all employers. Title VII (Equal Employment Opportunity) is a federal law passed in 1964 and amended in 1972 that prohibits discrimination in employment on the basis of race, color, religion, sex, or national origin. Based on this law, supervisors, sales managers, and upper management are responsible for EEO compliance because they represent the employer.

References provide a fourth way that sales managers can ascertain the abilities, credibility, and experience of applicants. The sales manager often uses references as a source of information in the evaluations of prospective sales representatives. However, it must be noted that references suggested by the candidate are often highly biased in favor of the prospective employee because they are typically friends and relatives. Quite often, the sales manager and his or her staff will check with the prospect's present and former employers, neighbors, present and former customers, present and former suppliers, bankers, and teachers, among others. The best way to obtain solid references is through face to face contact or by voice to voice contact on the telephone with each referent. More open dialogue occurs in these ways rather than by letter.

Psychological tests, a fifth valuable input to a sales manager's selection decision, are very popular among businesses in attempting to determine the potential successes of prospective employees. The four most common tests are (1) personality tests, (2) sales aptitude tests, (3) interest tests, and (4) intelligence tests. **Personality tests** attempt to measure a person's affability, confidence, poise, aggressiveness, etc. **Sales aptitude tests** are designed to measure a person's verbal ability, tactfulness, persuasiveness, tenacity, memory, and social extroversion-introversion, among many other traits. **Interest tests** are designed to identify a person's vocational and avocational inclinations. **Intelligence tests** attempt to measure three interacting components in a person's general mental ability: (1) *learning ability,* which is the mental ability to acquire information and remember it; (2) *critical ability,* which enables a person to assess the rationality of messages and thereby accept or reject a message on a logical basis; and (3) *ability to draw inferences,* which is the ability to interpret messages and make sound implications based on the facts in a message.

Sales managers should consider these tests as useful inputs to their decisions, but not as final hiring decisions. The sales manager's *judgment* is the final test of which prospective candidates to hire. A good sales manager tempers the results of measurement tools with his or her judgment and intuition.

In recent years the polygraph (lie-detector test) has been administered to prospective employees. In many cases prospects have been ruled out because of failure to pass this examination. Examples of companies that use this test are K-Mart and Zippy Mart. The authors make no judgment regarding either the ethics or the legality of such tests; rather, they try to report what is happening in the hiring market.

Directing the Sales Force

Direction of the sales force requires a multifaceted approach. This function involves sales training of new recruits, continuing education of existing personnel, and motivational and incentive plans for all sales personnel. This section describes briefly the elements of sales force direction.

Sales Training for New Recruits   Sales training for new members of the sales force does not differ significantly from the refresher courses that current sales people should undergo. Thus, this discussion overlaps to some degree the comments that will follow in the section titled "Developing Sales Personnel." The training of both new and current personnel varies from company to company according to "(1) the complexity of the product line and product applications, (2) the nature of the market in terms of buyer sophistication, (3) the pressure of competition and the resulting need for nonsales service, and (4) the level of knowledge and the degree of the sales experience of the trainee."[24]

Objectives of Training   The general objectives of sales training should be to (1) reduce salesperson turnover, (2) improve salesperson morale and attitude, (3) establish expected salesperson behavior (and, therefore, control), (4) improve customer relations, (5) lower selling costs, and (6) show salespeople how to use time efficiently. These broad sales management objectives for a sales training program should then be broken down into specific objectives for the sales representatives. These objectives may include training sales representatives to fill out reports, to demonstrate how management uses reports, to provide salespeople with methods on how to keep records, how to allocate their selling time with and among customers, how to improve prospecting, and how to handle objections.[25]

Personnel for Training   There are three basic sources of trainers: *line personnel* (e.g., district sales manager), *staff trainers* (either ones already within the existing structure of the company or ones hired for the exclusive purpose of training sales personnel), and *outside training specialists* (hired consultants who either provide general training programs or specialize in particular aspects of sales techniques).

Content of Training   The content of the sales training program varies, of course, from company to company depending on the level of sophistication among the firm's sales personnel. Also, the content varies according to whether new sales personnel or veteran sales personnel are the audience. Generally, however, the content focuses on corporate policies, selling techniques, product knowledge, and self-management skills.

---

[24]James F. Engel, Martin R. Warshaw, and Thomas C. Kinnear, *Promotional Strategy* (Homewood, IL: Richard D. Irwin, 1983), pp. 428–429.

[25]Stanton and Buskirk, *Management of the Sales Force*, pp. 186–188.

Location of Training   Some initial training is conducted in the classroom, with additional training done in the field. The classroom setting is usually either in the home or district office.

Timing of Training   Companies vary in their philosophies regarding when training should take place. Some companies feel that extensive training in basic product knowledge, sales techniques, company policies, etc. should be concentrated in the first several weeks after a person is hired. Then, the person is qualified to go out and sell. Other companies prefer to give new hirees a quick, basic course, have the applicants go into the field and gain some practical experience, and then provide them with an intensive period of training. Some companies schedule several one- to two-day training seminars per year, whereas others schedule several intensive one- to two-week training programs per year. Consistency in the schedules of training programs is perhaps the key in timing.

Training Techniques   The training techniques a company uses depend upon the objectives sales managers want to accomplish and the amount of time the trainer has to achieve these objectives. For example, the lecture method would be better than the role-playing technique for conveying company policies and procedures.

The basic training techniques are lectures, discussion, demonstration, role playing, and on-the-job training. *The lecture method* is the most efficient way to present company policies, procedures, and selling concepts and principles. Lectures provide the new salesperson with an initial orientation toward the company and the subject of selling. *The discussion method* provides salespersons with the opportunity to state their ideas and opinions on a variety of subjects in personal selling and company policies. These thoughts are most often expressed through pedagogical devices such as *cases, round table discussions, and panels.* By using the discussion method, the group leader can often draw out experiences from the new sales representatives that are informative and useful to other members who have had or are having similar problems in the field. *Demonstration* is showing rather than telling about how to sell a product. Sales representatives can see how the job is to be done, as opposed to hearing about it. *Role playing* places sales trainees nearer the actual situation by having them sell a product in a hypothetical situation. Given that the situation and the prospect are presented realistically, the trainee learns how to translate lectured concepts and principles into real-life presentations. A technological tool that trainers often use in this teaching method is a videotape machine. Seeing and reviewing one's nonverbal behavior in a selling situation and listening to one's voice and presentation mode can be very enlightening to the sales trainee. Finally, *on-the-job training* presents the final test in the most realistic situations. The sales trainer accompanies the sales trainee in actual selling situations and discusses his or her experiences in either selling or not selling the prospect.

Developing Sales Personnel   This section emphasizes the company's need to train and to educate existing sales personnel continually. Although many of the training techniques described can also be applied to experienced salespeople, experienced sales representatives may have special needs that sales management should address. The long-range success of a sales force depends not only on the training of new recruits but also on the continuing development of the existing sales force. Often, these programs are called refresher because they focus on the existing salespersons's bad habits, provide new company practices and up-to-date information, inform the salespeople of any changes in product, price, distribution, and promotion developments, policies, and strategies. Furthermore, refresher programs identify what changes and problems are occurring in personnel, in competition, and in federal, state, and local regulations. University continuing education programs also provide an avenue for further development of experienced sales personnel. Normally, companies fund employees who seek these additional, outside educational courses.

Motivating the Sales Force   In motivating the sales force, sales management can use both financial and nonfinancial incentives. Because the salesperson's job is often an isolated job (one requiring long hours in a car or plane), financial rewards are usually not enough.

Financial Incentives   Sales management uses three basic compensation plans: *salary plan, commission plan,* and a *combination plan* (salary plus commission). Within the three basic plans, there are many combination possibilities involving base earnings and incentive pay. Seven of the most common methods of paying the sales force are

- Straight salary
- Straight salary + discretionary bonus
- Straight commission
- Commission + bonus
- Salary + commission
- Salary + bonus
- Salary + commission + bonus[26]

Although administratively complex, combination plans are most commonly used by sales manangers because they provide sales representatives with a much broader range of earnings opportunities. Regardless of the plan that management selects, the plan should meet the following three criteria: (1) be competitive within the industry, (2) be equitable within the company, (3) be fair among members of the sales force.[27] Figure 10.7 provides a bar graph of the forms of compensation that companies use.

   Straight salary is often called a base salary. It provides sales representatives with a fixed amount of income regardless of sales productivity. This method of compensation gives management maximum control over the sales force's activities

---

[26]Steinbrink, "Field Sales Management," p. 992.
[27]Ibid.

FIGURE 10.7   **Method of Compensation Plans Used (By Percentage)**

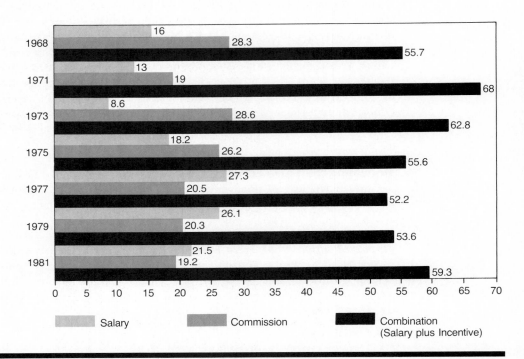

Source: John P. Steinbrink, "Field Sales Management," in Steuart Henderson Britt and Norman F. Guess (eds.), *Marketing Manager's Handbook* (Chicago: Dartnell Press, 1983), p. 993.

because management can dictate the activities salespeople must perform in servicing current customers, creating new merchandise displays, using new routes, making educational and missionary sells, and filling out reports for the home or district office. Thus, this plan is best for companies who have a large amount of work devoted to nonselling activities and routine selling tasks. Such selling jobs are found in the pharmaceutical, beverage, and fast-food industries.

A straight salary provides little incentive for sales representatives to increase sales. However, it is a good plan for new salespeople who are still learning the ropes.

A **straight commission** is payment based directly on performance. There are two basic commission plans: straight commission and draw against commission. Straight commissions can be based on a fixed percentage of a sales representative's dollar sales, product units sold, type of product sold, season sales, dollars of profit, etc., or can be based on a multiple percentage rate that increases as dollar sales volume or some other performance measure increases. Draw accounts are accounts from which the sales representative receives (or draws) a fixed sum of money on a regular time basis. The money in a draw account comes from either earned or unearned commissions. A salesperson, for example, may "draw" $1,000 per pay period but may have earned $800 or $1,200 during the same period. If there were an underage, the salesperson would owe the company money. If there were an overage, the salesperson may take the extra commission, apply it against past underages, or defer the amount to the future.

A **bonus** is usually a lump sum payment the company makes to its sales representatives who have exceeded a set sales quota. However, management may use bases other than sales, such as acquired new accounts, gross margin on sales, reduction in expenses, divisional profits, etc., to set the requirements for a bonus.

Financial incentives can come in many forms. Overall, straight salary provides a maximum of control over the sales representative's routine duties, whereas the straight commission plan provides maximum financial incentive to sell the company's line of products. Most companies use some combination of salary plus commission (and bonus).

Nonfinancial Incentives   Job satisfaction and motivation rest strongly on nonfinancial rewards. *Achievement* or *recognition* awards are commonly presented to sales representatives at sales meetings and award banquets to give sales representatives psychological rewards. Companies also frequently use newsletters, publicity in local media (such as newspapers), published sales results, personal letters of commendation, and other psychological rewards for the sales force. Sales managers can motivate sales force members by giving face-to-face encouragement, telephone calls of commendation, and individual help with responsibilities. Some companies also award honorary job titles to outstanding sales representatives, induct them into honor societies, and present distinguished sales awards, such as plaques or certificates.[28]

Sales managers often conduct annual sales meetings in exotic places to deliver their sales pitch on how exciting the new product lines are. The company may take their sales representatives (and spouses) to Acapulco for sales meetings in the morning and either golf or tennis in the afternoon. During the morning meetings, the sales managers generate enthusiasm for the new lines of products the company is introducing. Generally, the sales representatives remain extremely enthusiastic for weeks and, perhaps, months following the meeting. This form of away-from-home-base sales meeting is often overlooked by management but can be highly motivating.

Overall, sales managers must find ways to meet not only the immediate financial needs of their sales representatives but also (and perhaps more importantly) their security needs, their opportunities for advancement, their personal ego and status needs, their personal power needs, their desires for a meaningful job, their beliefs

---

[28]Steinbrink, "Field Sales Management," p. 992.

in self-determination, and their requirements for pleasant working conditions. These sales management considerations both attract and maintain a sales force.

Determinants of Salesperson's Performance

Salespeople's performance results from (1) their perception of their job (or role perceptions), aptitude, skill levels, and motivation level and (2) the ways management provides functional support (refer to Figure 10.1). This chapter has already described the sales management functions and now will briefly examine the determinants of a salesperson's performance.

Role Perceptions

Salespeople must know what is expected of them and have accurate role perceptions in order to perform their jobs well. Their jobs are defined by people both within and outside the organization, including family, sales managers, company executives, and customers. Thus, how well people perform in sales jobs depends on the accuracy of their perceptions of management's stated goals, demands, policies, procedures, and organizational lines of authority and responsibilities.

Very often salespeople face role conflicts that inhibit their sales performance. For example, a customer may want special advertising concessions that the company has policies against. Salespeople have been trained to meet customers' needs; however, they have also learned to obey company policies, especially where profits are concerned. They are put in the role of customer satisfier but also of company satisfier. What do sales representatives do? If a salesperson can negotiate differences between the two parties he or she may be able to resolve the conflict and make the sale.

Another example of role conflict is a situation in which the sales manager expects a sales representative to travel on weekends, but the salesperson's spouse and children desire to picnic or go to a movie. Once again, what is this person to do?

Aptitude

An individual's ability to perform certain tasks depends greatly on his or her interests, intelligence, and personality. Because different salespeople have different tasks and activities to perform, some people are better suited to one type of sales job than another. Sales managers must recognize these differences and make assignments accordingly.

Skill Levels

"Whereas role perceptions determine how well the salesperson knows what must be done in performing a job and aptitude determines whether the person has the necessary native abilities, skill level refers to the individual's *learned proficiency at performing the necessary tasks."*[29] These skills include *salesmanship skills* (such as how to close a sale), *interpersonal skills* (such as how to cope with and resolve conflict), and *technical skills* (such as knowledge about the product's features, performance, and benefits).[30]

Motivational Level

Motivational level refers to the amount of time and energy a person is willing to expend on performing tasks and activities associated with a job. These tasks may include filling out reports, calling on new accounts, and creating new sales presentations. A good sales manager determines which combination of financial and nonfinancial rewards are best suited to his or her sales force and to the individual members of the entire sales team. That is, certain keys turn some people on, but not others.

Performance Evaluation and Control

Given the overall view of the company's environment, its marketing strategy, and the interaction between sales management functions and salesperson potential, certain outcomes (performances) can be measured to determine the entire system's effectiveness. This management function (control) requires the sales manager to monitor *actual* salesperson and sales force performance against *planned* performance standards. Performance standards include the sales representative's sales volume, percentage of quota met, selling expenses, profit contributions, and customer services rendered. Through sales analysis, cost analysis, and personal evaluations, sales managers can often determine key differences in the performances of good salespeople and poor salespeople. Although a salesperson may have a low ratio of selling expenses to sales volume, he or she may be failing to call on new accounts. Thus, the low ratio may be misleading in terms of overall performance.

When the actual and planned performances of a salesperson are significantly different, the sales manager must seek the underlying reasons and take the appropriate corrective actions. As examples, a union strike in a particular territory may have affected the salesperson's sales, a salesperson may have come down with an extended illness, a salesperson may be experiencing marital difficulties, or a salesperson may have a sales quota that is not attainable. These and other factors should be taken into consideration by the sales manager in evaluating a sales representative's performance and in determining which measures are necessary to control behavior.

[29]Churchill, Ford, and Walker, *Sales Force Management,* p. 237.

[30]Ibid.

Summary

Sales management involves the process of planning, organizing, staffing, directing, and controlling a company's sales force. A good sales manager will determine sales opportunities, analyze his or her resources, set goals and objectives, develop good recruiting and selection procedures, set up clear lines of authority and responsibilities, create sales training programs, utilize sound motivational approaches, and thoroughly analyze sales and costs, among many other activities. All of these functions must be performed within the context of both the external and internal environment of the firm. Furthermore, these functions must be coordinated with the firm's other elements of its overall marketing strategy.

Good sales management also includes a clear understanding of the determinants of a salesperson's performance. These determinants include the salesperson's view of his or her job requirements and his or her aptitude, skill levels, and motivation level.

Finally, the sales manager must evaluate the performance of the sales force by examining the outcomes of their efforts. This stage of the sales management process includes an analysis of sales volume, selling expenses, customer service reports and overall profitability. These and other performance evaluations help the sales manager to control and therefore direct (or redirect) the sales force. Needless to say, the sales management process is truly a complex and time-consuming job.

Discussion Questions

1. What is involved in developing a strategic sales management program? How would the strategic plan differ between a company that sells detergents and one that sells heavy industrial equipment?

2. Define the following terms:

   a. environmental variables
   b. market opportunity analysis
   c. role perceptions
   d. motivation level
   e. sales analysis
   f. sales force quotas
   g. customer service reports

3. The field of sales management is just beginning to expand into charitable organizations. How do you account for this delay? What would sales management in a charitable organization involve?

4. What are the shortcomings of evaluating sales representatives' performance solely on unit sales?

5. Discuss the relationship between sales territory design and sales force morale.

6. Describe the relationship between the measurement and control of sales management activities and geographically defined areas.

7. How do sales managers design sales territories? How often should sales territories be changed? For what reasons?

8. What is the relationship between a sales quota and a compensation plan?

9. What is the relationship between aptitude and skill level?

10. How may sales training objectives vary from firm to firm? Explain.

11. Sometimes salespeople are placed in conflicts that result from customers having expectations that are counter to a sales manager's expectations. How can sales training help to reduce this conflict?

12. What are the possible drawbacks to the use of sales contests in motivating salespeople?

13. Describe the relationship between sales analysis and cost analysis. Which should come first? Explain.

14. Why do many objective measures of performance evaluation focus on effort rather than results?

Exercises

1. Call, write, or personally interview three sales managers, each from a different industry, and describe their methods of managing their sales forces. Compare their approaches to the ideas you learned in this chapter.

2. Interview either a local football coach, basketball coach, tennis coach, baseball coach, band director, etc. to find out the methods they use in their "sales management" efforts. That is, how do they recruit personnel, motivate team members, evaluate performance, etc.? Compare their methods with those of a profit-oriented business sales manager.

CHAPTER 11

Personal Selling

Everyone is in the business of personal selling. Politicians try to sell their constituents on broad-ranging issues; preachers, priests, and rabbis espouse religious beliefs to their followers; athletes express their side of an argument with a referee, umpire, linesman, or other sports official; employees bargain with employers on their points of view; and agents for businesses (salespeople) attempt to exchange products and services with prospective customers for money. All these examples point to the universality and pervasiveness of personal selling in people's daily lives.

This chapter explores several dimensions of personal selling. First, the chapter discusses the importance of personal selling, society's attitudes toward this activity, categories of salespeople, the reasons people should consider selling as an occupation, and the kinds of duties and responsibilities salespeople have. Then the chapter examines several practical and conceptual thoughts and approaches on how salespeople do, and perhaps should, perform their selling tasks effectively. The order in which these various ideas and approaches are discussed does not imply that one is better than another. Instead, the text attempts to present the reader with a broad array of ideas from which to choose (and to integrate) for the purpose of adapting sets of techniques to a specific selling situation.

Personal Selling: An Overview

In business, **personal selling** may be defined as *a form of person-to-person communication in which a seller attempts to persuade prospective buyers to pur-*

chase his or her company's (organanization's) product(s) and/or service(s). The personal selling function in an economy cannot be overstated. In the United States approximately 6 million people (i.e. 1 out of 16 workers) sold $1/2 *trillion* worth of goods and services in 1984! Employers spend thousands of dollars per new employee annually in training, travel, and various other expense accounts. The average cost of training one industrial salesperson, for example, is approximately $20,000.

Unfortunately, even with its economic contributions to societies throughout history and throughout the world, selling has developed a bad reputation. This reputation is primarily due to the fly-by-night, one-time salesperson who promises people the moon and delivers little or nothing. These con men rely on deception, false promises, trickery, and misrepresentation to talk people into buying products and services they do not need or into buying items that do not work. Although this still happens today, it represents an extremely small percentage of the personal selling business.

Overall, selling benefits the U.S. economy in several ways. First, personal selling influences *product innovation* through continual salesperson feedback to company management concerning customer questions, needs, and problems. Second, it promotes a *higher standard of living* by changing and improving dissatisfied consumers' consumption patterns. And third, personal selling enhances *business activity and economic growth* by encouraging consumption of improved products, and therefore mass production, more jobs, and greater capital investment.[1] These societal benefits also translate into job opportunities, the reason many people consider choosing a sales career.

Opportunities in Personal Selling

Although there is a lot of criticism of personal selling, the opportunities are enormous, some of which follow:[2]

1. *A variety of jobs* (e.g., retailing, wholesaling, manufacturing, sales engineering, and servicing).
2. *Chances for advancement* (e.g., moving into a district sales manager's job at Procter & Gamble, Xerox, etc.).
3. *Rewards* in financial and nonfinancial terms (such as salary plus bonus, travel, a feeling of self-worth for a job well done, and the satisfaction that you provided the customer with a product or service that best met his or her needs).
4. *Job freedom* (i.e., little direct supervision, except by one's self). Salespeople may go days and even weeks without seeing their bosses. They can spend

[1]Charles A. Kirkpatrick and Frederick A. Russ, *Effective Selling* (Cincinnati: South-Western Publishing Co., 1981), pp. 4–7.

[2]Charles M. Futrell, *Fundamentals of Selling* (Homewood, IL: Richard D. Irwin, 1984), pp. 7–13.

twenty hours per week or seventy hours per week, as they see fit. In the eyes of their bosses, it is performance that counts.

5. *Job challenge.* Managing one's own time presents a challenge that professional salespeople enjoy. It is similar to operating your own business and means that you can invest as much of yourself into it as you want to and generate as much income as you are willing to.

Personal selling provides ample opportunities. In what has been a traditionally male-dominated field, professional selling has rapidly undergone changes. Today, women constitute approximately one-third of the nation's professional sales force. About 600,000 women sell real estate, 400,000 are manufacturers' representatives, and 200,000 sell stocks and bonds. Additionally, approximately 26 percent of insurance salespeople are women, and 48 percent sell advertising. These figures are up from 14 percent and 28 percent, respectively, since 1975. The typical saleswoman is between 25 and 29, is single, and makes between $25,000 and $30,000 per year, with an average of three years of selling experience.[3]

Salesperson Categories

There are several ways to categorize salespeople. None is perfect; however, one of the more comprehensive schemes is the following:[4]

1. *Route Salespeople.* Route salespeople deliver such items as bread, heating oil, newspapers, etc. Although not in the business of persuasive selling, these people are technically involved in selling because their job is related to a sale to the final consumer.
2. *Retail Salespeople.* Retail salespeople are mainly in retail outlets and are primarily order takers. They ring up sales as would a person at a fast-food restaurant (e.g., McDonalds). Of course, retail sales positions for some product categories (e.g., major appliances, furniture, and automobiles) require sales skills beyond mere order taking. Salespeople for these products are often as skillful as people who occupy more glamorous selling positions (such as industrial sales representatives, sales engineers, and creative salespeople).
3. *Detail People.* Detail people normally do not ask for orders but instead promote a product with the idea that the consumer will order from one of the company's vendors. For example, a representative from a cosmetics firm may demonstrate to customers in a department store how to properly apply

[3]Carol Kleiman, "Carving Out a Niche: Women Finding Rewards, Success and Sexual Equality in Sales," *Chicago Tribune* (reprinted in *The State,* Columbia, S.C., May 15, 1983, pp. 1-G, 6-G).

[4]Adapted from William P. Dommermuth, *Promotion: Analysis, Creativity, and Strategy* (Boston: Kent Publishing Company, 1984), pp. 309–310.

makeup. The customer would then be enticed to purchase the company's brand from one of the retailers carrying their merchandise.

4.   *Account Representatives.* Account representatives usually call on retailers and wholesalers who currently do business with them. Their function is to ensure that their customers are being properly serviced and that they receive reseller support.

5.   *Industrial Sales Representatives.* Industrial salespeople normally provide products that are already used by their clients, such as raw materials, supplies, etc. Although they may not have a high level of technical training in the products and services they sell, they tend to possess very good negotiating skills.

6.   *Sales Engineers.* Sales engineers are highly trained in the technical aspects of the products they sell. Their customers are mainly preexisting industrial accounts. With their expertise, they are able to help customers solve their problems with current products their companies offer or with specially designed products. Thus, most of these salespeople are in the high tech and heavy industry fields.

7.   *Creative Salespeople.* Since some customers require highly specialized and innovative products and services, a group of salespeople has emerged that supplies creative products and services to companies. Advertisers, for example, employ creative individuals to sell their company's ideas. Consulting, executive development programs, sales programs, and insurance also fall into this category.

Duties and Responsibilities of Salespeople

Although a salesperson's job is to create a sale, his or her duties and responsibilities far extend that notion. Simply getting an order is myopic. The salesperson must have long-range views for himself or herself, the company, and the customer. To be successful in selling, a person must be willing to perform the following duties and accept the following responsibilities:[5]

1.   The salesperson should provide *service to the buyer* after the sale. Neither salespeople nor companies make money from a single sale. They make it through *repeat sales.* Thus, it is important to continue to make the sale after the sale.

2.   The salesperson should provide *service to the company.* Within the context of the marketing concept, a salesperson is responsible not only for satisfying

[5]Carlton A. Pederson, Milburn D. Wright, and Barton A. Weitz, *Selling: Principles and Methods* (Homewood, IL: Richard D. Irwin, 1984), pp. 35–38.

the needs of customers but also for satisfying the needs of the company. Business transactions must be made to ensure the survival of the company. Consumer needs and company profits cannot exist without each other. A balance must exist between the two. Therefore, salespeople must try to meet consumer needs but at a reasonable profit.

3.   The salesperson should *prospect for new customers, increase sales to existing customers, make sales presentations, demonstrate products and services, quote prices and terms, and write orders.*

4.   The salesperson should try to *maintain and improve the company's good name* by advising and counseling the customer in merchandising and marketing problems, handling customer complaints, and attending periodic sales meetings to learn about new products, policies, and sales activities.

5.   The salesperson should carefully perform *nonselling and reporting activities.* These activities and reports include calls made, expenses, sales made, travel distance, orders lost, routes scheduled, services provided, and competitive and business conditions. Additionally, these nonselling and reporting activities include *collecting* money from clients who have purchased merchandise, *giving assistance to the credit department* on customer business for purposes of credit ratings, *organizing* time for optimal route scheduling, *working enthusiastically with management, traveling* throughout one's sales territory (counties, states, regions, or the entire country), and *studying* new information about the company, its products, and customer needs and problems.

The following sections examine several approaches to the profession of personal selling: traditional ideas on personal selling, a dyadic interaction approach to selling, a relational communications approach, a neurolinguistic approach, and a contingency approach. Though they overlap somewhat, each merits separate consideration.

Traditional Approaches to Personal Selling

As mentioned at the beginning of this chapter, personal selling has existed in many forms since the beginning of time. Over this vast period of time, people's experiences have dictated the best ways (rules of thumb) to sell. These people did not do scientific research to determine the best way to sell; they sold on instinct and trial and error. Dale Carnegie was such a person. He not only told people how to sell themselves and their products, he also sold millions of copies of books, which are still widely read today. Figure 11.1 summarizes some of the selling principles he advocated.

Upon close examination, we can see that Carnegie's thinking was consistent with the marketing concept and many of the psychological principles in personal selling that have been researched since he wrote his book. One of the steps in scientific

FIGURE 11.1 **Conventional Ideas on Personal Selling**

1. Become genuinely interested in other people.

2. Smile.

3. Remember that a person's name to him is the sweetest and most important sound in any language.

4. Be a good listener. Encourage others to talk about themselves.

5. Talk in terms of the other person's interest.

6. Make the person feel important—and do it sincerely.

7. The only way to get the best of an argument is to avoid it.

8. Show respect for the other person's opinion. Never tell someone he or she is wrong.

9. If you are wrong, admit it quickly and emphatically.

10. Begin in a friendly way.

11. Get the other person saying "yes, yes" immediately.

12. Let the other person do a great deal of the talking.

13. Let the other person feel that the idea is his or hers.

14. Try honestly to see things from the other person's point of view.

15. Be sympathetic with the other person's ideas and desires.

16. Appeal to the nobler motives.

17. Dramatize your ideas.

18. Throw down a challenge.

19. Begin with praise and honest appreciation.

20. Call attention to people's mistakes indirectly.

21. Talk about your own mistakes before criticizing the other person.

22. Ask questions instead of giving direct orders.

23. Let the other person save face.

24. Make the other person happy about doing the thing you suggest.

Source: Dale Carnegie, *How to Win Friends and Influence People* (New York: Pocket Books, 1964), pp. 110, 185, 217.

investigation is observation and, in terms of human behavior, he displayed a keen sense of what was around him.

Out of human experience and the need to understand how selling works, some people began to try to explain and systematize the personal selling process. What are the steps in making a sale? What are the characteristics of the successful salesperson? These questions led to written descriptions of, research on, and approaches to personal selling.

The Basic Steps in Personal Selling

Numerous practitioners and scholars have, over the years, presented their views on the sequential steps that salespeople take in attempting to make a sale.[6] Dubinsky's review of the literature and his own insights led to the conclusion that there are seven basic steps:[7]

1. Locating and prospecting for customers
2. The preapproach
3. The approach
4. The sales presentation
5. Handling objections/sales resistance
6. The close
7. The postsale follow-up

The first step, **locating and prospecting for customers,** involves "searching for and identifying potential buyers who have the need, willingness, ability, and authority to buy."[8] That is, the salesperson looks for names, addresses, telephone numbers, and other general facts about prospective customers. This involves using internal sources of information (e.g., company records, membership lists, and other written documents) and external sources of information based on referrals from existing customers, sales leads from organizations, friends, noncompeting salespeople, and so on.

The second step, **the preapproach,** requires the salesperson to arrange a meeting with the prospective customer and to acquire, prior to the meeting, more specific information about him or her and his or her business. The initial sales meeting is arranged in a variety of ways: by asking mutual friends to set up the meeting, by sending personal letters to prospects, or by having a present customer send a letter that introduces the salesperson and requests a sales interview.

Acquiring meaningful information about prospective customers and their business is an essential aspect of the preapproach. For example, the salesperson may learn that the prospective customer is a golfer, a tennis player, or a bridge player. Also, he or she may learn that the prospect's business is expanding rapidly and therefore could need the salesperson's product to accommodate the growing business. Salespeople use a variety of sources for obtaining information about prospective customers, including acquiring information about particular prospects from

---

[6]See, for example, Robert F. Spohn and I. Herbert Wilson, *Selling Dynamics* (New York: McGraw-Hill Book Company, 1984); and Danny Bellenger and Thomas N. Ingram, *Professional Selling* (New York: Macmillan Publishing Company, 1984).

[7]Alan J. Dubinsky, "A Factor Analytic Study of the Personal Selling Process," *The Journal of Personal Selling & Sales Management,* Vol. 1, Issue 1, pp. 26–33. The following discussion borrows freely from Dubinsky's excellent review and analysis of the steps in the selling process.

[8]Ibid, pp. 26–27.

current customers, obtaining useful information from local newspapers, observing the prospect's business facilities while waiting to meet with the prospect, etc.

The third step, **the approach,** is the beginning of the sales presentation. The first few moments and initial impressions are critical to making the sale. The sale is unlikely to occur if the salesperson has failed to do homework in the preapproach stage. It is imperative that the salesperson gain and hold the prospect's attention and interest. Salespeople use a variety of different approach techniques, often in combination with one another. A few of the more widely used approaches are (1) using a present customer's name as a reference to the prospect, (2) giving the prospect a token gift, (3) offering a benefit that has appeal to the prospect's curiosity, (4) opening the sales interview with a question to get the prospect's attention and interest, and (5) handing the product to the prospect for him or her to inspect.

The **sales presentation,** step four, is the basic part of the selling activity. The salesperson presents the product, explains what it will do for the prospective customer, demonstrates its strengths, and so forth. Efforts are made to arouse the prospect's interest and desire for the product. The salesperson can accomplish these objectives by adhering to some long-established rules for making effective sales presentations. Using product demonstrations, showing empathy with the prospect's special needs, employing language that the prospect can understand (rather than using technical language), and using dramatic efforts to emphasize a point are just some of the essentials of effective sales presentations.

In many, if not most, selling situations, prospects feel they have reasons not to buy the product or service offered by the salesperson. The salesperson must be prepared to **handle objections and sales resistance,** step five of the selling process. At this point the salesperson must reiterate how the product meets the customer's needs and problems, what benefits the product offers, and how the prospect can most easily make the decision (credit terms, for example). Also, the salesperson should make statements that help the customer reduce any perceived risk in making the buying decision.

Different methods are used to handle objections and reduce resistance. For example, the salesperson may stall the objection by telling the prospect that the question will be handled later in the presentation. The salesperson may also dispute the objection and provide solid reasons for the disputation. On the other hand, the salesperson may concede to parts of the objection and then dispute other parts of the objection in an inoffensive fashion. Also, salespeople sometimes use humor to relieve the pressure associated with an objectionable part of a sales presentation or simply dismiss the objection with a smile or other nonverbal gesture.

In step six, **the close,** the salesperson attempts to gain a commitment from the customer to purchase the product or service. In other words, the salesperson asks for the order. To close a sale, salespeople use different techniques to make it easier for the prospect to commit himself or herself to a purchase. For example, the salesperson may (1) tell the prospect about a previous customer whose needs were similar to the prospect's and who benefitted from the salesperson's product, (2) present the prospect with two or more product versions and ask which he or she prefers, (3) assume the prospect is ready to buy and focus on purchase details such as the delivery date and credit terms, (4) ask for the order in a straightforward fashion, or (5) offer some incentive to get the prospect to buy now.

Finally, in step seven, **postsales follow-up,** the salesperson attempts to reduce the consumer's postpurchase doubt (especially for products requiring a high level of effort, time, or money), suggest additional products and accessories, determine problems the customer may be having with the product, and develop a firmer relationship with the customer with the view of creating future sales.

Effective follow-up is critical for establishing long-term relationships with customers. Successful salespeople do not discontinue contact once they have made a sale. They assure that the product truly fits the customer's needs, that it is being used properly, that customer complaints are remedied expeditiously, and so on. Follow-up includes (1) sending letters of appreciation to customers, (2) training the customer's employees in the proper use of the product, (3) addressing the customer's complaints or product-related problems, and (4) making adjustments if the product does not meet the customer's expectations.

Characteristics of the Super Salesperson

The traditional view of what makes a very successful, or "super," salesperson has been described and studied for many years. Some of the colloquialisms have been, "He has a gift for gab," "She has charisma," etc. Research and practitioner intuitions on the mystique of the super salesperson are summarized in this section.

Through his business experience and research, Robert McMurry has described eight characteristics that he believes super salespeople possess.[9] These characteristics, along with some corroborating evidence from other researchers, are discussed briefly.

According to McMurry, a super salesperson

1. *Has a compulsive need to win.* The super salesperson is extremely competitive and views the sale as a conquest over his or her customer.
2. *Needs to hold the affection of others.* The super salesperson feels unloved, unwanted, and insecure and therefore must "buy" the attention and affection of others. He or she "seeks and enjoys recognition from others for selling accomplishments."[10]
3. *Has great empathy toward others.* The super salesperson is very sensitive to how other people feel and can put himself or herself "into their shoes." Because of this empathy, he or she can react quickly and accurately to sudden and minor changes in what customers say and do. If a salesperson has the

[9]Robert N. McMurry, "The Mystique of Super Salesmanship," *Harvard Business Review,* Vol. 39, March-April 1961, pp. 113–122.

[10]Lawrence W. Lamont and William J. Lundstrom, "Identifying Successful Industrial Salesmen by Personality and Personal Characteristics," *Journal of Marketing Research,* Vol. 14, November 1977, p. 525.

ability to put himself or herself mentally into the prospect's place and understand things from that viewpoint, then the salesperson is in a position to understand the prospect's needs and to satisfy those needs in a better way than a competing salesperson who does not have empathy. Furthermore, this perceptual skill "makes feedback from the customer much more likely."[11] That is, there is a mutual empathy that tells the salesperson what the customer's needs and feelings are.

4. *Has a high level of energy.* The super salesperson is a self-starter with a great deal of drive and energy. He or she is often described as a workaholic. The super salesperson's energy propels him or her into 10- to 14-hour workdays. Weekends and holidays are also part of super salespeople's work regimen. Even when they appear to be relaxing by the pool or watching television, their minds are quite often on their work. They think, eat, sleep, and live their work. They love work and have an intense need for success. They acquire energy from their desire for success.

5. *Displays tremendous self-confidence.* Super salespeople firmly believe that they have the ability to make a sale. This apparent self-confidence, however, is often a compensation for suppressed feelings of inadequacy, insecurity, and lack of self-confidence.

6. *Has a continuous desire for money.* The super salesperson aspires for material things in life and loves to show off. Money allows the salesperson to drive an expensive car, wear expensive clothes and jewelry, and to tip heavily (in front of prospects and other people) at restaurants and bars. This super salesperson does not want money for money's sake, but for what it can do for him or her in front of clients and other people. He or she is not a Midas in search of gold for gold's sake, but a person in search of using the gold to gain recognition and appreciation from clients and friends.

7. *Has a well-developed and disciplined habit of industry.* The super salesperson feels uncomfortable when he or she is not working. This salesperson has good work habits, works long hours, is perservering, and likes solving problems.[12] This salesperson also has the need to achieve and to work hard at the job at hand.

8. *Considers each objection and obstacle as a challenge.* Because of the super salesperson's competitive spirit and experiences, the thrill of victory in overcoming the prospect's objections and resistance in closing the sale is a triumph.

McMurry believes that a salesperson should have all of these characteristics to be a super salesperson. However, he feels the last five characteristics are the most important.

In a longitudinal study spanning seven years, Mayer and Greenberg found two essential qualities necessary to a person's becoming a good salesperson: *empathy*

---

[11] Bellenger and Ingram, *Professional Selling,* p. 95.

[12] Lamont and Lundstrom, "Identifying Successful Salesmen."

and *ego drive*. They also conclude that the good salesperson must have both qualities because they act in a synergistic fashion.[13] Lamont and Lundstrom, however, found that empathy and ego drive were negatively related to success in personal selling. The contradiction between these studies may be the result of the differences in the selling jobs the salespeople had to perform. Whereas Mayer and Greenberg studied life insurance salesmen, Lamont and Lundstrom examined industrial salesmen selling highly technical products.[14] Perhaps one explanation for these discrepant findings is that life insurance salespeople sell on emotion, whereas industrial salespeople sell on facts.

Other Characteristics of Successful Salespeople

Possesses Certain Physical Traits   Some physical characteristerics of successful salespeople go beyond the obvious personal grooming and hygiene requirements, such as shined shoes, clean teeth, fresh breath, a good haircut, clean body, a nice smile, and clothing (i.e., dress for success). Although these traits are important in any social interaction, research has shown that "tall, physically impressive, and energetic" people seem to have the edge over others without these traits.[15]

Broad Range of Interests   Successful salespeople must be able to talk on a broad range of issues, including sports, politics, medical practices, the economy, etc., because these topics often affect their business.[16] Although this person does not have to be highly educated in a formal sense, he or she must be intellectually capable.[17]

Views Selling as Professional Career   The successful salesperson see selling as a profession and does not have interest in achieving a status beyond that status.[18] In fact, he or she sees personal selling as an end unto itself. In general, many practitioners believe that good salespeople make very poor sales managers.

Has Positive (Optimistic) Attitude   A salesperson is more successful if he or she has a positive self-concept, likes his or her product and company, and looks forward to meeting prospects. A salesperson who does not have self-confidence will seldom be successful in selling. Furthermore, a salesperson must have a positive attitude toward the product, company, and sales message. A person who does

---

[13]David Mayer and Herbert M. Greenberg, "What Makes a Good Salesman?" *Harvard Business Review,* Vol. 42, July-August 1964, pp. 119–125.

[14]Lamont and Lundstrom, "Identifying Successful Salesmen."

[15]Ibid.

[16]"The New Super Salesman: Wired for Success," *Business Week,* January 6, 1973, pp. 44–49; and Robert B. Woodruff, Gerald E. Hills, and David W. Cravens, *Marketing Management* (Homewood, IL: Richard D. Irwin, 1976), pp. 365–376.

[17]Lamont and Lundstrom, "Identifying Successful Salesmen."

[18]Ibid.

not fully believe in what he or she does will be seen as insincere. After all, if the salesperson does not believe in his product, how can the customer?

Has Favorable Attitude toward Customers

Finally, the succesful salesperson exhibits a favorable attitude toward his or her customers. That is, the sales representative shows a genuine interest in the prospect's needs, problems, and concerns. Also, the salesperson demonstrates respect for customers and does not talk down to them. People are quick to notice a sales representative's positive attitude toward them, and they react favorably to it.

One author summarizes the credo of one very successful business person:

- I believe in myself.
- I believe in the goods I sell.
- I believe in the firm for which I work.
- I believe in my colleagues and helpers.
- I think of myself as a success.
- I am enthusiastic in helping buyers (service-oriented).
- I am positive about my life and my job.

Optimism is a key building block for success.[19]

Has Good Listening Skills

Too often a discussion of personal selling centers on speaking skills at the expense of listening skills. Listening is one means by which the sales representative obtains *feedback* from prospects. It enables him or her to understand the needs of the customer and to adjust the sales message accordingly. Not only does listening provide the sales representative with information useful to selling efforts, but it can also provide information useful to the company in designing products and marketing programs. The sales representative has a responsibility to channel such information back to his or her company. "God gave you two ears and one mouth, and He meant for you to do twice as much listening as talking."[20] These are the words on a sign on the office wall of a man who sold over *$1 billion* of life insurance in one year.

Listening is a rare skill, the most often used yet least understood and researched of the communications processes. People listen all day long, usually without even thinking about it, yet they do not always do it well.

Listening is a rare skill because it is difficult. But why is this so? One reason is that people are usually absorbed in their own lives and activities, and listening to someone else becomes boring and painful for them. Only when another person in a conversation is through talking and we can start talking do most of us enjoy a conversation. The fact that so many people look upon listening as something irksome indicates the scarcity of really good listeners.

[19]Futrell, *Fundamentals of Selling,* p. 65.

[20]Robert L. Shook, *Ten Greatest Salespersons* (New York: Harper & Row, 1978), p. 65.

In personal selling, the salesperson who is a perceptive listener has the edge. When customers ask about a product, a good salesperson can tell whether they are interested in a good bargain, a status item, or something in between. Does the customer for a new television want "only the one on special" or "one that will last" or "a nice piece of furniture"? Whatever the television has to offer can be highlighted to appeal to a particular customer's expectation of the product. Again, the shrewd salesperson listens carefully when the customer asks to see a certain product and lets the customer sell himself or herself. Figure 11.2 states several basic and practical ideas on listening skills.

Develops Lasting Relationships   Perhaps one of the most important statements that can be made about the successful salesperson is that he or she must establish a lasting sales relationship with the customer. The salesperson must be willing to treat customers fairly and honestly, develop a good working relationship, and provide outstanding service for them.[21] "A top marketing executive at International Business Machines Corp., which is one of the companies that has spearheaded the development of superselling, claims that today's salesman must develop a 'long-range partnership' with his clients. 'The installation of a data-processing system,' he emphasizes, 'is only the beginning, not the end, of IBM's marketing effort.' "[22]

Has Patience, Persistence, and Social Responsibility   The successful salesperson takes his or her time to cultivate customers. "It may take a year just to get to know a new customer and his problems."[23] Also, good salesmanship requires persistence and perseverance. Top selling often means staying with the job and the customer for long periods of time. Occasionally, it means going to the top of the executive ladder to make the sale. And finally, the good salesperson displays the characteristic of social responsibility. Personal selling revolves around a continuing relationship with satisfied buyers.

The Dyadic Approach to Personal Selling

The typical selling situation involves the smallest possible group, referred to as a **dyad,** or a group of two persons interacting with each other. Any dyad (such as a sales representative and a prospective customer) can be described as a + + (reciprocal positive), + − (mixed), or − − (reciprocal negative) relationship. Where the members of the dyad are in a + + relationship (i.e., each has a positive attraction to the other), communications between the pair tends to be open and relatively free of restraints. For members of a − − dyadic relationship (i.e., each has a negative attraction or set of attitudes toward the other), communications is quite

---

[21]Futrell, *Fundamentals of Selling,* p. 23.
[22]Woodruff, Hills, and Cravens, *Marketing Management,* p. 369.
[23]Ibid.

FIGURE 11.2   Personal Selling and Listening Ability

1. **Good listening is a key to selling.** If customers make objections, they prove they are listening. Therefore, they should be listened to.

2. **Stop talking.** You can't listen while you are talking.

3. **Empathize with the prospect.** Try to put yourself in customers' place so that you can see what they are trying to get at.

4. **Ask questions.** When you don't understand, when you need further clarification, when you want prospects to like you, when you want to show you are listening, ask questions.

5. **Don't give up too soon.** Don't interrupt prospects; give them time to say what they have to say.

6. **Concentrate on what the prospect is saying.** Actively focus your attention on words, ideas, and feelings related to the subject.

7. **Leave your emotions behind.** Try to push your worries, your fears, your problems, outside the room. They may prevent you from listening well.

8. **Control your anger.** Try not to get angry at what prospects say about your company and products. Your anger may prevent you from understanding words or meaning.

9. **Get rid of distractions.** Put down any papers, pencils, etc., that may distract you.

10. **Get the main point.** Concentrate on the main ideas your prospect expresses.

11. **Don't argue mentally.** When you are trying to understand prospects, it is a handicap to argue with them mentally as they speak. This sets up a barrier between you and speakers.

12. **Listen for what is not said.** Sometimes you can learn just as much by determining what people leave out or avoid in talking as you can by listening to what they do say.

13. **Listen to how something is said.** Salespeople frequently concentrate so hard on what is said that they miss the importance of prospect's emotional reactions and attitudes related to what is said. Prospect's attitudes and emotional reactions may be more important than what is said.

14. **Listen for the prospect's personality.** One of the best ways of finding out information about people is to listen to them talk; as they talk, you begin to find out what they like and dislike, what their motivations are, what their value systems are, what they think about everything and anything, what makes them tick.

15. **Listening calls for an attitude of eagerness to gain through listening.** Salespeople must be hungry to hear what their prospects have to say in order to profit from their comments regarding their needs, problems, and goals.

16. **Poor listening is the result of not caring about the prospect.** In many, and perhaps most, instances salespeople fail to listen because of their own predispositions, preoccupations, and biases. As examples, salespeople may fail to listen to prospects because (a) they assume the prospect is uninteresting, (b) they mentally criticize the prospect's comments, (c) they are too enamored with their own products or themselves, (d) they let their minds wander, and (e) they listen for only factual data and ignore body language, intonations, and gestural codes.

17. **Let your body give positive signs of listening.** Body language can tell prospects that you are listening to what they are saying. Make sure your body reflects an understanding and interest in their problems. Don't fidget or keep distant from your prospects. Keep eye contact and let your posture indicate you are listening.

Source: Adapted from William M. Morgenroth, Sr., "Are You Listening," an unpublished seminar paper.

restrained. And finally, in the $+ -$ relationship (i.e, one member is attracted to the other, but the other is not attracted to him or her), communications tends to resemble the $- -$ situation. In summary, as the relationship becomes more positive between the dyad members (i.e., the attraction is high), communications flows more easily, but as a relationship becomes more negative (i.e., greater adversity), communications is more restrained.

Predictably, as the level of attractiveness between a sales representative and a client becomes more positive, the probability of a sale is enhanced. Evans found that there was a greater probability that a sale would be made as the *perceived* similarity between a sales representative and his or her client increased.[24] From an earlier discussion on the topic of source factors in marketing communications (Chapter 6), the reader will recall that people who perceive others to be similar to themselves tend to *like* them more than people they perceive as dissimilar (i.e, there is greater positive attraction between people who perceive themselves as similar than between those who perceive themselves as dissimilar). An implication of this principle for salespeople is that the more structured the selling situation is (in terms of similarity between the sales representative and the prospect), the greater the likelihood of a sale. Thus, the success of the selling situation depends, in part, upon the interpersonal interaction between sales representative and client. Similarity can be viewed along several dimensions, such as personal traits (humor, modesty, quietness, etc.), physical characteristics (height, age, dress, etc.), ethnic characteristics (religion, place of birth, etc.), status, political preference, personal habits (such as smoking), and a host of other dimensions.[25]

Allport suggests that personal traits are the most important in the dyadic relationship.[26] Evans found that the perceived similarity in religion and politics was most crucial to the successful sale in his experiment.[27] The following discussion looks at several avenues that researchers have taken in their quest to uncover specific dimensions of the buyer-seller dyad to increase the likelihood of a sale.

Similarity

The Evans study cited earlier opened new doors to the study of dyadic relationships in the personal selling process. His study illustrates how the *perceived* similarity between the sales representative and his or her prospect can enhance communications interaction and the probability of a sale. Additional evidence has been obtained by other researchers to support the same hypothesis in the marketplace.

---

[24]Franklin B. Evans, "Selling as a Dyadic Relationship: A New Approach," *The Behavioral Scientist,* Vol. 6, May 1963, pp. 76–79.

[25]See Evans, "Selling as a Dyadic Relationship"; see also G. W. Allport, *Pattern and Growth in Personality* (New York: Holt, Rinehart, and Winston, 1961).

[26]Allport, *Pattern and Growth in Personality.*

[27]Evans, "Selling as a Dyadic Relationship," p. 79.

Brock found that perceived similarity between paint salesclerks and their customers was very important in their attempts to persuade prospective buyers to purchase higher- and lower-priced paints than customers originally intended to purchase.[28]

Woodside and Davenport used a music store as the setting of their experiment, in which a sales representative attempted to sell customers a kit that cleaned 8-track tape players. In the *similar* condition the sales representative informed customers that she had purchased the same tapes the customers were purchasing, followed by a recommendation that they try the tape cleaner. In the *dissimilar* condition, the sales representative indicated to customers that she preferred a different type of music, followed by a recommendation that they try the tape cleaner. The researchers found that the similar condition produced significantly higher sales of the tape head cleaner than the dissimilar condition.[29] Other marketing researchers have obtained similar results of the positive effects of *similarity* between sales personnel and customers in producing sales.

Credibility

Source credibility, which was examined closely in Chapter 6, suggests that a source is generally more persuasive when *perceived* as being high in credibility than when *perceived* as being low in credibility. Recall also that credibility is a multifaceted concept, which may be established by the source's perceived *prestige, expertise, power, or trustworthiness,* etc. However, to the extent that the salesperson has something to gain by his or her persuasive attempts, his or her persuasiveness is reduced. Prospective customers recognize a sales representative's intentions to manipulate and the gains he or she will derive from a sale.

A sales representative, therefore, must fight an uphill battle to establish some degree of credibility in the eyes of a customer. A sales representative who can project confidence in what he or she says and who can demonstrate a high level of expertise for the product enhances his or her chances of being perceived as a credible source.

Woodside and Davenport, who were mentioned previously as having studied the issue of similarity, also studied the question of sales representative expertise in a selling situation. Their study involved a sales representative presenting a brief, prepared sales pitch to customers on the use of a cleaning kit for tape decks. In her presentation, the sales representative demonstrated a high level of product knowledge (the *expert* condition) by describing the *technical features* and use of the kit in cleaning "the dirt and tape oxide from the guides, the head, and especially the drive wheels of your tape player."[30] In the *nonexpert* condition, the sales repre-

[28]Timothy C. Brock, "Communicator-Recipient Similarity and Decision Change," *Journal of Personality and Social Psychology,* Vol. 1, June 1965, pp. 650–654.

[29]Arch G. Woodside and J. William Davenport, "The Effect of Salesman Similarity and Expertise on Consumer Purchasing Behavior," *The Journal of Marketing Research,* Vol. 11, May 1974, pp. 198–202.

[30]Ibid., p. 200.

sentative showed the kit to the customer but said that she did not know how it worked or anything about the tapes at all but that it was supposed to help the tape player somehow. As would be predicted, the *expert* condition produced significantly greater sales than the *nonexpert* condition.

In comparing the results of the effects of similarity and expertise on the purchase of the cleaning kits, the researchers learned that perceived expertise "produced a greater proportion of purchases than the perceived similarity of the salesperson."[31] Busch and Wilson also found that a salesperson's perceived expertise has a greater influence on making a sale than perceived similarity.[32] They learned that gaining the customer's trust is one of the most important aspects challenging the salesperson in making a sale.

Although expertise appears to be a more important determinant in selling than similarity (a referent power relationship), there is evidence that salespeople should also develop a strong referent power relationship with customers. In particular, a salesperson "who continually uses rewards, such as gratification of customer's ego, entertainment, and 'favor-doing' for customers, eventually may develop a referent power base of influence over the customer. This is particularly important in industrial selling where long-term buyer-seller relationships are common."[33] This comment can be expanded to include virtually any selling job in which repeat sales and repeat business are important.

Traditionally, practitioners and academicians have viewed sales performance as a function of job satisfaction, motivation, product knowledge, and salesperson attributes. Today, however, they focus more attention on the dyadic interaction between the salesperson and the prospect. They have discovered that the same salesperson, using the same selling techniques, is not always successful in making a sale to prospects with the same kind of needs.[34] The following sections will expand on this notion.

A Neurolinguistic Approach

One way a salesperson can develop a positive dyadic relationship with a prospect is to establish similarity by using neurolinguistic programming (NLP). This method, which psychotherapists developed to create rapport with clients, can be useful to salespeople in building rapport with clients. Successful salespeople appear to have the ability to observe their clients' eye movements, breathing patterns, body pos-

[31]Ibid., p. 201.

[32]Paul Busch and David T. Wilson, "An Experimental Analysis of a Salesman's Expert and Referent Bases of Social Power in the Buyer-Seller Dyad," *Journal of Marketing Research,* Vol. 13, February 1976, pp. 3–11.

[33]Ibid., p. 10.

[34]Edward A. Riordan, Richard L. Oliver, and James H. Donnelly, Jr., "The Unsold Prospect: Dyadic and Attitudinal Determinants," *Journal of Marketing Research,* Vol. 14, November 1977, pp. 530–537; see also Peter H. Reingen and Arch G. Woodside (eds.), *Buyer-Seller Interactions: Empirical Research and Normative Issues* (Chicago: AMA Proceedings Series, 1981).

ture, and skin tones to determine their prospects' thought processes. Through these observations, salespeople can match their customers' moods and behaviors to create perceived similarities, and therefore rapport. Some research indicates that successful salespeople can detect differences in personality styles of consumers and adapt accordingly through their use of an increased perceptiveness of consumers' verbal and physical cues. Visual, auditory, and kinesthetic senses are the basic senses in NLP, while the olfactory and gustatory senses play a lesser role.[35]

As an example, Nickels, Everett, and Klein describe how a prospect's eye movements can be observed by the salesperson to discover how his or her client thinks. Imagine the following:

> *The buyer is asked to recall the last time he or she purchased a product that really satisfied his or her needs. The buyer looks up and to the left and says, "I remember this great copy machine we bought six months ago. It* looked *very promising and I* saw *a great opportunity to save money." Then, looking down and to the right, the buyer says, "It* felt *right from the start"—and, looking left—"I can* hear *now all the secretaries* saying *how much they enjoy using it."*[36]

Using NLP the salesperson realizes that the prospect makes buying decisions by *looking* at new products, *feeling* what it would be like to use, and finally *listening* to what others *say* about it after the purchase. General guidelines regarding people's eye movements are the following:[37]

1.   When people look *up and left,* they are visualizing something from the past. They are *picturing* it in their minds.
2.   When people look *up and right,* they are *constructing* an image, visualizing what it would eventually look like.
3.   When people look *down and right,* they are either recalling or imagining *feelings.*
4.   When people look *sideways to the left,* they are hearing *sounds* from the past.
5.   When people look *sideways to the right,* they are *constructing* a future conversation, thinking of the right words.
6.   When people look *down and to the left,* they are *talking* with themselves in a kind of internal dialog.

The objective in NLP is for the salesperson to "match" the behavior of the prospect in both terms of verbal and nonverbal behavior. Therefore, in this example, the seller might say, "'Let's take a *look* at what this product will do and you'll *see*

---

[35]William G. Nickels, Robert F. Everett, and Ronald Klein, "Rapport Building for Salespeople: A Neuro-Linguistic Approach," *The Journal of Personal Selling & Sales Management,* Vol. 3, November 1983, pp. 1–2.

[36]Ibid., pp. 2–3.

[37]Ibid., p. 3.

that it fits your need perfectly. I'm sure it will *feel* right to you and you'll *hear* lots of good things about it from others.' "[38]

For this matching, or mirroring, behavior to be effective, it must be done as subtly as possible. These skills can be learned in a rather short period of time.

The Relational Communications Approach

Buyers and sellers usually do not say exactly what they mean and hear more than what was said. Therefore, salespeople and buyers attempt to interpret other people's intentions by using informational cues that go beyond the content of their verbal messages. That is, they realize that what people say in a personal selling situation is further influenced by *how it was said and the relative position* each person created in terms of either their *relative dominance, deference, or equality* (see Figure 11.3).

How these interrelational positions occur is addressed by the concept of **relational communications** (literally, "communication about communication"). This concept examines the message's form more than the message's content.[39] Specifically, relational communication directs attention to "message exchanges indicating the right to direct, structure, or dominate the interpersonal communication system."[40]

In personal selling, consider the following example:

Salesperson: With all considered, this product has great value for the money; don't you agree?

Prospect: What about a guaranty?

At the content level, the salesperson extols the product's benefits in terms of value, whereas the prospect wants information regarding the product's guaranty. However, in a relational communication sense, the salesperson and prospect are trying to *control* the interaction.

By avoiding the salesperson's question and instead posing one, the prospect creates a *dominant* position. If, at this point, the salesperson answers the prospect's question, he or she accepts the prospect's bid for the dominant position. The salesperson, on the other hand, can counter the prospect's attempt at dominance by

---

[38]Ibid.

[39]Gary F. Soldow and Gloria Penn Thomas, "Relational Communications: Form Versus Content in Sales Interactions," *Journal of Marketing,* Vol. 48, Winter 1984, p. 84.

[40]Donald G. Ellis, "Relational Control in Two Group Systems," *Communication Monographs,* Vol. 46, August 1979, p. 154.

FIGURE 11.3   **Relational Combinations Classified Regarding Agreement**

Salesperson

	Dominance	Deference	Equality
Dominance	− a	+ b	− c
Deference	+ d	− e	− f
Equality	− g	− h	+ i

(Buyer, vertical axis label)

Key:
+ Agreement regarding the definition of relationship
− Disagreement regarding the definition of relationship

Source: Gary F. Soldow and Gloria Penn Thomas, "Relational Communication: Form Versus Content in Sales Interaction," *Journal of Marketing,* Vol. 48, Winter 1984, p. 87.

proposing another assertion, "We can get to that in a moment; but how do you feel about the price?"[41]

Relational communication has potential importance for personal selling because it affects the control process. And, the salesperson's ability to influence (and perhaps control) the selling situation positively contributes to his or her negotiations

[41]Soldow and Thomas, "Relational Communications," p. 85.

TABLE 11.1   Dialogs Exemplifying Relational Combinations

		Dominance	SALESPERSON Deference	Equality
BUYER	**Dominance**	Salesperson: You are the most knowledgeable buyer I've met. Buyer: Actually, I know very little. Initiation/Disconfirmation	Buyer: Your prices are really quite high. Salesperson: Do you really think so? I guess they are. Initiation/Question, Confirmation	Buyer: Your prices are really quite high. Salesperson: Yes they are, but so are everybody's in this inflationary economy. Initiation/Extension
	Deference	Salesperson: You are the most knowledgeable buyer I've met. Buyer: Do you really think so? Initiation/Question	Buyer: Your product really meets our needs. Salesperson: Do you really think so? Buyer: Yes, don't you? Support, Question/Support, Question	Buyer: Your prices are really quite high. Salesperson: Yes they are, but so are everybody's. Buyer: Do you really think so? Extension/Support, Question
	Equality	Salesperson: You are the most knowledgeable buyer I've met. Buyer: Thank you. I've had 17 years of experience. Initiation/Extension	Salesperson: You are the most knowledgeable buyer I've met. Buyer: Thank you. I've had 17 years of experience. Salesperson: Oh really! Extension/Question, Support	Buyer: Your product really meets our needs. Salesperson: You're right. It is beautifully designed. Buyer: Yes. So is most of your line. Extension/Extension

Source: Gary F. Soldow and Gloria Penn Thomas, "Relational Communication: Form Versus Content in the Sales Interaction," *Journal of Marketing,* Vol. 48 Winter 1984, p. 88.

and sales outcomes. In this regard, Soldow and Thomas offer the following propositions:[42]

- Proposition 1: When the salesperson and prospect agree on the relationship, there is greater mutual satisfaction and a greater probability of a sale than when they disagree on the relationship.
- Proposition 2: Salespeople who have the abilities to *recognize* and to *manipulate* relational communication are more effective in personal selling than salespeople who have a lesser degree of these abilities.
- Proposition 3: Relational communications is *more important* than the content level in controlling the sales interaction.

Table 11.1 provides examples of the nine dialog relational combinations.

[42]Ibid., pp. 87–89.

Whereas other models of salesperson effectiveness have concentrated on the content level exchanged between a salesperson and prospective customers and the perceived similarity between customers and salespersons, the relational communication theory suggests that another level of interaction occurs between these two parties. Specifically, the interaction involves a combination of relative power positions between the salesperson and the prospective buyer. These interactive positions involve *dominance, deference, and equality.*

To be effective in selling, the salesperson must be a good negotiator. According to the ideas presented in this section, the good negotiator (salesperson) must have an ability to adjust to the relational communication level effectively.

A Contingency Approach to Personal Selling

In the past, research has focused on narrow views of the personal selling situation. That is, personal selling effectiveness has been viewed in terms of either the specific characteristics of the salesperson or the dyadic relationships that would ultimately lead to sales success. However, a broader view is that selling effectiveness depends on the *total situation* in which the transaction takes place. Weitz suggests that "the effectiveness of sales behaviors across customer interactions is contingent upon or moderated by (a) the salesperson's resources, (b) the nature of the customer's buying task, (c) the customer-salesperson relationship and interactions among (a), (b), and (c)."[43] Figure 11.4 displays a contingency model of salesperson effectiveness.

In Figure 11.4, there are several constructs in this contingency framework. *Effectiveness* in this model is defined in terms of the salesperson. That is, salesperson effectiveness is measured by long-term sales of the company's products and services. Customer satisfaction is implicit in this measurement because short-term strategies would not meet long-term sales goals.

Again, looking at Figure 11.4, *selling behaviors* are an important set of factors influencing the outcome of a potential sale. Some of these behaviors include (1) adapting to customers, (2) establishing influence bases, (3) the use of influence techniques, and (4) controlling the sales interaction. *Characteristics of the customer's buying task* include (1) an examination of how people buy according to their needs and beliefs, (2) their knowledge of the alternatives, and (3) the characteristics of the buying task. Additionally, the salesperson has both financial and personal *resources* in (1) company prestige, (2) product and customer knowledge, (3) analytical and interpersonal skills, and (4) the availability of alternatives. Finally, the characteristics of the *salesperson-customer relationship* also moderate the salesperson's effectiveness. This set of variables includes (1) the level of con-

---

[43]Barton A. Weitz, "Effectiveness in Sales Interactions: A Contingency Approach," *Journal of Marketing,* Vol. 45, Winter 1981, pp. 85–103.

FIGURE 11.4   **A Contingency Model of Salesperson Effectiveness**

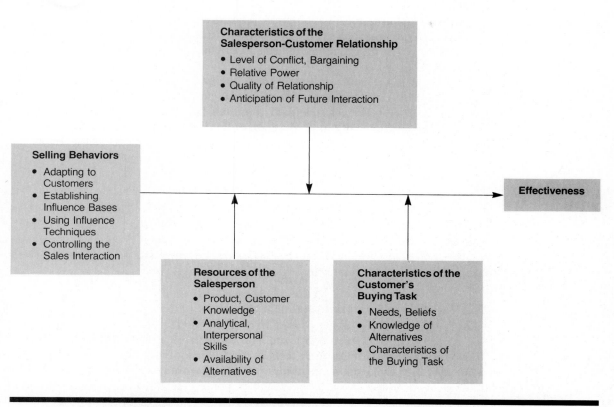

Source: Barton A. Weitz, "Effectiveness in Sales Interactions: A Contingency Framework," *Journal of Marketing*, Vol. 45, Winter 1981, p. 90.

flict and bargaining, (2) relative power, (3) quality of the relationship, and (4) the anticipation of future interaction.

Selling Behavior

One key to personal selling appears to be in the salesperson's ability to adapt to the customer and the selling situation. At one extreme is the canned presentation; at the other extreme is the salesperson who encounters a unique situation with every customer. All situations in between still require a degree of adaptability and flexibility. Additionally, salesperson behaviors include establishing credibility, using such influence techniques as one-sided versus two-sided messages, and knowing how to control the sales interaction (discussed in previous section).

Customer's Buying Task

An effective salesperson must modify his or her selling behavior according to the customer's buying task. Customers may engage in either new buy, modified buy, or straight rebuy situations. The **new buy task** is one that is new to customers and one in which they have no experience. They are undoubtedly nervous and, perhaps, defensive. The **straight rebuy,** on the other hand, is routine and already well structured. Each buying condition requires a different sales approach. "The degree to which the product requirements are known by the customer, the degree to which a variety of products could satisfy the customer's needs, and the degree to which the customer is able to evaluate the performance of the product after the sale"[44] determine how the salesperson must adapt to the customer's buying task.

The Salesperson's Resources

The salesperson enters a sales situation with a set of skills and abilities and a level of knowledge about the products, the company, the industry, and the customer. Additionally, the salesperson is shrouded by the company's reputation, the range of alternatives the company allows him or her to offer, and his or her ability to alter the terms of the sale to match customers' needs.

The Customer-Salesperson Relationship

Dyadic interaction and relative power, which have been described earlier, fall under the customer-salesperson relationship part of the contingency approach. Additionally, the salesperson must know how to handle such *conflicts* as policy differences, hostility, stress, anxiety, and customer aggression in any and all kinds of sales situations. Finally, the salesperson must be able to understand the "nature of the present customer-salesperson relationship and the anticipation of future interactions. One important aspect of the salesperson-customer relationship is whether the salesperson represents an 'in' or an 'out' supplier. An 'in' salesperson is presently selling the product to the customer, while an 'out' salesperson is attempting to make an initial sale."[45] Therefore, the salesperson must realize that he or she should perform different functions and sales behaviors according to whether he or she is in an "in" or an "out" selling situation.

With regard to future interactions, research indicates that bargaining behavior varies according to the anticipation of future interactions. "For example, one would expect that effective retail and industrial salespeople typically engage in

[44]Ibid., p. 93.
[45]Ibid., p. 94.

different behaviors because industrial salespeople typically have continuing relationships with customers, while the retail salespeople do not."[46]

In summary, the contingency approach strongly advocates that a salesperson must be flexible and adaptable to a wide array of selling situations in order to be successful. That is, successful salespeople can be characterized by the degree to which they alter their sales behavior during a customer interaction or across customer interactions. However, simply engaging in adaptive behavior does not guarantee high sales performance. Salespeople must also have skills that help them make appropriate adaptations. Many of these skills, both verbal and nonverbal, have already been discussed.

The contingency model, therefore, provides the reader with an all-encompassing view of the personal selling situation because it incorporates all of the previous approaches into one framework. This model shows that many variables interact in the personal selling situation. Thus, a significant key to successful personal selling is *adaptability.*

Summary

It is true that everyone is in the business of personal selling: husbands, wives, politicians, friends, preachers, and businesses. The primary concern of this chapter has been to concentrate on personal selling in business, although the same concepts apply outside of business.

Some of the features of personal selling are (1) it is the most effective, but least efficient, form of promotion, (2) it is financially and personally rewarding, (3) it provides job freedom, (4) it offers chances for advancement, and (5) it provides a challenge.

There are several kinds of salespeople: (1) route salespeople, (2) retail salespeople, (3) detail people, (4) account representatives, (5) industrial sales representatives, (6) sales engineers, and (7) creative salespeople. Good salespeople are those who provide service to the buyer and service to the company. They do this by prospecting for new accounts, providing services to current accounts, doing what is necessary to maintain and improve the good name of the company, and performing nonselling and reporting activities.

The basic steps in the selling process are (1) locating and prospecting for customers, (2) the preapproach, (3) the approach, (4) the sales presentation, (5) handling objections, (6) the close, and (7) the postsale follow-up.

Several characteristics of the super salesperson have also been discussed. They include a compulsiveness to win, the need to hold the affection of others, a strong empathy toward others, a high level of energy, a tremendous display of self-confi-

---

[46]Ibid.

dence, a continuous desire for money, a habit of industry, and the belief that each objection is a challenge.

The selling situation is described in terms of dyadic interaction, neurolinguistics, relational communications, and a contingency approach. Each contributes in a different way to understanding the personal selling process.

Discussion Questions

1. There is a popular belief that personal selling has a negative image. What can the personal selling profession do to reverse this image?
2. Explain why personal selling is the most *effective* marketing communications tool. Specifically, describe the kinds of products and services for which personal selling is best.
3. Discuss selling as a two-way communications process.
4. How would you evaluate the canned sales presentation? What are the advantages and disadvantages of this form of presentation? When may it be used and when should it not be used?
5. What are your opinions on what makes a super salesperson? What other factors may describe the super salesperson?
6. What are some nonverbal cues (other than those mentioned in the chapter) that may aid the salesperson in making the sale?

Exercises

1. Interview three sales representatives, all from different lines of work, and describe the differences in their approaches to personal selling. Compare these results with the ideas presented in the text.
2. Describe a good salesperson you have met and the way it affected your purchase decision. Also, describe a poor salesperson you have met and the way it affected your purchase decision.
3. Write a two- to three-page essay on why you would or would not be a good salesperson.

CHAPTER 12

An Overview of Advertising

This is the first of four chapters devoted to the subject of advertising. This chapter examines the economic and social aspects of advertising. Discussion then turns to managerial issues. The various participants in the advertising process (agencies, media, etc.) are described and a general framework of the overall process is presented. The bulk of the chapter focuses on two basic, yet critically important, aspects of advertising management: *objective setting* and *budgeting.*

Economic and Social Aspects of Advertising

Because we are surrounded by advertising in our day-to-day lives (especially in the United States) nearly everyone has firm impressions and feelings about how advertising works and how it serves the economy and society. Before discussing some of these views, this section will establish what advertising is and will examine what functions it performs.

 Advertising is "paid, nonpersonal communication through various media by business firms, nonprofit organizations, and individuals who are in some way identified in the advertising message and who hope to inform or persuade members of

a particular audience."[1] In comparison with the other tools of promotion management, advertising has four relatively distinct characteristics:[2]

1. *Public presentation.* Advertising is massive and public in nature; it is out
   where everyone can see it.
2. *Pervasiveness.* Advertising is nearly ubiquitous; it seems to be everywhere all
   the time.
3. *Amplified expressiveness.* Through its utilization of music, dramatic visualizations, and creative expressiveness, advertising dramatizes and sometimes ex-
   aggerates product offerings.
4. *Impersonality.* Advertising is a relatively impersonal form of communication
   because it is transmitted via mass media and not person to person.

Functions Performed by Advertising

Advertising in its most basic sense is an *economic investment,* an investment that
is, in fact, regarded very favorably by numerous businesses, as well as not-for-profit
organizations. Advertising expenditures in the United States alone exceeded $75
billion in 1983 and are estimated to exceed $86 billion in 1984.[3] The top 100 U.S.
advertisers themselves invested nearly $19 billion in advertising in 1983.[4] Table
12.1 presents these top 100 advertisers, their rankings, and their total advertising
expenditures. For example, Proctor & Gamble, the number one advertiser in the
United States since 1964, had expenditures exceeding $773 million. Even the U.S.
government is a heavy advertiser; its expenditures were nearly $229 million, mak-
ing it the twenty-eighth leading advertiser in 1983.

Businesses would not make the massive investmments shown in Table 12.1 unless advertising performed useful functions. What are these functions and how does
advertising serve consumers as well as businesses? Practitioners and scholars generally recognize the following five advertising functions: (1) informing, (2) persuading, (3) reminding, (4) adding value, and (5) assisting other company efforts.[5]

Informing   Advertising makes consumers aware of new products, informs them
about specific brands, and educates them about particular product features and
benefits. Because advertising is an efficient form of communication (i.e., it is capable of reaching mass audiences at a relatively low cost per contact), businesses are
better able to introduce new products and increase demand for existing products.

---

[1]S. Watson Dunn and Arnold M. Barban, *Advertising: Its Role in Modern Marketing,* 4th ed. (Hinsdale,
IL: The Dryden Press, 1978), p. 8.

[2]Sidney J. Levy, *Promotional Behavior* (Glenview, IL: Scott, Foresman and Company, 1971), pp. 64, 65.

[3]Robert Coen, "Final Figures: Advertising Surged in '83," *Advertising Age,* May 14, 1984, p. 62.

[4]R. Craig Endicott, "Leaders Rebuild Sales, Hike Advertising 10.5%," *Advertising Age,* September 14,
1984, p. 1.

[5]These functions are similar to those identified by the noted advertising pioneer James Webb Young.
See, for example, "What Is Advertising, What Does It Do," *Advertising Age,* November 21, 1973, p. 12.

TABLE 12.1   The 100 Leading U.S. Advertisers, 1983 ($000)

Rank	Company	Advertising	Rank	Company	Advertising	Rank	Company	Advertising
1	Procter & Gamble Co.	$773,618.3	35	Gillette Co.	$185,604.4	67	Du Pont	102,637.0
2	Sears, Roebuck & Co.	732,500.0	36	Mattel Inc.	179,934.8	68	Trans World Corp.	101,503.3
3	Beatrice Cos.	602,775.4	37	Kellogg Co.	176,306.9	69	American Motors Corp.	100,800.7
4	General Motors Corp.	595,129.5	38	Sterling Drug	171,828.1	70	Sony Corp. of America	97,283.2
5	R. J. Reynolds Industries	593,350.3	39	CBS Inc.	167,711.0	71	CPC International	96,627.3
6	Philip Morris Inc.	527,481.8	40	Tandy Corp.	156,728.0	72	Miles Laboratories	89,063.8
7	Ford Motor Co.	479,060.0	41	Richardson-Vicks	150,813.9	73	Union Carbide Corp.	88,000.0
8	American Telephone & Telegraph	463,095.5	42	Quaker Oats Co.	148,441.7	74	S.C. Johnson & Son	86,970.3
9	K mart Corp.	400,000.0	43	Batus Inc.	146,076.9	75	Greyhound Corp.	83,564.0
10	General Foods Corp.	386,134.2	44	Gulf & Western Industries	145,500.0	76	AMR Corp.	80,000.0
11	Nabisco Brands	367,530.4	45	American Cyanamid Co.	142,400.0	77	Kimberly-Clark Corp.	77,460.0
12	PepsiCo Inc.	356,400.0	46	Chesebrough-Pond's	141,324.5	78	UAL Inc.	77,200.0
13	Warner-Lambert Co.	343,553.5	47	Eastman Kodak Co.	141,318.9	79	American Brands	75,590.1
14	American Home Products Corp.	333,485.0	48	Loews Corp.	135,115.1	80	MCA Inc.	74,543.6
15	Unilever U.S.	324,865.8	49	ITT Corp.	134,229.0	81	Mazda Motors of America	74,500.0
16	McDonald's Corp.	311,378.0	50	Beecham Group p.l.c.	134,126.8	82	Stroh Brewery Co.	73,532.4
17	Johnson & Johnson	295,328.8	51	Texas Instruments	129,042.0	83	Pfizer Inc.	72,084.3
18	Mobil Corp.	294,932.5	52	Campbell Soup Co.	126,000.0	84	Brown-Forman Distillers	70,500.0
19	J.C. Penney Co.	292,451.0	53	Revlon Inc.	123,968.9	85	GTE Corp.	70,179.9
20	Anheuser-Busch Cos.	290,616.4	54	Nissan Motor Corp. in U.S.A.	122,848.0	86	Eastern Air Lines	70,000.0
21	Ralston Purina Co.	285,667.4	55	Mars Inc.	120,350.5	87	Cosmair Inc.	69,955.0
22	Coca-Cola Co.	282,150.0	56	Time Inc.	119,785.0	88	Clorox Co.	69,429.0
23	General Mills	268,690.2	57	Jos. E. Seagram & Sons	119,604.4	89	Hershey Foods Corp.	68,257.4
24	Colgate-Palmolive Co.	268,000.0	58	International Business Machines Corp.	119,222.5	90	Wendy's International	64,445.0
25	Warner Communications	251,049.6	59	Schering-Plough Corp.	117,914.2	91	Wm. Wrigley Jr. Co.	63,948.2
26	Bristol-Myers Co.	235,000.0	60	American Honda Motor Co.	115,182.3	92	Delta Air Lines	63,944.3
27	Chrysler Corp.	230,020.1	61	Nestle Enterprises	114,957.0	93	Adolph Coors Co.	63,621.3
28	U.S. Government	228,857.2	62	Toyota Motor Sales U.S.A.	113,649.0	94	Noxell Corp.	58,264.4
29	RCA Corp.	212,300.0	63	Volkswagen of America	112,500.0	95	Canon U.S.A.	58,032.9
30	Dart & Kraft	210,279.4	64	IC Industries	112,100.0	96	Goodyear Tire & Rubber Co.	57,831.7
31	H.J. Heinz Co.	202,400.0	65	Xerox Corp.	110,101.8	97	GrandMet U.S.A.	55,566.2
32	General Electric Co.	196,506.6	66	American Express Co.	107,571.0	98	Coleco Industries	55,216.4
33	Consolidated Foods Corp.	195,858.0				99	Carnation Co.	54,284.6
34	Pillsbury Co.	190,944.3				100	American Broadcasting Cos.	49,167.5

Figures are a composite of measured and unmeasured advertising.

Source: Advertising Age, September 14, 1984, p. 1. Copyright 1984 Crain Communications, Inc.

Persuading   Beyond gaining awareness and facilitating comprehension, advertising also predisposes prospective customers to purchase advertised brands, at least on a trial basis. Sometimes persuasion in advertising takes the form of influencing **primary demand** for an entire product category; other times, and more frequently, it involves persuasion to try a specific company brand (**selective demand**).

Reminding   Advertising also keeps a company's brand to the fore of the consumer's memory so that when a need arises related to the advertised product category the consumer will consider seriously the company's brand. As discussed in Chapter 3, there is a tendency for increased familiarity to result in favorable disposition to a product (the mere exposure hypothesis). Consumers tend to develop some degree of confidence in heavily advertised brands compared with those that are rarely, if ever, advertised.

Adding Value   Advertising adds value to products and to specific brands by influencing consumer's perceptions. Thus, some brands are, as a result of effective advertising efforts, viewed as more elegant than, more stylish or prestigious, or superior to competitive offerings. Another way that advertising adds value is by reducing the cognitive dissonance that consumers experience after making important and risky buying decisions.

Advertisers use a variety of procedures to add value to their brands. One interesting application is **vicarious modeling,** which attempts to influence consumer's perceptions and behaviors by having them observe the actions of others (e.g., models in advertisements) and the consequences of the models' behaviors.[6] For example, the makers of Aviance perfume show its users enjoying an "Aviance night"; Coca-Cola routinely depicts the users of its brands as experiencing fun and excitement; and Beefeater gin (Figure 12.1) portrays itself as a drink for elegant occasions.

Assisting Other Company Efforts   Advertising facilitates other company efforts in the marketing communications process. In particular, it provides a vehicle for sales promotions (coupons, sweepstakes, etc.) and assists sales representatives by generating leads to prospective customers and by preselling customers before a salesperson calls upon them.

One major study analyzed data from more than 1,000 advertising schedules for 26 different products and concluded that "advertising acts as a valuable introduction for the salesman to his prospective customers."[7] The study also reported that selling costs were from 2 percent to 28 percent lower in those instances where customers had been preexposed to advertisements. Sales effort, time, and costs are reduced because of leads provided by advertising and because less time is required to inform prospects about product features and benefits. Moreover, advertising legitimizes or makes more credible the sales representative's claims.[8]

---

[6] For further discussion of the procedures and principles underlying vicarious modeling, see Walter R. Nord and J. Paul Peter, "A Behavior Modification Perspective on Marketing," *Journal of Marketing,* Vol. 44, Spring 1980, pp. 36–47.

[7] John E. Morrill, "Industrial Advertising Pays Off," *Harvard Business Review,* March-April 1970, p. 4.

[8] The synergism between advertising and personal selling is not always a one-way flow from advertising to personal selling. In fact, one study has demonstrated a reverse situation, in which personal sales calls appear to pave the way for advertising. See William R. Swinyard and Michael L. Ray, "Advertising-Selling Interactions: An Attribution Theory Experiment," *Journal of Marketing Research,* Vol. 14, November 1977, pp. 509–516.

FIGURE 12.1   **Illustration of the Value-Added Role of Advertising**

Source: Reprinted with permission of Kobrand Corporation. Sole U.S. Importers of Beefeater Gin.

Besides supporting the efforts of sales representatives, advertising also may enhance the results of other marketing communications. For example, because of advertising exposure, consumers can more easily identify product packages in the store and recognize the value of a product (thereby justifying the price).

Advertising's Economic Role

The preceding discussion focused on advertising's micro role, i.e., the functions it performs for individual advertisers. The macro role of advertising, i.e., the impact it has on the economy in general, is explored in this section. There are two divergent schools of thought on advertising's role: "advertising = market power" versus "advertising = information." Table 12.2 summarizes these two perspectives.[9]

TABLE 12.2   Two Schools of Thought on Advertising's Role in the Economy

Advertising = Market Power		Advertising = Information
Advertising affects consumer preferences and tastes, changes product attributes, and differentiates the product from competitive offerings.	Advertising	Advertising informs consumers about product attributes and does not change the way they value those attributes.
Consumers become brand loyal and less price sensitive, and perceive fewer substitutes for advertised brands.	Consumer Buying Behavior	Consumers become more price sensitive and buy best "value." Only the relationship between price and quality affects elasticity for a given product.
Potential entrants must overcome established brand loyalty and spend relatively more on advertising.	Barriers to Entry	Advertising makes entry possible for new brands because it can communicate product attributes to consumers.
Firms are insulated from market competition and potential rivals; concentration increases, leaving firms with more discretionary power.	Industry Structure and Market Power	Consumers can compare competitive offerings easily and competitive rivalry is increased. Efficient firms remain, and as the inefficient leave, new entrants appear; the effect on concentration is ambiguous.
Firms can charge higher prices and are not as likely to compete on quality or price dimensions. Innovation may be reduced.	Market Conduct	More informed consumers put pressures on firms to lower prices and improve quality. Innovation is facilitated via new entrants.
High prices and excessive profits accrue to advertisers and give them even more incentive to advertise their products. Output is restricted compared to conditions of perfect competition.	Market Performance	Industry prices are decreased. The effect on profits due to increased competition and increased efficiency is ambiguous.

Source: Paul W. Farris and Mark S. Albion, "The Impact of Advertising on the Price of Consumer Products," *Journal of Marketing,* Vol. 44, Summer 1980, p. 18.

[9]The following discussion follows closely the excellent review in Paul W. Farris and Mark S. Albion, "The Impact of Advertising on the Price of Consumer Products," *Journal of Marketing,* Vol. 44, Summer 1980, pp. 17–35.

Advertising = Market Power   The view that advertising yields market power is founded on one major premise: advertising has the ability to *differentiate* physically homogeneous products. It follows from this that advertising may create brand-loyal customers who are less price sensitive than they would be in the absence of advertising and that price elasticity of demand is less elastic than it otherwise would be. In turn, it becomes more difficult for new firms to enter the industry (i.e., entry barriers are increased) because new firms must spend relatively more on advertising to overcome established brand loyalty patterns. Thus, established firms are relatively insulated from potential rivals, their market shares or concentration levels increase, and they are left with more discretionary power to increase prices and to influence the market in other ways. In other words, firms are less likely to compete on the basis of price or quality, and product innovation may be reduced. The result, ultimately, according to the advertising = market power position, is that firms charge high prices, earn excessive profits, and restrict output.

Advertising = Information   The advertising-equals-information perspective purports that advertising informs consumers about product attributes and increases their price sensitivity and ability to obtain the best value. Barriers to entry (for prospective new firms) are reduced because advertising enables these new firms to communicate their product attributes and advantages to consumers. Advertising allows consumers to compare competitive offerings easily, which results in increased competitive rivalry. Industry prices are decreased because consumers, informed by advertising, put pressure on firms to lower prices. Product innovation is facilitated via new entrants, and quality is improved.

A Reconciliation   The world is never as simple and straightforward as the two views of advertising would lead us to believe. Neither view is, in fact, entirely correct or adequate by itself. Critics of the advertising = market power view contend that a number of factors other than advertising (e.g., superior product quality, better packaging, better distribution) may account for both brand loyalty and price insensitivity.[10] Advertising is not the sole marketing force responsible for a firm's market power.

Similarly, advertising does not possess all the virtues that advocates of the advertising = information school would lead one to believe. Critics of this view contend that advertising goes beyond merely providing consumers with information and, in fact, influences consumers' relative preferences for different product attributes. It follows from this contention that advertising, if indeed it does influence consumers' attribute preferences, may create the same undesirable consequences (i.e., market concentration, price insensitivity, entry barriers, etc.) claimed by the advertising = market power proponents.[11]

---

[10]For more discussion, see ibid., p. 19.

[11]For more discussion, see ibid., p. 20.

In sum, advertising's economic role is neither all good nor all bad. The exact role varies from situation to situation, and generalities are meaningless. On balance, advertising has negative economic effects (as claimed by the market power school) to the extent that only one or a few advertisers in a given product-market situation possess differential advantages over competitors in terms of advertising spending ability or effectiveness. If, however, any one advertiser's efforts can be counter-vailed by other advertisers, then the positive effects of advertising (as claimed by the information school) would outweigh the negative.[12]

Advertising's Social Role

The role of advertising in society has been debated for centuries. Advertising is claimed by its practitioners to be largely responsible for much of what is good in life and is criticized by its opponents as guilty for the bad. A noted social scientist has offered a succinct, yet elegant, account of why advertising is so fiercely criti-cized:

> *As the voice of technology, [advertising] is associated with many dissat-isfactions of the industrial state. As the voice of mass culture it invites intellectual attack. And as the most visible form of capitalism it has served as nothing less than a lightning-rod for social criticism.*[13]

A variety of specific criticisms have been leveled against advertising. Because the issues are complex, it is impossible in this chapter to treat each criticism in great detail. The purpose of this discussion is, instead, merely to introduce the basic issues.[14] The following criticisms are illustrative, rather than exhaustive.

Advertising Is Deceptive   As discussed in Chapter 9, deception is said to occur when an advertisement falsely represents a product or service to consumers who believe the false representation. Is advertising deceptive according to this general definition? *Some* advertising *is* deceptive—the existence of governmental regula-tion and industry self-regulation attests to this fact. However, it would be very naive to assume that all or most of advertising is deceptive. The advertising indus-try is not much different than any other institution in a pluralistic society. Lying, cheating, and outright fraud are universal, occurring at the highest levels of gov-

---

[12]Kent M. Lancaster and Gordon E. Miracle, "How Advertising Can Have Largely Anticompetitive Effects in One Sector But Largely Procompetitive Effects in Another," University of Illinois Working Paper No. 7, Urbana, IL, November 1979.

[13]Ronald Berman, "Advertising and Social Change," *Advertising Age,* April 30, 1980, p. 24.

[14]The reader is encouraged to review a text on principles of advertising or advertising management for additional discussion of the issues. Two particularly good sources are David A. Aaker and John G. Myers, *Advertising Management,* 2nd Ed. (Englewood Cliffs, NJ: Prentice-Hall, 1982), chap. 15; and Dunn and Barban, *Advertising,* chap. 5.

ernment (e.g., Watergate) and in the most basic human relationships (e.g., husbands and wives). Advertising is not without sin, but neither does it have a monopoly on it.

Advertising is Manipulative   The criticism of manipulation asserts that advertising has the power to influence people to perform certain behaviors that they would not perform were it not for advertising. Taken to the extreme, this suggests that advertising is capable of moving people against their own free wills. How could advertising possibly have such power? What psychological principles would account for such power to manipulate? The evidence (discussed in detail in the next chapter) certainly does not support subliminal motivation, which is probably the most frequent and provocative explanation underlying the claim of advertising manipulation.

In general, the contention that advertising manipulates is without substance. Advertising does attempt, undeniably, to persuade consumers to purchase particular products and brands. Persuasion and manipulation are not the same, however. Persuasion is a legitimate form of human interaction that all individuals and institutions in society perform. The ability to persuade cannot be arrogated to advertising alone, and the power to manipulate should not be attributed to advertising at all.

Advertising Is Offensive and in Bad Taste   Advertising critics contend that much advertising is insulting to human intelligence, is vulgar, and is generally offensive to the tastes of many consumers. Several grounds exist for this criticism: (1) inane commercials of the "Mr. Whipple" and "ring around the collar" genre, (2) sexual innuendo in all forms of advertisements, (3) television commercials that advertise unpleasant products (hemorrhoid treatments, feminine hygiene products, etc.), and (4) repetitious usage of the same advertisements *ad infinitum, ad nauseam.*

Undeniably, much of advertising *is* disgusting and offensive. Yet, in its defense, the same can be said for all forms of mass media presentations. For example, many network television programs verge on the idiotic, and theater movies are often egregious in their use of sex and violence.

Advertising Creates and Perpetuates Stereotypes   The contention at the root of the criticism that advertising promotes stereotyping is that advertising tends to portray certain groups in very narrow and predictable fashion: Blacks and other minorities are portrayed disproportionately often in working-class roles rather than in the full range of positions they actually occupy, women are too often stereotyped as housewives or as sex objects, and senior citizens are frequently characterized as feeble and forgetful people.

Advertising *is* guilty of perpetuating stereotypes. It would be unfair, however, to blame advertising for creating these stereotypes, which, in fact, are perpetuated by all elements in sociey. Spreading the blame does not make advertising any better, but it does show that advertising is probably not any worse than the rest of society.

Advertising Causes People to Buy Things They Really Do Not Need   A frequently cited criticism suggests that advertising is responsible for people's buying items or services for which they have no need. This criticism is a value-laden judgment. Although advertising most assuredly influences consumer tastes and encourages people to undertake purchases they may not otherwise make, it is difficult to determine what consumers need or do not need.

Advertising Plays upon People's Fears and Insecurities   Some advertisements appeal to the negative consequences of not buying a product—rejection by members of the opposite sex, bad breath, failure to have provided for the family if one should die without proper insurance coverage, etc. Some advertisers must certainly plead *mea culpa* to this charge. However, once again, advertising possesses no monopoly on this transgression. For example, educators are known occasionally to play upon students' fears, and the church has made a science out of threatening sinners with years in purgatory or eternal damnation in hell for failure to perform certain behaviors.

In sum, the institution of advertising is certainly not free of criticism. What should be clear, however, is that advertising reflects the rest of society, and any indictment of advertising probably applies to society at large. Responsible advertising practitioners, knowing that their practice is particularly susceptible to criticism, have a vested interest in producing advertisements that are beyond reproach. Advertising, when done honestly and ethically, can serve society well.

Advertising Management Overview

A completed advertisement, such as a television commercial, is often the final product of the efforts of various research, production, creative, media, and other services. Most national and regional advertisements and some local advertisements reflect the collective work of various advertising services and institutions.[15] About half the dollars spent on advertising are spent through advertising agencies, while companies who prepare their own ads (supermarkets, department stores, and other local rather than national advertisers) spend the other half.[16]

Five major groups are involved in the total advertising process:[17] (1) advertising associations (e.g., the Advertising Research Foundation), (2) companies and other organizations that advertise (e.g., Procter & Gamble, the U.S. government), (3) advertising agencies (e.g., Tokyo-based Dentsu, the world's largest advertising agency), (4) advertising production companies (independent businesses that pho-

---

[15]William M. Weilbacher, *Advertising* (New York: Macmillan Publishing Co., 1979), p. 62.

[16]Edmund W. J. Faison, *Advertising: A Behavioral Approach for Managers* (New York: John Wiley & Sons, 1980), p. 63.

[17]Ibid., p. 65.

tograph, film, and otherwise produce advertisements), and (5) advertising media (newspapers, television, etc.).

Although the advertising industry involves a number of collective efforts, the focus of this chapter is restricted to the second group, advertisers themselves. A general model of the advertising process is presented, followed by in-depth treatment of two aspects of advertising management: objective setting and budgeting.

The Advertising Management Process

Advertising management entails a variety of strategic and tactical activities, both of which extend from a company's overall corporate and marketing strategies. The overall process is presented in Figure 12.2.

Corporate and Marketing Strategies   **Corporate strategy** is set by top management and represents the long-range (typically three to five years) objectives, plans, and budgets for all corporate units and departments. Corporate strategy (1) is based on situation analyses of economic, competitive, social, and other pertinent factors that represent opportunities and threats for a business enterprise and (2) is formulated in view of the enterprise's inherent strengths and weaknesses.

Marketing strategy is an extension of corporate strategy and involves plans, budgets, and controls needed to direct a firm's product, promotion, distribution, and pricing activities. The purpose of the marketing strategy is to coordinate the various marketing mix elements and to assure that marketing efforts are in line with corporate strategy. *target mkts / positioning / marketing mix + its coordination*

FIGURE 12.2   **The Advertising Management Process**

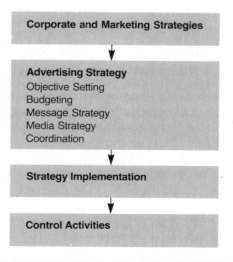

Advertising Strategy   **Advertising strategy** is guided, in theory at least, by corporate and marketing strategies. These more general strategies determine how much can be invested in advertising, at what markets advertising efforts need to be directed, how advertising must be coordinated with other marketing elements, and, to some degree, how advertising is to be executed.

An advertising campaign introduced in 1984 by Pepsi-Cola USA illustrates these strategic relations.[18] Corporate officers at Pepsi-Cola dedicated the company to tapping the youth market in a fashion unprecedented in the soft drink industry. In tune with this marketing reorientation, Pepsi-Cola moved away from its past half-century of using jingles and image-oriented campaigns ("Join the Pepsi generation," "Have a Pepsi day") to a new campaign ("Pepsi, the choice of a new generation") that conveyed a young, contemporary theme. In line with this theme, Pepsi-Cola invested millions of dollars to identify itself with Michael Jackson, the entertainer who supposedly embodied "the spirit of today's youngsters."[19] The company is estimated to have paid $7 million for two commercials by the Jackson brothers and the rights to identify itself with Michael Jackson and his concert fans. Pepsi-Cola invested an additional $47 million in media advertising to air and print its new campaign.[20] Synopses of a Jackson brothers commercial and five others in Pepsi-Cola's 1984 advertising campaign appear in Figure 12.3.

Advertising strategy involves, in general, five major activities (see Figure 12.2). The first two, *objective setting* and *budgeting,* are described later in this chapter. Pepsi-Cola's objective, for example, was to create a contemporary image that appealed to youth. The company budgeted over $50 million to achieve this general objective.

A third aspect of advertising strategy is *message strategy.* Pepsi made its messages compatible with its advertising objective by using themes (e.g., the *E.T.* take-off in the "Basement Visitor" commercial, Figure 12.3) that had near universal appeal and topical interest for contemporary youth. Message strategy is treated fully in the following chapter.

Media strategy, the fourth aspect of advertising strategy, involves the selection of media categories and specific vehicles to deliver advertising messages. Pepsi's campaign, for example, placed particular emphasis on television commercials. Chapter 14 covers media strategy in depth.

A final aspect of advertising strategy, *coordination,* involves the necessary steps to ensure that all advertising efforts are properly coordinated and that advertising is integrated with the other marketing mix elements. In the case of Pepsi-Cola's advertising, this meant that point-of-purchase materials had to be tied in and coordinated with the advertising themes.

---

[18]The following discussion is based on various sources but borrows most heavily from Fred Danzig, "Pepsi-Cola Gambles on the Young," *Advertising Age,* March 5, 1984, pp. 3, 62.

[19]Ibid., p. 3.

[20]Ibid.

FIGURE 12.3   **Pepsi-Cola's 1984 Ad Campaign**

"Street" (30 and 60 seconds; Bob Giraldi, director; Michael Peters, choreographer): As 12-year-old Alfonso Ribeiro, of Broadway's "The Tap Dance Kid," emulates Michael Jackson and dances into a city street with his friends, young Mr. Ribeiro bumps into his idol, Michael Jackson, and the other Jackson brothers. They merge their dancing into a street carnival.

"Spaceship" (30 and 60 seconds; Ridley Scott, director): A spaceship hovers over a rural gas station as a boy and dog watch in awe (the spot is a derivative of "Close Encounters"). After cans of Coca-Cola and Pepsi-Cola are drawn up into the spaceship from the station's vending machines—presumably for a taste test?—the Pepsi machine is lifted into the spaceship's hold.

"Basement Visitor" (30 and 60 seconds; Ridley Scott, director): Derivative of "E.T.," this commercial, with no music, has a mother questioning her little daughter about a nearly-empty Pepsi liter bottle she has found in the refrigerator. It turns out that the girl is harboring a visitor from outer space who is also part of the Pepsi generation, squeaky voice and all.

"Sound Truck" (30 and 60 seconds; Barry Myers, director): A van with speakers overwhelms sun worshipers at a beach with thirst-quenching sounds. Slowly they react to the sounds of a bottle being opened, Pepsi being guzzled and the vendor's "Aaah." The van's "deejay" turns to face the crowd approaching his counter. "Okay. Who's first?" he asks.

"Shark" (30 seconds; Barry Myers, director): A derivative of "Jaws," the spot shows a black "shark fin" making its way amid a beach umbrella-filled screen, headed toward a lone umbrella with the Pepsi logo. As suspense builds, viewers finally see that the fin is really the keel of a surfboard and there's a bottle of Pepsi waiting for the surfer under that Pepsi umbrella.

"Reflections" (30 seconds; Tony Scott, director): A speeding motorcyclist roars across a desolate purple, pink and golden desert road. His gleaming, chrome-fitted, mirrored machine and helmet reflect the passing landscape. A Pepsi vending machine shows up. He zooms past it, but, as the reflection lingers, goes into a fast U-turn and pulls up to that Pepsi oasis.

Strategy Implementation   Strategy implementation deals with the tactical, day-to-day activities that must be performed to carry out an advertising campaign. For example, whereas the decision to emphasize television over other media is a strategic choice, the selection of specific types of programs and times at which to air a commercial is a tactical matter, one of strategic implementation. Chapter 13 (which deals with message strategy) and Chapter 14 (which discusses media strategy) touch on implementation issues.

Control Activities   Control activity is a critical aspect of advertising management that ensures that objectives and plans are being accomplished. Control activities involve comparing actual results with intended or projected results. This often requires that baseline measures be taken before an advertising campaign begins (to determine, for example, what percentage of the target audience is aware of the brand name) and then afterwards to determine whether the objective was, in fact, achieved. Because research is fundamental to advertising control, a separate chapter (Chapter 15) is devoted exclusively to evaluating advertising effectiveness.

Setting Advertising Objectives

Advertising objectives are goals that advertising efforts attempt to achieve. The issues involved in establishing advertising objectives are complex; therefore, it will be useful first to review, from the perspective of the individual buyer or consumer, the process by which advertising influences people to undertake a course of action advocated by the advertiser.

The traditional model of how advertising and other forms of marketing communications work is known as the *hierarchy of effects*. Actually, there are a variety of hierarchy of effect models, but one of the earliest and best known is by Lavidge and Steiner.[21] Their model proposes that advertising works by moving people through a series of stages: awareness → knowledge → liking → preference → conviction → purchase. This sequence portrays the consumer as initially unaware of a particular product or brand until advertising informs him or her of its availability. Subsequent advertising exposures provide the consumer with knowledge of specific brand attributes and benefits, leading eventually to some degree of liking for the brand, perhaps preference for it, and a possible conviction that the advertised brand is the only one to purchase. The process culminates when the consumer purchases the brand that he or she perceives most favorably. Thus, advertising is presumed by the traditional hierarchy model to create a sequence of effects from *cognition* (awareness, knowledge) to *affect* (liking, preference, conviction) to *conation* (intention and purchase).

[21]Robert J. Lavidge and Gary A. Steiner, "A Model for Predictive Measurements of Advertising Effectiveness," *Journal of Marketing,* Vol. 25, October 1961, pp. 59–62.

This traditional view of advertising has been widely criticized as being too restrictive and applicable only under limited conditions, that is, in instances of high-involvement behavior in which the purchase decision is important and has significant risks associated with it. Critics of the traditional (cognitive → affective → conative) sequence have developed alternative models. Two of the more notable are Preston's "association model"[22] and Smith and Swinyard's "integrated information response model."[23] This text will discuss only the latter, because it is more straightforward and therefore more appropriate for present purposes.

see Engel text

The Integrated Information Response Model

The integrated information response model (Figure 12.4) provides for several different patterns of response to advertising.[24]

The Cognition → Affect → Commitment Sequence The pattern of cognition → affect → commitment, which is essentially the same as the traditional (Lavidge and Steiner) hierarchy of effects model, is shown in Figure 12.4 by the dashed arrow from *advertising* to *high information acceptance* and on, in turn, to *higher order beliefs, higher order affect,* and ultimately to *commitment.* This sequence represents information-processing situations in which consumers accept advertising message claims, consequently form attitudes toward the advertised brand, and become firmly committed to purchasing the advertised product. This response pattern, though a theoretical possibility, is certainly the exception rather than the rule, because advertising has *limited ability* to form higher order beliefs, that is, strongly held beliefs that an advertised brand indeed does possess some desired attribute or will provide some wanted benefit.

The Cognition → Trial → Affect → Commitment Sequence The sequence from cogniton to trial to affect and to commitment is captured in Figure 12.4 by the flow of solid arrows from *advertising* to *low information acceptance,* on through *lower order beliefs* and *lower order affect* to *trial,* and ultimately on to *commitment* as a function of *direct experience* and the *higher order beliefs* and *affect* that result therefrom. This response pattern captures the notion of *low-involvement learning,*[25] which purports that much advertising processing occurs

[22]Ivan L. Preston, "The Association Model of the Advertising Communication Process," *Journal of Advertising,* Vol. 11, No. 2, 1982, pp. 3–15; and Ivan L. Preston and Esther Thorson, "Challenges to the Use of Hierarchy Models in Predicting Advertising Effectiveness," in Donald W. Jugenheimer (ed.), *Proceedings of the 1983 Convention of the American Academy of Advertising* (Lawrence, KA: American Academy of Advertising, 1983).

[23]Robert E. Smith and William R. Swinyard, "Information Response Models: An Integrated Approach," *Journal of Marketing,* Vol. 46, Winter 1982, pp. 81–93.

[24]The following discussion follows closely the discussion in Smith and Swinyard, "Information Response Models," especially pp. 86–90.

[25] Herbert E. Krugman, "The Impact of Television Advertising: Learning without Involvement," *Public Opinion Quarterly,* Vol. 29, 1965, pp. 349–356.

FIGURE 12.4   Integrated Information Response Model

Summary Labels

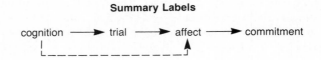

Detailed Sequence

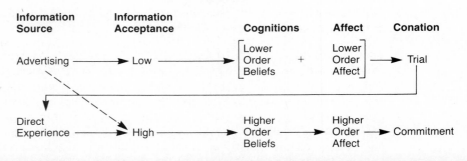

Source: Robert E. Smith and William R. Swinyard, "Information Response Models: An Integrated Approach," *Journal of Marketing,* Vol. 46, Winter 1982, p. 85.

under passive learning conditions and that affect is formed *after* purchasing and experiencing a product rather than *before* purchasing, which applies only to high-involvement learning.

The Cognition → Trial → Trial → Trial . . . Sequence   The pattern from cogniton to multiple trials is implicit in Figure 12.4 and suggests that in the case of relatively homogenous product categories there may be no such thing as affect-based brand preference either before or after purchase experience. Rather, in such instances, "The consumer may consistently switch brands, never forming sufficient differential affect for one to qualify as a preference."[26]

The alternative response patterns in the "integrated information response model" point out the need to set advertising objectives in accordance with the prevailing information response situation. For example, "influencing consumer beliefs" would represent a suitable advertising objective under high-involvement conditions (i.e., the first sequence) but would not be appropriate for the second or third sequences.

[26]Smith and Swinyard, "Information Response Models," p. 90.

Different Sets of Advertising Objectives

With the preceding introduction to how advertising works, it is now possible to begin examining the specifics of advertising objective setting. An initial consideration is, for what aspects of advertising decision making are objectives needed? The work of Rossiter and Percy aids in this discussion.[27] Rossiter and Percy have formulated a comprehensive explanation of how advertising communicates with and persuades people to action. Their formulation rests on the premise that effective advertising requires prospective buyers in the target audience to (1) be exposed, via media, to an ad or series of ads in a campaign, (2) process the elements of each ad in the manner intended by the advertiser so that the advertising results in (3) communication effects (awareness, interest, etc.), which ultimately will produce (4) purchase of the advertised brand.[28]

Four related sets of advertising objectives extend from this formulation: (1) *target audience* objectives, (2) *brand communication* objectives, (3) *ad processing* objectives, and (4) *media exposure* objectives. Specific objectives for each set of considerations are presented in Table 12.3. The various questions in Table 12.3 represent the types of decisions that advertising managers must address in order to develop intelligent advertising campaigns. These questions also provide guidelines for establishing systematic and coordinated advertising objectives.

Requirements for Setting Advertising Objectives

The purpose of advertising objectives is to direct advertising activity by identifying specific target audiences, by specifying the message arguments needed to move the audience effectively to action, and by selecting media that will reach the intended market. As one writer has said, "Advertising objectives are statements of what must be accomplished by advertising to overcome problems or realize opportunities facing the product . . . ."[29] All statements are not, however, good advertising objectives. Consider the following examples:

- *Example A:* The advertising objective for Brand A this year is to increase sales.
- *Example B:* The advertising objective for Brand B is to increase the target audience's brand awareness from 63 percent to 90 percent by July 31st.

These extreme examples differ in two important regards. First, Example B is obviously more specific. Second, whereas Example A deals with a financial objective, i.e., to increase sales, Example B involves a nonsales goal. The sections that

---

[27]John R. Rossiter and Larry Percy, "Advertising Communication Models," working paper, N.S.W. Institute of Technology, Sydney, Australia, September 22, 1983.

[28]Ibid., pp. 2–3.

[29]David W. Nylen, *Advertising: Planning, Implementation, and Control,* 2nd Ed. (Cincinnati: South-Western Publishing Co., 1980), pp. 211–212.

TABLE 12.3   **Advertising Communication Objectives**

Target Audience Objectives

1. Which households/companies/retailers are sales to come from? For example, should the target audience be trial users or brand switchers?
2. Who is the decision maker that the advertising must reach: initiators, influencers, deciders, purchasers, or users?
3. What is the personal profile of the decision maker in terms of demographics, psychographics, and other relevant characteristics?

Brand Communication Objectives

1. Should the advertising campaign be directed at reminding buyers about the *need for the product category,* selling the product category, or simply ignoring the product category and focusing on creating secondary (brand-specific) demand?
2. In terms of *brand awareness* objectives, should emphasis be placed on influencing brand recognition, brand recall, or both?
3. In terms of *brand attitude* objectives, should emphasis be placed on creating new attitudes, maintaining existing ones, or increasing present attitudes?
4. In terms of *brand purchase intentions,* should advertising efforts be "soft sell" (to deduce a subconscious decision) or "hard sell" (to induce a conscious, immediate decision)?

Ad Processing Objectives

1. What message points need to be stressed?
2. What emotion(s) should the ad attempt to elicit?
3. If a presenter is used, what characteristics should he or she possess in terms of credibility and attractiveness?

Media Objectives

1. What media are appropriate?
2. What exposure frequency is needed?
3. Which geographic markets should be emphasized?

Source: Condensed and adapted from John R. Rossiter and Larry Percy, "Advertising Communications Models," working paper, N.S.W. Institute of Technology, Sydney, Australia, September 22, 1983. For a complete checklist of advertising communication objectives, see John R. Rossiter and Larry Percy, *Advertising and Promotion Management,* New York: McGraw-Hill, in press.

follow describe why specific objectives are absolutely essential and why financial objectives are typically inappropriate.

Purpose of setting adv. objectives

Objective Specificity   Advertising objectives are useful by providing valuable *agendas for communication* among advertising and marketing decision makers and by offering *benchmarks against which to compare actual performance.* These functions are satisfied, however, only if objectives are sufficiently specific. Example B represents the desired degree of specificity and, as such, would give executives something meaningful to direct their efforts toward as well as a clear-cut benchmark for assessing whether the advertising campaign has accomplished its objectives.

Example A, by comparison, is much too general. Suppose sales have actually increased by 2 percent during the course of the ad campaign. Since the objective was to "increase sales," does this mean that the campaign was successful? If not, how much of a sales increase is necessary for the campaign to be regarded a success?

The preceding questions serve to indicate that advertising objectives must satisfy various requirements:

1. Objectives should be stated in *precise terms.* That is, objectives should minimally specify the target audience, indicate the communication objective, and indicate the relevant time frame in which to achieve the objective. Pepsi-Cola's "new generation" campaign discussed earlier in the chapter may be stated as follows: Within six months following the start of the new ad campaign, the objectives are that (1) at least 95 percent of all U.S. youth between the ages of 9 and 14 have been exposed to at least one new ad and can recall one or more specific advertising episodes; (2) at least 20 percent of loyal Coca-Cola consumers in the 13 to 19 age category have switched to Pepsi-Cola; and (3) at least 65 percent of 9– to 14-year-olds answer, "Pepsi-Cola," in response to the postcampaign question: "What is the new generation's soft drink?"

2. Objectives should be *measurable.* This requirement implies that ad objectives should be stated in quantitative terms, such as are the hypothetical objectives in number 1 for Pepsi-Cola.

3. Objectives should be *realistic.* Unrealistic objectives are as useless as having no objectives at all. An unrealistic objective is one that cannot be accomplished in the time allotted to the proposed advertising investment. For example, a brand that has achieved only 15 percent consumer awareness during its first two years on the market could not realistically expect that meager advertising expenditures would increase the awareness level to, say, 65 percent.

4. Objectives should be *compatible* with other objectives. Compatibility of objectives is a requirement of internal consistency. It would seem incompatible, for example, for a manufacturer of packaged goods to proclaim a 25 percent reduction in sales force size as one marketing communication objective while simultaneously stating that advertising's objective is to increase the number of shelf facings by 20 percent. These objectives are incompatible; without adequate sales force effort, it is doubtful that the retail trade will devote more shelf space to a particular brand.

5. Objectives should be *clear and in writing.* For objectives to accomplish their purposes of fostering communication and enabling evaluation, they must be stated clearly and be in writing so that they can be disseminated among their users and among those who will be held responsible for seeing that the objectives are accomplished.

Problems with Financial Advertising Objectives   A final objective-setting issue involves the matter of financial versus nonfinancial advertising objectives. Financial objectives involve sales or profits, but nonfinancial objectives deal with buyer responses that lead to sales and profits. Buyer responses, which are also called *communication goals,* include the brand communication objectives in Table 12.3—brand awareness, brand attitude, and brand purchase intentions.

Sales and profits are typically unsuitable goals for advertising efforts because these financial outcomes are the consequence of a host of factors in addition to advertising. A brand's sales and profits in a given period result from the prevailing economic climate, competitive activity, and all marketing mix variables—price level, product quality, distribution efficiencies, personal selling activity, and so forth. Because advertising is just one determinant of sales and profit performance, it is virtually impossible to determine precisely what role advertising has had in influencing sales in a given period. The following analogy makes the point vividly.

> *Some argue that evaluating advertising only by its impact on sales is like attributing all the success (or failure) of a football team to the quarterback. The fact is that many other elements can affect the team's record—other players, the competition, and the bounce of the ball. The implication is that the effect of the quarterback's performance should be measured by the things he alone can influence, such as how he throws the ball, how he calls the plays, and how he hands off. If, in a real-world situation, all factors remained constant except for advertising (for example, if competitive activity were static), then it would be feasible to rely exclusively on sales to measure advertising effectiveness. Since such a situation is, in reality, infeasible, we must start dealing with response variables that are associated more directly with the advertising stimulus.*[30]

A second reason sales response should not represent the objective for advertising effort is that the effect of advertising on sales is typically delayed or *lagged*. That is to say, advertising during any given period influences sales at later periods. Automobile advertising, for example, may have an immediate impact on consumers' attitudes toward the advertised models but not influence purchases until a later date, when the same consumers are actively in the market for a new car. Thus, advertising may have a decided impact upon consumers' brand awareness, product knowledge, attitudes, and ultimately purchase behavior, but this influence may not be evident during the period when advertising's effect is measured.

Financial objectives (sales and profits) are therefore not suitable measures of advertising effectiveness in most situations. One exception to this principle, however, is in marketing circumstances in which sales result immediately from advertising efforts and in which the time interval between advertising activity and sales is short enough to preclude interference from factors other than advertising.

Direct marketing and retail advertising are two marketing situations that satisfy the exceptional condition. In these instances, it is possible to pinpoint the actual impact advertising has had on sales volume. Take, for example, a local department store. The store knows precisely how much of a particular item, say Mikasa dinnerware, it sells each week. Therefore, when the store runs a special promotion

[30]Aaker and Myers, *Advertising Management*, pp. 93—94.

on Mikasa for a period of three days, any increase in sales volume (over baseline levels) is attributable almost exclusively to advertising.

Budgeting for Advertising

The advertising budgeting decision is, in many respects, the most important advertising decision. If too little is spent on advertising, sales volume will not be as high as it could be, and profits will be lost. If too much is spent, expenses will be higher than they need to be, and profits will be reduced.

The budgeting decision is also one of the most difficult advertising decisions to make. The difficulty in establishing budget size is due to the inability to determine precisely how effective advertising has been or will be in the future. Intelligent and prudent financial policy demands that management be able to identify the profits that alternative investment opportunities will earn and to invest only in those options which satisfy minimal return standards. But, this is the crux of the problem of advertising budgeting; it is hard to know with certainty the amount of sales (and thus profits) that advertising will generate. Because the *sales response function* to advertising is influenced by a multitude of factors (quality of advertising execution, the intensity of competitive advertising efforts, customer taste, and other considerations), it becomes nearly impossible to predict accurately how effective advertising will be.

Advertising Budgeting in Theory

Advertising budgeting is, in theory, a simple process, provided one accepts the premise that the best (optimal) level of any investment is the level that maximizes profits. This assumption leads to a simple rule for establishing advertising budgets: profit maximization occurs at the point at which *marginal revenue is equal to marginal cost.* From basic economics courses, the reader will recall that marginal revenue (marginal cost) is the change in total revenue (total cost) that results from producing/selling an additional item. The "profit maximization rule" is then a matter of simple economic logic: Profit maximization can occur only at the point where $MR = MC$. At any point below this (i.e., where $MR > MC$) profits are not maximized because at a higher level of output more profit can be earned. Similarly, at any point above this (i.e., where $MC > MR$) there is a marginal loss.

What this means in practical terms is that advertisers should continue to invest in advertising as long as the marginal revenue from that investment exceeds the marginal cost. For example, perhaps a company is currently spending $1 million on advertising and is considering the investment of another $200,000. Should the investment be made? The answer is simple: only if the additional advertising generates more than $200,000 additional revenue. Now say that the same company is contemplating an additional advertising expenditure of $300,000. Again, the company should go ahead with the advertising if it can be assured that the investment will yield more than $300,000 in additional revenue.

It is evident from this simple exercise that advertising budget setting is, in theory at least, a matter of answering a series of "if-then" questions—*if* $X are invested in advertising, *then* what amount of revenue will be generated? However, budgets are set a priori (before the fact). This requires that the "if-then" questions already have answers. In order to employ the profit maximization rule for budget setting, the advertising decision maker must know the advertising sales response function for every brand for which a budgeting decision will be made. Because such knowledge is rarely available, theoretical (profit maximization) budget setting is an ideal that is generally nonoperational in the real world of advertising decision making.

Practical Advertising Budgeting

Advertising decision makers must consider several different factors when establishing advertising budgets. The most important consideration should be the *objectives* that advertising is designed to accomplish. That is, the level of the budget should follow from the specific objectives established for advertising; more ambitious objectives require larger advertising budgets. If advertising is intended to increase a brand's market share, then a larger budget is needed than would be required if the task were simply to maintain consumer awareness of the brand name.

Competitive advertising activity is another important consideration in setting ad budgets. In competitive growth markets, this means that more must be invested in advertising in order to increase or at least maintain market position. A case in point was IBM's entry into the personal computer market in the early 1980s. IBM's heavy expenditures on the now famous "Charlie Chaplin" campaign forced competitors to increase their advertising expenditures in order to preserve their eroding market shares.

A third major consideration is the *amount of funds available.* In the final analysis, advertising budget setting is determined in large part by decision makers' perceptions of how much they can afford to spend on advertising. Because advertising budgets are often viewed with suspicion by top management and considered overinflated,[31] advertising managers face the challenge of convincing top management that proposed budgets are indeed affordable. Because this is no easy task, especially when hard data on advertising effectiveness is itself unavailable, advertising budget setters have tended to use simple decision rules (heuristics) for making budgeting decisions.

Budgeting Practices

In view of the inability to predict sales response to advertising investment accurately, management "must ordinarily depend on some blend of judgment, experience with analogous situations, and simple rules-of-thumb guidance in setting

---

[31]Nylen, *Advertising,* p. 233.

budgets."[32] The two most pervasive heuristics used by both industrial advertisers[33] and consumer goods advertisers[34] are the *percentage of sales* and the *objective and task* methods.

Percentage of Sales Budgeting   As the name suggests, the percentage of sales heuristic operates by setting the budget at a fixed percentage of sales. The sales base is either *past sales* or *anticipated sales.* A recent survey of the top 100 consumer goods advertisers in the United States found that 53 percent employ the "percent anticipated sales" method and 20 percent the "percent past sales" method.[35]

The actual percentage of sales devoted to advertising is highly variable. The third column in Table 12.4 shows the percentage of U.S. sales spent on advertising in 1983 by the top 100 consumer goods advertisers. Food advertisers, for example, allocated anywhere from 2.4 percent of sales (Carnation Co.) to 11.3 percent (Kellogg Co.). It is particularly interesting to compare differences in advertising expenditures from one product category to another. Toiletries and cosmetic companies spend an especially large percentage of sales on advertising (notice Noxell Corp.'s 22.8% of sales expenditure), but automobile companies invest a relatively small proportion (both GM and Ford spend less than 2% of sales).

The percentage of sales method is frequently criticized as being illogical. The argument often given for this criticism is that sales are actually a function of advertising, but this budgeting method reverses the causal order by setting advertising as a function of sales. That is, if sales are anticipated to increase, then advertising will also increase; if sales are expected to decline, then advertising will be reduced. However, if sales are expected to decline, a company may be wise to increase advertising to prevent further sales erosion. Thus, the problem with the percentage of sales heuristic is that, if used blindly, it substitutes a simple rule of thumb for sound business judgment.

The Objective and Task Method   The setting of ad budgets by the objective and task method focuses on communication goals, rather than sales effects. Applying the method involves the following steps:[36]

1.   Establish specific *marketing objectives* that need to be accomplished, such as sales volume, market share, and profit contribution.

2.   Assess the *communication functions* that must be performed to accomplish the overall marketing objectives.

---

[32]Gary L. Lilien, Alvin J. Silk, Jean-Marie Choffray, and Murlidhar Rao, "Industrial Advertising Effects and Budgeting Practices," *Journal of Marketing,* Vol. 40, January 1976, p. 21.

[33]Ibid.

[34]Kent M. Lancaster and Judith A. Stern, "Computer-based Advertising Budgeting Practices of Leading U.S. Consumer Advertisers," *Journal of Advertising,* Vol. 12, No. 4, 1983, p. 6.

[35]Ibid.

[36]These are adapted from Lilien et al., "Industrial Advertising and Budgeting," p. 23.

TABLE 12.4   Advertising Expenditures as a Percentage of U.S. Sales in 1983 ($000)

Rank/Company	U.S. Advertising Expenditures	U.S. Sales	Adv. as % of U.S. Sales	Worldwide Sales	Worldwide Earnings (loss)
Food					
3 Beatrice Cos.	$602,775.4	$ N/A	N/A	$13,442,885.0	$550,000.0
10 General Foods Corp.	386,134.2	6,407,500.0	6.0	8,599,800.0	317,100.0
11 Nabisco Brands	367,530.4	3,655,600.0	10.1	5,985,200.0	322,600.0
16 McDonald's Corp.	311,378.0	7,069,000.0	4.4	8,687,000.0	342,640.0
21 Ralston Purina Co.	285,667.4	3,848,600.0	7.4	4,900,000.0	256,000.0
23 General Mills	268,690.2	5,100,000.0	5.3	5,600,800.0	233,400.0
30 Dart & Kraft	210,279.4	6,905,300.0	3.0	9,714,000.0	435,100.0
31 H. J. Heinz Co.	202,400.0	2,555,368.0	7.9	3,950,000.0	237,500.0
33 Consolidated Foods Corp.	195,858.0	5,195,752.0	3.0	7,000,310.0	188,441.0
34 Pillsbury Co.	190,944.3	4,160,000.0	4.6	4,172,000.0	169,800.0
37 Kellogg Co.	176,306.9	1,560,000.0	11.3	2,381,100.0	242,000.0
42 Quaker Oats Co.	148,441.7	1,623,500.0	9.1	3,340,000.0	138,700.0
52 Campbell Soup Co.	126,000.0	2,760,000.0	4.6	3,292,433.0	250,000.0
61 Nestle Enterprises	114,957.0	2,508,000.0	4.6	13,400,000.0	N/A
64 IC Industries	112,100.0	3,375,000.0	3.3	3,730,000.0	92,700.0
71 CPC International	96,627.3	1,525,900.0	6.3	4,010,900.0	136,200.0
90 Wendy's International	64,445.0	1,908,000.0	3.4	1,922,913.0	55,220.0
99 Carnation Co.	54,284.6	2,221,081.5	2.4	3,365,275.0	194,759.0
Automotive					
4 General Motors Corp.	595,129.5	66,160,000.0	0.9	74,581,600.0	3,730,200.0
7 Ford Motor Co.	479,060.0	33,000,000.0	1.5	44,454,600.0	1,866,900.0
27 Chrysler Corp.	230,020.1	11,642,100.0	2.0	13,240,000.0	700,900.0
54 Nissan Motor Corp. in U.S.A.	122,848.0	14,417,183.0	0.9	14,417,183.0	293,883.0
60 American Honda Motor Co.	115,182.3	10,165,969.0	1.1	10,165,969.0	409,301.0
62 Toyota Motor Sales U.S.A.	113,649.0	5,300,000.0	2.1	20,386,099.0	839,050.0
63 Volkswagen of America	112,500.0	1,576,611.8**	7.8	16,027,530.6	(23,493.0)
69 American Motors Corp.	100,800.7	3,271,720.0	3.1	3,271,720.0	(146,730.0)
81 Mazda Motors of America	74,500.0	5,846,280.0	1.3	5,846,280.0	109,890.0
96 Goodyear Tire & Rubber Co.	57,831.7	6,794,200.0	0.9	9,735,800.0	305,500.0
Pharmaceuticals					
13 Warner-Lambert Co.	343,553.5	1,822,000.0	18.9	3,108,325.0	200,496.0
14 American Home Products Corp.	333,485.0	3,482,300.0	9.6	4,856,501.0	627,233.0
17 Johnson & Johnson	295,328.8	3,600,000.0	8.2	3,610,000.0	281.800.0
38 Sterling Drug	171,828.1	703,433.0	24.4	1,901,171.0	136,844.0
41 Richardson-Vicks	150,813.9	667,134.0	22.6	1,280,500.0	71,900.0
59 Schering-Plough Corp.	117,914.2	985,200.0	12.0	1,808,500.0	190,100.0
72 Miles Laboratories	89,063.8	784,000.0	11.4	1,115,400.0	35,500.0
83 Pfizer Inc.	72,084.3	1,950,000.0	3.7	3,750,000.0	447,100.0
Airlines					
68 Trans World Corp.	101,503.3	3,221,788.0	3.2	5,240,000.0	(7,700.0)
76 AMR Corp.	80,000.0	4,763,307.0	1.7	4,763,307.0	227,867.0
78 UAL Inc.	77,200.0	6,021,840.0	1.3	6,021,840.0	142,045.0
86 Eastern Air Lines	70,000.0	3,500,000.0	2.0	3,942,134.0	(183,667.0)
92 Delta Air Lines	63,944.3	3,616,413.0	1.8	3,616,413.0	(86,700.0)
Communications and Entertainment					
25 Warner Communications	251,049.6	2,715,940.0	9.2	3,425,272.0	(417,803.0)
29 RCA Corp.	212,300.0	8,010,000.0	2.7	8,977,300.0	240,800.0
39 CBS Inc.	167,711.0	3,900,000.0	4.3	4,540,184.0	187,198.0
44 Gulf & Western Industries	145,500.0	3,443,000.0	4.2	3,992,601.0	263,320.0*
56 Time Inc.	119,785.0	2,529,000.0	4.7	2,717,000.0	143,000.0
80 MCA Inc.	74,543.6	1,254,583.0	5.9	1,584,539.0	147,160.0
100 American Broadcasting Cos.	49,167.5	2,948,849.0	1.7	2,948,849.0	159,834.0
Tobacco					
5 R. J. Reynolds Industries	593,350.3	10,769,000.0	5.5	13,533,000.0	835,000.0
6 Philip Morris Inc.	527,481.8	9,303,100.0	5.7	12,975,900.0	903,500.0
43 Batus Inc.	146,076.9	6,064,000.0	2.4	6,064,000.0	259,000.0
48 Loews Corp.	135,115.1	5,260,075.0	2.6	5,260,075.0	341,242.0
79 American Brands	75,590.1	3,048,100.0	2.5	7,093,392.0	390,298.0
97 GrandMet U.S.A.	55,566.2	1,340,000.0	4.1	1,340,000.0	84,428.0

Rank/Company	U.S. Advertising Expenditures	U.S. Sales	Adv. as % of U.S. Sales	Worldwide Sales	Worldwide Earnings (loss)
Toiletries and Cosmetics					
26 Bristol-Myers Co.	235,000.0	2,889,300.0	8.1	3,917,000.0	408,000.0
35 Gillette Co.	185,604.4	1,020,000.0	18.2	2,183,297.0	145,876.0
46 Chesebrough-Pond's	141,324.5	1,310,242.0	10.8	1,685,417.0	127,878.0
50 Beecham Group p.l.c.	134,126.8	2,800,000.0	4.8	2,800,000.0	385,000.0
53 Revlon Inc.	123,968.9	1,660,930.0	7.5	2,378,867.0	111,203.0
87 Cosmair Inc.	69,955.0	480,000.0	14.6	600,000.0	N/A
94 Noxell Corp.	58,264.4	255,414.0	22.8	304,300.0	23,205.0
Wine, Beer, and Liquor					
20 Anheuser-Busch Cos.	290,616.4	6,658,500.0	4.4	6,658,500.0	348,000.0
57 Jos. E. Seagram & Sons	119,604.4	1,639,000.0	7.3	2,647,552.0	117,500.0
82 Stroh Brewery Co.	73,532.4	1,561,000.0	4.7	1,646,000.0	N/A
84 Brown-Forman Distillers	70,500.0	885,089.0	8.0	1,146,343.0	73,554.0
93 Adolph Coors Co.	63,621.3	1,110,406.0	5.7	1,110,406.0	89,261.0
Soaps and Cleaners					
1 Procter & Gamble Co.	773,618.3	9,554,000.0	8.1	12,946,000.0	890,000.0
15 Unilever U.S.	324,865.8	2,808,000.0	12.2	3,328,000.0	125,800.0
24 Colgate-Palmolive Co.	268,000.0	2,200,000.0	12.2	4,865,000.0	381,000.0
74 S.C. Johnson & Son	86,970.3	880,000.0	9.9	2,000,000.0	N/A
88 Clorox Co.	69,429.0	824,419.0	8.4	974,566.0	79,709.0
Chemicals and Gasoline					
18 Mobil Corp.	294,932.5	23,900,000.0	1.2	58,998,000.0	1,503,000.0
45 American Cyanamid Co.	142,400.0	2,388,662.0	6.0	3,535,500.0	166,400.0
67 Du Pont	102,637.0	25,832,000.0	0.4	35,378,000.0	1,127,000.0
73 Union Carbide Corp.	88,000.0	6,189,000.0	1.4	9,001,000.0	79,000.0
Gum and Candy					
55 Mars Inc.	120,350.5	N/A	N/A	2,083,000.0	N/A
89 Hershey Foods Corp.	68,257.4	1,700,000.0	4.0	1,700,000.0	100,160.0
91 Wm. Wrigley Jr. Co.	63,948.2	406,472.0	15.7	581,688.0	39,164.0
Retail Chains					
2 Sears, Roebuck & Co.	732,500.0	32,637,000.0	2.2	35,883,000.0	1,342,000.0
9 K mart Corp.	400,000.0	17,785,700.0	2.2	18,600,000.0	492,300.0
19 J.C. Penney Co.	292,451.0	11,565,000.0	2.5	12,078,000.0	467,000.0
Soft Drinks					
12 PepsiCo Inc.	356,400.0	6,714,000.0	5.3	7,895,936.0	284,111.0
22 Coca-Cola Co.	282,150.0	4,071,400.0	6.9	6,829,000.0	558,800.0
Electronics and Office Equipment					
40 Tandy Corp.	156,728.0	2,354,000.0	6.7	2,780,000.0	281,900.0
47 Eastman Kodak Co.	141,318.9	6,435,000.0	2.2	10,170,000.0	565,000.0
51 Texas Instruments	129,042.0	3,295,000.0	3.9	4,579,800.0	(145,400.0)
58 International Business Machines Corp.	119,222.5	23,100,000.0	0.5	40,180,000.0	5,485,000.0
65 Xerox Corp.	110,101.8	5,300,000.0	2.1	8,463,500.0	466,400.0
70 Sony Corp. of America	97,283.2	1,356,047.0	7.2	4,747,953.0	127,312.0
95 Canon U.S.A.	58,032.9	860,174.3	6.7	966,448.0	N/A
98 Coleco Industries	55,216.4	526,051.0	10.5	596,498.0	(7,433.0)
Telephone Equipment					
8 American Telephone & Telegraph	463,095.5	67,648,000.0	0.7	69,848,000.0	248,700.0
49 ITT Corp.	134,229.0	12,430,000.0	1.1	20,249,842.0	674,510.0
85 GTE Corp.	70,179.9	10,900,000.0	0.6	12,943,918.0	995,604.0
Miscellaneous					
28 U.S. Government	228,857.2	N/A	N/A	N/A	N/A
32 General Electric Co.	196,506.6	17,649,000.0	1.1	26,797,000.0	2,024,000.0
36 Mattel Inc.	179,934.8	840,000.0	21.4	989,495.0	(94,100.0)***
66 American Express Co.	107,571.0	7,352,000.0	1.5	9,770,000.0	515,000.0
75 Greyhound Corp.	83,564.0	2,625,031.0	3.2	2,625,000.0	105,500.0
77 Kimberly-Clark Co.	77,460.0	2,325,800.0	3.3	3,274,300.0	189,000.0

Source: AA's estimates and company sources; *Advertising Age,* September 14, 1984, p. 8. Copyright 1984 Crain Communications, Inc.
*Earnings from continuous operations.
**Includes Latin America.   ***Net loss from continuous operations.

3.   Determine *advertising's role* in the total communication mix in performing these functions.
4.   Establish specific *advertising goals* in terms of the levels of measurable communication response required to achieve marketing objectives.
5.   Establish the *budget* based on estimates of expenditures required to accomplish the advertising goals.

The objective and task method is generally regarded as the most sensible and defendable advertising budgeting method. In using this method, advertising decision makers are forced to clearly specify the role they expect of advertising and then set budgets accordingly. The inherent advantages of the objective and task method are recognized by advertising practitioners. Indeed, fully 80 percent of the respondents to the previously mentioned top 100 advertisers survey indicated that their companies use the objective and task method.[37] This percentage represents a dramatic increase in comparison with the 12 percent of respondents in a 1974 survey who indicated using the objective and task method.[38]

Other Budgeting Heuristics   The *match competitors* (also known as competitive parity) and *affordability* methods are additional heuristics used by industrial and consumer goods advertisers. These techniques, which operate as their names suggest, are used most frequently by smaller firms, who tend to follow industry leaders. However, affordability and competitive considerations influence the budgeting decisions of all companies. In reality, most advertising budget setters combine a variety of methods rather than depend exclusively on one heuristic. For example, an advertiser may have a fixed percentage of sales figure in mind when starting the budgeting process but subsequently adjust this figure in light of anticipated competitive acitivity, funds availability, and other considerations.

Summary

This chapter offers an introduction to advertising and an overview of the advertising management process. Advertising is shown to perform five major functions: informing, persuading, reminding, adding value, and assisting other company efforts. Advertising's economic role is examined by comparing two schools of thought—Advertising = Market Power versus Advertising = Information. The first perspective views advertising negatively and assumes that advertising has the power to influence brand loyalty, which, in turn, is assumed to lead to negative consequences such as price insensitivity, high industry concentration levels, barriers to entry, price increases, and excessive profits. An alternative perspective,

---

[37]Lancaster and Stern, "Computer-based Advertising."

[38]Andre J. San Augustine and William F. Foley, "How Large Advertisers Set Budgets," *Journal of Advertising Research,* Vol. 15, October 1975, p. 13.

Advertising = Information, presents a positive picture by portraying advertising as a useful purveyor of information, a role that allows consumers to compare competitive offerings, resulting in increased competitive rivalry, reduced prices, and more product innovativeness. Both schools of thought present extreme views on advertising's economic impact. Neither view is sufficient by itself because the actual role of advertising varies greatly from industry to industry.

An overview of the advertising management process is given, and two aspects, objective setting and budgeting, are described in detail. As is shown, objective setting depends on the specific response pattern to advertising. The "information response model" is presented, and three different response patterns are described. The need for specificity, measurability, and clarity of written objectives are discussed as the major requirements for developing effective advertising objectives. A final section describes the problems associated with using financial criteria (sales and profits) as advertising objectives.

The chapter concludes with an explanation of the advertising budgeting process. The budgeting decision is one of the most important advertising decisions and also one of the most difficult. The complication arises with the difficulty of determining the sales function response to advertising. In theory, budget setting is a simple matter, but the theoretical requirements are generally unattainable in practice. For this reason, advertising practitioners use various rules of thumb (heuristics) to assist them in arriving at satisfactory, if not optimal, budgeting decisions. Percentage of sales budgeting and objective and task methods are the dominant budgeting heuristics.

Discussion Questions

1. Of the five advertising functions described in the chapter, which is the most important?

2. Explain the differences between the Advertising = Market Power and Advertising = Information views on advertising's economic role.

3. Advertising strategy should flow from corporate and marketing strategy. Explain.

4. Let us assume that the lawn fertilizer industry consists of five manufacturers, all producing virtually identical products. One firm is, however, far superior to the others in advertising success. This firm has achieved a 45 percent market share and charges prices about 15 percent higher than its competitors. Explain this situation in terms of the Advertising = Market Power versus Advertising = Information views on advertising's economic role.

5. A manufacturer of office furniture has established the following advertising objective for next year: "The objective for next year's advertising is to increase sales by 20 percent." Evaluate this objective. Provide a better objective.

6. What reasons can you give for certain industries (e.g., food and pharmaceuticals) investing considerably larger proportions of their sales in advertising than other industries, such as automobiles? (Refer to Table 12.4.)

7. Why is it so difficult to measure precisely the specific impact that advertising has on sales and profits?

8. Some critics contend that the use of the percentage of sales budgeting technique is illogical. Explain.

9. Would it be possible for an advertising budget setter to use two or more budgeting heuristics in conjunction with one another? Describe how this could be done.

Exercises

1. Advertising is often accused of various "sins." The social criticisms of advertising that were mentioned in the text include claims that advertising is deceptive, manipulative, and offensive and that it plays upon people's insecurities and fears. Try to find evidence from print advertisements that support any of these claims. Point out specifically how each ad you have clipped is subject to criticism.

2. Interview three or four local businesses and identify their advertising objectives. Investigate whether they set formal ad objectives and, if not, whether they have some rather clear-cut, though implicit, objectives in mind.

3. While interviewing the same businesses from question 2, also investigate their advertising budgeting practices. Determine whether they establish formal ad budgets, and identify the specific budgeting methods used.

Advertising Messages and Creative Strategy

What do people think about advertisements? What makes a good advertising message? How effective are humor, sex, and subliminal cues in advertising? What is the process that leads to the creation of advertising messages? What are the different types of creative strategies and when and why are they used?

The preceding questions will be answered in this chapter. An earlier chapter (Chapter 5) introduced the subject of messages, but this was from the general perspective of all forms of marketing communications. The present chapter examines only those issues which involve advertising directly. First, the issue of advertising's image will be examined. Discussion turns next to advertising effectiveness. Then the underlying determinants of advertising messages, the advertisement development process (i.e., creative platform), creative strategies, and various specific advertising issues (humor and sex in advertising, corporate issue advertising, etc.) will be discussed.

The Image of Advertising

Most people have strong opinions about advertising. Some consider advertising to be informative and even enjoyable; others regard it as boring, misleading, and sometimes inane. Because feelings toward advertising differ so greatly, it would be unwise to draw general conclusions on the basis of one individual's experiences, impressions, and idiosyncracies. It would instead be preferable to know what others think about advertising. Two recent studies are insightful.

Selection Research Inc. (SRI) performs periodic image studies by interviewing a probability sample of 1,250 respondents from throughout the continental United States. SRI's study findings indicate, perhaps somewhat surprisingly, that advertising's image is generally rather favorable. In one SRI study, 88 percent of all respondents felt advertising was excellent, good, or fair in overall quality, while only 9 percent thought it was poor.[1] Fifty-nine percent said they enjoy the advertising they read, see, and hear and generally feel good about it. Nearly one-half of these respondents also thought that advertising was more creative than it had been the previous year. On the negative side, 44 percent of the respondents either disagreed or strongly disagreed in response to the statement, "Advertising is generally honest and trustworthy."

SRI asked consumers in a second study to rate the *believability* of three types of specific product claims: product tests using consumers (i.e., sample demonstrations), statistical claims (e.g., "three out of four doctors recommend"), and qualitative claims (e.g., "stronger," "more effective," "new and improved").[2] Ratings, which were based on five-point believability scales (5 = totally believable, 3 = neutral, 1 = totally unbelievable), fell toward the "unbelievable" end of the scales for all three types of claims, with mean scores of 2.49, 2.39, and 2.32 for the sample demonstrations, statistical claims, and qualitative claims, respectively. These results show that consumers are often skeptical of certain advertising claims.

In sum, although many people disbelieve certain types of advertising claims, a general conclusion from the two SRI studies is that advertising is held in favorable light by the majority of consumers. Of course, casual observation reveals that advertising messages are highly variable in quality. Some ads are incredibly trivial and stupid; others are ingeniously delightful and entertaining.

What is it that makes a good advertising message? What are the secrets to advertising effectiveness?

Advertising Effectiveness

Consider the following situation. Company X markets a product that has nearly universal recognition among consumers. Nearly all grocery stores stock it, and there are virtually no competitive brands or products. The product's sales activity, however, is stagnant with no prospects for growth. This is not a hypothetical description. It actually characterizes the situation that faced Arm & Hammer baking soda until around 1970. Arm & Hammer was a "sleepy, one-dimensional brand—albeit a staple on grocers' shelves—with an advertising budget of less than $500,000 a year, mostly in print."[3] Then Church & Dwight, the makers of Arm &

---

[1] Nancy Millman, "Consumers Rate Advertising High," *Advertising Age,* October 24, 1983, pp. 1, 18.

[2] Nancy Millman, "Product Claims Not Believable," *Advertising Age,* March 5, 1984, pp. 1, 32.

[3] Jack J. Honomichl, "The Ongoing Saga of 'Mother Baking Soda,'" *Advertising Age,* September 20, 1982, pp. M-2, M-3, M-22.

Hammer, made a dramatic move. They increased the advertising budget substantially and began advertising an extended use for baking soda, namely, as a refrigerator freshener/deodorant. At the outset of the ad campaign only 1 percent of U.S. households had ever used baking soda for this purpose, but within one year the number had increased to 57 percent and eventually reached 90 percent. In a period of three years, Arm & Hammer's baking soda sales increased by 72 percent, most of this increase due to the advertising campaign.[4]

Qualities of an Effective Ad

The Arm & Hammer campaign is surely an exceptional illustration of successful advertising. In general, there seem to be three factors underlying successful advertisements: newsworthiness, rational stimulus, and emphasis.[5] A good ad possesses at least one of these characteristics, although few ads boast all of them.[6]

Newsworthiness is the simplest way to create effective advertising. An advertisement that informs consumers about a valuable product feature or benefit is newsworthy and thus stands a good chance for success. This was the secret to Arm & Hammer's success. Consumers were provided with a convenient solution to the unpleasant task of cleaning their refrigerators. It is hard for advertising to fail when it has something important to say.

Advertisements that provoke consumers to evaluate, judge, and reach a purchase decision are said to possess *rational stimulus.* When involved in an important purchase decision (such as is the case with expensive and risky purchases), consumers are most likely to pay close attention to advertisements and to devote the necessary mental energy to process message arguments. Advertising under such circumstances is effective to the extent that it provides the type of product information (rational stimulus) that consumers desire.

The most difficult advertising situation occurs when consumers are not highly involved, because the purchase has relatively little importance and alternative brands are very similar to one another. In this situation, *emphasis* is critical to advertising success. "The advertiser in such cases is more likely to emphasize a single theme or one aspect of the product. Also, he repeats frequently to gain attention and make his message familiar to the public. . . . In short, advertising by emphasis aims for small, delayed effects, points that stick in the mind long enough to tip the scales in favor of Brand A over Brand B."[7]

---

[4]Ibid., p. M-2.

[5]Herbert E. Krugman, "What Makes Advertising Effective?" *Harvard Business Review,* March-April 1975, pp. 96–103. Krugman used the term *information* rather than *newsworthiness,* but the latter, in the authors' opinion, is a more descriptive term.

[6]Ibid., p. 97.

[7]Ibid.

Making an Impression

Effective advertising must somehow make a relatively lasting impact on consumers, which means getting past the clutter from other advertisements, activating attention, and giving consumers something to remember about the advertised product. Advertising must, in other words, make an *impression.* Research indicates that five major types of advertising impressions occur and that there exists a structured, well-defined hierarchy of impressions.[8]

1. *Brand name* is the most likely aspect of a commercial that viewers retain in memory. Consumers often remember what brands are advertised but little else.

2. The second most typical impression consists of *generics,* which represent major selling claims that are associated with the advertised brand (e.g., 7-UP is caffeine-free or Federal Express delivers overnight) or outstanding characteristics of an advertising campaign (e.g., Levi's commercials are psychedelic, Oscar Mayer has cute kids).[9]

    [handwritten: Nike — almost no copy or words / black & white — GUESS]

3. *Attitudinal response* is next in the impression hierarchy. A commercial has an attitudinal response when viewers retain an emotional or affective reaction. Specific types of attitudinal responses include impressions, positive and negative, that a commercial is funny, uplifting, enjoyable, disgusting, boring, silly, and so forth.

4. Retention of *commercial specifics* is the fourth most frequent form of impression. Commercial specifics involve elements in the execution of the advertisement such as the spokesperson (e.g., John Houseman for Smith Barney), the music (e.g., the music accompanying the "What the big boys eat" jingle for Wheaties cereal), the overall situation (e.g., an emotional ad for Hallmark greeting cards), and characters (e.g., Rodney Dangerfield, Bubba Smith, John Madden, and other personalities in the Miller Lite commercials; "Alex," the dog, in Stroh beer commercials; "Charlie Chaplin" in IBM's personal computer commercials).

5. The last thing that viewers retain is the *specific sales message.* Repeated exposures and persistence during the course of an advertising campaign can, however, enable a sales message to be retained as a "generic" element.[10] For example, Orson Welles, in his long-standing capacity as spokesman for Paul Masson wines, was probably the most outstanding impression initially, but over time, the sales message ("Paul Masson will not be sold before its time") probably became as well remembered as the commercial's inimitable spokesperson.

---

[8]Dave Vadehra, "Making a Lasting Impression: What Viewers Remember Leads to 'Outstanding' Commercials," *Advertising Age,* April 25, 1983, pp. M-4–M-38.

[9]Examples are those provided by Video Storyboard Tests. Vadehra, "Making a Lasting Impression," p. M4.

[10]Ibid., p. M-4.

Examples of Outstanding Commercials

Research by Video Storyboard Tests provides evidence of what consumers consider outstanding in television commercials. Over 22,000 interviews were conducted nationwide in 1982. Respondents were asked "to name the most outstanding TV commercial they have seen in the past four weeks. They are further asked to list the reasons that make their chosen commercial 'outstanding.' The word 'outstanding' is intentionally ambiguous, and its meaning is left to individual interpretation."[11] The ten outstanding television campaigns of 1982 were the following campaigns:

1. **Miller Lite.** This is the continuing "Everything you always wanted in a beer and less" campaign using Rodney Dangerfield, Mickey Spillane, and the cast of athletic personalities.

2. **Coca-Cola.** The "Coke is it" campaign achieved second place with its youthful characters, good jingles, good dancers, etc.

3. **Federal Express.** The "fast talking" spokesman routine along with a variety of other commercials impressed consumers and enabled Federal Express to promote successfully its claim of overnight service.

4. **McDonald's.** This fast-food marketer's advertising success continued with the "You deserve a break today" campaign.

5. **Pepsi.** Pepsi's "Now you see it. . . now you don't" campaign was memorable for its use of a catchy jingle and physically attractive product users.

6. **Burger King.** The "Aren't you hungry" campaign attracted consumers' attention by showing attractive food close-ups to support the campaign theme.

7. **Budweiser Light.** A lone Clydesdale galloping on sand (somewhat reminiscent of a scene from the movie *Chariots of Fire*) was used to convey aesthetically and effectively Budweiser's "Bring out your best" theme.

8. **Dr Pepper.** Dr Pepper's 1982 campaign contained three commercials targeted to 25- to 49-year-old women to present its "Ooh what a surprise" taste message and appearance benefit.[12]

9. **Atari Videogames.** Atari used the services of various well-known celebrities (Billy Martin, "Too Tall" Jones, E.T.) to position itself as a "family entertainment company."

10. **AT&T/Long Lines.** "Reach out and touch someone" was an emotionally moving campaign. These commercials "reach out to everyone and realistically portray emotions, human feelings and happiness that only a phone call can bring. However, there appears to be a growing feeling in some circles that the campaign is a masterpiece in manipulation, in psychological exploitation, by making viewers lonely."[13]

---

[11]Ibid.

[12]Vadehra, "Making a Lasting Impression," p. M-36.

[13]Ibid.

These commercial campaigns were, and still are, outstanding because they skill-fully and creatively combined elements that attracted viewers' attention and made lasting impressions.[14] Creativity alone is not sufficient, however, to make a suc-cessful advertising campaign. Research by Korgaonkar, Moschis, and Bellenger has identified ten major correlates of advertising success.[15] Questionaires were mailed to a national probability sample of 1,500 advertising agency executives, who were asked to evaluate one of their agency's successful or unsuccessful campaigns (with success defined as increasing sales, attitudes, or awareness) in terms of the ten success correlates hypothesized by Korgaonkar et al. A total of 375 usable ques-tionnaires were obtained, 200 of which dealt with successful advertising campaigns and 175 with unsuccessful campaigns. Results are summarized in Table 13.1.

TABLE 13.1   **Correlates of Successful Versus Unsuccessful Advertising Campaigns: Mean Values and Standard Deviations***

Variable	Successful (n = 200)	Unsuccessful (n = 175)	Significance of t-test
1. Product uniqueness	21.30 (32.85)	25.01 (30.92)	N.S.
2. Product cost	1.51 (0.50)	1.45 (.49)	N.S.
3. Product type	2.30 (1.13)	2.12 (1.01)	N.S.
4. Nature of the market	1.35 (.59)	1.29 (.58)	N.S.
5. Competition	19.74 (42.74)	17.62 (32.74)	0.01
6. Agency–Client Relationship	25.43 (21.41)	23.00 (31.44)	0.01
7. Market Research	22.99 (18.70)	33.91 (42.38)	0.01
8. Financial and Managerial Resources	17.26 (22.08)	24.69 (34.02)	0.01
9. Media selection	12.24 (12.82)	21.93 (40.76)	0.01
10. Message and Creativity	15.96 (18.84)	32.32 (61.65)	0.01

Source: Pradeep K. Korgaonkar, George P. Moschis, and Danny N. Bellenger, "Correlates of Successful Advertis-ing Campaigns," *Journal of Advertising Research,* Vol. 24, February-March 1984, p. 49. Reprinted from the *Journal of Advertising Research* © Copyright 1984 by the Advertising Research Foundation.
*Standard deviations are in parentheses.

[14]The interested reader is encouraged to examine the article by Vadehra, "Making a Lasting Impres-sion," for other illustrations of outstanding advertisements. Also, *Advertising Age,* a major marketing and advertising periodical, presents annually its list of outstanding commercials. See, for example, "Best TV Commercials of 1983," *Advertising Age,* April 2, 1984, pp. M-4–M-45.

[15]Pradeep K. Korgaonkar, George P. Moschis, and Danny N. Bellenger, "Correlates of Successful Adver-tising Campaigns," *Journal of Advertising Research,* Vol. 24, February-March 1983, pp. 47–53.

The results in Table 13.1 reveal *no* significant differences in the mean ratings of successful versus unsuccessful campaigns for four of the ten hypothesized correlates: product uniqueness, product cost, product type (durable versus nondurable), or nature of the market (consumer versus industrial). Statistically significant differences were found, however, for the six remaining correlates. An examination of Table 13.1 indicates that successful advertising campaigns had the following features: "they are backed with adequate financial and managerial resources; they are based on careful media planning; and, they are likely to use messages that are perceived to be creative and unique. On the other hand, the presence of competition and problems arising from agency-to-client relationships are likely to have a negative effect on the success of the campaign."[16]

Advertising Message Determinants and Creative Platform

Advertising messages (television commercials, magazine ads, etc.) represent the culmination of creative efforts, which in many instances have been directed or channelled by findings from consumer behavior studies or other forms of marketing research. A variety of factors play instrumental roles, in theory if not in practice, in determining the shape, content, and character of advertising messages. Figure 13.1 presents a simple model of advertising message determinants.

Message Determinants

Product Characteristics   The character of the product itself is a major determinant of the content of advertising messages. Industrial ads are likely to use factual presentations and "reason-why" arguments.[17] Consumer goods advertising, by comparison, varies greatly depending upon the type of product. Whereas style goods (clothing, furniture, etc.) tend to use emotional appeals or imitation appeals (i.e., references to the type of people who own the advertiser's product), mechanical goods (automobiles, computers, etc.) and services (e.g., financial and legal services) often employ the same types of informational and reason-why appeals used by industrial advertisers.[18]

Consumer Characteristics   The consumer is, or at least should be, the foremost determinant of advertising messages. The notion of a **means-end chain** provides a useful framework for understanding the relationship between consumer characteristics and advertising messages. A means-end chain is, as used in the present sense, the connection among product attributes, consumer consequences, and personal values.[19] *Attributes* are features or aspects of products, *consequences* (desir-

---

[16]Ibid., p. 49.

[17]Julian L. Simon, *The Management of Advertising* (Englewood Cliffs, NJ: Prentice-Hall, 1974), p. 185.

[18]Ibid., pp. 185–186.

[19]Jonathan Gutman, "A Means-End Chain Model Based on Consumer Categorization Processes." *Journal of Marketing,* Vol. 46, Spring 1982, pp. 60–72.

FIGURE 13.1   **Determinants of Advertising Messages**

able or undesirable) are received by consumers when consuming products, and *values* represent important beliefs that people hold about themselves and which determine the relative desirability of consequences.[20]

The linking (means-end chaining) of attributes to consequences to values in consumers' memories constitutes what is more typically referred to as a product or brand *image*. For this reason, the mean-ends concept is an important one, because creative advertising indeed is the practice of "image management."[21]

---

[20]Thomas J. Reynolds and Jonathan Gutman, "Advertising Is Image Management," *Journal of Advertising Research,* Vol. 24, February-March 1984, pp. 27–36.

[21]Ibid.

Advertising Classics

1984 Communication Arts Award of Excellence
Source: Courtesy of Volvo of America Corporation.
Agency: Scali, McCabe, Sloves/New York.

Imagine getting dressed and not knowing which one to put on first.

Each year thousands of Americans under 30 suffer severe head injuries that turn everyday objects into everyday problems. They survive the injury. But they find it hard surviving day-to-day.

Severe head injuries can cause long-lasting, mental, physical, or emotional handicaps. Now the National Head Injury Foundation offers these victims and their families help, hope and opportunity.

National Head Injury Foundation

Because life after head injury is never the same.

National Head Injury Foundation, Framingham, MA., 01701 (617) 879-7473

1984 2nd Place Hatch Award—Boston Ad Club; 1984 Communication Arts Award of Excellence; 1985 Andy Award; 1985 Art Directors Club of New York
Source: Courtesy of National Head Injury Foundation.
Agency: Rossin Greenberg Seronick & Hill/Boston.

Some of us have more finely developed nesting instincts than others.

INVEST IN *Karastan*

Some of us have more finely developed nesting instincts than others.

INVEST IN *Karastan*

1984 Communication Arts Award of Excellence
Source: Courtesy of Karastan Rug Mills.
Agency: Ally & Gargano, Inc./New York.

Apple announces a technological breakthrough of incredible proportions.

12" x 11¼" x 2¼".

The first transportable computer worth taking anywhere.

The sad truth is that most small computers are pea brains. With 8 to 16K of internal memory. Displays that look like a jogger's watch. And fewer good programs than Radio Tehran.

The Apple IIc, on the other hand, has more brains and talent in its 7-1/2 pound body than you'll find in some full-size office computers.

It can run a vast library of Apple II software. Over 10,000 programs.

With a full 128K RAM, it can run advanced business software. Like AppleWorks, a 3-in-1 program that integrates word processing, electronic filing and spreadsheets.

And even as we write this, seventy-nine leading software companies are writing new programs for the Apple II family. Including software that takes full advantage of the AppleMouse.

As a matter of fact, the Apple IIc can do almost everything the IBM PC can, and thousands of things the IBM PCjr can't.

You can add an extra disk

MousePaint Electronic Illustration

SubLogic's Flight Simulator II

Stickybear Shapes™ Educational Software

AppleWorks Integrated Business Software

Dollars & Sense™ Personal Finance

Access II Communications Software

drive so you can run advanced business software for accounting, payroll and taxes.

Not to mention specialized software for doctors, lawyers, contractors, farmers, brokers, screenwriters and just about every other profession that's legal.

And, of course, since the Apple II is the most popular computer in all levels of education from grade school to graduate school, the Apple IIc can run more educational software than any other computer in the world, save one—the Apple IIe.

Which makes the IIc the only computer that's as good for your kids as it is for you. And vice versa.

In fact, an Apple IIc can do everything you'd ever need a computer to do, sitting happily on your desk at work or at home.

But if someday you need it to do

something in some faraway hotel room, you'll remember what a superb traveling companion it can be.

It can use almost any TV for a monitor—even a hotel TV.

Or you can add an Apple IIc Flat Panel Display*—the very first LCD display that shows you as much information as a regular monitor—80 characters wide by 24 lines deep.

And when your work day is done and you're all alone far from home, it can do one more thing no other portable computer can do.

Play Zaxxon!™

Available Fall 1984.

1984 Communication Arts Award of Excellence
Source: Courtesy of Apple Computer, Inc.
Agency: Chiat/Day/Los Angeles.

1984 Communication Arts Award of Excellence
Source: Courtesy of BMW of North America.
Agency: Ammirati & Puris, Inc./New York.

1984 Communication Arts Award of Excellence
Source: Courtesy of Bertram Yacht.
Agency: Mike Sloan Advertising/Miami.

Art Directors Club 63rd Annual Exhibition 1984 Merit Award

Art Directors Show, Distinctive Merit Award
Source: Courtesy of National Federation of Coffee Growers of Colombia.
Agency: Doyle Dane Bernbach/New York.

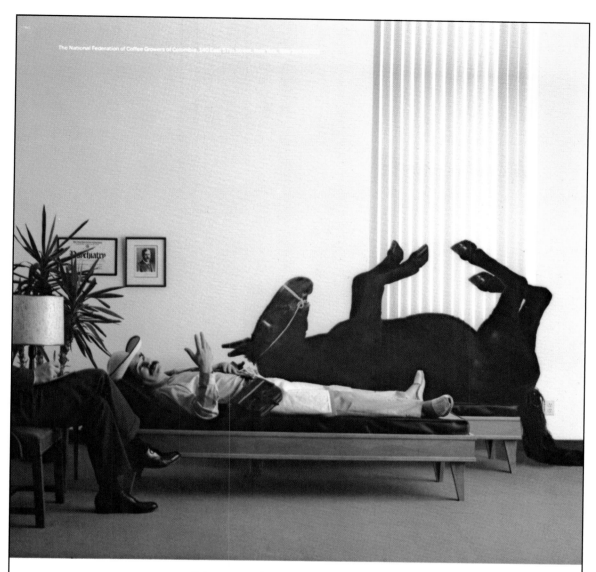

Fame has its price.

"Doctor, it's gotten to the point where people are constantly asking for my autograph. I can't even eat my chorizos in peace."

These words recently came from the fatigued form of Juan Valdez.® Along with his partner he's starting to feel the pressure of success.

The cause of it all, of course, is their huge television exposure for Colombian Coffee. In fact this year alone, Juan and his friend will be seen almost 2 billion times in American living rooms.

Frankly they've proven to be successful spokesmen. A recent survey indicates that most Americans now believe that Colombian Coffee is the best in the world. Which, unfortunately for Juan, makes him even more popular.

What this means to you is that if you're not making shelf space for 100% Colombian Coffee brands, it's time to start. Every day you delay you're losing potential profits.

And if you let that happen you'll end up like Juan. Spilling the beans to a psychiatrist.

100% Colombian Coffee

CLIO Statuette, Trade Advertising; Art Directors Show, Gold Award
Source: Courtesy of National Federation of Coffee Growers of Colombia.
Agency: Doyle Dane Bernbach/New York.

1984 Communication Arts Award of Excellence
Source: Courtesy of Pabst Brewing Company.
Agency: Young & Rubicam/Chicago.

TABLE 13.2   **MECCAs—Means-End Conceptualization of Components for Advertising Strategy**

Level	Definition
Driving Force	The value orientation of the strategy; the end-level to be focused on in the advertising.
Leverage Point	The manner by which the advertising will "tap into," reach, or activate the value or end-level of focus; the specific key way in which the value is linked to the specific features in the advertising.
Executional Framework	The overall scenario or action plot, plus the details of the advertising execution. The executional framework provides the "vehicle" by which the value orientation is to be communicated; especially the Gestalt of the advertisement; its overall tone and style.
Consumer Benefit	The major positive consequences for the consumer that are to be explicitly communicated, verbally or visually, in the advertising.
Message Elements	The specific attributes, consequences, or features about the product that are communicated verbally or visually.

Source: Reprinted by permission from the publisher from *Advertising and Consumer Psychology* edited by Larry Percy and Arch G. Woodside, (Lexington, Mass.: Lexington Books, D. C. Heath and Company). Copyright 1983, D. C. Heath and Company.

The relationship between advertising strategy and means-end chains has been labeled MECCAs, an acronym standing for "Means-End Conceptualization of Components for Advertising Strategy."[22] Table 13.2 presents and defines the various levels of the MECCAs model.

An illustration of a MECCAs model can be provided using the long-standing advertising campaign for Maytag appliances, which, as you may recall, has concentrated on the "lonely repairman" theme. Maytag has attempted to create an image of reliable, dependable, and trouble-free products. The *driving force,* or end-level, for this campaign (refer to Table 13.2) would seem to be the value that consumers place on trust, i.e., the desire to be able to depend on other people and objects. The *leverage point* in the Maytag commercials is the activation of consumers' desire for trust by emphasizing that Maytag appliances always work and rarely require repairs. The rather pathetic, "lonely repairman," who has nothing to do but anxiously await consumers' calls for repairs, represents the *executional framework,* or vehicle, for communicating trust, the key value orientation embodied in the ad. The obvious *consumer benefit* conveyed is the positive consequence of dependable product performance and the associated relief from the inconvenience and expense of product repairs. Finally, the key *message elements,* or product attributes, that convey dependability are the claims that Maytag products are made with great care, precision, and quality.

This example demonstrates how an image is created by linking product attributes in advertising messages to consumers' desired consequences and important

---

[22]Jerry Olson and Thomas J. Reynolds, "Understanding Consumers' Cognitive Structures: Implications for Advertising Strategy," in L. Percy and A. Woodside (eds.), *Advertising and Consumer Psychology* (Lexington, MA: Lexington Books, 1983), pp. 77–90.

values. Advertising's role is "to enhance physical attributes and their relative importance with respect to how the consumer sees him/herself, essentially providing psychological benefits through the image-creation process."[23] Developing successful advertising messages requires insight into the memory linkages among consumers' values, consequences, and product attributes.

Competitive Considerations   A third determinant of creative advertising messages (refer again to Figure 13.1) is the amount and type of competitive advertising. Although there is a strong tendency toward "me-tooism" among advertisers, there also are persistent efforts to carve out distinct forms of creative expression. Television advertisers are especially motivated to create unique techniques, with hopes of attracting consumer attention and distinguishing their messages from the general clutter.[24] For example, Apple Computer Inc. spent $400,000, which is four times the average cost of a 30-second commercial, to produce its dramatic, Orwellian advertisement that introduced the Macintosh computer.[25]

Economic Considerations   Advertisers have traditionally increased advertising budgets during periods of economic affluence and cut back during recessionary periods.[26] Advertising messages tend, as a result, to vary in their elaborateness depending upon the economic climate.

Technological Considerations   Advertising creativity is constrained by the state of technology. Advances in audio and video technologies (including noise synthesizers, laser-based holography, and computer graphics) have extended creative horizons and made possible a variety of ingenious and artistically appealing advertising productions.

Philosophical Considerations   A final determinant of advertising creativity is advertising philosophy. Philosophy in this sense refers to practitioners' views of what is essential for effective advertising. Several philosophies have been particularly dominant during the modern, post-1940s' marketing era, including Rosser Reeve's notion of "unique selling propositions,"[27] David Ogilvy's "brand image" formulation,[28] and Ries and Trout's "positioning" philosophy.[29] These philosophies are elaborated upon in a subsequent section on creative strategies.

[23]Reynolds and Gutman, "Advertising Is Image Management," p. 27.

[24]"The New TV Ads Trying to Wake Up Viewers," *Business Week,* March 19, 1984, p. 46.

[25]Ibid.

[26]M. Wayne DeLozier, "Advertising in an Age of Recession," *Business and Economic Review,* April 1984, p. 17; Nariman K. Khalla, "Advertising as an Antirecession Tool," *Harvard Business Review,* January-February 1980, p. 158.

[27]Rosser Reeves, *Reality in Advertising* (New York: Alfred Knopf, 1961).

[28]David Ogilvy, *Confessions of an Advertising Man* (New York: Ballantine, 1963).

[29]Al Ries and Jack Trout, *Positioning: The Battle for Your Mind* (New York: McGraw-Hill, 1981).

The Creative Platform[30]

The creative process in advertising involves two stages: (1) formulating *a way to promote* the product and (2) *actually writing the advertising*. The focus of this discussion rests entirely with the first stage, which is known as the **creative platform.** The platform represents the blueprint for an advertising campaign and consists of five parts: objectives, target audience, key consumer benefit, other usable benefits, and creative strategy statement.

Objectives Advertising objectives, as discussed in the previous chapter, set the stage for all subsequent advertising activity. As part of the creative platform, objectives state the specific goal an advertisement is intended to accomplish. To increase brand awareness, to change consumer attitudes, or to reposition the brand against competitive offerings are just some of the many general objectives that may initiate a creative platform.

Consider the fictitious product Maxi-Wipes, which are disposable cleaning cloths that contain a liquid cleaning solution, are dispensed from a pop-up box, and are designed to clean most household surfaces.[31] Assume that the creative advertising objective for this hypothetical new product is to establish Maxi-Wipes as a totally new, modern way to clean household surfaces efficiently.

Target Audience The next aspect of the creative platform is to define the intended market. Advertisers ordinarily identify markets in terms of pertinent demographic, socioeconomic, and psychographic characteristics. The Maxi-Wipes campaign, for example, might be directed to reach homemakers who are concerned with maintaining clean homes but want to do so with a minimum of effort and inconvenience. These people are looking for an easier, yet effective, way to accomplish an unpleasant task. Demographically, the target audience may be defined as married women between the ages of 18 and 49 with children.

Key Consumer Benefit The key consumer benefit is the strongest claim the advertiser can make about its product. It should be the claim with the most meaningful appeal to the target audience. The key benefit of Maxi-Wipes is that it offers a faster and easier way to clean and eliminates the need for bottles, sprays, dirty rags, and sponges.

Other Usable Benefits Other benefits supplement the claims of key benefit. Some of the supplemental benefits of Maxi-Wipes might be the following: it deodorizes and disinfects, as well as cleans; it is economical because the consumer does not need a number of cleaning products; it eliminates risk of spilling cleaning liquids; it reduces waste because each towelette contains just enough cleaning solution; it is nonpolluting because the product is biodegradable.

---

[30]Much of the material in this section is adapted from A. Jerome Jewler, *Creative Strategy in Advertising* (Belmont, CA: Wadsworth Publishing Co., 1981); see especially chap. 2.

[31]This illustration is adapted from Jewler, *Creative Strategy in Advertising.*

Creative Strategy Statement   Creative strategy has been defined as "a policy or guiding principle which specifies the general nature and character of messages to be designed. Strategy states the means selected to achieve the desired audience effect over the term of the campaign."[32] The creative strategy statement lays out the focus for the entire campaign by explaining the common component or theme that will tie together all aspects of the creative program. It also explains how the same theme will accommodate spin-offs so that the same basic message, with periodic variations, can be delivered over and over to the target audience.

The creative strategy statement for Maxi-Wipes might be something such as the following: advertisements for Maxi-Wipes will stress cleaning ease, multiple usage applications, and the attractiveness of this product as a contemporary way to clean. Product users in television commercials will be shown pulling a Maxi-Wipe from its dispenser and wiping grease and grime away in one sweep. Prospects will be urged to use Maxi-Wipes throughout their homes. Potential users also will be urged to throw away their other cleaning materials and replace them with this new, modern, and effective cleaning product.

Creative Strategy Alternatives

Creative strategy is an integral part of the creative platform. Although there are numerous forms of creative strategies, Frazer has identified seven strategies, which aptly characterize the bulk of contemporary advertising. These are summarized in Table 13.3 and described in detail in the following sections.[33]

Generic Strategy

Generic strategy is manifest when an advertiser makes a claim that could be made by any company that markets the product. The advertiser makes no attempt to differentiate its brand from competitive offerings or to claim superiority. This strategy is particularly appropriate for a company that dominates a product category.

AT&T Long Line's "Reach out and touch someone" campaign epitomizes generic strategy, as does Campbell soup's "Soup is good food" campaign. A generic strategy is effective for firms with dominant market shares because such firms will enjoy a large share of any primary demand stimulated by the advertising.

Preemptive Strategy

Preemptive strategy is most used by advertisers in product or service categories where there are few, if any, functional differences or product differentiation among competitive brands. The strategy "is preemptive in the sense of forcing competi-

---

[32]Charles F. Frazer, "Creative Strategy: A Management Perspective," *Journal of Advertising*, Vol. 12, No. 4, 1983, pp. 36–41.

[33]For the following discussion the authors are indebted to Frazer's insightful treatment of creative strategies. See Frazer, "Creative Strategy." The present treatment borrows freely from Frazer's treatment but extends his coverage at various points.

TABLE 13.3   **Summary of Creative Strategy Alternatives**

Alternative	Most Suitable Conditions	Competitive Implications
Generic straight product or benefit claim with no assertion of superiority	monopoly or extreme dominance of product category	serves to make advertiser's brand synonymous with product category; may be combated through higher order strategies
Preemptive generic claim with assertion of superiority	most useful in growing or awakening market where competitive advertising is generic or nonexistent	may be successful in convincing consumer of superiority of advertiser's product; limited response options for competitors
Unique Selling Proposition superiority claims based on unique physical feature or benefit	most useful when point of difference cannot be readily matched by competitors	advertiser obtains strong persuasive advantage; may force competitors to imitate or choose more aggressive strategy (e.g., ''positioning'')
Brand Image claims based on psychological differentiation, usually symbolic association	best suited to homogeneous goods where physical differences are difficult to develop or may be quickly matched; requires sufficient understanding of consumers to develop meaningful symbols/associations	most often involves prestige claims, which rarely challenge competitors directly
Positioning attempts to build or occupy mental niche in relation to identified competitor	best strategy for attacking a market leader; requires relatively long term commitment to aggressive advertising efforts and understanding consumers	direct comparison severely limits options for named competitor; counterattacks seem to offer little chance of success
Resonance attempts to evoke stored experiences of prospects to endow product with relevant meaning or significance	best suited to socially visible goods; requires considerable consumer understanding to design message patterns	few direct limitations on competitor's options; most likely competitive response is imitation
Affective attempts to provoke involvement or emotion through ambiguity, humor or the like, without strong selling emphasis	best suited to discretionary items; effective use depends upon conventional approach by competitors to maximize difference; greatest commitment is to aesthetics or intuition rather than research	competitors may imitate to undermine strategy of difference or pursue other alternatives

Source: Charles F. Frazer, ''Creative Strategy: A Management Perspective,'' *Journal of Advertising,* Vol. 12, No. 4, 1983, p. 40.

tors into what is conventionally considered the weak position of echoing 'me too' in their advertising or of finding another advertising alternative.''[34]

Diet Pepsi advertises, ''Now you see it, now you don't.'' Competitors could not make the identical claim without appearing unimaginative at best or piratical at

[34]Ibid., p. 37.

worst. Another example of preemptive strategy is Visine eye drop's claim that it "gets the red out." All eye drops are designed to get the red out, but by making this statement first, Visine made a dramatic statement that the consumer will associate only with Visine. No other company would make this claim now for fear of being labeled a copycat.

Unique Selling Proposition Strategy

The unique selling proposition (USP) creative strategy is based on physical differentiation by promoting a product attribute that represents a meaningful, distinctive consumer benefit. A main feature of USP adverising is identifying an important difference that makes a brand unique and then developing an advertising claim that competitors either cannot or do not make. The translation of the unique product feature into a relevant consumer benefit provides the unique selling proposition.

The USP strategy is best suited for companies whose products possess relatively lasting competitive advantages, such as makers of technically complex items or providers of sophisticated services. Successful USP advertising can force competitors to make significant product improvements, to appeal to different market segments, or to utilize some other type of creative strategy.

Federal Express advertises a unique selling proposition when it guarantees delivery by 10:30 a.m. the next day. Eastman Kodak also has a unique selling proposition with its Disc camera, which permits nonprofessional photographers to take fast and easy pictures. Burger King's unique selling proposition is that only it (and not McDonald's, Wendy's, or other hamburger chains) broils, rather than fries, its hamburgers. Anacin has a USP in claiming that its headache remedy contains 800 milligrams of active, headache-fighting agent, whereas competitors' products only have 650 milligrams.

Brand Image Strategy

Whereas the USP strategy is based on promoting physical and functional differences between the advertiser's product and competitive offerings, the brand image strategy involves psychological, rather than physical, differentiation. Advertising attempts to develop an image or identity for a brand by associating the product with symbols and archetypes. For example, David Ogilvy, the "father" of image advertising, is renowned for the famous Hathaway shirt campaign in which Hathaway wearers are always shown with a black eye patch covering one eye. A current version of this long-standing campaign involves the use of famous business personalities wearing a Hathaway shirt and an eye patch. Figure 13.2 shows an ad with Ted Turner, the innovative and imaginative owner of the Turner Broadcasting System, the Atlanta Braves (baseball team), and other business interests.

Developing a brand image through advertising amounts to giving a product a distinct identity or personality. This is especially important for brands that compete in product categories where there is relatively little physical differentiation and all brands are relatively homogeneous (beer, soft drinks, cigarettes, etc.).

[handwritten margin note: Dannon Yoghurt - discovered it was the only yoghurt on the market w/ all nat. ingred.! or no additives or preservatives]

FIGURE 13.2   Illustration of Brand Image Advertising

Creating a brand image or changing an existing, but undesired, image is what much advertising attempts to accomplish. For example, in 1984 the National Coffee Association, an industry group, undertook a major, $20 million television campaign to change coffee's image among young people.[35] The campaign used the services of various sports and entertainment celebrities (e.g., professional quarterback Ken Anderson, actress Jane Curtin) who are recognized and admired by young people. These celebrities spoke in favor of coffee and attempted to convey the desired image that coffee is a drink for young achievers.

Another illustration of a brand image campaign is K Mart's investment of $40 million in its 1984 Olympic Games advertising and marketing programs to upgrade its image.[36] The advertising tag line, "K Mart. We've got it good," was used to promote K Mart's move toward higher quality, name brand merchandise.

Welch's Grape Juice provides another illustration of brand image creative strategy. The advertisement in Figure 13.3 attempts to fortify Welch's identity as a quality, traditional company that is still doing things the same way it has for over 100 years—the "Welch's Way."

Positioning Strategy

Successful advertising, according to the positioning strategy philosophy, must implant in customers' minds a clear meaning of what the product is, what benefits it offers, and how it compares to competitive offerings. These activities, referred to collectively as *positioning*, have much in common with more traditional marketing concepts such as market segmentation and product differentiation.[37] Selectivity in marketing efforts and concentrating on narrow market segments rather than attempting to reach the whole potential market represent the essence of positioning. Effective positioning requires that a company be fully aware of its competition and exploit competitive weaknesses. Looked at from a competitive perspective, a brand is positioned in the consumer's mind relative to competition.

Trout and Ries, who popularized the notion of positioning, describe the importance of competitive orientation: "To be successful today, a company must be 'competitors' oriented. It must look for weak points in the position of its competitors and then launch marketing attacks against those weak points."[38] Positioning strategy is particularly well suited for new entries in a product category or for brands with relatively small market shares that wish to challenge market leaders.[39]

[35]Judy Lisncott, "Coffee Gets Perky New Image," *The State,* Columbia, SC, November 10, 1983, p. 2-B. The remaining discussion is adapted from this source.

[36]"K Mart Breaks Olympic Drive," *Advertising Age,* October 24, 1983, p. 12.

[37]John P. Maggard, "Positioning Revisited," *Journal of Marketing,* Vol. 40, January 1976, pp. 63–66.

[38]Jack Trout and Al Ries, "The Positioning Era: A View Ten Years Later," *Advertising Age,* July 16, 1979, pp. 39–42.

[39]Frazer, "Creative Strategy," p. 38.

CHAPTER 13   *Advertising Messages and Creative Strategy*

FIGURE 13.3   **Another Illustration of Brand Image Advertising**

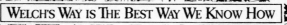

Numerous examples are available to illustrate positioning strategies. Before its demise, Intellivision used entertainer George Plimpton to compare itself with Atari and position itself as the more fun and more realistic home computer game alternative.[40] Another home computer marketer, Commodore, has always marketed to the general public at low prices and has positioned itself as providing value.[41] Positioning is also critical in the business computer industry; every computer advertiser is faced with the challenge of trying to distinguish itself from IBM.[42]

The fast-food industry is another business in which positioning plays an important role in marketing and advertising. For example, Wendy's established itself initially by competing head-on against McDonald's and other hamburger chains. It then expanded its menu with chicken sandwiches, salad bars, taco salads, and stuffed potatoes. A Wendy's executive described the strategy this way: "We're going to be positioning ourselves out of the kiddie hamburger wars."[43] Arby's, another fast-food chain, has traditionally positioned itself as an alternative to hamburgers. Its 1984 to 1985 advertising campaign used the theme, "Welcome to Arby's, you're right where you belong," which was designed to be a more upbeat and adult-oriented positioning strategy.[44]

The automobile industry is another that relies heavily on effective positioning. For example, the 1984 Continental Mark VII was positioned as a premium car to differentiate it from traditional American luxury models. A sporty version of the Mark VII was positioned against three European luxury sedans—Mercedes-Benz, BMW, and Volvo.[45]

Industrial marketers also utilize positioning strategies. McDonnell Douglas, for example, markets its line of MD-80 airplanes as "elegant investments" and is selling the MD-80 as a fashionable, yet sound, business investment. Advertisements in business and airline trade magazines are aimed at airlines, leasing companies, and individual entrepreneurs.[46]

Resonance Strategy

The resonance strategy has been described in the following manner:

> *Advertising based on this principle does not focus on product claims or brand images. Rather, it seeks to present circumstances, situations or*

---

[40]Ibid., pp. 38–39.

[41]Robert Raissman, "Frenetic Commodore Awaits New Agency Crew," *Advertising Age*, September 12, 1983, p. 12.

[42]Daniel Burstein, "Advertisers Seek That Breakthrough Strategy," *Advertising Age*, November 14, 1983, p. M-16.

[43]Nunzio Lupo (Knight-Ridder Newspapers), "Wendy's Stuffed Spuds Has Nation's Potato Producers Smiling," *The State*, November 17, 1983, Columbia, SC, p. 20-D.

[44]Scott Hume, "Arby's Finally Finds Strategy," *Advertising Age*, September 26, 1983, pp. 3, 82.

[45]"Mercury Marketing to Deliver Information," *Advertising Age*, September 12, 1983, p. 32.

[46]"McDonnell Invests in MD-80 Ads," *Advertising Age*, September 12, 1983, p. 28.

emotions which find counterparts in the real or imagined experiences of specific groups of consumers. The intended audience impact of advertisements based on this strategy is the matching of "patterns" in the commercial or ad with the stored experience of the prospect.[47]

[handwritten margin note: consumer identifies w/ the experience]

The term *resonance,* as used in the advertising-strategy sense, is analogous to the physical notion of resonance, which refers to noise resounding off an object. In similar fashion, an advertisement resonates (or patterns) the audience's life experiences. Resonant advertising strategy extends from psychographic, or life-style, research and structures an advertising campaign to pattern the prevailing life-style orientation of the intended market segment. The Miller Beer campaign ("Welcome to Miller time") is illustrative. Beer drinkers who are employed in blue-collar jobs can readily identify with the relaxing and pleasant experience of enjoying a beer after work with friends.

Affective Strategy

[handwritten margin note: this strategy is probably the one the copywriters for claims against it as manipulative. DuPont]

Much contemporary advertising aims to reach the consumer on an emotional level. Many advertising practitioners, as well as scholars, recognize that products are bought often on the basis of emotional factors and that appeals to emotion can be very successful if used appropriately and with the right products.[48] Emotional commercials and ads should work especially well for products associated with emotions (e.g., foods, jewelry, cosmetics, fashion apparel, soft drinks, long distance calls) in comparison with products associated with thinking (e.g., business computers, kitchen appliances), which are typically purchased on the basis of informed and rational decision making.

Examples of emotional advertisements abound; the following two are illustrative.[49] A Hallmark Cards 90-second commercial showed a schoolgirl dashing to her piano lesson and slipping a birthday card on the music rack to surprise her gruff music teacher, whose composure cracked, but only barely. A 60-second TV spot for Rainier National Bank portrayed a young black architect tracing his past— building Tinker Toys as a tot, building a tree house at 10, working as a short-order cook at college, and now persuading the bank to finance his new building.

In sum, seven general forms of creative strategies have been presented. These strategic alternatives, although they unavoidably overlap to some extent, should provide a useful aid to understanding the different approaches available to advertisers and the factors influencing the choice of creative strategy.

[47]Frazer, "Creative Strategy," p. 39.

[48]See, for example, "In 'Era of Emotion,' Researchers Should Count Feelings, Not Numbers," *Marketing News,* Vol. 14, September 19, 1980, pp. 1–10; David Berger, "A Retrospective: FCB Recall Study," *Advertising Age,* October 26, 1981, pp. S-36, S-38. Also refer to section on attitude-toward-the-ad in Chapter 4.

[49]Both illustrative ads received awards from *Advertising Age's* editors as among the best television commercials of 1983. See "Advertising Age Best TV Commercials of 1983," *Advertising Age,* April 2, 1984, pp. M-4–M-45.

Specific Advertising Message Issues

To this point the chapter has given a general overview of the creative advertising process. The final section focuses on specific advertising issues. Topics covered include humor in advertising, the use of sex and subliminal advertising, and corporate image and issue advertising.

It is useful at the outset to offer a perspective on the cyclical and somewhat faddish character of creativity advertising. Creative styles in advertising, particularly in the case of television commercials, vary over time and reflect the extant social, economic, and political climates. For example, television commercials during the 1970s mirrored the times by presenting their products in a straightforward and serious manner. However, with the economic recovery of the mid-1980s, a distinct trend toward less restrained, more innovative, and humorous commercials has taken place. There also now is more use of sexual themes in advertising, attributable in part to the trend toward less inhibition in society.

Aside from these economic and social developments, advertisers will use whatever techniques they are permitted to use in order to best represent their clients' products. This means finding ways to attract consumer attention and to overcome competitive clutter. Many advertising practitioners and commentators believe the public has become bored with advertising and that advertisers have been forced to find new ways to break through consumer apathy and cynicism.[50] Humor and sex in advertising are used increasingly to gain consumer attention and to accomplish other advertising goals.

Humor in Advertising

The topic of humor was introduced previously (Chapter 5) in the discussion of message factors in marketing communications. However, it is appropriate at this time to elaborate on some of these earlier points as they apply specifically to advertising.

Humor, if used correctly, can be an extremely effective advertising technique. The famous "Where's the beef?" campaign for Wendy's hamburgers transformed its spokesperson, Clara Peller, into a cult star, if only emphemerally, and also led to a phenomenal 15 percent increase in sales shortly after the ad was aired.[51] Other famous humorous ads include the long-standing campaign for Miller Lite beer (with Rodney Dangerfield and remaining cast of oddball characters) and the successful, "fast talker" advertisements for Federal Express.

Despite the frequent use of humor in advertising, relatively little is known, in a scientific sense, about its effects on customer behavior. Researchers, however, have

---

[50]"Goodbye, Mr. Whipple," *Newsweek,* March 26, 1984, p. 62.

[51]"Prime Ribbing," *Time,* March 26, 1984, p. 54.

deduced tentative generalizations about the roles and effects of humor in advertising. The following list is from Sternthal and Craig:[52]

1. Humorous messages attract attention.
2. Humor can inhibit consumers' comprehension or understanding of the intended meaning of a message.
3. Because humor is a pleasant form of distraction, it can produce an increase in persuasion by effectively "disarming" receivers' natural selective perception and reducing their tendencies toward counterarguing with persuasive selling claims.
4. Humor tends to enhance source credibility, thereby improving the persuasive impact of an ad message.
5. A humorous context may increase liking for the source and create a positive mood, which may enhance the persuasive effect of the message.
6. To the extent that a humorous context functions as a positive reinforcer, a persuasive communication placed in such a context may be more effective.
7. The effects of humor can differ due to differences in audience characteristics. Advertisers must use humor carefully since consumers display a variety of tastes in what is humorous and what is not. For example, what is funny in New York might not be funny in Minneapolis.

Because humorous appeals seem to inhibit comprehension but enhance message attention and acceptance, it has been suggested that humor in advertising should be used only in situations in which the audience is familiar with the product and brand attributes, but not in which the product is substantially new or when there are a large number of facts for consumers to understand.[53]

Humorous appeals are also not equally effective for all consumers. Using data on magazine readership patterns from the Starch magazine readership database (see Chapter 15 for details about Starch data), Madden and Weinberger determined that men had higher attention scores than women for humorous ads and that magazines with predominantly white audiences had higher attention scores for humorous ads than did those with predominantly black readers.[54]

Whatever the effects advertisers are trying to achieve, they should proceed cautiously because consumers display a variety of tastes in humor. Advertisers should carefully research audiences nationwide and internationally before venturing into humorous advertising.

[52]Brian Sternthal and C. Samuel Craig, "Humor in Advertising," *Journal of Marketing,* Vol. 37, October 1973, pp. 12–18.

[53]Brian Sternthal and C. Samuel Craig, *Consumer Behavior: An Information Processing Perspective* (Englewood Cliffs, NJ: Prentice-Hall, 1982), p. 272.

[54]Thomas J. Madden and Marc G. Weinberger, "The Effects of Humor on Attention in Magazine Advertising," *Journal of Advertising,* Vol. 11, No. 3, 1982, pp. 4–14.

Sex in Advertising

> *The scene: a bedroom. The action: a young woman pulls on silky bikini*
> *panties and a bra. While the camera slides seductively over the blonde's*
> *bare body, the woman coos that her underwear "brings out the best in*
> *me." No, this isn't an X-rated scene from "Love Kittens" but a new cable*
> *commercial for Berlei USA lingerie that [was] broadcast on independent*
> *network television.*[55]

Whereas the use of such explicit sex was unthinkable just a few years ago, it
now represents part of a new trend in American advertising. Whether such advertising is effective and under what conditions it may be effective or ineffective
remains largely an unexplored issue.[56] The following discussion will take a brief
look at some of the evidence on the issue. First, however, it will be useful to
describe what is meant by sex in advertising.

There are two aspects to sex in advertising: *nudity* and *suggestiveness*. Studies
have demonstrated that both nudity and suggestiveness generate reactions from
respondents, though there is lack of consensus which is more effective.[57]

Why is sex used in advertising, and what role does it play? There actually are
several potential roles for sex in advertising. First, the use of nudity or suggestiveness may serve to *elicit attention*. It is likely that sexual material in advertising
acts as an initial attentional lure and also holds attention for a longer period, given
that the models are attractive or the scene is pleasant.[58] This has been referred to
as the "stopping power" role of sex in advertising.[59]

A second potential role of sex is to *enhance recall*. The available evidence suggests that sexual content or symbolism will enhance recall only if it is appropriate
to the product category and the creative advertising execution.[60]

Richmond and Hartman found that sexual appeals produce significantly better
recall only if the advertising execution has a "functional," "fantasy," or "symbolic"
rather than "inappropriate" use.[61] A sexual advertising theme for a product such

---

[55]"Goodbye, Mr. Whipple," p. 62.

[56]For a review of the scientific issues involved in studying sex in advertising, see Robert S. Baron,
"Sexual Content and Advertising Effectiveness: Comments on Belch et al. (1981) and Caccavale et al.
(1981)" in Andrew Mitchell (ed.), *Advances in Consumer Research,* Vol. 9 (Ann Arbor, MI: Association
for Consumer Research, 1982), pp. 428–430.

[57]Michael A. Belch, Barbro E. Holgerson, George E. Belch, and Jerry Koppman, "Psychophysiological
and Cognitive Responses to Sex in Advertising," in Andrew Mitchell (ed.), *Advances in Consumer
Research,* Vol. 9 (Ann Arbor, MI: Association for Consumer Research, 1982), pp. 424–427.

[58]Baron, "Sexual Content and Advertising Effectiveness," p. 428.

[59]B. G. Yovovich, "Sex in Advertising—The Power and the Perils," *Advertising Age,* May 2, 1983,
p. M-4.

[60]Larry Percy, "A Review of the Effect of Specific Advertising Elements upon Overall Communication
Response," in J. H. Leigh and C. R. Martin, Jr. (eds.), *Current Issues and Research in Advertising,* Vol.
2 (Ann Arbor, MI: Graduate School of Business Administration, 1983), p. 95.

[61]David Richmond and Timothy P. Hartman, "Sex Appeal in Advertising," *Journal of Advertising Research,* Vol. 22, October–November 1982, pp. 53–61.

as perfume or lingerie (see Figure 13.4) would probably reflect an appropriate use of sex, whereas the use of sex in an ad for industrial equipment would likely be inappropriate and result in diminished recall of copy points.

A third role performed by sexual content in advertising is to evoke an *affective response* from receivers. "A positive affective reaction to a sexual ad (such as lust or attraction) should increase persuasive impact via classical conditioning, with the opposite occurring if the ad elicits negative feelings (such as disgust, embarrassment, or uneasiness)."[62] Research suggests that whether sexual content elicits a positive reaction or a negative one depends on the appropriateness or relevance of the sexual content to the advertised subject matter. *+ the viewer's gender!*

A study by Peterson and Kerin experimentally varied magazine ads for two products, a ratchet wrench set (a product for which a sexual appeal is irrelevant) and a body oil (a relevant sex appeal product.).[63] The study also manipulated three versions of dress for the female model who appeared in the ads: in the "demure model" version, she was shown fully clothed in a blouse and slacks ensemble; in the "seductive model" version, she wore the same clothing as in the demure version, but the blouse was completely unbuttoned and knotted at the bottom, exposing some midriff and cleavage; in the "nude model" version, she was completely undressed. Study findings revealed that the seductive model/body oil treatment combination was perceived most favorably by all respondents, males and females combined, whereas the nude model/body oil combination was perceived *surprising* as the least appealing advertisement. When results were separated for males and females, it was found that females regarded the nude model/ratchet set as least appealing.

Similar results were obtained from focus group research involving television commercials for Underalls pantyhose.[64] One commercial focused on the derrières of two women, one of whom, according to the research report, had a "terrific looking rump" and the other had panty lines that looked awful. The woman with the panty lines tells viewers that "Underalls make you look like I wish I looked." Focus group tests on this commercial revealed that respondents liked the commercial and did not find it offensive. Reactions were very unfavorable, however, to a second version of this commercial that differed from the first by using the tagline "Underalls make me look like I'm not wearing nothing." This ad was viewed as offensive, because looking like one is not wearing "nothing" is not regarded as a primary product benefit.[65]

The implication to be drawn from the research cited is that sexual content stands little chance of being effective unless it is directly relevant to an advertising

[62]Baron, "Sexual Content and Advertising Effectiveness," p. 428.

[63]Robert A. Peterson and Roger A. Kerin, "The Female Role in Advertisements: Some Experimental Evidence," *Journal of Marketing,* Vol. 41, October 1977, pp. 59–63.

[64]This research was performed by the research department of the Needham, Harper, and Steers advertising agency and is described in B. G. Yovovich, "Sex in Advertising," p. M-5.

[65]Ibid.

FIGURE 13.4   **Use of Sex in Advertising**

message's primary selling point. When used appropriately, however, sexual content in advertising has the potential to elicit attention, enhance recall, and create a favorable association with the advertised product.

Subliminal Advertising

The word *subliminal* refers to the perception of stimuli at a level below the conscious threshold. That is, stimuli that cannot be perceived by the conscious senses may nonetheless be perceived subconsciously. This possibility has generated considerable concern from advertising critics and has fostered much speculation from scientific and not-so-scientific researchers. One particularly outspoken commentator, Wilson Key, has perhaps generated the most controversy on the topic of subliminal advertising with his three provocatively titled books: *Subliminal Seduction, Media Sexploitation,* and *The Clam Plate Orgy.*[66]

Key and others claim that subliminal advertising techniques are used extensively and that these techniques have the power to influence consumers' choice behaviors. What does the scientific evidence have to say on this matter? Three considerations need to be addresssed to answer this question: (1) the nature of subliminal stimulation, (2) the evidence dealing with subliminal perception, and (3) the connection between subliminal advertising and buyer behavior.[67]

Subliminal Stimulation   There are three forms of subliminal stimulation. A first form, which is limited to scientific research rather than practical applications, is accomplished by presenting *visual stimuli* at a very rapid rate (say, 1/3000th of a second) by means of a device called a tachistoscope. A second form is the use of *accelerated speech in low volume auditory messages.* The third form is the *embedding of hidden symbols* (such as a sexual images or words) in print advertisements. The latter two means of subliminal stimulation do have potential practical applications. However, even if accelerated speech and symbolic embeds are attempted, is there evidence that people do indeed perceive messages subliminally?

Subliminal Perception   Though it is beyond the scope of this chapter to delve into the scientific literature on the topic, a reasonable conclusion is that there *is* indeed evidence to support the phenomenon of subliminal perception. People can perceive some subliminal cues under certain conditions. In fact, one study pur-

---

[66]Wilson B. Key, *Subliminal Seduction: Ad Media's Manipulation of a Not So Innocent America* (Englewood Cliffs, NJ: Prentice-Hall, 1972); *Media Sexploitation* (Englewood Cliffs, NJ: Prentice-Hall, 1976); *The Clam Plate Orgy: And Other Subliminal Techniques for Manipulating Your Behavior* (Englewood Cliffs, NJ: Prentice-Hall, 1980).

[67]The following discussion is patterned after the thorough review on subliminal advertising in Timothy E. Moore, "Subliminal Advertising: What You See Is What You Get," *Journal of Marketing,* Vol. 46, Spring 1982, pp. 37–47.

ports to show that truly subliminal stimuli can influence people's liking for objects.[68]

The Connection between Subliminal Advertising and Behavior
Despite the evidence supporting the phenomenon of subliminal perception, there are a variety of practical problems that have to be overcome before it could work in a practical advertising context.

> *One problem has to do with individual differences in threshold. There is no particular stimulus intensity or duration that can guarantee subliminality for all viewers. In order to preclude detection by those with relatively low thresholds, the stimulus would have to be so weak that it would not reach viewers with higher thresholds at all. Lack of control over position and distance from the [TV] screen would further complicate matters. Finally, without elaborate precautions, supraliminal material (i.e., the film or commercial in progress) would almost certainly wash out any potential effects of a subliminal stimulus. In order to duplicate the results of laboratory studies that have shown subliminal effects, it is crucial to duplicate the conditions under which the effects were obtained. From a practical standpoint, this is virtually impossible.[69]*

Even if subliminal advertising stimuli were processed by consumers under natural advertising conditions, there remains the issue of whether subliminally implanted information would have sufficent impact to affect consumer choice behavior. Standard (superliminal) advertising information itself has a difficult time influencing consumers. There is no theoretical reason to expect that subliminal information is any more effective.

In sum, the topic of subliminal advertising (particularly the Wilson Key variety of symbolic embeds) makes for interesting speculation and discussion, but scientific evidence in support of its practical effectiveness in advertising is nonexistent. Moore has summarized the issue quite lucidly:

> *A century of psychological research substantiates the general principle that more intense stimuli have a greater influence on people's behavior than weaker ones. While subliminal perception is a bona fide phenomenon, the effects obtained are subtle and obtaining them typically requires a carefully structured context. Subliminal stimuli are usually so weak that the recipient is not just unaware of the stimulus but is also oblivious to the fact that he/she is being stimulated. As a result, the potential effects of subliminal stimuli are easily nullified by other ongoing stimulation in the same sensory channel or by attention being focussed*

---

[68]W. Kunst-Wilson and Robert Zajonc, "Affective Discrimination of Stimuli That Cannot Be Recognized," *Science,* Vol. 207, No. 1, pp. 557–558. Refer to Moore, "Subliminal Advertising," for additional discussion on subliminal perception.

[69]Moore, "Subliminal Advertising," p. 41.

on another modality. These factors pose serious difficulties for any possible marketing application.[70]   *what about ethical issues?!*

Corporate Image and Issue Advertising

The type of advertising discussed so far in this chapter is commonly referred to as product– or brand-oriented advertising, the purpose of which is to increase the chances that consumers will purchase the advertiser's product/brand. An alternative form of advertising, termed either <u>corporate or institutional advertising</u>, performs a different role than product advertising and is growing in frequency of usage.[71] Sethi has described institutional advertising as follows:

> *Corporate image advertising is aimed at creating an image of a specific corporate personality in the minds of the general public and seeking maximum favorable images among selected audiences, e.g., stockholders, employees, consumers, suppliers, and potential investors. In essence, this type of advertising treats the company as a product, carefully positioning and clearly differentiating it from other similar companies and basically "selling" this product to selected audiences. Corporate image advertising is not concerned with a social problem unless it has a preferred solution. It asks no action on the part of the audience beyond a favorable attitude and passive approval conducive to successful operation in the marketplace.*[72]

Corporate advertising is thus designed "to increase the probability that people will *think* as the advertiser wishes them to, rather than to increase the probability that they will *act* in a particular way."[73] There actually are two rather distinct forms of corporate advertising: image and issue advertising.[74]

Image advertising attempts to gain name recognition for a company, to establish goodwill for it and its products, or to identify itself with some meaningful and socially acceptable activity. For example, an advertisement for E.F. Hutton declared, "After 73 years, E.F. Hutton & Company still has one name" (name recognition); AT&T proudly announced that it <u>sponsored</u> the running of the torch to Los Angeles for the ceremonial starting of the 1984 summer Olympics (goodwill, see Figure 13.5); and Phillips Petroleum identified itself as sponsoring United States Swimming and Diving (activity identification, see Figure 13.6).

---

[70]Ibid., p. 46.

[71]Barbara J. Coe, "The Effectiveness Challenge in Issue Advertising Campaigns," *Journal of Advertising,* Vol. 12, No. 4, 1983, pp. 27–35.

[72]S. Prakash Sethi, "Institutional/Image Advertising and Idea/Issue Advertising As Marketing Tools: Some Public Policy Issues," *Journal of Marketing,* Vol. 43, January 1979, pp. 68–78.

[73]William M. Weilbacher, *Advertising,* 2nd Ed. (New York: Macmillan Publishing Company, 1984), p. 475.

[74]This distinction is based on a classification by Sethi, "Institutional/Image Advertising," who actually labels these two subsets of corporate advertising as "institutional/image" and "idea/issue." We have shortened these for reading ease to *image* versus *issue* advertising. The following discussion is adapted from Sethi's presentation, especially pp. 72–75.

FIGURE 13.5   **Illustration of Goodwill Image Advertising**

Source: Courtesy of AT&T.

FIGURE 13.6   **Illustration of Activity Identification Image Advertising**

A ripple never stops.

It goes all the way to the edge of the water. And then comes back. Every time you reach out from yourself, you make a bright new one. U.S. Swimming and U.S. Diving are a chance for thousands of young people to find that you can reach even farther than you thought. And make ripples of your own. And every time you make a ripple, it touches everyone around you.

Phillips Petroleum has sponsored United States Swimming for twelve years; and United States Diving for six; helping with operating costs of national and international competitions leading to world championships. We continue to support them. Because their ideals touch the lives of everyone.

TABLE 13.4   **Thirty-One State Marketing Area Image Attributes for Selected Petroleum Companies Among Advertising-Aware Respondents**

	Phillips	Rank	Comp A	Comp B	Comp C	Comp D
Additional Energy Sources	7.4	1	6.8	7.1	6.5	6.6
Protecting the Environment	7.1	1	6.4	6.6	6.5	6.4
High Quality Products	7.6	1	7.2	7.2	7.4	7.0
New Developments	7.7	1	6.5	7.1	6.6	6.5
Public Service	7.3	1	6.7	6.9	6.7	6.8
New Sources of Petroleum	7.4	1	6.9	7.3	6.8	6.6
Good Company To Do Business With	7.7	1	7.2	7.1	7.4	7.0

Source: Paul R. Cleek, Richard C. Craiglow, and Richard W. Peters, Jr., "Tracking the 'Performance' Campaign," Phillips Petroleum Company, Bartlesville, OK, March 1981.

Phillips Petroleum, in addition to the specific advertising activity shown in Figure 13.6, has been one of the leading U.S. corporate advertisers.[75] Starting in the early 1970s following the Arab oil embargo and the consequent animosity toward oil companies, Phillips introduced the "performance" campaign as an alternative to traditional product/brand advertising. Phillips positioned itself to consumers as a performance company and backed this up with advertisements touting its innovative and socially beneficial products other than gasoline and oil. The objective of the continuing performance story campaign has been to convey the notion that Phillips is a good corporate citizen and a good company to do business with.[76]

The success of this particular campaign is evident in the results presented in Table 13.4, which compares Phillips to four other major oil companies in terms of seven corporate attributes (e.g., "high quality products"). Consumers evaluated Phillips and its competitors on ten-point scales (10 being the highest) along all seven attributes. The results show that Phillips ranked number one (as of 1980) on every attribute, clearly an exceptional advertising success story for a company that spent less on advertising than any of the four major competitors.[77]

The moral to be drawn from this illustration is that corporate image advertising, when done intelligently and with the consumer's needs in mind, can provide an excellent marketing communication device for achieving objectives that conventional product/brand advertising may be unable to accomplish.

The other form of corporate advertising is **issue advertising,** also sometimes termed *advocacy* advertising. Issue advertising "is concerned with the propagation of ideas and the elucidation of controversial social issues of public importance. It

[75]Ibid., p. 69.

[76]Paul R. Cleek, Richard C. Craiglow, and Richard W. Peters, Jr., "Tracking the 'Performance' Campaign," March 1981, Phillips Petroleum Company, p. 4.

[77]Ibid., p. 5.

does so in a manner such that [it] supports the position and interests of the sponsor while expressly or implicitly downgrading the sponsor's opponents and denying the accuracy of their facts."[78] An illustration of advocacy advertising is presented in the R. J. Reynolds Tobacco Company advertisement (Figure 13.7). R. J. Reynolds is taking a specific position on the issue of whether cigarette smoke is deleterious to nonsmokers.

Issue advertising is a topic of considerable controversy. Business executives are divided on whether this form of advertising represents an effective allocation of corporate resources. Critics of advocacy advertising question its legitimacy and challenge its status as a tax-deductible expenditure. Further discussion of these points is beyond the scope of this chapter, but the interested reader is encouraged to review the previously cited articles by Coe[79] and Sethi,[80] as well as the sources contained in the following footnote.[81]

Summary

Advertising messages and creative strategy formulation are determined by a variety of factors, including the nature of the product itself, consumer characteristics, competitive and economic considerations, and technological and philosophical factors. The creative advertising process must deal, explicitly or implicitly, with these diverse factors. Creating effective and successful advertisements requires the advertiser to gain the consumer's attention while overcoming competitive clutter.

A logical, systematic approach to advertising is accomplished by formulating a *creative platform.* Five interrelated stages are involved: establishing objectives for the advertisement or campaign, identifying the target audience, establishing the key consumer benefit, which will be stressed throughout the campaign, selecting other useful product benefits that can be identified in the advertising copy, and developing a creative advertising statement that indicates the overall procedure or strategy to execute the advertising campaign.

A variety of creative strategies are available. The chapter discusses seven strategies that have been particularly dominant in American advertising during the modern, post-1940s' marketing era: generic strategy, preemptive strategy, unique selling proposition strategy, brand image strategy, positioning strategy, resonance-strategy, and affective strategy. The specific nature of each strategy is discussed along with the conditions under which the strategy is most appropriate.

The final section of the chapter described four specific advertising topics that have considerable practical significance, as well as research importance: the role

---

[78]Sethi, "Institutional/Image Advertising," p. 70.

[79]Coe, "The Effectiveness Challenge."

[80]Sethi, "Institutional/Image Advertising."

[81]Louis Banks, "Taking on the Hostile Media," *Harvard Business Review,* March-April 1978, pp. 123–130; David Kelley, "Critical Issues for Issue Ads," *Harvard Business Review,* July-August 1982, pp. 80–87; Ward Welty, "Is Issue Advertising Working?" *Public Relations Journal,* November 1981, p. 29.

FIGURE 13.7   **Illustration of Advocacy Advertising**

Second-hand smoke: Let's clear the air.

Can cigarette smoke in the air cause disease in non-smokers?

That's an emotional question for smokers and non-smokers alike. So we'll try to set the record straight in the most direct way we know.

There is little evidence—and certainly nothing which proves scientifically—that cigarette smoke causes disease among non-smokers.

You don't have to take our word for it.

U.S. Surgeon General Julius B. Richmond—who was no friend of smoking—said in his 1979 Report: "Healthy non-smokers exposed to cigarette smoke have little or no physiologic response to the smoke, and what response does occur may be due to psychological factors."

And in the 1982 Report, Surgeon General C. Everett Koop could not conclude that passive smoking is a cause of cancer in non-smokers.

The director of the National Heart, Lung and Blood Institute, Dr. Claude Lenfant, has been one of the tobacco industry's sharpest critics. Yet Dr. Lenfant stated in 1980 (and we believe it remains true today) that "the evidence that passive smoking in a general environment has health effects remains sparse, incomplete and sometimes unconvincing."

We've decided to speak out on passive smoking because there is so much rumor and rhetoric on this subject today. And we intend to continue, from time to time, to speak out on other topics of concern to you and to us.

Our critics may try to discredit these messages as self-serving. In a sense, they will be right. We will challenge allegations that are unproven and attacks we think are unfounded. If that is self-serving, so be it.

The questions that surround smoking raise many important issues. We believe that you're entitled to hear all sides of these controversies.

R.J. Reynolds Tobacco Company

Source: Courtesy of R. J. Reynolds Tobacco Company.

of humor in advertising, the use of sex in advertising, the nature and effects of subliminal advertising, and the role of corporate image and issue advertising.

Discussion Questions

1. Research has shown that television commercials evoke a relatively standard pattern, or hierarchy, of impressions. Describe this hierarchy and explain why brand name is at the top of the hierarchy while specific sales points are at the bottom.

2. Explain the meaning of the MECCAs model and describe an advertising campaign of your choice in terms of this model.

3. Krugman has described three necessary ingredients for a successful advertisement: newsworthiness, rational stimulus, and emphasis. Explain what each of these means and support your explanations with illustrations from actual advertisements.

4. Explain the differences between unique selling proposition and brand image strategies and indicate the specific conditions under which each is more likely to be used.

5. The use of humor in advertising is a potentially effective way to promote a product. Humor must be used with caution, however. Explain the specific conditions when humor may be used effectively and when it probably should not be used.

6. Comment on the following statement: The use of sex in advertising is gauche at best and unethical at worst.

7. Subliminal perception is a reality, but it is unlikely that subliminal advertising "works." Reconcile this seeming inconsistency.

8. Some critics contend that advocacy, or issue, advertising should not be treated as a legitimate tax deduction expenditure. What is your opinion on this matter?

9. There are signs of a trend toward the use of shorter television commercials (15 seconds and less) and the use of so-called split-30 commercials, which are 30 second commercials in which the advertiser promotes two separate brands. Many advertising practitioners do not support such practices. What do you think accounts for their criticism?

Exercises

1. Select an advertising campaign that has been on television for a least one year and describe in detail what you believe its creative platform to be.

2. Identify three or four illustrations of humor in advertising and argue for each why you think the use of humor is effective or ineffective.

3. Identify three or four illustrations of sex in advertising and argue for each why you think the use of sex is effective or ineffective.

4. Review magazine advertisements and locate specific examples of the seven creative strategies that were discussed in the chapter. Be sure to justify why each ad is a good illustration of the strategy with which you identify it.

5. Locate specific illustrations of corporate image and issue advertising.

CHAPTER 14

Media Selection in Advertising

The role of media selection in advertising is similar to that of merchandising in retailing. Conventional retailing wisdom holds that "merchandise well displayed is half sold," which is to say that items sell beter if displayed attractively and located conveniently. Likewise, creative advertisements are more effective when placed in media whose characteristics enhance the value of the advertising message and reach the advertiser's targeted customers. Improper media selection can doom an otherwise promising advertising campaign.

Media selection is, in many respects, the most complicated of all marketing communication decisions. This is because a variety of decisions must be made when choosing media. In addition to determining which general media categories to use (television, radio, magazines, etc.), the media selector must also pick specific vehicles within each medium, i.e., choose particular radio stations, select specific magazine issues, and so forth. Also to be decided is how to allocate the available budget among the various media and vehicle alternatives. Additional decisions involve determining when to advertise, choosing specific geographical locations, and deciding how to distribute the budget over time and across geographic locations. Thus, media selection involves, at minimum, five interrelated decisions:

1. Selecting general media categories
2. Picking specific vehicles within media
3. Determining when and how often to advertise
4. Deciding where (geographically) to advertise

FIGURE 14.1   **Overview of the Media Planning Process**

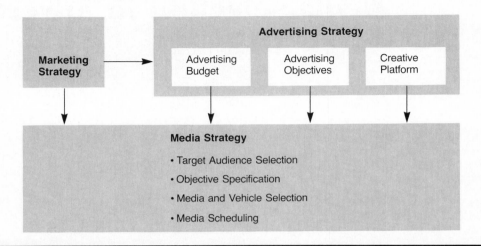

5.   Allocating the budget over time and across media, vehicles, and geographic locations

Intelligent media selection demands the use of planned, systematic approaches instead of ad hoc, seat-of-the-pants judgments. The formal approach to media selection is called *media planning,* an overview of which is presented in Figure 14.1. This chapter first reviews the media planning process and then provides detailed analyses of five major advertising media: television, radio, magazines, newspapers, and outdoor advertising. Discussion of a sixth major medium—direct mail—is delayed until Chapter 16, which provides in-depth coverage of various direct marketing techniques.

The Media Planning Process

As shown in Figure 14.1, media planning involves coordination of three levels of strategy formulations: marketing strategy, advertising strategy, and media strategy. The overall marketing strategy (consisting of target market identification and marketing mix selection) provides the impetus and direction for the choice of both advertising and media strategies. This is to say that the advertising budget, objectives, and creative platform extend naturally from the overarching marketing strategy. In similar fashion, media strategy necessarily evolves from the more general advertising strategy decisions involving budgeting, objective setting, and creative considerations. The media strategy itself consists of four sets of interrelated activities: (1) selecting the target audience, (2) specifying media objectives, (3) selecting media categories and vehicles, and (4) scheduling media.

Target Audience Selection

Successful media selection requires first that the target audience be clearly pinpointed. Failure to define the audience precisely results in wasted exposures, i.e., some nonpurchase candidates are exposed to advertisements, while some prime candidates are missed.

Four major factors are used in segmenting target audiences for media selection purposes: (1) geographic, (2) demographic, (3) product usage (e.g., heavy, medium, and light product users), and (4) life-style/psychographics.[1] Product usage information typically provides the most meaningful basis for segmenting target audiences.[2] Such information is often unavailable, however, and media planners are forced to rely on geographic, demographic, and psychographic data.

Geographic, demographic, and psychographic considerations are typically combined for purposes of target audience definition. For example, a manufacturer of small pickup trucks may define its target audience in this manner: working men between the ages of 25 and 44, who live in smaller towns and rural areas, participate in outdoor activities, enjoy hunting and fishing, are avid viewers of televised sporting events, and are politically conservative and patriotic. A target audience defined in such specific terms has obvious implications for media selection. Outdoor magazines and television sports programs would represent two attractive possibilities.

Media Objectives

The second media strategy step is establishing specific objectives. These include both *qualitative* objectives (e.g., place advertisements only in magazines with prestige images) and *quantitative* objectives (e.g., reach; frequency; gross rating points, or GRPs; and effective rating points, or ERPs).

Reach represents the percentage of an advertiser's target audience exposed to at least one advertisement over an established time frame, with a four-week period representing the typical time frame for most advertisers. Reach, which is also called *net coverage* or *unduplicated audience,* thus represents the number of target customers who see or hear the advertiser's message *one or more times* during the time period. Reach by itself is an inadequate objective for media planning because it tells nothing about how often target customers are exposed to the advertiser's messages.

Frequency is the media planning statistic that deals with how often prospects are reached by the advertiser's messages. In formal terms, frequency is the *average number of times the target audience is exposed.*

[1]Anthony F. McGann and J. Thomas Russell, *Advertising Media: A Managerial Approach* (Homewood, IL: Richard D. Irwin, Inc., 1981), p. 83.

[2]Henry Assael and Hugh Cannon, "Do Demographics Help in Media Selection?" *Journal of Advertising Research,* Vol. 19, December 1979, pp. 7–11; Hugh M. Cannon and G. Russell Merz, "A New Role for Psychographics in Media Selection," *Journal of Advertising,* Vol. 9, No. 2, 1980, pp. 33–36, 44.

An illustration will help clarify the relationship between reach and frequency.[3] An advertiser for a well-known national food brand has just purchased network television time on eight programs over a four-week period. Messages will appear in a variety of programs to achieve maximum reach. Pertinent information appears in Figure 14.2.

The audiences for the eight programs (A through H) are, respectively, 10 million, 9 million, 10 million, 8.5 million, 7 million, 18 million, 9 million, and 16 million. Thus, a total of 87.5 million homes will be exposed to at least one of the advertising messages during the four-week period. This total, called *gross impressions,* is *not* equivalent to actual reach because many of the 87.5 million households are duplicates—they will see more than just one of the eight programs. For example, program A is delivered to 10 million homes (see Figure 14.2) and program B reaches 9 million homes. However, program B adds only 4 million new homes to those already reached by program A. This is indicated by the vertical distance, *a,* in Figure 14.2.

The other vertical distances in the figure (*b, c, d,* etc.) indicate the unique, unduplicated audience that each program reaches. The total unduplicated audience—38 million—represents the collective reach for all eight programs. Assuming the advertiser's target audience consists of 60 million households, this then would represent a reach of 63.3 percent.

Frequency is determined by dividing the total gross impressions or duplicated audience (87.5 million) by the net coverage or unduplicated audience (38 million). As shown in Figure 14.2, the computed frequency, 2.3, represents the average number of times that the unduplicated audience of 38 million households will be reached during the four-week period.

Media planners normally combine reach and frequency statistics to form what is called **gross rating points** (GRPs). GRPs represent the mathematical product of reach times frequency. The media schedule in Figure 14.2 yields approximately 146 GRPs (63.3 × 2.3). The number of GRPs indicates the total weight of advertising during a time frame such as a four-week period. Media buyers often attempt to allocate the budget so as to maximize GRPs. Alternative media plans can be compared in terms of the number of GRPs each generates.

It is important to realize, however, that more GRPs does not necessarily mean better. Consider, for example, two alternative media plans, X and Z, both of which require the same budget. Plan X generates 180 GRPs, consisting of 90 percent reach and an average frequency of 2. Comparatively, Plan Z provides for 160 GRPs that result from a reach of 52 percent and a frequency of 3.08. Which is the better plan? The answer depends on the advertiser's objective. Plan X is clearly superior in terms of total GRPs and reach, but Plan Z has a higher frequency level. If the product in question requires a greater number of exposures in order for the advertising to have an impact, then Plan Z may be the superior plan even though it yields fewer GRPs.

---

[3]This illustration is adapted from William M. Weilbacher, *Advertising,* 2nd Ed. (New York: Macmillan Publishing Co., 1984), pp. 268–271.

FIGURE 14.2   **Illustration of Reach and Frequency**

Total Homes Delivered $= A+B+C+D+E+F+G+H = 87{,}500{,}000$ Homes

Average Time Each Home is Reached $= \dfrac{\text{Gross Homes Delivered}}{\text{Net Coverage}} = \dfrac{87{,}500{,}000}{38{,}000{,}000} = 2.3$

Net Coverage (Program Reach) $= 10{,}000{,}000 + a + b + c + d + e + f + g = 38{,}000{,}000$ Homes

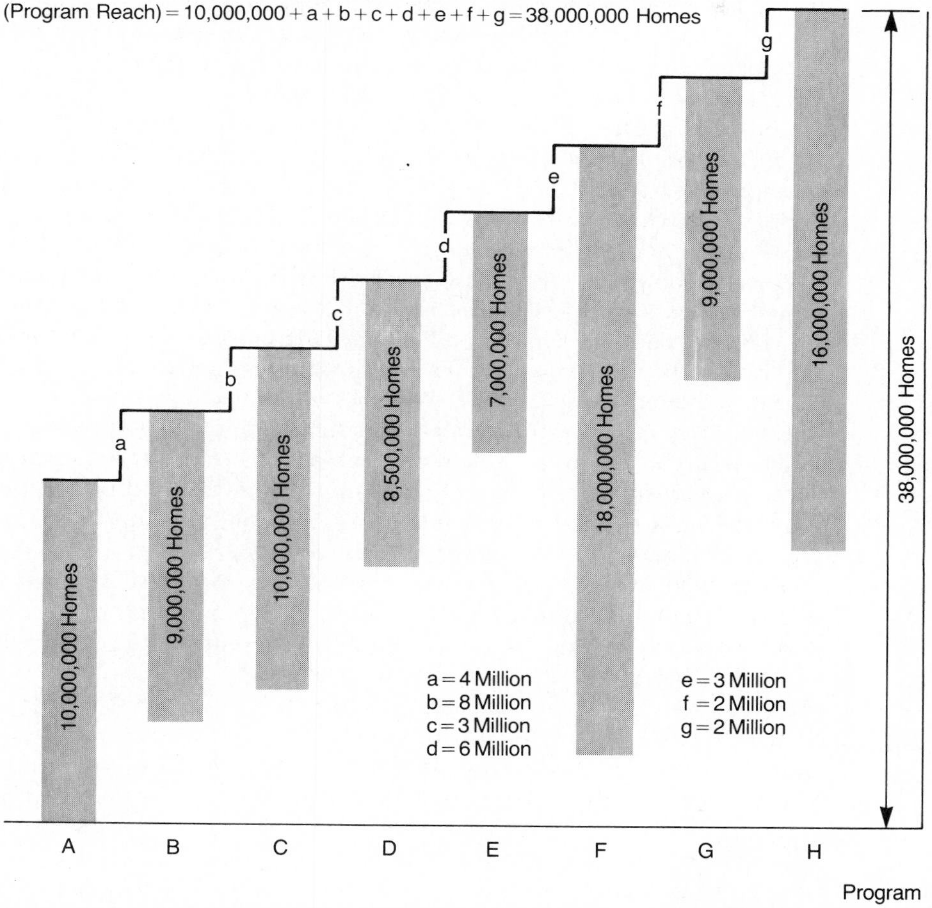

a = 4 Million		e = 3 Million
b = 8 Million		f = 2 Million
c = 3 Million		g = 2 Million
d = 6 Million		

A = 10,000,000 Homes
B = 9,000,000 Homes
C = 10,000,000 Homes
D = 8,500,000 Homes
E = 7,000,000 Homes
F = 18,000,000 Homes
G = 9,000,000 Homes
H = 16,000,000 Homes

38,000,000 Homes

Program

Media planners have become critical of the GRP concept in recent years. The basic criticism is that "it rests on the very dubious assumption that every exposure is of equal value, that the 50th exposure is the same as the tenth or the first."[4]

[4]A quote from advertising consultant Alvin Achenbaum cited in B. G. Yovovich, "Media's New Exposures," *Advertising Age,* April 13, 1981, p. S-7.

Media analysts are beginning to think more in terms of **effective rating points** (ERPs). The ERP concept is based on the idea that an advertising campaign may reach some consumers too few times and other consumers too many times. But what constitutes too few or too many exposures? On the low end, fewer than three exposures is generally considered ineffective, while more than ten exposures is considered excessive.[5] It is important to realize, however, that what is effective (or ineffective) for one product may not necessarily be so for another. Moreover, the creative strategy itself is a major determinant of effective exposure levels. For example, a reason-why type presentation may require four or more exposures to have any noticeable effect, but an emotional, feeling commercial may achieve its optimal impact after only one or two exposures.

The use of effective exposure rather than gross ratings as the basis for media planning can have a major effect on overall media strategies. In particular, the use of ERPs generally leads to *using multiple media* rather than depending exclusively on televison, which often is the strategy when using the gross rating point criterion. Prime-time television is especially effective in terms of generating reach (a desirable goal for achieving high GRPs) but may be deficient in terms of effective exposure (a necessary condition for high ERPs). Thus, using ERPs as the decision criterion often involves giving up some of prime-time television's reach to obtain greater frequency (at the same cost) from other media.

Table 14.1 illustrates the media alternatives with four different media strategies. The four strategies involve different combinations of media expenditures from an annual advertising budget of $12 million. Notice that the use of only network televison leads to the lowest levels of reach, frequency, GRPs, and percentage of target consumers who are exposed three or more times to the advertiser's message. An even split of $6 million to network television and magazines generates an especially high level of reach (91 percent), while combinations of network television with network radio and network television with outdoor advertising are es-

TABLE 14.1	Alternative Media Plans (Based on $12 Million Annual Budget and Four-Week Media Analysis)			
	Network TV Only ($12M)	Network TV ($8M) Network Radio ($4M)	Network TV ($6M) Magazines ($6M)	Network TV ($8M) Outdoor ($4M)
Reach	69%	79%	91%	87%
Frequency	2.8	5.5	3.2	6.7
GRPs	192	438	291	583
3+ Exposures	29%	48%	53%	61%

Source: Adapted from "The Muscle in Multiple Media," *Marketing Communications,* December 1983, p. 25.

[5]Ibid.

pecially impressive in terms of frequency, GRPs, and the percentage of consumers exposed three or more times.

Media and Vehicle Selection

The media planner must select general media categories and then pick specific vehicles within each medium that will effectively reach the target audience. Although a number of factors are involved in both determinations, the most important are target audience, cost, and creative considerations.

Target Audience Considerations   The most important task faced by media planners is that of picking media and vehicles to match the target audience's salient demographic, psychographic, and product usage characteristics. Ideally, subscribers to a magazine or viewers of a television program would match perfectly the characteristics of the advertiser's target audience. The actual match is determined by analyzing media users' characteristics that are made available to advertisers by such syndicated advertising research services as Nielsen (television) and Simmons Market Research Bureau (magazines).[6]

Figure 14.3, for example, is a *Cosmopolitan* magazine advertisement that is directed at media buyers. The ad points out that the *Cosmo* reader is younger, better educated, more urban, and more upscale than women in general. Furthermore, though not shown in Figure 14.3, the ad also indicates the *Cosmopolitan* reader to be a heavy user of various cosmetics, sporting goods, automobiles, and other items. The marketers of these products would probable consider *Cosmopolitan* an attractive vehicle in their efforts to reach young, upscale, and fashion-conscious women.

Cost Considerations   The most basic consideration in media selection is the cost of entering a medium. The relatively high cost of television advertising is often prohibitive for those national brands which have small market shares. Advertisers for these brands, who are unable to afford enough television time to have meaningful impact, are forced to use less expensive media. Cost considerations also play an important role in choosing specific vehicles. One vehicle (such as a specific magazine) may match an advertiser's target audience better than another magazine but may be considerably more expensive. The decision ultimately amounts to a trade-off between cost and value. A more expensive vehicle often represents a far better value by virtue of reaching the right audience, reflecting favorably on the advertiser's product, and leading ultimately to more sales.

Creative Considerations   Creative considerations represent another critical factor in media and vehicle selection. Each medium and vehicle has its set of unique characteristics and virtues (see Figure 14.4). This will almost certainly vary with

---

[6]These services are described in the following chapter.

FIGURE 14.3   **Use of Advertising to Appeal to Media Buyers**

Source: Cosmopolitan is a publication of Hearst Magazines, a division of The Hearst Corporation. Copyright 1985 The Hearst Corporation.

the judgment of the media planner, but advertisers do attempt to select those media and vehicles whose characteristics are most compatible with the advertised product and which will enhance the product's image. For example, magazines are particularly strong in terms of elegance, beauty, prestige, and tradition. The corresponding strengths of the other media are discussed in a subsequent section that offers detailed descriptions of all five major media.

Creative considerations play a particularly important role in vehicle selection decisions. Specific magazine issues and television programs are carefully selected to match a product's desired image. Consider, for example, home gyms, a product with high growth potential in view of today's fitness-conscious society. One marketer, Diversified Products, picked the following magazine vehicles to promote the

FIGURE 14.4   **Which Media Do It Best?**

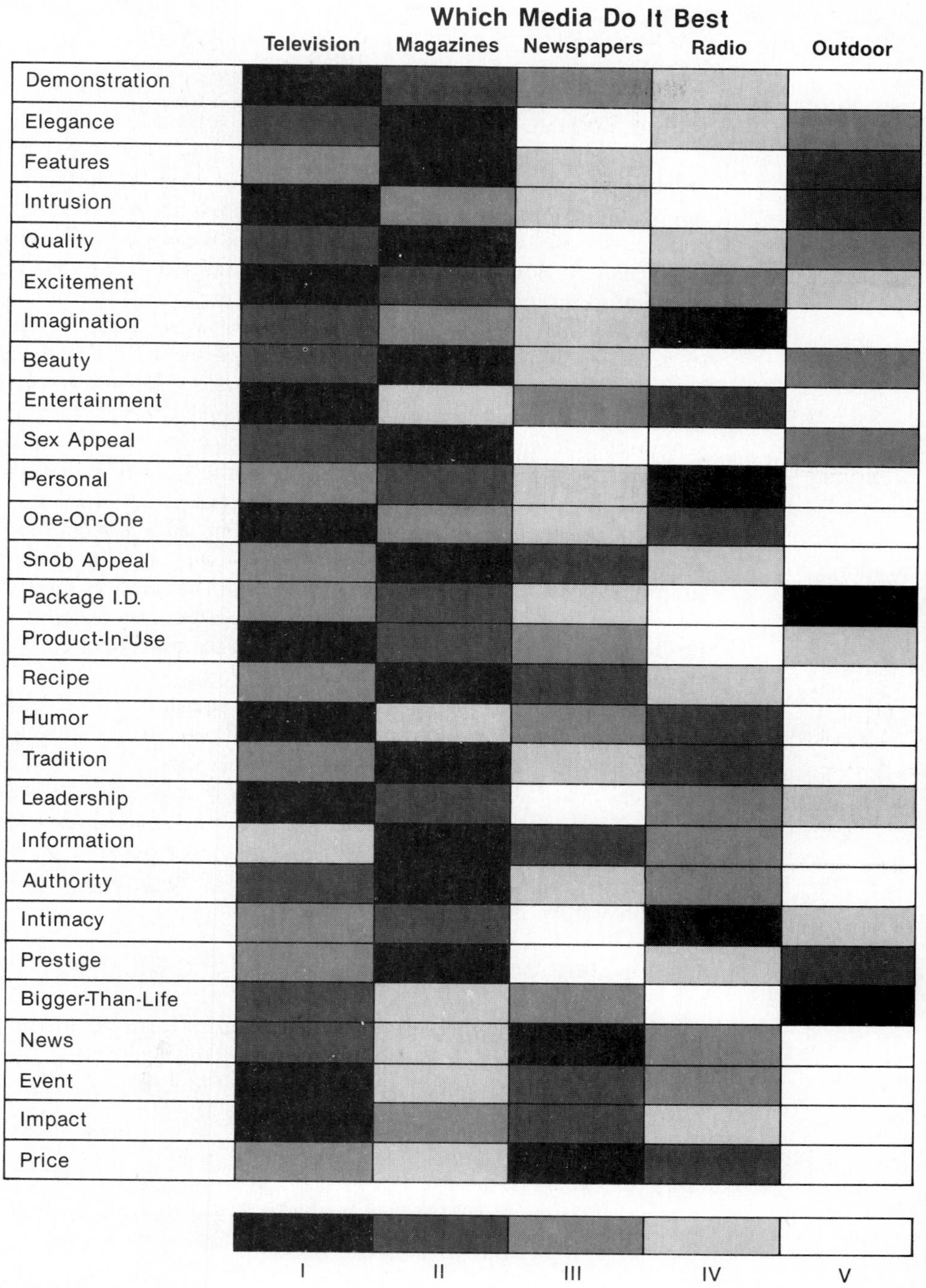

Which Media Do It Best

	Television	Magazines	Newspapers	Radio	Outdoor
Demonstration					
Elegance					
Features					
Intrusion					
Quality					
Excitement					
Imagination					
Beauty					
Entertainment					
Sex Appeal					
Personal					
One-On-One					
Snob Appeal					
Package I.D.					
Product-In-Use					
Recipe					
Humor					
Tradition					
Leadership					
Information					
Authority					
Intimacy					
Prestige					
Bigger-Than-Life					
News					
Event					
Impact					
Price					

I   II   III   IV   V

Source: Courtesy of Needham Harper Worldwide, Inc.

right image for its Gympac home gym: *Cosmopolitan, Gentlemen's Quarterly, Glamour, Good Housekeeping, Newsweek, People, Playboy,* and *Sports Illustrated.*[7]

Media Scheduling

Some products are advertised only at certain times of the year because of seasonal purchasing habits. The scheduling decision for such products is rather straightforward: advertise immediately in advance of and during the season when the product is consumed. But marketers of products that are demanded throughout the year face a more complicated scheduling decision. Should the media budget be distributed uniformly throughout the year, should it be spent in a concentrated period to achieve ultimate impact, or should some other schedule between these two extremes be used? As always, the determination of what is best depends on the specific product/market situation. In general, however, a uniform advertising schedule suffers from too little advertising weight at any one time. A heavily concentrated schedule, on the other hand, suffers from excessive exposures during the advertising period and a complete absence of advertising at all other times.

To avoid erring in either of these directions, advertisers often attempt to achieve a compromise by advertising intermittently for a period of several weeks, discontinuing advertising for a period of several additional weeks, returning to advertising for several more weeks, and so on. This practice, called *flighting,* enables advertisers to spread a limited budget over a longer period of time, yet have sufficient weight to achieve impact.

Flighting originated with television advertising, but recently it has been adapted to other media. This is illustrated by Gulf Oil Corp.'s flighting program.[8] Gulf underwrites four *National Geographic* specials that are telecast each year on public broadcasting stations. Gulf plans all media to run in conjunction with the on-air time of each special. "TV is concentrated within the four days preceding. Radio and newspaper are scheduled on the same day as the special. Weekly magazine ads run the week prior. All of this advertising is integrated with an extensive public relations effort."[9]

Media Plan for General Mills's Fruit and Blueberry Muffins

It will be useful now to examine an actual advertising media plan. The one discussed is the 1983–1984 plan developed by the advertising agency Needham, Harper & Steers for General Mills's fruit and blueberry muffins.[10] After successfully

[7]"Home Gym Market Flexing Ad Muscle," *Advertising Age,* August 15, 1983, p. 30.

[8]Merle Kingman, "Admen See Pulsing as Way To Beat Soaring TV Time Costs," *Advertising Age,* July 4, 1977, p. 29.

[9]Ibid.

[10]The authors are grateful to General Mills, Inc. and to Needham, Harper & Steers for providing this example. Permission to publish is granted by General Mills, Inc.

test marketing fruit muffins in the Dallas and Kansas City regions in March of 1982, General Mills began national distribution in September of 1983.

Media Objectives   The primary objective was to create high levels of product awareness among the target audience—women between the ages of 25 and 49. This was accomplished by introducing the product at the beginning of the traditional baking season (fall) when muffin sales are typically at their peak. A secondary objective was to sustain awareness levels through March and April of 1984 by initiating a second wave of advertising beginning the last week of January.

Media Strategies   Two media, television and magazines, were selected to accomplish the media objectives. *Network daytime television* was used due to its ability to (1) deliver a high *frequency* of message exposures and (2) provide a cost-efficient medium for reaching the target audience. *Network prime-time television* was used because of its ability to (1) build broad *reach* quickly and high levels of awareness, (2) reach light television viewers, and (3) place advertising messages within an all-family viewing environment. *Magazines* were appropriate because they provided (1) a selective vehicle for reaching the target audience and (2) an editorial environment that was compatible with the dissemination of food advertising information.

Figure 14.5 presents pertinent information for General Mills's 1983 to 1984 media schedule for blueberry and fruit muffins. This includes the dates of advertising placements in the three media, the number of target gross rating points during each advertising flight, and actual advertising expenditures. Note that the total budget was $2,763,100, of which 71 percent was spent for daytime and prime-time television and the remainder for magazines.

Table 14.2 provides the associated frequency information that corresponds to the media schedule information in Figure 14.5. Table 14.2 reveals that 400 GRPs were generated during the introductory advertising period (i.e., through 1983), while 362 GRPs were achieved during the January to April 1984 sustaining period. These totals were obtained by summing the GRP figures that appear in Figure 14.5.

It can be seen in Table 14.2 that 89 percent of the target audience was reached at least once during the introductory advertising campaign. The average frequency of exposure was 4.5 (i.e., 400 GRPs ÷ 89%). This means that target customers (women between the ages of 25 and 49) were exposed on average to 4.5 fruit muffin ads. No woman, of course, was reached 4.5 times exactly; this is just a statistical average. Some women would not have been reached at all, and others would have been exposed to many more than four fruit muffin ads.

The average frequency during the sustaining period was also 4.5, and for the total campaign the average frequency was 8.1. Overall, 94 percent of target customers were exposed to at least one ad, whereas 78 percent fell into the effective frequency range by being exposed to three or more ads during the course of the advertising campaign (see Table 14.2).

The previous section alluded to specific advertising media. The following sections, starting with television, provide a detailed analysis of each of five major advertising media: television, radio, magazines, newspapers, and outdoor advertising.

FIGURE 14.5   1983/84 Media Schedule for General Mills' Fruit Muffins

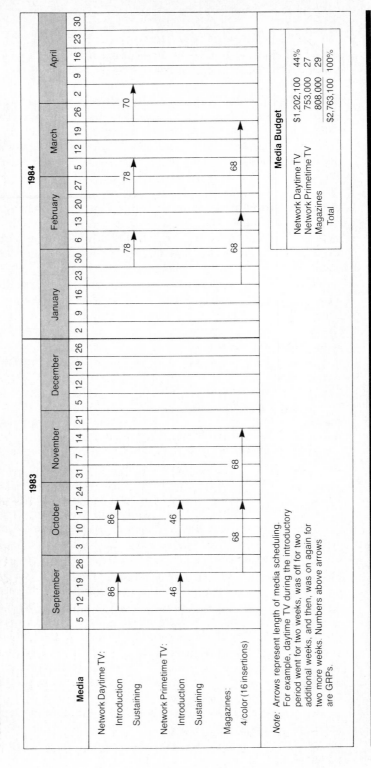

Source: The Department of Media Resources, Needham, Harper & Steers/Chicago.

TABLE 14.2   **Reach and Frequency Estimates for Target Audience**

Scheduling Period	Gross Rating Points	Average Frequency	Reach By Frequency			
			1+	2+	3+	4+
Introduction	400	4.5	89	75	60	47
Sustaining	362	4.5	81	64	50	38
Total	762	8.1	94	87	78	70

Source: The Department of Media Resources, Needhan, Harper & Steers Advertising, Inc., Chicago, Illinois.

Television

Television is a near ubiquitous communication medium in the United States as well as in much of the industrialized world. Television sets are present in almost 98 percent of American households, with half having two or more sets.[11] As an advertising medium, television is uniquely personal and demonstrative, yet it is also expensive and subject to considerable competitive clutter.

Television's specific strengths and weakness will be elaborated upon in a later section. First it will be instructive to examine two specific aspects of television advertising: (1) the different programming segments, or so-called dayparts, and (2) the alternative outlets for television commercials (network, spot, local, and cable).

Television Programming Segments

It would be simplistic to treat all television advertising as if it were equally expensive and effective. Advertising costs, audience characteristics, and programming appropriateness vary greatly at different times of the day and during different days of the week. In television parlance, the times of day are referred to as *dayparts,* of which there are three major segments: prime-time, daytime, and fringe time. Each segment has its own strengths and weaknesses.[12]

Prime Time   Prime time is the period between 8:00 p.m. and 11:00 p.m. (eastern time). The best and most expensive programs and actors are scheduled during this period. Audiences are largest during prime time, and the networks naturally charge the highest rates. Advertising rates during prime time have continued to increase year after year because many national advertisers apparently find prime-time advertising worthwhile. They are thus willing to pay increasing rates.

[11]McGann and Russell, *Advertising Media,* p. 109.

[12]The following discussion is adapted from McGann and Russell, *Advertising Media,* pp. 110–112.

Daytime   Daytime starts with the early morning news shows (e.g., "Today Show") and extends to 4:00 p.m. (eastern time). Early daytime appeals first to adults with news programs and then to children with special programs designed for this group. Afternoon programming, with its special emphasis on soap operas, appeals primarily to women working at home and, according to rumor, to college students in dormitories.

Fringe Time   Fringe time is the period preceding and following prime time. Early fringe starts with afternoon reruns and is devoted primarily to children, but it becomes more adult oriented as prime time approaches. Late fringe appeals primarily to young adults.

Network, Spot, Local, and Cable Advertising

Television messages are transmitted by local stations, which are either locally owned cable television systems or are affiliated with the three major commercial networks (ABC, CBS, NBC) or with an independent cable network (such as WTBS, the Turner Broadcasting System). This arrangement of local stations and networks makes possible different ways of buying advertising time on television.

Network Television Advertising   Companies that market products nationally often use network television to reach potential customers throughout the country. The advertiser, typically through an advertising agency, purchases desired time slots from one or more of the major networks and advertises at these times on all local stations that are affiliated with the network.

The cost of such advertising depends on the daypart that an ad is aired on as well as upon the popularity of the television program in which the ad is placed. For example, a 30-second ad on the prime-time "M*A*S*H" program was estimated to cost $170,000 during the 1982-1983 television season.[13] Comparatively, a 30-second spot on "Private Benjamin" during this same season cost only half as much at $85,000.[14]

In spite of these large figures, network television is frequently a cost-efficient means to reach mass audiences. Consider the $170,000 cost for "M*A*S*H." This program was estimated to have a rating of 33 in 1982-1983, which means that approximately one-third (about 27 million) of all television households (about 81 million) were tuned in to "M*A*S*H" when it was aired by CBS on Monday evenings. Thus, an advertiser on this program would have paid approximately $6.30 to reach every 1,000 households. This, the cost per thousand rate, is typically referred to as the CPM.

Another point in favor of the national advertiser's using network television advertising (rather than the alternative, spot television) is that network rates are

---

[13]"Ad Agencies Expert at Forecasting TV Fare's Fate," *Advertising Age,* September 27, 1982, p. 60.
[14]Ibid.

only 10 to 70 percent of the sum of the individual station (spot) rates, with the actual rate differential depending upon time of day and season.[15]

Network advertising is, however, inefficient, and in fact infeasible, if the national advertiser chooses to concentrate efforts on selected markets only. Some brands, though marketed nationally, are directed primarily at consumers in certain geographic locales—perhaps either larger cities or small towns and rural areas. This being the case, it would be wasteful to invest in network advertising, which would reach many areas where target audiences are *not* located.

Spot Television Advertising   The national advertiser's alternative to network television advertising is spot advertising. As the preceding discussion intimated and as the name suggests, this type of advertising is placed (spotted) only in selected markets.

In some situations network advertising is entirely infeasible for the national advertiser, who must then rely on spot television advertising. One such situation is when a company rolls out a new brand market by market before it achieves national distribution. Another is the case of the company whose product distribution is limited to one or a few geographical regions.

Local Television Advertising   Television advertising has historically been dominated by national advertisers, but local advertisers are turning to television in ever greater numbers. Local advertisers often find that the CPM advantages of television, plus the advantage of product demonstration, justify the choice of this advertising medium. Local television advertising is particularly inexpensive during the fringe times preceding and following prime-time programming.

Cable Advertising   Cable television has been available for a number of years, but only recently have advertisers turned to cable as a potentially valuable advertising medium. Though national advertisers are sill somewhat uncertain about the advertising potential of cable television and regard it as an "experimental buy,"[16] growing numbers are willing to experiment with cable. Cable television has enjoyed tremendous recent growth in advertising revenues. Total revenue, which amounted to only $58 million in 1980, is estimated to exceed $1 billion in 1986.[17]

What accounts for this tremendous growth rate? The major factor is the growth of cable television itself. A.C. Nielsen estimates that by 1983 cable television had penetrated 31 million American households, or over 37 percent of all television households and that by 1990 the penetration rate should exceed 60 percent.[18]

---

[15]John L. Peterman, "Differences between the Levels of Spot and Network Television Advertising Rates," *Journal of Business,* Vol. 52, No. 4, 1979, pp. 549–561.

[16]"Cable: An Experimental Buy," *Marketing Communications,* June 1983, pp. 16, 17.

[17]Joanne Cleaver, "The Medium is Potent, If the Message is Clear," *Advertising Age,* June 13, 1983, p. M-32.

[18]Susan Spillman, "Cable Gets Serious on Ads," *Advertising Age,* April 11, 1983, p. 1.

A second factor is advertisers' growing dissatisfaction with network television because of rapidly increasing advertising rates and declining network viewing audiences. Network advertising costs in 1982, for example, were over three and one-half times higher than they had been in 1967, only 15 years earlier.[19] Because of the tremendous rate increases, one advertising commentator has characterized network television as the "OPEC of Media."[20] At the same time, network prime-time share among all television viewers in 1982 was 81 percent, which represented a decrease of about 10 percent in only five years.[21] It is estimated that this share will fall to only 59 percent by 1990.[22] Thus, the combination of higher rates and smaller audiences has forced advertisers to experiment with new media alternatives.

A third reason for cable advertising's growth is the opportunity for advertisers to be more selective (than with network or spot television) in picking target audiences. There are literally dozens of national cable systems, each appealing to several million households.[23] These include, by way of example, Black Entertainment Television, Cable Health Network, ESPN (Entertainment and Sports Programming Network), MTV: Music Television, National Jewish Television, and Spanish Universal Network. The names of these systems illustrate the selectivity available to the national advertiser.

A final factor behind cable advertising's rapid growth is the demographic composition of cable audiences. Cable subscribers "are younger, better educated, more likely to be employed, married and have children, and more affluent than the population as a whole."[24] These characteristics have great appeal to many national advertisers.

Television Advertising: Strengths and Problems

Each advertising medium possesses relative strengths in comparison with other media. These involve both *quantitative* considerations (the number of target customers a particular medium reaches, its cost, and so on) and *qualitative* matters (e.g., how elegant or personal a medium is). The qualitative factors, though inherently more subjective, often play the determining role in advertisers' media decisions. Figure 14.4, which was introduced earlier in the chapter, illustrates the types of qualitative considerations that advertising practitioners consider when making media selections and shows the relative strengths of television, as well as the other major advertising media.

---

[19]Robert J. Coen, "Next Year's Cost Increases May Average Only 6%," *Advertising Age,* November 7, 1983, p. M-20.

[20]John O'Toole, "Network Television: The OPEC of Media," *Marketing Communications,* June 1983, p. 96.

[21]Les Luchter, "The Cabling of America," *Marketing Communications,* September 1982, p. 31.

[22]Ibid.

[23]See Luchter, "The Cabling of America," p. 35–85, for a directory of national cable services.

[24]Luchter, "The Cabling of America."

Television's Strengths   Beyond any other consideration, television possesses the unique capability to *demonstrate* a product in use. No other medium has the ability to reach consumers simultaneously through both auditory and visual sensory modes. Viewers can see and hear a product being used, identify with the product's users, and imagine themselves using the product.

Television also has *intrusion value* unparalleled by other media. That is, television advertisements engage one's senses and attract attention even when one would prefer not to be exposed to an advertisement. Comparatively, it is much easier to avoid a magazine or newspaper ad by merely flipping the page or to avoid a radio ad by changing channels. But for a television program, it is often easier to sit through a commercial rather than attempt to avoid it either physically or mentally.

A third relative advantage of television advertising is its combined ability to *provide entertainment and generate excitement.* Advertised products can be brought to life or made to appear even bigger than life. Products advertised on television can be presented dramatically and made to appear more exciting and less mundane than they actually are.

Television also has the unique ability to reach consumers *one on one,* as is the case when a spokesperson or endorser espouses the merits of a particular product. Like a personal sales presentation, the interaction between spokesperson and consumer takes place on a personal level.

More than any other medium, television also has the ability to use *humor* as an effective advertising strategy.

In the final analysis, the greatest relative advantage of television advertising is its ability to achieve *impact.* Impact is that quality of an advertising medium which activates a "special condition of awareness"[25] in the consumer and which "enlivens his mind to receive a sales message."[26]

Problems with Television Advertising   Television, as an advertising medium, suffers from three distinct problems. First, and perhaps most serious, is the rapidly escalating advertising cost. As noted in a previous section on cable television, the cost of network television advertising has more than tripled from the late 1960s to mid-1980s. A dramatic illustration of this is the increasing cost of buying advertising time for the Super Bowl. In 1975, the cost was $110,000 for a 30-second commercial. By 1985 the cost had increased to $525,000 (see Table 14.3). In addition to the soaring media costs, there has also been a substantial increase in the cost of producing television commercials. A commonplace cost for a simple 30-second commercial is $80,000 or more.[27]

A second problem is the erosion of television viewing audiences. Video cassette recorders, cable television, and other leisure and recreational alternatives have

---

[25]Richard C. Anderson, "Eight Ways to Make More Impact," *Advertising Age,* May 17, 1982, p. M-23.

[26]Raymond Rubicam quoted in Anderson, ibid.

[27]Miner Raymond, "How Much Should a Commercial Cost?" *Marketing Communications,* June 1983, p. 40.

TABLE 14.3   Super Bowl Advertising Costs, 1975 to 1985

This chart shows the year-by-year increases in the average cost of a 30-second commercial on the Super Bowl broadcast over the past 10 years. While the average rating of audience has remained relatively constant, the prices have escalated more than 400% since 1975 and cost-per-thousand rates have increased threefold.

This year, the average Super Bowl commercial will cost between $500,000 (on a package or exclusivity deal) and $525,000 for a single unit. The 1985 Super Bowl price hike is the greatest since 1982, the first Super Bowl after the NFL season was interrupted by the players' strike. *Source:* Lord, Geller, Frederico, Einstein and J. Walter Thompson USA, New York.

Year	Game (winner in bold)	Cost	CPM	Rating
1975	**Pittsburgh** vs. Minnesota	$110,000	3.74	42.4
1976	**Pittsburgh** vs. Dallas	125,000	3.96	42.3
1977	**Oakland** vs. Minnesota	162,000	4.72	44.4
1978	**Dallas** vs. Denver	185,000	5.27	47.2
1979	**Pittsburgh** vs. Dallas	222,000	6.28	47.1
1980	**Pittsburgh** vs. Los Angeles	225,000	6.39	46.3
1981	**Oakland** vs. Philadelphia	275,000	7.98	44.4
1982	**San Francisco** vs. Cincinnati	335,000	8.31	49.1
1983	**Washington** vs. Miami	400,000	9.94	48.6
1984	**Los Angeles** vs. Washington	445,000	11.41	46.4
1985	**Unknown**	525,000	13.00	48.0

Source: Advertising Age, November 26, 1984. Copyright 1984 Crain Communications, Inc.

diminished the number of people viewing network television. Projections are that the share of audience for prime-time network television will decline from 80 percent in 1982 to only 60 percent by 1990.[28]

Clutter is a third serious problem with television advertising. Clutter refers to the growing amount of nonprogram material—commercials, public service messages, and promotional announcements for stations and programs. Clutter has been created by the networks' increased use of promotional announcements to stimulate audience viewing of heavily promoted programs and by advertisers' increased use of shorter commercials. Whereas 60-second commercials once were prevalent, now the vast majority are 30 seconds or less. Moreover, some advertisers are experimenting with "split-30" commercials, where two different brands are advertised during a single 30-second commercial.

Regardless of cause, the effectiveness of television advertising has suffered from the clutter problem. One study showed that the percentage of viewers who could correctly recall commercials within five minutes after they aired dropped from 18 percent in 1965 to 7 percent in 1981.[29] A series of experiments by Ray and Webb revealed that the amount of attention devoted to commercials, the degree of con-

[28]O'Toole, "Network Television."

[29]Leo Bogart and Charles Lehman, "The Case of the 30-Second Commercial," *Journal of Advertising Research,* Vol. 23, February-March 1983, pp. 11–19.

tent recall, and the extent of brand name recognition all suffered from increased levels of clutter.[30] For example, the percent of subjects who paid full attention to any part of the tested commercials decreased from 56 percent in the least cluttered experimental condition to 46 percent in the most cluttered condition. Correct brand name recognition dropped from 22 percent in the least cluttered version to 10 percent in the most cluttered version.[31]

The Ray and Webb research also determined that the extent to which clutter has negative effects on commercial effectiveness depends critically on a commercial's position in a series or stream of continuous commercial messages. The middle position is worst, the first postion is best, and the last position is next best.[32]

Radio

The second broadcast medium, radio, is both an attractive advertising alternative to television and a useful complement to television and other advertising media. Like television, radio is a nearly ubiquitous medium: 99 percent of all homes in the United States have radios, 77 percent of the homes own four or more radios, 95 percent of all cars have a radio, and more that 50 million radios are purchased in the United States each year.[33] These impressive figures indicate radio's strong potential as an advertising medium.

Radio Is Red Hot

Promotional efforts by the Radio Advertising Bureau, an industry trade association, claim that radio is the "red hot" medium. Trade puffery aside, the fact remains that radio is indeed a "hot" advertising medium. Though radio has always been a favorite of local advertisers, it is only in recent years that national advertisers have begun to appreciate radio's relative advantages as an advertising medium. The following section examines these advantages and also explores some of the problems with radio advertising.

Radio Advertising: Strengths and Problems

Radio's Strengths   Radio is second only to magazines in its ability to reach segmented audiences. Radio thus personifies the notion of narrowcasting. An extensive variety of radio programming enables advertisers to pick specific formats and stations to be optimally compatible with their target audience and creative mes-

---

[30]For a review of these studies, see Peter H. Webb and Michael L. Ray, "Effects of TV Clutter," *Journal of Advertising Research,* Vol. 19, June 1979, pp. 7–12.

[31]Ibid., p. 9.

[32]Ibid., p. 11.

[33]Burt Manning, "Friendly Persuasion," *Advertising Age,* September 13, 1982, p. M-8.

sage strategies. In Los Angeles alone, there are over 80 radio stations. One media director explains radio's narrowcasting versatility this way:

> *There's classical music to reach the same kind of educated, high income adults [who] read* Smithsonian *or* Travel and Leisure, *only at less cost. You've got a yen to reach working women? Try an all news station in a.m. drivetime. Blacks? Stations like WBLS in New York reach them more efficiently than TV's "Soul Train" or black magazines such as* Ebony *and* Essence. *You've got teen stations, old lady stations, stations which reach sports nuts, young adults and middle-of-the-roaders. So don't think of radio as a mass medium unless sheer tonnage at the lowest CPM is your game. The radio networks are made up of hundreds of stations with different formats, audiences, signal strengths, coverage, etc.*[34]

Table 14.4 illustrates the diverse radio formats that are available to advertisers and the breakdown of average quarter hour audiences by age category. It can be seen that the 18 to 24 age group, for example, is most likely to listen to adult contemporary, golden oldies, progressive, soft contemporary, or top 40 formats. The 65 or over age category, by comparison, is most likely to listen to all news or talk programming formats. Other dramatic differences in programming preferences are apparent upon further perusal of Table 14.4.

A second major advantage of radio advertising is its ability to reach prospective customers on a *personal and intimate level.* The CEO of J. Walter Thomson USA, the largest advertising agency in the United States, has metaphorically described radio as a "universe of private worlds" and as "communication between two friends."[35] What he means by this is that people select radio stations much in the same fashion that they select personal friends, namely, by associating with others with whom their attitudes and interests are compatible. In similar fashion, people listen to those radio stations with which they closely identify. Because of this, radio advertising is likely to be received when the customer's mental frame is most conducive to persuasive influence. Radio advertising in this sense, then, is a personal and intimate form of "friendly persuasion."[36]

Economy is a third advantage of radio advertising. In terms of CPM per target audience, radio advertising is considerably cheaper than other mass media. This is shown in Table 14.5, which presents media CPM trends in index terms. For example, spot radio's 1983 index was only 207 (in 1967 dollars) in comparison to network television's and newspaper's indices of 318 and 314, respectively.

Flexibility is another relative advantage of radio advertising. Because radio production costs are typically inexpensive and scheduling deadlines short, copy

[34]Cyril C. Penn, "Marketing Tool Underused," *Advertising Age,* September 25, 1978, p. 122.

[35]Manning, "Friendly Persuasion."

[36]Ibid.

TABLE 14.4   Average Quarter Hour Audiences by Formats

Total Adults in U.S. 6 a.m.–midnight, Monday–Friday	U.S. Total	Total Radio	Adult Contemporary	All News	Beautiful Music	Black	Classical/ Semi-Classical	Country	Golden Oldies	Middle of the Road	Progressive	Soft Contemporary	Standard	Talk	Top 40
18 to 24															
Percent of composite	18.3	21.7	38.8	6.6	5.7	37.0	9.1	11.8	49.8	14.9	39.0	41.1	9.3	5.0	39.1
Index	100	119	212	36	31	202	50	64	272	81	213	225	51	27	214
25 to 34															
Percent of composite	22.0	24.4	30.7	14.6	15.2	30.8	12.4	21.2	29.8	28.5	43.9	36.8	13.8	8.0	30.7
Index	100	111	140	66	69	140	56	96	135	130	200	167	63	36	140
35 to 44															
Percent of composite	15.6	17.4	10.5	13.3	23.1	18.6	28.6	27.8	11.9	18.3	8.1	6.5	21.3	14.1	14.9
Index	100	112	67	85	148	119	183	178	76	117	52	42	137	90	96
45 to 54															
Percent of composite	15.7	15.4	8.0	24.3	22.8	10.9	33.2	15.9	3.1	19.6	2.3	6.5	23.3	26.8	8.3
Index	100	98	51	155	145	69	211	101	20	125	15	41	148	171	53
55 to 64															
Percent of composite	13.6	12.0	6.9	19.0	20.3	1.6	11.2	15.2	2.8	10.6	6.1	6.9	16.6	21.1	3.9
Index	100	88	51	140	149	12	82	112	21	78	45	51	122	155	29
65 or over															
Percent of composite	14.8	9.1	5.1	22.2	12.8	1.2	5.4	8.2	2.3	8.2	0.7	2.6	15.7	25.3	3.2
Index	100	61	34	150	86	8	36	55	16	55	5	18	106	171	22
18 to 49															
Percent of composite	63.0	69.8	83.0	46.0	54.1	92.4	57.7	69.8	93.7	70.2	91.7	87.8	53.8	36.0	87.6
Index	100	111	132	73	86	147	92	111	149	111	146	139	85	57	139
35 to 49															
Percent of composite	22.7	23.7	13.6	24.8	33.2	24.7	36.1	36.8	14.1	26.8	8.8	9.8	30.7	22.9	17.9
Index	100	104	60	109	146	109	159	162	62	118	39	43	135	101	79

Source: Reprinted with permission, Simmons Market Research Bureau, copyright 1978.

TABLE 14.5   **Media CPM Trends, 1967 = 100***

	1980	1981	1982	1983	1984†
Newspapers	235	263	288	314	340
Magazines	173	188	205	221	236
Network TV	238	261	292	318	350
Spot TV	201	223	248	268	298
Network radio	178	202	220	244	264
Spot radio	164	182	195	207	222
Outdoor	222	242	262	286	309
Direct mail	235	234	275	265	264
Composite	217	231	261	272	288

Source: McCann-Erickson, *Advertising Age,* November 7, 1983, p. M-20.
*1967 used as base year (100) for measuring all media.
†Estimated.

changes can be made quickly to take advantage of important developments and changes in the marketplace.[37]

Problems with Radio Advertising   Radio has some of the same weaknesses and problems that television has. Foremost, perhaps, is that both broadcast media are cluttered with competitive commercials and other forms of interference.

A second limitation is that radio is the only major medium that is unable to employ visual images. Because pictures are more concrete than words and concrete information is more effective than less concrete material (refer to Chapter 3 for further discussion), radio advertising has less impact than any major medium except outdoor advertising. It is important to note, however, that many advertising campaigns use radio as a supplement to other media, rather than as a stand-alone medium. This reduces radio's task from one of creating visual images to one of reactivating images that have been created already via television or magazines.

A third problem with radio advertising results from the difficulty of buying radio time. This is particularly acute in the case of the national advertiser who wishes to place spots in different markets throughout the country. There are more than 8,000 commercial radio stations operating in the United States,[38] and buying time is complicated due to unstandardized rate structures, which include a number of different combinations of fixed and discount rates.

A Note on Buying Radio Time

Radio advertisers are interested in accomplishing reach, frequency, and GRP requirements while assuring that the station format is compatible with the advertised product and its creative message strategy. Several considerations influence the

[37]McGann and Russell, *Advertising Media,* p. 148.
[38]Weilbacher, *Advertising,* p. 337.

choice of station.[39] Station format (black, country, top 40, etc.) is a preeminent consideration. Certain formats are obviously inappropriate for particular products and brands.

A second consideration is the choice of geographic areas to cover. National advertisers buy time from stations whose audience coverage matches the advertiser's geographic areas of interest. This typically means locating stations in preferred Standard Metropolitan Statistical Areas (SMSAs) or in so-called Areas of Dominant Influence (ADIs), which are approximately 200 areas in the United States that correspond to the major television markets.

A third consideration in buying radio time is the choice of daypart. Most stations offer anywhere from two to five dayparts. Following is a typical radio time schedule, with different dayparts designated by letter combinations:

> *AAAA—Monday through Saturday, 5:30 to 10:00 a.m.*
> *AAA—Monday through Saturday, 3:00 to 8:00 p.m.*
> *AA—Monday through Friday, 10:00 a.m. to 3:00 p.m.; Saturday and*
> *   Sunday, 6:00 a.m. to 8:00 p.m.*
> *A—Monday through Sunday, 8:00 p.m. to midnight.*
> *B—Tuesday through Sunday, midnight to 5:30 a.m.*

Rate structures vary depending on the attractiveness of the daypart, with AAAA in the preceding illustration obviously higher priced than B. Information about rates and station formats are available in *Spot Radio Rates and Data,* a source published by the Standard Rate and Data Services.

Magazines

Magazines have historically been considered a mass medium, but this is less true today. Now there are literally hundreds of special interest magazines, each appealing to audiences that manifest specific interests and life-styles. In fact, Standard Rate and Data Services, the technical information source for the magazine industry, identifies nearly 1,300 "consumer magazines" and divides these into dozens of specific categories such as "automotive" (e.g., *Motor Trend*), "general editorial" (e.g., *The New Yorker*), "sports" (e.g., *Sports Illustrated*), "women's fashions, beauty, and grooming" (e.g., *Glamour*), and many others. There are, in addition to consumer magazines, hundreds of other publications that are classified as farm magazines or business publications. Advertisers obviously have numerous options when selecting magazines to promote their products.

Buying Magazine Space

A number of factors influence the choice of specific magazines in which to advertise. Most important is selecting magazines that reach the type of people who constitute the advertiser's target market. However, because the advertiser typically

---

[39]See McGann and Russell, *Advertising Media,* for additional discussion, especially pp. 149–153.

has several vehicle alternatives that satisfy the target market objective, economic considerations become paramount in comparing the cost of advertising in different magazines. This evaluation is aided by the use of a well-known formula, called cost per thousand (CPM), to compare different magazine buys. It is computed as follows:

$$\text{Cost per thousand (CPM)} = \frac{\text{page rate} \times 1{,}000}{\text{circulation}}$$

Table 14.6 presents the CPM figures for a four-color page in various leading magazines aimed at men. The four-color cost per thousand figures (4/c CPM) are broken down according to total men and then into more specific categories. It is

TABLE 14.6   Comparative CPM Rates

Total Men

Publication	Audience (000)	4/c CPM
Field & Stream	7,243	$5.46
Newsweek	8,919	8.26
Sports Illustrated	10,786	6.13
Time	12,322	8.26
U.S. News & World Report	5,710	8.56
Mechanix Illustrated	4,123	6.96
Popular Mechanics	4,977	6.52
Popular Science	3,801	8.23
Sports Afield	2,585	5.98
Outdoor Life	3,876	7.01
Penthouse*	4,378	7.77
Playboy*	7,908	6.80

Men 18–49

Publication	Audience (000)	4/c CPM
Field & Stream	5,264	$ 7.52
Newsweek	6,804	10.83
Sports Illustrated	8,929	7.41
Time	9,181	11.09
U.S. News & World Report	3,755	13.02
Mechanix Illustrated	2,890	9.93
Popular Mechanics	3,500	9.28
Popular Science	2,685	11.65
Sports Afield	1,872	8.26
Outdoor Life	2,850	9.54
Penthouse*	3,960	8.59
Playboy*	6,908	7.78

Men 25–49

Publication	Audience (000)	4/c CPM
Field & Stream	4,007	$ 9.87
Newsweek	4,685	15.73
Sports Illustrated	6,029	10.97
Time	6,370	15.99
U.S. News & World Report	2,982	16.40
Mechanix Illustrated	2,359	12.17
Popular Mechanics	2,764	11.75
Popular Science	1,960	15.96
Sports Afield	1,459	10.59
Outdoor Life	2,219	12.25
Penthouse*	2,715	12.52
Playboy*	4,805	11.19

Male Homeowners

Publication	Audience (000)	4/c CPM
Field & Stream	5,798	$ 6.82
Newsweek	6,492	11.35
Sports Illustrated	7,700	8.59
Time	9,078	11.22
U.S. News & World Report	4,534	10.79
Mechanix Illustrated	3,313	8.66
Popular Mechanics	4,063	7.99
Popular Science	3,088	10.13
Sports Afield	2,040	7.58
Outdoor Life	3,008	9.04
Penthouse*	2,519	13.50
Playboy*	5,129	10.48

Source: Simmons Market Research Bureau, 1983.
*Based on adjusted '83 audience.

interesting to note the considerable variability in CPM across the various vehicles. *Field & Stream* is consistently the least expensive across all categories. This, however, does not necessarily mean that this publication is the best choice. Other factors such as appropriateness of editorial content, quality of reproduction, and prestige must also be considered. Moreover, if an advertiser is interested in reaching a more specific group of men (say only those with incomes greater than $35,000), considerable waste circulation may result from advertising in *Field & Stream*. In short, cost per thousand information is a useful aid in making magazine vehicle selection decisions, but many other factors must also be taken into account.

Magazine Advertising: Strengths and Problems

Magazine's Strengths   The ability to pinpoint specific audiences (termed *selectivity*) is a distinct magazine advertising advantage. If a potential market exists for a product, there is most likely at least one periodical that reaches this market. The advantage of selectivity is that it enables an advertiser to achieve effective, rather than wasted, exposure. This translates into more efficient advertising and lower costs per thousand.

Magazines are also noted for their *long life*. Unlike other media, magazines are often used for reference and are kept around the home for weeks or even longer. One study found that over three-fourths of all men and women referred back to, or reread, something in a magazine issue that they had previously read.[40] Moreover, magazine subscribers often pass their copies to other readers, which further expands a magazine's life.

In terms of qualitative considerations (refer again to Figure 14.4), magazines as an advertising medium are exceptional with regard to elegance, quality, beauty, prestige, and snob appeal. These features result from the high level of reproduction quality and from the surrounding editorial content that often transfers to the advertised product. Magazines also are a particularly good source for providing detailed product information and for conveying this information with a sense of authority.

Problems with Magazine Advertising   Two distinct limitations are associated with magazine advertising. First, advertisers must often buy *waste circulation* when advertising in magazines. This is because a magazine may reach geographically beyond the advertiser's primary market. For example, a regional meat packer whose primary markets are in the two Carolinas and Georgia would experience considerable waste circulation by advertising in a magazine circulated throughout the Southeast. Many magazines have overcome this problem by offering special advertising editions (called regional editions) that enable advertisers to designate

[40]S. Watson Dunn and Arnold M. Barban, *Advertising: Its Role in Modern Marketing,* 4th Ed. (Hinsdale, IL: The Dryden Press, 1978), p. 553.

specific geographic areas in which to advertise. The meat packer, for example, might advertise in *Southern Living* and pay for circulation only in the three states that represent the company's primary market.

A second limitation is *lack of flexibility.* In newspapers and the broadcast media, it is relatively easy to change ad copy on a fairly short notice and in specific markets. Magazines, by comparison, have long closing dates that require advertising materials to be on hand many days or weeks in advance of publication. *Reader's Digest,* for example, has a nine-week closing date.[41]

Newspapers

Newspapers received $20.6 billion, or nearly 36 percent, of the $58 billion spent in the United States in 1983 on consumer media advertising.[42] The total $20.6 billion in newspaper advertising revenues consisted of $11.8 billion in revenue for retail ads, $6 billion for classified ads, and $2.7 billion for national ads.

Local advertising is clearly the mainspring of newspapers. However, newspapers have become more proactive in their efforts to increase national advertising. These efforts have been facilitated by the Newspaper Advertising Bureau (NAB), a non-profit sales and research organization. The NAB offers a variety of services that assist both newspapers and national advertisers by simplifying the task of buying newspaper space and by offering discounts that make newspapers a more attractive medium.[43]

Buying Newspaper Space

Whereas buying space in magazines is done on the basis of full and fractional pages, space in newspapers is identified in terms of *agate lines* and *column inches.* An agate line is $\frac{1}{14}$ inch in depth and one column wide, regardless of the width of the column. The formula for transforming rates charged by different newspapers to a common denominator is called the **milline rate,** which stands for cost per line of advertising space per million circulation. The formula is as follows:

$$\text{Milline rate} = \frac{\text{line rate} \times 1{,}000{,}000}{\text{circulation}}$$

What this formula accomplishes is to adjust individual line rates in terms of a newspaper's circulation. Obviously, a higher line rate in one newspaper may well be a better value than a lower rate in another paper if the circulation in the former

[41]Ibid., p. 554.

[42]"Newspapers Lead in Media Expenditures," *Marketing News,* March 30, 1984, p. 6.

[43]See McGann and Russell, *Advertising Media,* pp. 166–169, for further discussion.

newspaper is proportionately large enough to offset its proportionately higher line rate.

Another consideration in buying newspaper space is the choice of position for an advertisement. Agate line rates apply only to advertisements placed r.o.p. (run-of-paper), which means that the ad appears in any location, on any page at the discretion of the newspaper. Premium charges may be assessed if an advertiser has a preferred space positioning, such as at the top of the page in the financial section. Whether premium charges are actually assessed is a matter of negotiation between the advertiser and the newspaper.

Newspaper Advertising: Strengths and Problems

Newspaper's Strengths   Because people read newspapers for news, they are in the right mental frame to process advertisements that *present news* of store openings, new products, sales, and so forth.

Mass audience coverage is a second strength of newspaper advertising. Newspapers cover as many as 70 percent of all households in some major markets.[44] Coverage is not restricted to specific socioeconomic or demographic groups but rather extends across all strata. Special-interest newspapers also reach large numbers of potential consumers. For example, it is estimated that 83 percent of college students read a campus newspaper.[45]

Flexibility is perhaps the greatest strength of newspapers. National advertisers can adjust copy to match the specific buying preferences and peculiarities of localized markets. Local advertisers can vary copy through in-paper inserts targeted to specific zip codes. Short closing times is another element of newspaper flexibility, which permits advertisers to tie in advertising copy with local market developments or newsworthy events. A further element of flexibility is achieved by locating advertising copy in a newspaper section that is compatible with the advertised product. Retailers of wedding accessories advertise in the bridal section, sporting goods stores advertise in the sports section, and so forth.

The ability to use *long copy* is another strength of newspaper advertising. Detailed product information and extensive, editorial passages are used in newspaper advertising to an extent unparalleled by any other medium.

Problems with Newspaper Advertising   *Clutter* is a problem in newspapers, as it is in all of the other major media with one exception. Outdoor advertising is not as highly susceptible to clutter as are other forms of advertising media.

Newspaper is not a highly *selective* medium. Newspaper is able to reach broad cross sections of people, but with few exceptions (such as campus newspapers), it is unable to reach specific groups of consumers effectively.

---

[44]Ibid., p. 181.

[45]"Mediawatch," *Marketing Communications,* February 1983, p. 9.

Occasional users of newspaper space (such as national advertisers who infrequently advertise in newspapers) pay higher rates than do heavy users and have difficulty in securing preferred, non-r.o.p. positions.

Newspaper does not offer the same quality of reproduction that can be obtained in magazines. For this and other reasons, newspaper is not generally known to enhance a product's perceived quality, elegance, or snob appeal, as do magazines and television.

Buying difficulties is a particularly acute problem in the case of the national advertiser who wishes to secure newspaper space in a variety of different markets. Each newspaper must be dealt with individually, and on top of this, the rates charged to national advertisers are typically higher than those charged to local advertisers.

The National Advertising Bureau (NAB) is, as noted earlier, making great strides toward making it easier for national advertisers to buy newspaper space. One program, called Standard Advertising Units (SAUs), has established 25 basic ad sizes that can be used in all broad-sheet newspapers (not tabloids) regardless of their column format or page size. Over 1,400 newspapers have accepted this program.[46] Another NAB program goes by the acronym *CAN DO,* which stands for Computer Analyzed Newspaper Data On-Line System. This program provides national advertisers with pertinent information about newspapers in terms of CPMs and demographic information on age, household income, and household size.[47]

Cooperative Advertising

Cooperative (co-op) advertising is, as the name suggests, a cooperative arrangement between manufacturers and retailers whereby the manufacturer pays a set allowance (anywhere from 50 to 100 percent) of the retailer's advertising cost. The actual amount of total advertising cost a manufacturer pays depends on the amount of merchandise a retailer purchases from the manufacturer during a specified period. The retailer receives (earns, in a sense) from the manufacturer an advertising fund, called an *accrual,* against which advertising costs are charged.

For example, suppose a certain appliance retailer purchases $200,000 from a particular manufacturer in one year. Suppose further that the manufacturer's cooperative program allows 3 percent of purchases to accrue to the retailer's cooperative advertising account. Thus, the retailer would have accrued $6,000 worth of cooperative advertising dollars. Now suppose that the manufacturer's co-op program pays 50 percent of individual advertising charges and that the retailer buys a $1,000 newspaper ad featuring the manufacturer's brand of appliances. The manufacturer would pay 50 percent of this amount, $500, and the retailer would have $5,500 remaining in its accrual account for future advertising.

[46]"Shedding the Local Image," *Marketing Communications,* September 1982, p. 43.
[47]Ibid.

Most cooperative advertising programs work in a similar fashion. Manufacturers develop specific programs that lay out the contractual obligations that the retailer must satisfy in order to be eligible for co-op dollars. These programs typically require retailers to feature the manufacturer's product(s) and not other brands in order to be eligible for reimbursements. Sometimes the co-op arrangements specify the percentage of accrued co-op dollars that must be spent in different advertising media, for example, X percent for newspapers, Y percent for television, and Z percent for radio. It should be noted that newspapers have been the dominant cooperative advertising medium.

Why is cooperative advertising used and how does it serve both manufacturers and retailers? There are several reasons.[48] First, manufacturers know that potential consumers for infrequently purchased goods (e.g., appliances, expensive wearing apparel) are responsive to retailer advertisements, especially preceding a major buying decision. Co-op advertising is thus a stimulant to immediate consumer purchases.

Second, manufacturers have found that cooperative advertising stimulates greater retailer buying and merchandising support. Retailers, knowing that they have accrued co-op dollars, are more eager to promote and merchandise a manufacture's specific brands and items aggressively. From the manufacturer's perspective, this amounts to greater stocking and more display space for its brands, as well as more retail advertising support.

A third advantage of co-op advertising is that it enables manufacturers to have access to local media at an advertising rate that is lower than would be paid if the manufacturer advertised directly rather than through retailers. This cost premium extends from the fact that local media, particularly newspapers, charge lower advertising rates to local advertisers than to national advertisers. Thus, by using cooperative advertising, a manufacturer is able to advertise locally at a lower rate.

Cooperative advertising, from the retailer's perspective, is a relatively inexpensive form of advertising. The advertising is not truly free, however, because the manufacturer's cooperative advertising costs are actually built into the price of the merchandise. Failure to take advantage of accrued co-op dollars means that the retailer is effectively paying more for the same merchandise than retailers who do utilize co-op funds.

Much cooperative advertising accruals are never spent by retailers. It is estimated that of about $7 billion available annually in co-op funds, only about half is used.[49] Recent research by the Newspaper Advertising Bureau shows that only about 40 percent of all retailers take advantage of co-op accruals.[50] For this reason manufacturers are developing new cooperative advertising programs to make it easier and more lucrative for retailers to utilize co-op funds. The objective is to

[48]Stephen A. Greyser and Robert F. Young, "Follow 11 Guidelines to Strategically Manage Co-op Advertising Program," *Marketing News,* September 16, 1983, p. 5.

[49]Renee Blakkan, "Savory Deals Tempt Hungry Retailers," *Advertising Age,* March 7, 1983, p. M-11.

[50]Ibid.

FIGURE 14.6   **An Example of Outdoor Advertising**

Source: Courtesy of NIKE. Photographer: Chuck Rogers.

make the plans simpler to read and easier to use. Advertising media are also offering new programs to attract more co-op dollars. For example, the Newspaper Advertising Bureau, in conjunction with the co-op services division of Standard Rate & Data Services, has developed a program whereby newspaper space salespeople are able to identify all the products that carry co-op being sold in a retailer's store, determine how much the retailer has accrued for each product, and then run an ad for the retailer that will use the accrued co-op funds.[51]

Outdoor Advertising

Outdoor advertising, the oldest form of advertising, includes a variety of advertising mechanisms. "T-shirts on joggers, skywriting, bus shelters, taxicabs, giant inflatables, construction site fences, and ads painted on the sides of cars and trucks all fall under the outdoor umbrella, but the ubiquitous billboard is the leading example of the medium."[52] An award-winning advertisement for Nike running shoes in Figure 14.6 shows outdoor advertising at its best. In the markets where the campaign has run, Nike sales have increased an average of 30%, distribution has swung back toward high-end retailers, and considerable enthusiasm has been generated in management and the sales force at Nike (*Marketing News*, June 7, 1985, p. 7).

Outdoor advertising, which is regarded as a supplementary, rather than primary, advertising medium, receives about 2.8 percent of U.S. advertising expenditures, a

[51]Ibid.

[52]Kevin Higgins, "Often Overlooked Outdoor Advertising Offers More Impact and Exposures Than Most Media," *Marketing News*, Vol. 17, July 22, 1983, p. 1.

figure that has been static for years.[53] There are about 275,000 U.S. billboards,[54] of which nearly 40 percent advertise cigarettes or liquors.[55]

Buying Outdoor Advertising

Outdoor advertising is purchased through individual operators, which are called *plants.* There are approximately 600 plants nationwide that offer outdoor advertising in more than 900 markets.[56] National outdoor buying organizations enable national advertisers to purchase outdoor space at locations throughout the country.

Just like television and radio, outdoor advertising space is sold in terms of gross rating points (GRPs). However, the notion of GRP is somewhat different in the case of outdoor advertising. Specifically, one outdoor GRP means reaching 1 percent of the population one time. Outdoor GRPs are based on the daily *duplicated audience* as a percentage of the total potential market. For example, if four billboards in a community of 200,000 population achieve a daily exposure to 80,000 persons, the result is 40 gross rating points. GRPs are sold in units of 25, with 100 and 50 being the two most purchased levels.[57]

Outdoor Advertising: Strengths and Problems[58]

Outdoor Advertising's Strengths   A major strength of outdoor advertising is its *broad reach and high frequency levels.* Outdoor advertising is effective in reaching virtually all segments of the population. The number of exposures is especially high when signs are strategically located in heavy traffic areas.

Another advantage is *geographic flexibility.* Outdoor advertising can be strategically positioned to supplement other advertising efforts in select geographic areas where advertising support is most needed.

Low cost per thousand is another advantage. Outdoor advertising is the least expensive advertising medium on a CPM basis.

Outdoor advertising is also *bigger than life,* and *product identification* is substantial. The ability to use large representations offers marketers excellent opportunities for brand and package identification.

Outdoor advertising also provides an excellent opportunity to reach consumers as a last reminder before purchasing.

---

[53]Ibid., p. 10.

[54]Ibid.

[55]Kenneth Wylie, "What's Good, What's Bad, What's Beautiful," *Advertising Age,* August 8, 1983, p. M-14.

[56]McGann and Russell, *Advertising Media,* p. 227.

[57]Ibid., p. 235.

[58]The following discussion is an adaptation of the presentation in McGann and Russell, *Advertising Media,* pp. 227–233.

Problems with Outdoor Advertising   One significant problem with outdoor advertising is *nonselectivity*. Outdoor advertising can be geared to general groups of consumers (e.g., inner-city residents), but it is incapable of pinpointing more specific market segments (say, professional black men between the ages of 25 and 39).

In addition, *short exposure time* is a drawback. "Now you see it, now you don't" appropriately characterizes the fashion in which outdoor advertising engages the consumer's attention. For this reason, outdoor messages that have to be read are less effective than predominantly visual ones.

It is also difficult to measure outdoor advertising's audience. The lack of verified audience measurement is regarded by some as a significant impediment to outdoor advertising's becoming a more widely used advertising medium.

Developments in Outdoor Advertising

A number of technological advancements are enhancing outdoor advertising's attractiveness. Fiber optics, which uses light-transmitting glass fibers to give special illumination effects, is an appealing technology. Fiber optics are being used as borders around panels and as tracing around letters in company and brand names. This technology is a cheaper and more flexible substitute for conventional neon lighting.[59]

Some additional innovative developments in outdoor advertising include the following:[60]

1. Reflective discs, which vibrate when the sun hits them. This technology was used to introduce Camel Light cigarettes and to promote a Linda Ronstadt record album.
2. Backlighting, which involves an open container on one side that is filled with fluorescent lighting and covered over the open side with a sheet of transparent sheeting that is hand painted with an advertising message. Coca-Cola, Budweiser, and other companies have experimented with this method.

Media Impact

The objective of all advertising, stated simply, is to attain *impact,* to attract the prospective customer's attention and to give him or her a meaningful reason to invest the time and effort necessary to examine an advertisement. The message itself, as was already discussed in the previous chapter, is largely responsible for accomplishing this objective, but the strategic selection of media can further enhance advertising impact.

---

[59]"Fiber Optics and Other Technologies Add 'Wow Appeal' to Outdoor Ads," *Marketing News,* Vol. 17, July 22, 1983, p. 10.

[60]Wylie, "What's Good," p. M-15.

A media executive for a large advertising agency—Needham, Harper & Steers, New York—has proposed an innovative set of eight media strategies to enhance advertising impact.[61] These strategies, listed in no particular order, are saturation, omnipresence, matching the medium to the message, doing the unexpected, extreme continuity, unusual use of the facilities of a medium, short-term blitzes, and shifting from one medium to another.

Saturation

Saturation involves very heavy advertising in a particular medium. Chrysler Corporation typified saturation strategy in the early 1980s when it spent nearly $10 million to advertise its rebate program ("Get a car, get a check"), which was, in many respects, a last-ditch effort to save the company. "The impact of 200 spots a week on network radio and another 200 in spot radio made it virtually impossible to escape the Chrysler message."[62] Apple computer saturated a November 1984 issue of *Newsweek* by buying all of the advertising space in that magazine issue.

Omnipresence

A counterpart to saturation, omnipresence involves simultaneous advertising in multiple media. "The theory is to come in with all flags flying, with the avowed purpose of achieving instant popularization of product or service."[63] Many companies follow an omnipresence strategy when introducing new products.

Matching Media to Message

The placement of advertisements in certain media or media vehicles may serve to enhance the importance of a company and its messages. Local (nonnational) companies accomplish this when they advertise in prestigious publications such as regional issues of *Time* magazine. In general, this strategy's objective is to find a medium whose own prestige and appeal will augment the credibility, importance, and appeal of the advertiser's message. The choice of medium depends, of course, on the specific product/market situation involved.

Unexpected Media Placement

Another strategy involves placing advertising in a medium or vehicle that is atypical for the advertised brand or service. The International Ladies Garment Workers' Union achieved tremendous impact by spending all of its limited advertising

---

[61]The following discussion borrows liberally from Anderson, "Eight Ways." Readers are encouraged to read the original source for additional detail and examples.

[62]Ibid., p. M-24.

[63]Ibid.

budget on a dozen commercials in the Academy Awards show.[64] The early choice of cable television as an advertising medium by a few pioneering national brands (e.g., Budweiser) further illustrates this strategy.

Extreme Continuity

Extreme continuity is the strategy of continued advertising over the years in the same time slot on radio or television or in the same newspaper or magazine pages. The value of such advertising is that it builds a strong association (a form of conditioning effect) between the advertised brand and the program or publication in which the advertising occurs. There are numerous familiar illustrations of this strategy. One that particularly stands out in the authors' minds is Saturday afternoon college football scores on television sponsored by Prudential (the "Prudential College Scoreboard").

Use of Facilities of a Medium

Another advertising strategy involves coalescing a brand's primary selling proposition with the peculiar features or strengths of a given medium. When Honda, for example, first began marketing its automobiles in the United States, it needed to use a medium that would overcome American suspicions about the quality of Japenese cars. Honda's media strategy was the use of good color magazine spreads to display the quality and appeal of its cars.[65]

Short-Term Blitzes

Short-term blitzes are the strategy of buying saturation for a short period of time. This is an especially effective way of creating impact for the small advertiser whose budget does not permit continued saturation. Rather than spreading a limited budget over time, with the possibility that none of the limited advertising will have impact, a blitz campaign can generate impact for a short period at the least.

Shifting Media

The shifting media strategy is intended to overcome boredom that customers may experience when they repeatedly see or hear the same brand advertised in the same medium. This strategy seeks to create some novelty value through media selection. Advertising by the Quasar Co. is illustrative.

> *[Quasar] spends a small amount of money on advertising relative to the total electronics category. In addition, Quasar budgets remain static*

---

[64]Ibid.
[65]Anderson, "Eight Ways," p. M-24.

from year to year, and in the face of rising media cost, maintaining awareness becomes an increasingly difficult task. Quasar's objectives were to boost its media visibility, to dominate competitive advertising levels whenever possible and to stimulate distributors and the field sales force into thinking "Quasar" on a day-to-day basis. The advertising strategy developed was to consolidate all funds in a single medium at one time and to rotate the chosen media to hype consumer attention. Plans from 1978 to date have alternated in six-month intervals from all-magazine to all-TV plans and for one six-month period included an exclusive Sunday supplement plan, which ran for 13 consecutive weeks.[66]

In sum, these eight media strategies illustrate, but certainly do not exhaust, the strategic possibilities that can be implemented to increase advertising impact. Message creativity is critical, but it alone is not sufficient. Creative media selection must work in tandem with creative message development to accomplish impact objectives.

Agency-Client Relations

The subject of agency-client relations is a fitting chapter conclusion because the media strategies and decisions discussed to this point are most often the joint work of advertisers (clients) and their advertising agencies. This section will examine first the advertising agency role and then the issue of agency compensation.

Advertising Agency Role

Companies have three alternative ways to perform the advertising function. First, a company can maintain its own, *in-house* advertising operation. This necessitates employing an advertising staff and absorbing the overhead required to maintain the staff and its operations. Such an arrangement is unprofitable unless a company does a relatively large and continuous amount of advertising.

An alternative arrangement is to contract for advertising services with a *full-service advertising agency*. Full-service agencies perform research, creative, and media-buying services. They are also involved in the advertiser's total marketing process and, for a fee, may perform a variety of other marketing services including sales promotion, publicity, package design, strategic marketing planning, and sales forecasting.

The advantages of using a full-service agency include (1) acquiring the services of specialists with in-depth knowledge of current advertising and marketing techniques, (2) obtaining negotiating muscle with the media, and (3) being able to

[66]Ibid.

coordinate advertising and marketing efforts. The major disadvantages are (1) some control over the advertising function is lost when it is performed by an agency rather than in house, (2) agencies sometimes cater to larger advertiser clients, and (3) agencies sometimes are inefficient in media buying.[67]

A third alternative is to purchase advertising services *à la carte.* That is, rather than depending entirely on a single full-service agency to perform all advertising and related functions, an advertiser may recruit the services of a variety of "individual firms with particular specialties, such as creative, media, production, research, sales promotion, publicity, new product development, etc."[68] The advantages of this arrangement are (1) the ability to contract for services only when they are needed, (2) availability of high caliber creative talent, and (3) potential cost efficiencies. The disadvantages include (1) a tendency for specialists (so-called "boutiques") to approach client problems in a stereotyped rather than innovative fashion, (2) lack of cost accountability, and (3) financial instability of many smaller boutiques.[69]

Many advertisers actually employ a combination of the different advertising options rather than use one exclusively. For example, a firm may have its own in-house agency but contract with boutiques for certain needs. Although in-house agencies and boutiques experienced considerable growth during the late 1960s and early 1970s, the trend today is toward full-service agencies and away from in-house agencies—especially among larger advertisers.[70]

Agency Compensation

An interesting pricing system for compensating advertising agencies has evolved over the years. This system involves a flat 15 percent commission paid to agencies for all advertising that is placed in behalf of the advertiser in a major commissionable media (newspapers, magazines, radio, and television).[71] To illustrate, suppose the XYZ Advertising Agency buys $100,000 of space in a certain magazine for its client, ABC Company. When the invoice for this space comes due, XYZ would submit payment of $85,000 to the magazine publisher ($100,000 less the 15 percent discount) and then bill ABC for the full $100,000. The $15,000 in revenue realized by XYZ Advertising Agency has historically been regarded as a fair amount of compensation to the agency for its creative expertise, media-buying insight, and ancillary functions performed in behalf of its client, ABC Company.

The 15 percent compensation system has, as one may suppose, been a matter of some controversy between company marketing executives and managers of adver-

---

[67]George Donahue, "Evaluating Advertising Services: Part II," *Marketing Communications,* April 1982, p. 61.

[68]Ibid., p. 63.

[69]Ibid., p. 64.

[70]George Donahue, "Evaluating Advertising Services: Part I," *Marketing Communications,* March 1982, p. 46.

[71]The discount paid to advertising agencies for outdoor advertising is typically 16.67 percent. The extra 1.67 percent is used by outdoor companies (plants) to lure business away from the other major media.

tising agencies.[72] The primary topic of disagreement is the matter of whether 15 percent compensation is too much (marketing executives' perspective) or too little (ad agencies' perspective). The disagreement has spurred the growth of an alternative compensation system, called the *fee system.* This system involves price negotiations between advertisers and agencies such that the actual rate of compensation, which may be more or less than 15 percent, is based on mutual agreement concerning the worth of the services rendered by the advertising agency.

A recent survey by the Association of National Advertisers has revealed slippage in the use of the traditional compensation system. Whereas 52 percent of respondents (national advertisers) to a 1983 survey compensated their agencies using the traditional commission system, the percentages for previous surveys were 57 percent in 1979 and 68 percent in 1976.[73] The 1983 survey shows further that 29 percent of respondents reported using a fee arrangement, and 19 percent use some variation of the traditional commission system.[74]

Despite these results, most agency executives believe that the 15 percent commission system will never die.[75] The following quote from an agency executive summarizes well the argument in favor of the traditional commission system:

> *The best part about the commission system is that it is easy to understand and operates almost automatically. It can be reviewed periodically. Service can be improved or increased. Or concessions can be made. But the commission system actually reduces the chance of friction, which sooner or later can destroy even a productive agency-client relationship.*[76]

A counterperspective is offered in the following quote from a marketing executive:

> *A standard 15% is not always equitable since for some big billing brands it's too much and for other smaller brands [which demand] an inordinate amount of work it's not enough.*[77]

In many respects, the matter of agency compensation boils down to an issue of what is fair and workable. Agencies and clients are not in complete harmony on this issue. A survey of 158 members (agency representatives and clients) of an influential group called the Sounding Board offers insight into the perceptions of agencies and advertisers concerning the fairness and workability of various compensation systems.[78] Agencies' and advertisers' views are somewhat divergent with

---

[72]For an insightful review of different perspectives on the issue, see Herbert Zeltner, "Sounding Board: Clients, Admen Split on Compensation," *Advertising Age,* May 18, 1981, pp. 63–76.

[73]"The 15% Media Commission Plans," *Marketing News,* June 10, 1983, p. 9.

[74]Ibid.

[75]Merle Kingman, "To Fee or Not to Fee," *Advertising Age,* August 29, 1983, p. M-24.

[76]Ibid.

[77]Zeltner, "Sounding Board," p. 63.

[78]Ibid.

regard to the fairness/workability of various compensation plans. In general, agencies prefer standard media commissions with additional fees for extra services rendered, whereas advertisers most prefer the standard media commission system with maximum (ceiling) and minimum (floor) percentage adjustments for additional services rendered or not rendered.

Summary

Selection of advertising media and media vehicles is one of the most important and complicated of all marketing communication decisions. Media planning must be coordinated with marketing strategy and with other aspects of advertising strategy. The strategic aspects of media planning involve four steps: (1) selecting the target audience toward which all subsequent efforts will be directed; (2) specifying media objectives, which typically are stated in terms of reach, frequency, gross rating points (GRPs), or effective rating points (ERPs); (3) selecting general media categories and specific vehicles within each medium; and (4) scheduling media.

The last two steps represent the core of media strategy. Media and vehicle selection are influenced by a variety of factors, the most important being target audience, cost, and creative considerations. Media planners select media vehicles by identifying those that will reach the designated target audience, satisfy budgetary constraints, and be compatible with and enhance the advertiser's creative messages. There are numerous ways to schedule media insertions over time, but media planners are increasingly using some form of pulsed or flighted schedule whereby advertising is on at times, off at others, but never continuous.

Advertising media planners have available five major media: television, radio, magazines, newspapers, and outdoor advertising. Each medium has its unique qualities and strengths and weaknesses. The chapter provides a detailed analysis of each medium.

Achieving impact is the ultimate concern in any advertising undertaking. Impact is largely a function of message quality, but media placement can also play an important role. Eight specific media strategies for enhancing impact are examined: saturation, omnipresence, matching media to message, unexpected media placement, extreme continuity, use of facilities of a medium, short-term blitzes, and shifting media.

A concluding chapter topic is the role of an advertising agency. Companies basically have three ways to perform the advertising function: set up an in-house advertising operation, use a full-service advertising agency, or buy advertising services on an à la carte basis from specialized advertising services called boutiques.

Discussion Questions

1. Why is target audience selection the critical first step in formulating a media strategy?
2. Explain the problems associated with using GRPs as a media selection criterion. In what sense is the concept of ERPs superior?

3. Why is reach also called net coverage or unduplicated audience?

4. As noted in the text, it cost advertisers $525,000 for 30 seconds of advertising during the 1984 Super Bowl. This price is three or four times more expensive than most network television charges. Does this mean that the Super Bowl viewing audience would have to be three or four times larger than other program audiences in order for an advertiser to justify buying Super Bowl time?

5. What are the advantages and disadvantages of cable television advertising?

6. Assume you are brand manager for a product line of thermos containers. Your products range from thermos bottles to small ice chests. With reference to Table 14.6, select two magazines from the list and justify your choice to advertise your products in these magazines.

7. How does cooperative advertising work? What are its advantages to both manufacturers and retailers?

8. It was noted in the text that cigarettes and liquors are credited with nearly 40 percent of all billboard advertising. Why do you think these two product categories dominate the billboard medium?

9. Pretend you are a manufacturer of various jewelry items, one of the most important in your product line being graduation rings for high school and college students. Suppose you are in the process of developing a media strategy aimed specifically at high school students. You have an annual budget of $3 million. What media and vehicles would you use and how would you schedule the advertising over time?

Exercises

1. Examine a copy of the most recent *Spot Radio Rates and Data* available in your library, and compare the advertising rates for three or four of the radio stations in your home town or university community.

2. Interview several retailers, both large and small, to determine how extensively they use cooperative advertising. Ascertain their motivations for using (or not using) co-op funds. Determine when they are most and least likely to use co-op funds. Request an extra copy of a co-op program from the retailers and summarize the manufacturer's requirements contained in the program.

3. Select any five magazines and apply the criteria in Figure 14.4 that are especially relevant to magazines (e.g., "elegance"). On the basis of this application, construct a rank ordering from best magazine to worst. Justify your rankings.

4. Pick your favorite clothing store in your university community (or home town) and justify the choice of one radio station that the clothing store should select for its radio advertising. Do not feel constrained by what the clothing store may already be doing. Focus instead on what you think is most important. Be certain to make explicit all criteria used in making your choice and all radio stations considered.

CHAPTER 15

Assessing Advertising Effectiveness

Companies and not-for-profit organizations annually invest billions of dollars in advertising, but much (if not most) of these expenditures are made without undertaking efforts to determine whether the advertising actually accomplishes the objectives for which it is intended. Some firms refuse to assess advertising effectiveness formally because they consider such an undertaking unnecessary. Other organizations neglect to measure advertising effectiveness because they consider the task too expensive. Still others bypass efforts to assess advertising effectiveness formally because they consider the task hopeless.

Measuring advertising effectiveness is indeed a difficult and often expensive task, but the value gained from undertaking the effort typically outweighs the expense incurred and difficulty encountered. In the absence of formal research, most advertisers could not know whether their advertising is doing a good job nor could they know what should be changed so that their future advertising could do an even better job.

Advertising Effectiveness Measurement

The Ideal

The role, importance, and difficulty of assessing advertising effectiveness can perhaps best be appreciated by first examining what an ideal system of advertising effectiveness measurement would contain.

First, an ideal measure would *provide an early warning signal,* i.e., a "reading" of ad effectiveness at the earliest possible stage in the advertisement development process. The sooner an advertisement is found to be ineffective, the less time, effort, and financial resources will be wasted. Similarly, early detection of effective advertisements enables marketers to hasten the developmental process so that the ads can generate return on investment as quickly as possible.

Second, an ideal measurement system would evaluate advertising effectiveness in terms of *sales response,* the ultimate advertising objective. A measure of advertising effectiveness becomes less valuable the further removed it is from the advertisement's potential for generating sales volume.

Third, an ideal measurement system would also satisfy the standard research requirements of *reliability and validity.* Advertising measures are *reliable* when the same results are obtained on repeated occasions, i.e., the results are replicable. Measures are *valid* when they predict actual marketplace performance.

Finally, an ideal system would permit *quick* and *inexpensive* measurement.

The Reality

The ideal conditions just discussed are rarely satisfied. In fact, several are inconsistent. For example, a measurement system capable of predicting sales potential is unlikely to be inexpensive. Similarly, one that provides an early warning signal is less likely to be reliable and valid. Thus, advertising research must necessarily deviate from the ideal circumstances described previously.

The following sections describe a variety of actual research techniques that are used for assessing advertising effectiveness. First, however, it will be useful to examine a major recent public statement that was prepared jointly by 21 leading U.S. advertising agencies. This document, called PACT for short, represents a consensus of the advertising community on fundamental copy testing principles.

Positioning Advertising Copy Testing (PACT)[1]

Advertising effectiveness research, or, more simply, *copy research*, involves two stages. *Copy development research*, which often precedes copy testing, is performed to aid the direction of creative strategy and selection of executional elements. *Copy testing* is performed to determine whether an advertisement or commercial should run in the marketplace. The PACT document deals with copy testing only and, although relevant to testing advertising in all media, is directed primarily at television advertising. PACT consists of nine copy testing principles:

---

[1]Material for this section is extracted from the PACT document, which is published in its entirety in the *Journal of Advertising,* Vol. 11, No. 4, 1982, pp. 4–29.

Principle 1   A good copy testing system provides measurements that are relevant to the objectives of the advertising. The specific objective(s) that an advertising campaign is intended to accomplish (creating brand awareness, influencing brand image, encouraging product trial, etc.) should be the first consideration in determining the copy testing methods to assess advertising effectiveness. For example, if the objective for a particular campaign is to encourage product trial, then a measure of emotional response would be inappropriate.

Principle 2   A good copy testing system is one that requires agreement about how the results will be used *in advance* of each specific test. Specifying how research results will be used before data are collected ensures that all parties involved (advertiser, agency, research firm) agree on the research goals and reduces the chance of conflicting interpretations of test results. This principle's intent is to encourage the use of decision rules or action standards that, in advance of actual testing, establish the test results which must be achieved for a test advertisement to receive full media distribution. An action standard is stated similarly to the following illustration: Commercial X must receive a minimum Burke-rated Day-After Recall score of 40, or the commercial will not be run.[2]

Principle 3   A good copy testing system provides *multiple* measurements because single measurements are generally inadequate to assess the performance of an advertisement. Because the process by which advertising influences customers is complex, multiple measures are more likely to capture the various advertising effects and are therefore preferred over single measures.

Principle 4   A good copy testing system is based on a model of human response to communications—the *reception* of a stimulus, the *comprehension* of the stimulus, and the *response* to the stimulus. Because advertisements vary in impact they are intended to achieve, a good copy testing system is capable of answering a number of questions. Table 15.1 provides a listing of the types of questions that may be addressed in copy testing.

Principle 5   A good copy testing system allows for consideration of whether the advertising stimulus should be exposed more than once. This principle addresses the issue of whether a single test exposure (i.e., showing an ad or commercial to consumers only once) provides a sufficient test of potential impact. Because multiple exposure is often required for advertisements to accomplish their full effect,[3] copy testing procedures should expose a test ad to respondents on two or more occasions when the communication situation calls for such a procedure. For ex-

---

[2]The Burke Day-After Recall (DAR) testing method is discussed in a later section.

[3]Herbert E. Krugman, "Why Three Exposures May Be Enough," *Journal of Advertising Research,* Vol. 12, December 1972, pp. 11–14.

TABLE 15.1	**Illustrative Copy Testing Questions**

Reception

Did the advertising get through?
Did it catch the consumer's attention?
Was it remembered?
Did it catch his eye? his ear?

Comprehension

Was the advertising understood?
Did the consumer get the message?
Was the message identified with the brand?
Was anything confusing or unclear?

Response

Did the consumer accept the proposition?
Did the advertising affect attitudes toward the brand?
Did the consumer think or feel differently about the brand after exposure?
Did the advertising affect perceptions of the brand?
Did the advertising alter perceptions of the set of competing brands?
Did the consumer respond to direct action appeals?

Source: PACT Document, *Journal of Advertising,* Vol. 11, No. 4, 1982, p. 17.

ample, a single-exposure test is probably insufficient to test whether an advertisement successfully conveys a complex benefit. On the other hand, a single exposure may be adequate if an advertisement is designed solely to create name awareness for a new brand.

Principle 6   A good copy testing system recognizes that the more finished a piece of copy is, the more soundly it can be evaluated, and a good system requires, at minimum, that alternative executions be tested in the same degree of finish. "Experience has shown that test results can often vary depending on the degree of finish of the test executions. Thus, careful judgment should be used in considering the importance of what may be lost in a less than finished version. Sometimes this loss may be inconsequential; sometimes it may be critical."[4]

Principle 7   A good copy testing system provides controls to avoid the bias normally found in the exposure context. The context in which an advertisement is contained (e.g., the clutter or lack of clutter in a magazine) will have a substantial impact on how the ad is received, processed, and accepted. For this reason copy testing procedures should attempt to emulate the actual context that an advertisement or commerical may eventually have.

[4]PACT document, *Journal of Advertising*, p. 21.

Principle 8   A good copy testing system is one that takes into account basic considerations of sample definition. Any good research requires that the sample be representative of the target audience to which test results are to be generalized and that the sample size be sufficiently large to permit reasonably precise statistical conclusions.

Principle 9   A good copy testing system is one that can demonstrate reliability and validity. Reliability and validity are basic requirements of any research endeavor. As applied to copy testing, a reliable test is one that yields consistent results each time an advertisement is tested, and a valid test is one that is predictive of marketplace performance.

The foregoing principles establish a high set of standards for the advertising research community. Yet, they should not be regarded in the same sense that the earlier discussion of research ideals were. Rather, these principles should be viewed as mandatory for meaningfully testing advertising effectiveness.

Copy Testing Techniques

Literally dozens of copy testing techniques have evolved over the years for measuring advertising effectiveness. Some of these techniques are similar in methodology and intent, and others serve entirely different purposes, are used to test different advertising objectives, and may not be substituted for one another. The following sections discuss the important and most frequently used procedures in advertising copy testing. A meaningful framework for the discussion is the Association Model shown in Figure 15.1.[5]

An Overview of the Association Model

The association model is one in a long stream of so-called hierarchy-of-effect models. Like its predecessors, it is designed to explain the process by which advertisements move consumers to make a buying choice. The association model is distinguished from the other models, however, because it is more comprehensive and because it is the only model that is able to incorporate all of the major measures of research commonly used in advertising.

The model, as adapted in Figure 15.1, consists of seven major levels, or hierarchies, of advertising effect: exposure, awareness, association evaluation, perception, evaluation, stimulation, and action. Each level is reviewed briefly to provide the necessary backdrop for the discussion of specific research techniques in the following section.[6]

---

[5]Ivan L. Preston, "The Association Model of the Advertising Communication Process," *Journal of Advertising*, Vol. 11, No. 2, 1982, pp. 3–15.

[6]The discussion follows Preston's presentation, ibid., pp. 3–7.

FIGURE 15.1   The Association Model of Advertising

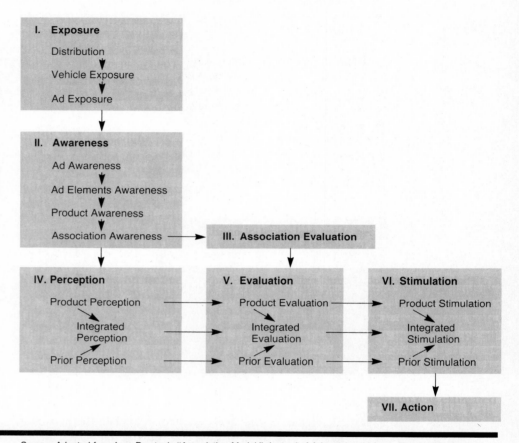

Source: Adapted from Ivan Preston's "Association Model," *Journal of Advertising,* Vol. 11, No. 2, 1982, p. 4.

Exposure   The initial task an advertiser faces is to assure that sufficient numbers of potential customers are actually exposed to its advertisements. This requires that (1) media vehicles (television programs, magazine issues, etc.) be distributed to carry advertisements, (2) customers be exposed to these vehicles (by watching a television program, by reading a specific magazine issue, etc.), and (3) customers be exposed to the advertiser's specific advertisement(s) carried in these vehicles.

Commercial advertising research firms regularly conduct studies to measure exposure levels. *Nielsen* measures audience exposure to television programs, *Simmons* monitors magazine readership, and *Arbitron* measures local radio listening habits. The services provided by these research companies are described in the section that follows this general overview of the Association Model.

Awareness   After a consumer is exposed to an advertisement, several levels of awareness may occur. *Ad awareness* involves simply noticing an ad without noticing specific executional elements. *Ad elements awareness* involves the consumer's becoming aware of specific parts, elements, or features of an ad. *Product awareness* involves recognizing the specific product, brand, or service being advertised. *Association awareness* involves the receiver's recognition of specific copy points or other executional elements that have been included in the advertisement by the advertiser with hopes that the receiver will indeed associate them with the advertised product/brand.

Thus, various types of awareness are needed in order for consumers to make the necessary associations (hence the name *Association Model*) that the advertiser intends them to make. *Starch readership studies* and *Burke Day-After Recall measures* are the best known commercial services for measuring various aspects of advertising recognition and awareness. These methods will be described in a later section.

Association Evaluation   Advertisers intend consumers to evaluate positively those aspects of an advertisement which the advertiser has associated with the product or brand. This does not always occur, of course; some consumers make no evaluations or make ones that are negative or neutral. Knowing the association evaluations that consumers make in response to advertisements is important in principle, yet most commercial research firms do not undertake efforts to measure these evaluations.[7]

Perception   Figure 15.1 shows that *integrated perception* results from *product perception* and *prior perception.* Prior perception is the consumer's existing knowledge and beliefs about a product or brand before exposure to an advertisement. Product perception is the total picture of a product or brand that the consumer forms from processing an advertisement. Integrated perception represents the combination of past inputs (prior perception) with present inputs (product perception). Integrated perception is what a consumer actually believes about a product or brand following exposure to an ad. The integrated perception of today will become tomorrow's prior perception.

Evaluation   Evaluation represents the consumer's affective reaction to the advertised product or brand. Paralleling the process described previously for perception, *integrated evaluation* represents the outcome of the consumer's pre-ad exposure evaluation *(prior evaluation)* combined with his or her ad-based evaluation *(product evaluation).* Integrated perception is the consumer's *feeling* toward the ad itself or toward the advertised product or brand that results from processing an advertisement.

[7]Ibid., p. 5.

Two facets of feelings are measured by advertising researchers. First, a variety of methods are employed to measure consumers' emotional reactions to advertisements. A second type of study uses standard verbal measures to assess consumers' attitudes. Both types of measures are discussed later in this chapter.

Stimulation   Stimulation is the motivation or intention toward the final step, *action.* The intention before exposure to an ad *(prior stimulation)* is augmented (or perhaps mitigated) as a result of being exposed to an advertisement. The result is *integrated stimulation.*

Various so-called "theater tests" are conducted by commercial advertising researchers to assess how effective advertisements are in motivating consumers to act. Two particularly well known theater testing methods, *Audience Studies, Inc. (ASI)* and *Competitive Environment Tests,* are discussed later.

Action   Integrated stimulation prompts the final step, *action,* which typically translates as purchase behavior. Exciting new research techniques that combine the use of supermarket optical scanners and split cable television for purposes of measuring actual purchase response to advertising are described later.

Advertising Research Techniques

The specific advertising research methods that were alluded to previously will be discussed in this section. The presentation naturally extends from the overview of the Association Model. Table 15.2 categorizes specific research techniques into the major stages of the Association Model and provides the framework for the following presentation.

Exposure Measurement   It is common practice in advertising research to infer *ad exposure* from *vehicle exposure.* Consumers who are exposed to a particular media vehicle are assumed also to be exposed to advertisements within that vehicle. This assumption is made of necessity, due to the impossibility of determining the actual advertisements or commercials to which consumers have been exposed.

A number of commercial advertising research services measure vehicle exposure.[8] Three that are particularly well known and widely used are the Nielsen Television Index (network television), Simmons Market Research Bureau (magazines), and Arbitron (local radio).

Nielsen Television Index   In the Nielsen Television Index, television sets in a national sample of 1,250 households are equipped with electronic meters that continuously monitor set usage and station choice and transmit this information to a central computer. A supplemental Nielsen service is provided by having another

[8]For review, see Udayan Gupta, "The Ratings Game," *Advertising Age,* November 8, 1982, pp. M-10–M-18.

TABLE 15.2   **Advertising Research Techniques**

I. Exposure
Simmons Media Studies
Local Arbitron Radio
Nielsen TV Index and Audience Composition

II. Awareness
Starch Readership Studies
Burke DAR

III. Perception
Image Studies

IV. Evaluation
TRACE
Physiological Measures
Standard attitude measurement

V. Stimulation
Audience Studies, Inc. (ASI)
Competitive Environment Tests

VI. Action
BehaviorScan
AdTel

random sample of 2,400 households maintain diaries on their television viewing practices. Subscribers to these services (advertising agencies, networks, advertisers) receive information concerning viewers' network and program preferences along with detailed geographic and demographic breakdowns. This information is crucial to advertisers and media decision makers in choosing specific programs as vehicles for carrying advertising messages.

Simmons Market Research Bureau (SMRB)   The SMRB service assesses magazine vehicle exposure for over 100 consumer magazines. A national probability sample of approximately 19,000 individuals are interviewed, and their magazine reading habits examined. Interviewees are shown representations of the logos of all the magazines and are asked to identify those they may have read or looked through during the last six months. For each magazine logo correctly identified, respondents then are asked to look through a stripped-down version of a recent magazine issue. Through a series of questions, interviewers attempt to determine whether respondents have truly been exposed to the particular magazine issue. Statistical inference procedures are used to generalize total vehicle exposure from the sample results. Advertisers and media planners use the readership information along with detailed demographic and product usage data to evaluate the absolute and relative value of different magazines.

It should be noted that considerable controversy surrounds the SMRB research results. A competitive service, Mediamark Research (MRI), uses substantially different research procedures and obtains results that often differ considerably from

SMRB's. The uncertainty facing media planners is not knowing which service is "right" or whether both are wrong in their estimates of magazine audience size.

Local Arbitron Company   Arbitron measures radio listening patterns in over 250 local markets based on data from 250 to 13,000 individuals age 12 or over who are randomly selected in each market. Respondents maintain diaries of their listening behavior. Subscribers to the Arbitron service (over 5,000 radio stations, advertisers, and agencies) receive detailed reports involving listening patterns, station preferences, and demographic breakdowns. This information is invaluable for selecting stations whose listener composition matches the advertiser's target market.

Awareness Measurement   Having gained exposure, the advertiser's task is to assure that consumers become aware of specific parts of the advertisement, recognize the specific product/brand being advertised, and associate the key advertising elements with the advertised item. Accomplishing these tasks is critical to advertising success. Recent research by the Strategic Planning Institute, which operates the prestigious Profit Impact of Marketing Strategy (PIMS) program, has established a clear link between consumer brand awareness and a company's market share, which itself has a strong influence on profitability.[9] Figure 15.2 shows the relationships between awareness and market share and between market share and pretax return on investment.

Several syndicated research services provide advertisers with information on how well their ads perform in terms of generating awareness. Starch Message Report Service and Burke Day-After Recall Tests are two of the better known research services.

Starch Message Report Service   The Starch MRS reports on reader awareness of advertisements in consumer magazines and business publications. Over 75,000 advertisements are studied annually based on interviews with more than 100,000 people involving over 140 publications. Sample sizes range from 100 to 150 individuals per sex per issue, with most interviews conducted in respondents' homes or, in the case of business publications, in offices or places of business. Interviewing begins three to six days after the on-sale date of a magazine issue and continues for one to two weeks.

Starch interviewers locate eligible readers of each magazine issue studied. An eligible reader is one who has glanced through or read some part of the issue prior to the interviewer's visit and who meets the age, sex, and occupation requirements set for the particular magazine. Once eligibility is established, interviewers turn the pages of the magazine, inquiring about each advertisement being studied. Respondents are first asked, "Did you see or read any part of this advertisement?" If a respondent answers, "Yes," a prescribed questioning procedure is followed to

[9]"Brand Awareness Increases Market Share, Profits: Study," *Marketing News*, November 28, 1980, p. 5.

FIGURE 15.2   Awareness-Market Share and Market Share-ROI Relations

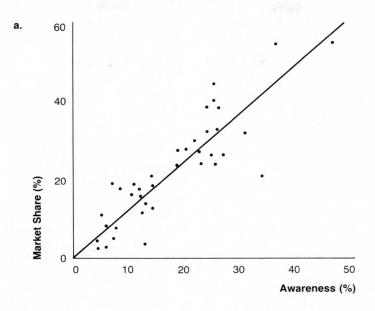

a.

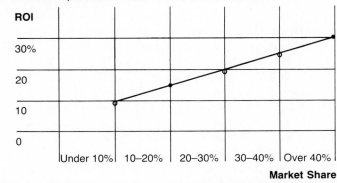

b.   Relationship between Market Share and Pretax ROI

Source: "Brand Awareness Increases Market Share, Profits: Study," *Marketing News,* November 28, 1980, p. 5.

determine the respondent's awareness of various parts of the ad (illustrations, headline, etc.). Respondents are then classified as follows:

- Nonreader: A person who did not remember having previously seen the advertisement in the issue.
- "Noted" Reader: A person who remembered having previously seen the advertisement in the issue.

- "Associated"   A person who not only "noted" the advertisement but also
  Reader: saw or read some part of it that clearly indicates the brand or
                     advertiser.
- "Read-Most"   A person who read half or more of the written material in the
  Reader: ad.

Figure 15.3 illustrates a Starch-rated advertisement with actual scores for a Molson Ale ad that ran in *Sports Illustrated.* It can be seen that 24 percent of the male (M) respondents remembered having previously seen the ad (i.e., noted it), 24 percent associated it, 2 percent read most of it, 10 percent read the headline, and so on.

A basic assumption of the Starch MRS procedure is that respondents accurately remember whether they did in fact see a particular ad in a particular magazine issue. Some misreporting undoubtedly occurs. This, however, represents a form of systematic (nonrandom) bias that applies to all magazine issues studied. Consequently, the absolute scores may be misleading, but the relative scores (among different magazine issues) are the most relevant and important. Starch has been performing these studies for well over 50 years and has compiled a wealth of baseline data from which advertisers and media planners can make informed decisions concerning the relative merits of different magazines.

Burke Day-After Recall Tests   Burke's DAR testing is undertaken to assess consumer awareness of new television commercials. Test commercials are run in several television markets, and the following day telephone interviews are conducted with a sample of 200 consumers. Contacted individuals are first qualified as having watched the program in which the test commercial was placed and as having been physically present at the time the commercial was aired. Once qualified, individuals receive a product or brand cue, are asked whether they saw the test commercial in question, and then are asked to recall all they can about it.

Findings are reported as (1) *claimed recall* scores, which indicate the percentage of respondents who recall seeing the ad, and (2) *related recall* scores, which indicate the percentage of respondents who accurately describe specific advertising elements. Advertisers and agencies use this information, along with verbatim statements from respondents, to assess the effectiveness of test commercials and to identify commercial strengths and weaknesses. On the basis of this information, a decision is made to advertise the commercial nationally, to revise it first, or possibly even to drop it.

The Recall Measurement Controversy   Many national advertisers pretest new commercials using day-after recall procedures. However, in recent years considerable controversy has surrounded the use of DAR testing. David Ogilvy, a famous advertising practitioner, contends that recall testing "is for the birds."[10] Coca-Cola

---

[10]David Ogilvy, *Ogilvy on Advertising* (New York: Crown Publishers, 1983).

FIGURE 15.3   **An Illustrative Starch-Scored Magazine Ad**

executives reject recall as a valid measure of advertising effectiveness because, in their opinion, recall simply measures whether an ad is received but not whether the message is accepted.[11]

The strongest challenge to day-after recall testing comes from a study performed by Foote, Cone & Belding, a major advertising agency. The FCB agency claims that DAR copy tests significantly understate the memorability of commercials that employ emotional or feeling-oriented themes.[12] This is because the test procedures emphasize respondents' ability to verbalize key copy points, which biases the results in favor of rational or thought-oriented commercials and against emotional or feeling-oriented commercials that rarely make explicit selling points.

The Foote, Cone & Belding study involved three thinking and three feeling commercials. The six commercials were copy tested with two methods: the standard DAR measurement described previously and a masked recognition test. The latter test involves showing a commercial to respondents on one day, telephoning them the next, requesting that they turn on their television sets to a given station where the commercial is shown once again (but this time masked, i.e., without any brand identification), and then asking them to identify the brand. FCB defines correct brand name identification by this masked recognition procedure as "proven recognition" or "true remembering."[13]

The research results (Table 15.3) demonstrate clearly the day-after recall procedure's bias against emotional, feeling commercials. For example, Commercial B's DAR score was only 21 percent, but its masked recognition score was considerably higher at 37 percent. Overall, the masked recognition method revealed that proven recognition for the three feeling commercials was 68 percent higher (see Table 15.3) than the traditional recall scores. The implication for standard recall testing is this: "When remembering the commercial is an important evaluative concern, and when imagery or feeling is important in the strategy of the commercial(s), masked recognition should be the evaluative test of first recourse."[14]

Perception Measurement Perception involves the consumer's cognitive, non-evaluative response to an advertisement and is typically measured in terms of the consumers' beliefs regarding product attributes. There are no known commercial advertising research services that focus exclusively on measuring perceptions. Rather, most perception research is done as part of companies' periodic brand image studies. Consumer beliefs are measured with respect to important product attributes, and advertising effectiveness is assessed by comparing preadvertising beliefs (i.e., those measured before an advertising campaign begins) against postadvertising beliefs. Advertising is successful to the extent that it makes consumers' brand-specific beliefs more positive.

---

[11]"Recall Not Communication: Coke," *Advertising Age*, December 26, 1983, p. 6.

[12]Jack Honomichl, "FCB: Day-After-Recall Cheats Emotion," *Advertising Age*, May 11, 1981, p. 2; David Berger, "A Retrospective: FCB Recall Study," *Advertising Age*, October 26, 1981, pp. S-36, 38.

[13]Honomichl, "FCB," p. 82.

[14]Ibid.

TABLE 15.3   **Day-After Recall versus Masked Recognition Research Findings**

"Thinking" Commercials	Day-After Recall	Masked Recognition	Index: Masked Recognition To Recall
A	49%	56%	114
D	24	32	133
E	21	24	114
Average	31	37	119
"Feeling" Commercials			
B	21%	37%	176
C	25	36	144
F	10	23	230
Average	19	32	168

Source: "FCB Says Masked-Recognition Test Yields Truer Remembering Measures Than Day-After Recall Test," *Marketing News,* June 12, 1981, p. 1.

Measurement of Evaluation   Evaluation, from the consumer's perspective, represents affective responses to advertisements, which, from the advertiser's perspective, translates into persuasive impact. There are various degrees of evaluation. At its most basic level, evaluation represents the feeling consumers are left with after processing an advertisement; at a more advanced level, evaluation represents consumers' attitudes toward advertised products. Standardized measures of evaluation are uncommon.[15] However, many advertising researchers assess persuasive impact by measuring attitudes both before and after an advertising campaign.

Efforts to measure consumers' feelings toward advertisements is complicated by the fact that many people have difficulty verbalizing their feelings. One research firm, Market Facts Inc., has attempted to overcome this problem by using computer-aided technology.[16] The system, called TRACE, enables consumers to reveal their feelings toward what they are seeing in a television commercial by pressing a series of buttons on a hand-held microcomputer. Responses are synchronized with commercial content, and the microcomputer then plays back the consumer's feelings, expressed as a TRACEline across the television screen, which moves up when the consumer feels good about what he or she saw and down when he or she feels bad about it. At points of critical change in the TRACEline, consumers are asked to discuss why their feelings changed at that point. Consumers seem willing, in light of these vivid changes, to talk about their feelings.

[15]Preston, "The Association Model," p. 6.

[16] "New Technology 'TRACES' Reaction to TV Ads," *Marketing News,* May 25, 1984, p. 3.

Advertising researchers have also turned to a variety of sophisticated *physiological testing* devices to assess emotional responses (evaluative reactions) and to avoid the problem of having to ask people directly about their feelings toward advertisements. These include such techniques as the psychogalvanometer (which measures minute levels of perspiration in response to emotional arousal), pupillometric tests (pupil dilation), and voice-pitch analysis. Psychologists have concluded that these physiological functions are indeed sensitive to psychological processes of concern in advertising.[17]

All of the bodily functions cited are controlled by the *autonomic nervous system*. Because individuals have little voluntary control over the autonomic nervous system, changes in bodily functions can be used by advertising researchers to indicate the actual, unbiased amount of emotional arousal resulting from advertisements.

In order to appreciate the potential value of such physiological measurement, consider the case of a (sexist) advertisement intended for a male audience that portrays a product in association with a scantily clad young lady. In pretesting this ad, some men, when asked what they think about it, may feign disgust or aggravation in order to make a favorable impression on the interviewer. These men may actually enjoy the ad, and their true emotional reactions could not be hidden when measured by sensitive physiological devices.

The Psychogalvanometer   The psychogalvanometer is a device for measuring galvanic skin response. When the consumer's autonomic nervous system is activated by some element in an advertisement, one bodily function affected is the activation of sweat glands in the palms and fingers, which open in varying degrees depending on the intensity of the arousal. "When the sweat glands open, the skin resistance drops, and by sending a very fine electric current through one finger, out the other, and completing the circuit through the galvanometer, the instrument can measure both the degree and frequency with which [an advertisement] sparks responses."[18] Thus, the psychogalvanometer assesses the degree of emotional response to an advertisement by indirectly measuring minute amounts of perspiration.

Pupillometric Tests   Although it has not gone unchallenged, there has been scientific evidence since the late 1960s to suggest that pupillary responses are correlated with people's arousal to stimuli and perhaps even with their likes and dislikes. Pupillometric tests in advertising are conducted by measuring respondents' pupil dilation as they view a television commercial or focus on a printed advertisement. Respondents' heads are in a fixed position to permit continuous

[17]Paul J. Watson and Robert J. Gatchel, "Autonomic Measures of Advertising," *Journal of Advertising Research*, Vol. 19, June 1979, pp. 15–26.

[18]"Psychogalvanometer Testing 'Most Predictive,' " *Marketing News*, June 17, 1978, p. 11.

electronic measurement of changes in pupillary responses. Responses to specific elements in an advertisement are used to indicate positive reaction (in the case of greater dilation) or negative reaction (smaller relative dilation).

Voice-Pitch Analysis   A complaint leveled against the psychogalvanometer, pupillometric tests, and other physiological measurement devices is that they are capable of indicating the amount of emotional arousal but not the direction of arousal. One advertising commentator stated it this way: "The problem . . . is that once you have the data, you don't know what to do with it. All you have is a reading of physiological changes in a person. You have to get from there to whether that is good or bad."[19]

Voice-pitch analysis (VOPAN) is one physiological measurement device that purportedly overcomes the preceding criticism. It works as follows.[20] A specially programmed computer analyzes a person's voice pitch in response to a question about a test commercial to see whether the pitch differs in relation to the individual's normal or baseline pitch levels. When an individual has emotional commitment, the vocal chord, which is regulated by the autonomic nervous system, becomes abnormally taut, and the pitch is higher than normal. Thus, the voice-pitch reading indicates the amount of emotional involvement, and the person's response (yes or no) to a question about an advertisement is used to identify whether the emotion is positive or negative. "The veracity of the response is established if changes in voice pitch over the respondent's preinterview levels fall within an empirically defined range. Studies conducted by several universities and governmental agencies document that changes in voice pitch greater than the empirically defined range indicate a lie (either conscious or unconscious) or a confused response."[21]

The potential value of voice-pitch analysis is revealed in the following case.[22] A New York advertising agency developed three different commercials for a new, nonfood product. Traditional verbal testing revealed that the three commercials did not vary statistically in their ability to register purchase interest from consumers (see Table 15.4). Voice-pitch analysis revealed, however, that commercial Z was a clear winner over the other commercials (see Table 15.4). Actual test market results supported the VOPAN predictions, as the product received a significantly higher market share when advertised with commercial Z than with the other test commercials.

---

[19]Comment by William Wells as quoted in Mark Liff, "Cataloging Some Tools," *Advertising Age*, October 31, 1983, p. M-54.

[20]The following discussion is based on material from several sources: Glen A. Brickman, "Voice Analysis," *Journal of Advertising Research*, Vol. 16, June 1976, pp. 43–48; Ronald G. Nelson and David Schwartz, "Voice Pitch Gives Marketer Access to Consumer's Unaware Body Responses," *Marketing News*, January 28, 1977, p. 21; Ronald G. Nelson and David Schwartz, "Voice-Pitch Analysis," *Journal of Advertising Research*, Vol. 19, October 1979, pp. 55–59.

[21]Nelson and Schwartz, "Voice-Pitch Analysis," p. 55.

[22]This case is described in Nelson and Schwartz, "Voice Pitch Gives Marketer Access," p. 21, and in Nelson and Schwartz, "Voice-Pitch Analysis," p. 56.

TABLE 15.4   VOPAN Test Results Compared with Traditional Verbal Test Results

Commercial	Verbal Purchase Interest Data (%)	Voice Response Score	Market Share
X	59	168	1.2
Y	65	172	1.4
Z	58	251	11.0

Source: Ronald G. Nelson and David Schwartz, "Voice-Pitch Analysis," *Journal of Advertising Research,* Vol. 19, No. 5, 1979, p. 56. Reprinted from the *Journal of Advertising Research* © Copyright 1979 by the Advertising Research Foundation.

Stimulation (Purchase Intention) Measurement   Though no commercial advertising research firm offers services to measure purchase intentions alone, several research organizations conduct tests that tap purchase stimulation in addition to measuring brand preference and other related measures. The two leaders in the area of what is referred to as "theater testing" are Audience Studies, Inc.'s (ASI) measurements and Dancer, Fitzgerald, and Sample advertising agency's Competitive Environment Tests.

ASI Measurements   ASI recruits approximately 300 consumers from shopping centers and invites them to attend a preview of new television programs. Once they are in the ASI theater, consumers are told that prizes from various product categories will be awarded in a drawing, and they are asked to identify for each product the specific brand they would prefer receiving if their name should happen to be drawn. They are then exposed to a pilot television program followed by test commercials for each of the product categories mentioned in the drawing. After being exposed to a second pilot television program, the participants are led to believe that one product was inadvertently omitted from the list of products for which the drawing will be held and that they will have to complete a new brand preference sheet that includes the omitted product as well as the others.

Commercial effectiveness is determined by comparing the two sets of brand preferences. A commercial is considered effective to the extent that more consumers indicate a higher preference for the test commercial on the second preference sheet (i.e. after they have been exposed to a commercial for the brand) than on the first sheet (before they were exposed to the test commercial). Based on numerous past studies, ASI has been able to develop norms indicating the actual magnitude of shifting in brand preferences that advertisers in particular product categories should expect. In addition to the brand preference measurement, ASI theaters are equipped with electronic "Instantaneous Reaction Profile Recorder" dials, which permit respondents to register continuously their likes and dislikes regarding the pilot programs and the test commercials. These specific likes and dislikes concerning commercial elements are used to explain the brand preference shifts.

Competitive Environment Test   The Competitive Environment Test procedure represents an adaptation of the ASI methodology. Two hundred respondents are recruited from shopping centers and taken to an adjacent research test site (such as a specially equipped mobile trailer). Once they are at the test location, respondents are asked to allocate ten hypothetical purchases among competitive brands in the test product category. They then are exposed to a test commercial for one of the brands (which, unbeknown to respondents, is the one being tested) and to commercials for two or three competitive brands. (The ASI method, by comparison, does not expose respondents to competitive commercials.) Following the commercial exposure, respondents are again asked to allocate ten hypothetical purchases among the competing brands in the product category.

Advertising effectiveness is determined by the shift in brand preference, just as it was in the ASI test. The difference here, however, is that the Competitive Environment Test portrays reality more accurately by exposing respondents to several commercials within a product category rather than to a single commercial.

Measurement of Action   The ultimate issue in measuring advertising effectiveness is whether advertising leads to increased sales activity. Determining the sales impact of advertising is, as explained previously in Chapter 12, a most difficult task. However, substantial efforts have been made in recent years toward the development of research procedures that are able to assess the sales-generating ability of advertising.

The most fascinating of the new techniques are procedures in use by two Chicago-based research services (AdTel and BehaviorScan). Both services measure the sales impact of advertising by combining three technologies: supermarket checkout scanning equipment, split cable television, and household panels. Here is how it works:[23] AdTel and BehaviorScan operate test markets in a number of small cities around the United States (e.g., Pittsfield, MA; Marion, IN; Midland, TX). The cities must be relatively small, because all grocery stores have to be equipped with automatic scanning devices that read UPC symbols from grocery packages. A panel of 2,500 consumers are recruited in each city, and each member receives a coded identification card that must be used each time the shopper visits the supermarket. Panel members are eligible for prize drawings (BehaviorScan) or receive a 1 percent rebate from their grocery purchases (AdTel) as remuneration for their participation.

Now suppose a company is interested in testing a new television commercial. AdTel or BehaviorScan would do the following: (1) stock the company's product in all supermarkets in two or three test markets, (2) selectively broadcast the new commercial using special split cable television so that the commercial is received by only a portion of the panel members in each market, (3) record electronically grocery purchases made by all panel members, and (4) compare the purchase

---

[23]For further discussion, see Joseph Poindexter, "Shaping the Consumer," *Psychology Today*, May 1983, pp. 64–68; "Shifting Sales into High Gear," *Marketing Communications*, January 1984, pp. 15–21.

behavior of those panel members who were potentially exposed to the new commercial with those who were not exposed. If the advertising is effective, then a greater proportion of the panel members exposed to the test commercial should buy the promoted item in comparison to those members not exposed to any advertising.

AdTel and BehaviorScan research procedures represent a major step forward in advertising research. These services are not restricted to testing the effects of advertising, however. They can be used to examine other marketing mix variables such as price, sales promotions, and in-store merchandising activity. There is no question that this new technology will facilitate a more sophisticated understanding of how marketing communications and other marketing variables interact to affect consumer choice behavior.

Summary

Measuring advertising effectiveness, though difficult and often expensive, is essential so that advertisers can better understand how well their ads are performing and what changes need to be made to improve performance. The actual conduct of advertising copy testing should adhere to strict measurement procedures. A group of representatives from leading U.S. advertising agencies recently proposed a set of nine principles to guide copy testing efforts. One principle, for example, makes the critical point that the choice of copy testing techniques(s) for assessing the effectiveness of advertising campaigns depends first and foremost on the specific objective an advertising campaign is intended to accomplish.

Literally dozens of copy testing techniques have evolved over the years for measuring advertising effectiveness. The reason for this diversity is that advertisements perform a variety of functions, and multiple methods are needed to test different indicators of advertising effectiveness. The Association Model provides a useful framework for categorizing the diversity of copy testing methods. The model consists of seven major levels of advertising effect: exposure, awareness, association evaluation, perception, evaluation, stimulation, and action.

The Nielsen Television Index, Simmons Market Research Bureau, and Arbitron are three well-known and widely used commercial services for measuring advertising exposure in television, magazines, and local radio, respectively. Starch Message Report Service and Burke Day-After Recall Tests are techniques for measuring various aspects of awareness. Advertising-related perceptions are measured as part of standard image studies, while evaluations generated by advertising are assessed with attitude questions and the measurement of various bodily functions (pupil dilation, perspiration, voice pitch, etc.) regulated by the autonomic nervous system. Theater testing is performed to measure consumer purchase stimulation, while the impact of advertising on actual purchase behavior (action) is assessed by integrating the use of controlled consumer panels with supermarket optical scanning equipment and split cable television.

No single copy testing technique is ideal, nor is any particular technique appropriate for all occasions. The choice of technique should depend on the specific objective an advertising campaign is intended to accomplish. Moreover, it is typically preferable to use multiple measurement methods rather than any single technique in order to answer the diversity of questions that are typically involved in attempts to assess advertising effectiveness.

Discussion Questions

1. It is desirable that the measurement of advertising effectiveness focus on sales response rather than upon some precursor to sales, yet measuring sales response to advertising is typically infeasible. Explain why sales response measurement is desirable but typically infeasible.

2. PACT principle 2 states that a good copy testing system should establish how results will be used in advance of each copy test. Explain the specific meaning and importance of this copy testing principle.

3. In reference to PACT principle 9, explain in your own words what "valid" measurement means. Suppose a research firm offers television advertisers an inexpensive method of testing commercials by merely having consumers evaluate photographed pictures of key commercial scenes. Comment about the probable validity of this approach.

4. Advertising research often uses measurements of vehicle exposure to indicate advertising exposure. What is the difference between these two types of exposure, and why do researchers measure the former when advertising decision makers are really interested in the latter?

5. If you were an account executive in an advertising agency, what would you tell clients to convince them to use (or not to use) the Starch Message Report Service?

6. An advertising agency is in the process of arranging research services to assess advertising effectiveness for two clients: one advertising campaign is for a unique financial service that is advertised with a number of specific selling points; the other campaign involves a very touching family scene used to advertise the company's food product. The agency proposes that day-after recall tests be conducted for both clients. Comment.

7. As advertising manager for a brand of toothpaste, you are considering using a physiological measurement technique to assess consumers' evaluative reactions to your new advertisements. Present an argument in favor of using VOPAN rather than pupil dilation testing or galvanic skin response measurement.

8. Present an argument in favor of using the Competitive Environment Test rather than the Audience Measurement, Inc.'s testing procedure.

9. A scanner-cable test performed by AdTel or BehaviorScan will cost you, as brand manager of a new brand of cereal, approximately $150,000. Why might this be a prudent investment in comparison to spending $50,000 to perform an image study?

Exercises

1. Visit your library and examine the most recent Arbitron local radio ratings for the various stations that are located in your university town or city. Before the visit, construct a demographic profile for each station, and then compare the correspondence between your subjective profile and Arbitron's objective, measured profile.

2. Arrange a meeting at a local advertising agency with an account executive for purposes of getting his or her views toward the following commercial research services: Burke Day-After Recall measurement, Starch magazine readership studies, and Arbitron local radio ratings.

3. Select two or three national television commercials, identify the objective(s) each appears to be attempting to accomplish, and then propose a procedure for how you would go about testing the effectiveness of each commercial.

PART IV

Promotion Management: Direct Marketing, Sales Promotion, and Other Promotion Management Tools

Part IV explores a variety of increasingly important areas of promotion management, including direct marketing, telemarketing, sales promotion, public relations, publicity, specialty advertising, and point-of-purchase communications. Today these promotion management tools have become primary forces in creating brand awareness, maintaining brand awareness, promoting trial purchase behavior, encouraging impulse purchasing, and much more.

Chapter 16, which deals with direct marketing, describes the tremendous growth that is occurring in nonstore marketing and looks at some of the major developments in this field. Chapters 17 and 18 deal with the growing area of sales promotion. Chapter 17 introduces the topic—its nature, growth rate, and purposes—and then describes the use of sales promotions for stimulating the trade and the sales force. In Chapter 18 sales promotion is covered from the perspective of the ultimate consumer. Samples, coupons, premiums, sweepstakes, and group promotions are some of the topics treated in this chapter. The coverage then turns in Chapter 19 to a review of public relations, publicity, and specialty advertising. These communication tools serve to build goodwill and to enhance brand and corporate images. In this respect, public relations, publicity, and specialty advertising differ in emphasis from other forms of promotion. The last chapter in Part IV, Chapter 20, looks at point-of-purchase materials (displays, banners, wall posters, plastic reproductions of products, etc.) as a special form of marketing communications that plays an important role in influencing the consumer's in-store product and brand choices.

CHAPTER 16

Direct Marketing Communications

The preceding chapters introduced various aspects of advertising communications and management with emphasis on the major advertising media: television, magazines, newspapers, radio, and outdoor advertising. Advertising in these media is, as previously described, commissionable, measurable, targeted to large and often highly undifferentiated audiences, and designed to either build or reinforce a brand's image.

There are, however, a variety of communication objectives and tasks that firms need to accomplish but for which the major advertising vehicles are not particularly well suited. For this reason, alternative forms of marketing communications have evolved and have grown particularly rapidly in recent years. This chapter focuses on two special forms of marketing communications, direct marketing and telemarketing, both of which are vital to many firms' promotion management operations.

Direct Marketing

Direct marketing is a term that is often misunderstood and used imprecisely. To clarify the confusion, let us offer the following definition by the Direct Marketing Association:

> *Direct (response) marketing is the total of activities by which products and services are offered to market segments in one or more media*

for informational purposes or to solicit a direct response from a pre-sent or prospective customer or contributor by mail, telephone or other access.[1]

The confusion arises because the word *direct* appears in two related notions, direct response advertising and direct mail. There are, however, several important distinctions. First, *direct marketing* encompasses the other terms; that is, direct marketing is a special form of marketing that involves direct response advertising and the use of direct mail delivery. **Direct mail** is a specific medium employed by direct marketers, and **direct response advertising** is the use of any medium (direct mail, television, etc.) with the intent of creating immediate action from customers. General advertising (i.e., nondirect response) intends, by comparison, to create consumer awareness and to build company and brand images.

There are three distinct characteristics of a direct response advertisement: (1) it makes a definite offer, (2) it contains all the information necessary to make a decision, and (3) it contains a response device (coupon, phone number, or both) to facilitate immediate action.[2]

An illustration of direct response advertising is one for Casio watches in Figure 16.1. This ad satisfies the requirements of direct response advertisement in its appeal to readers of *Runner's World Magazine.* Note the detailed information and the conspicuous toll-free number. The ad provides prospective customers with solid reasons to buy a Casio watch *and* a convenient mechanism, the toll-free number, to actualize their purchase desires. The ad further promises satisfaction, a one-year warranty, and an offer to return the watch within 30 days if the purchaser is not satisfied fully. The consumer has little to lose when responding to this offer, which is essential for successful direct marketing.

Direct marketing, then, is an interactive system whereby the marketer solicits orders from customers who order directly from the seller, and the seller ships the product directly to the buyer.[3] The direct marketer's purpose is to establish a direct relationship with a customer to initiate immediate and measurable responses. Response measurability is an important aspect of direct marketing because customer responses reveal something about the drawing power and effectiveness of a direct response advertising effort. These responses also reveal important information about customers. By keeping records for each customer, a company knows how frequently a customer orders by mail, how recent his or her last order was, and how much he or she spends on average. This information indicates each customer's potential future purchases.

---

[1] Bob Stone, *Successful Direct Marketing Methods* (Chicago: Crain Books, 1979), p. 3.

[2] Bob Stone, "For Effective Direct Results," *Advertising Age,* March 28, 1983, p. M-32.

[3] Chaman L. Jain and Al Migliaro, *An Introduction to Direct Marketing* (New York: Amacom, 1978), p. 7.

FIGURE 16.1 **Illustration of Direct Response Advertising**

Brand New
CASIO
165 Foot Watertight
Runner's Multi-alarm Chronograph

Announcing Casio's New Watersports Wonder
. . . With 50 meter water-resistance
. . . 5-year battery
. . . Pro stopwatch
. . . Plus 4 independent alarms and countdown timer.

Casio's prototype watersports runner's alarm chronograph was a runaway best seller for us last summer and fall. It was so popular that we sold out and orders were returned unfilled. Now, Casio has improved it. Made it more versatile with extra convenience features.

You get 50 meters of depth-tested protection. A professional 1/100 second stopwatch, countdown timer alarm, dual time, 12/24 hour time, night light, electronic calendar and 4 independent daily alarms. All for under $30.00

5-YEAR NON-STOP CHRONO
This waterproof wonder boasts a 5-year lithium battery with a full-function 1/100 second stopwatch which repeats every hour. A unique feature of this watch allows you to see time in every mode. The time of day automatically appears in the corner of the display. Now you'll have no need to push a button to switch modes to see the time while you're running (and risk clearing the stopwatch).

ALARMS THAT ORGANIZE YOUR LIFE, DUAL TIME AND MORE
This electronic genius has an extraordinary organizing talent. It reminds you of important daily events. There's an alarm to wake you up and a "snooze" function which chimes five and ten minutes after the preset time. Another alarm chimes five and ten minutes before the preset time to get you to the starting line on time. Two other independent alarms can be set to sound day or night at precisely the minute you choose. Yet another alarm can be set as a pleasant chime to sound every hour. And a 12-hour countdown timer alarm is perfect for curtailing lengthy meetings or appointments.

If you love to travel, this Casio allows you to simultaneously display your local time and another time of your choice — in 12- or 24-hour time. An electronic calendar displays month, day and date. A night light is standard. Time is accurate to 1/2 second per day. Own the 50-meter water-resistant **W-25** for only **$29.95** or the 200-meter (over 660 feet) water-resistant model **DW200** for **$39.95**. Both are constructed of lightweight black polysulfone for the case and band.

THREE OTHER TOP CHOICES
PUT A THERMOCHRONOMETER ON YOUR WRIST FOR JUST $49.95.
Here's a gifted marine timepiece that gives

MODEL W-25

you an electronic thermometer that reads in Celsius or Fahrenheit (-10°C (13°F) to 60°C

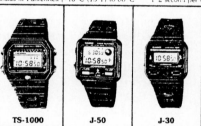

TS-1000 **J-50** **J-30**

(140°F)] in or out of water. Watertight to over 330 feet, this beauty also gives you time and calendar, accuracy to 1/2 second per day. 12/24 hour formats, thermo-alarm function, daily alarm, time signal, one-hour 1/100 second stopwatch with repeat, 8 world time zones and night light. Available in lightweight black polysulfone model **TS 1000** for **$49.95** or all-stainless model **TS 3000** for **$79.95**.

PACE WATCH WITH DISTANCE COMPUTER
Here's the top-rated watch in *Runner's World Magazine*'s latest survey of runner's quartz watches. Pace is the secret to success in training and the Casio **J-50** signals each step (30 different pace levels). It then gives you your daily performance level by registering stride length, distance covered and elapsed time. You also get two precision chronos. One works with the pacer up to 24 hours. The second gives you 1/100 second timing which repeats every hour. Regular time is accurate to 1/2 second per day. You also get a

countdown timer alarm, calendar, daily alarm and time signal. The model **J-50** is constructed of lightweight black polysulfone and is only **$29.95**

DEPTH-TESTED COMPACT PACER
This 50-meter water-resistant genius allows you to set your pace for training from 15 different levels. You also get 2 chronographs. The first works with or without the pacer function to 24 hours. The second is a full-function 1/100 second stopwatch which repeats every hour. Regular time is accurate to 1/2 second per day. You also get a countdown timer alarm, calendar, daily alarm and time signal. Constructed of lightweight black polysulfone, this compact beauty fits male or female wrists equally well on the road or in the water. Model **J-30** is only **$29.95**

OUR DOUBLE GUARANTEE
You get an included 1-year warranty with each Casio. Secondly, we guarantee your satisfaction. If not delighted with your new Casio, return it within 30 days for a full refund.

We're one of the largest Casio timepiece dealers in the U.S. and we're as close as your phone. Order now and be delighted.

CREDIT CARD HOLDERS ORDER TOLL-FREE TODAY
To order, call toll free number below, or send a check or money order for the total amount **plus $2.50** for the first watch, $1.00 for each additional watch for shipping and insurance. Add an additional $2.00 for U.P.S. air delivery. ND residents add 4% tax.

800-437-4385
On The Run

107 Roberts Street, Department 7 P.O. Box 67, Fargo, ND 58107 Telephone (701) 232-9400

1983 ON THE RUN

Source: Runner's World Magazine, July 1983.

The Growth of Direct Marketing

Historically, direct marketing represented a relatively small part of most companies' marketing efforts. However, by 1984, American consumers were estimated to have spent $200 billion through mail and telephone-order sales.[4] Furthermore, it is estimated that direct marketing accounts for nearly one-third of all U.S. advertising expenditures.[5] Mail order buying is growing 50 percent faster than store retailing in the United States.[6] Mail order is, in fact, the fastest growing form of product distribution in the United States. It may come as a surprise to learn that the higher one's socioeconomic status, the greater the likelihood one buys through mail order; in fact, nearly 55 percent of college graduates are mail-order buyers compared with only 34 percent of those who are not high school graduates.[7]

A variety of factors help to explain direct marketing's growth. For consumer goods, direct marketing provides shoppers with an easy, convenient, and relatively hassle-free way to buy. The tremendous increase in the number of women working outside the home is another important factor that has contributed to the rapid growth of direct marketing and nonstore buying.[8]

Business-to-Business Direct Marketing   In addition to the growth of consumer-oriented direct marketing, there has been a tremendous increase in applications of direct marketing for businesses that market to other businesses. Many firms are turning to direct marketing as a means of reaching and effectively serving their business customers. One reason for this trend is the cost of an industrial sales call, which in 1983 was estimated to exceed $200 per call.[9] Direct marketing in some companies actually replaces the sales force, whereas in other cases it is used to supplement the sales force's efforts by building goodwill, generating leads, and opening doors for salesmen.[10]

A direct marketing program developed by an Atlanta advertising agency illustrates how a creative direct marketing program can accomplish various objectives.[11] The agency developed the direct mail promotion to attract interest in a series of data processing seminars conducted by its client, the Merlyn Corp. These seminars are presented to data processing professionals and involve detailed information for various data processing products. Videotaped sales presentations spon-

---

[4]"Industry Sales Put at $200 Billion," *Advertising Age,* October 18, 1984, p. 6.

[5]David Astor, "Perfecting the Direct Sell," *Marketing Communications,* October 1982, pp. 48–51.

[6]"Sroge Lists Leading Mail Order Firms," *Marketing News,* June 12, 1981, p. 3.

[7]Bob Stone, "Now, a Bigger Bargain," *Advertising Age,* May 30, 1983, p. M-28.

[8]Larry J. Rosenberg and Elizabeth C. Hirschman, "Retailing Without Stores," *Harvard Business Review,* July-August 1980, pp. 103–112.

[9]Ibid.

[10]Dylan Landis, "Taking Care of Business," *Advertising Age,* January 19, 1981, pp. S-4–S-10.

[11]This case is described in Kevin Higgins, "Ad Agency's 'Talking Shoe' Promotion Effectively Reaches Seminar Prospects," *Marketing News,* February 19, 1982, p. 15.

sored by companies selling data-processing products are used as teaching tools. Merlyn Corp. funds the seminars by finding companies to sponsor the videotape presentations.

The direct mail task of Merlyn Corp. was to locate sponsors; only 12 prospects could be identified, however, because the product category is so narrow. A direct mail program was designed to reach and elicit interest from these 12 prospects. Here is how it was done: A shoebox was delivered by Federal Air Express to each prospect. Inside the box was a man's shoe with a microcassette recorder attached. The recorded message read: "Good morning, Mr. (recipient's surname), my name is Vaughn Merlyn, and I'd like to point out that I just got my foot in your door for under $100, and, if my calculations are correct, that's about one-tenth of what it costs you everytime one of your salespeople makes a call on a qualified prospect." The tape continued for over three minutes by explaining how sponsorship of a videotaped segment could enable the sponsor to reach up to 300 qualified buyers (i.e., the data-processing professionals who would be seminar attendees) at a cost of only $35 per person.

All of the shoebox recipients responded when follow-up sales calls were made, and six of the 12 prospects bought the idea. This program was a success because it found a unique, but meaningful, way to gain the attention and interest of busy executives.

Business-to-business direct marketing can substantially reduce marketing costs and provide firms with larger potential markets. Consider the case of General Binding Corp. (GBC), a marketer of printing-related machines and other printing products.[12] GBC's sales force consisted of more than 300 salespersons who sold to tens of thousands of small, medium, and large businesses throughout the country. Escalating sales costs forced the company to find ways other than direct sales contact to do business with its many smaller customers. GBC found that mail order provided it with an efficient distribution method for serving the many customers that make small purchases individually but represent huge sales potential collectively.

General Binding Corp.'s experience is similar to that of many other businesses. Mail-order selling and other forms of direct marketing provide attractive options for firms who either prefer to avoid the tremendous expense of a sales force or desire to supplement sales force effort with supportive marketing communications.

Direct Response Advertising Media

Direct response advertising has a variety of media from which to choose. The direct marketer's objective is to select a medium (or multiple media) to achieve maximum ability to segment the market at a reasonable cost. Effective direct response media selection demands that the marketer have a clearly defined target market in mind and specific media objectives. For example, with reference to the

---

[12]This illustration comes from a description in Jack Miller, "Several Factors Converge to Spawn Mail Order's Business-to-Business Sales Growth," *Marketing News,* July 8, 1983, p. 8.

TABLE 16.1   **Total Estimated Direct Advertising Expenditures, 1977–1983 (Millions of Dollars)**

	1983	1982	1981	1980	1979	1978	1977
Coupons	182.1	127.1	94.6	84.2	72.0	61.0	84.0
Direct mail	12,692.2	11,359.4	10,566.7	9,998.7	8,876.7	7,298.2	6,966.7
Consumer magazines	188.7	167.0	150.0	135.0	123.0	99.8	86.2
Business magazines	73.9	66.0	59.0	53.0	47.0	49.4	49.4
Newspapers	80.5	70.6	73.0	60.6	54.4	58.0	42.8
Newspaper preprints	2,850.0	2,500.0	2,288.5	2,032.4	1,779.5	1,390.0	1,086.0
Telephone	13,608.3	12,935.6	11,467.0	9,845.0	8,555.6	8,555.6	7,699.0
Television	386.5	339.0	295.0	253.0	217.0	265.0	340.7
Radio	37.0	33.0	29.0	26.0	23.0	N/A	N/A
Total	30,099.2	27,597.7	25,022.8	22,487.9	19,748.2	17,777.0	16,354.8

Source: Copyright 1984, Direct Marketing Association, Inc., 6 E. 43rd Street, New York, New York 10017. Reproduced with permission.

Casio example provided earlier (Figure 16.1), the target market is serious joggers and runners (those who read *Runner's World Magazine*), and a possible objective might be to generate 24,000 orders at an average cost of $2.00 each.

Table 16.1 presents the various direct response advertising media and traces the changes in media expenditures from 1977 to 1983. The total advertising investment increased from roughly $16.4 billion in 1977 to over $30 billion in 1983. Direct mail expenditures (approximately $12.7 billion) and telephone marketing expenditures (approximately $13.6 billion) are clearly the dominant media; their combined expenditures amounted to 87 percent of the total direct response advertising investment in 1983.

Direct Mail   Direct mail advertising is any advertising matter sent through the mail directly to the person whom the marketer wishes to influence; these advertisements can take the form of letters, postcards, programs, calendars, folders, catalogs, blotters, order blanks, price lists, or menus.[13] Direct mail's primary advantages are that it enables companies to pinpoint messages to specific market segments and to measure success immediately by knowing how many customers actually respond.

Additional positive features of direct mail are that it permits greater personalization than does mass media advertising; it can gain the prospect's undivided attention because it is not subject to competing adjacent ads, such as other print and broadcast media; it has no constraints in terms of form, color, or size (other than those imposed by cost and practical considerations); and it is relatively simple and inexpensive to change direct mail ads.[14]

[13]"Direct-Mail—Quiet Medium," *Advertising Age,* November 21, 1973, p. 116.

[14]Richard Hodgson, *Direct Mail and Mail Order Handbook* (Chicago: Dartnell Publishing Corp., 1974).

An alleged disadvantage of direct mail is that it is more expensive than other media. On a cost per thousand (CPM) basis, direct mail *is* more expensive. For example, the CPM for a particular direct mailing may be as high as $250, whereas a magazine's CPM may only be $4. However, compared with other media, direct mail is much less wasteful and will usually produce the highest percentage of responses. Thus, on a *cost per order* basis, direct mail is often less expensive and a better bargain.

Success with direct mail depends greatly upon the quality of mailing *lists* and upon the effectiveness of advertising *copy.* Each of these topics will be discussed in the following pages.

Three types of lists are used: house lists, mail response lists, and compiled lists. **House lists** are generated from a company's own internal records. Because these lists contain the names of customers who previously responded, they are generally more valuable than the other types of lists. House lists are often divided along lines of active, recently active, long-since active customers, or merely inquiries. A list may be segregated by the recency of a customer's purchase, the frequency of a customer's purchase, the monetary value of each purchase, or the type of products purchased. Customers may be categorized by geographic, demographic, or psychographic characteristics.[15]

Mail response lists are house lists of other companies bought by a firm to promote its own products. These lists are effective because they comprise the names of people who have responded to another company's direct response offer. The greater the similarity of the products offered by both the buyer and the seller of the list, the greater the likelihood that the purchased list will be effective.

Compiled lists are prepared from a variety of data sources, such as census reports, telephone directories, and car registrations. Compiled lists are not as desirable as the preceding two types of lists, however, because they do not contain information about the willingness of a person to purchase by mail. The characteristics of the members of compiled lists may also be too diversified to serve the purposes of the direct mailer.[16] However, some compiled lists are put together with considerable care and may serve the direct mailer's specific needs.

Figure 16.2 presents an advertisement from one such list supply company, the Lifestyle Selector, whose list file consists of 5 million people who have supplied information pertaining to hobbies and interests (psychographic information) and have provided important demographic data. The Lifestyle Selector permits a mailer to order a list with any combination of life-style and demographic information. A manufacturer of mens' sporting goods, for example, would be able to request a list matching its desired target market. For example, this might be something such as males between the ages of 25 and 44 who play golf and enjoy fashion clothing, who are business executives, professionals, or technicians

---

[15]Stone, *Successful Direct Marketing Methods,* p. 80.
[16]Ibid.

FIGURE 16.2   Advertisement for a Compiled Mailing List

earning $30,000 or more annually, and who possess an American Express credit card.

Effective copy is the other critical element in direct mail advertising. As with all forms of advertising, it is essential that direct mailers pattern their communications to match the backgrounds and interests of target customers. Certain generalizations apply, however, regardless of the audience. These include striving for clarity, insisting on brevity, being courteous and polite, and writing believable copy.[17] John Caples, who has been characterized as representing to direct response advertising what Abner Doubleday was to baseball,[18] offers the following principles underlying successful direct mail advertising:[19]

1. *Get attention.* This is usually done by stating in a few words a believable promise or by showing a picture of the reward that the advertised product offers potential customers.
2. *Hold attention.* Subheads, subillustrations, or the first paragraph are used to hold attention.
3. *Create desire.* Benefits in the copy create desire.
4. *Make it believable.* Facts, figures, testimonials, and guarantees are just some of the methods used to establish believability.
5. *Prove it's a bargain.* Price reductions and advertising copy that builds up the value of the selling proposition serve to prove the offer is a bargain.
6. *Make it easy to buy.* This is done by telling potential customers how to order and by making it easy for them to order.
7. *Give a reason to buy now.* Rewards for promptness and special offers are used to promote quick ordering.

So far, this chapter has focused on the role of direct mail advertising from the direct marketer's perspective. It is important to look also at direct mail from the consumer's perspective. The factors that influence consumers to purchase by mail and the items they are most willing to buy are interesting subjects that were examined in a recent survey.[20] Table 16.2 lists the 16 major factors that are important to consumers in deciding to purchase by mail. Nearly 82 percent of the 1,120 respondents to the survey indicated that it is important or very important that merchandise be from trustworthy companies. Other major reasons for purchasing by mail are the availability of money-back guarantees if one is dissatisfied with product purchases, better product quality than what is available from retail stores, product unavailability in retail outlets, speedy delivery, and more adequate buying information than they can obtain from retail stores.

---

[17]Bodo Von Der Wense, "Planning, List Selection, Copy, Layout, Timing, Testing Can Make or Break Direct Mail Pieces," *Marketing News,* November 14, 1980, p. 7.

[18]Bob Stone, "Long Narrative Copy: A Marketer's Views," *Advertising Age,* August 25, 1980, p. 48. (By the way, Abner Doubleday invented baseball.)

[19]Ibid.

[20]A.R. Pironti, Morton M. Vitriol, and Andrew Thurm, "Consumer Interests in Mail Order Purchasing," *Journal of Advertising Research,* June 1981, pp. 35–38.

TABLE 16.2   **Factors Influencing Customers to Purchase by Mail**

Factor	Percent Rating Factor: Very Important or Important[a]
1. Products are from companies I can trust	81.9%
2. Money-back guarantee	77.5
3. Better quality	75.2
4. Products were from well-known companies	71.0
5. Can't find product anywhere else	70.9
6. Speedy delivery	66.4
7. More adequate buying information	65.5
8. Convenience	62.6
9. Greater variety of choices	61.5
10. Mail-order prices are lower	61.2
11. Free trial period to examine merchandise	54.7
12. Free telephone ordering service	53.6
13. Major credit cards acceptable	45.1
14. Coupons for order information	43.0
15. Fun of anticipating arrival of merchandise	23.2
16. Enjoy buying by mail	20.9

Source: A.R. Pironti, Morton M. Vitriol, and Andrew Thurm, "Consumer Interests in Mail Order Purchasing," *Journal of Advertising Research,* June 1981, p. 36. Reprinted from the *Journal of Advertising Research* © Copyright 1981 by the Advertising Research Foundation.
[a]Percentages based on 1,120 responses.

The same survey also identified the specific items that consumers are most interested in purchasing through the mail.[21] The top two categories are books and magazines; over 40 percent of the respondents indicated that they are interested or very interested in buying books and magazines by mail. Garden supplies, hobby and craft items, and gift merchandise are other products for which over one-third of the respondents indicated mail-order purchase interest. More than one-fourth of the respondents also indicated interest in purchasing clothing and housewares by mail.

Mail-order buying is experiencing phenomenal growth in the United States, where it is growing 50 percent faster than is conventional retailing.[22] Mail order's share of consumer expenditures for department store goods alone is projected to increase by 500 percent by 1990.[23] Table 16.3 lists the leaders in seven mail-order industry segments. Ready-to-wear is the leading segment and accounts for over $5 billion in sales. The marketing of food by mail (including steaks!) accounts for a surprisingly high $500 million annual sales volume.

[21]Ibid.

[22]"Sroge Lists Leading Mail Order Firms."

[23]Ibid.

TABLE 16.3   **Leaders in Seven Mail-Order Industry Segments (Millions of Dollars)**

Ready-to-Wear
Segment volume $5.1 billion
1. New Process, Warren, Pa. $233
2. Lane Bryant, New York   152
3. The Talbots, Hingham, Mass.   56
4. Avon Fashions, New York   40
5. Haband, Paterson, N.J.   40

General Merchandise
Segment volume $4.1 billion
1. Sears, Chicago $1,646
2. Penney's, New York   1,139
3. Wards, Chicago   686
4. Spiegel, Chicago   412
5. Aldens, Chicago   250
    (* = includes only
    nonstore catalog sales)

Insurance
Segment volume $4 billion
1. Colonial Penn, Philadelphia $800
2. Geico, Washington, D.C.   726
3. National Liberty, Valley Forge, Pa.   274
4. Physician's Mutual, Omaha, Neb.   110
5. Union Fidelity, Trevose, Pa.   95

Books
Segment volume $1.4 billion
1. Time-Life, New York $432
2. Reader's Digest, Pleasantville, N.Y.   350
3. Doubleday, Garden City, N.Y.   140
4. Grolier, Danbury, Conn.   104
5. Meredith, Des Moines, Iowa   25

Collectibles
Segment volume $920 million
1. Franklin Mint, Franklin Center, Pa. $360
2. Bradford Exchange, Northbrook, Ill.   50
3. Glendinning, Norwalk, Conn.   38
4. Paramount International,
    Engelwood, Ohio   23
5. Calhoun Collectors, Minneapolis   20

Sporting Goods
Segment volume $780 million
1. L. L. Bean, Freeport, Maine $104
2. Eddie Bauer, Seattle   34
3. Austad, Sioux Falls, S.D.   20
4. Goldberg's Marine, Philadelphia   16
5. Orvis, Manchester, Vt.   15

Foods
Segment volume $500 million
1. Swiss Colony, Monroe, Wis. $35
2. Harry and David, Medford, Ore.   34
3. Figi's, Marshfield, Wis.   30
4. Omaha Steaks, Omaha, Neb.   18
5. Crest Fruit, Alamo, Texas   12

Source: Maxwell Sroge Co. as printed in "Sroge Lists Leading Mail Order Firms," *Marketing News,* June 12, 1981, p. 3.

Catalog Marketing   Though catalog marketing is part of direct mail, its growth and distinctiveness justifies a separate section.[24] For clarity, it should be noted that there are actually four types of catalogs: *retail* catalogs designed by retailers to create increased in-store traffic, *full-line merchandise* catalogs (e.g., Sears, J.C. Penney), *consumer specialty* catalogs (e.g., the L.L. Bean sporting goods and ready-to-wear catalog), and *industrial specialty* catalogs, which have gained much acceptance in recent years from industrial companies who want to reach smaller customers and free up the sales force's time to devote to larger, more promising customers.

[24]The growth in catalog marketing is typified by the number of catalogs distributed. The average American household is estimated to receive 40 catalogs per year. See "Catalogue Cornucopia," *Time Magazine,* November 8, 1982, p. 75.

A number of factors account for the growth of catalog sales: (1) catalogs save time because people do not have to find parking spaces and deal with in-store crowds, (2) catalog buying appeals to those consumers who are afraid, due to increasing crime rates, to shop in downtown locations and in shopping malls, (3) catalogs allow people the convenience of making purchase decisions at their leisure and away from the pressure of a retail store, (4) the availability of toll-free 800 numbers has made it particularly easy for people to order from catalogs.[25]

Catalog marketing in England offers an interesting comparison with that in the United States. British mail-order companies use catalog agents to solicit orders. One out of every ten housewives is an agent. Agents order merchandise for neighborhood friends and acquaintances and fulfill functions for catalog companies such as performing credit checks and making collections. Agents are compensated by the catalog companies with discounts on personal purchases. The British approach has proven very successful; 85 percent of all direct marketing sales in the United Kingdom are created in this fashion.[26]

Other Media for Direct Marketing   Direct marketing is not limited to mail and catalog vehicles. Magazines, newspapers, and television, though minor vehicles of direct marketing in comparison with direct mail, provide direct marketers with alternative means to achieve specific objectives.

Magazines are potentially useful to direct marketers because this medium offers a tremendous diversity of vehicles that appeal to specialized consumer groups. Effective direct marketing demands an ability to pinpoint audiences. Magazines, in addition to providing selectivity, also offer good color reproduction, relatively low cost, and the capability of testing different creative approaches by running one ad version in one magazine edition and a different version in another.

Newspapers represent another useful direct marketing medium, the major advantages being geographic selectivity, a variety of formats and reproduction methods, and the ability to position an ad in a section (financial, fashion, sports, etc.) that matches the interests of the designated market segment. On the other hand, advertisements placed in the regular newspages (i.e., ROP locations) may be lost among the editorial content and attract minimal attention. For this reason, direct response advertising is often placed in special locations such as syndicated newspaper supplements, mail-order shopping sections, inserts or preprints, and comic sections. The comic section is, in fact, a surprisingly good location. The comics attracts a variety of readers, with the statistical norm being an individual who is 39.2 years old, who possesses at least a high school education, and who earns an above-average income.[27]

---

[25]For additional factors underlying the growth of catalog marketing, see Bob Stone, "Factors in the Growth of Catalog Sales," *Advertising Age,* March 26, 1979, p. 61.

[26]Andrew Burne, "Behind Successful UK Catalog Stands a Catalog Agent," *Direct Marketing,* May 1980, pp. 40–44.

[27]Stone, *Successful Direct Marketing Methods.*

Television represents a relatively minor medium for direct response advertising and accounts for a little over 1 percent of the total media expenditures in 1983 (see Table 16.1). However, developments in cable television and two-way interactive systems portend considerable growth for direct marketing on television.[28] Television is particularly useful in performing a support function for other direct response media. In addition, it can perform a valuable role by making a direct sales offer or by generating leads for salespersons, who may then convert prospects into customers.

Summary

The tremendous growth in direct marketing shows promise of continuing. Analysts expect nonstore sources to obtain as much as one-third of retail sales in the United States by 1990, and retailers are being warned to prepare for the challenge.[29] Conventional marketers realize direct marketing's potential. Many companies have responded to the rapid growth in direct marketing by establishing their own direct marketing departments.[30]

Telemarketing

Telephone marketing (telemarketing) is a special form of direct marketing; however, it is treated separately in this chapter because of its distinct characteristics and importance. The telephone was, in fact, the dominant direct marketing medium in 1983, with expenditures of over $13.5 billion. But what exactly is telemarketing? The following is how one source describes it:

> *Telemarketing is a low cost, highly efficient method of conducting business. Applied properly, telemarketing can increase sales, open new accounts, qualify advertising leads, establish new markets and efficiently service existing business, i.e., reorders and customer service. Telemarketing can be used in conjunction with advertising, direct mail, catalogue sales, face-to-face selling, plus other communication modes. When used properly, telemarketing enables a business or individual to target market his message, at low cost, to customers and prospects. It enables a salesman to carry on a two-way conversation, thus allowing him to answer any questions, and eventually close a sale without leaving his office.*[31]

---

[28]Mary McCabe English, "Videotech Brightens Marketers's Screens," *Advertising Age,* January 19, 1981, pp. S-14–S-17.

[29]Mike Slosberg, "Direct Marketing and Retailing in the 80's," *Direct Marketing,* October 1980, pp. 100–110.

[30]Cecilia Lautini, "A Basic Part of the Plan," *Advertising Age,* July 19, 1981, pp. S-1, S-39.

[31]This description is contained in the undated promotional literature of *Telemarketing* magazine, which characterizes itself as "the magazine of electronic marketing and communication." *Telemarketing* is a publication of the Technology Marketing Corp., Norwalk, CT.

The preceding description indicates that telemarketing can accomplish a variety of tasks. Telemarketing's versatility applies to both consumer-oriented products and business-to-business marketing.

Two forms of telemarketing are practiced extensively. One involves *outbound* calls from telephone salepersons to customers and prospects, and the other involves handling *inbound* orders, inquiries, or complaints. The distinction between outbound and inbound telemarketing is somewhat analogous to the personal selling distinction between order getting and order talking. Outbound telemarketing is proactive in soliciting orders and servicing accounts. Inbound telemarketing takes orders that have been generated by other media. A later discussion will point out that inbound telemarketing is not, however, limited to order taking.

Outbound Telemarketing

Consider these facts: A sales contact made to a client face to face in 1983 was estimated to cost approximately $200 on average; a telephone sales call, by comparison, cost between $6 and $10.[32] For this reason, many companies are using the telephone to support or even replace their conventional sales forces. A survey of over 500 industrial salespeople found that 88 percent use a combination of telephone and in-person selling; 6 percent use in-person selling exclusively; and 6 percent rely entirely on the telephone.[33] The survey revealed further that telephone applications include generating or qualifying leads, arranging face-to-face sales calls, upgrading orders or cross-selling (i.e., encouraging a customer who has purchased one product to buy another item), prospecting for new accounts, reactivating old accounts, and full account management.[34]

IBM, for example, uses telemarketing to cover its small- to medium-sized accounts, to generate incremental sales, to enhance the productivity of traditional sales representatives via the leads and information that it provides, and to ensure customer satisfaction and buying convenience. IBM has a fully integrated system of mail, catalog, and inbound and outbound telephone activity for its hardware, software, supplies, and services. The strategy is to transform a prospect or a dormant account into an active account, then to service the account with as little in-person sales contact as possible. Junior and senior college students are used as telephone salespersons. They work a maximum of 20 hours a week and are paid on an hourly basis supplemented with incentive rewards.[35]

[32]Neesa Sweet, "Let the Salesmen Do the Talking," *Advertising Age,* June 20, 1983, pp. M-18–M-21.

[33]Hubert D. Hennessey, "Matters to Consider Before Plunging into Telemarketing," *Marketing News,* July 8, 1983, p. 2.

[34]Ibid.

[35]This description is an adaptation of remarks from Peter DiSalvo in "3 Telemarketers Tell How to Hire, Train, Organize for This Profitable Direct Medium," *Marketing News,* July 8, 1983, p. 4.

Implementing an Outbound Telemarketing Program Telemarketing is not appropriate for all sales organizations. One practitioner has suggested the following eight-step process for evaluating the suitability of introducing a telephone sales force:[36]

1. An initial consideration is an evaluation of how essential face-to-face contact is; the more essential it is, the less appropriate telemarketing is.

2. A second consideration is geographical concentration. Telephone selling may represent an attractive alternative to in-person sales if customers are highly dispersed; if, however, customers are heavily concentrated (e.g., apparel manufacturers in Manhattan), minimal travel time is required and personal selling is probably preferable.

3. Economic considerations involving average order size and total potential should be estimated to determine whether in-person sales is cost-effective. It may not be in cases of small and marginal customers, who are served more economically by telephone.

4. A fourth area for evaluation is customer decision criteria. Telephone sales may be sufficient if price, delivery, and other quantitative criteria are paramount, but in-person sales may be essential in instances where product quality, dealer reputation, and service are uppermost in importance.

5. A fifth step is to determine the number of decision makers typically involved in purchasing a company's product; the more decision makers involved (e.g., when an industrial engineer, a purchasing agent, and the finance department are all involved), the more essential is face-to-face contact.

6. A next consideration is the nature of the purchase. Routine purchases (say, office supplies) can be handled easily by phone.

7. The status of the major purchase decision maker is a seventh factor to be evaluated. The telephone is acceptable for buyers, purchase agents, and engineers, but probably not for owners, presidents, and vice-presidents.

8. A final consideration is an evaluation of the specific selling tasks that telephone sales is and is not capable of performing. For example, telephone representatives may be particularly effective for prospecting and postsale follow-ups, whereas in-person sales effort is needed for the intervening sales tasks—preapproach, approach, presentation, objective handling, and closing.

These eight steps make it apparent that telephone selling is appropriate and effective in certain situations but not others. A systematic application of this eight-step process should enable a company to determine whether and to what extent telemarketing is appropriate for serving its customers.

Establishing a telephone marketing department requires solid management support and may also require drastic changes for a company to make the system work. For example, the electronics division of one Fortune 500 company replaced an

---

[36]Hennessey, "Matters to Consider."

entire field sales organization with an inside telephone sales team. The effort paid off, however, as the move resulted in an increased market share, a tremendous reduction in sales costs, and a 30 percent increment in sales productivity.[37]

Inbound Telemarketing

There are two general forms of inbound telemarketing. One form involves the nearly ubiquitous toll-free, or 800, number. The other is the Dial-It, or 900, number service, which is not a free call for the user. Both forms of inbound telemarketing will be discussed, with particular emphasis on the former because toll-free numbers are used more widely and have greater potential as a marketing communication tool.

Toll-Free (800 Number) Telemarketing

800 numbers are nearly ubiquitous. Everytime someone opens a magazine, turns on the television, or picks up a newspaper, one hears, "Call 1-800-xxx-xxxx." Currently, about one-third of the ads in major magazines contain 800 numbers. For example, Hewlett Packard urged readers to call its toll-free number for information concerning the nearest dealer of its new personal computer; Porsche-Audi encouraged readers to call its 800 number for information about a new 24-month/unlimited mileage warranty; and *Money* magazine listed its toll-free number so that interested parties might call for an immediate subscription.

An 800 number telecommunication program uses an *incoming* WATS (wide area telecommunication service) telephone system to encourage potential customers to phone a publicized number (an 800 number) in response to media advertising or other marketing communications. This 800 number, correctly inserted in advertisements, can be used by motivated, self-qualified consumers to request product or service information, place direct orders, express complaints or grievances, request coupons or other sales promotion materials, and inquire about the nearest dealers or outlets. Researchers estimate that at least 90 percent of Americans have already used 800 numbers or are familiar, at least, with their existence.[38]

Customer service representatives who receive 800 calls can provide immediate responses to requests for merchandise and product information and can handle complaints. Additionally, representatives can record callers' names and addresses to initiate immediate follow-ups by sending promotional materials. Also, the effectiveness of an advertising campaign can be measured quickly.

WATS line usage has grown at an annual rate of 25 percent, and the market is expected to increase to almost 4 billion calls by 1985.[39] At present, the 800 market

---

[37]Richard L. Bencin, "Telemarketing: The Answer to Rising Cost of Cold Calls," *Direct Marketing,* December 1981, pp. 51–55.

[38]James Venuto, *Telephone Marketing for Consumer Goods Product Introductions with Insight into Sampling, Couponing, and Sweepstakes* (Omaha: Team Telephone Inc., 1982).

[39]Murray Roman, *Telephone Marketing* (New York: McGraw-Hill, 1976).

has realized only one-third of its potential.[40] The many successful applications of 800 programs can almost assure continued rapid growth. Success stories include the following:

- The use of 800 numbers in print advertising and direct mail consistently adds incremental sales of 25 to 30 percent.[41]
- When combined with direct mail, telephone marketing generates an incremental response rate from 2.5 to 7 times greater than mail alone.[42]
- When broadcast commercials offer customers the opportunity to order either by writing in or phoning in, the latter outpulls the former threefold.[43]
- When an 800 system is in use, the conversion rate of inquiries to completed sales is reported to climb 28 to 30 percent.[44]
- In terms of specific applications, the following are illustrative of the effective use of 800 numbers. Brown and Williamson Tobacco Company sent coupons redeemable for a free carton of Barclay cigarettes to all people who called its 800 number. Due in part to this program, Barclay gained an impressive 3 percent market share, worth $375 million in sales volume per year.[45] Procter & Gamble responded to consumers' product complaints and requests for information by including 800 numbers on the packages of all of its brands. Approximately 500,000 customers contacted the company during the first year of the program's operation.[46]

Toll-free numbers are widely used and will be used increasingly because they are valuable adjuncts to marketing communication programs. Although there are distinct benefits with 800 numbers, there are problems as well. Table 16.4 summarizes the benefits and problems. The benefits are self-explanatory, but a few comments should help in better understanding the problems.

One major problem with toll-free numbers is the failure to define program objectives; this leads to severe limitations in evaluating the program's effectiveness and future potential. Another problem may arise because communicators assigned to work 800 number telephone lines require skills somewhat different from operators used in initiating calls. The 800 service communicators must be able to provide consumers with all of the data necessary for a completed call and have an inherent sales ability. A third potential problem is that there may be an insufficient

---

[40]"WATS Strikes Back," *Sales and Marketing Management,* August 17, 1981, pp. 20, 22.

[41]Roman, *Telephone Marketing.*

[42]Chuck Wingis, "Telemarketing: A Great Idea Whose Time Has Come," *Industrial Marketing,* August 1981, pp. 71–79.

[43]Roman, *Telephone Marketing.*

[44]Frank Spiro, "Toll-Free '800' Number Speeds Inquiries from Ads," *Industrial Marketing,* June 1977, p. 124.

[45]Venuto, "Telephone Marketing for Consumer Introductions."

[46]John A. Prestbo, "At Procter and Gamble, Success Is Largely Due to Heeding the Consumer," *Wall Street Journal,* April 29, 1980, pp. 1, 35.

TABLE 16.4   Benefits and Problems with 800 Numbers

Benefits	Problems
1. Permits quick, effective media tracking	1. Failure to define the goals and objectives of the program
2. Invites instant action	
3. Enables direct order taking	2. Lack of specialized planning
4. Reassures customers/provides better service	3. Failure to assess staff skills and provide adequate training
5. Assists sales promotion activities	
6. Identifies nearest dealer	4. Failure to make cost comparisons among options, vendors versus in-house, and usage rates
7. Can be used to accept memberships/reservations	
8. Aids market analysis through segmentation	5. Lack of integration into the marketing program of the company
9. Enables product information dissemination	
10. Can be used to obtain demographic and psychographic information	6. Inability to determine the number of lines needed to handle incoming calls during peak periods
11. Enables credit screening	7. Failure to be flexible
12. Adds to firm's prestige and credibility	8. Inadequate equipment used in the 800 program
13. Permits price quotations	9. Inability to provide services quoted over the 800 number
14. Assures the message is being reached in different segments	

---

number of lines to handle all incoming calls, since the 800 system cannot delay, or stack up, calls. Finally, failure to integrate the 800 number carefully into a company's marketing program can be extremely wasteful. Advertising, sales promotions, and 800 numbers need to be coordinated carefully to achieve their maximum, synergistic effects.

Dial-It (900 Number) Telemarketing   The Dial-It, or 900 number, service was introduced by AT&T to permit callers to pay a fee to phone a central number and register an opinion on a particular issue. The first major use was during the Carter-Reagan debate on October 28, 1980, when over 700,000 people spent 50 cents each to call the 900 number and register their opinions about who won the debate.[47] Another example is the "dramatic" poll conducted by NBC-TV's "Saturday Night Live" to determine whether "Larry the Lobster" should be boiled. Nearly a half million viewers participated, at 50 cents each.[48]

In addition to these novel applications, the 900-number technology offers various marketing communications possibilities. One possibility would be to use a 900 number to encourage customers to call for product information.[49] Such a service could possibly replace pamphlets and information guides that companies mail to consumers. The telephone information is immediate, and callers have a

---

[47]Theodore J. Gage, "900 Is Batting 1.000," *Advertising Age,* January 19, 1981, pp. S-33, 34.

[48]Bernie Whalen, "Marketers Expand Applications of Dial-It 900 Technology," *Marketing News,* November 26, 1982, p. 23.

[49]Gage, "900 Is Batting 1.000."

chance, unlike in mailed literature, to ask additional questions. Furthermore, the telephone cost incurred by a company (if it chooses to pay the fee rather than have customers pay it) could, quite possibly, be less than the cost of printing and mailing literature.

Another application for 900 numbers is to update customers about services that are subject to frequent changes. For example, the American Bankers Association sponsors a 900 number service to inform callers of the most recent interest rates on various financial instruments.[50]

Dial-It numbers can also be used by advertisers to test the effectiveness of their media buys. The calls generated by an ad tagged with a 900 number can be delineated by geographical area to determine where the ad had its greatest impact.[51] By cutting in and talking live with callers, advertisers can acquire additional useful information, such as demographic data, product usage characteristics, and advertising recall measures for recent television commercials.[52]

A 900 number can also be used during corporate emergencies. Johnson & Johnson instituted an immediate Dial-It service when its product, Extra-Strength Tylenol, was linked to seven deaths in the Chicago area. J & J developed a recorded message that informed callers about the problem and encouraged them to call a toll-free number for further questions.[53]

Although the use of 900 numbers is in its infancy, this technology is certainly another potentially valuable tool for marketing communicators. The whole field of telemarketing is developing rapidly, and many exciting and effective applications are available to companies that are willing to diverge from conventional business conduct.

Summary

Direct marketing is the most rapidly growing aspect of marketing activity in the United States. Total sales volume in 1981 exceeded $125 billion. Direct mail is the dominant direct marketing advertising medium. The outstanding advantages of this medium are that marketers can target messages to specific market segments and determine success (or failure) virtually immediately. Direct mail also permits greater personalization than does mass media advertising and is not subject to competing ads such as those that appear in other print and broadcast media. On a cost per order basis, direct mail is often less expensive and more efficient than alternative media.

Magazines, newspapers, and television are additional media used by direct marketers. Catalog marketing is a facet of direct marketing that is enjoying spectacular

---

[50]Whalen, "Marketers Expand Applicatons."

[51]Ibid.

[52]Ibid.

[53]Ibid.

success. A number of factors account for this growth, a few of which are consumer time savings, buying freedom, greater disposable income, and increased confidence in mail-order buying.

Telemarketing is a special form of direct marketing. As of 1983, the telephone was the major direct marketing medium, with expenditures in excess of $13.6 billion. Two forms of telemarketing are practiced. One involves outbound calls from telephone salespersons to customers and prospects; the other involves handling inbound calls for orders, inquiries, and complaints. The growth of outbound telemarketing is attributable in large part to the enormous expense of in-person sales contacts, which in 1983 cost approximately $200 per contact on the average. A telephone call, by comparison, cost only between $6 and $10. Telemarketing can be used to support or even replace a conventional sales force.

Inbound telemarketing includes the well-known toll-free, or 800 number, programs and the lesser known Dial-It, or 900 number, service. Toll-free programs have experienced tremendous growth, with the market growing at an annual rate of 25 percent. Dial-It (900 number) telemarketing was introduced initially by AT&T to permit callers to pay a fee for a phone call to register an opinion on a particular issue. Beyond this, Dial-It service offers marketing communicators additional possibilities. One possibility, for example, would be to encourage customers to call a designated 900 number and request product information.

Discussion Questions

1. Explain the differences between direct marketing, direct response advertising, and direct mail.
2. Why has direct marketing enjoyed such rapid growth in recent years?
3. For what kind of products is business-to-business direct marketing most appropriate?
4. What are the major advantages and disadvantages of direct mail advertising?
5. What is television's role as a direct response advertising medium?
6. Distinguish between telemarketing and direct marketing.
7. Distinguish between outbound and inbound telemarketing.
8. Under what conditions should a firm implement an outbound telemarketing service to replace its sales force?
9. Compare and contrast 800 and 900 number telemarketing programs.

Exercises

1. Gather two illustrations of direct mail advertisements and critique each using Caples's seven direct mail advertising principles.
2. Clip two or three direct response advertisements from magazines and apply Caples's principles to these ads.
3. Assume you are a direct marketer of a line of merchandise imprinted with the names and logos of major universities. These items are targeted to the

fans and supporters of the universities' athletic programs. Detail how you would compile a mailing list. Use your college/university for illustration.

4. Conduct interviews with five to ten consumers and investigate their attitudes toward catalog usage. Why, specifically, do these people use (or not use) catalogs? What products are they most likely to purchase by catalog? How satisfied have they been with past catalog purchases?

5. Go through a recent magazine and list every advertiser that employs a toll-free 800 number. Describe the specific function that the 800 number is apparently intended to serve for each advertiser.

CHAPTER 17

An Overview of Sales Promotion

In the past many businesses viewed sales promotion as playing a minor, supporting role in the total promotional program. Today, however, numerous companies, particularly those that market consumer goods, devote larger percentages of their budgets to sales promotion than to advertising.[1] Because of its growing importance, two chapters will be devoted to sales promotion. This chapter gives a broad overview of the subject, discusses reasons for sales promotion's growth, and explains the role of sales promotion in motivating the sales force and stimulating the trade (i.e., wholesalers and retailers). The following chapter continues with an in-depth treatment of consumer-oriented sales promotion techniques.

The Nature of Sales Promotion

The term **sales promotion** is often used as a catchall to encompass all promotional activities (excluding advertising, personal selling, and public relations/publicity) that stimulate short-term behavioral responses from consumers, retailers, and the company's own sales force. *Promotional inducement* has been offered as a more descriptive term, and it probably is, but this chapter will retain the more

[1]Roger A. Strang, *The Promotional Planning Process* (New York: Praeger Publishers, 1980), p. 1.

445

FIGURE 17.1   Illustrations of Outstanding Sales Promotions

Revlon Inc.

Revlon's Grand Prix sweepstakes is an innovative promotion in a category that seldom veers from purchase-with-purchase premiums. Men—virtually a minority in terms of target markets—constituted the primary audience for this promotion, which featured Tom Selleck as spokesman. Mr. Selleck, star of "Magnum P.I.," drives a Ferrari sportscar in the TV series, which makes his involvement and the Grand Prix grand prize—a Ferrari—particularly relevant.

Objectives: Increase sell-in and sell-through. Stimulate excitement among the sales force and trade.

Basic idea: Distribute instant-winner, scratch-off game pieces as bind-in cards. Require participant to visit store display to determine prize. Award a custom Ferrari as grand prize. Barter $50,000 worth of prizes—including Ferrari Custom Leather Luggage, Carrera/Porsche 18-carat gold sunglasses, Nikon cameras, Alpine audio systems and Seiko watches—in exchange for publicity. Advertise in *Newsweek, Playboy,* and *Sports Illustrated,* for a combined circulation of 16 million. Time promotion to coincide with Father's Day and graduations. Use TV star Tom Selleck as spokesman. Support at the point of sale with 30,000 counter cards with second change entry blanks. Conduct separate sweeps for trade and—excluding Ferrari—award matching prizes. Enclose the trade sweeps entries in point-of-sale kits. Motivate sales force to exceed sell-in quotas with additional prizes.

Budget: Media, approximately $750,000. Promotion, $115,000. Total, about $865,000.

Results: Sell-in increased more than 40%; sell-through increased 35%. Received 1,502,000 entries, 100,000 of which were facsimiles. Received 355,000 requests by mail for second chance entries. Ten percent of the game pieces were redeemed.

Polaroid

Polaroid teamed up with Delta Airlines to increase the sale of Polaroid's Series 600 cameras, priced from $40 to $200 at retail. This unique offer—involving marketers of quite diverse products—generated awareness for both. During the "Buy a Polaroid 600, Fly Delta Free" promotion, hundreds of thousands of fliers and college students did just that.

Objectives: Increase share and sales at Christmas. Broaden trial among affluent air travelers and college students.

Basic idea: In exchange for proof of purchase, offer a free Bonus Transportation Certificate. Camera purchasers may redeem the certificate for a free round-trip ticket to anywhere Delta Airlines flies when they buy a ticket of equal or greater value. Support with national advertising in more than 80 newspapers, including *The Wall Street Journal,* for a combined circulation of more than 30 million. Advertise on network TV; reach 90% of the households an average of 15 times. Promote on college campuses with posters. Supply dealers with point-of-sale kits including counter cards with tear-off order forms for the certificate. Encourage dealers to advertise via co-op programs.

Budget: Multi-million-dollar campaign representing 35% of Polaroid's fall expenditures. Delta bartered the premium (airfare) in exchange for advertising exposure.

Results: Polaroid estimates sales of more than $1 million. About 33% (300,000) of the certificates have been redeemed, at least a portion of which indicates Polaroid generated incremental sales. Represents Polaroid's biggest Christmas sell-through in more than 10 years. Dealers participating in the co-op ad program are thought to have increased ad exposure by 200% to 300%.

Source: William A. Robinson, "Best Promotions of the Year," *Advertising Age,* May 9, 1983, pp. M-54–M-59. Copyright 1983 Crain Communications, Inc.

---

traditional label, *sales promotion.*[2] Sales promotion has also been characterized as "sales engineering," that is, influencing the trade and the company's own sales force to deliver sales on a predictable basis.[3] It is useful, however, to think of sales promotion as "those activities which provide an incentive, additional to the basic benefits provided by a product or service, and which temporarily change the perceived price/value relationship of that product or service."[4]

---

[2]Eugene R. Beem and H. Jay Shaffer, *Triggers to Customer Action—Some Elements in a Theory of Promotional Inducement* (Cambridge, MA: Marketing Science Institute, Report No. 81-106, December 1981).

[3]Joel Harnett, "$60 Billion Can't Be Wrong," *Marketing Communications,* May 1983, p. 48.

[4]Roger A. Strang, "Sales Promotion Research: Contributions and Issues," unpublished paper presented at the AMA/MSI/PMAA Sales Promotion Workshop, Babson College, May 1983.

The practice of sales promotion can perhaps be understood best by examining the specific techniques marketers use to induce action. There are twelve major sales promotion inducements: trade allowances; trade coupons; samples; consumer coupons; price-offs; in–, on–, or near-pack premiums; free-in-the-mail premiums; self-liquidating premiums; contests and sweepstakes; refund offers; bonus packs; and stamp and continuity plans.[5]

Each of these techniques will be discussed extensively in this and the following chapter; however, an illustration of sales promotion in action will be presented first. Figure 17.1 presents two successful programs that were implemented by the Revlon and Polaroid companies. These promotions are examples of excellent campaigns that cut through competitive clutter, appealed to specific markets, and accomplished desired results. It is unlikely that advertising could have accomplished the same results in such a cost-effective manner.

Sales Promotion's Rapid Growth

Expenditures on sales promotion have increased dramatically in recent years. Figure 17.2 displays year-to-year growth from 1975 to 1983. The amount spent on sales promotion grew from $27.7 billion in 1975 to $71.7 billion in 1983, with an average annual increase in expenditures of 12 percent.

Reasons for Sales Promotion's Growth

Several factors account for the growing sales promotion expenditures. Following are the eight major reasons:[6]

1. *Sales promotion has become more acceptable to corporate executives.* Successful use of couponing, rebates, and other techniques has increased sales promotion's legitimacy and has shown management that these techniques can complement advertising messages and sales force efforts.

2. *Sales promotion facilitates product introductions by encouraging the sales force to devote more time to new products, by giving retailers an incentive to handle these products, and by providing consumers with tangible reasons to undertake trial purchases.* Successful new product introductions require marketing techniques that move merchandise into distribution networks and, ultimately, into the hands of consumers—tasks for which sales promotion is suited particularly well.

[5]William A. Robinson, "What Are Promos' Weak and Strong Points? *Advertising Age,* April 7, 1980, pp. 53–54.

[6]For further discussion, see Russell D. Bowman, "Advertising and Promotion Expenditures: Third Annual Report," *Marketing Communications,* September 1982, p. 36; "Creative Sales Promotion Vital in Marketing Mix," *Marketing News,* November 30, 1979, p. 8; Bud Frankel, "Sales Promotion Is Marketing Giant, But It's Misunderstood, Underestimated, and Mishandled," *Marketing News,* October 7, 1977, p. 6; Harnett, "$60 Billion Can't Be Wrong," p. 48; Strang, *The Promotional Planning Process,* p. 7.

FIGURE 17.2   Year-to-Year Growth of Sales Promotion

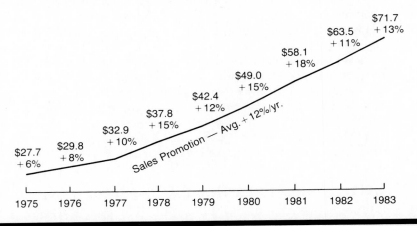

Source: Association of National Advertisers. Reprinted in Russell D. Bowman, "Advertising and Sales Promotion Report," *Marketing Communications,* August 1984, p. 6.

3.   *The expansion in product and brand management organizational struc-tures has fostered sales promotion growth.* Sales promotion is able to gen-erate relatively quick sales activity, and short-term sales response (rather than slow, long-term growth) is more compatible with the reward structures operative in many U.S. firms.

4.   *Sales promotion helps companies to avoid competitive clutter and to stand out in the crowd.* Increased competition and a tendency toward product parity have exerted pressures on firms to seek unique competitive advan-tages. Because real, concrete advantages are often difficult to obtain, more firms have turned to sales promotion to achieve at least temporary advan-tages over competitors.

5.   *Rapidly escalating media costs, particularly for network television, have led many executives to reduce advertising expenditures and to devote pro-portionately larger budgets to what often is more cost-effective sales pro-motion.*

6.   *Economic turmoil, with simultaneous recession and inflation, has acted as a major stimulant for firms to seek ways of providing dealers and consum-ers with reasons for buying their brands rather than competitive alterna-tives.* Attractive sales promotion deals provide such a reason.

7.   *Beset by economic turmoil and heightened competition, retailers (espe-cially large, sophisticated chains) have exerted pressure on product manu-facturers to offer trade allowances, cooperative advertising dollars, and other promotional inducements that lead to cost cutting and greater profits.*

8.   *Consumers respond favorably to money-saving opportunities.*

Sales promotion will, in all likelihood, continue to grow. However, too much emphasis on sales promotion can harm both an individual brand and a product category, because excessive promotional activity can damage a product's image, diminish brand loyalty, and possibly even reduce consumption.[7] The important point, stressed throughout the text, is that no single promotional tool is a panacea; rather, the various promotional tools must be blended together intelligently without inordinate emphasis on any one.

The Role of Sales Promotion in the Marketing Mix

Chapter 1 introduced the concept of "Three Modes of Marketing" as a framework for the text.[8] To review this concept, there are three ways marketers seek to manage the demand for their offers. The first mode, the *basic offer,* is a company's product or service that is designed to meet the needs of target customers. *Persuasive communications,* the second mode, is intended to stimulate consumer wants. The third mode, *promotional inducement* (sales promotion), is the means used by marketers to trigger customer action by offering extra substantive benefits beyond the basic offer. Each mode performs a different function. Sales promotion attempts to induce action directly; the other modes influence action less directly. The three modes overlap and are interrelated, but this discussion will focus on the third mode, promotional inducement, to amplify the specific tasks of sales promotion and to describe the factors that influence the choice of sales promotion over advertising to expand a product's sales.

Specific Tasks of Sales Promotion

Sales promotion is well suited for accomplishing certain tasks but incapable of achieving others. It is instructive to examine first the tasks that sales promotion *cannot* accomplish.[9]

1. Sales promotion incentives (samples, coupons, etc.) cannot, by themselves, give the consumer any compelling long-term reason to continue purchasing a promoted brand.

2. Sales promotion cannot permanently stop an established product's declining sales trend.

3. Sales promotion cannot change the basic nonacceptance of an undesired product.

4. Sales promotion cannot create an image for a brand.

---

[7]Strang, *The Promotional Planning Process,* p. 7.

[8]Beem and Shaffer, *Triggers to Customer Action.*

[9]Charles Fredericks, Jr., "What Ogilvy & Mather Has Learned About Sales Promotion," *The Tools of Promotion* (New York: Association of National Advertisers, 1975).

Sales promotion cannot work wonders, but it *is* ideally suited to accomplish the following tasks:[10]

1. Sales promotion can stimulate sales force enthusiasm for a new, improved, or mature product.
2. Sales promotion can create trade (primarily retailer) awareness for new products.
3. Sales promotion can help to gain distribution and build inventories.
4. Sales promotion can increase on– and off-shelf merchandising space.
5. Sales promotion can reinforce advertising.
6. Sales promotion can elicit a trial purchase from consumers.
7. Sales promotion can hold current users by encouraging purchase habit building.
8. Sales promotion can preempt competition by loading consumers. That is, some sales promotion techniques (e.g., bonus packs) encourage consumers to purchase larger quantities of a particular item than they would normally. This, then, takes consumers temporarily out of the marketplace for competitive brands.
9. Sales promotion can increase product usage by loading consumers. That is, consumers tend to use more of certain products (e.g., snack foods) as a function of how much they have available in their homes.

We have merely listed the tasks that sales promotion can accomplish. At later points in this chapter and in the next chapter we will elaborate on these objectives in the context of the specific techniques that are most often used to achieve the objectives of sales promotion.

Determinants of Promotional Strategy

Advertising and sales promotion both play important roles in most companies' marketing mixes. What, however, determines which receives greater emphasis and budgetary support in a given company? A recent study has provided some answers to this important and interesting question.

Strang performed both in-depth interviews and mail surveys with two samples of marketing executives who represented a variety of grocery, personal care, toiletry, and household products.[11] Some of the more important findings were (1) advertising plays a dominant role in the promotional mixes of more profitable

---

[10]The following list has been compiled from a variety of sources, but three were particularly useful: Fredericks, ibid.; William A. Robinson, "Plan to Avoid Wheel-Spinning," *Advertising Age,* November 8, 1982, p. M-50; Tony Spaeth, "Planning Matrix Gives Boost to Today's Promotion," *Advertising Age,* October 3, 1977, pp. P2–P4.

[11]Strang, *The Promotional Planning Process.*

brands, (2) premium-price brands also place greater reliance on advertising, (3) low-growth brands place greater emphasis on sales promotion. These findings, considered collectively, suggest that successful brands support their success with advertising, and brands that desire greater success (i.e., faster growth, larger market shares, etc.) attempt to achieve it with relatively greater emphasis on sales promotion.

In addition to the preceding findings, Strang also detected several "environmental" factors that influence the sales promotion versus advertising allocation decision. As depicted in Table 17.1, these environmental factors include product life-cycle stage, market dominance, purchase frequency, and other factors. The interviewed executives consider product life-cycle stage to be the single most important consideration in their allocation decisions, with advertising being more critical in the introductory and growth stages and sales promotion dominating the promotional mix in later stages. Additionally, sales promotion is regarded as more important (1) for regional brands that cannot afford to compete in advertising against dominant national brands, (2) when competitors emphasize sales promotion over advertising, and (3) when a brand is especially vulnerable to losing retail distribution. Comparatively, advertising receives a larger share of the promotional budget for (1) highly differentiated products, (2) products with high purchase frequencies, and (3) situations in which competitors emphasize advertising.

It should be apparent that the allocation of the promotional mix between advertising and sales promotion varies from situation to situation; there is no best solution. Rather, the best allocation depends upon the specific conditions a brand encounters in the marketplace.

TABLE 17.1   Major Environmental Determinants of the Advertising versus Sales Promotion Allocation Decision

| | Impact on Allocation | |
Factor	Increase Advertising	Increase Sales Promotion
Stage in brand life cycle		
Introduction	X	
Growth	X	
Maturity		X
Decline		X
Regional brand		X
Market dominance	X	
Promotion-oriented competitor		X
Advertising-oriented competitor	X	
High differentiation	X	
High purchase frequency	X	
Distribution vulnerability		X

Source: Roger A. Strang, *The Promotional Planning Process* (New York: Praeger Publishers, 1980), p. 94.

Sales Promotion Planning

Business practice requires that systematic planning precede decision making. Sales promotion has traditionally suffered from informal, seat-of-the pants decision making. Significant changes are taking place, however, and there is a notable trend toward professional planning.[12] Industry representatives generally agree that planning is essential for successful sales promotion campaigns. Figure 17.3 depicts the fundamental elements of a formal sales promotion planning process.[13]

The first step, environmental analysis, includes the dual activities of performing a situation analysis and, from the information generated, identifying the problems and opportunities facing the target brand (i.e, the brand under consideration). The output of such an analysis is a determination of the possibilities of using sales promotion in view of the identified problems and opportunities confronting the brand. For example, a soft drink company may establish from its environmental analysis that consumption of the product category (say, non-colas) is declining and that cola competitors are in the process of launching major advertising campaigns. These results may suggest an opportunity for creative sales promotion activity.

The next step, internal analysis, involves an introspective assessment of the firm's promotional philosophy and an evaluation of the role of sales promotion in the target brand's marketing mix. One determination may be that sales promotion is incompatible with the image the firm desires for the brand. Alternatively, management may decide that certain forms of sales promotion, say, premiums or sweepstakes, are acceptable but coupons are not. Regardless of the specific determination, a formal evaluation of the specific role that sales promotion should have in the overall marketing mix is a valuable exercise.

The two background analyses, environmental and internal analyses, lead to the all-important third step, the establishment of objectives for the contemplated sales promotion campaign. Is the objective to generate trial purchases, establish repeat purchase behavior, preempt competition, or something else? It is critical that the specific objective(s) be established at the early stages of the planning process.

The fourth step involves setting the budget for the proposed campaign. The budget and objectives are interdependent activities, as indicated by the two-headed arrow in Figure 17.3. That is, program objectives determine how much will be needed to accomplish desired goals, yet budgetary restrictions impose limits as to how grandiose the objectives can be in view of limited funds. Thus, setting budgets and establishing objectives are interactive activities.

The development of strategies, step five, follows from the budgetary and objective-setting activities. At this point, the planner must determine which sales promotion technique or combination of techniques will accomplish the designated

---

[12]See Robinson, "Plan To Avoid Wheel-Spinning," p. M-50.

[13]Figure 17.3 represents an amalgamation of ideas from Frankel, "Sales Promotion Is Giant"; Robinson, "Plan To Avoid Wheel-Spinning"; Spaeth, "Planning Matrix."

FIGURE 17.3   Sales Promotion Planning Process

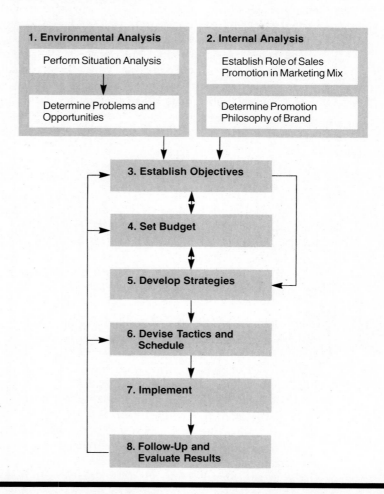

objectives. Suppose the objective is to generate (trial usage) for the target brand. Strategic options include coupons (with many alternative delivery systems), price-offs, refunds, and samples. The strategist must decide which of these is best suited to the task at hand in light of budgetary restrictions. Once the strategy is formulated, management often must reevaluate, and perhaps revise, the proposed budget.

Steps six and seven represent the detailed, operational aspect of promotion planning: devising tactics, setting the time schedule for the campaign, and implementing it. Here, creativity and timing are essential. The challenge is to devise delivery instruments (for instance, coupons or samples) that can break through the tremendous competitive clutter,[14] attract consumer attention, and produce the desired response. It also is important that the program be timed to coordinate with advertising campaigns, to tie in with sales force incentive compensation, and to be compatible with retailers' requirements.

The final activity in formal sales promotion planning, follow-up and evaluation of results, is a continuing process, which involves comparing results with objectives, evaluating whether or not the program was accomplished within budget, and determining whether or not the schedule was followed as closely as possible. This information provides a measure of performance, which is useful in the evaluation of personnel responsible for the execution of the program.

Sales Promotion Techniques

This section discusses the specific sales promotion techniques listed at the beginning of the chapter. A brief evaluation of sales promotion's role in motivating the sales force is provided, followed by a rather detailed treatment of trade-oriented techniques. (Chapter 18 covers fully the consumer-oriented techniques of sales promotion.)

Sales-Force Motivation[15]

Purpose of sales promo.

The primary purpose of sales promotion is to induce desired behavior from consumers and the trade. However, sales promotion can, secondarily, enhance sales force enthusiasm and effort. Consider the many salespeople who call daily upon grocery and drugstore buyers and managers. These salespeople represent product lines that typically are not vastly different from competitive offerings in terms of product quality, price, and other relevant attributes. Yet, their job is to motivate buyers to stock their company's brands, if the store does not already, or, if the store does stock the company's brands, to purchase larger quantities or to provide better shelf positions or more space. Sophisticated buyers look for hard evidence for engaging in behavior that a salesperson attempts to effect. The salesperson's job is to provide the concrete, tangible evidence to motivate the buyer to engage in the desired behavior. Sales promotion can, indeed, play an important role to support a salesperson's efforts. Armed with the knowledge that his or her company is scheduled to launch a major sampling campaign, to offer an attractive sweep-

---

[14]A good discussion of the magnitude of the problem is provided in Louis J. Haugh, "A Crisis in Creativity: Promos Lose to Clutter," *Advertising Age,* September 17, 1979, pp. 64, 68.

[15]The topic of sales force motivation is much broader than what is presented here. A host of compensation programs, travel awards, gifts, and recognition programs are used to motivate salespeople. Some of these were discussed in Chapter 11. For an in-depth treatment see John C. FitzMaurice, "Sales Incentives," *The Tools of Promotion* (New York: Association of National Advertisers, 1975).

stake, or to introduce a bonus-pack deal, the salesperson has additional tools to make an important sale or to obtain extra shelf space.

Trade-Oriented Techniques

There are two basic forms of sales promotions: *internal* sales promotions attempt to push goods from the manufacturer to wholesalers and retailers, and *external* sales promotions are directed at pulling the product through the distribution channels by creating consumer demand.[16] Sales promotion managers in the United States have historically invested larger percentages of their promotional dollars in internal (trade) promotions than in external (consumer) promotions. Although there has been a recent trend toward greater investment in consumer promotions and less investment in trade promotions,[17] trade promotions represent the first step in any marketing effort. Consumer promotions are likely to fail unless trade promotion efforts have been successful in getting wholesalers to distribute the product and retailers to stock adequate quantities.

The objectives of trade-oriented sales promotions are many: (1) to introduce new or revised products, (2) to increase distribution of new packages or sizes, (3) to build retail inventories, (4) to increase the manufacturer's share of shelf space, (5) to obtain displays outside normal shelf locations, (6) to reduce excess inventories and increase turnover, (7) to achieve product features in retailers' newspaper advertising, and (8) to break competitive exclusivity.[18]

Three major categories of trade-oriented sales promotions are used by marketing practitioners. Each has its own distinct set of objectives, advantages, and disadvantages.

Allowance Promotions   Several different forms of promotion provide allowances to the trade in terms of free goods or price reductions in return for purchasing specific quantities of goods. For example, Shell Fire & Ice Motor Oil offered its retailers 5 free cases (120 free quarts) with every purchase of 45 cases. The makers of ACTIFED, a nasal decongestant/antihistamine, provided a trade allowance of 16 2/3 percent off the retail invoice price for all purchases during the deal period.

Manufacturers find allowance promotions attractive for several reasons: They are easy to implement, can successfully stimulate initial distribution, are well accepted by the trade, and can increase trade purchases during the allowance period. How-

---

[16]William Robinson and Don E. Schultz, *Sales Promotion Management* (Chicago, IL: Crain Books, 1982), p. 9.

[17]"Consumer Promotions Continue Strong," *Supermarket Business,* July 1983, p. 9.

[18]These objectives and much of the material in this section are adapted from a consumer promotion seminar conducted by Ennis Associates, Inc., and sponsored by the Association of National Advertisers, Inc., New York, undated.

ever, one disadvantage is that allowances may induce the trade to stockpile a product in order to take advantage of the temporary price reduction. This merely shifts business from the future to the present.

In practice, marketers use various forms of allowances. *Count-recount allowances* offer the trade a specified payment on each case of product moved from the warehouse to retail during the allowance period. Such allowances are effective if the objective is to encourage trade support for the brand or to reduce trade inventories, but these allowances may accomplish little more than increasing store inventories.

Retail merchandising performance offers (RMPOs), by comparison, offer allowances to the trade for moving merchandise from the warehouse to retail outlets, but only when store inventories are supported with special advertising or display efforts. Thus, RMPOs are designed to encourage greater trade cooperation than that which is accomplished with count-recount allowances. However, retailers often fail to devote sufficient effort to move merchandise into consumers' hands.

Advertising Allowances and Display Allowances   Advertising and display allowances are designed to overcome the lack of retailer commitment to a product by requiring retailers to actively support the promoted brand. *Advertising allowances* provide retailers with a specified payment per case for supporting the manufacturer's brand in newspaper features. *Display allowances* work in a similar fashion by offering retailers an opportunity to earn a discount for each case that is actually displayed. Although both types of allowances are effective in stimulating in-store activity, a potential problem is the difficulty manufacturers have in verifying that retailers have performed in accordance with the allowance program.

Display Material Promotions   Display material promotions, which often are used in conjunction with trade allowances, provide retailers with special in-store display materials. These materials include dump bins, motion pieces, stand-up racks, end-of-counter displays, posters, shelf cards, and a variety of other materials—all of which are designed to attract consumer attention by enhancing either the conspicuousness or the attractiveness of the displayed merchandise.

Marketers must, in general, use some incentive to obtain trade support for display promotions, especially for more elaborate promotions such as the center-of-the-aisle displays one often encounters in grocery stores. These incentives typically include buying allowances of one form or another, as described previously, a free gift to consumers (such as a sample or a premium offer), or prizes as part of a trade sweepstakes.

Display promotions are particularly effective for brands that the trade accepts as good display brands, namely, those with strong consumer franchises. Display promotions are relatively ineffective for small-volume brands. Another significant problem is that many displays, especially posters, shelf cards, and other smaller items go unused. They often are delivered to retailers but are never brought out of storage areas or, worse yet, immediately end up in retailers' trash bins. Robinson and Schultz estimate that only 25 percent of all display materials sent by manufacturers are eventually used in retail stores. The reasons are that (1) display materials often are poorly planned by manufacturers and are unsuitable for retailers, (2) the materials take up too much space for the amount of sales generated, and (3) they are too difficult to manage and set up.[19]

Seller Beware!   Trade-oriented promotions are effective in gaining retail distribution and in encouraging retailers to devote more or better shelf space and displays to the manufacturer's brand; however, trade promotion is fraught with problems, mainly because some retailers take advantage of allowances without performing the services for which they receive credit. In fact, some manufacturers estimate that perhaps as much as two-thirds of trade-promotion dollars are wasted.[20]

One study determined that large chain retailers are particularly likely to take advantage of manufacturers' trade allowances without passing the savings along to consumers.[21] Table 17.2 shows that large chains accounted for 29 percent of all retail sales for merchandise *not* sold on deal (i.e., nondeal sales) but only accounted for 17 percent of total sales for merchandise purchased on allowance. By comparison, medium-size chains' sales of featured merchandise were exactly proportionate to their nondeal sales (providing a trade performance index of 100, Table 17.2), and small chains and independents took advantage of manufacturers' deals and sold proportionately more feature items.

The reason large chains are disproportionately more likely *not* to pass the price reductions they receive from manufacturers along to consumers is that they, unlike smaller chains and independents, merchandise their own private brands. Because private brands offer chain stores better profit margins than do manufacturers' brands, it appears that large chains enjoy the best of both situations by receiving discounts from manufacturers for services unrendered while earning larger profits

TABLE 17.2	**Deal versus Nondeal Sales by Store Size**		
Store Size	Nondeal Sales (1)	Feature Sales (2)	Trade Performance Index (2 ÷ 1)
Large chains	29%	17%	59
Medium chains	7	7	100
Small chains and independents	64	76	119
	100%	100%	

Source: Adapted from *Insights: Issues 1–13, 1979–1982* (New York: NPD Research, 1983), p. 9.

[19]Robinson and Schultz, *Sales Promotion Management,* p. 278.

[20]*Insights: Issues 1–13, 1979–1982* (New York: NPD Research, 1983), p. 8.

[21]Ibid.

from their own private brands. This certainly is not meant to imply that all large chains exploit manufacturers and consumers. It does, however, point out a serious problem that manufacturers must deal with when offering trade promotions. Many manufacturers have, in fact, responded to this problem by tightening performance requirements and requiring retailers to do more to earn their allowances.[22]

Summary

The topic of sales promotion was introduced. Sales promotion is gaining in stature, sophistication, and magnitude. The major reasons underlying sales promotion's growth were described. The specific tasks that sales promotion can and cannot accomplish were discussed. Sales promotion cannot, for example, give the consumer compelling long-term reason to purchase. It is suited ideally, however, to generating trial-purchase behavior.

An eight-step, formalized sales promotion process was illustrated and explained. Two of sales promotion's major objectives, motivating the sales force and eliciting action from wholesalers and retailers, were discussed in depth. The following chapter picks up with a detailed treatment of sales promotion's third major objective, influencing the behavior of ultimate consumers.

Discussion Questions

1. The term *promotional inducement* has been suggested as an alternative to *sales promotion*. Explain why this new term is more descriptive than the established term.
2. Describe the factors that have accounted for sales promotion's rapid growth. Do you expect sales promotion to continue its rapid growth over the next ten years?
3. Four specific tasks that sales promotion is *incapable* of accomplishing were given without explanation. Provide the explanation.

4. The allocation of promotional dollars to advertising and sales promotion is influenced by a variety of factors, including life-cycle stage, the degree of brand differentiation, and the degree of brand dominance. Explain how these factors influence the allocation decision.
5. Figure 17.3 depicts double-headed arrows between objectives and budget and between budget and strategies. Explain the nature of these reciprocal relations.
6. Why is it important that objectives be specified clearly when formulating a sales promotion program?

---

[22]Eugene S. Mahany, "Food Industry Jitters Bring Intensified Promotion Efforts," *Advertising Age,* October 30, 1978, p. 101.

7. How can sales promotion techniques generate enthusiasm and stimulate improved performance from the sales force?

Exercises

1. Interview a marketing executive of a manufacturing company (preferably a consumer goods firm) and analyze the company's sales promotion activity that is directed at retailers.
2. Interview two or three salespeople who represent grocery, drug, or general merchandise products and attempt to determine the sales promotion techniques their firms use. Evaluate whether these techniques are effective motivating devices.
3. Conduct interviews with two or three retail managers or buyers and question them about trade allowances and display programs currently in effect in their stores.

CHAPTER 18

Consumer-Oriented Sales Promotion

The previous chapter introduced sales promotion. It discussed the different techniques marketers use, the objectives they want to accomplish, the growth sales promotion has experienced, and the specific application of sales promotion for purposes of stimulating sales force enthusiasm and inducing trade action. The present chapter continues the discussion and focuses on consumer-oriented sales promotions. A variety of techniques are available to promotion managers; each accomplishes a specific set of objectives, each encounters certain obstacles to implementation, and each incurs varying costs. This chapter will demonstrate the unique character of each sales promotion technique and will show the specific objectives that each is intended to accomplish.

Table 18.1 provides the organizational framework for the discussion in the chapter. The table classifies consumer-oriented sales promotion techniques both in terms of the reward offered to consumers, which may be either immediate or delayed, and in terms of the primary objective underlying a manufacturer's use of a particular sales promotion, whether trial impact, franchise holding, or image reinforcement.

Cell 1 in Table 18.1 includes two sales promotion techniques, sampling and instant coupons, which are used to induce trial purchase behavior by providing consumers with an immediate reward. The reward is either monetary savings, in the case of instant coupons, or a free product, for sampling.

Media– and mail-delivered coupons and free-in-the-mail premiums, found in cell 2, are techniques that produce trial impact yet delay the reward to consumers.

TABLE 18.1   **Typology of Sales Promotion Techniques**

Consumer Reward	Manufacturer Objective		
	Trial Impact	Franchise Holding	Image Reinforcement
Immediate	1. • Sampling • Instant coupons	3. • Price-offs • Bonus packs • In-, on-, and near-pack premiums	5.
Delayed	2. • Media and mail-delivered coupons • Free-in-the-mail premiums	4. • In- and on-pack coupons • Refunds	6. • Self-liquidating premiums • Contests and sweepstakes

Cells 3 and 4 contain franchise holding tools of sales promotion. Marketing communicators design these techniques to keep existing customers from switching to competitive brands, to reward present customers, and to encourage repeat purchasing in general. Immediate reward/franchise holding methods (cell 3) are price-offs; bonus packs; and in–, on–, and near-pack premiums. Delayed reward/franchise holding techniques, those in cell 4, are in– and on-pack coupons and refund offers.

Building a brand's image is primarily the task of advertising; however, sales promotion tools may support advertising efforts by reinforcing a brand's image. By nature, these techniques are incapable of providing consumers with an immediate reward; therefore, cell 5 is empty. Cell 6 classifies self-liquidating premiums and contests/sweepstakes in terms of delayed reward and image reinforcement; these techniques, in addition to performing other tasks, serve to strengthen a brand's image.

Immediate Reward/Trial Impact Techniques

Sampling

Consider the following situation. General Mills planned to introduce Yoplait, the yogurt of France, in southern California. Because this area has a population that is demographically diverse and because there are a number of strong regional yogurt brands, successful introduction necessitated building both trade (i.e., wholesaler and retailer) and consumer awareness quickly and creating high trial purchase levels among targeted customers. Several legal issues, however, hindered the achievement of these goals; it is illegal in California to offer coupons for dairy products or to use trial-size samples.

The solution executed by General Mills was a promotion strategy that supported its advertising effort and enabled it to distribute samples legally. The promotion utilized refrigerated vans that were decorated to look like French cafés on wheels from which full-size samples were distributed at fairs, beaches, baseball games, and other sites. In addition, General Mills held the Yoplait Bicycle Challenge, a takeoff of the Tour de France, which represented a healthy activity with which the target audience could identify and provide another site for sampling. In less than three months Yoplait was number one in a market that has expanded by 25 percent since Yoplait's introduction.[1]

This case illustrates the power of sampling as a promotional technique. Most practitioners agree that sampling is the premier sales promotion device to generate trial purchase behavior. In fact, some observers believe that sample distribution is almost a necessity when introducing new or improved products or when seeking new markets for established products (as in the case of Yoplait).

Sampling, by definition, includes any method of distribution that can be used to deliver an actual– or trial-size product to the consumer. Marketers deliver samples in a variety of ways: (1) by direct mail, either alone or in cooperation with other brands; (2) through flat samples included in print media; (3) door to door by special distribution crews; (4) via another product, in– or on-pack, which serves as the sample carrier; (5) at high-traffic locations, such as shopping centers or special events; (6) and in store, where demonstrator samples are available for trial.

When the objective is to reach a broad cross section of consumers, door-to-door and mail delivery are the most effective means of sampling. The other sampling methods cost substantially less but do not reach nearly as many consumers. Consequently, practitioners recommend using those other techniques only when funds are limited.[2]

Sampling Problems   Despite its apparent advantages, there are several problems associated with the use of sampling. First, sampling is an expensive technique. Second, mass mailings of samples can be mishandled by the postal service; furthermore, direct mail is efficient only for products weighing less than six ounces. Third, door-to-door sampling and distribution at high-traffic locations can be relatively slow, and controlling distribution quality is difficult. Fourth, in– or on-package sampling is subject to limited distribution; the sample is never available to consumers who do not buy the carrying brand. Finally, in-store demonstrators often receive poor handling and inadequate distribution.

Due to its expense and because of waste and other problems, the use of sampling decreased in the early 1970s as many marketers turned to offering coupons as a cheaper alternative.[3] However, with the development of creative solutions and innovations in sampling, marketers have again become enthusiastic about sampling.

---

[1]This case is adapted from Edward D. Meyer, *Promotion Update '82,* a publication of the Promotion Marketing Association of America Inc., New York, 1982.

[2]*ANA Consumer Promotion Seminar Fact Book* (New York: Association of National Advertisers, undated).

[3]George Donahue, "Sampling Update, Part I: Direct Response Offers, New Distribution Methods, and Co-op Promotions Help Improve Sampling Efficiency," *Marketing Communications,* September 1980, pp. 61–63.

Sampling has become more efficient with regard to reaching specific target groups, results are readily measured, and the rising costs of media advertising have increased the relative attractiveness of sampling.

Sampling Trends   Six major trends have evolved in conjunction with the renewed use of sampling.[4]

Increased Selectivity   The distribution of samples has become very selective in recent years. This is due largely to the emergence of sampling services that specialize in rifle-shooting, or precision, distribution rather than the shotgun approach. For example, John Blair Marketing offers the "JBM Sample Pack," a service that pinpoints and selectively delivers samples to consumers who are either product nonusers or users of competitive brands. Sample recipients are surveyed initially by questionnaire and identified by deomographic and product/brand-use characteristics. Then individual sample packs are assembled specifically for each person such that he or she receives only those products which match her or his product and brand consumption patterns. Sampled products are delivered directly by mail to recipients' homes.

Another specialized service, Cinema Marketing, distributes samples in movie theaters. This service offers both geographic flexibility and demographic selectivity and assures that the sample brand is delivered only to the desired target market. Cinema Marketing claims to be able to distribute samples to approximately 46 million movie-goers in the top 100 U.S. markets in 21 days.[5]

Greater Customization   Successful sampling requires considerable advance planning in order to tailor the sampling program effectively to the objectives established for a particular brand. This involves determining the appropriate market positioning for the brand, deciding upon the proper size and package design for the sample, and coordinating all supporting advertising, publicity, and other forms of sales promotion.[6]

More Promotional Integration   Sampling is, to a greater extent than ever before, becoming integrated with advertising, with sales force activity, and with other sales promotion techniques such as coupons, sweepstakes, and refunds. A promotional campaign for Nescafe coffee illustrates such integration. Nescafe, in order to secure broad consumer trial and to get users of competitive brands to switch, advertised coupons worth 19¢ each. Along with this effort, Nescafe provided retailers with

---

[4]George Donahue, "Sampling Update, Part II: A Guide to Distribution Methods and Services," *Marketing Communications,* October 1980, pp. 82–87.

[5]JBM Sample Pack, Cinema Marketing, and a number of other specialized services are given a more detailed treatment in George Donahue, "Sampling Update, Part III: Who's Who—Profile of the Industry's Top Firms," *Marketing Communications,* November 1980, pp. 64–76.

[6]Roy Harris, "Sampling," *The Tools of Promotion* (New York: Association of National Advertisers, 1975).

displays that carried 19¢ trial-size samples of this coffee brand. The coupons enabled consumers to get either the trial size free or to apply the 19¢ coupon against any regular-size jar of Nescafe.[7]

New Techniques and Ideas   Numerous creative ideas are being applied in an effort to get sample merchandise into the hands of targeted consumers. Any college student who has traveled to Florida over spring break is familiar with the product sampling techniques Miller Brewery and Anheuser-Busch use.

Another innovative sampling program is one that was designed for R.J. Reynolds' Camel Lights. Choices of advertising media are, of course, limited for cigarettes; furthermore, Camel Light's target users, young adults, are difficult to reach by means of conventional sampling. Reynolds' solution was to use specially trained crews to distribute samples to young adults at locations where they gather, such as night clubs and bowling alleys.

Increased Testing and Evaluation   As with other sales promotion techniques, follow-up research is being conducted more frequently to assess the results of sampling campaigns. This chapter concludes with a discussion of methods used for measuring the success of sampling and other sales promotion methods.

Continued Growth   Sampling experts expect that the rise of sampling will experience continued growth for the following reasons: (1) sampling produces immediate sales results, (2) innovations in sampling distribution have lowered most manufacturers' costs of implementing sampling programs, (3) sampling programs are becoming more effective in inducing trial purchase behavior from product nonusers and competitive users, (4) sampling is used increasingly by established brands to combat efforts of new brands, (5) psychographic sampling is becoming a reality, making sampling more effective.[8]

Empirical Evidence   How effective is sampling in influencing trial purchase behavior? Moreover, what influence does it have on stimulating repeat purchase behavior? Recent evidence has shed light on these questions. NPD Research, Inc., a firm that collects data from a panel of over 30,000 households who maintain continuous diaries of their package goods purchases, evaluated many new product introductions involving free samples. Their composite results for eight brands show that of the households who did not receive free samples (the control group), an average of 11.4 percent made trial purchases of the eight brands. By comparison, 16 percent of the recipients of free samples made trial purchases. Moreover, 35.7 percent of the families who purchased after receiving a sample repurchased the brand, whereas only 31.8 percent of the control group triers repurchased.[9]

---

[7]This case is adapted from Meyer, *Promotion Update '82.*

[8]These ideas are described in Donahue, "Sampling Update, Part I", p. 63.

[9]*Insights: Issues 1–13, 1979–1982* (New York: NPD Research, 1983), pp. 6–7.

The repeat purchase results are particularly interesting because they run somewhat contrary to more theoretically based research, which detected a tendency for sampling to diminish repeat purchasing.[10] Attribution theory was used by the researchers to explain why free samples might diminish rather than increase the likelihood that consumers will repeat purchase a brand that they tried previously in response to a free sample. According to attribution theory, sampling should diminish repeat purchasing because the sample user is inclined to infer that the only reason he or she consumed the sample product was because it was free. The user is said to make an external attribution. That is, sample trial users are thought to form unfavorable attitudes toward sampled products and, instead, to discount their personal liking for the item in favor of an alternative explanation, namely, that they tried it only because it was free. Volitional trial users, those who try a product without first receiving a sample, are presumed to attribute their trial to a personal liking for the item (an internal attribution). This internal attribution fosters a positive attitude and enhances the probability of repeat purchasing.[11]

When Should Sampling Be Used?   Promotion managers use sampling to induce consumers to try either a brand that is new or one that is moving into a different market. While it is important to encourage trial usage for new brands, sampling is not appropriate for all new or improved products. The ideal circumstances for sampling are the following:[12]

1.   *When a new or improved brand is either demonstrably superior to other brands or when it has distinct relative advantages over other products it is intended to replace.* For example, freeze-dried coffee, when introduced in the 1960s, had distinct advantages over conventional coffees. Therefore, sampling was a viable means through which to attain high trial rates.

2.   *When the product concept is so innovative it is difficult to communicate by advertising alone.* Freeze-dried coffee also illustrates this point.

3.   *When promotional budgets can afford to generate consumer trial quickly.* Broad-scale sampling is terribly expensive. Imagine the expense incurred by Lever Brothers when it distributed samples of Sun Light dishwashing liquid to over 50 million households. (See Figure 18.1 for additional information about this product.)

4.   *When the product class has almost universal usage.* Broader product usage makes sampling easier because selectivity is not as critical, and waste is not a problem.

---

[10]Carol Scott, "Effects of Trial and Incentives on Repeat Purchase Behavior," *Journal of Marketing Research,* Vol. 13, August 1976, pp. 263–269. See also Joe A. Dodson, Alice M. Tybout, and Brian Sternthal, "Impact of Deals and Deal Retraction on Brand Switching," *Journal of Marketing Research,* Vol. 15, February 1978, pp. 72–81.

[11]For more discussion of applications of attribution theory in marketing and consumer behavior, see Richard W. Mizerski, Linda L. Golden, and Jerome B. Kernan, "The Attribution Process in Consumer Decision Making," *Journal of Consumer Research,* Vol. 6, September 1979, pp. 123–140.

[12]Charles Fredericks, Jr., "What Ogilvy & Mather Has Learned about Sales Promotion," *The Tools of Promotion* (New York: Association of National Advertisers, 1975).

FIGURE 18.1   **Murphy's Law in Sampling**

As with all forms of marketing communications, things sometimes do not work in sampling the way they are designed. Take the previously mentioned case of Sun Light dishwashing liquid, a product of Lever Brothers. This product, which smells like lemons and contains 10 percent lemon juice, was extensively sampled to more than 50 million households. However, for some odd reason in Maryland, nearly 80 adults and children became ill after consuming the product, having mistaken the dishwashing liquid for lemon juice! According to a Lever Brothers' marketing research director, there is always a potential problem of misuse when a product is sent to homes rather than purchased with prior product knowledge at a supermarket.

Source: Lynn G. Reiling, "Consumers Misuse Mass Sampling for Sun Light Dishwashing Liquid," *Marketing News,* September 3, 1982, pp. 1, 2.

Instant Coupons

Most coupon distribution methods have delayed impact on consumers because the coupon is received and held for a period of time prior to its redemption. Instant coupons, however, represent an immediate reward that can spur the consumer to undertake a trial purchase of the promoted brand. Wheaties cereal provides an illustration of instant couponing. General Mills, the makers of Wheaties, wanted a promotional program that would provide a significant price reduction and an immediate point-of-purchase incentive for consumers. Rather than use a price-off deal, which often creates problems for retailers, General Mills offered a 15¢ peel-off coupon attached to the front of the Wheaties package. The coupons were designed to be removed by the consumer and redeemed concurrently with the purchase of Wheaties. The program gained strong retailer acceptance and high coupon redemption levels.[13]

Although the instant coupon is a relatively minor form of coupon, it has emerged in recent years as a popular technique. A major advantage is that it costs less than price-off deals, in which case every package must be reduced in price. Moreover, the redemption level, around 25 percent in 1981, is considerably higher than those for other couponing techniques.[14]

Delayed Reward/Trial Impact Techniques

Media— and mail-delivered coupons and free-in-the-mail premiums are the two major techniques that delay the reward to consumers, yet are quite effective trial-inducing tools.

---

[13]This case is adapted from Richard H. Aycrigg, *Promotion Update '82,* a publication of the Promotion Marketing Association of America, Inc., New York, 1982.

[14]Ed Meyer, "It's on the Package," *Advertising Age,* May 17, 1982, p. M-27.

Media– and Mail-Delivered Coupons

Coupons provide cents-off savings to consumers when the coupon is redeemed. The major delivery modes are direct mail, the mass media, and packages—in or on either a brand's own package or another brand's package. Not all methods have the same impact, however. Although marketers use instant coupons, as discussed previously, to provide immediate rewards to consumers and to encourage trial purchases, mail– and media-delivered coupons delay the reward, although they also generate trial purchase behavior. In comparison, package-delivered coupons are used to accomplish franchise holding rather than product trial. This section will discuss media– and mail-delivered coupons. First, however, it will be helpful to examine the growth and magnitude of offering coupons before discussing any specific delivery mode.

Growth and Trends in Coupons   In 1970 manufacturers distributed fewer than 17 billion coupons in the United States.[15] By 1982, they distributed nearly 120 billion. Figure 18.2 displays graphically the growth in coupon distribution over the period from 1972 to 1982.

The rising trend of coupons offers reflects not only the increase in the absolute number of manufacturers using coupons as an intregral part of their promotional activities but also the growing importance of coupons to these companies.[16] While major users of coupons are package goods manufacturers, coupon use has spread to producers of appliances and other durables, apparel, and numerous other products. Perhaps the most innovative of all applications of coupons was one devised by the airline industry. Following a devastating 55-day strike, United Airlines introduced half-fare coupons. The company reportedly regained its prestrike market share in only 11 days, rather than the seven months that company financial executives had predicted that it would take for recovery.[17]

Concurrent with the rising trend in the use of coupons, significant developments have taken place in the manner in which coupons are distributed. Changes have been instigated primarily by the need to avoid competitive clutter. In order for this promotional tool to be successful, coupons must stand out so that they will be clipped and ultimately redeemed by consumers. Table 18.2 compares total coupon distribution across the major media for the years 1979 and 1981. Two major

---

[15]Roger A. Strang, "The Economic Impact of Cents-off Coupons," *Marketing Communications,* March 1981, pp. 35–44.

[16]"Couponing Distribution Trends and Patterns," specially prepared by the Nielsen Clearing House for *Promotion Update '82,* a publication of the Promotion Marketing Association of America, Inc., New York, 1982.

[17]"The Toothpaste Tube That Saved United," *Advertising Age,* October 29, 1979, p. 14. The interesting title to this article provides a clue as to the reason that United decided upon its couponing campaign. It seems that corporate executives were having difficulty coming up with a major promotional program to regain market share until one employee entered a meeting with a tube of toothpaste, claiming that just that morning he had gone to the store for his wife to get toothpaste and rather than buying her regular brand he switched to another brand that offered a 50¢-off coupon. So, why can't United do the same to get customers to switch back to it?

FIGURE 18.2   Growth in Coupon Distribution by Manufacturers

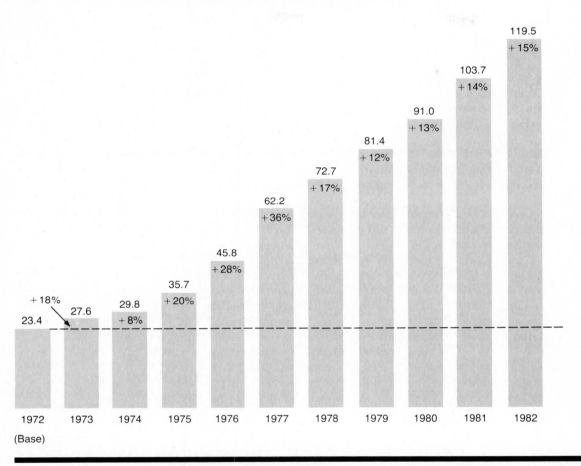

Source: A. C. Nielsen Company. Reprinted in "Best Food Day Build-Up May Spurt New Coupon Usage," *Marketing Communications*, March 1983, p. 47.

developments are apparent. First, the percentage of coupons delivered individually (i.e., solo) in separate run-of-press (ROP) ads[18] fell from 36.2 percent of all coupons distributed in 1979 to 27.3 percent in 1981. During the same time period, the percentage of coupons distributed via freestanding inserts[19] in Sunday papers rose from 14.9 percent in 1979 to 26.2 percent in 1981. The reason for these

[18]A run-of-press (also called run-of-paper) ad is one whose positioning location is at the discretion of the newspaper, with or without regard to the advertiser's position requests.

[19]Freestanding inserts are loose ads that fall in your lap or on the floor when you are trying to enjoy the newspaper.

TABLE 18.2   **Changes in Coupon Distribution by Media: 1979 and 1981**

Medium	1979	1981
Newspapers		
ROP solo	36.2%	27.3%
Co-op	16.1	17.7
Sunday paper	9.5	7.3
Sunday freestanding insert	14.9	26.2
Magazines	12.2	11.8
Direct Mail	3.2	3.3
In/On Pack	7.9	6.4
	100.0%	100.0%

Source: Adapted from A.C. Nielsen Company, "Couponing Distribution Trends and Patterns," *PMAA Promotion Update '82* (New York: Promotion Management Association of America, Inc., 1983).

changes should be obvious; freestanding inserts capture the consumer's attention more readily and therefore are superior to ROP solo ads in overcoming competitive clutter.

Another major trend in coupon distribution has been the establishment of cooperative (co-op) coupon programs. These are syndicated programs that attract participation from manufacturers, who wish to expand their coupon reach and to gain the economies of scale resulting from shared distribution costs.[20] Some illustrative cooperative programs are "Newspaper Co-op Couponing" by the Marketing Corporation of America (a daily newspaper distribution program), "Blair Inserts" by John Blair Marketing (a Sunday insert program), "Thermatics" by Synergistic Marketing (a magazine insert program), "Carol Wright" by Donnelly Marketing (direct mail), and "Intercept" by Stratmar Systems (store handouts).[21]

Economic Impact   The growth in coupon offers has not occurred without criticism. On average, fewer than 5 percent of all distributed coupons are redeemed; therefore, some contend that coupons are wasteful and may actually increase prices of consumer goods. Furthermore, according to one food industry consultant, coupons have become an economically intolerable and unjustifiable cost of doing business.[22] This same consultant contends that the primary value of coupons to manufacturers is in coercing food retailers, rather than persuading consumers, to buy their products. "By flooding the country with their coupons, our suppliers can force us to carry merchandise we don't want," claimed a skeptical Chicago grocer, "but they can't force our customers to buy it and they are not."[23]

Whether or not coupons are wasteful and inefficient remains problematic. The idea that coupons are an expensive proposition, however, is undeniable. The total

[20]"Couponing Distribution Trends and Patterns."

[21]Ibid.

[22]William Nigut, Sr., "Is the Boom in Cents-off Couponing Going to Burst?" *Advertising Age,* December 15, 1980, pp. 41–44.

[23]Ibid., p. 42.

costs for production, distribution, and redemption of coupons in 1978 were estimated to be $855.4 million.[24] To get a better feel for coupon costs, consider the case of a hypothetical cake mix marketer that offers a 25¢-off coupon to consumers. However, the actual cost to the manufacturer is considerably more than 25¢ per coupon. Table 18.3 presents an estimate of the full cost structure for this coupon offer. The actual cost of nearly 52¢ per coupon indicates that coupon activity requires substantial investment to accomplish desired objectives. Obviously, programs that aid in reducing costs, such as cooperative delivery programs, or in enhancing redemption rates, as in the case of freestanding inserts, are eagerly sought. One should expect to see marketers develop various creative and innovative coupon programs in the near future.

The preceding discussion has probably given the reader the impression that the costs of coupons exceed the benefits. This certainly is not the case. Coupons offer several benefits to both manufacturers and consumers:[25]

1. Coupons, because they stimulate trade and consumer action, play a major role in the promotional programs for either a new product or a product line extension.

TABLE 18.3   **Estimated Costs per Redeemed Coupon: Hypothetical Case for One Company[a]**

1. Distribution cost:
   10,000,000 coupons circulated
   @ $5 per thousand $50,000
2. Redemption rate = 4.2%[b]   420,000 redeemed coupons
3. Redemption cost:
   420,000 redemptions
   @ 25¢ face value $105,000
4. Handling cost:
   420,000 redemptions @ 7¢ each[c] $29,400
5. Total program cost: 1 + 3 + 4 $184,400
6. Cost per coupon redeemed:
   $184,000 ÷ 420,000   43.9¢
7. Actual product sold on redemption
   (misredemption estimated at 15%): 420,000 × 85%   357,000
8. Cost per redeemed product:
   program cost ($184,400) ÷ actual number of redeemed
   products (357,000)   51.65¢

---

[a]This illustration is an adaptation of a case presented by Louis J. Haugh, "How Coupons Measure Up," *Advertising Age,* June 8, 1981, p. 58.
[b]4.2% is an average redemption rate estimated by the research department, A.C. Nielsen Clearing House, 1978, as printed in Roger A. Strang, "The Economic Impact of Cents-Off Coupons," *Marketing Communications,* March 1981, p. 35.
[c]A handling charge is the amount paid by manufacturers to retailers to compensate them for their costs incurred to handle coupons. The current charge of 7¢ per coupon will probably go up to 10¢ in the near future.

[24]Strang, "Economic Impact," p. 35.

[25]Ibid., pp. 39, 40, 42, 44.

2. Because coupons facilitate new product introductions through encouraging product trial, they serve to accelerate the manufacturer's return on investment.

3. Coupons strengthen the position of manufacturers relative to that of large, integrated retail chains.

4. Coupons, unlike trade allowances and other forms of trade promotions, ensure that manufacturers' price reductions are, in fact, passed along to consumers.

5. Coupons benefit consumers by lowering prices. It is interesting to note with respect to this point that coupon critics charge that prices would actually be lower in the absence of coupons. However, it could be argued that manufacturers will employ some means, whether it be coupons or something else, to induce product trial. Hence, prices would not necessarily drop were the use of coupons discontinued.

Coupons are indeed costly, some are clearly wasteful, and other promotional devices may be better. However, the extensive use of coupons either suggests that there are a large number of incompetent marketing executives or that better promotional tools are not available or are economically infeasible. The latter explanation is the more reasonable one because of how the marketplace operates: If something does not work, it will not be used; when something better is available, it will replace the previous solution to a marketing problem.

The Role of Media- and Mail-Delivered Coupons   To this point, the discussion has dealt with coupons in general. The focus turns now to media- and mail-delivered coupons, the two delivery modes that initiate trial purchase behavior by offering delayed rewards to consumers. As previously shown in Table 18.2, direct-mail-delivered coupons represented only 3.3 percent of the manufacturer-distributed coupons in 1981. Mass media modes, newspapers and magazines, are clearly dominant, carrying about 90 percent of all coupons distributed in 1981. While there are advantages and disadvantages to employing either mode, each performs a different function.

Mail Coupons   Marketers typically use mail coupons to introduce new or improved products. Mailings can be directed either at a broad cross section of the market or targeted to specific demographic segments. Mailed coupons achieve the highest household penetration. Whereas coupon distribution via magazines rarely reaches more than 60 percent of all homes, mail can reach as high as 95 percent.[26] Moreover, when consumers receive coupon offers in the mail, they are able to make a purchase decision at home, away from the competitive influences of the supermarket. Furthermore, direct mail achieves the highest redemption rate of all

[26]Fredericks, "What Ogilvy & Mather Learned," p. 4.

mass-delivered coupon techniques.[27] A.C. Nielsen estimated the 1980 direct-mail redemption rate to be 11.6 percent. Comparatively, the estimated redemption rates for ROP solo newspaper, Sunday freestanding inserts, and ROP magazine were 3.1, 5.1, and 2.6 percent, respectively.[28]

The major disadvantage of direct-mailed coupons is that they are relatively expensive compared with other methods of distributing coupons. Another disadvantage is that direct mailing is a particularly inefficient and expensive method of distributing coupons for brands that enjoy a high market share. This is because a large proportion of the coupon recipients may already be regular users of the coupon brand, thereby defeating the purpose (namely, to generate trial purchasing) for which the couponing is undertaken in the first place.[29]

A particularly good way for companies to increase the impact of mailed coupons is by tying the coupon in with another product or program. Procter & Gamble did this in a mailing delivered by Publishers Clearing House, which reached about 50 percent of U.S. households. In this particular instance, the coupon offer was tied in with a worthy cause, the Special Olympics athletic program for mentally handicapped children. Households were told that P & G would donate 5¢ to the Special Olympics for every coupon redeemed within a specified period of time. P & G sales personnel and Special Olympics volunteers encouraged the grocery trade to build mass displays of the couponed brands. Awareness of the event was bolstered through concurrent network television advertising support. The program was successful in accomplishing the dual objectives of stimulating retailer support and increasing coupon redemption.[30]

Media-Delivered Coupons   Most coupon distribution is achieved through various newspaper delivery modes (ROP solo, co-op, Sunday paper, and freestanding inserts) and magazines (see Table 18.2). The major advantage of media coupons is their broad exposure; they are limited only by media circulation. Media coupons also can be directed to specific market segments. While magazines and newspapers both permit geographical selectivity, magazines enable demographic and psychographic pinpointing as well. Freestanding inserts have an added advantage in that coupons are delivered to the target population on the same day; this can effectively force the retail trade to maintain sufficient inventories to cover a surge in consumer demand as a result of coupon redemption. Moreover, while freestanding inserts cost only 50 to 60 percent of the cost of direct-mail coupons, their redemption rate is upwards of 80 percent of that of direct mail.[31]

---

[27]*ANA Consumer Promotion Seminar Fact Book,* p. 10.

[28]Louis J. Haugh, "How Coupons Measure Up," *Advertising Age,* June 8, 1981, p. 58.

[29]*ANA Consumer Promotion Seminar Fact Book,* p. 10.

[30]This case is adapted from Joseph S. Maier, *Promotion Update '82,* a publication of the Promotion Marketing Association of America, Inc., New York, 1982.

[31]*ANA Consumer Promotion Seminar Fact Book,* p. 11.

The disadvantages of media-delivered coupons, however, are that they generate relatively low levels of redemption; do not, with the exception of freestanding inserts, generate much trade interest; and suffer from considerable misredemption. The latter problem is so significant to all parties involved in couponing that it deserves a special section.

The best way to understand how misredemption occurs is to examine the redemption process. A customer presents coupons to the checkout clerk along with merchandise, the total bill is added, and the face value of the coupons is subtracted from this total. Certain conditions and restrictions must be met: the consumer must buy the merchandise specified on the coupon in the size, brand, and quantity directed; only one coupon can be redeemed per item; cash may not be given for the coupon; and if there is an expiration date, the coupon must be redeemed before that date.

Retailers must, in turn, redeem the coupons they have received in order to obtain reimbursement from the manufacturers that sponsored the coupons. Retailers typically hire another company, called a *clearinghouse,* to sort and redeem the coupons in return for a fee. Clearinghouses, acting on behalf of a number of retail clients, consolidate coupons by redemption address before forwarding them. Legitimate clearinghouses maintain controls by assuring that their clients are legitimate retailers and are likely to sell the products in the amounts they are submitting for redemption. Clearinghouses forward the coupons to *redemption centers,* which serve as agents of the manufacturer that issued the coupons. The redemption center pays off on all properly redeemed coupons. If a center questions the validity of certain coupons, it may go to its client, a manufacturer, for approval on redeeming suspected coupons.[32]

The system is not quite as clear-cut as it may appear from the foregoing description. Some large retailers act as their own clearinghouses, some manufacturers serve as their own redemption centers, and some independent firms, e.g., the A.C. Nielsen Co., offer both clearinghouse and redemption center services. However, regardless of the specific mechanism by which a coupon is ultimately redeemed (or misredeemed), the retailer is reimbursed for the amount of the face value paid to the consumer and for payment of a handling charge, which currently is 7¢ per coupon. Herein rests the potential for misredemption: A single coupon with, say, a face value of 40¢ pays the unscrupulous person 47¢. One hundred such misredeemed coupons are worth $47!

Now that the reader has a grasp of the redemption mechanism, the discussion of how misredemption occurs and who participates can be continued. As noted previously, misredemption has become a major problem; however, it is very difficult to measure the magnitude of the problem. Even spokesmen for A.C. Nielsen Clearinghouse, the industry's largest, are uncertain of the extent of misredemption. Estimates range from a low of 15 percent to a high of 40 percent. Many product managers are reported to estimate a 20 to 25 percent rate of misredemption when

---

[32]"The Route to Redemption," *Advertising Age,* May 30, 1983, p. 57.

budgeting for coupon events.[33] Misredemption of coupons in the United States in 1982 was estimated at $350 million.[34]

Misredemption occurs at every level of the redemption process. Sometimes consumers at the checkout counter present coupons for items not purchaed, for a smaller-sized product than that specified by the coupon, or for which the expiration date has passed. Some clerks take coupons to the store themselves and exchange them for cash without making a purchase. At the store management level, retailers may boost their profits by submitting extra coupons to those redeemed legitimately. A dishonest retailer can buy coupons on the black market, age them in a clothes drier, mix them with legitimate ones, and then mail in the batch for redemption.

Some professional, large-scale misredeemers operate what are called "green chicken" stores. These "stores" operate exclusively for the purpose of redeeming illegally huge quantities of coupons.[35] These illegal coupons are often the result of someone's gang cutting or tearing mint-condition coupons from numerous copies of the same issue of a newspaper or magazine. Nor are the clearinghouses beyond dishonesty. Shady clearinghouses mix illegally purchased coupons with real ones and certify the batch as legitimate. Other fraudulent practices include the counterfeiting of coupons, the printing of extra quantities from genuine plates, and the salvaging and collecting of coupons by garbage collectors and others for sale on the black market.[36]

The following examples illustrate the scope of the misredemption problem. Jimmy's Coupon Redemption Center was the front for a six-man misredemption ring. Jimmy's acquired bulk coupons from sources such as scrap dealers, newspapers, and charity groups. They designated fictitious stores as payees for redemption of the coupons. The gang managed to acquire $750,000 from nearly 200 national companies before they were caught.[37] Another case involving coupon fraud was discovered by employees of Colgate-Palmolive's coupon redemption center in Kentucky. The redemption center received coupons that had been printed but had never been used in a promotion. The discovery of these stolen coupons led investigators to a large-scale fraud scheme run by four supermarket operators, who during an 11-month period defrauded companies of about $½ million.[38] A Los Angeles accountant recruited newspaper coupon clippers, who worked for California charities, and paid them $5 per pound of coupons. Needless to say, he accu-

[33]Louis J. Haugh, "What Are the Added Costs of Coupon Misredemption?" *Advertising Age,* February 6, 1978, p. 42.

[34]Jennifer Alter and Nancy Giges, "Industry Losing $350 Million on Coupon Misredemption," *Advertising Age,* May 30, 1983, pp. 1, 57.

[35]Vincent Coppola and David Friendly, "Coupon Caper," *Newsweek,* November 27, 1978, pp. 89–90.

[36]Ibid., p. 90.

[37]Louis J. Haugh, "Feds Smash Profitable Coupon Fraud Operation," *Advertising Age,* June 9, 1975, p. 27.

[38]Coppola and Friendly, "Coupon Caper," pp. 89–90.

FIGURE 18.3   **Advertisement and Coupon for Fictitious Essent Shampoo**

Source: *Advertising Age,* May 30, 1983, p. 1.

mulated huge quantities of coupons and was able to redeem millions of dollars of coupons before his scheme was detected.[39]

Due to the pervasiveness of the coupon misredemption problem, and especially because of the part played by organized crime in coupon fraud, postal authorities and local governments have been forced to take action. Two celebrated sting operations have been undertaken in an attempt to identify fraudulent coupon redemption schemes. In both cases, coupons for fictitious products have been advertised heavily in newspapers. The first undercover operation was undertaken by the Brooklyn district attorney's office and involved a fictitious detergent brand, Breen, which was advertised with 25¢-off coupons. Of course, because Breen was a fictitious brand, any redemption of the coupons amounted to misredemption. Twenty-six retailers, who collected more than $122,000 from a variety of coupon refunds, including over $100,000 paid out by A.C. Nielsen, were indicted on various charges of larceny and fraud.[40]

The most recent sting operation was implememted in both New York and Chicago by a private industrial-security association. The bait this time was a 50¢-off coupon for fictitious Essent shampoo. An ad for Essent (Figure 18.3) was run for the first time on May 15, 1983, in inserts in the *Chicago Tribune* and the *New York Daily News;* it was run again later that week in those same newspapers as a large ROP display in best food day sections.[41] The results of the operation are not known at the time of this writing. It is worth noting, however, that this type of sting operation has been criticized as unfair to the consumers who attempt to redeem a coupon for an unavailable brand and as undermining the credibility of legitimate coupon programs. The fact remains, however, that misredemption is a serious problem that requires the concerted efforts of all participants to the redemption process in order to maintain coupons as an effective promotional device.

The Advent of In-Store Coupons

Media— and mail-delivered coupons are widely accepted by promotion managers. However, as discussed previously, these delivery modes suffer from such problems as low redemption levels, clutter, and misredemption. In response to these problems, several companies are introducing in-store coupon-distribution schemes.[42] For example, a Massachusetts-based company plans to place its in-store coupon vending machines nationwide by the end of 1987. This company's machine ("the Coupon Counter") dispenses a strip of coupons to consumers who insert a special

---

[39]Ibid.

[40]"Coupon Fraud Indictments Termed 'Only Tip of Iceberg,'" *Advertising Age,* December 18, 1978, pp. 1, 77.

[41]Nancy Giges, "New Coupon Trap Set," *Advertising Age,* May 30, 1983, pp. 1, 57.

[42]The following discussion is adapted from "In-store Pioneers Clip Coupon Competition," *Advertising Age,* January 24, 1985.

access card. Another company, Actmedia, distributes coupons in person rather by machine. Yet another company, Retail Insight, has devised a machine that employs laser-disc technology. The machine displays up to 32 different products, and the consumer simply presses buttons next to products for which he or she wishes to receive coupons.

It is problematic at this time whether these new coupon-distribution schemes will eventually achieve wide acceptance by marketers, consumers, and retail outlets. On the negative side, marketers must pay more for this form of coupon redemption in comparison to conventional distribution modes. On the other hand, in-store distribution offers the advantages of increasing redemption rates while cutting down on the clutter and misredemption problems.

Free-in-the-Mail Premiums

Premiums, broadly defined, are either articles of merchandise or services (e.g., travel) offered by manufacturers to induce action on the part of the sales force, trade representatives, or consumers. The present concern is with consumer motivation, as the other objectives were touched upon in Chapter 17. Many types of premium offers are used. These include in–, on–, or near-pack premiums, reusable containers, self-liquidating premiums, and free mail-ins.

The free mail-in premium is one we all remember as kids—"With 10 box tops, we'll send you . . . ." By definition, a free-in-the-mail premium is a promotion where consumers receive premium items from the sponsoring manufacturer in return for submitting the required number of proofs of purchase. Such premiums have potential for stimulating high levels of consumer trial, especially for products aimed at children.[43]

Although free mail-ins may be viewed as trial-impacting promotional devices (see Table 18.1), this type of premium offer can accomplish other objectives as well. In fact, when directed at adult audiences, these premiums can accomplish franchise-holding objectives by rewarding consumers' brand loyalties and encouraging repeat purchase behavior.

Relatively few consumers who are exposed to free mail-in offers actually avail themselves of the opportunity. The national average redemption rate is estimated to be between 2 and 4 percent.[44] However, these premiums can be extremely effective if the premium item is appealing to the target market. Some successful applications of free-in-the-mail premiums include the following: Kraft's Velveeta cheese offered a recipe booklet upon receipt of two front panels from any Velveeta product. S.C. Johnson & Son's offered a household repair book in return for the purchase of Shout brand laundry soil and stain remover. Kool-Aid offered children

---

[43]Ed Meyer, "Do Your Sales Promotions Lack Impact," *Advertising Age,* October 27, 1980, p. 74.

[44]William R. Dean, "Irresistible But Not Free of Problems," *Advertising Age,* October 6, 1980, p. S-1–S-12.

a free Kool-Aid man video game worth $20 in return for 60 Kool-Aid proofs of purchase.

Immediate Reward/Franchise-Holding Techniques

Often, the objective of sales promotion is, not to induce trial purchasing, but rather to reward and reinforce the behavior of present customers and to generate repeat purchasing of the marketer's brand. These are known collectively as *franchise-holding* objectives. Sales promotional techniques that are primarily a means of holding franchises are the subject of this and the following section. Price-offs; in–, on–, and near-pack premiums; and bonus packs attempt to secure brand franchises by offering consumers immediate, point-of-purchase rewards. In– and on-pack coupons and refunds/rebates attempt to accomplish this same objective, but the reward to the consumer is delayed.

Price-offs

Price-off promotions entail a reduction in a brand's regular price. Typical price-offs range between 10 to 25 percent. This type of promotion is effective when the marketer's objective is any of the following: (1) to reward present brand users; (2) to get consumers to purchase larger quantities of a brand than they normally would (i.e., to "load" them), thereby effectively preempting the competition; (3) to establish a repeat purchase pattern after an initial trial; (4) to ensure that promotional dollars do, in fact, reach consumers (no such assurance is possible with trade allowances); (5) to obtain off-shelf display space provided that display allowances are offered to retailers; and (6) to provide the sales force with an incentive to obtain retailer support.[45]

Price-offs cannot reverse a downward sales trend, produce a significant number of new users, or attract as many trial users as sampling, coupons, or premium packs. Furthermore, retailers often dislike price-offs because they create inventory and pricing problems, particularly when a store has a brand in inventory at both the price-off and regular prices. Despite trade problems, price-offs have strong consumer appeal.

FTC Price-off Regulations   Manufacturers cannot indiscriminately promote their products with continuous or near-continuous price-off labeling. The Federal Trade Commission controls price-off labeling with the following regulations: (1) price-off labels may only be used on brands already in distribution with established retail prices; (2) there is a limit of three price-off label promotions per year per brand size; (3) there must be a hiatus period of at least 30 days between price-off label promotions on any given brand size; (4) no more than 50 percent of a

---

[45]See Fredericks, "What Ogilvy & Mather Learned," p. 11; and William A. Robinson, "What Are Promos' Weak and Strong Points?" *Advertising Age,* April 7, 1980, p. 54.

brand's volume over a 12-month period may be generated from price-off label promotions; (5) the manufacturer must provide display materials to announce the price-off label offer; and (6) the dealer is required to show the regular shelf price in addition to the new price reflecting the price-off label savings.[46] The purpose of these regulations is to protect consumers and competitors from unscrupulous manufacturers who may attempt, with price-off labeling, to mislead consumers into thinking falsely that they will receive a true savings by purchasing the promoted brand.

Bonus Packs

Bonus packs are extra numbers or quantities of a product a company gives consumers at the regular price (e.g., a sleeve of four Tourney golf balls for the price of three; 20 percent more Planter's peanuts at the regular price). Bonus packs are sometimes used as an alternative to price-off deals when the latter are either overused or resisted by the trade. The extra value offered to the consumer is readily apparent and for that reason can be effective in loading current users and thereby removing them from the market as a defensive tactic against aggressive competitors. Perhaps the biggest drawback of bonus packs is that a large proportion of the bonus-packed merchandise will be purchased by regular customers who would have purchased the brand anyway.

In–, On–, and Near-Pack Premiums

In– and on-pack premiums offer a premium item inside or attached to a package. Reusable containers also fall into this category. Near-pack premiums, by comparison, provide the retail trade with specially displayed premium pieces, which retailers then give to consumers when they purchase the promoted product. These types of premium offers provide consumers with an immediate value, the intent of which is to encourage increased product consumption. Retailers find these techniques to be reasonably attractive, and they are difficult for competitors to duplicate quickly. Near-pack premiums have the added advantage of being less expensive than on-pack premiums because additional packaging is not required. Furthermore, near-pack premiums can also effectively build sales volume in stores that put up displays and participate fully.

Disadvantages of these techniques are a long lead time of 12 to 18 months is often required to develop and implement these types of promotions, extra manufacturing and packaging effort is required in the case of in– and on-pack premiums, and both on– and near-pack premiums are susceptible to mutilation and pilferage.[47] Another major problem with in– and on-pack premiums is that a poor premium can actually reduce sales by preventing regular purchasers from buying.[48]

---

[46]*ANA Consumer Promotion Seminar Fact Book,* p. 7.

[47]"Premiums and Incentives in the Strategic Plan," *Marketing Communications,* June 1983, pp. 8, 9.

[48]Fredericks, "What Ogilvy & Mather Learned," p. 13.

Delayed Reward/Franchise-Holding Techniques

In– or on-package coupons and refunds/rebates are two techniques that stimulate repeat purchasing and build franchises in other ways.

In– and On-Pack Coupons

In– or on-pack coupons are distributed by inclusion either inside the package or attached to the outside of the package. Frequently, a coupon for one brand is promoted by another brand. For example, General Mills promoted granola bars by offering cents-off coupons in its cereal products. This practice is known in the trade as *crossruffing,* a term borrowed from bridge and bridge-type card games where partners alternate trumping one another when they are unable to follow suit.

Though marketers use crossruffing to create trial purchases or to stimulate purchase of products that are not staple items, such as granola bars, in– and on-pack coupons carried by the same brand are generally intended to stimulate repeat purchasing. That is, once consumers have exhausted the contents of a particular package, they are more likely to repurchase that brand of product if an attractive inducement, such as a cents-off coupon, is available immediately. The coupon has, in other words, *bounce back* value. Bounce back is another trade term that implies that an initial purchase, the "bounce," may stimulate another purchase, the "bounce back," when a hard-to-avoid inducement such as an in-package coupon is made available.

A major advantage of in– and on-pack coupons is that there are virtually no distribution costs. Moreover, redemption rates are much higher (typically 30 to 60 percent higher than media-delivered coupons) because most of the package-delivered coupons are received by brand users.[49] The major limitations of these coupons are that they offer delayed value to consumers, they do not reach non-users of the carrying brand, and trade interest is relatively low due to the delayed nature of the offer.

Refunds and Rebates

Refunds, which are used to promote package goods, and rebates, which are used for durable goods, offer consumers delayed value. Consumers are, nevertheless, generally very responsive to attractive offers. All kinds of companies promote their products in this manner. Automotive companies offered attractive rebates in the early 1980s; appliance manufacturers and sporting goods companies often promote their products with rebates; and, of course, numerous makers of packaged goods use refund offers to appeal to the savings-conscious consumer.[50] The tremendous

---

[49]*ANA Consumer Promotion Seminar Fact Book,* p. 14.

[50]Louis J. Haugh, "What Is the Hot Promotion of the '80's? Cash Refunds!" *Advertising Age,* October 6, 1980, p. 68.

FIGURE 18.4   **Illustrative Cash-or-Coupon Refund Promotion**

Source: Courtesy of Coca-Cola Foods, a division of The Coca-Cola Company.

growth in manufacturers' use of refunding has led to the formation of hundreds of consumer refund clubs nationwide and to the evolution of "round robin" chain letters—one member starts the letter, including refund certificates, and each member receiving the letter removes the refunds he or she needs and replaces them with new refund offers.[51]

Two types of refunding that marketers use are cash refunds and free coupons. Both are used frequently, primarily to stimulate repeat purchasing or to encourage users of other brands to switch. The makers of Pampers disposable diapers use both types of refunds. Their refund offers consumers the choice of a $1.00 cash refund or $2.00 in Pampers coupons. To receive a refund, the consumer must mail in a completed certificate and proof of purchase. The refund offer is doubled, $2

---

[51]Ed Meyer, "Refunds: The Offers Few Can Refuse," *Advertising Age,* October 6, 1980, p. 68.

cash or $4 in coupons, if the consumer also includes a tear-off "refund doubler" certificate obtained from a Pampers display at a grocery store. When manufacturers promote products in this manner, the trade is more likely to provide display support. Thus, the product is highly visible, which increases the likelihood that consumers will come into contact with the brand being promoted.

Another creative refund offer, tied in to the 1984 Olympics, was from Minute Maid's Real Lemonade (Figure 18.4). Consumers received either a $1.25 cash refund or $2.00 in coupons. The refund alternative had the added feature of allowing consumers to designate that Minute Maid donate 25¢ to the U.S. Olympic team. Thus, consumers were doubly rewarded by receiving monetary savings and gaining a sense of patriotism as well.

Overall, refunds represent a useful technique; they reinforce brand loyalty, provide the sales force with something to talk about, and enable the manufacturer to flag the package with a potentially attractive deal. However, because of the delayed reward, interest is limited among many consumers and much of the retail trade.

Image Reinforcement Techniques

The primary role of sales promotion is *not* to create or reinforce a product's image; this is the job for which advertising is particularly well suited. However, self-liquidating premiums and contests/sweepstakes are two techniques that, in addition to accomplishing other objectives, reinforce a brand's image.[52] Returning once again to the typology of sales promotion techniques (Table 18.1), it may be noted that both of these techniques provide consumers with delayed rewards and that no sales promotion method influences a brand's image and simultaneously rewards consumers (i.e., cell 5 in Table 18.1 is empty).

Self-Liquidating Premiums

The self-liquidating premium gets its name from the fact that the consumer mails in a stipulated number of proofs of purchase along with sufficient money to cover the manufacturer's purchasing, handling, and mailing costs of the premium item. The premium object is generally a product other than the brand that promotes the deal. However, the premium may be related to the sponsoring brand (e.g., a cooking utensil as a premium for a processed food product), but it need not be.

For example, Castle & Cooke Foods increased display support among the trade and boosted retail sales of Dole bananas with a self-liquidating offer of a yellow jacket, priced at $7.95, that folded into a pouch resembling a banana that bore the Dole logo. Scott paper promoted its Waldorf and Family Scott tissue brands to the trade with 14,000 displays and to consumers with a self-liquidating Kodak Camera that could be acquired by the consumer for $9.95 and three proofs of purchase.[53]

[52]Meyer, "Do Your Sales Promos Lack Impact," p. 74.

[53]Paul Howard, "Dangling the Right Carrot," *Marketing Communications,* January 1983, pp. 16–20.

In additon to their ability to reinforce and strengthen a brand's image by improving the brand's price/value relationship and by associating it with an attractive premium object, self-liquidating premium offers are also very effective in obtaining store displays and encouraging trade support for the brand. An additional positive feature is that this type of promotion does not require extensive packaging changes and, therefore, can be executed relatively simply at the factory level.[54]

The limitations of self-liquidators are that they do not generate trial usage, and fewer than 10 percent of all households have ever sent for a premium.[55] Low redemption is another limitation. Companies generally expect only 0.1 percent of self-liquidators to be redeemed. A circulation of 20,000,000, for example, would be expected to bring about 20,000 redemptions.[56]

Industry specialists generally agree that the most important consideration in developing a self-liquidator program is that the premium be appealing to the target audience and represent a value. Most sources agree that consumers look for a savings of at least 50 percent of the suggested retail price.[57]

Contests and Sweepstakes

Both contests and sweepstakes offer consumers the opportunity to win cash, merchandise, or travel prizes. In a sweepstakes, winners are determined purely on the basis of chance. Accordingly, proofs of purchase cannot be required as a condition for entry. In a contest, however, the consumer must solve the specified contest problem (e.g., a puzzle) and may be required to submit proofs of purchase. Sweepstakes, because they require less effort from consumers and generate greater response, are much preferred to contests.

Recently, sweepstakes have experienced a tremendous increase in popularity; the apparent reason is that they are, when compared with many other sales promotion techniques, relatively inexpensive and simple to execute and are able to accomplish a variety of marketing objectives.[58]

In addition to reinforcing a brand's image and attracting attention to advertisements, well-designed sweepstakes can accomplish several additional objectives: sweepstakes promote distribution and retailer stocking, increase the interest of the sales force, provide extra incentives in combination with other promotions, and reach specific groups, such as ethnic markets, through a prize structure that is particularly appealing to those groups.[59]

---

[54]"Premiums and Incentives in the Strategic Plan," p. 8.

[55]Robinson, "What Are Promos' Points?" p. 54.

[56]Francine Schore, "Inflation Hurts Cheaper Items," *Advertising Age,* October 6, 1980, pp. S-19, 20.

[57]Ibid.

[58]Thomas J. Conlon, "Sweepstakes Rank As Tops," *Advertising Age,* October 6, 1980, pp. S-6, 7; Don Jagoda, "It's Not What You Give But What You Get," *Marketing Communications,* April 1984, pp. 27–31.

[59]Stanley N. Arnold, "Consumer Sweepstakes and Contests," *The Tools of Promotion* (New York: Association of National Advertisers, 1975), pp. 4, 5.

The majority of sweepstakes promotions offer a prize or group of prizes to entrants, who mail an entry blank along with a proof of purchase (or a facsimile, since purchase cannot legally be required) to the manufacturer's judging agency. Award winners are drawn randomly. Print advertising and point-of-purchase displays usually support the sweepstakes promotion.

A promotion by Green Giant brand vegetables provides an example of the manner in which sweepstakes operate. Green Giant's objectives were several: to expand retail displays for its vegetables, to enhance sales force enthusiasm, and to increase sales. They promoted their sweepstakes in full-page ads in the comics section of Sunday newspapers. Prizes included 10-speed Schwinn bicycles, stereos, and radios. The promotion resulted in an increase in retail displays, case shipments, and even market share.

The effectiveness and appeal of sweepstakes or contests, by themselves, is generally limited; however, when tied in with advertising and other promotional tools such as coupons, these devices can work effectively to produce significant results.

Overlays and Group Promotions

Discussion to this point has concentrated on individual sales promotion techniques. As a result, it may seem as if a single brand may be promoted by only one technique. In practice, sales promotion techniques are often used jointly to accomplish a number of objectives that any one promotional tool could not accomplish alone; furthermore, these techniques, individually or in conjunction with one another, are frequently used to promote simultaneously two or more brands either from the same company or from different firms. Joint sales promotion efforts are known as *overlays,* or *combination,* programs; simultaneous promotion of multiple brands is called a *group,* or a *tie-in,* promotion.

A campaign by Welch's Jam & Jelly illustrates the use of overlay and group promotions in conjunction with one another. Welch's primary objectives were to load existing customers and to induce users of competitive brands to make a trial purchase. Their strategy consisted of overlaying coupons with a self-liquidating premium. At the same time, the promotion was tied in with two natural partners, the Quality Bakers of America and the American Dairy Association.

Welch's selected a family-oriented vehicle, a Sunday comics co-op with a circulation of 37 million, as a means of delivering the coupon and announcing a free milk offer. Consumers received a free half-gallon of milk for submitting the net weight statements from any three jars of Welch's grape jelly or strawberry jam *and* from any Quality Bakers of America brand bread. In addition, display materials in stores offered consumers a soccer ball with $27 retail value in return for only $11.95 and the UPC Codes from any two jars of Welch's jams or jelly. Moreover, a trade-oriented contest was run in an effort to stimulate retailer support. Prizes included a Nassau vacation for two people and 500 soccer balls for store managers to give to their children.

As a result of this creative and well-coordinated program, initial sales exceeded levels forecasted to the trade by 30 percent, the increase in in-store display activity

FIGURE 18.5   Illustration of the Joint Use of Overlay and Group Promotions

was double that originally estimated, and Welch brands experienced a 3.9 percent increase in market share over the eight weeks following the promotion.[60]

Another illustration of a combined overlay program and group promotion is provided by Kellogg's. This program (see Figure 18.5) featured Rice Krispies and three lesser known "Talking Krispies" brands. A 15¢ off coupon for Rice Krispies and 30¢ off coupon for any of the other three brands was accomplished by an attractive sweepstakes offer; 5,551 Texas Instruments prizes were to be given away.

Purpose of Overlay Programs

Media clutter is an ever-growing problem facing marketers. When used individually, sales promotion tools, particularly coupons, may never be noticed by consumers. A combination of tools, such as Kellogg's overlay of a coupon offer and a sweepstakes, increases the likelihood that consumers will read an advertisement that contains the sales promotion offer. The joint use of several techniques in a well-coordinated promotional program equips the sales force with a strong sales tool. Overlays are more attractive to the trade and, as a result, can induce higher levels of purchasing and increased display activity. In short, overlay programs are synergistic.

Successful Group Promotions

A growing number of companies are using tie-ins (group promotions) to generate increased sales, to stimulate trade and consumer interest, and to gain optimal use of their promotional budgets.[61] By encouraging consumers to purchase each of several participating brands, a group promotion can lead to greater total sales volume, since consumers who ordinarily would have purchased only one brand, such as Rice Krispies in the Kellogg's example, purchase others as well. In addition, cost of a group promotion is less than it would have been had each brand been promoted separately. For example, an individual brand's expenditure on a coupon offer and ad space in a freestanding insert with distribution of 20 million could be $60,000. Were five brands to participate in the same group promotion, each might invest only $40,000.[62]

---

[60]This case is adapted from Joseph S. Maier, *Promotion Update '82,* a publication of the Promotion Marketing Association of America, Inc., New York, 1982.

[61]For an additional illustration, see Ed Brutman, "Tying the Knot with the Tie-in," *Advertising Age,* May 4, 1981, pp. S-1, 19.

[62]Louis J. Haugh, "How Group Promos Work," *Advertising Age,* April 27, 1981, p. 56.

An in-house study conducted by a large packaged goods company discovered a number of important conclusions and implications regarding the use of group promotions:[63]

1.   Group events, when compared with single brand promotions, tend to build share for all participating brands, large and small.
2.   Group promotions contribute to the accomplishment of marketing objectives primarily because they are more successful in obtaining trade support in terms of advertising features and display space.
3.   The sales force consistently supports group promotions.
4.   There is little evidence to suggest that interbrand cannibalization results from joint promotions.
5.   Requirements for successful group promotions are (a) the group of participating brands must complement each other; (b) every group event should have one major brand that serves as a principal focus for trade merchandising and upon which less well known brands can ride (Rice Krispies served this role in Kellogg's group promotion, Figure 18.5); (c) the overlay event must be simple in concept so that it will be readily understood by the sales force and the trade (the Welch and Kellogg promotions both satisfy this requirement); (d) all the brands involved should be targeted toward similar consumer groups.

As a closing comment, a notable trend in group promotions is the use of worthy causes as tie-ins. Procter & Gamble donated 5¢ with every redeemed coupon to the Special Olympics for mentally handicapped children; Bristol-Myers made use of a similar tie-in with the United Cerebral Palsy Association, Inc.;[64] Minute Maid donated 25¢ to the U.S. Olympic team as part of a refund offer. These tie-ins have dual attraction by appealing simultaneously to consumers' need for monetary savings and altruistic spirit. Brotherhood and merchandise can be sold together!

An Unsuccessful Group Promotion

As with all aspects of promotion management, a group promotion can go awry if it is not fully thought out prior to its implementation. A classic illustration is the 1984 tie-in promotion between Trans World Airlines Inc. and Polaroid Corp.[65] These two companies entered into an arrangement whereby purchasers of Polaroid cameras would receive a coupon worth 25 percent off the price of a TWA ticket. The tie-in was intended to move Polaroid's camera and film during the 1984 Christmas season and to sell TWA airline tickets during the slow, postholiday period. Anyone buying specified cameras or film during the period between October

---

[63]Ibid.

[64]Maier, *Promotion Update '82.*

[65]The following discussion is a summary of points from "How Polaroid and TWA Created a Monster," *Business Week,* January 21, 1985, p. 39.

1, 1984, and January 31, 1985, was eligible to receive the TWA discount. The discounts applied to all coach fares, including international flights, except those to London.

This tie-in promotion held promise of being an excellent promotion for both companies; unfortunately, from TWA's perspective, there was one major oversight—TWA neglected to put a "one per customer" limit on the offer. Consequently, commercial customers (corporate travel departments and travel agencies) purchased Polaroid cameras by the hundreds in order to take advantage of the attractive coupon offer. For example, a St. Louis travel agency bought 10,000 cameras so that it could offer attractive flight discounts to its commercial customers. Even Polaroid's own travel department purchased 2,000 of the company's own cameras in order to obtain discounted TWA tickets.

Although Polaroid has benefitted greatly from this poorly executed promotion, it is doubtful that TWA has realized equivalent benefits. In fact, TWA executives expect that more than 150,000 coupons will ultimately be redeemed, each at a 25 percent discount from the airline's normal rates. Beyond the sheer number of discounted flights, an additional fact is that the promotion was intended to increase domestic flight activity when, in actuality, customers took primary advantage of international flight discounts. The moral is clear: Be extremely careful in designing sales promotions so that there are no loopholes for customers to exploit.

Testing and Evaluating Sales Promotions

Chapter 15 reviewed a variety of techniques useful in evaluating advertising effectiveness. The same justification for advertising research applies equally well to sales promotion. Historically, however, sales promotion research has been relatively neglected; there are signs that this is changing. One important indication of such change is the evolution of research specialists who are filling the sales promotion research void.[66]

Two basic types of sales promotion research are *planning research*, which develops sound promotional strategies, and *evaluation research*, which monitors the performance of promotions during and after execution.[67]

The Sales Promotion Research Process

A formal process for evaluating sales promotion is an invaluable aid in developing sales promotion programs. Schultz and Robinson proposed the following three-step process:[68] (1) clearly specify the sales promotion objectives, (2) gain agreement

---

[66]Louis J. Haugh, "Service Companies Filling Void in Promotion Research Frontier," *Advertising Age,* April 21, 1980, p. 56.

[67]Ibid.

[68]Don E. Schultz and William A. Robinson, "Rating Sales Promos Easy as One, Two, Three," *Advertising Age,* November 17, 1980, pp. 64, 66.

among all involved parties with the objectives established in the first step, and (3) use the following five-point evaluation system to rate any sales promotion program or idea:

1. How good is the general idea? If the objective is to increase product trial, a sample would be rated favorably and so would a coupon, but a sweepstake would flunk this initial evaluation.
2. Will the sales promotion idea appeal to the target market? A contest might, for example, be great with children, but for certain adult groups it would have disastrous results.
3. Is the idea unique or is the competition doing something similar?
4. Is the promotion presented clearly so that the intended market will notice, comprehend, and respond to the deal?
5. How cost-effective is the proposed idea? This requires an evaluation of whether or not the proposed promotion will achieve the intended objectives at an affordable cost.

Specific Research Methods

Marketers use various research methods to plan a proposed sales promotion program. Some of the better known methods are ballot tests, show tests, and market tests.[69]

The sole purpose of *ballot tests* is to measure the relative drawing power of mail-in premium items. Item descriptions are mailed to a sample of known premium redeemers, offering the item at a self-liquidating price or for free. The inclusion of a benchmark premium item in the test (i.e., one which has been used previously in an actual promotion and for which redemption results are known) makes it possible to calculate an index of how well a potential premium item draws compared with the known drawing power of the benchmark premium. Ballot testing is reasonably reliable and inexpensive; however, it is an incomplete test of a promotional program because sales force and trade reactions are not assessed.

Show testing is another method of assessing the drawing power of premium items. Consumers are screened on the basis of demographic characteristics and are shown premium items or facsimiles, which they rate in terms of preference. A benchmark premium, such as that described for ballot testing, is usually included in the test for comparison. Show testing is quick and inexpensive, but it is, at best, a rough indicator of how consumers will respond under natural, in-home conditions.

More realistic testing is accomplished with *market tests*. This type of testing is comparable in purpose and procedure to new product testing. Testing in isolated

[69]*ANA Consumer Promotion Seminar,* pp. 61–77; Carole E. Boudreau, "Testing Plays Vital Role in Premiums Promotion," *Advertising Age,* October 1, 1979, p. S-6; and Haugh, "Service Companies Filling Void."

markets under real world conditions (i.e., with advertising support, in-store competition, etc.) provides a more accurate assessment of how successful a sales promotion technique will be. Market tests, however, require the greatest amount of time and expense.

In addition to these methods of research, which are useful in the planning stage, there are various data sources that can be used to evaluate the success of a promotional program. First, companies can study their own internal data on product shipments. Additionally, they can use syndicated research (e.g., Nielsen store audits) to assess product movement, inventory levels, and other in-store data relevant to sales promotion performance. They can also conduct special trade studies or consumer research to assess specific aspects of a sales promotion program.

Summary

This chapter has attempted to demonstrate that sales promotion techniques are invaluable in terms of a company's marketing communication activities. A number of points have been made, some of which are worth repeating, and some new points are worth mentioning.

The first and most critical requirement for a successful sales promotion is that it be based on clearly defined objectives.

Second, the program must be designed with a specific target market in mind. It should also be realized that many consumers, perhaps most, desire to maximize the rewards gained from participating in a sales promotion while minimizing the amount of time and effort invested. Consequently, effective sales promotion, from a consumer-response perspective, must make it relatively easy for consumers to obtain their reward, and the size of the reward must be sufficient to justify the consumer's efforts.

A third essential ingredient for effective sales promotions is that programs must be developed with the best interests of retailers, and not just consumers, in mind. Manufacturers must understand and appreciate retailers' basic needs (increasing profit per square foot of space, providing consumers fair value, building store traffic, etc.) and respond to these needs by treating the retailer as an equal business partner. Effective promotions, from the retailers' perspective, are ones that are promoted aggressively by the manufacturer in an effort to build store traffic. In addition, retailers prefer promotions that do not require that they expand inventory unnecessarily and which, ideally, promote a line of related brands or products, thereby simplifying their advertising and display activities.

Discussion Questions

1. Describe the specific objectives of sales promotion and compare these with the role of advertising.
2. Compare and contrast sampling and media-delivered coupons in terms of objectives, consumer impact, and overall roles in marketing communication strategies.

3. Six major sampling trends were described in this chapter. Explain whether or not you expect each of these trends to continue.

4. A packaged goods company plans to introduce a new bathroom soap that differs from competitive items by virtue of a distinct new fragrance. Should sampling be used to introduce the product?

5. Compare instant coupons, freestanding inserts, and in-package coupons in terms of purpose and consumer and trade impact.

6. Explain the rationale for cooperative couponing programs and obtain an illustration of a co-op program from your daily or Sunday newspaper or from a magazine.

7. Compare free mail-in premiums with self-liquidators in terms of purpose and impact.

8. Discuss coupon misredemption in terms of what parties are involved and of how and why it occurs.

9. What is the purpose of the FTC price-off regulations?

10. Compare bonus packs and price-off deals in terms of impact on consumers.

11. What is crossruffing in sales promotion, and why is it used?

12. There are literally hundreds of refund clubs in the United States. Is this desirable from the perspective of manufacturers who offer refunds?

13. How can sales promotion reinforce a brand's image? Is this a major objective of sales promotion?

14. Compare contests and sweepstakes in terms of how they function and in terms of relative effectiveness.

15. What are the purposes, advantages, and potential problems of overlays and tie-in programs?

Exercises

1. Conduct interviews with two store managers to get their views on the causes and magnitude of coupon misredemption in their stores. Determine what actions their stores take to minimize misredemption.

2. Go through old copies of major magazines and clip examples of at least ten different sales promotions. For each example, analyze what you think the objectives and target markets are.

3. Go to a major supermarket and obtain at least two or three specific examples of each of these forms of sales promotions: bonus packs; price-offs; in–, on–, or near-pack premiums; on-package coupons; and saleable samples.

4. Conduct interviews with three or four nonstudent adults and investigate whether or not they have participated in any sweepstakes, contests, refund offers, or mail-in premium deals within the past year or so. Also, evaluate their personal attitudes towards each of these sales promotion methods.

5. Find at least two examples of group (tie-in) promotions and, for each, evaluate why you think the different brands are involved in a joint promotion.

CHAPTER 19

Public Relations, Publicity, and Specialty Advertising

The conventional tools of promotion management (advertising, sales, and sales promotion) are capable of accomplishing a variety of marketing communication objectives: creating awareness, influencing attitudes, generating trial purchasing, servicing customers, and so on. The same tools are not, however, entirely suitable for accomplishing an additional critical objective, that being the maintenance of *goodwill* between an organization and the various publics with which it interacts.

Public relations, publicity, and, to a lesser degree, specialty advertising, are the promotion management elements that build and foster goodwill between a company and its customers, employees, stockholders, and other publics. This is not to say that these auxiliary promotion tools are restricted to creating goodwill. On the contrary, public relations, publicity, and specialty advertising also serve to supplement media advertising, sales, and sales promotion in creating product awareness, building favorable attitudes toward a company and its products, and encouraging purchase behavior. The ensuing discussion examines these objectives as well as the more traditional task of creating goodwill.

Public Relations and Publicity

Initially, it is important to clarify the distinction between **public relations** and **publicity.** These terms often are inappropriately used interchangeably. As has been noted elsewhere, public relations is to publicity what marketing is to sales-

FIGURE 19.1   **The Various Publics with Which Public Relations Interacts**

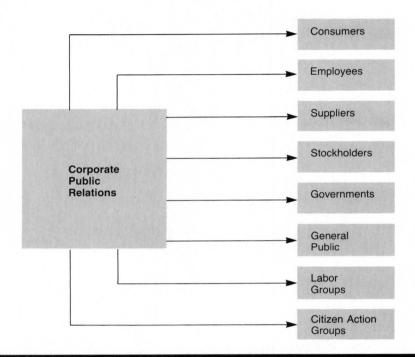

manship.[1] Public relations is, in other words, a more general practice that emcompasses publicity. Public relations, or PR as it is typically truncated, includes all nonadvertising and nonselling activities that are designed explicitly to engender a desired corporate image. This corporate-image engineering is directed at promoting harmonious relations with various publics: consumers, employees, suppliers, stockholders, governments, the general public, labor groups, and citizen action groups (see Figure 19.1).

Managing Public Relations

Specific public relations duties and activities vary greatly across organizations, but there are four basic management systems for handling the public relations func-

[1]Edmond W. J. Faison, *Advertising: A Behavioral Approach for Managers* (New York: John Wiley & Sons, 1980).

tion: (1) internally, undelegated; (2) internally, delegated; (3) externally, delegated; and (4) internal and external combined.[2]

Internally, Undelegated   Some organizations handle public relations in an informal fashion without utilizing personnel trained specifically in public relations. A chief executive or top policy official performs public relations duties when the situation calls for it.

Internally, Delegated   Most major organizations that deal regularly with many publics have PR departments or staffs that perform the public relations function. The staff may consist of many people or only one person, but the common feature is that the public relations function is conducted professionally rather than in an ad hoc fashion.[3]

Externally, Delegated   Large organizations often go outside their own firms to contract with a public relations counseling firm or a public relations department of an advertising agency. Rationale for using professional firms is that these external professionals deal with numerous clients and have greater expertise than can be acquired internally.

Internal and External Combined   Many large organizations have their own internal public relations departments but also retain external public relations counseling firms. These counseling firms are often able to provide services that the internal department is unable to perform.

Public Relations Activities and Functions

The PR function, whether performed internally or externally, entails a variety of specific duties. The following represent the functions and activities considered most important:[4]

1. *Advice and counsel.* Public relations input is required in any decision that has significant implications for any of an organization's publics. For example, a decision to construct a new manufacturing facility in a geographic area where wildlife may be disturbed would require public relations advice and counsel to know how best to deal with environmentalists and other concerned citizen groups.
2. *Publications.* Public relations departments routinely prepare publications for important publics. Newsletters are distributed to employees, information is

---

[2]Raymond Simon, *Public Relations: Concepts and Practices* (Columbus, OH: Grid Publishing, 1980), p. 75.

[3]Ibid., p. 76.

[4]Ibid., pp. 86, 87.

disseminated to stockholders, and letters are directed to governmental agencies.

3. *Publicity.* The PR department serves as the prime source of an organization's contact with the news media. Publicity involves the planning of press conferences and the preparation of press releases in conjunction with any newsmaking events affecting the organization. Publicity is especially important for new product introductions or during periods of corporate crisis. More will be said about this in a later section.

4. *Relations with publics.* It is the job of public relations personnel to deal with the company's various publics in matters involving any company decisions, policies, or impending actions that have ramifications for these publics.

5. *Institutional advertising.* Corporate image advertising, as discussed in Chapter 13, is often the work of the public relations department in coordination with the organization's advertising department.

6. *Research.* Public relations departments work closely with marketing research departments or do the research themselves in matters involving public opinion. Because public opinion is often volatile, it is important that public relations departments spot emerging trends that may have significance for corporate policies and actions.

7. *Miscellaneous.* In addition to the preceding functions and activities, public relations departments sometimes have responsibility for handling speaker's bureaus, corporate donations, scholarship and awards programs, and other programs.

Marketing Public Relations

Promoting goodwill with an organization's various publics is public relations' overarching function. This, however, is not its sole role. Public relations, in fact, can and should work in conjunction with advertising, sales promotion, and personal selling to assist new product introductions, to promote product revisions, and to help ward off trouble for products in times of emergency or crisis. These product-oriented functions are more akin to the functions performed by the more conventional marketing communication tools (advertising, etc.) than they are to the general public relation tasks characterized previously. The label *marketing PR* distinguishes this aspect of public relations.[5] Subsequent discussion is restricted to this specific facet of public relations.

Marketing PR is used with other promotional devices to give a product additional exposure, newsworthiness, and credibility. News releases, feature or human interest stories, photo pages, broadcast public service announcements, prepackaged talk shows, and broadcast clips are various forms of marketing PR and publicity that marketers use to achieve exposure for new products and to enhance the credibility of established or new brands.[6]

[5]Theodore J. Gage, "PR Ripens Role in Marketing," *Advertising Age,* January 5, 1981, p. S-10.
[6]Ibid.

The following cases illustrate the effective use of marketing PR:

Beech-Nut Baby Food   In the mid-1970s consumer activists demanded that the major baby food manufacturers, which included Beech-Nut, remove salt and sugar from their products. Beech-Nut, agreeing with the critics, made necessary changes and developed "naturally good" products. A major marketing PR program was formulated to project Beech-Nut as credible, dynamic, and responsive to consumer interests.

At a major news conference in 1977, Beech-Nut's CEO announced that from that time on Beech-Nut would "make baby food for baby's taste, not for mother's matured tastes." All three television networks carried the announcement; print coverage was extensive; articles appeared in the *Washington Post,* the *New York Times, Newsweek,* and elsewhere. The favorable media coverage effectively enhanced Beech-Nut's credibility at a time when the baby-food industry was under attack. It is doubtful that other marketing communication tools would have been nearly as effective as this marketing PR campaign turned out to be.[7]

Raid Bug Killer   Johnson Wax undertook a publicity campaign directed at making consumers more aware of a nasty household problem, roaches. Raid bug killer, manufactured by Johnson Wax, was the product that stood to gain from heightened consumer awareness. The campaign's major objective was to remove the guilt feelings associated with having roaches in one's house and to remove the misconception that poor cleaning practices and household filth breed roaches.

Johnson Wax's public relations agency devised an award-winning campaign. Public service announcements (PSAs) were distributed through the National Homeowners Association to 650 television stations and 2,400 cable television outlets. Pamphlets, brochures, and consumer education booklets about roach problems were developed and delivered to media representatives by Johnson Wax's home economists. Efforts to gain broadcast time and newspaper space were facilitated by using a 250-pound actor dressed as a humanoid cockroach.

During a three-month period the PSAs reached 115 million households, and numerous newspapers carried roach-related articles. The advantages of obtaining media support for a PR campaign such as this were detailed vividly by an account executive for Johnson Wax's PR agency: "Getting the media to disseminate PR information creates the added allure of a third party endorsement. When a magazine or newspaper runs an article on how to get rid of bugs and attributes it to Raid, it's almost like them saying 'go out and buy Raid.' You can't beat that kind of endorsement."[8] The point of this is that consumers tend to view publicity as a form of news; as a result, information received via publicity appears objective and

[7]Jeanne Gumm, "Public Relations Is Primary Element in Beech-Nut Food's Marketing Program," *Advertising Age,* February 6, 1978, p. 39.

[8]Gage, "PR Ripens Role," p. S-11.

gives consumers the impression that the transmitting medium supports the information. This provides a level of credibility that is missing from advertising.[9]

Cabbage Patch Kids   Cabbage Patch Kids dolls, by Coleco Industries, were the selling sensation of the 1983 and 1984 Christmas seasons. Retailers could not keep the dolls in stock. Some people traveled long distances to locate the dolls, and there were reports of people actually fighting over a last available doll. What accounted for this phenomenal success? The product itself was largely responsible, but beyond this, advertising and marketing PR played a very important role in creating consumer interest and demand for the Cabbage Patch Kids.

Here are some of the things that Coleco's public relations agency did to promote the dolls: (1) the agency sent a doll to Jane Pauley of the "Today" television program, who devoted five minutes of program time to discussing the Cabbage Patch Kids; (2) a number of women's magazines were encouraged to mention the dolls as good Christmas gift ideas in their November magazine issues; (3) the dolls were featured several times on Johnny Carson's "Tonight" show; (4) a number of newspapers and radio stations were encouraged to use the dolls as prizes for their readers and listeners; (5) children's hospitals were given free dolls to give to their young patients; this, of course, generated favorable media coverage for Coleco. These and other programs generated an enormous amount of publicity. All of this was accomplished with a PR budget of less than $500,000, a virtual pittance in comparison to what it would have cost to generate the same amount of product interest and demand via media advertising.[10]

Business-to-Business Marketing PR   The examples up to this point have dealt only with consumer goods. It would be incorrect to think that only consumer good companies engage in marketing PR; thus, an illustration of business-to-business PR is provided. The Shakespeare Corp. aimed a publicity campaign at electrical utilities, architects, and electrical contractors. Shakespeare is the largest U.S. maker of fiberglass light poles, but many buyers do not give fiberglass serious consideration when choosing a supplier. The objective of Shakespeare's publicity campaign was to reach influential decision makers and to enhance the credibility of fiberglass light poles by comparing the relative advantages of fiberglass with metal poles, which dominate the light pole market.

Shakespeare's strategy was to inform engineers, architects, and other target markets by publishing articles in leading engineering and building trade journals. Shakespeare then distributed reprints of these articles to its sales representatives, who gave them to potential buyers as hard evidence that fiberglass poles work.

[9]Ibid.

[10]For further discussion, see "Behind Scenes Look At Cabbage Patch PR," *Advertising Age,* December 26, 1983, pp. 2, 18.

Sales representatives credited the publicity reprints for the gains in serious buying consideration from prospective customers.[11]

Publicity

The preceding cases were presented as illustrations of marketing PR. Publicity played a major role in all of these success stories. Publicity involves, in general, the use of press releases, press conferences, photographs, editorials, films, and other communication tools to disseminate information about companies' products, personnel, and other newsworthy events.

Publicity's general purpose is not unlike that of advertising and sales promotion; publicity attempts also to create consumer awareness, change attitudes, and influence purchase behavior. The difference is, however, that marketing communicators must pay for advertising space and time and for sales promotion materials, but publicity is a *nonpaid* form of communications. Moreover, consumers tend to regard publicity as more *credible* than advertising, because advertising is perceived as inherently manipulative whereas the news media that publish or air publicity releases are considered to be nonmanipulative and more objective.

Publicity can be either planned or unplanned. Where it is planned, some measure of control can be exercised by a company to cast itself and its products in a favorable position. Companies use press releases, press conferences, and other publicity modes, as noted previously, to control their publicity. A large company will normally send out hundreds of news releases about new products, modifications in old products, and other stories it feels may be newsworthy. The press conference is used to announce major news events that may be of interest to the public. Photographs, tapes, and films are useful for illustrating product improvements, new products, advanced production techniques, and so forth. Of course, all forms of publicity are subject to the control and whims of the news media. However, by disseminating a large volume of publicity materials and by preparing materials that fit the needs of the news media, a company increases its chances of obtaining beneficial publicity.

Brandstanding   Brandstanding is a special form of publicity and is an effective and inexpensive way to promote *mature products.* Brandstanding, which is a blend of the words *brand* and *grandstanding,* links a product to an event, issue, or idea inherently interesting to consumers, thus creating a rapport between consumers and the product.[12] A major advantage of brandstanding is its minimal cost. Whereas a 30-second network television spot may cost $150,000 to $400,000, an

---

[11]Arch G. Woodside, "Industrial Marketers Can Gain Credibility and Impact from Public Relations by Following These 10 Guidelines," *Marketing News,* December 10, 1982, p. 7.

[12]Art Stevens, "Don't Retire Mature Products, Promote Them with 'Brandstanding' PR Technique," *Marketing News,* March 18, 1983, pp. 2, 14.

effective brandstanding campaign can cost as little as $50,000 annually and still increase brand awareness and use.[13]

A survey among a cross section of national brand managers found that over three-fourths of them planned to use brandstanding in the future, and 60 percent had already used it.[14] Some of the best known brandstanding campaigns have been linked with sporting events: the Colgate Women's Games, Avon Tennis Championship, the Volvo Classic, the Ford College Cheerleading Championship, and Hertz Corp.'s "No. 1" campaign, which selects the number one high school athletic performer in each of the 50 states. Another well-known brandstanding campaign is McDonald's support of Ronald McDonald Houses that help families who have serious or terminally ill children in nearby hospitals.

Negative Publicity   The kind of publicity discussed so far is planned, and some measure of control can be exercised by a firm to cast its products in a favorable position. Companies are also subject to negative publicity. Where unplanned, the results can be extremely harmful to the firm and its products.

Several cases are illustrative. Kero-Sun Inc. was, as of 1982, the nation's largest seller of kerosene space heaters. The company had grown in just seven years from a single retail outlet into a $100 million-a-year business. Then, in September 1982, the cover story in the influential publication *Consumer Reports* claimed that kerosene heaters were fire hazards and emitted dangerous levels of toxic fumes. The story was disseminated throughout the country by newspapers and television stations. This negative publicity, together with an abnormally warm winter in 1982 to 1983, had a devastating impact on Kero-Sun's sales.[15]

The alcoholic beverage industry is also beset by bad publicity. Antiadvertising sentiment is extensive, particularly with regard to television commercials for beer and wine. Grass-roots movements such as Mothers Against Drunk Driving (MADD) have provided the impetus for what is now widespread antiadvertising sentiment. The exact impact this negative publicity will have on alcoholic beverage sales and advertising is unclear, but it is likely that the advertising of beer, wine, and spirits will not be permitted to continue to grow at its past, phenomenal rate—nearly a threefold increase from 1970 to 1981.[16]

A final negative publicity illustration is the celebrated case involving Extra-Strength Tylenol. Seven people in the Chicago area died in 1982 from cyanide poisoning after ingesting Tylenol tablets. Johnson & Johnson, the makers of Tylenol, removed the product from store shelves to prevent the possibility of further incident. Many analysts predicted that Tylenol would never regain its previously sizable market share. One well-known Madison Avenue advertising agency execu-

[13]Ibid.

[14]Ibid.

[15]"Kero-Sun Firm Faces Critical Test of Survival," *The State,* Columbia, SC, August 18, 1983, p. 12-D.

[16]Joseph M. Winski, "Pressures Mounting to Curtail Liquor Advertising," *Advertising Age,* July 18, 1983, pp. 1, 74.

tive predicted that Johnson & Johnson would never be able to sell another product under the Tylenol name.[17]

Johnson & Johnson proved the analysts wrong. Their handling of the Tylenol affair represents an exemplary illustration of both corporate responsibility and outstanding publicity and public relations. Rather than denying the problem, as other companies have done, Johnson & Johnson acted swiftly by removing Tylenol from retail shelves, appearing on television and cautioning consumers not to ingest Tylenol tablets, designing a tamper-proof package, and ultimately offering free replacements to consumers for products they had disposed of in the aftermath of the Chicago tragedy.

Figure 19.2 presents a Tylenol advertisement that offered consumers a $2.50 certificate for obtaining a free bottle of Tylenol. This advertisement reflects a responsive and astute company that dedicated itself to rebuilding consumer confidence and regaining lost market share. Tylenol regained its market share shortly after this campaign began, even though its major competitor, Datril, had launched an intensive advertising campaign and cents-off deal to steal Tylenol consumers.

Negative publicity can hit any company at any time. The extent of damage depends on how a company responds to the publicity. The Tylenol tragedy cost Johnson & Johnson millions of dollars, but the actual cost was a fraction of what it could have been had Johnson & Johnson not been as adept as it was in handling the problem. The lesson to learn from this incident is that quick and positive response to negative publicity are imperative.[18]

Developing a Formal Plan for Publicity   A number of brand and product managers eschew the use of publicity for promoting their products. They complain that publicity is difficult to control, is unsophisticated, and is impossible to measure for effectiveness.[19] Although these criticisms may apply to past practices, they do not appropriately characterize the current practice of publicity in some companies. Sophisticated users of publicity follow a formal plan, rather than conduct publicity in an unsystematic fashion. A formal plan should include the following elements:[20]

1.   *Analysis.* The first step in designing a product's publicity program is to analyze the situation with regard to present marketing strategies, competitive activity, public opinion, and other relevant factors.

2.   *Objectives.* Once a company has a clear understanding of what the situation is like, a next step is to formulate specific publicity objectives that are real-

[17]Jerry Knight, "J & J: Lesson in PR and Responsibility," *The State,* Columbia, SC, October 12, 1982, p. 6-B.

[18]For practical suggestions for how to handle negative publicity, see David P. McClure, "Publicity Should Be Integrated into Marketing Plan," *Marketing News,* December 10, 1982, p. 6.

[19]Gerald S. Schwartz, "Public Relations Gets Short Shrift from New Managers," *Marketing News,* October 15, 1982, p. 8.

[20]McClure, "Publicity Should Be Integrated."

FIGURE 19.2   **Illustration of PR and Corporate Responsibility At Their Best**

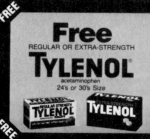

istic, measurable, and consistent with other marketing communication objectives.

3. *Methods and media.* In light of the situation analysis and objectives, specific methods can be created and media selected for disseminating publicity materials.

4. *Measurement.* A long-standing complaint with publicity programs is that there is no way of knowing how effective they are in accomplishing objectives. The traditional method for assessing effectiveness has been to count the number of column inches that publicity releases have obtained in print publications and to measure the time given by broadcast media. But these methods alone do not indicate whether the publicity has been effective. There are, however, other methods available for assessing publicity's effectiveness. For example, marketers can use controlled market comparisons whereby sales results in test markets that use publicity as part of the communications mix are compared with markets where publicity is absent. Also, marketers can gauge effectiveness by performing pretests to establish benchmarks; prior to undertaking a major publicity program, a company should measure customers' brand awareness or attitudes (or whatever the objective criterion is), and then use postprogram measurements to reveal whether the publicity program accomplished its objectives.

Specialty Advertising

Specialty advertising is, in certain respects, a hybrid form of marketing communications. On the one hand, it is very much like direct mail, as both pinpoint their communication efforts toward specifically defined audiences. On the other hand, specialty advertising is like public relations in that both are able to engender goodwill.

In more specific terms, **specialty advertising** is the use of articles of merchandise imprinted with an advertiser's message and distributed without obligation to designated recipients. Specialty advertising complements other forms of advertising by providing another way to keep a company's name before customers and prospects.[21] Special advertising expenditures are small in comparison with expenditures in other advertising media, but marketing communicators still spend over $4 billion each year on specialty merchandise.

Over 10,000 different articles of merchandise are used in specialty advertising. This merchandise is broadly classified into three groups: *advertising specialties* (imprinted items such as ball-point pens and T-shirts,), *business gifts* (items that seldom carry the advertiser's imprint and are usually distributed as goodwill gestures), and *advertising calendars.*[22]

---

[21]George L. Herpel and Richard A. Collins, *Specialty Advertising in Marketing* (Homewood, IL: Dow Jones-Irwin, 1972).

[22]"The Case for Specialty Advertising," Specialty Advertising Association International, Irving, TX, undated.

In addition to fostering goodwill, specialty advertising can help companies achieve a variety of other marketing communication objectives: (1) promotion of branch openings, (2) introduction of new products, (3) motivation of salespeople, (4) establishment of new accounts, (5) development of trade show traffic, (6) improvement of client or customer relations, and (7) activation of inactive accounts.[23] Two illustrations of how specialty advertising works to accomplish specific objectives follow.[24]

WQRS FM radio in Detroit wanted to promote its station as a prominent classical music source to advertising agencies and listeners. Therefore, the station mailed ad agency media buyers Rubik Cubes specially imprinted with the station's call letters. They followed up by sending puzzles to the same media buyers, who, upon solving a special design related to the Rubik Cube, won floral arrangements that were delivered directly to the person of their choice. The station also created a series of bumper stickers for distribution to its listeners. These and other promotions enabled the station to achieve a 70 percent increase in cash sales over an eight-month period.

Eastern Airlines opened a new terminal for its air-shuttle service at New York's La Guardia International Airport. The task was to create awareness of the terminal so that passengers would be directed to the new, rather than the old, terminal. Because 60 percent of all passengers arrive by taxi, taxi drivers became the primary target for the specialty advertising portion of the promotional campaign. Clipboards, imprinted with the announcement of the new air-shuttle terminal, were distributed to 7,000 cab drivers. Directing advertising to the highly specific market segment of cab drivers provided an ideal application of specialty advertising. Other media would have been very inefficient and wasteful.

Structure of the Specialty Advertising Industry[25]

The specialty advertising industry consists of a number of typically small businesses that fall into three groups: *Suppliers* manufacture, import, imprint, or otherwise convert the many varieties of specialty merchandise. The Zippo Company is, for example, a major supplier of imprinted cigarette lighters and other specialty items. *Distributors* work with customers to develop ideas for specialty advertising products and then purchase desired items from suppliers, who, based on standard industry practice, typically drop-ship products directly to customers. This method of distribution saves shipping expenses and eliminates the distributor's need to maintain inventories. *Direct-selling houses* combine the functions of suppliers and distributors. These organizations manufacture their own products and sell them

[23]Ibid.

[24]These cases are adapted from various printed materials supplied by the Specialty Advertising Association International, Irving, TX.

[25]George Herpel, "A Study in Industry Marketing Structure, Problems, and Image," Case 302, Specialty Advertising Association International, Irving, TX, undated.

through their own sales forces directly to specialty advertising customers. Industry experts estimate that there are nearly 2,500 suppliers and direct selling houses in the United States and approximately 3,500 distributors.

Summary

Public relations involves a variety of functions and activities that are directed at fostering harmonious interactions with an organization's publics (customers, employees, stockholders, governments, etc.). Publicity is a nonpaid form of marketing communications that is able to accomplish some of the same objectives as advertising. The outstanding advantage of publicity is that it, unlike advertising, is not perceived as intentionally manipulative but rather is seen as a credible and objective form of marketing communications.

Brandstanding is a variant of publicity that is used to link a mature product to an event, issue, or idea of inherent interest to consumers. Brandstanding enables a company to create a special rapport between itself and consumers. Brandstanding is particularly attractive because it is cost-effective in comparison with advertising.

A detailed discussion was devoted to the problem of negative publicity and ways to handle such publicity. The Tylenol case, which involved cyanide poisoning, was presented as an exemplary illustration of corporate responsibility and astute public relations. Specific guidelines for handling publicity were presented.

Specialty advertising is similar to public relations in that both are able to foster goodwill with an organization's various publics. Specialty advertising involves the use of articles of merchandise imprinted with an advertiser's message and distributed without obligation to designated recipients. Though not as well known as other media, advertisers spend over $4 billion each year on specialty advertising. A number of different marketing communication objectives can be facilitated with specialty advertising. Introducing new products, motivating salespeople, and improving customer relations are just a few.

Discussion Questions

1. What role might specialty advertising perform for a nationally distributed consumer goods product such as a brand of soft drink? How might a new architectural firm use specialty advertising?

2. It is said that public relations is to publicity what marketing is to salesmanship. Explain.

3. Explain the similarities and differences among public relations, marketing PR, and publicity.

4. What are the advantages of publicity in comparison with advertising? What are some of the same objectives performed by both of these marketing communication techniques?

5. Some marketing practitioners consider publicity to be too difficult to control and to measure. What is the reason for this negative view?

6. As the brand manager of Planter's Peanuts, an old and mature brand, how might you use brandstanding to create some inexpensive brand exposure?

Exercises

1. Go through your personal possessions and identify specialty advertising items. Evaluate what objectives you think these items were intended to accomplish and present your view of how effective each item has been in accomplishing its objective.

2. Identify several examples of brandstanding other than those presented in the text.

3. Review recent magazines and newspapers and provide illustrations of three or four instances of publicity. Evaluate the objectives you think these publicity efforts were intended to accomplish.

CHAPTER 20

Point-of-Purchase Communication and Merchandising

The point of purchase in a retail store represents the time at which the consumer makes product and brand choices. The point of purchase is a time when the marketer can have a major influence on the choices made; it is the time and place at which all elements of the sale (the consumer, the money, and the product) come together.[1] Marketers hope to influence consumers' buying decisions by using various communication vehicles at the point of purchase—displays, packaging, sales promotions, in-store advertising, and salespeople.[2]

Point of purchase (POP) performs four important marketing functions. *Informing* consumers is POP's most basic communication function. Outdoor store signs inform consumers that a certain product or brand is available, and indoor signs, posters, and displays alert consumers to specific items. A second communications function is *reminding* consumers of brands they have been informed about previously via broadcast, print, or other advertising media. *Persuading* consumers to buy a specific item or brand is POP's third communication function. The actual presentation of the product itself to facilitate customer inspection and to enable

---

[1]John A. Quelch and Kristina Cannon-Bonventre, "Better Marketing at the Point of Purchase," *Harvard Business Review,* November-December 1983, pp. 162–169.

[2]Ibid. It is important to note that the focus of this chapter is on *displays* as the primary POP communication vehicle. The remaining vehicles are discussed in other chapters with related subject matters.

retailers to utilize floor space effectively is the *merchandising* function of point of purchase.

Marketers use an array of items in point-of-purchase promotions, including various types of signs, mobiles, plaques, banners, shelf tapes, mechanical mannequins, lighted units, mirror units, plastic reproductions of products, checkout units, freestanding display units, wall posters, and numerous other forms. Many of these materials are *temporary* items, with useful life spans of only weeks or months, whereas others are *permanent* fixtures that can be used for many months or years. Whereas temporary displays are particularly effective for promoting impulse purchasing, permanent POP units compartmentalize and departmentalize a store area to achieve high product visibility, facilitate customer self-service, prevent stock-outs, and help control inventory.[3]

General Electric's Quick-Fix System and the Minnetonka Shower Mate display represent good illustrations of functional, attractive, and effective POP (see Figure 20.1). General Electric's display encourages dealers to feature the Quick-Fix unit in selling-space areas. Usually, products such as these, major appliance replacement parts, are stored in inaccessible storage areas. The display is organized to allow consumers easily to identify specific repair parts and to enable retailers to restock immediately. Color coordination attracts the consumer's attention, and a gravity feed feature keeps the display looking full and appealing.

Minnetonka, Inc. used its display to introduce Shower Mate Soap. This product's unique molded hook-cap permits suspending the bottle from shower heads, towel bars, and other convenient locations. The POP display dramatizes this revolutionary concept by serving as a giant replica of the product container.

Point of Purchase's Marketing Communication Role

Returning to the discussion in Chapter 1 in which the "Three Modes of Marketing"[4] (basic offer, persuasive communications, and promotional inducements) were identified, the general roll of point-of-purchase materials is embodied in the second mode, *persuasive communications*—the creation or stimulation of wants among target customers for the marketer's basic offering. POP can serve as a very strong motivator because it reaches the right people at the right place and time.

POP is positioned only where the item or service it is communicating is available for sale. Since consumers tend to patronize stores where they can afford to shop, the target audience is highly receptive to the selling message presented by

---

[3]"Merchandising Power: Maximizing Consumer Potential at Retail," *Marketing Communications,* January 1983, p. 12P.

[4]Eugene R. Beem and H. Jay Shaffer, *Triggers to Customer Action: Some Elements in a Theory of Promotional Inducement* (Cambridge, MA: Marketing Science Institute), 1981.

FIGURE 20.1   Illustrations of Permanent and Temporary POP Displays

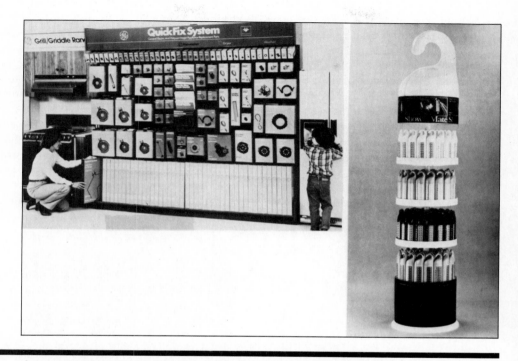

Source: 1980 POPAI Merchandising Awards (New York: Point-of-Purchase Advertising Institute, 1982), pp. 8, 20.

the POP display or material. In contrast, television commercials and other forms of advertising often fail to reach those consumers whose attention is focused on other things.[5]

Point-of-purchase materials provide a useful service for all participants in the marketing process.[6] For a *manufacturer,* POP keeps the company's name and the brand name before the consumer and reinforces the product's brand image as previously established through advertising. It calls attention to special offers such as sales promotions and helps stimulate impulse purchasing. It also helps to enhance the manufacturer's position with retailers.

[5]"Merchandising Triangle: Retailers, Advertisers, and Manufacturers Make P-O-P a Promotional Powerhouse," *Marketing Communications,* July 1983, pp. 1P–10P.

[6]The following discussion borrows from two sources: "Merchandising Triangle" and "Merchandising Power."

POP serves *retailers* in that it attracts the consumer's attention, increases his or her interest in shopping, and extends the amount of time spent in the store—all of which mean increased sales for the retailer. Point of purchase can help retailers utilize available space to the best advantage by displaying several manufacturers' products in the same unit (e.g., many varieties of vitamins and other medicinal items all in one well-organized unit). It enables retailers to better organize shelf space and to improve inventory control, volume, stock turnover, and profitability.

Consumers are served by point-of-purchase units that deliver useful information and simplify the shopping process by setting products apart from similar items.

In addition to benefiting all participants in the marketing process, point of purchase plays another important role. It serves as the capstone for an integrated promotional program. POP by itself may have limited impact, but when used in conjunction with other marketing communications (advertisements, sales promotions, and sales clerks), POP can create a synergistic effect. In fact, point-of-purchase tehcniques have been so effective that manufacturers are using media advertising to focus consumer attention on in-store promotional and display vehicles.[7]

POP in Action

The following illustrations are presented to demonstrate how effective point-of-purchase materials can be when they are designed with clear objectives in mind and are directed at specific target markets.

The ALIGN Singles Server II[8]   The Seven-Up Company undertook the development of a modular device in an effort to facilitate the stocking and displaying of single soft drink cans in convenience stores. Their research indicated that 60 percent of soft drinks sold in convenience outlets were single can sales, the consequences of which were broken six packs, disorganized coolers, and reduced sales. The research further indicated that convenience store executives desired a total soft drink system whereby they could achieve better cooler management. The ALIGN Singles Server II (Figure 20.2) was the solution to their problems.

Seven-Up's objectives in developing the ALIGN system were to increase consumers' purchase convenience and to improve retailers' inventory control and eliminate dead space on soft drink shelves. As shown in Figure 20.2, the ALIGN system provides retailers with individual injection-molded dispensers. Each row holds eight cans, or 24 cans per dispenser, and up to five full 24-can cases when five dispensers are snap-locked together. The system is intended not only to stock Seven-Up but to provide space for various brands, with allocations ideally proportional to each brand's historic sales performance in local markets.

---

[7]"Merchandising Triangle," p. 8P.

[8].This case is adapted from "Marketing Textbook: Seven-Up Company's ALIGN Singles Server II," *POPAI News,* Vol. 6, No. 2, 1982, p. 3.

FIGURE 20.2   Seven-Up's ALIGN Singles Server II Modular System

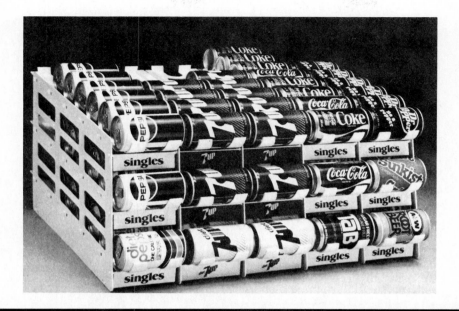

Source: "Marketing Textbook: Seven-Up Company's ALIGN Single Server II," *POPAI News,* Vol. 6, No. 2, 1982, p. 3.

Market test results clearly demonstrated the system's effectiveness. Consumer purchase units in Singles Server II stores outperformed control stores by an average of 23.5 percent, and gross profits in the Singles stores exceeded the control stores' profits by an average of nearly 22.7 percent.

Clairol's Haircoloring Information Center[9]   Clairol developed its information center (Figure 20.3) for a virtually undeveloped market segment consisting of women who are uninformed about hair-coloring products or who have been dissatisfied with these products. Clairol designed the information center to educate customers about the major questions women have concerning hair-coloring products. This information appears on large, colorful header signs above the actual products on in-line gondola shelves (see top of Figure 20.3). The information cen-

[9]This case is adapted from "Marketing Textbook: Clairol's Haircoloring Information Center," *POPAI News,* Vol. 7, No. 1, 1983, p. 3.

FIGURE 20.3   **Clairol's Haircoloring Information Center**

Source: Courtesy of Clairol.

ter also makes product selection easy; color-coded labels identify product subcategories, and shelf dividers separate the various products. Moreover, the center invites customers to call Clairol's hair-coloring consultants on a toll-free 800 number for additional assistance.

Clairol sales increased an average of 32 percent in retail outlets that installed the information center, and shelf space devoted to Clairol products averaged 15

FIGURE 20.4   **Thomas Flexible Paint Accessories System**

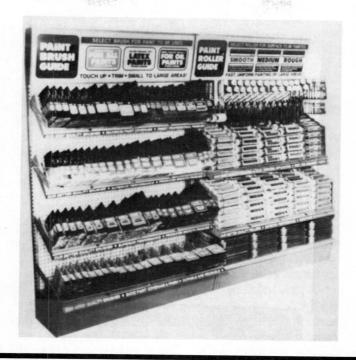

Source: Point of Purchase Advertising Institute. Undated.

---

percent more linear feet in those retail accounts. Furthermore, the 800 telephone number received more than 400,000 calls in the first year of operation from consumers seeking additional information about hair coloring and Clairol products.

The Thomas Flexible Paint Accessories System[10]   Paintbrushes and other painting accessories are often poorly displayed and merchandised in a confusing and cluttered fashion. The Thomas Paint Accessories System (Figure 20.4) was created to remove clutter and confusion, promote brand image, and reduce out-of-stock problems. The eight-foot-wide unit separates different product areas to display a full line of painting accessories. Retailers can adjust the shelves and partitions to meet their own specific merchandising needs. The Thomas display system has boosted sales by an impressive 30 percent.

[10]This case is adapted from "Case Histories: Analyzing What Makes this Display Work," *POPAI News,* Vol. 8, No. 3, 1984, p. 6.

Research on Point of Purchase

The previous illustrations suggest that POP can be extremely effective in certain specific applications. It would be useful, however, if additional evidence were available to support point of purchase's more general marketing communications role. Fortunately, two studies provide insight in this regard.

McKinnon, Kelley, and Robison examined the effects of in-store signs on sales of department store products. They found that when merchandise was priced regularly, the use of a sign with price information (i.e., a price sign) did not increase sales over the amount reported when no sign was used. The price sign did, however, increase sales for sale merchandise. Signs describing product benefits (benefit signs) were found to increase sales regardless of whether the merchandise was regular price or sale price, although sales increased at a greater rate for sale merchandise. The major conclusion from this research is that POP signs can stimulate sales activity, particularly when solid reasons for purchase (sale prices, product benefits) exist and need to be highlighted to motivate consumers to make a purchase at that time.[11]

A more far-reaching study is the most recent in a long line of famous DuPont buying-habit studies. Because of its importance, this research deserves an entire section in this chapter.

The POPAI/DuPont Consumer Buying Habits Study[12]

The POPAI/DuPont study is a successor to studies previously conducted by DuPont. The earlier studies were published every five years during a thirty-year period from 1935 to 1965. The most recent study, like its predecessors, was conducted in an effort to determine the percentage of total supermarket purchases that are preplanned and to compare the preplanned percentage with the percentage of purchases that are influenced by something that happens after the consumer enters the store. The study was conducted in 1977 and involved the recording of 53,000 purchases made by 4,000 shoppers at 203 nationwide supermarkets. Upon entering the supermarket, consumers were interviewed to ascertain what purchases they intended to make (the preplanned purchases). Next, for each consumer, actual purchase behavior was compared with the initial data obtained regarding preplanned purchase intentions. Purchases were classified item by item into the following four categories by comparing intended (preplanned) purchases with actual purchases:

---

[11]Gary F. McKinnon, J. Patrick Kelley, and E. Doyle Robison, "Sales Effects of Point-of-Purchase In-Store Signing," *Journal of Retailing*, Vol. 57, Summer 1981, pp. 49–63.

[12]The Point-of-Purchase Advertising Institute (POPAI) has released results of this study in a variety of special reports copyrighted in 1978. The following discussion has borrowed from various reports with particular emphasis on "POPAI/DuPont Consumer Buying Habits Study" (New York: The Point-of-Purchase Advertising Institute), 1978.

1. *Specifically planned.* This category represents purchases where the consumer indicated that he or she intended to purchase a specific brand and proceeded to buy that brand. For example, a purchase in which a consumer said that he or she intended, among other purchases, to buy Diet Pepsi would be classified as a specifically planned purchase if the consumer actually bought this brand.

2. *Generally planned.* This classification applies to purchases for which the shopper had a particular product in mind (say, soft drinks) but specified no particular brand. The purchase of Diet Pepsi in this case would be classified as generally, rather than specifically, planned.

3. *Substitute purchases.* This category includes purchases where the shopper changed his or her mind and did not buy the product or brand that had been specifically planned. If, for example, the hypothetical consumer said that he or she would buy Diet Pepsi but actually purchased Tab, or no diet soft drinks at all, this would have constituted a substitute purchase.

4. *Unplanned purchases.* Under this heading are purchases that the consumer did not plan to buy. If, for example, he or she bought Diet Pepsi without having informed the interviewer of this intent, then the behavior would have been recorded as an unplanned purchase.

It is necessary to address a technical point at this time. Unplanned purchases are often considered the same as "impulse purchases." By definition, an *impulse purchase* is one that the consumer has no prior intention of making; the purchase decision is, in other words, made spontaneously in the store. It is important to recognize, however, that not all of the "unplanned purchases," as defined in the POPAI/DuPont study, are truly impulse purchases. An alternative possibility is that some unplanned purchases were recorded as such simply because consumers occasionally were unable or unwilling to make the effort to recall precisely everything that they had intended to purchase. This would mean, in effect, that a purchase may have been recorded as unplanned (on impulse) when in fact the consumer actually had planned to buy an item but failed to inform the interviewer of his or her intent to do so.

The point of this discussion is not to imply that the POPAI/DuPont approach was wrong, but rather that the measurement of unplanned purchases probably was overstated somewhat due to the unavoidable bias just described. Furthermore, it should be noted that the other categories may be biased as well. For example, the percentage of specifically planned purchases probably was, by the same logic, somewhat understated. In any event, the findings are important even if they are not precisely correct.

A summary of the 1977 POPAI/DuPont findings for select product categories is presented in Table 20.1. Notice, first, at the top of the table that the generally planned, substitute, and unplanned purchases are summed to form another column labeled "1977 % Total Store Decision." The three categories representing purchases that were not specifically planned all represent decisions influenced by in-store factors. (The proportion of total store decisions in 1965 is presented for comparison purposes as the last column in the table.) Note also that at the very

TABLE 20.1   Classification of Purchases, 1977 POPAI/Dupont Consumer Buying Habits Study (Select Products Only)

Product Purchased	% Specifically Planned	% Generally Planned +	% Substitute Total +	% Unplanned =	1977 % Total Store Decision	1965 % Total Store Decision
General Merchandise						
Alcoholic beverages	33.0	13.3	2.2	51.5	67.0	69.3
Housewares, hardware	18.5	13.6	0.3	67.6	81.5	83.8
Oral hygiene, remedies and vitamins	42.7	3.9	2.1	51.3	57.3	64.6
Other health and beauty aids	27.9	8.6	2.3	61.2	72.1	71.3
Tobacco products and accessories	43.3	5.8	0.4	50.5	56.7	61.0
Pet foods and supplies	44.3	13.8	3.9	38.0	55.7	66.0
Other nonfoods	14.9	7.8	0.4	76.9	85.1	85.4
Groceries						
Baby foods and baby care products	39.0	27.2	2.9	30.9	61.0	80.0
Baking mixes	25.6	9.3	2.9	62.2	74.4	78.3
Baking needs except sugar and mixes	36.9	17.9	2.3	42.9	63.1	70.1
Canned and bottled fruits	23.0	17.0	4.6	55.4	77.0	80.9
Canned and bottled fruit juices and drinks	31.3	11.8	4.7	52.2	68.7	77.5
Canned and bottled vegetable juices	35.2	9.0	3.4	52.4	64.8	75.9
Canned beans, tomatoes, paste, puree, sauce	27.0	12.5	4.1	56.4	73.0	74.6
Canned fresh vegetables except tomatoes	27.3	19.7	4.6	48.4	72.7	80.8
Canned entrees, gravy, gravy mixes, bouillon	22.6	10.5	3.9	63.0	77.4	80.8
Canned soups and mixes	31.8	13.3	2.3	52.6	68.2	75.5
Catsup, chili, barbeque, steak, etc., sauces	30.2	8.7	3.4	57.7	69.8	73.3
Cold cereal	32.4	19.8	2.9	44.9	67.6	73.6
Entree mixes, meat extenders	24.4	7.3	2.0	66.3	75.6	85.3

bottom of Table 20.1 the average percentages across all products covered in the POPAI/DuPont study are given. (Due to space limitations, Table 20.1 has not presented all of the products from the POPAI/DuPont study but has presented instead a reasonable sampling of diverse products.)

The percentage of "total store decisions" across all products (64.8% in 1977) at the bottom of the table is the major finding of the POPAI/DuPont study. This indicates, to the extent that the figure is accurate, that nearly two out of every three supermarket decisions are influenced by in-store factors. *Environmental marketing* is an apt term characterizing what takes place. A variety of in-store, environ-

TABLE 20.1   *Continued*

Product Purchased	% Specifically Planned	% Generally Planned	+	% Substitute Total	+	% Unplanned	=	1977 % Total Store Decision	1965 % Total Store Decision
Ethnic, diet foods	16.7	15.1		2.3		65.9		83.3	80.6
Evaporated, condensed, powdered milk, coffee creamers	43.6	12.1		5.5		38.8		56.4	58.1
Herbs and spices	18.5	23.3		4.1		54.1		81.5	82.4
Hot cereal and other breakfast foods	30.2	11.1		1.0		57.7		69.8	66.7
Mayonnaise and salad dressings	36.9	6.8		3.7		52.6		63.1	65.5
Mustard and relishes, olives, pickles, vinegar	18.3	17.4		2.7		60.6		80.7	82.8
Oils and shortenings	43.8	8.1		3.2		44.9		56.2	57.5
Pastas, cereal grains	26.9	17.5		1.6		54.0		73.1	76.7
Soda, bottled or canned	44.1	8.0		3.9		44.0		55.9	61.3
Spreads	33.0	12.1		3.8		51.1		67.0	75.9
Sugar and sugar substitutes	38.6	20.5		2.2		38.7		61.4	69.2
Household Supplies									
Air fresheners, other cleaning supplies, waxes	30.5	7.3		3.1		59.1		69.5	65.6
Bags and wraps	29.0	10.7		4.0		56.3		71.0	75.1
Bath, hand, facial soaps	34.5	7.5		1.3		56.7		65.5	62.2
Bleaches, fabric softeners, other laundry products	44.7	6.8		4.9		43.6		55.3	60.8
Dishwashing products, cleansers, oven cleaners	38.9	8.6		3.7		48.8		61.1	63.5
Facial tissues	40.7	8.9		4.4		46.0		59.3	68.8
Laundry detergents and soaps	56.2	4.6		3.9		35.3		43.8	51.3
Napkins, tablecloths, plates and cups	24.9	20.2		0.8		54.1		75.1	80.6
Paper towels	26.1	17.8		5.3		50.8		73.9	69.7
Toilet tissue	37.3	14.7		4.7		43.3		62.7	72.6
ALL PRODUCTS	35.2	14.8		3.0		47.0		64.8	68.9

Source: "POPAI/DuPont Consumer Buying Habits Study," The Point-of-Purchase Advertising Institute, 1978, New Jersey. Reprinted with permission.

mental influences (POP displays, signs, packages, etc.) capture consumers' attention and affect their purchase decisions.

It should also be noted in Table 20.1 that the percentage of "total store decisions" varies considerably by product. Staple items (e.g., laundry detergents and soaps) represent a relatively low percentage of total in-store decisions (43.8%), whereas with less frequently purchased items (e.g., ethnic and diet foods), an extremely high proportion of decisions (83.3%) are made in the store. It is also interesting to note that the percentage of in-store decisions declined across all products (from 68.9% to 64.8%) during the period from 1965 to 1977. This holds true for most product categories. A number of factors may account for this. The most likely appear to be that more consumers used shopping lists in 1977 than in 1965 and that, because supermarket prices nearly doubled during this period, consumers in 1977 were somewhat more deliberate in their purchasing decisions.[13]

In summary, the POPAI/DuPont study has shown that a large proportion of all behavior in supermarkets is influenced by in-store factors. POP displays represent a very important determinant of consumer product and brand choice behavior.

The Role of Motion in Point-of-Purchase Displays

Point-of-purchase displays come in two general forms, static and motion displays. Motion displays, though typically more expensive than static displays, can represent a sound business investment by virtue of attracting significantly higher levels of shopper attention and by moving more merchandise. Research evidence from three studies shows that motion displays are often worth the extra expense.[14]

Olympia Beer   Researchers tested the relative effectiveness of motion and static displays for Olympia beer by placing the two types of displays in a test sample of liquor stores and supermarkets in California. Each of the sampled stores was stocked either with static or motion displays. Another sample of stores received no displays and served, therefore, as a control group. Over 62,000 purchases of Olympia beer were recorded during the four-week test period.

Static displays in liquor stores increased Olympia sales by 56 percent over stores with no displays (the control group), whereas in supermarkets, static displays improved Olympia sales by a considerably smaller amount (18%), although this was substantial nonetheless. More dramatic, however, was the finding that motion displays increased Olympia sales by 107 percent in liquor stores and by 49 percent in supermarkets.

S. B. Thomas English Muffins   Two groups of 40 stores each were matched by store volume and by customer demographics. One group was equipped with S. B. Thomas English muffin displays that utilized a post sign that moved from side to side. The other 40 stores used regular floor displays with no motion. Follow-up interviews indicated that motion displays aided shoppers in recalling what they had seen and heard in an accompanying media advertising campaign. Records of product movement revealed that sales in the stores stocked with motion displays increased by 473 percent! Part of this increase was due, of course, to the concurrent advertising effort; yet the sales increase in stores using static displays was only 370 percent, a full 103 percent below that of the sales generated by motion displays.

---

[13]For elaboration on these and other points, see "POPAI/DuPont Consumer Buying Habits Study."

[14]"The Effect of Motion Displays on the Sales of Beer"; "The Effect of Motion Displays on Sales of Baker Goods"; "The Effect of Motion Displays on Sales of Batteries." All from the Point-of-Purchase Advertising Institute, New York, undated.

Eveready Batteries   A study of motion displays for Eveready batteries was conducted in both Atlanta and San Diego. In each city, six drugstores, six supermarkets, and six mass merchandisers were studied. The stores were divided into two groups, as in the English muffin study. Some newspaper advertising appeared during the test period, but special pricing was the primary promotional element. For mass merchandisers, the static display increased sales during the test period by 2.7 percent over the base period, but surprisingly, sales in the drug and food outlets utilizing the static displays were slightly less (each 1.6% less) than those not using the static displays. By comparison, the motion displays uniformly increased sales by 3.7 percent, 9.1 percent, and 15.7 percent in the drug outlets, supermarkets, and mass merchandisers, respectively.

Evaluation of Test Results   The results from the preceding studies convincingly demonstrate the effectiveness of motion displays. The consumer information processing rationale (see Chapter 3) is straightforward: motion displays attract attention. Attention, once attracted, is directed toward salient product features, including recognition of the displayed brand's name. Brand name information may activate consumers' memories pertaining to brand attributes previously processed from media advertising. Information on brand attributes, when recalled, supplies a reason for the consumer to purchase the displayed brand. Thus, a moving display performs the critical in-store function of bringing a brand's name to active memory, and if the consumer is favorably disposed toward the brand because of past personal experience or media exposure, the probability of purchasing the brand increases, perhaps substantially, as in the case of S. B. Thomas's English muffins. The Eveready display was less effective apparently because the selling burden was placed almost exclusively on the display. Without prior stimulation of demand through advertising, the static display was ineffective, and the motion display was not as effective as it might have been.

Point-of-Purchase Trends

Expenditures on point-of-purchase materials amounted to almost $7 billion in the United States in 1983.[15] A number of factors have stimulated the increase in spending on point of purchase, and the same factors promise its continued growth: (1) The trend toward the employment of fewer salespeople in retailing requires that POP materials help perform the in-store selling function. (2) The rising cost of mass media advertising has forced executives to allocate larger percentages of marketing budgets to non–mass media communication vehicles. To place the cost factor in better perspective, Table 20.2 offers some comparative cost per thousand (CPM) figures for various media. The tremendous differences in CPMs should be noted carefully. (3) A third, and perhaps most important, factor contributing to POP's growth is the realization that, for many companies, point of purchase is an

[15]"P-O-P Power Grows as Annual Business Volume Passes $6.8 Billion Mark," *POPAI News,* Vol. 8, No. 3, 1984, p. 1.

TABLE 20.2   **Approximate Cost to Reach Each 1,000 Adults**

Medium	Approximate CPM
Network Television (30-second spots)	$4.05–$7.75
Radio (one-minute spots)	$3.50–$4.75
National Magazines (full-page, 4-color)	$2.50–$4.00
Newspaper (1,000-line ad)	$3.50–$4.50
Outdoor Billboard	
Painted Bulletin	$1.25–$1.50
30 Sheet Poster	$ .45–$ .50
Outdoor Metal Sign (3′ × 5′ wall—mounted sign, $20 cost, 500 daily adult exposure, 3-year life)	$ .04
Outdoor Metal Curbstand Sign ($50 cost, 2,500 daily adult exposure, 3-year life)	$ .03
In-store Permanent Product Merchandiser or Sign (Cost range of $5 to $20, exposure range 200 to 1,000/day depending on type of outlet, 1-year life)	$ .03–$ .37
In-store Temporary Product Merchandiser or Sign (Cost range $2.50 to $10, exposure range 200 to 1,000/day depending on type of outlet, 2-week life	$ .18–$3.00

Source: "Merchandising Power: Maximizing Consumer Potential At Retail," *Marketing Communications,* January 1983, p. 8P.

indispensable component of an integrated communication program—advertising creates awareness and interest, sales promotion provides inducements on top of the basic offer, and POP materials remind, reinforce, and direct consumer choice to the marketer's brand.

Major Trends

Four major trends are apparent in point-of-purchase merchandising:[16]

1. Promotions and display vehicles are being supported to a greater extent by media advertising. This is typified best by the growing tendency for television commercials and magazine ads to include shots of POP displays. This practice effectively cues consumers and facilitates memory activation at point of purchase.
2. Semipermanent and permanent product merchandisers and shelf-management systems (such as Clairol's Haircoloring Information Center, Seven-Up's Align Single Server System, and Thomas's Flexible Paint Accessories System)

are becoming increasingly prevalent. Permanent displays are especially appealing to marketers due to their extremely low (relative to mass media advertising) cost-per-thousand exposures.

3. Promotion and displays are being incorporated into the marketing mix with increasing sophistication on the part of POP producers. Top marketing management, at both manufacturer and retail levels, recognize POP's important role and accordingly have become more actively involved in POP programs.

4. Increased attention is also being paid to POP programs that are geared to specific market segments. Segmented POP materials can be especially effective in reaching markets that may not be reached economically through mass media advertising. For example, POP makes it possible to target Hispanic neighborhoods with Spanish-language messages, to direct messages with country themes to rural areas, and to appeal specifically to blue-collar workers.[17]

Summary

Point of purchase performs both communication and merchandising functions. A variety of POP materials are used, and these are distinguished broadly as either temporary (e.g., signs) or permanent (e.g., integrated merchandising systems). Permanent displays are becoming more common for two principal reasons: they offer the manufacturer substantial savings, and they enable the retailer to merchandise the product more effectively.

Major research has documented the high incidence of in-store decision making and, thus, the importance of POP materials. The POPAI/DuPont study classified all consumer purchases into four categories: specifically planned, generally planned, substitutes, and unplanned decisions. The last three categories represent, collectively, in-store decisions that are influenced by POP displays and other store cues. The POPAI/DuPont study found that in-store decisions represent nearly two out of every three purchase decisions.

Research results were presented that demonstrated the impressive impact motion displays have on sales volume. This impact was demonstrated for three products: beer, English muffins, and batteries. The chapter concluded with a discussion regarding the growth in the use of point-of-purchase techniques and the emergence of four major trends.

Discussion Questions

1. What functions can point-of-purchase materials accomplish that mass media advertising cannot?

2. Explain the consumer information processing rationale underlying the synergistic effect between advertising and POP.

---

[17]*POPAI News,* Vol. 6, No. 2, 1982, p. 6.

3. Explain why the POPAI/DuPont study results probably overestimate the percentage of unplanned purchases and underestimate the percentage of specifically planned purchases.

4. Suggest an alternative measurement procedure (i.e., different methods and different measurements) that would answer the same question addressed by the POPAI/DuPont study, yet would avoid the biases you identified in response to the previous question.

5. Note in Table 20.1 that the percentage in 1977 of total store decisions was 55.7 percent for "pet foods and supplies." The comparable percentage for 1965 was 66 percent. How would you account for the major decrease in in-store decision making for this particular product category? Also, the 1977 percentage of total store decisions for "herbs and spices" was 81.5 percent. What accounts for the 26 percent difference in in-store decision making between this product category and pet foods/supplies?

6. What role does point of purchase perform for retailers? for consumers?

7. The discussion of the S. B. Thomas English muffin study pointed out that in stores using motion displays, sales increased by 473 percent. By comparison, sales of Eveready batteries, when promoted with motion displays, increased anywhere from 3.7 percent to 15.7 percent, depending on type of store. How would you account for the tremendous disparity in sales impact of motion displays for English muffins vis-à-vis batteries?

8. Table 20.2 shows that the CPM range for network television is estimated at $4.05 to $7.75, with a midpoint of $5.90. For in-store permanent merchandisers or signs with a one-year life, the CPM range and midpoint are $.03 to $.37 and $.20, respectively. Thus, the average cost of the permanent fixture is 29.5 times less than that for network television (i.e., $5.90/$.20). Does this mean that permanent fixtures as marketing communication vehicles are, on average, 29.5 times better than network television? Justify your response.

9. Why were motion and static displays considerably more effective in increasing Olympia beer sales in liquor stores than in supermarkets?

Exercises

1. The best way to appreciate point of purchase is to systematically examine its use. Visit a supermarket and provide an accounting of the types and number of point-of-purchase materials used for five different product categories.

2. Use the same accounting approach in a drugstore or general merchandise store (e.g., K-Mart).

3. Interview two or three proprietors/managers of small retail stores (e.g., a camera shop, a sporting goods store) and determine what their experiences have been with point-of-purchase materials provided by manufacturers. (Develop a specific list of four or five questions before you go on your interviews.)

Nonpromotional Tools in Marketing Communications

Part V examines the nonpromotional elements of the marketing mix from a marketing communications perspective. Marketing scholars and practitioners have become increasingly aware that product, price, and place variables perform valuable marketing communications functions in addition to their other marketing roles. These nonpromotional communications variables are often as important (or more important) than the promotional tools that are used in marketing goods and services.

Chapter 21 looks at product characteristics, packaging, and brand symbolism. These product features communicate a variety of messages, such as strength, quality, value, status, and so on. The communications roles of price and place variables are discussed in Chapter 22. A product's price does more than merely inform the customer how much it will cost to acquire the product. Beyond this, the price can communicate snob appeal, quality, prestige, and a variety of other meanings which influence consumer choice behavior. In similar fashion, the place in which a brand is sold can evoke specific meanings. Architecture, size, store signs, interior layout, and store personnel are some of the important features of a store that communicate meaning to consumers.

CHAPTER 21

Product, Package, and Brand Symbolism

Chapter 2 discussed the role that codes (verbal and nonverbal) play in communicating meaning between senders and receivers. Marketing communicators employ a variety of codes and symbols to encode messages to prospective customers. For instance, elements in a product's packaging—color, shape, design, material, and labeling—provide consumers with important information cues about a product. Moreover, the brand name and the physical characteristics of the product itself contribute to an overall picture (or image) of the marketer's offering.

In a communications sense, products can be viewed as *symbols* that communicate meaning and help consumers to express their life-styles.[1] Consumers do not purchase a physical product per se; they purchase psychological satisfaction. For example, people do not purchase cosmetics but instead the promise of beauty. As symbols, products "carry all kinds of connotations, including respectability, conservatism, youthfulness, membership in a certain group, and being cheap or being expensive."[2]

This chapter examines how people respond to various product cues: color, design, shape, physical materials, and labels. Though the discussion centers on indi-

[1]Joseph W. Newman, "New Insights, New Progress, for Marketing," *Harvard Business Review,* Vol. 35, November-December 1957, p. 100.

[2]Harper W. Boyd, Jr., and Sidney J. Levy, *Promotion: A Behavioral View* (Englewood Cliffs, NJ: Prentice-Hall, 1967), p. 17.

vidual elements in the product message, bear in mind that the true test of a product's communications effectiveness is how consumers respond to the *total* product.

The Package

The package is the most important component of the product as a communication device. The growth of supermarkets and other self-service retail outlets has demanded that the package assume marketing functions beyond the traditional role of containing and protecting the product. One of packaging's most important jobs is establishing perceptual cues "to drive associations established in advertising into the consumer's mind."[3] The package further serves as the final vehicle to (1) close the sale, (2) break through competitive clutter at the point of purchase, and (3) justify price/value to the consumer.[4] The package is clearly a vital element in the marketing communications mix.[5]

Known as the "silent salesman," the package can often make or break a producer in the consumer goods market of today. Even products that require personal selling must be packaged in a way to reinforce the salesperson's claims and to continue to resell itself once the consumer has the product in the home.

The importance of packaging can best be illustrated with examples. Research has shown on numerous occasions that the package itself influences brand preferences. In one study, consumers declared preference for a brand of soap two to one over another brand, even though both were the same soap. The only difference was the package.[6] A more graphic illustration is offered by the case of a cleaning solution, Fantastik, which experienced a 40 percent sales increase after introducing a new package and went from the number two in sales to industry leader.[7]

In general, where a product is homogeneous, unexciting, or distasteful in appearance, packaging becomes a useful way to differentiate the product from available substitutes. Packaging accomplishes this by serving as a "continuous communicator." That is, "it works uninterruptedly in store and home to present the product: to say what it is, how it is used, and what it can do to benefit the user."[8]

---

[3]"Packaging Remains an Underdeveloped Element in Pushing Consumer Buttons," *Marketing News,* October 14, 1983, p. 3.

[4]"Package Research Probes Stopping Power, Label Reading, and Consumer Attitude among the Targeted Audience," *Marketing News,* July 22, 1983, p. 8.

[5]A. V. L. Brokaw, "Effective Packaging Talks," *Advertising Age,* December 28, 1980, p. S-4.

[6]Louis Cheskin and L. B. Ward, "Indirect Approach to Market Reactions," *Harvard Business Review,* Vol. 26, September 1948, pp. 572–580.

[7]"Texize Says New Package Boosted Fantastik to Lead," *Advertising Age,* November 17, 1975, p. 141.

[8]John Deighton, "A White Paper on the Packaging Industry," Dennison Technical Papers, December 1983, p. 5.

Many times with new or untried brands the consumer is looking, consciously or unconsciously, for a cue that tells him or her what the brand is all about. The tendency to equate the brand with an information cue, such as the package, is called **sensation transference.** Consumers impute information from the package to the product itself. Consumers are typically unaware of this association; instead, they believe they have made a selection on a purely rational basis. A thoroughly rational selection is improbable, however, because the consumer is simply confronted with too many alternatives to investigate and must rely upon simplifying cues.

The marketing communicator's task is to transmit desired meaning by designing, coloring, and shaping packages that are compatible with what the consumer is looking for in the product. It is importnt to note, however, that although the package is capable of communicating quality, economy, prestige, and other desirable attributes, a product will generate repeat purchases only if the product delivers what the package promises.

Package Symbolism

The package relies upon the use of **symbolism.** A symbol is any form, shape, or color that is meaningful within the consumer's societal context. In general, marketing communicators should use symbols that are familiar to consumers rather than require consumers to learn the connotations of new symbols. The Coca-Cola company, for example, finally settled on a new package (after 150 attempts) for its line extension Diet Coke. The chosen package was very similar to regular Coke and differed primarily by simply reversing the red and white colors. This assured consumer association with the well-known and easily recognized Coke symbol.[9]

No matter what the product category, the marketer's objectives in the use of package symbolism should be reflected in the company's total product positioning strategy. For example, the package for Miller's Lite beer was designed to create a feeling that this light beer had plenty of taste. Its type face, with a very German quality, helped to evoke a "real" beer feeling. The words, "A fine pilsner beer," embossed on a regal seal rounded out the impression of a quality product. This design helped position Miller Lite into a new category—light beer with taste.[10]

Even a successful package with favorable symbolism will not assure product success. In one instance, for example, a new product dropped from 25 percent to 10 percent share of market because the product had been cheapened. Although the new package communicated that the product was of superior quality, it was, in fact, inferior. From then on the package symbolized low quality, not high quality.

[9]"After 150 Tries Comes a Winning Design," *Advertising Age,* October 18, 1982, pp. M-4–M-5.

[10]Christopher Dingman, "The Obvious Point of Purchase Tool," *Advertising Age,* December 17, 1979, p. S-2.

The producer had downgraded the product, which was inconsistent with the quality communicated by the package.[11]

Packaging's Communication Components

Components of package communication are color, design, shape, size, brand name, physical materials, and product information labeling. All these components must interact harmoniously to evoke within buyers the set of meanings intended by the firm. The notion underlying good packaging is **gestalt.** That is, people react to the whole, not to the individual parts of a situation. The whole is greater than the sum of its parts when the parts interact synergistically. Sometimes, however, inconsistent package elements negate each other and produce a poor package communication. The following package components are discussed individually to facilitate analysis. However, throughout the discussion, bear in mind that the consumer perceives these components within their total context.

The Use of Color in Packaging   Color is an ancient symbol. Through the ages people have associated colors with aspects of their physical environments. Yellow signified the sun, red became associated with fire, and blue symbolized the sky and water. These associations, and many more subtle ones, are passed from generation to generation and learned by members of each society.[12]

Colors affect people *emotionally* rather than rationally. *Yellow* is a warm color with a cheerful effect on consumers and is a good attention getter. *Green* connotes abundance, health, and coolness. It is frequently used in packaging for mentholated products. *Blue* also suggests coolness but has the widest appeal of all colors. *Orange* is an appetizing color that is often associated with food. Finally, *white* signifies purity and is used in a variety of products.

Colors have the ability to communicate many things to prospective buyers, including quality, smell, taste, and the product's ability to satisfy the consumer's psychological needs. Research studies have documented the important role that color plays in affecting our senses. In one study, a panel of women were asked to use two face creams, one pink and the other white, not knowing that the two creams were exactly alike. The women were categoric in saying that the pink cream was milder compared with the white cream and that the pink cream was for more sensitive skins.[13] In another experiment, 200 people were served *identical* coffee from four different color pots—red, blue, brown, and yellow. Perceptions of coffee flavor differed drastically depending upon the color of pot from which the coffee was served. Subjects believed that coffee served from the *brown*

[11]Louis Cheskin, *Business without Gambling* (Chicago: Quadrangle Books, 1963), p. 23.

[12]Faber Birren, *Color Psychology and Color Therapy* (New Hyde Park, NY: University Books, 1961), p. 3.

[13]Jean-Paul Favre and Andre November, *Color and Communication* (Zurich, Switzerland: ABC Verlag, 1979), p. 64.

pot was too strong, coffee from the *red* pot was perceived as rich and full bodied, from the *blue* pot it was perceived as having a milder aroma, and the coffee from the *yellow* pot was considered to be a weaker blend. Unbeknown to the subjects, the coffee was all the same.[14]

In addition to the emotional impact of color, elegance and prestige can be added to products by the use of polished reflective surfaces and color schemes using whites and blacks or silvers and golds.[15] An example of the effective use of a white and black color scheme is found in the elegantly simple package utilized by Chanel perfumes (see Figure 21.1). Another example of prestige-enhancing packaging is that for LeSueur peas, which for years have stood out on grocery store shelves in their metallic silver labels. Cigarettes and liquor are two additional product categories that seem particularly fond of using silver, gold, and white and black color schemes in their package designs.

The use of color in evoking moods and connotative associations is a large field of study. The intent here has been simply to point out the communicative nature of color. Much more could be said about good color combinations, contrast, and the like. However, it is hoped that this brief discussion has suggested the usefulness and importance of color as a cue in package communication.

Design and Shape Cues in Packaging   Variations in the design and shape of a package communicate differences in the product to consumers. *Design* refers to the organization of the elements on a package. A good package design is one that permits good eye flow and provides the consumer with a point of focus. Package designers bring various elements together in a package to help define a brand's image. These elements include shape, size, and label design. The package design for many products can establish brand personality and help cut through the clutter at the point of purchase.[16] The design can be used to convey a feeling of modernity, to "play upon nostalgia and a yearning for the more simple and forthright days of yesteryear,"[17] to suggest that the producer is serious and technical minded,[18] or to convey a variety of other feelings in consumers.

One way of evoking different connotations and reactions is through the choice of length, thickness, and slope of lines on a package. *Horizontal lines* suggest restfulness and quiet and evoke feelings of tranquility. There appears to be a physiological reason for this reaction; namely, it is easier for people to move their eyes horizontally than vertically. Vertical movement is less natural and produces greater strain on eye muscles than horizontal movement. The muscles that move our eyes

---

[14]Ibid.

[15]Dennis J. Moran, "Packaging Can Lend Prestige to Products," *Advertising Age,* January 7, 1980, pp. 59–60.

[16]Kate Bertrand, "Shaping Packaging for Impact," *Advertising Age,* July 26, 1984, pp. 43–44.

[17]Moran, "Packaging Can Lend Prestige," p. 60.

[18]B. V. Yovovich, "Designers Make Their Mark on the Shelves," *Advertising Age,* October 10, 1983, p. M-37.

FIGURE 21.1 **Illustration of Prestige Package**

FIGURE 21.2   **The Use of Upward Slanting Lines in Packaging**

Source: Courtesy of The Coca-Cola Company.

from side to side are stronger and more conditioned to this movement. *Vertical lines* evoke feelings of strength, confidence, and even pride. *Slanted lines* suggest upward movement to most people. This is explained by the fact that people in the Western world read left to right and thus view sloped lines as ascending rather than descending. Diet Coke's packaging illustrates the use of upward slanting lines (see Figure 21.2). Perhaps the intent is to represent symbolically the product as fitting into the ambitious and upwardly mobile life-styles of the many "yuppies" (refer to Chapter 9), who are a prime market for Diet Coke and other weight-conscious products.

Line *thickness* can connote masculinity or femininity. Bold stripes evoke masculine feelings, whereas a pattern of thin lines suggests femininity. Combining a thin line pattern with white, pink, or other pastel colors enhances a package's message of femininity to prospective buyers. To combine bold stripes with pastel colors would, on the other hand, present an inconsistent message to prospective buyers, thereby confusing them as to the "correct" response to make. Design and color must combine harmoniously to achieve the desired effects. Inconsistent package elements tend to cancel each other.

Shapes, too, arouse certain emotions and have specific connotations. In general, round curving lines connote femininity, whereas sharp, angular lines suggest masculinity. The oval shape of the L'eggs package (refer back to Figure 2.6) is an example of true femininity. The egg-shaped L'eggs package elicits perceptions of a fragile and yet protected product and connotes fashion and perhaps even sex appeal.[19]

The shape of a package also affects the apparent volume of the container. In general, for two packages having the same volume but a different shape, the taller of the two will appear to hold a greater volume. Height is usually associated with volume. Another common figure, the circle, is also quite prevalent as a shape either for the package or on the package. By changing the color of the circle, the package designer can make the circle appear either larger or smaller. Generally, the same size circle will appear smaller if it is colored a darker color and if the contrasting background becomes lighter. In addition, if the packaging specialist draws several curved lines within the circle, the circle will appear to be an oval. Therefore, the same basic figure of a given size package can be made to appear larger, smaller, or of a different shape merely by changing the background or by adding a few lines.

Brand Name   The brand name is, perhaps, the single most important element found on the package. It identifies the product and differentiates it from others on the market. The brand name and graphics work together to communicate and position the brand's image.[20] A good brand name can evoke a feeling of trust, confidence, security, strength, durability, speed, status, and many other desirable associations.

Through brand names, a company can create excitement, elegance, exclusiveness, and various sensory perceptions. Ninety-nine percent of the customers of Polo brand clothing have never seen nor will ever play a polo game, yet Ralph Lauren was able to "establish a feeling of moneyed elegance and adventure in one word."[21] A peanut butter taste test reveals how a brand name alone can affect taste perceptions. When a certain brand of peanut butter was test marketed under the name "Superman" peanut butter, consumers described it as "watery" and as having other negative sensory properties. The same peanut butter fared well, however, in a blind taste test, and it did even better when it was subsequently labeled "Jif."[22]

---

[19]"Packaging Remains an Underdeveloped Element."

[20]Lorna Opatow, "Packaging Is Most Effective when it Works in Harmony with the Positioning of a Brand," *Marketing News,* February 3, 1984, p. 4.

[21]Moran, "Packaging Can Lend Prestige," p. 59.

[22]"Packaging Remains an Underdeveloped Element."

There are several fundamental requirements in selecting a brand name. A brand name should (1) *distinguish* the product from competitive items, (2) *describe* the product or its benefits, (3) *motivate* the consumer to want to purchase the product, (4) be *compatible* with the product, (5) help *create and support a brand image*, (6) be *brief, readable, memorable, and easy to pronounce,* (7) *connote the appropriate meaning when said aloud* (e.g., the detergent name "BOLD" when pronounced aloud sounds strong and powerful), and (8) *tell the consumer what to expect inside the product or what to expect from its use* (e.g., the coffee "DECAF" tells the consumer that he or she is buying a decaffeinated coffee).[23] Perhaps the key question the marketer must ask when selecting a brand name is, "Does the name fit the product?"[24]

One particularly interesting application of branding by American marketers is the widespread use of animal names. For example, automobile companies use names such as Mustang, Thunderbird, Bronco, Cougar, Lynx, Skyhawk, Skylark, Firebird, and Jaguar.[25] Because animal names are among the earliest words a child learns, their meaning and associations are strongly engrained within us all. We learn, for example, that a jaguar is sleek, has speed, strength, stamina, and power—all attributes that the makers of "Jaguar" hope consumers will associate with this automobile. We also learn that tigers are sure-footed animals; thus Uniroyal's choice of the "Tiger Paw" name for its tires is appropriate for implying the ability to grip the road (with an overtone of safety and reliability).

In addition to being memorable, animal names can also conjure up vivid images. This is very important to the marketing communicator because, as discussed in Chapter 3, concrete and vivid images facilitate consumer information processing. Consider, for example, the following brand names and their associated imagery. Lever Brothers' "Swan" soap suggests softness, grace, gentleness, and purity. "Billy Goat" vacuum cleaners and "Eagle Claw" fishhooks also elicit sharp, indelible pictures in the minds of consumers and suggest distinct brand benefits. Animal names, and their associated imagery, have been used successfully with children's products. Tiger Bread, Bunny Bread, Giraffe Cookies, and Pink Panther Flakes are but a few of the myraid animal names used in the children's market.[26]

Some words and combinations of words are more strongly associated with certain product categories than other words or word combinations. For example, plural words are associated with cereals (as the preceding names for children's cereals indicate), whereas singular words are associated with such products as laundry detergents (Tide, Wisk, Bold, Cheer, etc.).[27]

[23]Items 1 to 3 are from Walter P. Margulies, "Animal Names on Products May Be Corny, but Boost Consumer Appeal," *Advertising Age,* October 23, 1972, p. 78. The other items represent a summary of views from a variety of other sources.

[24]Dennis J. Moran, "How a Name Can Label Your Product," *Advertising Age,* November 10, 1980, p. 53.

[25]Ibid.

[26]Margulies, "Animal Names," p. 78.

[27]Robert A. Peterson and Ivan Ross, "How To Name New Brands," *Journal of Advertising Research,* Vol. 12, December 1972, p. 32.

In summary, a company should select a brand name that evokes the intended meanings and supports a desired image. The name should have positive and meaningful connotations that are easily remembered and compatible with the total package.

Physical Materials in Packaging   An important consideration in packaging that is often overlooked is the materials that make up a package. Often, cost is the prime consideration. The selection of package materials according to cost is the result of an engineering, production, or accounting decision. This may seem reasonable until the ramifications of selecting package materials solely on the basis of cost are considered. In many instances, increasing the expense of packaging materials will lead to increased sales, which more than compensate for the cost. The profitability criterion is based on what the market desires. Admittedly, sometimes a high cost for packaging materials will not be offset by increased sales and thus will reduce profits. In any event, cost should not be the sole criterion for material selection; it should instead be viewed in its relationship to sales. Here the economic concept of marginal analysis is applicable.

From a behavioral viewpoint, materials used to construct a package can arouse consumer emotions, usually subconsciously. Packages constructed of metal evoke feelings of strength, durability, and coldness, and plastics connote newness, lightness, cleanliness, and perhaps cheapness.[28] Materials that are soft, such as velvet and fur, are associated with femininity. Foil has a high-quality image and can evoke feelings of prestige.[29] Wood arouses feelings of masculinity. Consider, for example, the men's cologne English Leather, which has been successful with its wooden box as a secondary package and its bottle with a large wooden knob as a cap. The name and the rectangular package design present an example of total masculinity—the blend of design, shape, brand name, and materials achieve a consistent consumer image.

The importance of the choice of packaging materials is demonstrated in a study that tested different bread wrappers. The experiment was designed to determine whether consumers perceive a difference in the freshness of bread when it is wrapped in wax paper as opposed to cellophane. The results showed that bread wrapped in cellophane was perceived to be fresher than bread wrapped in wax paper.[30] This study illustrates the importance of *tactile* communications, since shoppers squeeze bread to determine its freshness.

Product Information on Packages   Product information can come in several forms. In a sense, all the previous package components—color, design, brand

[28]Burleigh B. Gardner, "The Package as Communication," in M. S. Moyer and R. E. Vosburgh (eds.), *Marketing for Tomorrow . . . Today* (Chicago: American Marketing Association, 1967), pp. 117–118.

[29]Kevin Higgins, "Foil's Glitter Attracts Manufacturers Who Want Upscale Buyers," *Marketing News,* February 3, 1984, p. 1.

[30]Robert L. Brown, "Wrapper Influence on the Perception of Freshness in Bread," *Journal of Applied Psychology,* Vol. 42, August 1958, p. 260.

name, and so forth—inform consumers about what is inside the package. Product information, however, refers to key words on the package, information on the back panel, ingredients, warnings, pictures, and illustrations. An example of the effectiveness of information included on packages comes from a field experiment measuring weekly sales of bread. When the "Made with 100% Natural Ingredients: No Artificial Additives" statement was affixed to the package, both penetration and buying frequency increased. When the message was removed, sales returned to their prior level.[31]

All of us have seen the words *new, improved,* and *free* on packages. These words are designed to stimulate immediate trial purchases or to restore a brand purchase pattern for consumers who have previously tried but have since switched to other brands. Often these are placed on existing brands to revive a faltering brand or to stave off new entries. The underlying reason for using these words is the belief that their use favorably influences the consumer's evaluation of the brand. Furthermore, these key words presumably offer consumers what they want—something new, improved, or free.

There is some question whether the key words just cited have been overworked in the marketplace. One study suggests, in fact, that the "new" and "improved" claims on packages do not significantly affect consumer evaluations of certain household and personal care products.[32] However, more research is necessary to support this point. Perhaps there is a need to find new motivating words. Some examples may be the use of numerals in Gleem II (toothpaste) and Clorox 2 (laundry bleach). These brand names names are apparently intended to tell consumers there is a new and improved version of an old product without directly using hackneyed words such as *new* and *improved.*

One of the most effective means of providing consumers information about a brand, as well as projecting the appropriate image, is the use of pictures and illustrations. Today printing techniques have improved to a point that realistic pictures and illustrations of a product can be imprinted on the package with high fidelity. Pictures are far more effective than words in projecting the desired image for a brand. For example, Nabisco redesigned its Fig Newton package by displaying an appetizing photograph, which emphasized that Fig Newtons were a fruit product. The new package tells the consumer what is inside and conveys an image of a healthy snack.[33]

Sometimes a good marketing tactic is to put short, memorable slogans on a package. These are best used when a strong association has been built between the brand and the slogan through extensive and effective advertising. The slogan on the package, by virtue of being a concrete reminder of the brand's advertising,

[31]William H. Motes and Arch G. Woodside, "Field Test of Package Advertising Effects on Brand Choice Behavior," *Journal of Advertising Research,* Vol. 24, February-March 1984, pp. 39–45.

[32]Edward H. Asam and Louis P. Bucklin, "Nutrition Labeling for Canned Goods: A Study of Consumer Response," *Journal of Marketing,* Vol. 37, April 1973, pp. 36–37.

[33]Charles Moldenhauer, "Packaging Designers Must Be Cognizant of Right Cues If the Consumer Base Is To Expand," *Marketing News,* March 30, 1982, p. 14.

can facilitate the consumer's retrieval of advertising content and thereby enhance the chances of a trial purchase.

One part of a package that is often neglected is the back panel. The back panel serves at least three important functions: (1) to incorporate ad copy and product information, (2) to promote a company's other products, and (3) to provide product usage ideas (such as recipes and cooking hints).[34] Using recipes and cooking ideas on back panels causes the consumer to handle the package more frequently, thereby becoming more familiar with the brand. The consumer may, to some degree, also come to depend upon cooking and recipe ideas suggested on the back panel and purchase the brand regularly for that purpose.

Fitting Packaging into the Consumption System

Studying how the consumer uses the product in the home can suggest important package changes and improvements. For instance, boxes of facial tissues are normally set in plain view in the bedroom, in the bathroom, and in other rooms. Having noted this, marketers designed attractively styled boxes that fit into a room's decor. Peanut butter and jelly producers discovered that consumers often use leftover jars as drinking glasses. Consequently, they began to put their jellies into decorative jars to promote the use of their packages as drinking glasses. Similarly, marketers of margarine changed their packages to plastic margarine containers to encourage reuse. There are numerous other illustrations of packaging developments that occurred because marketers wished to fit their product packages to the consumer's consumption system.

Recently, Quaker State Oil Refining Corp. realized consumers' difficulties with opening motor oil cans and pouring the oil into automobile engines and developed an easy-to-open plastic container with an easy-to-pour spout to simplify product usage.[35] (See Figure 21.3.) A further example of studying consumers' use of products and packages concerns toothpaste manufacturers, who finally responded to the problem of arguments within families over who left the cap off the toothpaste and who squeezed the tube in the middle. Makers of such familiar brands as Crest, Aim, and Colgate now offer toothpaste in convenient pump dispensers.

A final example of the importance of brand name, product design, and consumer desires is the story of "Long-Haul" jeans for truck drivers. The Jonbill Company learned that professional truck drivers wanted to wear jeans on their long drives but could not fit comfortably into the lean, slim cuts that are most often available. Therefore, they designed jeans cut from an oversized pattern, which had extra ease for sitting comfort on long drives. Moreover, the company (1) made it known that the jeans were made by a domestic manufacturer (truckers are responsive to products "made in America"), (2) designed the jeans to have an enlarged back pocket

---

[34]Asam and Bucklin, "Nutrition Labeling," pp. 36–37.

[35]Robert Raissman, "Quaker Converts to Plastic Bottles," *Advertising Age,* March 12, 1984, p. 6.

FIGURE 21.3   Illustration of a Workable Package

(truckers' wallets are often oversized), (3) named the jeans "Long Haul" (to characterize the jeans' intended use), and (4) gave the jeans a western style and placed a stagecoach on the label, since the trucker is, in certain respects, the last American cowboy.

Marketers can, and indeed must, develop and promote new packages and products to solve the problems and meet the needs of consumers. Simply observing consumer behavior yields useful ideas on how to improve products and packaging.

Evaluating the Package: The VIEW Model

A number of individual factors have been discussed in regard to what a package communicates to buyers. The most important concern, however, is whether the overall package is an effective marketing communication vehicle. Twedt has developed a simple verbal model that nicely integrates the material presented in this chapter.[36] Twedt's model goes by the acronym *VIEW,* which stands for the four criteria he recommends for evaluating a package: visibility, information, emotional appeal, and workability.

Visibility represents the ability of a package to attract attention at the point of purchase. Visibility is determined by a variety of factors. For example, brightly colored packages are more visible than dull packages. Novel packaging graphics, sizes, and shapes are additional means whereby package designers may enhance a package's visibility. The objective is to have a package stand out on the shelf, yet not be so garish that it detracts from a brand's image.

The second consideration, *information,* deals with product usage instructions, claimed benefits, slogans, and supplementary information (e.g., cooking recipes, sales promotion offers) presented on or in a package. Package information is useful for (1) stimulating trial purchase behavior, (2) encouraging repeat purchase behavior, and (3) providing correct product usage instructions. The objective is to provide the right type and quantity of information and not to clutter the package with excessive information, which could interfere with the primary information or cheapen the look of the package.

Emotional appeal, the third component, concerns the ability of a package to evoke a desired feeling or mood. In Chapter 2, the importance to marketing communicators of using emotional appeals was discussed. Emotional appeals for product packaging represent the connotative meaning conveyed by a package, compared with the denotative meaning conveyed by the previous component, information. It is undeniable that the role of packaging in many situations is to evoke positive feelings and associations in the prospective buyer's mind. For example, a soap package may convey a feeling of softness and femininity, a record album jacket may suggest sensuousness, and a jewelry item container may transmit a feeling of elegance. There are innumerable ways by which package designers at-

---

[36]Dik Warren Twedt, "How Much Value Can Be Added Through Packaging," *Journal of Marketing,* Vol. 32, January 1968, pp. 61–65.

tempt to evoke specific feelings and moods—through the use of color, shape, packaging materials, and so on. The objective is for a package to convey a personality that is compatible with the image a brand is attempting to project.

The final component of the VIEW model is *workability.* This deals more with function in packaging rather than with communications. Several aspects are involved: (1) Does the package protect the product contents? (2) Does it facilitate easy storage on the part of both retailers and consumers? and (3) Does it simplify the consumer's task in getting to and using the product?

Workability is, of course, relative. For example, the new Quaker State motor oil package mentioned earlier (Figure 21.3) is more workable than the old-fashioned container it replaced. As can be seen from the example, the objective is to design a package that is as workable as possible yet economical for the producer and consumer. Consumers prefer food packages, for example, that completely prevent food from getting stale or spoiling, but the manufacturer's ability to provide this degree of "workability" is limited by cost. At the other extreme, some marketers skimp in their package design and use inexpensive packages that are clearly unsuitable.

Most packages do not perform well on all criteria. In fact, packages need not always be exemplary on all four VIEW components because the relative importance of each criterion varies greatly from one product to another. Emotional appeal dominates for some products (perfume, for example), information for others (e.g., directions for using a new food processor), while visibility and workability are generally important for all products (especially frequently purchased self-service items). In the final analysis, the relative importance of packaging requirements depends, as always, on the particular market and the product's competition. Marketing communicators hope that their packages appeal to target audiences and yield an advantage over competitors.

Physical Characteristics of the Product

The product itself has characteristics that communicate with buyers. It has color, shape, size, and other physical features that consumers perceive as important in their buying decisions. Instead of reiterating much of the previous discussion, this section will simply look at several examples to illustrate the importance of a product's characteristics.

One of the best examples of a product whose physical characteristics communicate with buyers is the Contac cold capsule. Recognizing the value of product communications, the company designed a package with a small circular window to reveal one of the cold capsules. The capsule itself has a clear plastic end, which allows the consumer to see the "tiny little time pills" of red, yellow, and white colors. When Contac first came on the market, it was the only 12-hour cold capsule; all others were 4-hour tablets. The advertising message told consumers that Contac has "tiny little time pills," which release their medicinal powers periodically over a 12-hour period. The company evidently intended for the consumer to imagine one of the pill colors, say red, taking immediate effect for the first four hours, followed by, say, the yellow ones and then the white ones. The multicolored pills apparently served to reinforce the advertising-induced belief that Contac capsules work for 12 full hours. There is little doubt that the manufacturer could have colored these little pills all one color.

Detergent manufacturers have capitalized on the same idea with their multicolored flakes, with each color supposedly performing its wash-day function. One color flake gets the dirt out, while the other bleaches. Again, everytime a homemaker empties a cupful of detergent into his or her wash, he or she is reminded of the advertiser's message and the functions performed by the detergent.

Product *color* plays an important communications role. For example, the color of bathroom soap reinforces the brand name, as green does for Irish Spring soap, and also provides the consumer with a choice of colors to match the bathroom decor. Coffee provides yet another example, with some companies emphasizing their coffee's "dark, rich color."

In appliances, stereos, and certain other products, the number of knobs, switches, and buttons provides information about a product's technological sophistication and complexity. Items with large numbers of knobs are frequently perceived by consumers as technically advanced and perhaps high quality. This is not necessarily true, but as always, it is the consumers' subjective reality that determines perceptions and choice behavior rather than the objective reality.

Shape is often used in products as a communicator. Animal and cartoon characters are used in children's vitamin pills and cereals, for example.

The *taste* of a product also has communication value. The Listerine "taste bad" advertising reinforces the belief that a medicinal product must taste bad to be effective. Here the company is utilizing the prior learning exeriences that many people have from childhood that medicine which tastes bad is effective. A similar example relates to tactile communications. Antiseptics used in treating cuts have for a long time produced a sting when applied to an open wound. One company succeeded in producing an antiseptic solution that did not sting, but the product failed because consumers did not believe it was an effective germ killer.

There are hundreds of examples of how physical characteristics of a product communicate various messages to consumers. The purpose here has been to illustrate the importance of recognizing this form of communications when formulating and designing products.

Summary

This chapter explains how the product, its package, and brand name all perform important communication roles. Color, design, shape, size, physical materials, and information labeling are just some of the product-related cues that convey information and symbolic meaning to consumers.

The package is perhaps the most important component of the product as a communication device. The package serves to reinforce associations established in advertising, to break through competitive clutter at the point of purchase, and to justify price/value to the consumer. Packaging is a particularly important communication device when a product is homogeneous, unexciting, or distasteful in appearance.

Package design relies upon the use of symbolism to support a brand's image and to convey desired information to consumers. A number of package cues are used for this purpose, including color, design, shape, brand name, physical materials, and product information labeling. These cues must interact harmoniously to evoke within buyers the set of meanings intended by the marketing communicator. Sometimes, however, inconsistent package elements negate each other and produce a poor package communication.

The brand name is perhaps the most important single element found on a package. The brand name works with package graphics and other product features to communicate and position the brand's image. The brand name identifies the product and differentiates it from others on the market. A good brand name can evoke a feeling of trust, confidence, security, strength, durability, speed, status, and many other desirable associations. A good brand name must satisfy a variety of fundamental requirements: It must describe the product and its benefits, help create and support a brand image, be brief, be memorable, be easy to pronounce, and so on.

Aside from the package and brand name, the product itself has physical characteristics that also perform significant communication functions. The product has color, shape, size, and other features that consumers perceive as important in their buying decisions.

Discussion Questions

1. One of packaging's jobs is to "drive associations established in advertising into the consumer's mind." Offer a specific explanation of what this means and use several marketplace illustrations to support your explanation.
2. What is "sensation transference?" Provide two specific examples to support your answer.
3. The notion underlying good packaging is "gestalt." Explain what this means and provide one example of an actual package that embodies this packaging ideal.
4. In what sense does the use of animal names for products (e.g., Thunderbird) facilitate consumer information processing? Refer to Chapter 3 for specific concepts around which to answer this question.
5. Why, in your opinion, do so many marketers use the words *new* and *improved* on their product packages? Support your answer with reference to appropriate concepts from Chapters 3 and 5.
6. The text described how packages for some products have been designed to fit into the consumer's consumption system. Explain specifically what this means and describe at least one product category or specific brand that in your opinion has not done a particularly good job of fitting the package to the consumer's consumption system.

Exercises

1. Pick two competitive brands within a particular product category and describe the meaning that the *physical features* (not the packages or brand names) of each brand communicates. Be specific with reference to color, shape, or other pertinent characteristics.

2. Select a different product category than you selected for exercise 1 and apply the VIEW model to three competitive brands within that category. Specifically, you should do the following:

   a. Discuss all four components of the model (i.e., define each component and how it applies to your selected product).

   b. Weigh each component in the model in terms of your perception of its relative packaging importance in your chosen product category; do this by distributing ten points among the four components, with more points meaning more importance and the sum of the allocated points totalling exactly 10. (*Note:* this weighting procedure involves what marketing researchers refer to as a constant sum scale.)

   c. Next, evaluate each brand in terms of your perception of its performance on each packaging component by assigning a score from 10 ("performs extremely well") to 1 ("does not perform well").

   d. Combine the scores for each brand by multiplying the brand's performance on each component by the weight of that component and then summing the products of these four weighted scores. The summed score for each of your three chosen brands will reflect your perception of how good that brand's packaging is in terms of the VIEW model—the higher the score, the better the packaging in your opinion. Summarize the scores for the three brands in terms of an overall assessment of how good each brand's packaging is.

3. Select yet another product category and analyze the brand names for three competitive brands in that category. Analyze each brand name in terms of the fundamental requirements that were described in the text. Order the three brands in terms of which has the best, next best, and worst brand name. Support your ranking with specific reasons.

4. Identify five brand names (other than the ones used in the text) that, in your opinion, are especially notable in terms of their concreteness and vividness of the imagery which the names evoke.

Price and Place Communications

The purpose of this chapter is to examine the roles price and place play in marketing communications. In particular, the chapter will describe how each of these variables evokes meanings within consumers and how they interact with other marketing communications variables. Both price and place contribute to the image of the firm's *total product offering*.

The Role of Price in Marketing Communications

The primary concern in this section is to describe *how* and *when* price can be used as a communications cue to customers. Under *all* circumstances price communicates at a minimum the firm's asking rate of exchange for its product. However, firms also use prices to communicate status, snob appeal, quality, low purchase risk, and other ideas.

According to basic economics, the firm should ideally set its price at the point where its marginal revenue is equal to its marginal costs. However, business executives seldom, if ever, know exactly what their demand or cost functions are. Therefore, price setters must typically rely upon more practical pricing methods, such as cost-oriented and competition-oriented pricing. Although these pricing practices are useful and necessary approaches to the pricing problem, they should not be viewed as a final answer. In fact, marketers must consider *noneconomic* as well as economic factors when pricing their products. This means that it is essen-

FIGURE 22.1   **The Traditional Demand Curve**

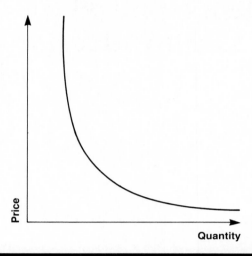

Source: M. Wayne DeLozier, *The Marketing Communications Process* (New York: McGraw-Hill, 1976), p. 191.

tial to examine how buyers respond to prices and how prices influence buyers' perceptions of the worth of a product.[1] The noneconomic factors that influence the pricing decision will be examined, and the circumstances under which price becomes an important communications cue will be discussed. First, however, a brief review of the basic economic view of price will be presented.

Economic View of Price

Traditionally, price has been viewed as a rate of exchange. Price is the amount of money a seller asks for a product and a buyer is willing to give up to acquire the product. For an exchange to take place, the buyer and seller must mutually agree upon a set rate. This interaction between buyers and sellers is summarized by economists in their **law of demand.** It says that as the price of a commodity rises, the quantity demanded by consumers declines, and vice versa. This inverse relationship defines the negatively sloped demand curve shown in Figure 22.1.

Although the law of demand is applicable to many products in the marketplace, particularly for undifferentiated products such as agricultural commodities, the traditional economic viewpoint fails to consider the impact that many marketing practices have upon consumer demand. Firms know that price can be used as a communications cue to differentiate product offerings and to satisfy consumers'

---

[1]Kent B. Monroe, Albert J. Della Bitta, and Susan L. Downey, "Contextual Influences on Subjective Price Perceptions," *Journal of Business Research,* Vol. 5, December 1977, p. 277.

FIGURE 22.2   **Illustration of the Backward-Bending Demand Curve**

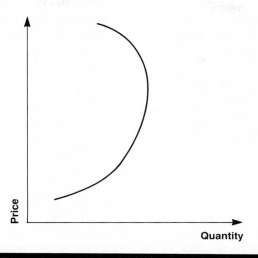

Source: M. Wayne DeLozier, *The Marketing Communications Process* (New York: McGraw-Hill, 1976), p. 192.

informational and psychological needs. When viewed in this manner, demand curves take on quite a different look from the one in Figure 22.1.

Quite often consumers use price as an indicator of quality.[2] Under such circumstances the demand curve for a product may look like the one shown in Figure 22.2. Part of the curve is positively sloped and indicates a direct relationship between price and quantity demanded over some portion of the price range. That is, a higher price is related to higher demand for the product. This phenomenon is often found for luxury items such as furs, jewelry, and cars. For example, Mercedes Benz correctly predicted that with costs rising and thus the cost of their cars rising, the Mercedes cars would be perceived as "items of even higher prestige and quality" and demand would rise. In a similar situation, the Rolls Royce had a two-year waiting list when its price doubled.[3]

The question for marketers to consider is, Under what circumstances is price used as a cue to quality? The following section attempts to answer this question by looking at two general categories of factors—*product* and *consumer* characteristics—that are favorable to the use of price as a communications cue.

---

[2]See Harold J. Leavitt, "A Note on Some Experimental Findings about the Meaning of Price," *The Journal of Business,* Vol. 22, July 1954, pp. 205–210; and Donald S. Tull, R. A. Boring, and M. H. Gonsior, "A Note on the Relationship of Price and Imputed Quality," *The Journal of Business,* Vol. 37, April 1964, pp. 186–191.

[3]Mary Louise Hatten, "Don't Get Caught with Your Prices Down: Pricing in Inflationary Times," *Business Horizons,* Vol. 25, March-April 1982, pp. 23–28.

Noneconomic View of Price

Characteristics of the Product   Price serves as an important communications cue to consumers for some products. The purpose of this section is to discuss the product characteristics that suggest when price becomes an important cue for consumers in evaluating a brand and in making a brand choice.

Perceived Variance in Product Quality   When consumers perceive a high *brand-to-brand variance in quality* within a product category, they are inclined to use price as a cue to quality in evaluating the brands.[4] Consumers perceive salt, for example, as having little or no quality variation across brands. That is, one brand of salt is about the same (in quality) as another brand of salt. In this case, price would *not* serve as an indicator of quality; thus, consumers would not be very likely to pay a premium price for one particular brand.

Products that consumers do perceive as having wide brand-to-brand variations in quality are cosmetics and medicine. Most consumers believe there are important quality differences between brands of cosmetics, for example, even though the differences may not be perceptible. One facial cream may be the same as another; yet, women who are very concerned about skin care will be prone to select a high-priced brand because they believe the higher price reflects "hidden qualities."

The Product as a Component   Where a product is used as an additive, an ingredient, or a component of another product, the consumer may rely on price as an important cue to quality. An experienced cook who is preparing an ethnic dinner, e.g., Chinese or Greek, at home is undoubtedly aware that the spices will affect the quality of the finished food as much as will the meat, vegetables, and other items. In fact, the cook may perceive the contribution of the spices to be much higher than their cost, and thus will pay a higher price for quality spices to decrease the risk of a poor-tasting dinner without significantly increasing the cost.[5] Similarly, a person who is buying an expensive sports car will not be too concerned about paying more for one brand of AM-FM stereo cassette when a less expensive brand is perceived as lower in quality. Where a product is viewed by the consumer as an *important* component of a larger product or where its use contributes significantly to the quality of the final product, the consumer will be inclined to use price as an indicator of product quality.

The Product as a Gift   Some products are purchased as gifts more frequently than others. For these products a high price serves to reduce the purchaser's risk of embarrassment in giving a poor-quality gift to another person. A man who gives his fiancée a bottle of perfume for her birthday will be inclined to use price as an

---

[4]Benson Shapiro, "The Psychology of Pricing," *Harvard Business Review,* Vol. 46, July-August 1968, p. 25.

[5]This example is adapted from Shapiro, ibid.

indicator of quality in making his brand selection. Of course, the price of the perfume is only one cue among several, such as fragrance, brand name, and packaging. But price becomes an important informational cue in the selection of a gift because the gift giver feels that the higher price gives the giver greater assurance that he or she will gain the desired approval of the recipient. Put another way, the higher-priced gift affords the giver a means of protecting and enhancing his or her self-image.

Other "gift" products are ones that are used for special occasions or for entertaining. Consumers often purchase more expensive products and brands for holidays, social gatherings, and other special occasions. By purchasing higher-priced brands, particularly those that are conspicuous, a person can enhance his or her self-image of being a good host(ess) and reduce the risk of giving or serving an inferior brand.

Brand Name   Another variable that affects the importance of the price cue is the familiarity and strength of the brand name. When brands of a product are physically homogeneous and brand names are unfamiliar to consumers, price becomes a powerful cue for consumers in evaluating the quality of a brand.[6] In fact, a familiar brand name is often as important or more important than the price cue in communicating product or service quality.[7]

Olson summarizes several studies describing the interaction of price and brand name in providing consumers with information cues. By varying levels of brand name familiarity, such as from low (lack of meaningful brand name information), to medium, to high, he concludes that "price cues should have an increasingly powerful effect on product evaluations as brand familiarity decreases. . . . That is, in cases of low brand familiarity or in the absence of a brand name, price cues should provide additional useful information unavailable through the brand name cue."[8] Basically, then, price becomes a strong communications cue in the absence of other product cues such as brand name.

New Products   A new product offers the marketer a good opportunity to use price to communicate product quality. Since the product is new, it has no traditional price and is, therefore, likely to be assessed by the market largely on the basis of its initial price.

Quite often marketers use a **skimming** pricing strategy in the introductory stage of a product's life cycle. Skimming refers to the strategy of setting a high

---

[6]J. Douglas McConnell, "An Experimental Examination of the Price-Quality Relationship," *The Journal of Business,* Vol. 41, October 1968, p. 442.

[7]Kent B. Monroe, "Buyers' Subjective Perceptions of Price," *Journal of Marketing Research,* Vol. 10, February 1973, p. 73.

[8]Jerry C. Olson, "Price as an Informational Cue: Effects on Product Evaluations," in A. G. Woodside, J. N. Sheth, and P. D. Bennett (eds.), *Consumer and Industrial Buying Behavior* (New York: Elsevier North-Holland, 1977), p. 278.

price to catch the relatively price-inelastic segment of the market. If the strategy is successful, the firm can gain a quick return on its initial investment. Furthermore, if consumers perceive the high price as an indicator of product quality, the firm can continue to use this strategy to reinforce consumers' beliefs about its quality. If the market rejects the product because of its high price, the firm is still in a position to lower its price and stress the "value" of its product offering.

At the other end of the continuum is **penetration pricing.** In penetration pricing the firm elects to introduce the product at a low price because management believes that demand is fairly elastic. The communications value of price in this case is quite low except to tell the consumer that the product is either a "popularly priced" brand or a "value" brand.

Durable Versus Nondurable Products   There appears to be a relatively strong positive relationship between consumers' price-quality perceptions of *durable goods* and the sales of durable goods, even under recessionary economic conditions. However, for nondurable goods, the same relationship is weak. A study of 10,162 brands tested by *Consumer Reports* over a 15-year period showed a positive correlation between price and sales due to "quality imputations." The relationship between price and quality for nondurables was weak.[9] Another study found that the price-quality relationship is poorest for convenience foods, especially frozen foods. Correlations between price and quality for packaged food products was near zero.[10]

One possible explanation for these findings is that higher-income consumers are much less affected by shifts in economic conditions than are lower-income consumers. That is, higher-income consumers can continue to purchase based on price as a cue to quality, status, snob appeal, etc., whereas consumers with lower incomes are generally hit hardest by recession and inflation and therefore begin to substitute lower-priced nondurables and forestall purchases of durables, particularly higher-priced ones.

Characteristics of the Consumer   As with product characteristics, several generalizations can be made regarding various consumer characteristics that are important in price communications. This section discusses these generalizations.

Product Experience   For consumers who lack experience and information about a product, price becomes an important informational cue for evaluating the product. Carpet, for example, is a product that people buy on an infrequent basis. Thus, carpet qualifies as a product with which people have relatively little buying expe-

[9]Peter C. Riesz, "Price Versus Quality in the Marketplace, 1961–1975," *Journal of Retailing,* Vol. 54, Winter 1978, pp. 15–28.

[10]Peter C. Riesz, "Price-Quality Correlations of Packaged Food Products," *The Journal of Consumer Affairs,* Vol. 13, Winter 1979, pp. 236–247.

rience. Price should therefore represent an important cue in consumers' quality perceptions. Research supports this expectation.[11]

A mother who wants to buy her daughter a fishing rod and reel for her birthday may not know what makes one rod and reel better than another. If she is shopping in a store where there is no personal selling assistance, the price becomes important to her in evaluating the quality of alternative rod and reels. Even in stores where she receives help from a salesperson, the price may serve to reinforce his or her advice. Likewise, a husband and father who is attempting to protect his family from intruders may decide to buy dead-bolt locks for the home. Most likely he will not be aware of brand names. Therefore, price becomes an important cue to the sturdiness and dependability of different brands of locks.

Products that are affected by rapid changes in *technology* or products that are subject to changes in *style* and *fashion* confront consumers with new situations. Major changes in product features, functions, or style place consumers in less informed positions than they were before encountering the product. Thus they make consumers more sensitive to information cues such as price in order to evaluate product quality.

Snob Appeal   Some consumers use the price of a product as a means of expressing status or prestige. The price appeals to the snobbishness in the purchaser. "A person may know that the more expensive model is no better than the cheaper one and yet prefer it for the mere fact that it is more expensive. He may want his friends and neighbors to know that he can afford spending all that money, or he may feel that his prestige and social position require that he should always buy the most expensive of everything."[12] Products that are conspicuous are more likely to be purchased for their snob appeal.

Although a high price may enhance a brand's image, it may also price the brand out of the market for substantial groups of consumers.[13] Therefore, the costs of lost consumer groups must be weighed against the potential benefits of greater exclusivity, and thus higher status and snob appeal.

Confidence in One's Judgment   A consumer who has little confidence in his or her ability to make a good product choice will rely on price and other cues to a greater extent than will a more confident person. In purchasing a component stereo system, the confident and knowledgeable consumer is less likely to rely on price as an indication of quality, whereas the consumer who is unsure of himself

[11]John J. Wheatley and John S. Y. Chiu, "The Effects of Price, Store Image, and Product Respondent Characteristics on Perceptions of Quality," *Journal of Marketing Research,* Vol. 14, May 1977, pp. 181–186.

[12]Tibor Scitovsky, "Some Consequences of the Habit of Judging Quality by Price," *Review of Economic Studies,* Vol. 12, No. 2, 1944–1945, p. 103.

[13]K. V. Ventataraman, "The Price-Quality Relationship in an Experimental Setting," *Journal of Advertising Research,* Vol. 21, August 1983, p. 51.

or herself will tend to rely on price in making his or her evaluation of the stereo system's quality.

Those who tend to be the least confident in their ability to evaluate products are the poorer consumers and those with little education. These individuals are highly susceptible to price connotations.[14]

Psychological Effects in Pricing[15]

There are a number of observable, yet unsatisfactorily explained, phenomena of price effects on demand. They run contrary to the traditional economist's explanation of the price-demand relationship. Furthermore, they do not fall into the price-quality category just discussed.

One such phenomenon is called the **quantum effect** in pricing. The quantum effect is observed when increases in price up to a point do not result in a loss of sales volume, but a price beyond that point produces a rapid drop in sales. The point at which this quick change in sales occurs is called the *quantum point.* Consumers are insensitive to prices up to the quantum point but are highly sensitive to prices even slightly above this point. For example, a product can be priced at $9.55, $9.65, $9.75, or $9.95 without a drop in retail volume. However, a price of $10.05 results in a drastic drop in sales volume. In this case, $10 is the quantum point. The quantum effect is illustrated in Figure 22.3.

Another psychological pricing situation is **reverse direction price perception.** As the name implies, consumers reverse the numerical price scale and perceive lower prices as being higher than higher prices. For instance, a price set at $1.95 may appear lower than a price set at $1.45. This phenomenon can be explained in terms of reference points. Rounded dollar figures serve as reference points and tell the consumer that the $1.95 price is 5 cents *below* $2. On the other hand, the $1.45 price is 45 cents above $1. Thus, one price may appear higher, and the other lower because of their relationship to their reference points.

Another psychological effect in pricing deals with what consumers perceive as a fair price for a product. Consumers form a "fair price" for a product, which then serves as a **fair price standard.** Even for new products, consumers use similar products to judge what a fair price range should be. For example, many consumers probably use the price of a blender as a reference point in determining the fair (reasonable) price for a food processor. A price above the market's conception of the fair price will result in reduced sales. A price below the fair price standard is considered to reflect poor quality and also results in a low sales volume. The most acceptable price is one that falls within the consumer's fair price range, closest to the fair price standard.

---

[14]Shapiro, "The Psychology of Pricing," p. 25.

[15]This section is based largely upon Chester R. Wasson, "The Psychological Aspects of Price," *The Economics of Managerial Decisions: Profit Opportunity Analysis* (New York: Appleton-Century-Crofts, 1965), pp. 130–133.

CHAPTER 22   *Price and Place Communications*

FIGURE 22.3   **Illustration of the Quantum Effect Showing (a) the Relationship between Price and Volume and (b) the Relationship between Price and Dollar Sales**

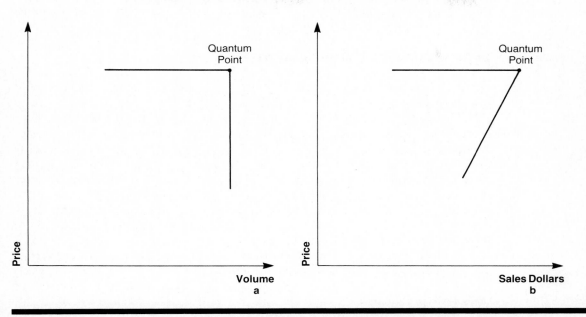

Source: M. Wayne DeLozier, *The Marketing Communications Process* (New York: McGraw-Hill, 1976), p. 196.

Consumers also use the concept of fair price with sale items. The perception of a sale price may depend on the position of the price in the range. If the price is below other offerings, buyers may perceive the item to be a bargain or they may not believe that the sale price is actually a reduction from the advertised original. It is possible, for example, that consumers may react more favorably if a $500 videocassette recorder were on sale for $350 than if it were advertised for $199.[16] Thus, the standard price range serves as an anchor, or reference point, for consumers' judgments. The end points of this range are clear in the consumer's mind and therefore can accentuate his or her perceptions of what is a bargain (or a piece of junk) and what is truly high quality (or overpriced).[17]

The final psychological aspect of price is the **cost price standard.** When consumers believe they can judge the producer's cost of a product, they develop a fair price estimate based on their judgment of the producer's cost plus a reasonable profit. For many industrial products, buyers have knowledge of the approximate costs in producing the product and refuse to pay a price above their estimate of

[16]Monroe, "Buyers' Subjective Perceptions of Price," p. 77.

[17]Ventataraman, "The Price-Quality Relationship," pp. 51–52.

the cost plus a reasonable profit. This is also true for some consumer products such as automobiles. Well-informed consumers can learn the cost of a car to the automobile dealer and offer, say, $150 above dealer cost for the car they want. Various consumer publications are available to assist consumers in their evaluations of what a fair or reasonable price is.

Desensitizing the Consumer to Price

As has already been discovered, many of the conventional economic notions about pricing are not appropriate to a total understanding of a consumer's response to price. In many cases consumers seem to be insensitive to variations in prices for brands of the same product category. The chapter has already explained that under various circumstances consumers use price as an indicator of quality, particularly in the absence of other meaningful cues. However, other conditions also affect consumer response to price; these conditions are the result of marketing activities that make consumers less sensitive to price. That is, in economic terms, price elasticity of demand becomes less elastic due to marketing efforts that effectively differentiate the marketer's offering. In these instances consumers tend to ignore price to some degree in arriving at a purchase decision.

One marketing activity that desensitizes consumers to price is *sales effectiveness.* An effective sales representative can often sell a product whether it is priced at $24.95 or at $39.95. The price difference is overcome by the persuasiveness of the sales representative.[18]

Another desensitizing factor is the effectiveness of the *local promotion and services.* Although a product may be supported by national advertising and sales promotions, local variations and supplements can often provide the additional impact necessary to make the sale, even though the brand may have a higher price than competitive brands. Amway and Avon both use this approach. The door-to-door and personal sales touch isolate them from competitors and allow them to extol the advantages of their products. The same sort of influence on the level of price sensitivity can result from variations in local service for a brand. Many consumers are willing to pay a higher price because a retailer provides local service on the product. Similarly, the reputation of serviceability of one local firm as opposed to another is a desensitizing factor. If one automobile dealership has a much better reputation than others in town, a higher price for the car will become a less important factor in the buyer's purchase decision.

A Summary of Noneconomic Factors in Pricing

The purpose of this first chapter section has been to emphasize the noneconomic factors affecting the pricing decision, especially those bearing on the communicative nature of price. A good pricing decision must necessarily rest upon a qualita-

---

[18]Richard T. Sampson, "Sense and Sensitivity in Pricing," *Harvard Business Review,* Vol. 42, November-December 1964, pp. 101–103.

tive and subjective assessment of both economic and noneconomic sets of information. The following list of questions is concerned primarily with noneconomic information that is useful in determining a product's price. A thorough evaluation of the market target should be made to answer questions such as the following:

1. To what extent do consumers perceive brand-to-brand variation in quality within the product category?
2. Is the product an important ingredient or component of another product?
3. Is the product purchased as a gift? If so, how frequently and when?
4. Is the product perceived by consumers as a new product? If so, how new?
5. Is the product purchased for special occasions? If so, for what occasions and when?
6. How strong is the brand's image within the market?
7. How knowledgeable and experienced are consumers with the product?
8. Does the brand have snob appeal and status possibilities for consumers?
9. How complex do consumers perceive the product to be?
10. What price does the market expect to pay for such a product?

The Role of Place in Marketing Communications

The distribution component, or *place* variable, in marketing deals with such matters as channels of distribution, middlemen, and the types of retail outlets that carry manufactured products. The discussion in this chapter section is restricted to the place variable's role as an important form of marketing communications. For this reason, the discussion focuses on the retailing component of place. The store performs an important marketing communications role by affecting the consumer's perception of the merchandise carried in the store, as well as the overall perception of the store itself.

All stores project a personality, or image, to consumers. Furthermore, the same store can have different images to different consumers. To the low– and middle-income groups, a high-fashion store may communicate extravagance, waste, and snobbishness. Furthermore, if these groups shop in this kind of store, it may evoke feelings of uneasiness. In contrast, a high-income group may perceive the same store as elegant, prestigious, and high styled.

A store's image is composed of many dimensions, each interacting with the others to influence the image various consumer groups hold for the store. Among the more important dimensions of a store's image are its architecture and exterior design, its interior design, its personnel, its lines of merchandise, its signs and logos, its advertising and sales promotions, its location, its postpurchase communications, and its services, displays, reputation, clientele, and name. How these dimensions interact with each other and the various consumer publics defines the store's image for each of these groups.

The various determinants of a store's image will be examined in the following section. Note that these dimensions are perceived within the context of all other dimensions of a store and may vary according to the characteristics of different consumer groups.

Dimensions of Store Image

Architecture and Exterior Design   Several aspects of a store's architecture and exterior design tell the consumer what to expect on the inside. The exterior is, in a sense, like the package on a product. And like the product inside the package, the inside of a store must deliver what the outside of the store promises to deliver to the consumer. A store's façade communicates considerable information to the prospective customer, such as the type and caliber of merchandise sold.[19]

Some of the components that make up the architecture and exterior design of a store are the physical size, the shape, the building materials used, the store front, and the lighting. *Physical size* can communicate strength, power, and security. In one large Midwestern city, a study revealed that consumers perceived bank X to be the strongest financially from among the other large city banks. In reality, bank X was the third largest bank in the city; however, it had recently completed the tallest building in town, and it could be seen from miles around.

A store's *shape* can communicate subtle meanings to consumers. Transamerica constructed its 853-foot-tall structure in the shape of a pyramid. The purpose of the building's shape was to create a suitable image for a previously "obscure" company and make it more widely known.[20] This structure, hovering over San Francisco, communicates that Transamerica is progressive and perhaps even ahead of its time (see Figure 22.4).

A *store's front* is usually the first part of the store with which consumers come in contact. The store front serves, in a sense, as the store's permanent advertisement. It provides information to consumers and conveys an impression about the store.[21] For example, the store front for Harrods, the famous London department store, evokes a feeling of grandeur and stateliness (see Figure 22.5).

Outside lighting also contributes to a store's beauty and image. The obvious reasons for outside lighting are adequacy for seeing, safety, and security. However, the proper lighting can contribute much in the way of aesthetics. Lighting must complement a store's architecture and clarify a store's form and texture. Outside lighting can create a specific buying atmosphere by telling prospective consumers that they are entering "an elegant place, a fun place, a homey place, an exciting place, a secure place, or a number of other kinds of settings a developer or retailer may think conducive to selling goods."[22]

A store's exterior appearance is determined to a large extent by the building *materials* used in constructing the store. The Royal Bank in Toronto communicates financial strength and solid banking security by the building it occupies. The

---

[19]Adolph Novak, *Store Planning and Design* (New York: Chain Store Publishing Corp., 1977), p. 51.

[20]Lloyd Shearer, "San Francisco's New Landmark—A Corporate Pyramid," *Parade,* January 14, 1973, p. 10.

[21]Novak, *Store Planning and Design.*

[22]"Outdoor Lighting: Six Checkpoints to the Best System for Your Center or Store," Crouse-Hinds Lighting Products Division, Bulletin 2876.

FIGURE 22.4   **Transamerica Building in San Francisco: Illustration of How a Building's Physical Size and Shape Communicate with Consumers**

Source: Courtesy of Transamerica Corporation.

FIGURE 22.5   **Harrods in London: Illustration of the Communication Role of a Store's Exterior**

Source: Courtesy of the British Tourist Authority, 40 West 57th Street, New York, New York 10019.

Royal Bank has an exterior of glass. The interesting feature about this glass is that each pane has been dipped in actual gold dust! The communication value is obvious (see Figure 22.6).

One last exterior feature deserving mention is customer *entrances.* In general, customer entrances should be wide and inviting, telling customers that they are welcome to the store.[23]

Interior Design   Once the prospective customer is in the door, the store must continue to communicate an image consistent with that of the store's exterior. Some of the components of the store's interior design are color scheme, fixtures, lighting, and aisles.

The *color scheme* in a store is one of the prime factors affecting buyer moods. As mentioned in the previous chapter, colors have different emotional qualities, and these emotional qualities must be appropriate for the kind of clientele served, as well as the class of merchandise being sold. For example, a store with a sophisticated clientele would probably be advised to use more subtle colors than an average middle-class store would use.[24]

Hot colors such as red, orange, and peach affect the autonomic nervous system and therefore increase blood circulation, heart rate, muscular activity, and even sociability. These colors can also stimulate appetite and thirst. Thus, many fast-food restaurants use these appealing colors. Nightclubs frequently use the more relaxing colors of blue and associated hues to calm their customers and induce them to stay awhile. Bright orange and yellow colors are suggested for retailers who sell bland-colored products, such as those often found in hardware stores.[25]

The colors of the walls in a store should not be neutral or white. Instead, the colors should be strong, and they should vary from wall to wall so that people will move around to see the variety of products the store has to offer. An exception, however, is for the high-fashion store, where customers wish to take their time in a calmer atmosphere (cooler colors). Finally, the colors in a store should also be related to the colors of the merchandise and what is in fashion.[26]

Colors can modify physical characteristics in a store. It has been suggested that light, cool tones (of the blue family) be used to give the appearance of additional spaciousness to a small store, while deep warm tones (such as brown) on a narrow distant wall and light cool tones on long side walls can be used to make a long narrow store appear shorter and wider.[27]

In general, colors are useful in highlighting particular areas of a store and in displaying merchandise. Moreover, color can create a pleasant working and shop-

---

[23]Delbert J. Duncan, Charles F. Phillips, and Stanley C. Hollander, *Modern Retailing Management* (Homewood, IL: Richard D. Irwin, 1972), p. 107.

[24]Eric P. Danger, *How To Use Color To Sell* (Boston: Cahners Publishing Company, 1969), p. 91.

[25]Nory Miller, "Spaces for Selling," *American Institute of Architects Journal,* Vol. 67, July 1978, p. 38.

[26]Ibid.

[27]Louis Cheskin, *Color for Profit* (New York: Liveright Publishing Corporation, 1951), pp. 65–66.

FIGURE 22.6 **The Royal Bank in Toronto: Illustration of the
Communication Role of Building Materials**

ping atmosphere by reflecting a store's friendliness and concern for its salespeople and customers.

In-store *fixtures and lighting* can communicate elegance, traditionalism, conservatism, and a host of other feelings. Fixtures come in wood, metal, and glass. The kind of fixtures a store selects should be based on the clientele it wishes to attract. The following example illustrates the importance of fixtures and lighting in contributing to a store's personality.

> *A leading Southern department store originally possessed a distinctive image emphasizing the traditionalist values of its city. The lighting and fixtures were old-fashioned, and the total store atmosphere was congruent with the city-wide interest in antiques, old families, old homes, old restaurants, and historical monuments. Then the women's apparel merchandiser modernized his department. He introduced new fixtures and lighting, more high-fashion styling, and a promotional flavor similar to any aggressive store in this field. The fortunes of the store declined in a definite progression—first women's apparel, then children's, then men's, and finally all hard-line departments. A management consultant determined that the store had dissipated the strongest component in its image, the key to which lay in the women's apparel department. It had become indistinguishable from any other store. On his advice, the store set about restoring its traditionalist, distinctively period personality. The old-fashioned lights and fixtures and ultra-conservative styling were brought back. As management reformulated the symbolic meaning which had given the store distinction and character, its fortunes changed sharply for the better in the same progression as they had declined—first women's apparel and ultimately the hard-lines.*[28]

Interior *lighting*, like outside lighting, has several obvious functional features. Customers must have ample illumination to see the merchandise the store is offering, and lighting can serve to reduce shoplifting. Moreover, lighting should highlight specific areas of the store and increase the effectiveness of store displays. In particular, retailers should use lighting in much the same way theatres and dramatic plays do—to accentuate major departments and boutiques while diminishing the intensity of aisle lighting.[29]

From a communications viewpoint, lighting must be coordinated with color schemes and store design to create the intended atmosphere. Lights too intense can create consumer discomfort and irritation. Therefore, proper light intensity, direction, and color should be used to contribute to a store's desired image.

Other interior design considerations need only be mentioned. Store counters can be inviting or awesome. Counters that are built too high overwhelm some

---

[28]Pierre Martineau, "The Personality of the Retail Store," *Harvard Business Review,* Vol. 36, January-February 1958, pp. 50–51.

[29]Novak, *Store Planning and Design,* p. 145.

shoppers and make customers feel as though they are being crushed.[30] Aisles that are spacious and uncluttered can be significant in producing a relaxed and pleasurable shopping experience. On the surface, these factors and others mentioned earlier may appear unimportant; however, all of them contribute to the way a customer *feels* during a shopping experience.

One study summarizes this section well. Donovan and Rossiter conducted research on store atmosphere and its relationship to other store image variables. They found that consumers view store atmosphere (composed of a combination of such variables as lighting, layout, color, and music) as relatively important compared with shopping hours, parking access, travel time, product assortment, price, and service. They also found that degree of arousal and perceived pleasantness of the store atmosphere influenced (1) enjoyment of shopping, (2) time spent browsing, (3) willingness to talk to sales personnel, (4) tendency to spend more money than originally planned, and (5) likelihood of returning to the store.[31] Such research suggests that if store surroundings are pleasant, increasing customer levels of arousal may increase patronage. Conversely, if pleasantness is not a characteristic of the store (such as is the case with some factory outlets) arousal should be kept at a low level (low lights, soft music, etc.).

Store Personnel Perhaps the most important determinant of a store's image is its personnel. Salespeople interact directly with customers and by their actions can alter considerably the image projected by other image determinants. If the salespeople are friendly, courteous, and knowledgeable, customers are much more likely to develop a favorable image toward the store. The importance of sales personnel in building a store's image cannot be overstressed. Studies have documented the importance of sales personnel in contributing to the consumer's total impression of retail stores.[32]

Factors other than a salesperson's personality affect the customers' impression of the store. For instance, a salesperson's age, sex, and physical mannerisms may affect customers' image of a store. A mature customer may not want a youthful person waiting on him or her. Under some circumstances, some people are embarrassed or uncomfortable when members of the opposite sex wait on them. In general, when salespeople are similar to customers and live up to their customers' expectations, those customers are more likely to view the retail store in a favorable way. Discussion in Chapter 6 previously elaborated on the importance of source and receiver similarity

Not to be overlooked under the topic of *store personnel* are the checkers, stock clerks, and baggers at supermarkets and the service and maintenance personnel at nearly all stores. A department store, for example, can spend considerable amounts

---

[30]Martineau, "The Personality of the Retail Store," p. 51.

[31]Robert J. Donovan and John R. Rossiter, "Store Atmosphere: An Environmental Psychology Approach," *Journal of Retailing,* Vol. 58, Spring 1982, pp. 34–57.

[32]For example, see Martineau, "The Personality of the Retail Store," p. 53; Michael Perry and Nancy J. Norton, "Dimensions of Store Image," *Southern Journal of Business,* Vol. 5, April 1970, pp. 1–7.

of money on image building through its advertising, hiring and training of sales personnel, store decor, and so on and can have one repairman destroy all these efforts in one day on a service call.[33] Thus, all of a store's personnel play an integral part in building a store's image.

The implication of this discussion is that store management should devote more effort toward careful selection and training of all personnel. All the money put into making the exterior and interior of a store attractive to customers, the careful selection of the appropriate merchandise for its clientele, and the other efforts to create the desired store image can be negated through improper selection and training of store personnel.

Merchandise   The kind of merchandise a store carries reflects upon its image. The quality, price, assortment, and quantity of merchandise tell the consumer several things. A store that carries high-quality, high-priced merchandise may impress the customer favorably. For example, many supermarkets have specialty sections— delis, cheese shops, fresh seafood departments, wine shops, etc.—that enhance the store's image in the customer's eyes. In effect, the supermarket is saying, "We not only provide the necessities, we also provide the finer things in life."

A store that invests heavily in merchandise and has a wide assortment of merchandise, as well as depth in each line, is telling the customer, "We have everything imaginable and plenty of it. If we don't have it, nobody does." This phenomenon is termed **classification dominance.** For any given class of goods, hand tools for instance, a store that carries a wide assortment and has great depth in each line is practicing classification dominance. Consumers come to the store confident that they can find the right kind of hand tools to suit their needs. *Hypermarkets* are one example of stores' utilizing classification dominance.[34] These huge stores stack merchandise as high as 32 feet and seem to carry every conceivable line of merchandise. Although these stores are proliferating throughout France and other parts of Europe, there is some question about the application of the hypermarket concept to North American markets. Stein's in Montreal and Jewel in Chicago have adapted this concept. More recently, the first true hypermarket in the United States has been opened in Cincinnati.

Signs and Logos   Many retailers realize that the signs they put up in front of their establishments perform an important function beyond merely catching the consumer's attention and identifying their stores. A store's sign and its logo tell customers something about a store's personality. "A sign can say 'discount' or 'high fashion' with color and design as well as with words. More and more signs are geared to do just that."[35]

[33]James U. McNeal, *An Introduction to Consumer Behavior* (New York: John Wiley & Sons, 1973), pp. 217–218.

[34]See Bernice Finkelman, "New Intelligence System Keeps Tabs on Rapidly Changing Retail Scene," *Marketing News,* October 15, 1973, pp. 8–9.

[35]"Chains Sign Up for Proper Image," *Chain Store Age,* December 1972, p. 37.

J. C. Penney changed its logo to project a "family image" for its stores.[36] K Mart's sign tells consumers that its stores are "bright, big, and clean."[37] The new Holiday Inn sign projects a rather sophisticated, modern look in comparison to the previously garish, and somewhat carnival-looking, sign for this motel chain. Furthermore, the signs at most fast-food places such as McDonald's, Burger King, and Wendy's use "appetizing" colors that relate to food—red, yellow, orange, and brown.

Retail Advertising Retail advertising can develop consumer images of stores, even for consumers who are unfamiliar with a store. As an example, a study of retail grocery advertisements took characteristic advertisements of several Chicago chains to different parts of the country where the shoppers were totally unfamiliar with the stores. The judgments of women who knew nothing whatever about the stores were remarkably similar to the opinions of Chicago women who were familiar with the stores.[38]

Perhaps more important than the content of a store's advertisement is its general *style and tone.* Consumers forget much of what the advertiser says, yet they retain a general feeling about a store based on the overall style and tone of its advertisements. Consumers perceive various art styles, typography, and tones as cues to a store's personality. Thus, the symbolism used in a store's advertising is a cue to its overall image and must be consistent with the personality the store projects throught its design, store personnel, and other image cues. The symbolic meaning of the advertising must, in other words, be consistent with the character of the store itself.[39]

When deciding upon the content of a store's advertising message, a retailer must consider the image dimensions that best differentiate its store from competitors. Moreover, it should stress factors that are most likely to have a positive impact on its target market.

Store Location Location affects a store's image in two ways. First, a store's *geographic* location segments its market. If a store locates in a high-income suburban locality, its clientele are likely to be different than had the store located in a moderate-income area. To be successful, store management must tailor the store's image to the locale or select a location that fits the image management wants to project.

In addition to geographic location, the location within a shopping center and the adjacent stores affect a store's image. Sometimes shopping centers are simply a miscellaneous collection of stores put side by side without regard to the conflict-

---

[36]Ibid.

[37]Ibid.

[38]Martineau, "The Personality of the Retail Store," p. 52.

[39]Ibid.

ing images these stores may have. If the stores in a shopping center have conflicting images, the result is likely to be confusion for the shopper. When stores have consistent images within a shopping center, the effect is likely to be synergistic, resulting in greater success for all stores.

Postpurchase Communications

Postpurchase communications refers to the communications a company has with consumers after the sale is made. The primary purpose of this kind of communications is to help consumers reduce cognitive dissonance they may experience during the postpurchase period. Businesses do not thrive on initial sales to consumers; rather, they succeed on the basis of repeat business. Assurance of future purchases and a more favorable store image can result from retailers' taking time to communicate with buyers after a sale.

Retailers have primarily two ways to communicate with consumers after a sale—by letter and by telephone. Of the two methods, the posttransaction letter appears to be superior. One study that compared the two methods found that consumers who received a letter after their purchase were less dissonant, had more favorable attitudes toward the store, and were more likely to purchase from the store in the future.[40] This same study found posttransaction telephone calls to be counterproductive. People who had been called by telephone felt greater dissonance, held less favorable attitudes toward the store, and were less inclined to purchase from the store in the future. Many consumers have had unpleasant experiences associated with past telephone conversations with sales representatives, which may account for the negative responses to the telephone call.[41]

Other Factors Affecting Store Image

A few additional factors that affect store image will be mentioned. One is *store services*. Services such as credit, delivery, and return and exchange policies affect how a consumer will view a store. Store *displays* communicate a store's offering, as well as tell the consumer something about the store's personality. Still other information that helps consumers form their impressions of a store are word-of-mouth references and the customers they see shopping at a store. The latter two factors are somewhat beyond a store's control, except to the extent that the store can attract the desired clientele and make favorable impressions on them so that favorable word-of-mouth is fostered.

Store names, like brand names, can communicate valuable information to consumers about a store's image. A store's name is particularly important when the store is new to an area or when consumers move from other parts of the country to a new area. For example, the name Family Dollar Store effectively communicates what kind of store it is compared with the name Howard's Store. The name Parisian Dress Shop suggests a certain elegance in women's wear, which Jones's Dress Shop does not.

---

[40]Shelby D. Hunt, "Post-Transaction Communications and Dissonance Reduction," *Journal of Marketing,* Vol. 34, July 1970, p. 50.

[41]Ibid.

A final effective communication device many retail stores use is *background music.* Background music can improve a store's image, make employees happier, reduce employee turnover, and stimulate customer purchasing.[42] In addition to background music, many stores are experimenting with *foreground* music. This type of music is, as the name suggests, "out front" and intended to be heard as soon as the customer enters the store. The music is chosen to be compatible with the listening interests of the store's clientele. Thus, a store catering to teenagers may use loud rock music, whereas a store appealing to middle-aged professionals would perhaps select a repertoire of classical music.[43]

Summary

This chapter examines the marketing communications roles of two nonpromotional mix variables—price and place—by describing how these variables evoke meanings within consumers and how they interact with other marketing communications variables.

The marketing communications role of price stems from consumers' tendency to use price as an indicator of product quality. This tendency is most pronounced when (1) consumers perceive high brand-to-brand variance in quality within a product category; (2) the product is viewed by the consumer as an important additive, ingredient, or component of a larger product or its use contributes significantly to the quality of the final product; (3) the product is purchased as a gift; (4) brands of a product are physically homogeneous and brand names are unfamiliar to consumers; (5) the product is new to a market; (6) consumers lack experience and information about a product; (7) consumers wish to express status or prestige in using a product; and (8) consumers lack confidence in their ability to make a good product choice decision.

In addition to the price-imputed quality relationship, the chapter addresses several additional psychological effects in pricing: (1) the *quantum effect,* (2) *reverse direction price perception,* (3) the *fair price standard,* and (4) the *cost price standard.* This section of the chapter concludes with a discussion of factors that seem to desensitize consumers to product prices. These include salesperson persuasiveness, promotion and services, manufacturer reputation, and consumer loyalty.

Turning to the place variable, focus is directed to how retail stores project personalities and to what factors determine a store's image. Among the more impor-

---

[42]Ronald E. Millman, "Using Background Music To Affect the Behavior of Supermarket Shoppers," *Journal of Marketing,* Vol. 46, Summer 1982, p. 91.

[43]Information about foreground music was acquired from an interview conducted by National Public Radio with an executive from Audio Environments, a Seattle, Washington firm that specializes in developing foreground music for retail stores. The NPR program was broadcast on January 4, 1985. This same program revealed that according to a recent Gallup study, 91 percent of the respondents to a survey indicated that music in retail stores affects their shopping behavior.

tant dimensions of a store's image are its architecture and exterior design, its interior design, its store personnel, its lines of merchandise, its signs and logos, its advertising and sales promotions, its location, its postpurchase communications, and its services, displays, reputation, clientele, and store name.

Discussion Questions

1. Why do consumers rely upon price as an indicator of product quality?
2. How may advertising desensitize consumers to a high price? Give several examples to support your answer.
3. How may a price that consumers perceive to be too low suppress sales?
4. Do you feel the consumer is getting "cheated" when he or she purchases a brand that is "status-priced?" Why or why not?
5. Consider the following products: (a) an automobile, (b) a pair of running shoes, (c) a new navy blue suit for job interviewing, (d) a set of automobile tires, (e) a bag of nachos, (f) an electric pencil sharpener, (g) a video cassette recorder, (h) a diamond ring. Which of these products lend themselves to "quality pricing?" For those that do, what noneconomic factors may be present to permit such a pricing strategy?
6. To what extent can personal selling be an effective desensitizing factor in prices for the following products: (a) cameras, (b) microcomputers, (c) living room furniture, (d) automobiles, (e) tennis shoes?
7. A variety of factors influence the tendency for ultimate consumers to impute product quality from price cues. Which of the factors discussed in the text would also apply to industrial buyers? For example, would industrial buyers tend to rely upon price as an indicator of quality when there is brand-to-brand variance in quality within a product category?
8. What factors contribute to a retail store's image? Select a store in your college/university community and describe the factors that contribute to your image of that store.
9. In what ways can a retailer project a quality-store image? A value-store image? A discount-store image?
10. Why is postpurchase communications important to retailers? Other than letters and telephone calls, how else could retailers reduce postpurchase dissonance?

Exercises

1. Architectural and exterior design features play important roles in communicating meaning to consumers. For each of the following features, provide two illustrations of retail establishments in your university/college community and explain what the feature communicates to you: (a) physical size, (b) shape, (c) store façade, (d) outside lighting, (e) building materials, (f) signs and logos. (*Note:* You should use different retail establishments to illustrate each feature.)

2.   With reference to the first exercise, follow its directions, but this time select retail establishments to illustrate the following interior design features: (a) color schemes, (b) in-store fixtures, (c) in-store lighting.

3.   Identify five product categories in which there is one brand that charges premium prices in comparison with other brands in that category. For each product category, provide a detailed explanation of how the "premium pricer" is able to charge higher prices than competitors. Be sure to relate your explanations to the chapter's discussion of specific product and consumer characteristics that influence the likelihood that consumers will impute quality from price.

PART VI

Conclusion

Part VI of this book consists of Chapter 23 and is designed to provide a brief integration of the marketing communications and promotion management concepts and techniques that have been discussed throughout the text. An overall, strategic marketing communications framework is illustrated by a case description involving a not-for-profit organization. The case deals specifically with a fascinating and highly successful application of communications theory and tools by the U.S. Agency for International Development (AID). The AID assisted the governments of The Gambia and Honduras in lowering the number of infant deaths that occur in these countries from diarrheal dehydration. The case shows how all facets of promotion management can and should be integrated and also illustrates the suitability of applying conventional business tools to nonbusiness problems.

CHAPTER 23

Integrated Marketing Communications and Promotion Programs

This chapter provides a summary and an integration of the vast variety of marketing communications and promotion topics that have been presented throughout the text. To accomplish this, the chapter presents a detailed case history of an extraordinarily effective communications program that was designed by the U.S. Agency for International Development and was implemented in Honduras and The Gambia to combat diarrheal dehydration—a malady that annually kills 7 out of 20 infants in the developing world![1]

Although the text has focused thus far on commercial applications of marketing communications, it is appropriate to demonstrate how communications and promotional techniques can also be used to combat serious societal problems. Indeed, during the past two decades dozens of campaigns involving such topics as smoking, alcoholism, energy conservation, forest fires, venereal disease, and seat belts have attempted to inform, motivate, and change the behavior of millions of Americans.

Figure 23.1 provides the framework for the remaining discussion. This same framework, it may be recalled, was presented previously in Chapter 1. It now provides a very appropriate "bookend" to demonstrate how various marketing

---

[1]*After Twelve Months of Broadcasting: A Status Report on the Project in Honduras and The Gambia* (Washington, DC: Academy for Educational Development, Inc., January 1984).

FIGURE 23.1   The Promotion Management Process Revisited

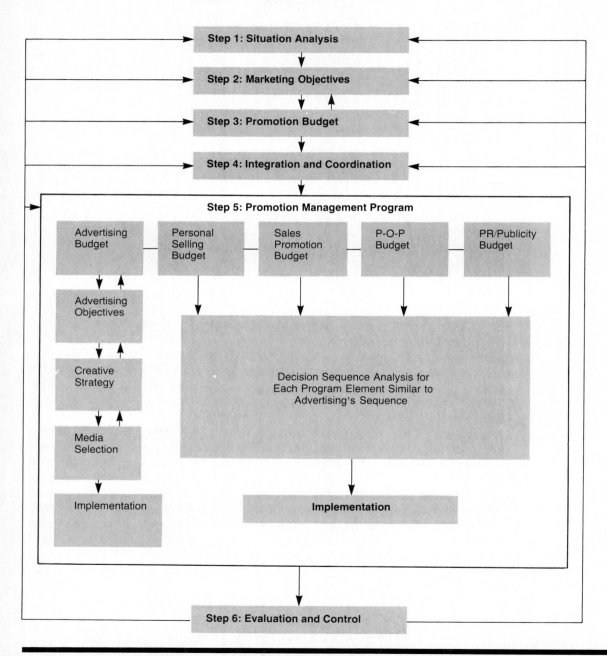

Source: Adapted from Michael C. Ray, "A Decision Sequence Analysis of Developments in Marketing Communication," *Journal of Marketing,* Vol. 37, January 1973, p. 31; and James F. Engel, Martin R. Warshaw, and Thomas C. Kinnear, *Promotional Strategy,* 5th. Ed. (Homewood, IL: Richard D. Irwin, Inc. 1983), p. 34.

communication and promotional tools can be coordinated to accomplish important social objectives.

Figure 23.1 represents the promotion management process in terms of six major steps: situation analysis, marketing objectives, promotion budget, integration and coordination, promotion management program, and evaluation and control. Each of these steps will be discussed as they apply to the oral rehydration programs implemented in Honduras and The Gambia. The chapter then concludes with a description of the procedure for designing a formal marketing communications plan.

Teaching Mothers Oral Rehydration Therapy

Diarrhea is one of the world's leading killers. Every year, 5 million children under the age of five die due to diarrheal dehydration.[2] Children in developing countries normally have diarrhea several times a year. Local practice often leads a mother to purge the child and to withhold food or stop breast-feeding when she realizes that the diarrhea bout is more severe than usual. The mother does not realize that dehydration, caused by the diarrhea, is the problem. Dehydration advances rapidly, and the child loses his or her appetite and the capacity to absorb vital liquids. Death can follow within hours.

Working with the Ministries of Health in Honduras and The Gambia, the U.S. Agency for International Development (AID), Bureau for Science and Technology, Offices of Education and Health, and its contractors (experts in health, communications, anthropology, evaluation and behavioral psychology) developed a public health education program to deliver oral rehydration therapy (ORT) to large numbers of rural and isolated people threatened by diarrheal dehydration. Using mass media, simple printed materials, and health worker training, rural women were taught what ORT is, how to use it in the home, and how to monitor their child's progress during the diarrheal episode.[3] The programs in Honduras and in The Gambia began in January 1980 and May 1981, respectively. Both programs extended for three full years.

The Situation Analysis

Oral rehydration therapy (ORT) is an established medical treatment for combatting an infant's loss of body fluid and electrolytes during a diarrheal episode. The therapy involves having mothers administer an oral rehydration solution to their children. The solution is either prepackaged or can be made simply at home by mixing appropriate portions of sugar, salt, and water. The solution is administered to a dehydrated child at the rate of approximately one liter per day.

---

[2]Anthony J. Meyer, Clifford H. Block, and Donald C.E. Ferguson, "Teaching Mothers Oral Rehydration," *Horizons,* Vol. 2, April 1983, pp. 14–20. The remaining discussion borrows liberally from this source.
[3]*After Twelve Months,* p. 1.

The key to effective ORT is the correct preparation and administration of the oral rehydration solution (ORS). Mothers must know how to mix the ingredients in exact proportions to avoid ineffective or potentially dangerous concentrations of sodium. They must also know how to give the solution correctly, i.e., slowly and continuously over a 24-hour period even if a child vomits or refuses the liquid.

The job confronting the AID was how to design a communications and promotional program that would teach mothers a new form of behavior. The Academy for Educational Development, the chief consultant to AID, characterized the task this way: "Our task is to alter the likelihood of people doing things [i.e., mixing and administering an oral rehydration solution] which are well within their capacities, but currently unlikely. The emphasis is on behavior. Attitudes, even those which may contribute to what people do, are of secondary importance."[4]

A number of important questions had to be answered: (1) Who in the total population should be selected as the principal audience? (2) What communication channels are most appropriate for these people? (3) What behaviors should be advocated? (4) What resources are needed to conduct the program? Preprogram research was conducted in both Honduras and The Gambia to assist planners in thoroughly understanding the problem that the subsequent communication and promotion programs would address.[5]

A combination of research methods (focus groups, surveys, in-depth interviews, product preference trials, etc.) were designed to provide answers to the preceding questions. Among the many findings, the research uncovered some traditional health beliefs with which the communication programs would have to deal. Rural Gambian mothers most often attributed diarrhea to some natural cause, such as dirt or wind, or to some supernatural cause. In Honduras, there was a widespread belief that diarrhea is caused by *"la bolsa,"* a sack believed to exist in everyone and to contain worms, which leave the sack after becoming agitated.

Another important research finding offered insight regarding how to promote ORS—whether as a fancy new medicine, as a traditional tea, or as a new local remedy. It had been assumed prior to the research that mothers would prefer a "product" that was similar to their existing method for treating diarrhea, namely, an herbal tea solution. This assumption was shown by the research evidence to be incorrect—mothers seemed to prefer a modern medicine for treating diarrhea rather than the herbal tea.

The research further revealed that mothers, contrary to preresearch fears, were able to mix the ORS solution in the correct proportions. They learned the mixing instructions very quickly, after only one or two explanations, even when the instructions were delivered via a tape recorder.

---

[4]Ibid., p. 7.

[5]The following description of the preprogram research is from Elizabeth M. Booth and Mark Rasmuson, "Traditional and Empirical Inputs in Program Design: The Role of Formative Evaluation in the Mass Media and Health Practice Project," Washington, DC: Academy for Educational Development, Inc. May 1984.

Overall, the preprogram research resulted in a detailed communications program consisting of (1) behavioral objectives, (2) target audience selection, (3) specific instructional messages, (4) culturally appropriate message formats, (5) plans for media use and integration, and (6) complete plan of action.

Objectives

Several local practices and beliefs that contribute to dehydration were singled out for modification. These included the practice of mothers' purging and withholding food from infants and the belief that breast milk causes diarrhea. Most important of all, however, was the goal to get mothers to administer the proper oral rehydration solution and thereby reduce the number of infant deaths caused by diarrhea.

In the final analysis, the success of the program depended on providing a large number of people with information they would find important and practical. To be successful, the program had to "make an impact on the consciousness of the intended audience by rising above the everyday clutter of advice and suggestions to become an important new priority in their lives. It must change what people do as well as what they think and believe. . . . It requires: a sensitive understanding of how people are affected by specific health problems, articulate crafting of useful and practical educational messages, and a coordinated distribution network that reaches each individual through various channels simultaneously."[6]

The Budget

The communication programs in Honduras and The Gambia were, as will be seen shortly, remarkably successful. Yet, the results were accomplished with very small budgets. Figure 23.2 illustrates the total costs and specific cost categories for each country. Costs exclude technical assistance from the U.S. Agency for International Development but include local salaries, benefits, travel, transportation, research, printing, production, and broadcast. Costs were significantly lower in The Gambia because (1) air time was provided free, (2) commercial printing costs were much lower, and (3) preprogram research costs were lower because the prior experience in Honduras permitted significant savings.[7]

The first-year expenditures in Honduras amounted to $135,000, of which $18,000 (approximately 13%) involved the combination of expenses for preprogram research and ongoing monitoring. The remaining $117,000 was spent on various communication media that were used to educate Honduran mothers about oral rehydration therapy. There were, for example, 29,000 radio broadcasts aired at a cost of $33,000 during the first year in Honduras.

[6]*After Twelve Months*, p. 8.
[7]Ibid., p. 25.

FIGURE 23.2   **First-Year Budgets for Honduras and The Gambia**

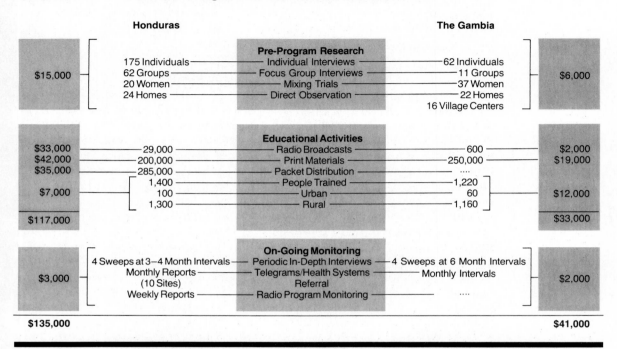

Source: After Twelve Months of Broadcasting: A Status Report on the Project in Honduras and The Gambia,
(Washington, DC: Academy for Educational Development, January 1984).

Total first-year expenditures in The Gambia amounted to $41,000. Approximately 20 percent ($8,000) was invested in preprogram research and ongoing monitoring, with the remaining $33,000 spent on educational activities.

Integration and Coordination

All successful marketing communication programs require that the various promotion mix elements work together to accomplish overall marketing objectives. To achieve optimal effectiveness, advertising campaigns, sales promotion techniques, and publicity releases must be integrated with one another and coordinated with personal selling efforts.

The success of the programs in Honduras and The Gambia depended on the combination of three communication media: radio broadcasts, print materials, and person-to-person communications using health workers and community volunteers. The careful integration of broadcast, print, and face-to-face support was essential. Radio alerted hundreds of thousands of Hondurans and Gambians about ORT. In Honduras, radio taught mothers how to measure a liter using local bottles. In The Gambia, radio taught mothers to understand the printed mixing instructions. Printed materials and graphics (posters and flags) helped mothers recall what to do at the actual time of using ORT. Health workers, who contacted mothers individually or in small groups, provided the needed credibility for key messages delivered by radio and in print.

Implementation and Program Management[8]

The Program in Honduras   The communications program in Honduras was directed to two target groups: (1) a primary audience of rural mothers/grandmothers with children under the age of five and to community volunteer health care workers called *guardianes* and (2) a secondary audience of physicians, nurses, fathers of children under five, rural schoolteachers and schoolchildren, and regional health promoters. The program was designed to teach the primary audience the proper preparation and administration of a prepackaged oral rehydration solution, called Litrosol, to children and to teach the secondary audience to support the primary audience by encouraging the use of ORT.

Litrosol, the prepackaged oral rehydration formula, was widely publicized through posters, pamphlets, and radio programs. A central campaign theme was developed around the concept of a loving image—a red heart was chosen as the central visual symbol to signify the love that mothers have for their children. Thousands of spot radio broadcasts and dozens of weekly programs were broadcast on carefully selected local stations. The programs built upon the loving theme that was used in print materials. Local health workers and health professionals were trained to use and promote Litrosol. A simple flag with the red heart symbol was given to each trained health worker. Radio programs announced that Litrosol was available at houses that displayed the red heart flag.

The integration of radio, graphics, and health workers proved to be a powerful combination.[9] Several dramatic results occurred within a year: (1) nearly half of the entire sample of mothers had tried Litrosol at least once; (2) recognition of Litrosol as a diarrheal remedy went from 0 percent to 93 percent; (3) knowledge levels concerning the procedure for mixing Litrosol received over 90 percent correct responses; (4) nearly 90 percent of mothers knew to continue breast-feeding during diarrheal bouts; and (5) a 40 percent drop in the percentage of deaths involving diarrhea was achieved.

The Program in The Gambia   The primary audience for the program in The Gambia was rural mothers, grandmothers, and older female siblings of children under five. The secondary market consisted of various health care workers (health inspectors, nurses, etc.). The communication program was designed (1) to teach the primary audience to mix a simple sugar and salt (S/S) rehydration solution properly and to administer the solution along with breastmilk and soft foods during

---

[8]The following discussion summarizes the presentation found in two sources: *After Twelve Months*, pp. 10–32 and Meyer, Block, and Ferguson, "Teaching Mothers Oral Rehydration," pp. 16–20.

[9]Summative evaluation was conducted under a AID contract to Stanford University Institute for Communication Research. This data is from their extensive evaluation activities and not the AEP formative research.

episodes of diarrhea and (2) to teach the secondary audience to mix and administer the S/S solution properly and to take care of moderate and severe diarrhea in the health centers.

Accomplishing these objectives required some creative thinking, because most people in The Gambia are unfamiliar with print materials of any kind. The creative solution involved a national contest, which began with the distribution of 200,000 copies of a color-coded flyer that provided instructions for the correct mixing and administering of the S/S solution. In conjunction with the flyers, radio announcements literally led listeners through each panel of the color-coded flyer. Mothers were repeatedly told how to mix the formula, how to administer it, what to do in the case of vomiting, and when to know they were getting results. Radio announcers also told them about other mothers with "happy baby" flags flying over their homes. These flags served as a symbol to people of the village that the "happy baby" home was a source of information on the diarrhea medicine.

Another element in the program was a prize giveaway contest. Any mother could win a prize—a plastic liter container or a bar of soap wrapped in a label with the "happy baby" symbol printed on it—by demonstrating to a health care worker that she could mix the S/S solution correctly. Winning mothers' names were included in a drawing for 15 radios. Follow-up radio programs used the testimonials of "happy baby" winners to continually reinforce the value and importance of the sugar, salt, and water solution. There was also a community prize each week for the village turning out the most mothers for the contest. The contest was concluded with a one-hour radio broadcast when The Gambian president's wife announced the names of grand prize winners.

The integrated communication program in The Gambia yielded some dramatic results, just as it had in Honduras. After eight months of the program, 66 percent of mothers knew the correct home mix solution, and 47 percent reported having used the solution to treat their children's diarrhea (Stanford data).

Evaluation and Control

Sophisticated promotion management requires that all programs be measured for effectiveness and that corrective action be taken when necessary. At six-month intervals, evaluation research was conducted to determine the amount of learning to date among target audiences and to identify strengths and weaknesses in the promotional campaign. Program monitoring in Honduras, for example, detected that mothers did not understand the concept of dehydration nor did they associate it with diarrhea and Litrosol. Therefore, subsequent promotional activity deemphasized the abstract concept of dehydration and focused instead on the physical manifestations of dehydration. This change in emphasis resulted in an increase from 20 percent to 77 percent of mothers who understood the signs of dehydration.[10]

[10]Booth and Rasmuson, "Traditional and Empirical Inputs."

A Wrap-up

The ORT programs in Honduras and The Gambia illustrate the use of some very sophisticated communication efforts. There are, in fact, four features of the oral rehydration program that could serve as models for any marketing communication endeavor.

Communication Grounded in Research   Marketing communicators sometimes jump immediately to the tasks of creating messages and selecting media before they have a thorough understanding of the marketplace. Such an approach stands a good chance of failure unless the intended audience is one with which the marketing communicator has had extensive prior experience. Many communication programs are doomed to failure because companies have not done their homework in adequately understanding the marketplace in terms of its culture, values, beliefs, stereotypes, and behavioral habits.

The project directors for the ORT program did not commit such a mistake. They conducted extensive preprogram research in both Honduras and The Gambia prior to designing communication programs for these countries. The information acquired from this research enabled the project directors to develop communication programs that were compatible with the beliefs, attitudes, and health care practices of both mothers and health care workers.

Use of Unifying Creative Message Themes   Another mistake committed by many marketing communicators is the failure to design communication programs around a central creative theme. In the absence of a unifying theme, programs tend to flounder and lack direction and meaning.

Such a mistake was not made in Honduras or The Gambia. The loving theme with the red heart symbol in Honduras and the happy baby theme in The Gambia provided unifying forces for the communication programs in these countries. By directing communication efforts around these themes, the chances were increased substantially that mothers would gain awareness of the ORT programs and become sufficiently motivated to learn how to mix the oral rehydration solution properly and administer it when necessary.

Coordination of Communication Efforts   Three communication channels—radio, print, and interpersonal—were carefully coordinated to accomplish communication objectives. Through radio, mothers learned about the oral rehydration solution, pamphlets and flyers provided instructions for its proper mixing and administration, and the availability of trained health care workers—with red heart and happy baby flags flying over their homes—enhanced the credibility of the ORT program and provided another source of information for mothers who required additional assistance.

Monitoring Program Performance   Another mistake marketing communicators commit is to fail to monitor communication programs to determine whether they are working as originally intended. Project directors in Honduras and The Gambia avoided this mistake by performing ongoing research to assure that the programs were, in fact, accomplishing objectives. This periodic monitoring identified several problems that were quickly corrected. The ultimate results were, as a result of the midcourse corrections, much more effective than they otherwise would have been.

Preparing a Marketing Communications Plan

It is fitting to conclude the text with a description of the process for preparing a marketing communications plan. A formal marketing communications plan is the first step toward an effective promotional program. The plan represents a written guideline for a company's overall communications program and provides at least three benefits: (1) it is tangible evidence that the marketing communications program is professionally organized, (2) it demonstrates that the marketing communications program is tied directly to overall marketing objectives, and (3) it provides a mechanism for both monitoring and documenting performance during the year.[11]

The process that one company, BF Goodrich, employs in developing its marketing communications plan will be described. This process, which is similar to that used by a number of other companies, entails five steps: the input phase, rough draft, final draft, approval phase, and follow-up activities.[12]

The Input Phase

The planning process begins at BF Goodrich—a manufacturer of a diversified line of industrial, transportation, and polymer products whose annual sales exceed $650 million—about five months before the company's budget is finalized. The first step is to have each product manager complete a *marketing communications questionnaire*. This ensures that the product managers have thoroughly considered their marketing communications needs prior to step two, which involves *a series of personal meetings* between each product manager and the marketing communications manager. The product manager discusses his or her specific advertising and promotional needs, informs the marketing communications manager about market trends, details the sales performance for the present year, and assesses the product's sales potential for the coming year.

These meetings serve two important functions. First, they ensure that the marketing communications plan is tied to the overall marketing strategy for each product line. Second, because product managers are involved in the formulation of marketing communications plans, this increases the chances that they will adhere to and pursue the finalized plan during the coming year.

[11]Douglas B. Limberg, "How To Develop a Marketing Communications Plan," *Marketing Communications,* May 1981, p. 62.

[12]This discussion is a summary of the presentation by Limberg, "Marketing Communications Plan," pp. 56–62.

The Rough Draft

In its final form, the written plan will contain three major sections: an introduction, a description of programs for each product line, and a budget statement. However, the rough draft is restricted to the program description section; the other sections are written later.

The *program description section* provides exact descriptions of the proposed programs for each product line and consists of three parts:

1. A *marketing analysis section* provides background information for each product. This includes information on market trends, analysis of competitive forces, and projected sales and market share for the coming year.
2. A *marketing communications strategy section* (1) states how the marketing communications projects will tie directly into overall marketing and sales objectives and (2) presents detailed plans for each major communication vehicle—advertising, sales promotion, trade shows, etc. The advertising strategy section, for example, describes the current ads that will be continued next year and explains the objectives and themes that will guide the development of new ads.
3. The marketing communications strategy is then summarized into a *budget statement and action plan.* A total budget is established for each communication vehicle. The plan of action then ranks each vehicle in terms of its importance in accomplishing overall marketing strategies and indicates the general completion date for each project.

The Final Draft

The rough draft is sent to the company's advertising agency, which has approximately one month to review the draft and make its creative input. The agency returns the draft with a proposed media advertising plan plus any additional recommendations it chooses to contribute. Minor changes are made in the rough draft to reflect the agency's inputs. Then an introduction and overall budget statement are added to the plan.

The *introduction* (1) addresses industrywide trends for marketing communications in terms of how the program compares with competitors, (2) evaluates past sales performance against the communication activities, and (3) assesses the future requirements for an effective communications program. In addition to its basic informational role, the introductory section to the final marketing communications plan performs an invaluable role in selling the plan to senior management.

The *overall budget statement* is the final section to be written. It summarizes the total marketing communications budget requirements for all product lines. The proposed budget for each product line is broken down in terms of how much is to be spent for advertising, sales promotion, trade shows, and other marketing communications activities. For each activity the statement shows both the proposed budget and the budget for the previous year.

TABLE 23.1   **The Marketing Communications Planning Process**

Step 1: Input Phase
1. Have product managers complete a marketing communications questionnaire.
2. Hold individual meetings between marketing communications manager and each product manager.

Step 2: Rough Draft
1. Perform marketing analysis.
2. Design marketing communications strategies.
3. Prepare budget statement and action plan.

Step 3: Final Draft
1. Send rough draft to advertising agency for its creative inputs.
2. Revise program descriptions on basis of ad agency inputs.
3. Write introduction to plan.
4. Construct overall budget statement.

Step 4: Approval Phase
1. Distribute plan to senior management for approval.
2. Ready approved plan for implementation.

Step 5: Follow-up
1. Track program performance throughout year.
2. Take corrective action when necessary.

Source: Adapted from Douglas B. Limberg, "How To Develop a Marketing Communications Plan," *Marketing Communications,* May 1981, p. 62.

The Approval Phase

Copies of the plan are forwarded to all managers in the company who influence the final budgeting decisions. A meeting between the marketing communications manager and senior managers who have received the plan is held shortly thereafter. The written and approved marketing communications plan is ready for implementation following this meeting.

The Follow-up

Because the marketing communications plan establishes specific objectives and details all program activities, it is possible to track the program's performance throughout the year and to take corrective action when necessary. In the final analysis, the written plan provides the opportunity for a marketing communications department to gain and maintain senior management support for marketing communications programs at the time of the annual budget review and during the course of the business year.

Table 23.1 summarizes the marketing communications planning process.

Summary

This chapter integrates the variety of marketing communication topics that have been covered throughout the text. The framework for accomplishing this is a detailed case history of a program developed by the U.S. Agency for International

Development to combat diarrheal dehydration in developing countries. Discussion focuses on experimental applications of the program in Honduras and The Gambia. The presentation centers on the six major steps of the promotion management process in their application to this major world problem: situation analysis, marketing objectives, promotion budget, integration and coordination of program elements, promotion management program, and evaluation and control.

The chapter concludes with a description of the process for preparing a formal marketing communications plan. The planning process at one company, BF Goodrich, provides a model for the discussion. The presentation covers five major steps in the process: gathering information, preparing the rough draft, writing the final report, gaining approval from senior management, and following up on the program to assure that it is achieving program objectives.

Discussion Questions

1. Why does the situation analysis represent a critical first step in the process of developing a marketing communications program?

2. What was the importance of using the "red heart" theme in Honduras and the "happy baby" theme in The Gambia as symbols of the ORT programs in these countries?

3. The Academy for Educational Development, the chief consultant to AID in the ORT program, characterized their task as one of changing mothers' behavior rather than attitudes. (See text for specific quote.) On the other hand, marketers of conventional products frequently place their promotional emphasis on creating favorable images for their brands. How can you account for this apparent contrast in communication objectives?

4. It can be argued that the communications task in, say, The Gambia was simpler than the promotional task faced by marketers of conventional products such as video casette recorders and personal computers. Take a position on this point and thoroughly support your position.

5. The communications program in The Gambia included a giveaway contest in which mothers could receive a prize by demonstrating an ability to mix the salt, sugar, and water solution correctly. Winners then became eligible to win a bigger prize in a drawing. Moreover, there was a community prize each week for the village turning out the most mothers for the contest. With reference to material presented in Part II of the text (especially Chapters 3, 4, and 5), what are the social-psychological principles that would justify the use of these promotional techniques?

6. A formal marketing communications plan performs a selling role as well as an informational role. Explain.

Exercises

1. Interview the marketing communications manager (or someone with a comparable position) in a manufacturing business and determine whether the company has a formal marketing communications plan and, if so, what it is.

Even if the company does not have a formal plan, still have the marketing communications manager describe the informal process that he or she uses. In either event, develop a flowchart of the planning process.

2. Select one of the social campaigns mentioned in the beginning of the chapter (antismoking, seat belt usage, forest fire prevention, etc.) and then perform a library search to acquaint yourself with the communication techniques that were used in promoting the program. Critique the techniques.

PART VII

Cases

The cases in this part of the text apply to discussions in various chapters or parts:

Case	Relevant Chapter or Part
Stanton Chemical Company	Chapters 3–5
CDs: The New Wave in Audio Technology	Chapter 8
BIC Disposable Razor Case	Chapters 8 and 9
Universal American Insurance Company, Inc.	Chapter 10
National Business Machines	Chapter 11
Missing Children of Greater Washington: Fund-Raising Strategy	Chapters 12–15
The Hydrosander Company	Chapters 12–16
Richtex Brick	Chapter 13
Pantera's Pizza	Chapters 12 and 15
Foster Care For Teens Program	Part III
Roy Rogers Case	Chapter 18
Pan Am Airlines	Chapter 19
Mead Products: The Trapper Keeper®	Parts III and IV
Pepsi. The Choice of a New Generation	Parts III and IV

Stanton Chemical Company*

Stanton Chemical Company produces and distributes a liquid laundry bleach under its own brand, Clo-White, on a regional basis. The company was founded in 1950 by its current president, Robert M. Stanton. From a modest beginning, the company has grown in size until it now has annual sales of over $12 million out of an estimated total industry sales of $250 million. Clorex, Purex, and Fleecy White, brands of three major consumer goods manufacturers sold nationwide, control about 55 percent of total industry sales. The remaining 45 percent is spread among some 26 companies, including Stanton Chemical, who primarily sell their products on a regional basis.

Laundry Bleach

Liquid laundry bleach is used primarily by homemakers to remove stains and whiten clothes. Bleach and detergents are also used to help take out stains and yellowing due to age.

The manufacture of bleach is simple, since it is merely sodium hypochlorite and water mixed together in a solution. All of the bleaches on the market contain 5.25 percent sodium hypochlorite and 94.75 percent inert ingredients (water), but bleach produced in this manner is subject to an "aging" problem. When first produced, laundry bleach has no odor and is at its highest potency level. However, once it has been on the shelf for a length of time (five to eight days), the solution begins to break down chemically. The chlorine in the mixture is given off as a gas, hence the strong smell that certain bleaches exhibit. When a bleach breaks down in this manner, it loses some of its potential for whitening and stain removal, but smells "stronger" to the consumer.

Stanton's Distribution Strategy

Because mixing and bottling plants are relatively simple to build and inexpensive to operate in cases where large volumes of a product are concerned, Stanton has built plants close to several of its major market areas. Another factor in this distribution strategy decision is the relatively low unit value and heavy weight per unit of product, which causes transportation costs to be characteristically high. Stanton's regional competitors have been reluctant to follow this strategy so far, choosing instead to place more emphasis in their marketing strategy on the promotion of their brands.

---

*This case was prepared by Daniel L. Sherrell, School of Business Administration, Louisiana State University. Copyright 1984 Daniel L. Sherrell. Permission granted by the author.

The management of Stanton Chemical has always emphasized a somewhat higher than average customer service level on the theory that "the consumer can't buy our products if they aren't on the shelves when they look for them!" In other words, top management feels that an efficient distribution system is just as important in the marketing of their bleach as price, promotion, or the product itself.

As a result of this emphasis, Stanton management has developed the capability to deliver its bleach more quickly and consistently than any of its competitors by locating mixing and bottling plants close to its markets. This capability has provided Stanton with a good reputation among retailers and helps make the job of Stanton's sales force easier.

Industry Conditions

The industry that Stanton is in may be described as extremely competitive. No one producer is able to command a price premium without risking the loss of substantial market share. Promotional activities consist of a heavy emphasis on advertising through broadcast and print media and the use of personal selling to gain distribution and retailer participation in company promotional campaigns.

Stanton's Distinctive Competence

Besides its ability to deliver its bleach quicker than its competitors, Stanton's distribution system has provided another advantage that management has been unwilling or unable to focus on until now. In tests, using samples of Clo-White, Snowy-White, and a third regional brand, Clo-White outperformed the other two bleaches in stain removal power and whitening ability.

As noted before, laundry bleach is identical in composition, regardless of the brand. The variation in performance is attributed to the lower average shelf age of Clo-White compared with its competitors. Clo-White is two to three days fresher when it arrives on the shelf due to Stanton's distribution system. Because it is fresher, it has more cleaning power for a short period of time before it, too, begins to break down.

The previous vice-president of marketing, who had helped found the company with Stanton and had retired five years earlier, had been unwilling to make use of this knowledge. His belief was that "consumers can't tell the difference in strength between bleaches. They are mainly interested in price." As a result, he had developed the current distribution system as a means to deliver the product quicker and cheaper to the retailer and thus gain a price advantage over competitors. This initially was the case, but the competition for market share quickly forced down prices to Stanton's level.

Consumers

Despite the availability of detergents with bleach additives, homemakers, according to industry estimates, still look to the chlorine-based laundry bleach as the means to remove stains and whiten clothes. The female who is married, has children, and has her own washer and dryer generally represents the heaviest-user segment of the laundry bleach market. Independent research studies suggest that a woman's attitude toward domestic activities and the degree of family orientation are primary determinants in brand selection. Women who possess a strong domestic orientation are more likely to perceive real or imagined differences in the quality of various bleaches, while women who possess weaker orientations will tend to rate all brands equal in quality and prefer to shop for the lowest priced brands.

Corporate Management's Concern

Top management has expressed concern over the apparent ability of Snowy-White to outsell Clo-White in the marketplace, particularly since the price and promotional expenditures for both products are approximately equal. In an effort to find a remedy for the situation, the vice-president of marketing recommended that a marketing research study be conducted to determine what consumers actually thought of Clo-White compared with other brands and, if possible, some reasons for the particular brand image.

As a result, a sample of 1,000 homemakers was selected at random from several large southern cities where Clo-White enjoyed a large market share. They were asked to rank pairs of leading regional brands in terms of perceived similarity, then to rank the brands according to their own individual preferences. Finally, the respondents were asked to give reasons why they ranked the bleaches in that particular order. While the answers to the final question did not represent "hard" enumerative data, nevertheless, it was felt that a consistent interpretation of the information might yield some useful results. The compared brands and the results of the data analysis are shown in Figure 1.

As shown, the top three brands come closest to the ideal point, representing the position of the ideal bleach. Of particular interest to the researchers at Stanton was the fact that Snowy-White was perceived by the respondents as being the strongest bleach on the market. In light of the results from the earlier laboratory tests, the respondents' reasons were examined to see if any possible explanations for the situation could be found. Some of the typical comments received from the respondents were

> *"All bleaches are the same. I just buy the cheapest one."*
> *"There's not much difference in price, so I usually buy the stronger bleach. It gets my clothes cleaner and that's what I want."*
> *"Well, you can take the cap off this one (Snowy-White), and smell the bleach. The other brands just don't have that kind of smell. I always buy the stronger bleach to get my clothes cleaner."*

Currently, Allison Products, the makers of Snowy-White, has launched its fall promotion campaign one month early this year, and preliminary indications are that a bigger-than-usual campaign is planned. The current campaign features television and magazine advertisements stressing the cleaning and whitening power of Snowy-White bleach. In addition, a 20¢-off deal on the gallon container of bleach is being run simultaneously with the advertising campaign.

FIGURE 1

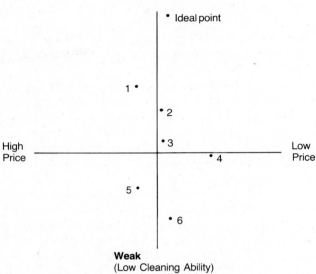

Relative Brand Image Position

Strong
(High Cleaning Ability)

• Ideal point

1 •

• 2

• 3

High   Low
Price   Price

• 4

5 •

• 6

Weak
(Low Cleaning Ability)

Composite Brand Ranking

1. Snowy-White
2. Blue Sky
3. Clo-White
4. Dixie Day
5. Miracle-White
6. Quality

Mr. Pearl, vice-president of marketing at Stanton, feels certain that Allison is starting an intensified promotional effort to increase Snowy-White's market share. Furthermore, he believes that it will succeed in further eroding Clo-White's position in the market unless Stanton reacts quickly. Pearl feels that what most consumers want is the strongest bleach on the market and that they are willing to pay at least the competitive price for it. He points out that the research proves Clo-White is the strongest bleach on the market due to Stanton's quick delivery time. Thus, he feels that Stanton should mount an advertising campaign that "educates" the consumer about the superiority of Clo-White over its competitors. "Tell them the research results and that smell doesn't make any difference. We must maintain our quality."

Mr. Lawrence, brand manager for Clo-White, feels that the research results indicate the importance the consumer attaches to smell as an indicator of strength. "Telling them that Clo-White is the strongest bleach won't convince them once they take the cap off and smell it. They just won't believe that kind of advertising."

Mr. Lawrence feels that Stanton Chemical must allow its bleach to "age" and to develop a stronger smell. "Most consumers go by the smell. Let's give them what they want." Lawrence's plan is to introduce "Clo-White Plus" and advertise it as a new and stronger bleach. "Shoot, we won't be lying to them; it will have a stronger smell and that's what they want. Gentlemen, we're dealing with consumer perceptions. How do you think Snowy-White got ahead of us?"

Mr. Stanton has heard both ideas. He doesn't want to reduce the product's quality; but, on the other hand, he does see the merits of Mr. Lawrence's arguments. He has asked Mr. Pearl and Mr. Lawrence to develop additional alternatives before making a decision.

Questions

1. What other promotional alternatives might Stanton Chemical consider?
2. What would be the short– versus long-run effects of each promotional strategy?
3. How important is olfactory perception in the consumer's evaluation of bleach and other similar products? How easy (difficult) would it be for a company to "educate" consumers about product characteristics which are contradictory to their own perceptions of the product?
4. Is Mr. Lawrence's suggestion ethical? Or is he right in giving consumers what they "want"?

*CDs: The New Wave in Audio Technology**

CDs (compact discs) are the latest innovation in audio technology. They offer the consumer unprecedented accuracy in recording and listening enjoyment. However, consumer awareness and acceptance of CDs have been extremely slow.

Conventional discs are stylus-to-groove systems, which use plastic or vinyl. More recently, magnetic tape has been used in cassette form. Each of these systems has faults. In particular, conventional discs break, scratch, and wear. Tapes hiss, stretch, pop, and crackle. Furthermore, there is a limited dynamic range (distance between the softest and loudest sounds).

Through digital audio technology, companies can provide the true audiophile with music, such as that provided in a professional recording studio. The CD is a hard plastic disc nearly 5 inches in diameter and can hold digital information of up to 74 minutes of stereo music, the equivalent of 10,000 five and one-quarter-inch floppy disks, or a total set of encyclopedias.

Using a CD playback system, the disc is decoded by a low-power laser beam. These data are immediately sent through a conventional sound system, producing phenomenal music.

With the introduction of CDs in early 1983, adoption was slow. The primary market for CDs was the classical-music lover, who tends to be highly educated, to have a great amount of concentration, to detect the slightest bit of noise in a recording, and to have a high salary. Some people, however, complained that digital music projected "artificial" sounds. But, by late 1984, these criticisms were quieted.

Approximately 40 manufacturers produce comparable sets and interchangeable formats for CDs. There is no need to worry about wow, flutter, turntable speed variations, etc. These advantages are in addition to the fact that CDs produce copy *identical* in quality to the original recording. So, the question is, Why is the awareness so low and the acceptance of CDs so slow?

Questions

1. Describe this new product in terms of the five perceived characteristics of an innovation. What does your evaluation suggest for the adoption and diffusion potential of this product?
2. Design a marketing communications program to increase the rate of adoption and diffusion of CDs. Defend.

---

*This case is adapted from Jim Pettigrew, Jr., "CDs: Audio's Newest Revolution," *Sky Magazine,* November 1984, pp. 36–43.

*BIC Disposable Razor Case**

Corporate Background

The BIC Corporation, headquartered in Milford, Connecticut, produces a line of reliable and inexpensive writing instruments, lighters, and shavers. Sales in 1984 totaled $246,862,000, representing the shipment of more than 1.5 billion BIC products in the United States.

BIC Corporation started in the United States in 1958, but its roots were in France. In 1945, a man named Marcel Bich, who had been the production manager for a French ink manufacturer, bought a factory outside Paris and set up business as a maker of parts for fountain pens and mechanical lead pencils. After years of development, Bich introduced his own ball point pen in 1949. He called the new pen BIC, a shortened, easy-to-remember version of his own name.

Realizing that a mass-produced disposable ball point pen had universal appeal, Bich turned his attention to the vast United States market. He bought out the Waterman Pen Company in 1958 and moved the new company in 1963 to its present site in Milford, Connecticut.

American consumers were initially skeptical of BIC pens because of their dissatisfaction with the many inferior brands that had already appeared on the market. To overcome this inherent resistance to disposable pens, BIC created an innovative national television advertising campaign to tell consumers that the BIC ball point was a pen that would "write the first time, every time." A series of "torture test" commercials was created to demonstrate the quality and durability of BIC pens. Commercial demonstrations revealed how BIC pens were able to write after being drilled through wallboards, scraped along ice, baked in a fire, and shot from a gun. These dramatic commercials sold BIC pens to millions of Americans.

Disposable Lighters

After establishing itself as the country's largest pen maker, BIC went on to capture another market, disposable lighters. The lighter was a perfect fit for the BIC philosophy of "commoditization," that is, mass marketing a no-frills product of high quality at the lowest price. The lighter was introduced at $1.49, but manufacturing efficiencies soon reduced the price to under $1.00.

---

*Material for this case was provided courtesy of the BIC Corporation and supplemented with information from the following sources: "The War of the Razors," *Esquire,* February 1980, pp. 28–30; "Disposable Razors Continue to Make Shaving News, *American Druggist,* April 1985, pp. 110–114; "Disposables Hone Shaving Products' Competitive Edge," *Non-Foods Merchandising,* May 1984, pp. 72–75.

The total market for disposable lighters was only 50 million units when BIC introduced its lighter in 1973. By 1984, the market had grown to nearly 450 million units, with BIC lighters accounting for nearly 55% of the market. A creative advertising campaign built around the catchy phrase, "flick your BIC," played a major role in contributing to a rapid sales increase for the BIC lighter.

The Introduction of Disposable Shavers

BIC also saw enormous potential for a disposable shaver that offered a quality shave at a fraction of the price of more traditional shaving systems. In the face of intense competition from Gillette and other companies, BIC introduced its first disposable shaver in the United States in 1976. Competitors criticized BIC's move and predicted that sales of disposables would never account for more than 10% of the market. The skeptics proved wrong, as disposable shavers account today for nearly 50% of the total wet-shave market. BIC enjoys an 18% share of the total market that includes nondisposables as well as disposable shavers.

The BIC Shaver for Sensitive Skin

The BIC Shaver for Sensitive Skin was introduced in 1985 as a line extension to the BIC Shaver and BIC Lady Shaver. The BIC Shaver for Sensitive Skin is the first blade product targeted specifically at men with sensitive skin. According to the BIC marketing manager, the company based its decision to launch the product on research showing that 42% of the men surveyed said that they have sensitive skin. The shaver, which has an orange handle in contrast to the white handle for the established BIC Shaver, was designed to offer smooth, comfortable shaves for men who are bothered by skin irritation and razor burn.

The BIC shaver for Sensitive Skin was marketed in Canada before its introduction in the United States. The shaver was launched in Canada in early 1984 and quickly accounted for one-third of the BIC Shavers sold there. Rather than cannabalizing sales of existing BIC items, the new shaver actually expanded the market because users saw the shaver as a unique way to meet their particular needs.

"We will promote BIC Shaver for Sensitive Skin heavily, using both couponing and sampling through higher target marketing vehicles," according to BIC's marketing manager, Keith Koski, in reference to the new product's introduction into the United States. Koski further pointed out that national television advertising would be used to promote product adoption.

John McEnroe, the famous yet frequently criticized tennis star, was retained to endorse the new shaver in a continuation of his role as endorser for the established BIC Shaver product. Illustrations of McEnroe's endorser role are shown in the magazine advertisement and television commercial in Figures 1 and 2.

It is uncertain whether the McEnroe advertising campaign for the Shaver for Sensitive Skin will live up to the successes accomplished with earlier advertisements for BIC products, namely, the "torture test" advertisements for ball point pens and the "flick your BIC" campaign for lighters.

FIGURE 1

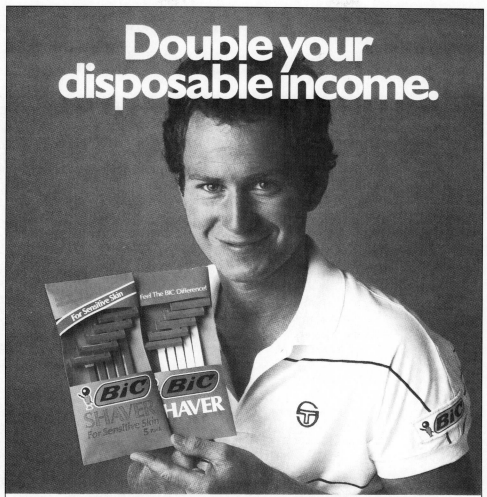

FIGURE 2

 **SHAVER**

WHITE FOR REGULAR AND ORANGE FOR SENSITIVE SKIN

"WORLD DIVIDED/U.S. VERSION"   XBOS 4309   :30 TV COMMERCIAL

JOHN McENROE: The world is divided in half.

Some can go to the net. . .

some can't.

There are good backhands. . .

and bad ones.

And most important to Bic. . . some guys have normal skin, while others have more sensitive skin.

So Bic made the new Bic Orange. It shaves sensitive skin gently and closely.

So for normal skin like mine the original Bic White shaver and for sensitive skin the new Bic Orange.

Oh by the way, some people love John McEnroe and some people. . .ehh.

Questions

1. Using concepts and theory from Chapter 6, evaluate BIC's choice of John McEnroe as endorser for its disposable shaver products. Specifically, is BIC's choice of Mr. McEnroe a wise choice? For what type of consumer is McEnroe likely to have positive appeal? negative appeal? Recommend a celebrity endorser other than Mr. McEnroe who, in your opinion, would be a superior endorser of BIC's products. Justify your choice using concepts and theories from Chapter 6.

2. With material from Chapter 15 as your source, recommend a procedure for testing the effectiveness of the advertising for BIC's Shaver for Sensitive Skin. Be sure to identify first what you believe to be BIC's advertising objective(s).

[handwritten marginalia: Comment on his credibility]

*Universal American Insurance Company, Inc.**

Jim Robinson was the Southwest Region Sales Manager of Universal American Insurance Company, Incorporated. Universal American was ranked among the top ten U.S. insurance corporations, with total assets in excess of $15 billion. The company sold life, homeowner's, automobile, and health insurance, along with annuities and mutual funds to both businesses and individuals. However, the backbone of the company's sales and profits was life insurance sales to individuals; personal selling was the exclusive promotional tool.

All sales agents worked out of a branch office under the supervision of the branch manager. The branch managers reported directly to the regional manager. Sales agents were compensated solely on a commission basis, as were the branch managers, who received an override commission on the sales of the agents they supervised in addition to the commission from their personal sales.

Jim was known and respected throughout his company as an innovative and dynamic manager. In fact, he had been the company's national sales manager for five years but had requested his own region again because he missed the day-to-day contact with his sales agents. The fact that he could also make more money as a regional manager played a part in his move back down from headquarters. Regional managers were paid an override commission on total sales in their region, whereas the national sales manager was paid a straight salary.

In order to motivate its sales force, the company organized two national sales contests each year. One was the President's Campaign in honor of the company president; the other was the Regional Director's Campaign in honor of each of the company's regional managers. The campaign gave individual recognition to sales agents with the highest sales over the five weeks each campaign lasted. Beyond the recognition that the winners received, bonus points were also awarded to determine who would attend the company's annual sales convention. The annual sales convention was always held at a special location and represented a paid vacation to the agents and their spouses, who were also invited. Attendance at the convention also provided recognition for the company's top producers in terms of annual sales. The most recent annual sales convention was held in Hong Kong, where attendees stayed for ten days with a three-day layover in Hawaii on the way to the convention site.

Jim Robinson knew that for the majority of his salespeople, the branch office played a vital role in their professional lives. It represented their business "home." Because sales agents spend nearly 90 percent of their time prospecting, either by phone from their homes or by "cold calls" in person, and in making sales presentations before prospects, the time they had at the branch office was very important

*This case was prepared by Stephen E. Calcich, School of Business, Norfolk State University. Copyright 1984 Stephen E. Calcich. Permission granted by the author.

Universal American Insurance Company, Inc.

TABLE 1 **Total Premium* Sales for 1984 by Branch Office: Southwest Region**

Branch Office	Number of Agents	Premium Sales $'s		
		President's Campaign	Regional Director's Campaign	Annual
Cauthen-Port Arthur	3	18,477	17,658	58,944
Simmen-Houston	22	64,174	68,288	412,104
Golden-Houston	14	44,114	42,462	300,552
Helsel-Las Cruces	4	15,500	14,248	69,716
Marantz-El Paso	7	41,916	43,211	155,958
Waggoner-San Antonio	11	31,559	34,540	233,761
O'Steen-Austin	7	23,576	23,870	129,304
Pitchford-Austin	9	47,934	53,487	174,924
Hilditch-Houston	5	15,285	14,645	93,535
Rea-Odessa	3	12,495	10,554	74,331
Griffith-Albuquerque	8	19,448	23,888	189,144
Akers-McAllen	3	10,278	8,826	48,873
Kubesch-Clute/Victoria	4	13,256	13,936	69,992
Mayfield-Lubbock	5	29,560	29,455	113,230
Nathan-Galveston	3	12,492	11,169	53,943
Basham-Corpus Christi	7	20,601	21,077	106,778
McInnerney-Houston	7	23,583	22,421	145,663
Rasor-San Angelo	2	10,328	9,438	38,854
Mack-Del Rio	2	12,486	10,716	44,070
Kristensen-Houston	3	8,811	9,744	69,348

*In the insurance industry, sales figures are usually expressed in volume. That is, a $50,000 insurance policy would be recorded as $50,000 in sales volume. However, depending on the type of policy issued, the premium paid by the policyholder may vary significantly. For a $50,000 whole-life policy on a 35-year-old male nonsmoker, the annual premium would be about $750, whereas for a $50,000 term policy, the annual premium would only be approximately $150. For management purposes, sales in terms of premium, which represents actual revenues to the company, is a more realistic measure of sales performance.

to them. Here they had their sales meetings and sales training sessions. There was the opportunity to relate their successes to their branch manager and fellow sales agents and also receive solace for the "big one" that slipped through the net.

Jim's immediate concern was the upcoming Regional Director's Campaign. Although his region's results were always comparable with those from other areas of the country, he nonetheless felt he was missing an opportunity to motivate his sales force for the sales campaign. He suspected the opportunity lay at the branch office level because of the key role the branch office played in the direct control and supervision of the sales force. Jim had found that the amount of interest shown by the managers of the branch offices for any particular policy was in direct proportion to the degree of acceptance of that policy among the sales agents. Perhaps sales agents' interest in the sales campaign was being affected by a lack of interest in them by some of the branches.

To investigate his suspicions further, Jim compiled sales figures from the previous year's campaigns along with yearly data for each branch office and the number of salespeople working out of each office. These data are shown in Table 1.

Questions

1. Analyze the sales figures to determine whether any data support the regional manager's suspicions of lack of interest in the sales campaigns on the part of branch offices.
2. Make recommendations to increase sales results in the southwest region.
3. Why is the job of Jim Robinson more challenging than that of sales managers in other types of industry?

Questions

1. How would you evaluate Brad's sales call at Harrison Brothers?
2. Why did Brad leave the demonstrator model? What was he hoping would happen when he returned?
3. What are Brad's chances of succeeding at NBM?
4. How can Brad improve his overall approach and presentation to be successful on future sales calls?

*Missing Children of Greater Washington: Fund-Raising Strategy**

"I don't know whether this family membership package is a good way to start a grass-roots fund-raising effort—$10 checks are O.K., but would we do better if we went after flat-out donations of any amount?" asked Terry Lowe-Edwards, Executive Director of Missing Children of Greater Washington (MCGW) in response to the proposed family membership concept.

The family membership concept (FMC) had been proposed as the central theme for all of MCGW's fund-raising efforts. Solicitation efforts would be directed at families throughout the greater Washington, D.C. area. For contributions of $10 or more, families would receive a one-year membership in MCGW that would entitle them to (1) membership cards for all family members along with MCGW's emergency hot line phone number, (2) file cards for child identification purposes (recent picture, fingerprints, etc.), (3) a brochure describing a prevention program and an action plan in the event a child is missing, (4) a subscription to MCGW's semiannual newsletter, and (5) an opportunity to vote for MCGW's Board of Directors.

Terry, along with influential members of MCGW's Board of Directors, had been in search of a vehicle for kicking off MCGW's fund-raising program. "Fund-raising has become a very competitive business," said Terry. "We have a series of services to sell—education, prevention, emergency referral, and victim assistance—and we have to convince our potential contributor that his or her dollar is better spent here than on other charities such as the Heart Fund, the Cancer Society, or even national organizations that deal with the missing children issue."

History and Activities of the Organization

MCGW was incorporated as a nonprofit organization in the District of Columbia in the summer of 1984. The organization was formed through the efforts of several Washington area residents. Some had personal family experiences involving a child abduction; others simply had compassion for the issue and its victims and wanted to do something about it. MCGW is not affiliated with any national organization that deals with the problems of missing children. All monies raised are channeled directly back into the greater Washington area. MCGW's programs are targeted toward the residents of the District of Columbia and surrounding counties in Maryland and Virginia.

---

*This case was prepared by Robert F. Dyer, who, at the time of this writing, was Professor of Marketing, The George Washington University.

The tragedy associated with America's missing children received national attention in October 1983 with the NBC television movie *Adam.* Adam Walsh was a six-year-old Ft. Lauderdale, Florida, youngster who was killed in July 1981, soon after being abducted from a department store. The October 24, 1983 issue of *U.S. News & World Report* highlighted the scope of the problem with the following statistics:

> *Experts estimate that some 1.8 million children are missing for various periods each year. About 90 percent run away for a few days and return home. But at least 100,000 are abducted by parents in custody fights, and 20,000 to 50,000 are snatched by strangers—most never to be seen again. Many of these children experience a tragic fate. Roughly 10 percent are sexually abused. Research collected by the Adam Walsh Center indicates that 80 percent of the children kidnapped by strangers are murdered within two days of their disappearance. Another expert on the issue has stated that we find more stolen cars and stray animals than missing children each year.*

MCGW'S Programs

During the first year of MCGW's operation, it was determined that the fundamental mission of MCGW should be to provide ongoing programs to educate parents and children about child abductions and to help them in preventing these abductions. For instance, one proposed program was to educate parents about the type of information they should have available about their children in the event of an abduction. MCGW's purpose was *not* actually to locate missing children, but rather to advise parents on the steps to take in the event their child does disappear and to refer parents to proper authorities and agencies equipped to handle various aspects of cases of missing children. In addition, MCGW saw itself as a potentially influential voice in the Washington community to advocate the well-being of children. Some of MCGW's proposed programs included the following:

1.   "Child Identification Days" at area schools and shopping malls. This program would be designed (a) to fingerprint children, (b) to provide parents with a form for listing pertinent information about their children, which would assist authorities in locating a missing child, and (c) to provide parents with a thorough action plan in case a child is missing.
2.   "Curriculum Guides" for use in elementary schools. These guides were proposed to increase recognition among children of danger signals leading to sexual abuse, molestation, and abduction.

Issues Regarding MCGW's Proposed Programs

Several jobs seemed of paramount importance to Terry as she looked at the challenges in front of her: (1) to build a volunteer network, (2) to develop a community hot line and law enforcement/social agency referral system, (3) to establish name recognition for MCGW through cultivating the local media with personal visits and distributing press kits, and (4) to create packages of community education materials to distribute to school systems, churches, civic groups, PTA organizations, etc.

As she reviewed this list of tasks, Terry pondered the upcoming board meeting. A key agenda item called for review of the family membership concept (FMC) that had been proposed prior to her assuming the executive director's position. Terry wondered whether families would consider the benefits offered by this program (a periodic newsletter, child fingerprinting, etc.) to be sufficiently meaningful. She thought that some people would probably donate with no benefits other than a receipt for tax deductions and a feeling that they had helped a worthy cause. "Why complicate the campaign?" Terry wondered.

Terry also had mixed feelings about the minimum $10 membership fee. She realized that a low fee, say $5, would probably not cover MCGW's costs, but she feared that the $10 minimum requirement would scare away potential donations in the $1 to $5 range. Terry believed, however, that family memberships at $10 or more would provide a spirit of belonging and fit the grass-roots nature of the organization. Families would receive tangible benefits, and MCGW's foot would be in the door for future (perhaps larger) donations using well-developed mailing lists and phone numbers for the following year's fund-raising.

Terry also considered an alternative fund-raising campaign: a combination of public service announcements (PSAs) on local radio and television stations that would be supplemented by direct mailing a fund-raising brochure. Terry had been assured by a MCGW board member that one or two local advertising/public relations firms would provide creative efforts gratis and that discounts could be arranged with printing companies.

Another possibility was door-to-door canvassing. Other charitable organizations used this approach with considerable success. This approach would involve getting a staff of volunteers who would canvass their neighborhoods for donations. Terry had several reservations about this approach: (1) she lacked the volunteer manpower; (2) she doubted whether she could compete against the established charitable organizations such as the Multiple Sclerosis Society, which was reported to use professional telephone solicitors to recruit over 10,000 volunteer canvassers in the Washington area; (3) she realized that the FMC program would not fit the door-to-door solicitation approach; and (4) she feared for the safety of canvassers in urban sections of Washington, D.C.

Terry realized that either approach, direct mail or door-to-door canvassing, would have to be carefully timed with publicity and public relations efforts. Her strategy was to put together a media event for reporters, newscasters, and station directors and to ask local broadcast media for PSA coverage to be launched a few weeks before the community fund-raising effort commenced. Terry contemplated several alternative creative strategies:

1. *An information and fund-raising campaign.* This campaign would announce the formation of Missing Children of Greater Washington with a

statement of the organization's objectives followed by a request for contributions.

2. *An information-only campaign.* This would be the same as the first strategy with the exception that there would be no request for contributions. MCGW's phone number and address would be given for the benefit of interested parties who desired further information or who needed assistance in the event their child was abducted.

   Several possibilities for creative format existed in either of these strategies. One format considered was to have the message announced by a well-known personality. Jackie Stone was one possibility. As a local newscaster on WTTG-TV, she had done an impressive multipart documentary on the missing children issue. John Walsh, the father of Adam Walsh, was another possibility. He had recently moved to Washington to organize a national missing children's group.

3. *A fear-appeal approach.* This approach would use a collage of headlines from local media about recent area child abduction cases followed by either message version 1 or 2.

Questions

1. Should MCGW adopt the FMC? What changes should be made in the program?

2. Which fund-raising approach should be used by MCGW? Support your reasoning with communication theory and concepts.

3. How should MCGW strive for "promotional synergism" in its fund-raising and education/prevention efforts?

4. Which message strategy and creative format would you suggest for MCGW? (You need not restrict your answer to the three strategies proposed in the case.)

*The Hydrosander Company**

Eastern Equipment and Chemical Company (EECC), formed in 1965, mixes and sells industrial degreasers and other cleaners to municipalities, manufacturing plants, and school systems in the Carolinas, Georgia, and Virginia. The company employs two manufacturing personnel, two shipping, five administrative and secretarial personnel, and three field salesmen.

In 1972, the owner of EECC, Otto Wemmer, recognized a need for graffiti-removing equipment. Several of his customers had tried graffiti-removing chemicals with no success and needed a better solution to their problem.

Otto's efforts to satisfy his customers' needs led to the development of the Hydrosander, a water-propelled sandblasting machine. With conventional sandblasting equipment, compressed air is passed through a chamber to create a vacuum and to pull sand into the airstream as it escapes. This method of sandblasting is extremely effective, but air contamination and high costs prevented its widespread use. The dust created with conventional sandblasting is a serious problem in meeting OSHA requirements.

The hydrosander uses a high-pressure jet of water, rather than compressed air, to pull the sand into the stream. The advantages of the water-propelled system are (1) the water-sand mixture totally eliminates the dust problem, and (2) the cost of the system is about one-third that of conventional air systems.

Several firms across the country recognize the problem that Otto has seen, and several have tried a water-sand combination as a remedy. Otto was the first, however, to design a reliable system. Other manufacturers had serious problems with wet sand plugs forming and clogging the system. Through a patented venturi (or vacuum) chamber, Otto totally eliminated the possibility of sand plugs.

As a machine designer, Otto was ingenious. He began to sell the Hydrosander to schools and other large facilities through his regular three-man sales force. He recognized that a nationwide market existed but was uncertain about how to penetrate that market.

He began with a series of nationwide direct mail programs to build awareness for the hydrosander concept. The positive responses confirmed Otto's belief in the market potential.

Hydrosander, Inc.

In 1980, Otto formed Hydrosander, Inc., as a separate business from EECC for financial and legal reasons, and shortly thereafter, he hired a marketing manager to coordinate the venture project. The two major tasks he addressed initially were

---

*This case was prepared by Karen L. Able, product manager of a large, international firm. The company name is disguised to provide anonymity for the company.

broadening the product line and securing market awareness. In January 1981, the Hydrosander product line consisted of one 12-horsepower unit. Three other units and various accessories were added that spring to broaden the line to serve a range of customer needs. The units ranged from 3½ to 12 horsepower, with accessories for high-pressure washing (with no sand), for high-pressure washing with chemical injection, and for water sandblasting.

An important criterion in product design was serviceability. All major components, the gasoline engine and the water pump, were major brands with service facilities nationwide.

The second task was communications and promotion. Potential customers had to be educated on the concept of water sandblasting, made aware of the proprietary advantages of the Hydrosander system, and sold on the equipment.

To educate and build brand awareness, Hydrosander launched both direct mail and trade advertising programs. They qualified sales leads by phone and by mail, and shipped equipment on a trial basis for customer evaluation.

This marketing communications program was relatively successful. Over the first eight months, they reduced average cost per lead from about $150 to $35, and average cost per sale from $890 to $220.

A More Focused Strategy

As Hydrosander established the product line and their market credibility, they began the second phase of market penetration in July 1981. At this stage, management defined the entire business strategy more narrowly and specifically. By targeting their resources in well-defined markets and products, Hydrosander believed they could maximize market penetration and sales.

Hydrosander identified four major markets for primary emphasis: paint contractors, waste disposal firms, municipalities maintaining large facilities, and shipyards. Their identification of these four markets provided a framework from which to make decisions about product development, distribution, and promotions. The implementation of these functions, subsequently, became more focused and efficient as Hydrosander's market position was clearly defined.

Product Development

Close contact with paint contractors revealed a need for portable, lightweight machines. The frames of the existing machines, therefore, were changed from steel to lightweight aluminum, and wheel kits were retrofitted for better portability.

A similar attention to customer needs led to the introduction of a hot water unit to clean the grease buildup from waste containers, and the introduction of a 45-horsepower diesel unit for the shipbuilding market.

Distribution

A key to better market penetration was distribution. The phone calls and trial shipments were successful only to a degree. In June of 1981 a major plan to establish industrial distributors was written and approved. Driving a Hydrosander van fully equipped with equipment for on-site demonstration, the marketing manager began travelling extensively to set up the distribution network.

Within one year, about 33 distributors were set up to build the Hydrosander business. The marketing manager worked with major stocking distributors extensively to train the distributor salesmen and coordinate sales lead follow-up.

Quantity discount price schedules also encouraged distributors to stock larger quantities of machines, which then placed added pressure to move the inventory.

Promotions

Marketing promotions continued to produce results as the focus became narrower. Advertising and direct mail were targeted to geographic areas where distribution was strong and to markets where sales potential was highest. Other promotional tools, like national trade shows, also helped to build Hydrosander success.

By the end of 1982, Hydrosander sales had tripled in two years. The product line had expanded from one to six major units with various accessories. An established distribution network formed a strong base for future sales growth. Advertising and promotions followed the customer orientation with better efficiency and effectiveness.

Questions

1. Evaluate the Hydrosander's marketing communications and promotion strategy during its introduction. What would you have done differently, if anything? Why?
2. Given Hydrosander's success with direct mail and trade advertising programs, why are they shifting (or should they shift) to an emphasis on the more expensive promotional mix element, personal selling?
3. What selling message would you use? Devise two alternatives.

*Richtex Brick**

The Richtex Corporation of Columbia, South Carolina, is now (circa 1982) in its seventh decade of operation. It is one of the top twelve brick manufacturers in the nation, and the largest brick manufacturing company in South Carolina. The company, founded in 1919, was known originally as the Richland Shale Products Company, but changed its name in 1969 to Richtex Corporation.

The abundance of raw materials (shale and kaolin) available to Richtex has allowed it to develop a variety of beautiful and enduring brick products. More than half of Richtex's mining efforts are performed on-site behind its plant. The styles of brick produced by Richtex range from contemporary to colonial and include many colors, textures, and sizes.

Between 1969 and 1979, the company experienced tremendous growth—over 65 percent in production and 110 percent in sales. Much of the growth was due to the population increase in South Carolina during this period. Currently, about 60 percent of Richtex's sales are in South Carolina. The remainder of sales are made in parts of Georgia, North Carolina, and Florida, as well as in cities along the eastern seaboard and in the Midwest. The majority of Richtex's brick is used for residential construction, although a good share is used for commercial construction.

Although there has been a growing trend recently towards consolidation through acquisitions and mergers, the majority of brick companies are still relatively small, family-owned businesses. The eight largest firms, in fact, account for only about one-third of total U.S. shipments. Most of the small brick companies have customer bases typically within a 50– to 70-mile radius of their plants due to transportation costs. While competition among the brick companies themselves has been keen, an even more pressing problem facing the industry is competition from alternative building products, the most significant being wood. Until recently, brick has been declining in importance as a siding material for single-family homes, with market share dropping from about 36 percent in 1972 to 29 percent in 1981.

Various theories have been offered to explain brick's relatively lackluster performance compared to wood's. The most often heard is that wood is cheaper than brick, at least in terms of initial cost. This fact, combined with the "disposable" mentality of the U.S. citizen, has tended to hurt brick sales. Other theories are that people are beginning to consider wood more fashionable than brick, that wood manufacturers spend more money advertising and promoting their products, and that contractors prefer to use wood because they have their own carpenters (and may have been carpenters themselves at one time) but must subcontract masonry work. All these theories are probably valid to varying degrees; because this is true,

*Permission granted by Mr. Robert L. Gandy, Jr., President of Richtex Corporation.

it is extremely difficult to measure the effect of one theory independently of the others.

Brick has some distinct advantages over other exterior building materials:

1. Maintenance. Brick doesn't rust, dent, fade, scratch, rot, peel, or warp, and it doesn't need painting.
2. Insurance Costs. Many insurance companies provide lower fire-insurance rates for brick homes, both on structure and content.
3. Pests. Brick is resistant to attack by pests, especially termites.
4. Resale Value. Most appraisal handbooks show that brick homes have a 2 to 5 percent higher resale value after 20 years than those built from other materials.

The president of the Richtex Corporation is concerned about the image that brick has, in general, and about Richtex's image in particular. For this reason, you have been hired to develop a creative advertising campaign to help Richtex regain market share that has been lost to wood.

*Pantera's Pizza**

Pantera's Pizza Company is a franchised pizza chain operating in the greater metropolitan area of St. Louis, and has 32 store locations. The management of Pantera's Pizza commissioned a survey to learn the level of awareness and buying behavior of consumers toward competing pizza restaurants in the St. Louis area. The results of the study are summarized in Figure 1.

FIGURE 1   **Research Report**

Unaided Awareness

Most respondents are aware of Pizza Hut (74%) and Pantera's Pizza (64%) when asked to name the pizza restaurants or chains in the greater St. Louis area that they know. Top-of-the-mind awareness (unaided first recall) is led by Pizza Hut (PH) followed by Pantera's Pizza (PP), 35% and 27%, respectively.

Among low-income households Pizza Hut has a very high unaided top-of-the-mind awareness (56%) versus Pantera's Pizza (11%). Persons in households with high incomes less often recalled PH and PP first and more often recalled single pizza restaurant locations first (40%).

Aided Awareness

Nearly all respondents have heard of PH (99%) and PP (95%). PP enjoys a very high word-of-mouth (32%) proportion of consumers reporting how they first learned about the restaurant. PH was first learned of by driving by the restaurants, according to 19% of the consumers. Thirty percent of the respondents report first learning about PP from the television ads compared with 31% for PH.

Eating at PH and PP

Nearly all (94%) of the respondents have eaten at least once at PH and 65% have eaten at least once at PP. Those who have eaten at PH have eaten there an average of 3.5 times in 1982. Consumption at PP among those persons who have ever eaten at PP was also 3.5 times in 1982.

Advertising Effect

Most respondents do remember something about PH's advertising (61%) and PP's advertising (65%).

A total of 42% of the respondents who did remember PP's advertising mentioned recalling the TV ads; 23% mentioned PP's five-minute lunch; and 10% recalled the 7½ lb. combo pizza. For PH, 17% who could recall the advertising mentioned the pitcher of Pepsi offer and 14% mentioned "super pan pizza."

"Your home town pizza restaurant" was recalled by 88% of the sample when asked if "you ever heard the following statement made." Among those recalling the statement, 84% identified its sponsor to be PH, and 93% of all respondents reported that "your home town pizza restaurant" was *not* "something you think about when going for a pizza."

(continued)

*This case was prepared by Arch G. Woodside, Malcolm S. Woldenberg Professor of Marketing, Tulane University. Copyright 1984 Arch G. Woodside. Permission granted by the author.

FIGURE 1   *Continued*

Eating at a Pizza Restaurant
   Most (75%) respondents report eating at a pizza restaurant during the past 30 days.
   The market is still fragmented with small pizza restaurants (single locations) in St. Louis: 41
   percent report going to such places in the past 30 days.
   PP was mentioned by 21 percent and PH by 18 percent as restaurants visited in the past 30
   days. Most St. Louis residents report 8 to 15 trips to pizza restaurants per year.

Evaluations of PH and PP
   Six attributes of both PH and PP were evaluated by the respondents. The quality of food at
   Pantera's is perceived to be very good (47%) more often than the quality of food at Pizza Hut is
   perceived to be very good (17%). Among persons who have eaten at both PH and PP,
   Pantera's is judged to have a higher quality of food.
   "The quality of food" is the major attribute that distinguishes PP from PH in the minds of
   persons who have eaten at both restaurants.

Evaluation by Age
   Teenagers have a very favorable opinion of the quality of food at PP. Teenagers rate PP higher
   in the quality of food and the variety of food than older customers. However, all age groups rate
   PP favorable on these dimensions. A weak halo effect on the other attributes evaluated appears
   to be created by the evaluation of the quality of food.

The senior management at Pantera's Pizza has read the report and is now seeking advice on how to use the report to make promotional decisions. Management wants to know what advertising campaign theme to use and what other devices to use in promoting their products.

Pantera's Pizza's management has requested that you read the research report and provide several recommendations for improving their promotional strategy.

*Foster Care For Teens Program**

In early January of 1983, Janet Franco, the newly appointed administrator of the Foster Care For Teens Program, was worried about how she would obtain temporary foster parents for the ever-growing number of teenagers matriculating into this program. Last year's promotional campaign had raised the total number of foster parents to twelve, but the projected number of foster parents needed for this next year was estimated at 25. Ms. Franco believed that the promotional program had to obtain this goal to remain a viable candidate for external funding. To accomplish this goal with a limited promotional budget of $2,200, Ms. Franco believed that she must first determine a target market for her message, a relevant copy platform appealing to the needs of these individuals, and an appropriate media mix before proceeding further with the development of the campaign.

Background Information: Youth Service Bureau

The Foster Care For Teens Program was just 1 of 12 programs sponsored by the Youth Service Bureau of Porter County, Indiana. The Youth Service Bureau is a United Way Agency that operates exclusively within Porter County through a unique combination of federal, state, and local funding, together with donated services and private philanthropy. An executive director, Raymond Bellicose, administers the 12 separate programs.

The Youth Service Bureau has four principle functions: (1) as a *referral agency* bringing together a young person and his or her family for counseling and diagnosis of service needs; (2) as a *catalyst* in the community bringing people and issues together through information, education, and experiental opportunities; (3) as an *advocate* with the direct purpose of both representing and protecting the rights of young people who are not able to speak for themselves; and (4) as a *direct service* organization offering a variety of programs designed to meet the needs of Porter County youth and their families.

The Indiana Criminal Justice Planning Agency (ICJPA) adopted a philosophy for funding that indicated that it was the responsibility of local communities to support their Youth Service Bureau financially after the first three years of organization. To that end, ICJPA funding was decreased by 50 percent for the fourth year of operations and only continued past the three-year limit because of positive evaluations by both the staff and the staff of the Indiana Juvenile Justice Task Force.

*This case was prepared by Robert J. Listman, Associate Professor of Marketing, Valparaiso University, as a basis for classroom discussion rather than to illustrate either effective or ineffective handling of an administrative situation. Presented at Midwest Case Writers' Association Workshop, Milwaukee, Wisconsin, 1983.

All other sources of funding are annual and only renewable if the programs meet their stated goals.

Description of Porter County

Porter County is a rural area in Northwest Indiana that encompasses 425 square miles. It lies between the areas of Lake Michigan to the north, the Kankakee River to the south, the city of LaPorte to the east, and the city of Hobart to the west.

During the past decade (1970 to 1980), the population of Porter County has increased by 29 percent. The estimated population in 1970 was 87,114, and in 1980 the estimated population was 112,600. More than half of the county's population resides in the following three areas: Chesterton (pop. est. 7,600), Portage (pop. est. 26,200), and Valparaiso (pop. est. 24,200).[1] Valparaiso, which is the largest city and county seat, contains the highest concentration of schools, churches, and business establishments and is one of the fastest growing cities in northwest Indiana.

Foster Care for Teens Program

The Foster Care For Teens Program has been in existence for seven years, but lack of external funding keeps the program quite small and understaffed. During the last two years the program has been greatly expanded, and a full-time program administrator, Janet Franco, has been appointed. In 1980, the Indiana Criminal Justice Planning Agency awarded the bureau a three-year grant to develop the program fully. The grant will run out in December of 1983. After this date, continued funding has to be obtained from other sources, which historically only financed those programs which attained their stated goals. The Foster Care For Teens Program was designed to provide alternative in-home foster parenting for teenagers between the ages of 13 and 17. These teenagers were generally status offenders[2] or disturbed teenagers, or abused and neglected children who did not come from a secure home environment. Some had repeated misdemeanor violations, like shoplifting, but the majority of the teens had not committed any criminal offenses. The program was designed to keep these teens out of the Youth Detention Center, which was a detention facility where children were placed prior to either a juvenile hearing or transferring of custody to another agency.

There were at least 9 to 13 children in the program at any one time, about 25 to 30 children placed within a year, and many more in need of placement. Janet

---

[1]Indiana State Board of Health, Division of Public Statistics, *Indiana Vital Statistics*—1979.

[2]A status offense is an offense that is only labeled a crime because the child is under 18 years of age (i.e., runaways, truant violators, etc.). Repeat status offenders were sent to the Youth Detention Center if they did not have a secure, caring home environment to be returned to after police apprehension.

Franco was not concerned about locating eligible teens for the program. Unfortunately, a dearth of troubled teenagers was not the problem; rather, the problem was in recruiting qualified applicants for positions as foster parents. To be eligible as a foster parent, an applicant had to be either single or married, emotionally sound, 21 or over, financially stable (although wealth was not necessary), and a resident of Porter County. The foster parents receive $10.00 per day per child for living expenses, and medical, dental, and clothing expenses were provided on an as-needed basis.

Ms. Franco was worried about the likelihood of the 1983 promotional campaign accomplishing its goal of recruiting, at minimum, 13 new foster parents. She believed the stated goal of 25 active foster parents was necessary because counselors were directed to match teenagers with the requirements of foster parents; consequently, a base of 25 was judged sufficient to facilitate this matching process. Some foster parents requested only girls or specified a certain grade in school or refused to accept a child who had a past run-in with the law, no matter how minor. Many of the foster parents had children of their own; therefore, they attempted to select teenagers based upon their family's demographic makeup.

Only $2,200 of grant money remained for the 1983 promotional campaign, and last year Janet spent slightly over $2,500 on promotional material, which generated about 75 inquiries. The 1982 promotional campaign relied upon a series of newspaper advertisements costing approximately $1,350; supplemental publicity announcements, scattered human interest stories in local newspapers, announcements in church bulletins, and formal presentations or addresses to civic and community groups augmented the newspaper advertising. The remaining dollars were spent on posters, bumper stickers, handouts, and balloons, which were distributed at the county fair and similar community events. Ms. Franco noticed that more qualified applicants came from the publicity announcements in church bulletins and the referrals from past foster parents than from the newspaper advertisements. This led her to the conclusion that perhaps there were specific segments of the community she should be appealing to rather than just concentrating on newspaper advertisements, which really did not appeal to any one group of people.

The idea of directing the promotional message to a more homogeneous group of prospects was very attractive to Ms. Franco. Intuitively, she believed she could reach a more qualified group of prospects and reduce both the expense and time associated in weeding out the nonqualified inquiries. However, she felt this targeted approach was risky because she had little experience in this form of promotion, and she was sure her immediate supervisor, Frank Bellicose, would not approve of this new campaign approach in this last year of the grant.

Questions

1. Is Janet Franco correct? Is there a target market profile for foster parents? If yes, describe this profile and explain why you feel the profile has that degree of homogeneity. Discuss how you would go about reaching this group of people with your promotional message.

2. List other types of behavioral information that need to be determined before proceeding further with the 1983 campaign. Discuss how you would obtain this information. Be specific in your recommendations.

3. Given the case information, comment upon the relative effectiveness of past types of promotion (newspaper advertisement, human interest stories, word-of-mouth referrals, etc.) in helping the Youth Service Bureau in obtaining foster parents.

*Roy Rogers Case**

The Vice-President of Marketing for the Roy Rogers Division of the Marriott Corporation pondered the 1984 expense report for the company's Roy Rogers fast-food division. The most salient figure was the percentage of the 1984 promotion budget taken up by sales promotion expenditures.

Background

The Marriott Corporation

The Marriott Corporation, a rapidly growing firm based in Washington, D.C., is organized into several strategic business units (SBUs): hotels and resorts, contract food services (e.g., airline catering and airport concessions), theme parks and cruise ships, and restaurants. The company's holdings consist of over 1,100 restaurants, 230 food service management accounts, 100 hotels and resorts, 85 airport facilities, 70 flight kitchens, and three cruise ships.

The growth of this food service giant, which began as a nine-seat root beer stand in 1927, is unsurpassed by that of any other major company in the industry except McDonald's. Industry analysts suggest that Marriott will grow at a rate substantially in excess of McDonald's in the future. Analysts project an average five-year growth rate of 25 percent in earnings per share.

The Fast-Food Industry

After over two decades of rapid expansion, the $10 billion U.S. fast-food business has entered a slow down. Some of the key trends are (1) America's love affair with the hamburger has tapered off; (2) choice store sites have been gobbled up, and few independent restaurants remain for the chains to drive out; (3) average per-store sales volume has actually fallen since the mid-1970s; (4) chains have expanded their menus in response to declining average unit volume and burger-bored customers; and (5) competitive advertising and sales promotion have become fairly commonplace as competitors engage in ever more intense efforts to protect and build market shares.

Thus, the fast-food business fits all the classic descriptors of an industry that has moved into the maturity/saturation phase of the life cycle: minimal growth in primary demand, a shakeout of marginal competitors, and intense competition for market share with heavy use of product differentiation, market repositioning, and heavy advertising and sales promotions.

*This case was prepared by Robert F. Dyer, Professor of Marketing, The George Washington University, and Richard F. Stark, Regional Marketing Manager, Roy Rogers Division of the Marriott Corporation.

One major indicator of the intense competition in the industry is the widespread use of a variety of sales promotions. Games, contests, scratch-and-win cards, premiums, coupons, and other efforts appear regularly at the point of sale. These sales promotions are used to achieve various objectives—to generate purchase trial, to induce switching behavior, to increase purchase frequency, and to stimulate lagging sales. Concerning the last objective, one industry marketing executive contends that the use of coupons has become analogous to heroin use. "When sales or share slump in an area, the regional marketing manager orders up a coupon drop. The 'high' takes the form of temporarily regaining sales and share, but like any fix, you've got to repeat the action over and over again."

Marriott's Roy Rogers Operation

Next to its hotels, Marriott's restaurant group, particularly the Roy Rogers fast-food division, offers the firm the greatest potential for growth. Marriott has, however, taken a very conservative expansionary approach to the fast-food market. This can be attributed in large part to the lessons learned when the company experienced great difficulties attempting to expand their Farrell's ice cream parlor concept across the nation.

Marriott's expansion of its Roy Rogers units has embraced a philosophy of three key success factors: (1) fostering consumer perceptions of a strong quality/value relationship, (2) developing a highly qualified store management system, and (3) concentrating in selected markets.

Marriott has been hesitant to go head to head against industry leaders (McDonald's, Burger King, etc.) unless it has at least a 15 percent market share in a given market. To provide such a position, Marriott initiated a buy out in 1982 of Gino's, an established regional fast-food chain, and converted 180 of the best Gino's sites in the Baltimore, Washington, D.C., Philadelphia, and northern New Jersey markets into Roy Rogers units.

By year-end 1983, Roy Rogers had the increased marketing leverage and consumer awareness it felt was required to compete aggressively in the "burger wars." The growth of store units and sales volume was particularly strong in Philadelphia and the New Jersey segment of greater New York. In 1984 the Roy Rogers system comprised 522 total units, consisting of 386 company-owned and 136 franchised outlets.

Roy Rogers units carry a broader product line than most competitive fast-food outlets. Items include fried chicken and roast beef sandwiches to complement a variety of burgers. Stores also offer a salad bar, topped baked potatos, and sundaes. Additionally, a crescent roll breakfast program is available in all stores in Baltimore and Washington and in 20 percent of the remaining stores.

Roy Rogers's 1984 Advertising and Sales Promotion Budget

By year-end 1984 Roy Rogers had achieved its marketing goal of establishing a strong presence in key markets in terms of number of sites and market share. Table 1 provides figures for Roy Rogers's 1984 media spending, sales, and market share

Roy Rogers Case

TABLE 1 **Roy Rogers's 1984 Media Spending, Sales, and Market Shares Across Five Major Markets**

	Washington	Baltimore	Philadelphia	New York	Connecticut	Total
1984 Media Spending	20.7%	14.6%	28.1%	29.3%	7.2%	100.0%
1984 Sales	33.5%	13.6%	26.4%	22.6%	3.8%	100.0%
1984 Share of Market	14.1%	25.0%	14.0%	7.0%	10.0%	

Source: Marriott Corporation, 1984.

for five key markets. It should be noted that Roy Rogers was a fairly late entry in the fast-food industry. Many of its outlets had, as of 1984, been open for only two years.

Roy Rogers was a heavy advertiser in its five key markets. During the first six months of 1984 it invested approximately $4,200,000 on television advertising in these markets. It had also become a very heavy spender on sales promotion tactics. Table 2 displays a percentage breakdown of Roy Rogers's 1984 total advertising and sales promotion budget.

TABLE 2 **Roy Rogers's Promotion Budget for 1984 and Proposed Promotion Budget for 1985**

	Percent of Total Promotion Budget (Actual for 1984)	Percent of Total Promotion Budget (Proposed for 1985)
Concept/Product		
Media	48	66
Media Production	7	9
Non–Media Production*	5	5
Subtotal	60	80
Promotional		
Media	26	12
Media Production	3	1
Non–Media Production*	11	7
Subtotal	40	20
Total Spending		
Media	74	78
Media Production	10	10
Non–Media Production*	16	12
Subtotal	100†	100‡

Source: Marriott Corporation, 1984.
*Point-of-sale materials, games, and premiums.
†Total promotional budget as a percent of sales = 4.9%
‡Total promotional budget as a percent of sales = 4.5%

It should be noted that concept/product expenditures cover advertisements in print and broadcast media and are intended to generate awareness of Roy Rogers, its diverse menu, and its high quality/value positioning. Expenditures directed at promoting products and concepts accounted for 60 percent of Roy Rogers's 1984 promotional budget. The promotional category in Table 2 covers media, media production costs, and non–media production costs for coupons, premiums, games, contests, and the like. Forty percent of the total promotional budget in 1984 was allocated to sales promotions (see Table 2).

The 1985 Advertising and Sales Promotion Budget

The date for completing the promotional budget section of Roy Rogers's 1985 Marketing Plan was fast approaching. Although no consensus existed about sales promotion's role for 1985, headquarters marketing was leaning towards a dramatic cutback in sales promotion expenditures. One alternative proposed (shown in Table 2) was a reallocation of total promotion spending to place much greater emphasis on concept/product advertising. This plan called for a split of 80 percent concept/product advertising and 20 percent sales promotion. Key strategy elements underlying this promotional alternative are presented in Table 3.

TABLE 3   **Key Strategy Elements for Roy Rogers's 1985 Promotional Program**

Overall Strategy Elements
1. Focus 80% of all media and production on product advertising to promote the Roy Rogers positioning strategy and concept.
2. In Washington and Baltimore, maintain consumer awareness of breakfast at, or near, levels achieved in 1984.
3. In all markets, establish that Roy Rogers's high-quality product offering makes it the best fast-food alternative for lunch and dinner:
   a. Rebuild awareness levels and quality perceptions for Roy Rogers's burgers and roast beef offerings.
   b. Maintain baked potato awareness and reinforce product use for dinner and lunch meal periods.
   c. Maintain chicken awareness and broadly establish product improvement, if appropriate.
4. Use appropriate concept/copy testing in development of creative materials.
5. Vertically integrate advertising throughout all media and in-store materials.

Creative Strategy Elements
1. Utilize "Slow Down—Fast Food You'll Want to Eat Slow" campaign creative format through 1985.
2. Continue development of the slow down campaign's ability to generate increased awareness for Roy Rogers's concept/products and to increase believability of the high-quality claims.
3. Continue to pursue alternative creative approaches that significantly improve communications effectiveness.

Media Strategy Elements
1. Focus all media on specifically targeted and defined audiences for each product and meal-part advertised.
2. Concentrate media plans and selections to achieve optimum balance of effective and efficient reach and frequency with effective registration of Roy Rogers's advertising messages.

In consideration of this alternative, Roy Rogers's Vice-President of Marketing expressed the following view: "Let's face it. We have to review what our huge sales promotion budget is doing for us. It seems that we've jumped on the industry bandwagon to scramble for share, trial, and volume. I'm wondering how much incremental new business the coupons and other promotional devices get us? Or are we really feeding our current customers at a lower price? Whatever the case, we've got a big educational process to undertake with our customers *and* our regional marketing people if we cut way back on sales promotion."

Questions

1. Should Roy Rogers reduce its heavy sales promotion expenditures in 1985? What research substantiation is needed to either maintain or reduce its current level of sales promotion spending?
2. If Roy Rogers does decide to reduce its sales promotion budget, what internal marketing within headquarters and with regional marketing staffs will be required? What external marketing with consumers will be needed to prevent them from switching to other fast-food outlets that offer a greater number of sales promotions?
3. Does the 1985 marketing plan's strategic direction seem sufficient to compensate for a movement away from heavy sales promotion expenditures? What risks is Roy Rogers taking?

Pan Am Airlines

The following letters describe a mishap that occurred with Pan American Airlines. Evaluate the customer's complaints and note the company's response.

September 24, 1984

Mr. William T. Seawell
Chairman of the Board and CEO
Pan American Worldways, Inc.
200 Park Avenue
New York, N.Y. 10166

Dear Mr. Seawell:

On September 10th, 1984, my wife, Mrs. Nita Gupta, my sister, Mrs. Shashi Kumar, and their four children boarded Pan Am flight 73 from New Delhi, India, for New York. From New York they were scheduled to connect with Pan Am flight 551 for Charlotte, North Carolina. Unfortunately, due to the late arrival of flight 73, they missed the connecting flight. The subsequent service they received from Pan Am's personnel at JFK was extremely poor. Furthermore, the representative's behavior was rude and unacceptable. I am providing for your information a description of the events that took place.

1. On September 10th, I along with my brother-in-law, Mr. Ravi Kumar, drove to Charlotte to receive our families. As the party did not arrive on flight 551, we approached Mr. Dave Sparrow, Pan Am's representative, with the problem (Mr. Sparrow works for United Airlines, which represents Pan Am at Charlotte). Since our family members were not on the passenger list, he suggested that they may have missed the connecting flight at JFK. Consequently, he gave us Pan Am's toll-free reservation number for information.

2. The reservation operator was not very helpful. She claimed that it was not possible for her to find out what happened at JFK. We asked her for Pan Am's phone number at JFK. Her response was, "I do not have the number; I do not know who you can contact; and I am sorry."

3. We then called some of our friends (we had to call them collect) in New York and requested them to, if they could, help us in tracing our family. One of our friends volunteered to go to JFK (this was at 10:30 p.m.) and subsequently left for the airport. Another friend of ours in New York told us that he would call JFK and find out what happened. After about 15 minutes he called us back and told us that, according to the Pan Am representative, no one on flight 73 had missed a connection and hence had not been overnighted.

4. We were now getting really concerned about the welfare of our family members. Consequently, we once again requested Mr. Sparrow to help. He was extremely helpful and obliged us by calling Pan Am operations. However, he seemed frustrated, as he could not get any satisfactory response. At this point we reached a conclusion that the only logical explanation was that our family must have missed their flight in New Delhi, India. For if they had missed the connecting flight at JFK, then at least Pan Am's JFK office would have informed Charlotte about the misconnection (we assumed that our family would have requested this). Having reached this conclusion, we returned (sans family) to our homes at 11:00 p.m.

5. After we reached home we tried to contact our family in New Delhi. Failing to get an international phone connection, we sent cables requesting their whereabouts.

6. At about 12:45 a.m. we received a collect call from my wife. She informed us that they missed the connecting flight at New York and had been overnighted. My obvious question to her was—knowing that we would be at Charlotte to receive you, why did you not inform us? She indicated that they repeatedly requested Pan Am's representative to inform Charlotte about their missing the connection and the representative's response was (a) this is not my problem; (b) such a service is not included in the airfare; and (c) if you want your family to know about your missing the connecting flight, then you call them from a public booth.

7. Furthermore, my wife told me that after Pan Am made arrangements for their stay at a hotel, the porter took them to a bus stop where a limo would come and pick them up. About an hour passed, and there was no sign of a limo. My wife went to the Pan Am representative for help. She was told that the porter took them to a wrong stop and that the correct stop was about half a mile from where they were and that it was their responsibility to go to the correct stop and Pan Am has nothing to do with how they get there. Anyway, knowing that they were safe in a hotel and had been booked on flight 551 for September 11, I asked my wife and sister to calm down and get some rest.

8. The next day I called Ms. Ramos at Pan Am's Consumer Affairs office and explained the incident. She assured me that such behavior was unacceptable and that a consumer affairs representative would contact me later during the day. (I am still waiting for the call.)

Mr. Seawell, we chose Pan Am for two major reasons. First, I had travelled with Pan Am last year and found the service adequate. Second, since our families would be travelling alone with small children, we wanted an airline in which you did not have to change terminals at JFK. However, as you can infer from the above incident, we seemed to have made a mistake in selecting Pan Am.

First of all, how do you expect two ladies with four tired children (who have been on the airplane for almost 24 hours) and 9 pieces of luggage to find out the phone number for Pan Am's office at Charlotte airport and inform us about the misconnection? (Note that we were unable to get your JFK number from reservations.) Second, having been taken to a wrong limo stop, how do you expect them to haul four children and 9 pieces of luggage? The least Pan Am's representative could have done was to show sympathy and courtesy and suggest that they can get a porter to move the luggage. Our family was prepared to pay the porter and was not asking for any freebies from Pan Am. All they expected was some courtesy and sympathy from your employees, who are supposed to be a company's goodwill ambassadors.

Finally, Mr. Seawell, I hope that this is not a norm but an isolated incident. Such experiences are bound to generate considerable ill will amongst your customers and result in negative word-of-mouth. We are enclosing copies of the cables we sent and the tickets. We hope you will look into the matter. We await your reply.

Sincerely,

Srinivas Gupta

Enclosures:
cc: Mr. Joseph H. Daley, V.P. Public Relations
    Mr. William R. Roy, V.P. Passenger Service

November 7, 1984

Mr. William T. Seawell
Chairman of the Board and CEO
Pan American Worldways, Inc.
200 Park Avenue
New York, NY 10166

Dear Mr. Seawell:

Enclosed is a copy of the letter explaining our experiences with Pan Am's service. I was under the impression that corporate management desires to stay close to the customer. At least this is the case with many firms. Since I did not receive any acknowledgement to my previous letter (September 24, 1984), I am assuming that Pan Am's management is not interested in the experiences of their consumers.

Sincerely,

Srinivas Gupta

Enclosure

Response from Pan Am

Donald L. Parker
Senior Vice-President
Passenger Services

November 27, 1984

Dear Mr. Gupta:

As I am responsible for all aspects of Pan Am's passenger services, your letter has been forwarded to me for my handling.

Pan Am Airlines

Please accept my sincere apologies for the inconvenience your family encountered. It is disheartening to learn that we sometimes fail to provide the professional and courteous service that has become Pan Am's standard.

The events you describe are of serious concern to me, as they are not in keeping with established practices. Allow me to take a moment to describe what our usual procedures are. When a flight is delayed or cancelled, a message is sent to our central reservations control office so the information can be disseminated to anyone calling. Whenever a delay or cancellation results in reaccommodating passengers on other flights or placing them in hotels, that information is recorded on a passenger manifest, and the station knows each passenger's disposition. In these situations, the station will make notifications upon request. It is therefore disturbing for me to learn that you experienced so much difficulty receiving accurate information and assistance.

As you know, in a marketing industry such as ours, customer service and customer satisfaction are essential to our success. Providing each of our passengers with thoughtful and courteous service is a basic function of all our employees. I am sorry that on this occasion the individuals involved did not fulfill this expectation. I want to assure you that this incident is being thoroughly investigated with the station personnel so that corrective action can be initiated.

This unfortunate experience is not representative of our usually high service standards. I do hope you will give us another opportunity to serve your travel needs. As a gesture of goodwill, we are enclosing a travel voucher in the amount of $200, which can be used toward future travel on Pan Am.

Thank you for taking the time to write. We are working hard to correct any deficiencies which may exist.

Sincerely,

Donald L. Parker

Attachment

Questions

1. How do you evaluate the efforts of the public relations division of Pan Am in this situation?
2. If you were in the position of Pan Am's public relations division, how would you have handled this situation differently?

*Mead Products: The Trapper Keeper®**

"You know, this just might be the most fantastic product we've ever launched. I think it's really going to shake up the school supplies market!" The man who spoke was Bryant Crutchfield, Mead Products' New Ventures manager.

Mr. Crutchfield had just concluded a meeting in Wichita, Kansas, with Bob Crandall, the regional sales manager, where the two men reviewed results of an August 1978 market test. The purpose of the test was to measure market acceptance of Trapper® Portfolio and the Trapper Keeper® Notebook.

As he prepared to depart Wichita Airport for Dayton, Ohio, Mr. Crutchfield felt good about the success of the test. A new unique product unlike anything else on the market—and a total sell-through in test market.

But Crutchfield also thought about plans for 1979 and the big questions yet to be resolved. "How many can we sell nationally?" "What promotional support will we need?"

Mead Products

A division of Mead Corporation, Mead Products (formerly Westab) is the largest U.S. manufacturer and marketer of school and college supplies, stationery, photo albums, and home/office supplies. Westab was founded in 1927 (as the Western Tablet and Stationery Corp.) and merged with Mead Corporation in 1966.

Since its inception, Mead Products has developed and marketed numerous items that stand as all-time best-sellers in the retail school supply and stationery markets. Perhaps it is most famous for its line of Spiral® brand wirebound school supplies that uses a unique method of wire-binding large quantities of tablet paper, which revolutionized the design and production of notebooks, theme books, and memo pads.

The Organizer®, a trifold pockets and pad binder introduced in 1972, was the industry's best-selling school supply item for three consecutive years. Other exclusive Mead Products' introductions include The System® (in 1973), The Spiral Organizer® (in 1974), the Data Center® (in 1975), and The Pinchless One® (in 1976). These also have been best-sellers.

Other well-known Mead Products include: The Big Chief® writing tablet, a best-seller for over seven generations; The Valet® tablet and envelope stationery line, which started a revolution in the 59¢ per item market; Academie^{T.M.} brand artists pads, books, watercolors and crayons; and Montag®, a famous name in quality, boxed stationery.

---

*This case was prepared by Peter S. Carusone, Marketing Department, Wright State University. Copyright 1982 Peter S. Carusone.

The company traditionally has been a trend setter in the industry. In 1966, for example, Mead Products was the first to replace the drab blue canvas coverings on loose-leaf binders with various fabrics in fashionable colors and designs. More recently, through innovative manufacturing techniques, photo-graphics have been applied to the covers of numerous school supply items.

Another industry first was Mead Products' decision twelve years ago to advertise on national network television. During the season the commercials are running (late August to early September), Mead Products becomes one of the largest TV advertisers in the country—of any product.

Today, Mead Products, with its own sales force, markets over 3,000 separate items. National distribution is obtained through wholesalers, distributors, and jobbers, as well as direct to chain discount, drug, variety, food and convenience stores, and department and college stores. The company operates seven plants and twelve sales offices/showrooms in ten states.

How The Trapper® and The Trapper Keeper® Originated

The idea for the Trapper® and The Trapper Keeper® was identified by extensive informal exploration of the school supplies market and its total environment. "Management requires us to do a complete situation analysis," Mr. Crutchfield points out. "We have to understand what's happening in the marketplace."

A situation analysis of Mead Products entails extensive study of everything that happens from production of products, through the channels of distribution, to their consumption. It includes analysis of educational trends, consumer trends, sales trends, product usage, competition, the trade, and pertinent external factors.

Consumer Definition   People of all ages involved in the learning process are the consumers of school supplies. The range is from the preschooler just learning how to hold a crayon up to and including the adult taking refresher courses to update professional skills.

Consumer Population   The total student population was projected to continue to increase over the next five years but at a lesser rate than in the past. While the number of grade, junior, and senior high school students was declining slightly, the decline would be more than offset by increases in two other consumer segments: (1) preschool kids who in just a few years will become primary customers and (2) college enrollment, and adult basic and occupational education.

Product Usage   Consumer product usage in the growth-market segments (except preschoolers) was basically the same as that of students in grade and high school: wirebounds, filler, binders, and portfolios. And, increasing in popularity were portfolios, wirebound notebooks, and selected binders. These select binders are those having pads and pockets that provide for versatile storage of a variety of materials. The demand for filler paper and ring notebooks was relatively flat.

Educational Trends   Important educational trends were identified, along with implications for future demand of various kinds of school supplies. It was learned, for example, that students were taking more courses, more advanced courses, and more individual instruction. Also uncovered were increased use of timely, special-ized portable materials, more use of shared classrooms, and smaller lockers. The impact of the energy shortage and emergence of a market for left-handed students also were assessed.

Trade Analysis   As changes in education were affecting the need for and usage of school supplies, so changes in retail shopping patterns were affecting the op-portunities for effective distribution of school supply products. Combination stores (food and drug) were growing. Independent drugstores were declining, while the drug chains were emerging. Growing rapidly and becoming very popular were the convenience food stores, particularly in certain markets. There were, for example, 864 convenience stores in Houston; 627 in Atlanta. In some cities, the number of convenience stores were twice the number of food stores. Another important retail type which was beginning to emerge is the minicombo (convenience and drug combination).

Competition   The school supplies market was very fragmented. Competition was mostly regional due to the high cost of freight. Only one or two companies other than Mead Products were selling nationally. Mead was the leader nationally, but this varied by product line and by region.

A Need Unfulfilled

The outcome of the situation analysis was that it led Mr. Crutchfield to formulate the following thesis: *There is a need for a notebook to hold and organize the portfolios.*

"We saw that students were taking more courses—some of these a variety of 'mini' courses. We saw an increase in the use of pocket portfolios—growth in excess of 20 percent annually. We knew from research that they were using one portfolio per subject or class. With the increased number of classes and portfolios, a student needs some place to keep them organized." "What's more," Mr. Crutch-field points out, "traditional ports with horizontal pockets have a tendency to spill their contents when mistakenly turned upside down. So, the Trapper® Portfolio and the Trapper Keeper® notebook would provide the student with both better portfolios *and* a place to keep them organized."

The best-selling portfolio on the West Coast (Pee-Chee®) has a vertical pocket, but it had never been popular east of the Rockies. It is interesting to note that the part of the rationale for the item occurred to Mr. Crutchfield as the result of a conversation at home with his 13-year-old daughter. In retrospect, he describes the experience as one of "creative listening." In asking his daughter about the usage of portfolios in her classes, Mr. Crutchfield thought he heard her relate how the teacher required the students to submit their assignments in portfolios as a timesaving device. The teacher wanted to use the ports both for collecting assignments and for redistributing them, along with handouts, so students could pick up their own portfolios and save class time. When a Mead researcher was dispatched by Mr. Crutchfield to talk with the teacher, he discovered that the teacher never said that. And when the 13-year-old daughter was questioned further, it was found that she never said that either. But, the results of the research were positive. The teacher thought the "nonexistent procedure" was a good one.

Questions

1. The Mead Corporation is an innovative company but requires some ideas regarding its promotional mix for new product introductions. What strategic concepts would you propose to Mead regarding its introduction of the Trapper portfolio and the Trapper Keeper? How do these ideas relate to their other products?
2. What weight would you put on advertising, personal selling, sales promotions, etc.? Explain. That is, what proportion of the budget would you put on each activity?

Pepsi. The Choice of a New Generation

PepsiCo proclaims its first Lionel Richie commercial, a BBDO-Bob Giraldi extravaganza, "the most talked about commercial of the year." The landmark three-part, three-minute music video starring pop singer/songwriter Lionel Richie debuted during the CBS Grammy awards telecast in late February 1985.

Building on the 1984 advertising theme "Pepsi. The Choice of a New Generation," the new commercial represented PepsiCo's most ambitious piece of advertising ever undertaken. The company hopes it will surpass the splash made by its Michael Jackson spots in 1984.

The commercial contains three distinct parts entitled "Style," "Heart," and "Beat." It features three Richie songs: the hits "Running with the Night" and "You Mean More to Me" plus an original composition written by Richie specifically for the commercial. Each part of the commercial also aired as separate 60-second commercials.

The commercial begins with Richie saying: "You know we're a whole new generation. A generation of new rhythms, new feelings and styles," then swings into the lively pop song he composed for the commercial:

> *You wear your style, and wear your smile so free,*
> > *so fine, so right.*
> *See the new generation. Flashing through the night.*
> *If looks could sing the sounds would ring across a*
> > *neon sky.*
> *We're a new generation. Living Pepsi style.**

*©PepsiCo, Inc., Brockman Music and Dyad Music Ltd. 1985. Reproduced with Permission.

After repeating the refrain, "We made our choice. Making it Pepsi," the commercial fades into a second segment, featuring the Richie ballad "You Mean More to Me." The pace then quickens in the third segment of the commercial with original lyrics set to the fast tempo of Richie's "Running with the Night," entertaining a crowd of 3,000 people at a block-party concert (see Figure 1).

"Today, music is the best way to communicate," said Roger Enrico, president and chief executive officer of Pepsi-Cola USA. "It's become part of the American language—and nobody speaks that language better than Lionel Richie."

PepsiCo signed Richie to what the company described as "the largest and most comprehensive agreement ever made between a performing artist and a corporation" in 1984. The deal included PepsiCo's exclusive sponsorship of Richie's

Sources: Jennifer Pendleton, "Pepsi: Richie Spot Truly a Winner," *Advertising Age*, February 25, 1985, pp. 3 and 84. Adapted with permission from *Advertising Age*. Copyright 1985 by Crain Communications, Inc., "Viewpoint: Editorial: Making Advertising—and News," *Ad Age*, April 1, 1985, p. 18.

Pepsi: The Choice of a New Generation

FIGURE 1   **Richie's Block Party for Pepsi-Cola**

The world's most popular performer gives you an inside look at the New Generation. Through his words and music, Lionel Richie exposes the pulsing beat that is "The Choice of a New Generation." "Block Party" is sure to become a Pepsi advertising classic.

1984–1985 concert tours, a series of commercials, and a joint donation of $100,000 to a program that encourages inner-city students to stay in school.

Commenting on the decision to produce and air a three-minute commercial, Enrico said: "Certainly three minutes of prime-time network advertising represents a major commitment on our part. But to present Lionel Richie's unique talents, we felt it was necessary to create a unique vehicle."

The Richie extravaganza drew from the brightest, creative talents in the industry: Pepsi-Cola USA's ad agency Batten, Barton, Durstine & Osborn; Bob Giraldi, the rock video whiz who directed Michael Jackson's Pepsi commercials; and Alan Pottasch, senior vice-president of creative services, Pepsi-Cola USA.

PepsiCo produced the elaborate spot with maximum hype in mind. To boost the spot, it placed newspaper ads in the top ten U.S. cities prior to the commercial's network debut. "In this jungle of jingles, if you don't do something impactful like create an event, it's very difficult to get attention," said Pottasch.

PepsiCo also received promotional help from MTV: Music Television. The music video cable network ran the three-minute commercial as a music news story the night following the Grammy awards telecast plus a special feature on the making

"Shuttle" Advertisement for Pepsi-Cola

The crew of astronauts is sweating out one of the inevitable delays in a space shuttle launch. The temperature in the cabin begins to rise. As the astronauts hear their friend at mission control pop a can of Pepsi, they can barely endure the tantalization. As the delay continues, the man from mission control talks his thirsty companions through a Pepsi—allowing them to enjoy their favorite drink in the only way possible. The controller describes the Pepsi and its irresistible taste so well that this just may be the shortest mission ever!

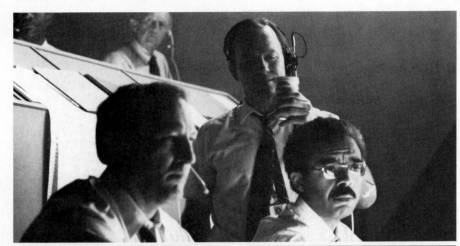

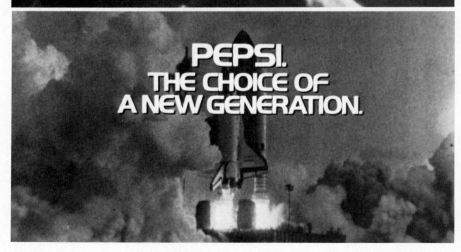

of the commercial. It also aired on VH1, MTV's new music service aimed at 25- to 54-year olds.

Six other new Pepsi ads joined the Richie commercial to form the brand's 1985 advertising campaign. Two commercials feature the Hispanic rock group Menudo; the other four are humorous looks at today's high-tech world. Examples of two of the humorous commercials are the following:

A "Space Shuttle" commercial shows an astronaut waiting for take off and longing for a Pepsi. A NASA official offers to guide him through the vicarious experience of enjoying a Pepsi by describing the slow pour, the water beads on the can, and the bubbles jumping (see Figure 2).

A group of people in the future encountering relics from earth sets the scene for the "Archaeology" commercial. A student finds an antiquated bottle of Coca-Cola and asks, "What is it?" The guide replies, "I have no idea." The commercial ends with the Pepsi theme "The Choice of a New Generation."

Questions

1. How would you describe the *kind* of advertising strategy that PepsiCo is using for its Pepsi soft drink in the 1984–1985 campaign? How would you evaluate the campaign? Compare PepsiCo's advertising with that of the current Coca-Cola advertising campaign.

2. How can PepsiCo pretest the effects of music in its commercial advertisements? How should the company post-test those advertising commercials?

3. Might the "new generation's" music and theme alienate "older" consumers of soft drinks? Should PepsiCo care? If so, Why? If not, Why?

4. Do superstars like Michael Jackson and Lionel Richie enhance the communications value of a product like Pepsi? The sales of the product? Explain.

5. In general, which is the more important element in advertising—the verbal content or the nonverbal content? Explain. How would you evaluate the importance of music versus the visual elements of television advertising? Could this latter issue vary with the type of product? Explain.

Glossary of Key Terms

Achievers (p. 151)
A group of outer-directed people who, according to the Values and Life-Styles typology, constitute 22 percent of the adult American population. They are the successful businesspeople, technocrats, and professionals in American society. Demographically, achievers are well-educated, middle-aged (median age of 42), and mostly white and married. Psychographically, achievers are highly self-confident, possess high need for achievement, and are very conservative.

Active-synthesis (p. 49)
The second stage of perceptual encoding, which involves a more refined perception of a stimulus than simply examining its basic features. The context of the situation in which information is received plays an major role in determining what is perceived and interpreted.

Activity quotas (p. 252)
Performance goals that emphasize such tasks as (1) daily calls, (2) new customers called on, (3) orders from new accounts, (4) product demonstrations made, and (5) displays built. This type of quota stimulates a balanced approach to sales representatives' jobs, however, it fails to show whether the activity was actually performed or whether it was done effectively.

Adoption process (p. 183)
The mental stages through which an individual passes in accepting and becoming a repeat purchaser of an innovation.

Advertising (p. 297)
A form of either mass communication or direct-to-consumer communication that is nonpersonal and paid for by various business firms, nonprofit organizations, and individuals who are in some way identified in the advertising message and who hope to inform or persuade members of a particular audience.

Advertising deception (p. 231)
An advertisement (or advertising campaign) that leaves the consumer with an impression and/or belief different from what would normally be expected if the consumer had reasonable knowledge, and that impression and/or belief is factually untrue or potentially misleading.

Advertising strategy (p. 308)
A plan of action that is guided by corporate and marketing strategies. Corporate and marketing strategies determine how much can be invested in advertising, at what markets advertising efforts need to be directed, how advertising must be coordinated with other marketing elements, and, to some degree, how advertising is to be executed.

Affect referral (p. 60)
A consumer strategy in which the customer calls from memory his or her attitudes (i.e., affect) toward relevant alternatives and picks the alterna-

tive with the most positive affect. This type of choice strategy is evident in frequently purchased items where risk is minimal (i.e., low-involvement items).

Affective component of attitude (p. 76)
The emotional component of an attitude.

Affectively based preference (p. 92)
A consumer's choice of a particular object based on his or her emotions toward the object or issue.

Anticlimax order (p. 103)
A message structure component in which the most important points are presented at the beginning of the message.

Aspirational group (p. 146)
A classification of people in which individuals do not, in fact, belong to the collective whole but wish to belong.

Associative bond (p. 125)
In congruity theory, attitude incongruity in which a message's source makes positive statements about the object in the message. Congruence is restored when the receiver holds the same attitude toward both the source and the object. *See* **Dissociative bond**

Attitude (p. 75)
A general and enduring positive or negative feeling about some person, object, or issue.

Behavioral component of attitude (p. 76)
The action component of an attitude. Also called conative component.

Behavioral modification (p. 92)
Methods that marketers use to change customers' preferences without first having to change customers' cognitions. Examples include classical and operant conditioning, modeling, and ecological modification.

Belongers (p. 151)
A group of outer-directed people who according to the Values and Life-Styles typology, represent 35 percent of the population and are an older group, with a median age of 52. The members of this group are deeply concerned with social acceptability and conformity. Belongers are mostly married, are white, and live in small towns or ru-

ral areas. They are satisfied with life, are averse to taking risks, and trust others.

Channel (p. 26)
The path through which the message moves from sender to receiver. Organizations use both broadcast and print media to channel their messages to current and potential customers.

Classification dominance (p. 561)
The practice in which a store heavily invests in merchandise and has a wide assortment of merchandise, as well as depth in each line. This procedure tells the customer, "We have everything imaginable and plenty of it. If we don't have it, nobody does."

Climax order (p. 103)
A message structure component in which a communicator presents the strongest arguments at the end of the message.

Cognitive component of attitude (p. 76)
The intellectual component of attitude. In marketing, the consumer's knowledge and thoughts about an object or issue.

Cognitive dissonance (p. 190)
A psychological state of tension or discomfort that results when two or more ideas, or cognitions, are perceived to be inconsistent within one another or with an individual's behavior. These cognitions consist of beliefs, feelings, and opinions a person holds about things in the environment.

Cognitive response (p. 82)
A self-generated thought that consumers produce in response to persuasive efforts.

Cognitive-based preference (p. 91)
A consumer's choice of a particular object based on his or her belief that the object is best able to satisfy his or her consumption needs.

Combination quotas (p. 252)
Performance goals that integrate the strengths of the four quota systems (sales volume quotas, profit quotas, expense quotas, activity quotas) and minimize their weaknesses. This system is complex and may be confusing to employees.

Communication goals (p. 20)
Statements of an organization's advertising objec-

tives. Examples of an organization's communication goals could be the following: (1) to create customer awareness of the product; (2) to facilitate customer understanding of the product, its attributes, benefits, and advantages; (3) to enhance the customer's attitude toward the offering; (4) to generate trial purchase behavior; and (5) to facilitate favorable word-of-mouth communication about the product.

Communications (p. 25)

Process whereby individuals share meaning and establish a commonness of thought. *See* **Marketing communications**

Comparative advertising (p. 100)

A message structure component in which advertisers directly compare their products or brands with competitive offerings, typically claiming that the advertised item is superior in one or several important purchase considerations. Comparative advertising may be either one- or two-sided.

Compatibility (p. 187)

The degree to which an innovation is perceived to fit into a person's ways of doing things. The more compatible an innovation is with a person's need structure, personal values and beliefs, and past experiences, the more rapid the rate of adoption.

Compensatory heuristic (p. 60)

A consumer strategy in which the customer ranks each of the criteria he or she would like to be met, decides how well each alternative will satisfy these criteria, and integrates this information to arrive at a "score" for each alternative. Theoretically the consumer selects the alternative with the highest overall score. This procedure is likely to be used in risky (high-involvement) circumstances; that is, when a decision involves considerable financial, performance, or psychological risk.

Compiled list (p. 429)

Customer names that are gathered from a variety of data sources, such as census reports, telephone directories, and car registrations.

Complexity (p. 187)

The degree of perceived difficulty of an innova-

tion. The more difficult an innovation is to understand or use, the slower the rate of adoption.

Conative component of attitude (p. 76)

The action component of an attitude; a person's behavioral tendency toward an object. In marketing, the consumer's intention to purchase a specific item. Also called behavioral component.

Conjunctive heuristic (p. 61)

One of three noncompensatory consumer strategies in which the consumer establishes cutoffs, or minima, on *all* pertinent criteria; an alternative is retained for further consideration only if it meets or exceeds *all* minima.

Consumer information processing (CIP) perspective (p. 41)

A model of consumer choice behavior in which marketers view the consumer as a logical, highly cognitive, and systematic decision maker. *See* **Hedonistic approach to consumption**

Continuous innovation (p. 182)

A new product or product change that represents a minor alteration from existing products and has limited impact on customer's consumption patterns. *See* **Discontinuous innovation**

Corporate strategy (p. 307)

A plan of action set by top management representing the long-range (typically three to five years) objectives, plans, and budgets for all corporate units and departments. Corporate strategy (1) is based on situation analyses of economic, competitive, social, and other pertinent factors that represent opportunities and threats for a business enterprise and (2) is formulated in view of the enterprise's inherent strengths and weaknesses.

Corrective advertising (p. 235)

A Federal Trade Commission program that is used when a firm misleads consumers to rectify any deceptive impressions it has created in consumers' minds.

Cost price standard (p. 551)

A psychological aspect of price that occurs when consumers believe they can judge the producer's cost of a product; they develop a fair price estimate based on their judgment of the producer's cost plus a reasonable profit.

Counterargument (p. 83)

A form of cognitive response that occurs when the receiver challenges message claims. *See* **Source derogation** and **Supportive argument**

Creative platform (p. 335)

The blueprint for an advertising campaign, consisting of five parts: objectives, target audience, key consumer benefits, other usable benefits, and creative strategy statement.

Culture (p. 146)

The collection of values, ideas, attitudes, and other meaningful symbols created by man to shape human behavior and the artifacts of that behavior as they are transmitted from one generation to the next. Culture is learned behavior and is not innate.

Decoding (p. 26)

The mental process of transforming message symbols into thought. *See* **Encoding**

Diffusion process (p. 183)

The channels through which an innovation is communicated and adopted by groups throughout the marketplace.

Direct mail (p. 424)

The use of mail deliveries sent to current or prospective customers. Examples include letters, postcards, programs, calendars, folders, catalogs, order blanks, and price lists.

Direct marketing (p. 423)

The total of activities by which products and services are offered to market segments in one or more media for informational purposes or to solicit responses from present or prospective customers or contributors by mail, telephone, or other access.

Direct response advertising (p. 424)

The use of any medium (direct mail, television, etc.) with the intent of creating immediate action from customers. Three distinct characteristics of direct response advertising are (1) it makes a definite offer, (2) it contains all the information necessary to make a decision, and (3) it contains a response device (coupon, phone number, or both) to facilitate immediate action.

Discontinuous innovation (p. 182)

A new product or product change that requires substantial relearning and fundamental alterations in basic consumption patterns. *See* **Continuous innovation**

Disjunctive heuristic (p. 61)

One of three noncompensatory consumer strategies in which the consumer accepts an alternative if it meets any one of his or her minimum standards; that is, an alternative is acceptable if it meets or exceeds choice criterion 1, *or* choice criterion 2, *or* choice criterion n.

Dissociative bond (p. 125)

In congruity theory, attitude incongruity in which a message's source makes negative statements about the object in the message. Congruence is restored when the receiver perceives equal polarization (i.e., -1 and $+1$) between the source and the object. *See* **Associative bond**

Dissociative group (p. 146)

A classification of people in which members eschew association with other members and view them negatively.

Distal stimulus (p. 33)

An activity-inciting object or agent that is not in contact with an individual. *See* **Proximal stimulus**

Dual-coding theory (p. 55)

A theory of memory that states that pictures are stored in an individual's memory in both verbal and visual form, whereas words are less likely to have visual representations.

Dynamically continuous innovation (p. 182)

A new product or product change that requires some disruption in established consumer behavior patterns, rather than fundamental alterations.

Effective rating points (ERPs) (p. 364)

A statistical measure of an advertising campaign based on the idea that each exposure to an advertisement is not of equal value. This system is used in media planning to achieve the maximum impact for a product; what is effective (or ineffective) for one product may not necessarily be so for another.

Emulators (p. 151)

A group of outer-directed people who, according to the Values and Life-Styles typology, represent 10 percent of the population, are a young group, with a median age of 28, live in urban areas, and tend to be somewhat dissatisfied with life because they perceive the system has somehow been unfair to them. They compensate for their felt inadequacies by emulating the behavior of higher status people.

Encoding (p. 26)
The mental process of putting thoughts into symbolic form. *See* **Decoding**

Expense quotas (p. 252)
Performance goals that relate the sales representative's expenses to his or her sales volume.

Experientials (p. 151)
A group of inner-directed people who, according to the Values and Life-Styles typology, are young (median age of 28), well-educated, and reasonably well-off financially. Experientials are interested in experiencing life. They tend not to become committed to any long-term relationships and are, instead, relatively liberated and impulsive. Experientials are unambitious and obtain their primary gratification, not from work, but from other life experiences.

External analysis (p. 18)
A process used in promotion management that involves a thorough review of environmental factors that are likely to influence promotional effectiveness and product success, primarily by assessing the economic and legal climates, the competition, sociocultural developments, and the channel of distribution. *See* **Internal analysis**

External environment (p. 245)
Factors outside an organization that affect sales management and sales performance, for example, the behavior of potential customers, the competition, the legal restrictions, the speed of change in technology, the abundance or lack of natural resources, and the social/cultural changes.

Feature analysis (p. 49)
The initial stage of perceptual encoding whereby a receiver examines the basic features of a stimulus (brightness, depth, angles, etc.) and from this makes a preliminary classification.

Formal group (p. 146)
A classification of people whose relationship is

based on specified membership requirements, bylaws, and the like.

Frequency (p. 361)
A media planning statistic that deals with how often prospective customers are reached by the advertiser's messages; the average number of times the target audience is exposed.

Gestalt (p. 528)
The notion that people react to the whole, not to the individual parts of a situation; the whole is seen as greater than the sum of its parts when the parts interact synergistically.

Gross rating points (GRPs) (p. 362)
A statistic that represents the mathematical product of reach times frequency. The number of GRPs indicates the total weight of advertising during a time frame, such as a four-week period.

Hedonistic approach to consumption (p. 41)
A model of consumer choice behavior in which marketers view the customer as driven not by rational and purely logical considerations, but rather by emotions. Also called Experiential approach. *See* **Consumer information processing (CIP) perspective**

Hedonistic consumption (p. 67)
Buying in which consumers' multisensory images, fantasies, and emotional arousal are elicited in using products. Products viewed from this perspective are more than mere objective entities and are, instead, subjective symbols representing love, pride, status, achievement, pleasure, and so forth.

Hierarchy of goals (p. 65)
A control mechanism in which consumers undertake various purposive behaviors to make a satisfactory purchase decision. A customer forms the hierarchy and then works to accomplish each goal.

House list (p. 429)
Names of customers that are generated from a company's own internal records. Customer's names are often grouped into active, recently active, long-since-active customers, or inquiry categories. A list may be subdivided by the recency

of a customer's purchase, the frequency of a customer's purchase, the monetary value of each purchase, or the type of products purchased. Customers may be categorized by geography, demography, or psychographic characteristics.

I-Am-Me's (p. 151)

A group of inner-directed people who, according to the Values and Life-Styles typology, represent the youngest group, with over 90 percent being younger than 25. Many are college students who are the children of the achievers group. They tend to be somewhat flamboyant and exhibitionistic and experiment with the unconventional.

Identification (p. 122)

Process whereby receivers perceive a source to be attractive and adopt the attitudes, behaviors, interests, or preferences of the source.

Image advertising (p. 351)

A paid communication that attempts to gain name recognition for a company, to establish goodwill for it and its products, or to identify itself with some meaningful and socially acceptable activity.

Informal groups (p. 146)

A classification of people whose relationship is loosely defined and without specified membership requirements.

Innovation (p. 181)

An idea, practice, product, or service that an individual perceives to be new. The consumers' view of the product is the critical factor.

Intelligence test (p. 260)

A psychological test that attempts to measure three interacting components in a person's general mental ability: (1) learning ability (which is the mental ability to acquire information and remember it), (2) critical ability (which enables a person to assess the rationality of messages and thereby accept or reject a message on a logical basis), and (3) ability to draw references (which is the ability to interpret messages and make sound implications based on the facts in a message).

Interest test (p. 260)

A psychological test that is designed to identify a person's vocational and avocational inclinations.

Internal analysis (p. 18)

A process used in promotion management that considers the organization's strengths and weaknesses, primarily by assessing its financial and personnel resources. *See* **external analysis**

Internal (organizational) environment (p. 245)

Factors within an organization that affect the operation of sales management, for example, an organization's objectives, the human and financial resources of the organization, its production capabilities and delivery schedules, its research and development capabilities, and its managerial philosophy.

Internalization (p. 128)

Phenomenon that occurs when the receiver learns and adopts the source's position or attitude as his or her own. Internalized attitudes tend to be maintained even when the source of the message is forgotten and even when the source switches to a new position.

Interrupt mechanism (p. 65)

A control mechanism that accounts for consumers' adaptation to changing conditions by his or her altering existing goals and structuring new ones.

Involuntary attention (p. 44)

Observation that requires little or no effort on the part of a receiver; the stimulus intrudes upon a person's consciousness even though he does not want it to.

Issue advertising (p. 354)

A paid communication that is concerned with propagating ideas and explaining controversial social issues of public importance. Also called advocacy advertising.

Law of demand (p. 544)

An economic principle that says that as the price of a commodity rises, the quantity demanded by consumers declines, and vice versa.

Lexicographic heuristic (p. 61)

One of three noncompensatory consumer strategies in which the consumer ranks his or her criteria according to relative importance. Alternatives are then evaluated on each criterion, starting with the most important. An alternative is selected if it is judged superior on the most important criterion. If two or more alternatives are judged equal on the most important criterion, the consumer examines these alternatives on the next most important criterion, then on the next most important, and so on until a tie is broken.

Line-item budgeting (p. 247)
Procedure that allocates funds in meticulous detail to each identifiable cost center, for example, office supplies, wages, research, and travel.

Luxury products (p. 166)
Goods that have a degree of exclusivity.

Mail response list (p. 429)
Customer names on the house lists of other companies bought by a firm to promote its own products.

Marketing (p. 4)
Process whereby businesses and other organizations facilitate exchanges, or transfers of value, between themselves and their customers and clients.

Marketing communications (p. 4)
Process whereby businesses and other organizations facilitate exchanges, or transfers of value, between themselves and their customers or clients by establishing shared meaning through the use of all elements in the marketing mix.

Marketing concept (p. 8)
Philosophy in which the marketer adapts to the customers' needs and wants. This is usually accomplished by satisfying the customer's needs and by offering superior value. *See* **Promotion concept**

Marketing strategy (p. 307)
A plan of action that is an extension of corporate strategy and involves plans, budgets, and controls needed to direct a firm's product, promotion, distribution, and pricing activities.

Membership groups (p. 146)
A classification of people in which the individuals do, in fact, belong because of some common attribute.

Mere exposure hypothesis (p. 43)
A marketing theory that asserts that a person's (or consumer's) repeated exposure to a stimulus may generate positive affect toward the object (or advertised brand) through enhanced familiarity.

Message (p. 26)
A symbolic expression of a sender's thoughts.

Message appeals (p. 106)
The contents of a message; specifically, the communicator's request for a favorable response toward the subject of the message.

Message codes (p. 110)
The system used for encoding thoughts into coherent and effective messages.

Message structure (p. 96)
The organization of elements in a message. Three structural issues have particular relevance to marketing communicators: (1) message-sidedness, (2) order of presentation, and (3) conclusion drawing.

New buy task (p. 294)
A situation in which customers have no experience; customers are unfamiliar with the product and are liable to be nervous and/or defensive.

Noise (p. 27)
Extraneous and distracting stimuli that interfere with reception of a message in its pure and original form. Noise occurs at all stages of the communications process.

Nonattention (p. 44)
Phenomenon that occurs when a person willfully selects a competing stimulus or is distracted by an intruding stimulus of greater strength.

Nonvoluntary attention (p. 44)
Observation that occurs when a person is attracted to a stimulus and continues to pay attention to the stimulus because it holds interest for him or her. A person in this situation neither resists the stimulus nor willingly attends to it initially. However, once his or her attention is attracted, the individual continues to give attention because the stimulus has some benefit or relevance. Also called spontaneous attention. *See* **Involuntary attention** and **Voluntary attention**

Observability (p. 189)
The extent of visibility or the degree to which other people can observe one's ownership and use of a new product.

Penetration pricing (p. 548)

Strategy whereby the organization elects to introduce its product at a low price because management believes that demand is fairly elastic.

Perceptual encoding (p. 49)

The process of interpreting stimuli, which includes two stages: feature analysis and active-synthesis.

Personal selling (p. 271)

A form of person-to-person communication in which a seller attempts to persuade prospective buyers to purchase his or her company's (organization's) product or service.

Personality test (p. 260)

A psychological test that attempts to measure a person's affability, confidence, poise, aggressiveness, etc.

Persuasion (p. 75)

In marketing, an effort by a marketing communicator to influence the consumer's attitude and behavior in some manner.

Phased strategies (p. 62)

Procedure in which consumers use a combination of heuristics in sequence or in phase with one another to make decisions.

Planning (p. 245)

One of the five basic management functions; the process of establishing a broad set of policies, procedures, and goals to achieve organizational objectives. Planning occurs at all levels of the organization.

Point-of-purchase communications (p. 5)

Promotional elements, including displays, posters, signs, and a variety of other in-store materials, that are designed to influence the customer's choice at the time of purchase.

Postdecisional dissonance (p. 191)

Refers to tension or discomfort that occurs after an individual makes an important decision; this state results from selecting one alternative from among several, all of which have both positive and negative characteristics. Postdecisional dissonance is greatest when the alternatives are very similar to each other.

Preference (p. 91)

A behavioral tendency that exhibits itself not so much in what the individual thinks or says about the object, but in how he or she acts towards it.

Primary demand (p. 299)

A consumer's want or need for an entirely new type of product. *See* **Selective demand**

Principle of cognitive consistency (p. 123)

Concept that states that the human mind has a persistent need to maintain harmony, congruency, balance, or consistency among the various cognitions, feelings, and behaviors recorded in the brain. When there are inconsistencies of these elements and structures, the human mind is compelled to adapt or to make changes.

Private products (p. 166)

Goods that are not readily identifiable, that is, others do not see the owner using these products.

Profit quotas (p. 252)

Performance goals based upon the total amount of revenue generated for the organization rather than the number of items sold.

Program budgeting (p. 247)

Procedure that provides each adminstrative unit with a lump sum of money that each administrative head can use as he or she sees fit to accomplish the stated objectives.

Promotion (p. 4)

In marketing, the activities that motivate customers to action.

Promotion concept (p. 8)

Philosophy in which the customer is adapted to the marketer's needs and wants. *See* **Marketing concept**

Promotion management (p. 5)

The practice of coordinating the various promotional mix elements, of setting objectives for what the elements are intended to accomplish, of establishing budgets that are sufficient to support the objectives, of designing specific programs to accomplish objectives, of evaluating performance, and of taking corrective action when results are not in accord with objectives.

Promotional mix (p. 5)

An organization's blend of advertising, personal selling, sales promotion, publicity, and point-of-purchase communications elements.

Proximal stimulus (p. 33)

An activity-inciting object or agent that is in contact with an individual. *See* **Distal stimulus**

Public products (p. 166)

Goods that other people can observe the owner using (e.g., an automobile).

Public relations (p. 493)

A practice that includes all nonadvertising and nonselling activities that are designed explicitly to engender a desired corporate image. This corporate-image engineering is directed at promoting harmonious relations with various publics: consumers, employees, suppliers, stockholders, governments, the general public, labor groups, and citizen action groups.

Publicity (p. 493)

Nonpersonal communication to a mass audience that is not paid for by an organization. Examples include news items or editorial comments about an organization's products or services.

Pyramidal order (p. 103)

A message structure component in which the most important points appear in the middle of the message.

Quantum effect (p. 550)

A consumer phenomenon that is observed when increases in price up to a certain point do not result in a loss of sales volume, but a price beyond that point produces a rapid drop in sales.

Reach (p. 361)

The percentage of an advertiser's target audience exposed to at least one advertisement over an established time frame, with a four-week period representing the typical time frame for most advertisers. Reach represents the number of target customers who see or hear the advertiser's message one or more times during the time period. Also called net coverage or unduplicated audience.

Receiver (p. 26)

The person or group of people with whom the sender of a communication shares thoughts. In marketing, the receivers are the prospective and present customers of an organization's product or service.

Reference group (p. 159)

An actual or imaginary individual or group of in-

dividuals that influences an individual's evaluations, aspirations, or behavior.

Refutational argument (p. 96)

A two-sided message structure component in which the communicator advocates one position while admitting either (1) to some weaknesses in his or her stand or (2) to the strengths of an opposing view.

Relational communication (p. 289)

The study of a message's form as opposed to its content; this study examines message exchanges in terms of who directs, structures, or dominates a communication.

Relative advantage (p. 186)

The degree to which an innovation is *perceived* as better than an existing idea or object.

Reverse direction price perception (p. 550)

A psychological pricing situation whereby consumers reverse the numerical price scale and perceive lower prices as being higher than higher prices.

Sales aptitude test (p. 260)

A psychological test that is designed to measure a person's verbal ability, tactfulness, persuasiveness, tenacity, memory, and social extroversion-introversion, among other traits.

Sales management (p. 243)

The process of planning, organizing, staffing, directing, and controlling an organization's selling function within the context of environmental limitations and corporate and marketing constraints. The purpose is to acquire, direct, and stimulate competent salespeople to perform tasks that move the company or organization toward its objective and mission.

Sales promotion (p. 445)

Marketing activities intended to stimulate quick buyer action by offering extra benefits to customers. Examples include coupons, premiums, free samples, sweepstakes and the like. Also called promotional inducements.

Sales quotas (p. 251)

Specific performance goals that management sets for sales representatives, territories, organizational branches, middlemen, and/or other marketing units.

Sales volume quotas (p. 252)

Performance goals that are based on geographical areas, product lines, individual customers, time periods, or a combination of these factors. Sales volume quotas do not, however, measure or control expenses, profits, nonselling activities, etc.

Scanner (p. 65)

A control mechanism that accounts for customers' adaptation to changing conditions by altering his or her existing goals and structuring new ones.

Selective demand (p. 299)

A consumer's want or need for a specific organization's brand. *See* **Primary demand.**

Sensation transference (p. 527)

The consumer's tendency to equate a brand with an information cue, such as the package; that is, the consumer imputes characteristics to the product from the package.

Shaping (p. 92)

A type of behavioral modification by which marketers attempt to elicit certain behaviors by arranging conditions that change the probable occurrence of certain behaviors; the elicited behaviors are not the ends themselves, but are a means of increasing the probabilities of target behaviors.

Sign (p. 29)

A stimulus that represents an object or idea; a label that is associated with the real object it represents. A sign has meaning only insofar as its association with the real-world object or idea is shared by other people.

Skimming (p. 547)

Pricing strategy of setting a high price to catch the relatively price-inelastic segment of the market.

Social group (p. 159)

A collection of people who interact on a regular basis, affecting each other psychologically, and who collectively have a distinct personality. They share values, needs, and attitudes and depend upon other members in the group for the achievement of common goals and satisfaction of common needs.

Socialization process (p. 147)

The process of learning one's own cultural heritage. Values, ideas, attitudes, and related artifacts are passed from generation to generation through the socialization process.

The societally conscious (p. 152)

A group of inner-directed people who, according to the Values and Life-Styles typology, are the oldest of the inner-directeds (median age of 37), are the most educated of all the VALS groups, and are second only to the achievers in income level. What most distinguishes this group is its concern for others and desire to improve life in general. They tend to support liberal causes and become involved in community affairs.

Source (p. 119)

In marketing communications, a person, a group, an organization, or a label that delivers a message. Marketing communication sources influence receivers by possessing one or more of three basic attributes: power, attractiveness, and credibility.

Source derogation (p. 83)

A form of cognitive response that occurs when the receiver disputes the source's ability to make certain message claims. *See* **Counterargument** and **Supportive argument**

Specialty advertising (p. 503)

Practice of imprinting merchandise with an advertiser's message and distributing them without obligation to designated recipients. Specialty advertising complements other forms of advertising by providing another way to keep a company's name before customers and prospects.

Straight commission (p. 264)

Payment based directly on sales performance. Straight commission can be based on a fixed percentage of a sales representative's dollar sales, product units sold, type of product sold, season sales, dollars of profit, etc. or can be based on a multiple percentage rate that increases as dollar sales volume or some other performance measure increases.

Straight rebuy (p. 294)

A situation with which the customer is familiar; the purchase is already well structured.

Straight salary (p. 263)
Payment that provides a sales representative with a fixed amount of income regardless of sales productivity. Also called base salary.

Subculture (p. 154)
A group of people who possess a social heritage distinct from the global culture's heritage. Marketing and consumer behavior scholars consider subcultures to be definable segments within the global culture that have relatively unique values and norms and manifest distinguishing modes of behavior.

Supportive argument (p. 83)
A form of cognitive response that occurs when a receiver agrees with a message's arguments. *See* **Counterargument** and **Source derogation**

Survivors (p. 150)
A group of need-driven people who, according to the Values and Life-Styles typology, represent about 4 percent of the adult population and who are the poorest group in American society. Many are separated or divorced. Survivors hold conventional attitudes toward morality.

Sustainers (p. 150)
A group of need-driven people who, according to the Values and Life-Styles typology, represent 7 percent of the population and consist predominantly of low-income families and minorities. Sustainers as a group are inclined to believe the system is against them and, accordingly, seek status and acceptance from among their peers rather than from the larger society.

Symbolism (p. 527)
In product packaging, the use of form, shape, or color that has meaning for the consumer.

Syntax (p. 31)
The set of rules that provides for the orderly presentation of words. Syntax is the result of common usage among people using the same word-signs.

Transceivers (p. 27)
Intermediaries (such as television networks and magazines) who receive and then retransmit an organization's message to the intended audience.

Trialability (p. 187)
The extent to which an innovation can be used on a limited basis. Trialability is tied closely to the concept of perceived risk.

Trier class (p. 183)
The group of consumers who actually try a new product; the second step in which an individual becomes a new brand consumer. Coupons, distribution, and price are the variables that influence consumers to become triers.

True cognition (p. 92)
A phenomenon that exists when a person is able to and is motivated to discriminate an object in terms of meaningful dimensions or features and can form perceptions or beliefs about specific items within the object category.

Values (p. 148)
Enduring, culturally determined beliefs that a specific mode of behavior or end-state of existence is personally preferable to alternate modes of behavior or end-states. Values are used when people attempt to establish standards, judge issues, debate options, plan activities, reach decisions, resolve differences, change patterns, or exert influence.

Vicarious modeling (p. 300)
A type of behavior modification in which advertisers attempt to influence consumers' perceptions and behaviors by having them observe the actions of others and the resulting consequences.

Vocalizations (p. 113)
Sounds that have no particular meanings in themselves but which do reflect certain emotions (e.g., yawning, sighing, 'um,' 'uh-huh,' etc.).

Voice qualities (p. 113)
Speech characteristics (e.g., speech rate, rhythm pattern, pitch of voice, precision of articulation, and control of utterances by the lips, tongue, and other articulators) that communicate meanings such as urgency, boredom, friendliness, sarcasm, and various emotional conditions.

Voluntary attention (p. 44)
Observation that occurs when a person willfully notices a stimulus. *See* **Involuntary attention** and **Nonvoluntary attention**

Name Index

Aaker, David A., 304, 316
Able, Karen L., 606
Abraham, D., 130
Achenbaum, Alvin, 363
Albion, Mark S., 302
Alessis, G., 136
Allen, Chris T., 91
Alter, Jennifer, 475
Ajzen, Icek, 62, 79, 87
Allport, Gordon W., 76, 285
Anderson, Ken, 340
Anderson, Richard C., 375, 391, 392
Armstrong, Gary M., 238, 239, 240
Arnold, Stanley N., 484
Aronson, E., 130, 131
Asam, Edward H., 535, 536
Ash, Stephen B., 100, 102
Assael, Henry, 77, 149, 361
Astor, David, 156, 426
Atkinson, J. W., 49
Atkinson, R. C., 52
Aycrigg, Richard H., 467

Bagozzi, Richard P., 76, 100
Bailey, Patricia P., 233
Banks, Louise, 355
Barban, Arnold M., 298, 304, 383
Barna, George E., 155, 156
Baron, Robert S., 346, 347
Baxter, James C., 112
Beales, Howard, 228
Bearden, William O., 166–167
Beem, Eugene R., 8–16, 446, 449, 508
Belch, George E., 44, 346
Belch, Michael A., 346
Belk, Russell W., 63
Bellinger, Danny, 246, 251, 257, 277, 280, 330
Bencin, Richard L., 438
Bennett, Peter, 131, 547
Berelson, Bernard, 198
Berger, David, 343, 412
Berkowitz, I., 107
Berlo, David K., 32, 34
Berman, Ronald, 304
Bertrand, Kate, 529
Bettinghaus, E. P., 111, 112, 113, 129
Bettman, James B., 42–44, 49, 51, 62, 63, 64, 66
Bianchi, Suzanne M., 226
Bierley, Calvin, 113
Birren, Faber, 528
Bither, Stewart W., 110
Blackwell, Roger D., 110, 146, 154, 155
Blakkan, Renee, 158, 387
Block, Clifford H., 571, 575
Bogart, L., 82, 376
Booth, Elizabeth M., 572, 576
Boring, R. A., 545
Boudreau, Carole E., 490
Bourne, Francis, 166, 168
Bowman, Russell D., 447, 448
Boyd, Harper W., 140, 525
Brickman, Glen A., 415
Britt, Steuart Henderson, 243, 264

Brock, Timothy C., 82, 119, 286
Brokaw, A. V. L., 526
Brooker, George W., 109
Brown, Kevin, 189
Brown, Robert L., 534
Brutman, Ed, 487
Bucklin, Louis P., 535, 536
Burke, Marian C., 91
Burne, Andrew, 434
Burnett, John J., 108
Burnkrant, Robert E., 160
Burns, George, 139, 143
Burstein, Daniel, 342
Busch, Paul 287
Buskirk, Richard H., 247, 251, 253, 254, 255, 256, 261

Cacioppo, John T., 76, 77, 83, 84, 85, 86
Calcich, Stephen E., 596, 599
Calder, Bobby J., 79
Cannon, Hugh, 361
Cantril, H., 50
Caples, John, 431
Capon, Noel, 136
Carlsmith, J. M., 105, 128
Carnegie, Dale, 275, 276
Carusone, Peter S., 626
Chaiken, Shelly, 82
Chaplin, Charlie, 318, 328
Cheskin, Louis, 526, 528, 557
Chiu, John S. Y., 549
Choffray, Jean-Marie, 319
Churchill, Gilbert A. Jr., 244, 246, 248, 249, 257, 267
Cialdini, Robert B., 8
Clark, Margaret, 50
Clarke, P., 77
Cleaver, Joanne, 373
Cleeck, Paul R., 354
Coe, Barbara J., 351, 355
Coen, Robert, 298, 374
Cohen, Dorothy, 233, 234
Coney, Kenneth A., 135
Conlon, Thomas J., 484
Connors, Jimmy, 141, 142
Cook, T., 136
Cooper, J., 80
Coppola, Vincent, 475
Cosby, Bill, 139
Cottingham, D. R., 107
Cousineau, Alain, 160
Craig, C. Samuel, 76, 108, 109, 345
Craiglow, Richard C., 354
Cravens, David W., 281, 283
Curtin, Jane, 340

D'Amico, Michael, 181
Danger, Eric P., 557
Dangerfield, Rodney, 139, 328, 329, 344
Danzig, Fred, 308
Davenport, J. William, 286
Davis, Harry, 168–171
Day, George S., 79
Dean, William R., 478

De Haan, H., 104
Deighton, John, 526
DeLay, Robert F., 212
Della Bitta, Albert J., 544
DeLozier, M. Wayne, 27, 28, 30, 334, 544, 545, 551
Deneuve, Catherine, 142
Deutscher, Terry, 79
De Wolf, A. S., 107
Dholakia, Ruby, 133, 134, 135
Dingman, Christopher, 527
DiSalvo, Peter, 436
Dodson, Joe A., 466
Dommermuth, William P., 273
Domzal, Theresa J., 131
Donahue, George, 394, 463, 464, 465
Donnelly, James H. Jr., 287
Donovan, Robert J., 560
Downey, Susan L., 544
Druckman, Daniel, 112
Dubinsky, Alan J., 277
Duncan, Delbert J., 557
Dunn, S. Watson, 298, 383
Dunn, William, 223, 304
Dyer, David C., 102
Dyer, Robert F., 602, 617

Eagly, Alice H., 82
Edell, Julie A., 91, 115
Ellis, Donald G., 289
Ellis, Elmwood A., 160
Endicott, Craig, 158, 298
Engel, James F., 17–18, 110, 146, 154, 155, 261, 570
English, Mary McCabe, 435
Enis, Ben, 214
Etgar, Michael, 103
Etzel, Michael J., 166–167
Evans, Franklin B., 285
Everett, Robert F., 288

Faison, E. W. J., 99, 306, 494
Farris, Paul W., 302
Favre, Jean-Paul, 528
Fazio, R. H., 79, 80
Ferber, Robert, 174
Ferguson, Donald C. E., 571, 575
Feshbach, S., 106
Festinger, L., 130
Finkelman, Bernice, 561
Fireworker, R. B., 123
Fishbein, Martin, 62, 79, 87
FitzMaurice, John C., 454
Flay, R., 136
Foley, William F., 322
Ford, Gary T., 51
Ford, Jeffrey D., 160, 244, 246, 248
Ford, Neil M., 244, 248, 249, 257, 267
Forkan, James P., 139
Francese, Peter, 224, 225
Frankel, Bud, 447, 452
Frankfurt, Stephen O., 224
Frazer, Charles F., 336, 337, 340, 343
Fredericks, Charles Jr., 449, 450, 466, 472, 479, 480

Name Index

Freedman, J. C., 105, 128
Friedman, H. H., 123
Friendly, David, 475
Futrell, Charles M., 247, 272, 282, 283

Gage, Theodore J., 440, 496, 497
Gaidis, William C., 92
Gandy, Robert L. Jr., 609
Gardner, Burleigh B., 534
Gardner, David, 110, 231
Garner, James, 140
Garreau, Joel, 219, 220
Gatchel, Robert J., 414
Gates, William H. III, 161, 162
Gaudet, Hazel, 198
Giges, Nancy, 475, 477
Gillig, Paulette M., 136
Girialdi, Bob, 630
Glock, Charles Y., 166
Golden, B., 131
Golden, Linda L., 466
Gonsior, M. H., 545
Goodwin, Stephen A., 103
Gorn, Gerald J., 90, 91, 116
Governale, C. N., 107
Granbois, Donald H., 172
Greenberg, B., 132
Greenberg, Herbert M., 280, 281
Greenwald, Anthony P., 136
Greyser, Stephen A., 387
Gruder, C., 136
Gubar, George, 172
Guess, Norman F., 243, 264
Gumm, Jeanne, 497
Gupta, Udayan, 406
Gutman, Jonathan, 331, 332, 334

Haaland, Gordon A., 110
Halamaj, J., 136
Hanan, Mack, 255
Hannah, Darlene B., 136
Harman, Robert P., 135
Harnett, Joel, 446, 447
Harris, Richard J., 53, 58
Harris, Roy, 464
Hartman, Timothy P., 346
Hastorf, A., 50
Hatten, Mary Louise, 545
Haugh, Louis J., 454, 471, 473, 475, 481,
    487, 489, 490
Heider, Fritz, 123
Hennessey, Hubert D., 436, 437
Hennigan, K., 136
Herpel, George L., 503, 504
Heslin, Richard, 97
Higgins, Kevin, 388, 426, 534
Hills, Gerald E., 281, 283
Hirschman, Elizabeth C., 41, 42, 67, 69,
    70, 155, 160, 426
Hodgson, Richard, 428
Holbrook, Morris B., 10, 41, 42, 67, 69,
    70, 160
Holgerson, Barbo E., 346
Hollander, Stanley C., 557
Holman, Rebecca H., 150
Honomichl, Jack J., 326, 412
Hope, Bob, 125, 126, 140
Houland, C. I., 96, 103, 104, 105, 136
Houseman, John, 139, 328

Howard, John, 106
Howard, Paul, 483
Hoyer, Wayne D., 50, 51
Hughes, Marie Adele, 172
Hulbert, James, 136
Hume, Scott, 140, 342
Hunt, H. Keith, 55, 115
Hunt, James M., 131
Hunt, Shelby D., 563

Ingram, Thomas N., 246, 257, 277, 280
Isen, Alice M., 50

Jackson, Michael, 308, 631, 633
Jacoby, Jacob, 50, 51
Jagoda, Don, 484
Jain, Chaman L., 424
Janis, I. L., 103, 104, 106
Jellison, J., 122
Jervey, Gay, 225
Jewler, A. Jerome, 335
Jones, S., 107
Jones, "Too Tall," 329
Joseph, W. Benoy, 123
Jugenheimer, Donald W., 311

Kamenetzky, J., 104
Kaplan, Abraham, 95
Karp, Lynn, 50
Kassarjian, H., 131
Kasulis, Jack J., 172
Katz, Daniel, 77
Kelley, David, 355
Kelley, H. H., 103, 104
Kelley, J. Patrick, 514
Kelman, Herbert C., 120
Kennedy, James N., 193
Kerin, Roger A., 226, 347
Kernan, Jerome B., 131, 466
Key, Wilson B., 349
Khala, Nariman K., 334
Kingman, Merle, 368, 395
Kinnear, Thomas C., 17–18, 91, 261, 570
Kirkpatrick, Charles A., 259, 272
Klein, Ronald, 288
Kleinman, Carol, 273
Kleppner, Otto, 232
Knight, Jerry, 501
Koop, C. Everett, 356
Koppman, Jerry, 346
Korgaonkar, Pradeep K., 330
Koski, Keith, 592
Kotler, Philip, 207, 210
Kramer, Arthur B., 363
Krishnamurhi, Lakshman, 168
Krugman, Herbert E., 311, 327, 401
Kucherov, Alex, 216
Kunst-Wilson, W., 350

LaBarbera, Priscilla A., 237, 240
Lamont, Lawrence M., 148, 149, 279,
    280, 281
Lancaster, Kent M., 304, 319, 322
Landis, Dylan, 426
Lauren, Ralph, 532
Lautini, Cecilia, 435
Lavidge, Robert J., 310
Lazersfeld, Paul F., 198
Leavitt, Clark, 133, 135

Leavitt, Harold J., 545
Lee, Lucy Chao, 174
Leff, Laurel, 210
Lehman, Charles, 376
Leigh, James H., 231, 346
Lenfant, Claude, 356
Lessig, V. Parker, 159, 160
Leuba, C., 49
Levitt, Theodore, 138
Levy, Sidney J., 160, 298, 525
Liff, Mark, 415
Lilien, Gary L., 319
Limberg, Douglas B., 578, 580
Lisncott, Judy, 340
Listman, Robert J., 613
Lucas, C., 49
Luchter, Les, 374
Lumsdaine, A. A., 96, 136
Lundstrom, William J., 226, 279, 280, 281
Lupo, Nunzio, 342
Lutz, Kathy A., 55, 56, 58, 115
Lutz, Richard J., 55, 56, 58, 76, 89, 115,
    201

McCarthy, E. Jerome, 207
McClelland, David C., 49
McClure, David P., 501
McConnell, J. Douglas, 547
McEnroe, John, 142, 592, 593, 594, 595
McGann, Anthony F., 361, 371, 380, 381,
    384, 389
McGuire, William J., 42, 43, 45
McKinnon, Gary F., 514
McMahon, Ed, 140
McMurry, Robert N., 258, 279, 280
McNeal, James U., 561
McNeill, Dennis L., 231, 235, 236
McSweeney, Frances K., 113
Madden, John, 328, 345
Madden, Thomas J., 91, 109
Maggard, John P., 340
Mahany, Eugene S., 458
Maier, Joseph H., 473
Maier, Joseph S., 487, 488
Mandell, W., 104
Manning, Burt, 377, 378
Margulies, Walter P., 533
Markus, Hazel, 91
Martin, Billy, 329
Martin, Claude R., 231, 346
Martineau, Pierre, 559, 560, 562
Mayer, David, 280, 281
Mazis, Michael B., 228, 230, 231, 235,
    236
Mellott, Douglas W. Jr., 108
Meredith, Don, 140
Merlyn, Vaughn, 427
Merz, Russell, 361
Metcalf, Barbara L., 231
Meyer, Anthony J., 571, 575
Meyer, Edward D., 463, 465, 467, 478,
    482, 483
Michaels, Ronald E., 184
Midgley, David M., 160
Migliaro, Al, 424
Miller, G. R., 82, 132
Miller, Jack, 427
Miller, James C. III, 232
Miller, Nory, 557

Milliman, Ronald E., 116, 564
Millman, Nancy, 326
Mills, J., 122
Miracle, Gordon E., 304
Mitchell, Anderson A., 51, 52, 58, 90, 91, 112, 346
Mitchell, Arnold, 150
Mizerski, Richard W., 51, 466
Moldenhauer, Charles, 535
Moniak, Jo, 430
Monroe, Kent B., 544, 547, 551
Moore, Timothy E., 349, 350
Moran, Dennis J., 529, 532, 533
Morgenroth, William M., 284
Morrill, John E., 300
Morris, Ben R., 224
Moschis, George P., 330
Motes, William H., 535
Moyer, M. S., 534
Munson, J. Michael, 148
Murchinson, C. A., 76
Murphy, Patrick E., 168, 172, 173
Myers, John G., 304, 316

Naisbitt, John, 150
Narasimham, Chakravarthi, 182, 183
Nelson, Ronald G., 415, 416
Newman, Joseph W., 525
Nickels, William G., 288
Nicklaus, Jack, 140
Nigut, William Sr., 470
Nord, Walter R., 92, 93, 300
Norton, Nancy J., 560
Novak, Adolph, 554, 559
November, Andre, 528
Nylen, David W., 313, 318

Ogilvy, David, 334, 338, 410
Oliver, Richard L., 108, 287
Olmsted, Michael S., 146
Olshavsky, Richard W., 184
Olson, Jerry C., 51, 90, 91, 333, 547
Opatow, Lorna, 532
Osgood, Charles, 32, 34, 125
Ostrom, Thomas M., 119
O'Toole, John, 374, 376
Ozanne, Julie L., 238, 239, 240

Packwood, Bob, 232
Paivio, Allan, 55
Park, C. Whan, 159, 160
Pauling, Linus, 161
Pederson, Carlton A., 274
Peller, Clara, 344
Penn, Cyril C., 378
Percy, Larry, 55, 58, 59, 84, 90, 112, 113, 115, 313, 314, 333, 346
Perlogg, Richard M., 82
Perrault, William D., 207
Perry, Michael, 560
Peterman, John L., 373
Peters, Richard W. Jr., 354
Peterson, Robert A., 347, 533
Pettigrew, Jim Jr., 590
Petty, Richard E., 76, 77, 83, 84, 85, 86, 119, 129
Phillips, Charles F., 557

Pironti, A. R., 431, 432
Pitts, Robert E. Jr., 148, 150
Plimpton, George, 342
Poindexter, Joseph, 417
Prasad, V. Kanti, 102
Prescott, Eileen, 201
Prestbo, John A., 439
Preston, Ivan L., 231, 235, 311, 403, 404, 413
Prunk, Tim, 430

Qualls, William, 184
Quelch, John A., 507

Raissmam, Robert, 342, 536
Rao, Murlidhar, 319
Rasmuson, Mark, 572, 576
Ray, Michael L., 17–18, 48, 77, 107, 300, 376, 377, 570
Raymond, Miner, 375
Redford, Robert, 143
Reeves, Rosser, 334
Regan, D. T., 79, 80
Reiling, Lynn G., 467
Reingen, Peter H., 287
Reynolds, Thomas J., 332, 333, 334
Richins, Marsha, 201
Richmond, David, 346
Richmond, Julius B., 356
Ricks, David A., 152, 153
Richie, Lionel, 631, 633
Ries, Al, 334, 340
Riesz, Peter C., 548
Rigaux, Benny P., 168–171
Rioloff, Richard M., 82
Riordan, Edward A., 287
Risen, James, 224
Roberts, Donald F., 45
Robertson, Dan H., 251
Robertson, Thomas A., 105, 146, 154, 160, 181, 193, 195, 196, 216
Robey, Bryant, 222
Robinson, William A., 189, 446, 447, 450, 452, 455, 457, 479, 484, 489
Robison, E. Doyle, 45
Roedder, Deborah L., 79
Rogers, Chuck, 388
Rogers, Everett M., 184, 185, 186, 190, 192, 193, 195, 199, 200
Rokeach, Milton, 148, 149
Roman, Murray, 438, 439
Rosen, Dennis L., 172
Rosenberg, Larry J., 426
Ross, Ivan, 533
Rossiter, John R., 55, 56, 58, 59, 90, 113, 115, 313, 314, 560
Rothschild, Michael I., 92
Rozelle, Richard M., 112
Rubicam, Raymond, 375
Russ, Frederick A., 259, 272
Russell, Cheryl, 222
Russell, J. Thomas, 361, 371, 380, 381, 384, 389
Russo, J. Edward, 231

Salop, Steven, 228
Sampson, Richard T., 552
San Augustine, Andre J., 322

Sawyer, Alan G., 97, 98
Scammon, Debra L., 234
Schore, Francine, 484
Schramm, Wilbur, 25, 45
Schultz, Don E., 455, 457, 489
Schwartz, David, 415, 416
Sciglimpaglia, Donald, 226
Scitorsky, Tibor, 549
Scott, Carol, 466
Scott, Jerome E., 148, 149
Sears, D. O., 105, 128
Semenik, Richard J., 234
Sen, Subrata K., 182, 183
Sethi, S. Prakash, 351, 355
Shaffer, H. Jay, 8–16, 446, 449, 508
Shalker, Thomas E., 50
Schumann, David, 85, 86
Schwartz, Gerald S., 501
Shapiro, Benson, 546, 550
Shearer, Lloyd, 554
Sheffield, F. O., 96, 136
Shepard, R. N., 115, 116
Sherrell, Daniel L., 585
Sheth, Jagdish, 106, 547
Shields, Brooke, 140
Shiffrin, Richard M., 52
Shimp, Terence A., 92, 102
Shook, Robert L., 282
Silk, Alvin J., 319
Simon, Julian L., 331
Simon, Raymond, 495
Singer, R. P., 107
Slosberg, Mike, 435
Smith, Bubba, 328
Smith, Jaclyn, 140, 142
Smith, Robert E., 81, 311, 312
Soldow, Gary F., 289, 290, 291
Soloman, Michael R., 160
Spaeth, Tony, 450, 452
Spain, Daphne, 226
Spielman, H. M., 122
Spillane, Mickey, 329
Spillman, Susan, 373
Spiro, Frank, 439
Spohn, Robert F., 277
Staelin, Richard, 115, 228
Stanton, William J., 247, 251, 253, 254, 255, 256, 261
Staples, William A., 168, 172, 173
Stark, Richard F., 617
Staubach, Roger, 140
Steinbrink, John P., 243, 259, 263, 264, 265
Steiner, Gary A., 310
Stephens, Debra, 231
Stern, Judith A., 319, 322
Sternthal, Brian, 76, 79, 108, 109, 133, 134, 135, 136, 345, 466
Stevens, Art, 499
Stone, Bob, 424, 426, 429, 431, 434
Strang, Roger A., 445, 446, 447, 449, 450, 451, 468, 471
Streep, Meryl, 142
Swinyard, William R., 81, 300, 311, 312
Szybillo, George J., 97

Tannenbaum, Percy H., 125
Thistlethwaite, D. L., 104

Name Index

Thomas, Gloria Penn, 289, 290, 291
Thorson, Esther, 311
Thurm, Andrew, 431, 432
Triandis, H. C., 121
Trout, Jack, 334, 340
Tull, Donald S., 545
Turner, Ted, 338
Twedt, Dik Warren, 538
Tybout, Alice M., 76, 100, 466

Vadehra, Dave, 328, 329, 330
Venkatesan, M., 110
Venkatesh, Alladi, 226
Ventataraman, K. V., 549, 551
Venuto, James, 438, 439
Vinson, Donald E., 148, 149
Vitriol, Morton M., 431, 432
Von Der Wense, Bodo, 431
Vosburg, R. E., 534

Walker, Orville C. Jr., 244, 246, 248, 249, 257, 267
Walster, E., 130, 132
Ward, L. B., 526

Ward, Scott, 146, 154, 181, 195, 196, 216
Warshaw, Martin R., 17–18, 261, 570
Wasson, Chester R., 550
Watson, Paul J., 414
Webb, Peter H., 48, 376, 377
Wee, Chow-Hou, 100, 102
Weilbacher, William M., 306, 351, 362, 363, 380
Weinberger, Marc G., 109, 345
Weitz, Barton A., 274, 292, 293
Wells, Orson, 328
Wells, William D., 172, 415
Welty, Ward, 355
Whalen, Bernie, 227, 440, 441
Wheatley, John J., 108, 549
White, Hooper, 212
Wicker, A. W., 79
Wilkie, William L., 107, 231, 235, 236
Wilson, David T., 287
Wilson, J. Herbert, 277
Wingis, Chuck, 439
Winski, Joseph M., 500
Woodruff, Robert B., 281, 283

Woodside, A. G., 84, 148, 150, 286, 287, 333, 499, 535, 547, 611
Wright, Milburn D., 274
Wright, Peter L., 60, 83, 108, 133, 201
Wylie, Kenneth, 389, 390

Yalch, Richard, 51
Yankelovich, Daniel, 149, 175
Young, James Webb, 298
Young, Robert B., 184
Young, Robert F., 387
Yovovich, B. G., 346, 347, 363, 529
Yuspeh, Sonia, 152

Zajonc, Robert B., 44, 91, 350
Zaltman, Gerald, 154
Zanna, M. P., 80
Zanot, Eric J., 237
Zeithaml, Carl P., 207, 208
Zeithaml, Valerie A., 207, 208
Zeltner, Herbert, 395
Zielinski, Joan, 146, 154, 181, 195, 196, 216
Zikmund, William, 181

Subject Index

Adopter categories, 192–194
Adoption process, 183–191
Adtel, 417–418
Advertising
  agency-client relations, 393–394
  agency compensation, 394–396
  budgeting, 317–322
  corrective, 235–236
  defined, 4, 297–298
  economic and social aspects, 297–306
  functions performed by, 298–302
  objectives, 20, 310–317
  self-regulation, 236–237
  sex in, 346–349
Advertising effectiveness, 326–331, 399–418
Advertising management process, 307
Advertising strategy, 307–310
Affective strategy, 343. See also Creative strategy
Anticlimax order, 103
Arbitron, 408
Associative bond, 125–128. See also Congruity
  model
Association model, 403–406
Attitude
  affective component, 76
  behavioral component, 76
  cognitive component, 76
  conative component, 76
  defined, 76
  ego-defensive function, 78
  knowledge function, 78
  measurement considerations, 79–80
  nature and role of, 75–81
  utilitarian function, 77–78
  value-expressive function, 78

Balance model, 123–125
Behavior Scan, 417–418
Behavioral modification, 92. See also Preference
Bonus packs, 480
Brand image strategy, 338–340. See also Creative
  strategy
Brand name, 532–534
Budgeting for advertising, 317–322
Burke Day-After Recall Tests, 410

Channel, 26
Classification dominance, 561
Climax order, 103
Cognitive dissonance, 190–191
Cognitive response theory, 133, 134–135
Cognitive responses, 82–83
Communication modality, 82
Communications
  defined, 4, 25
  goals, 20
  interpersonal, 28
  mass, 28–29
  models, 27, 28
Comparative advertising, 100–103
Compliance, 120–121. See also Source
Conclusion drawing, 104–106
Congruity model, 125–128
Consumer information processing (CIP)
  CIP perspective, 42–43

defined, 41
  information processing stages, 43–63
  integrated CIP model, 63–66
Consumption system, 536–538
Contests, 484–485
Cooperative advertising, 386–388
Copy testing techniques, 403–418. See also
  Advertising effectiveness
Corporate image advertising, 351–355
Corporate issue advertising, 354–355
Corporate strategy, 307
Cost price standard, 551–552. See also Pricing
Counterargumentation, 133
Coupons, 467–479, 481
Creative platform, 331–343
Creative strategy, 21
Creative strategy alternatives, 336–343

Decoding, 26
Diffusion process, 183, 192–202
Direct mail, 424, 428–434
Direct marketing, 423–441
Direct response advertising, 424, 427–435
Dissociative bond, 125–128
Distribution, 109–110. See also Message

Elaboration Likelihood Model, 83–85
Encoding, 26
Environmental management
  defined, 207–208
  demographic, 214–228
  regulatory, 228–240
  technological, 208–214
Experiential approach, 41–42. See also Hedonistic
  approach
Expertise, 129. See also Source

Fair price standard, 550–551. See also Pricing
Family decision making
  autonomic, 169–171
  husband dominant, 169–171
  syncratic, 169–171
  wife dominant, 169–171
Family life cycle, 172–174
Fear appeals, 106–108. See also Message
Federal Trade Commission, 231–232
Feedback, 28
Flow of influence, 197–198

Generic strategy, 336. See also Creative strategy
  alternatives
Groups
  aspirational, 146
  black, 155–158
  cultural, 146–153
  dissociative, 146
  family, 168–174
  formal, 146
  hispanic, 158–159
  informal, 146
  membership, 146
  primary, 146
  reference, 159–168
  religious, 155
  secondary, 146

social, 159
subculture, 154

Hedonistic approach, 41–42, 67–72
Hired promoters, 139–140
Humor, 108–109, 344–345. *See also* Message
Hypermarkets, 561

Identification, 120, 121–128. *See also* Source
Image
  company, 138
Innovation
  continuous, 182
  defined, 181
  degree of, 181–182
  discontinuous, 182
  dynamically continuous, 182
Integrated information response model, 311
Internalization, 120, 128–137

Law of demand, 544–545

Magazines
  buying space, 381–383
  strengths and problems, 383–384
Marketing
  defined, 41
  establishing objectives, 19
Marketing communications
  defined, 4
  plan, preparing, 578–581
  purposes, 3
  sources, 137–141
Marketing concept, 8
Marketing strategy, 307
Meaning
  connotative, 35–36
  contextual, 36–37
  denotative, 35
  dimensions of, 35–37
  how learned, 32–35
  meaning of, 32
  structural, 36
Means-end chain, 331–336
Media
  impact, 390–393
  objectives, 361–364
  planning process, 360–370
  scheduling, 368–370
  selection, 21, 365–368
  as a source, 139
Mediation process, 34
Message
  appeals, 95, 106–110
  arguments, 81–82
  codes, 95, 110–116
  defined, 26
  structure, 95, 96–106
Message sidedness, 96–100. *See also* Refutational
    argument
Modeling, 93. *See also* Preference
Motivation, 65. *See also* Consumer information
    processing
Music, 116

NAD/NARB process, 238–240
Newspapers
  buying space, 384–385
  strengths and problems, 385–386

Nielsen Television Index, 406–407
Noise, 27
Nonverbal codes, 112–116

Opinion leaders, 199–201
Opinion leadership, 197–202
Order of presentation, 103–104. *See also* Message
Outdoor advertising, 388–390
Overheard conversation, 130

Package, 526–540
PACT (positioning advertising copy testing), 400–403
Penetration pricing, 548
Peripheral cues, 82
Personal selling
  basic steps in, 277–279
  categories of, 273–274
  contingency approach, 292–295
  defined, 4, 271–272
  duties and responsibilities of, 274–275
  dyadic approach, 283–287
  neurological approach, 287–289
  opportunities in, 272–273
  relational communications approach, 289–292
  super salesperson, 279–283
  traditional approaches to, 275–279
Persuasion
  fundamentals of, 81–83
PIMS (profit impact of marketing strategy), 408
Place communications, 553–564
Point-of-purchase communications
  defined, 5, 507–521
POPAI/DuPont Consumer Buyer Habits Study,
    514–518
Positioning strategy, 340–342. *See also* Creative
    strategy
Postdecisional dissonance, 191
Preemptive strategy, 336–338. *See also* Creative
    strategy
Preference
  affectively based, 92
  cognitive-based, 91
  defined, 91
  nature and formation of, 91
  true cognition, 92
Premiums, 478–479
Price communications, 543–553
Price-offs, 479–480
Price skimming, 547–548
Pricing, psychological effects, 550–553
Primary demand, 299
Principle of cognitive consistency, 123
Processing capacity, 63–65. *See also* Consumer
    information processing
Product communications, 525–540
Promotion
  defined, 4
  evaluation and control, 21–22
  setting budget, 19
Promotion concept, 8–9
Promotion management
  defined, 5
  implementing the program, 20–21
  the process, 16–22
Promotional inducements, 10–13, 445–446. *See also*
    Sales promotion
Promotional mix
  defined, 5
Psychogalvanometer, 414

Public relations, 493–499
Publicity, 5, 493–494, 499–503
Pupillometrics, 414–415
Pyramidal order, 103–104

Quantum effect in pricing, 550–551. *See also* Pricing

Radio, 377–381
Receiver, 26
Receiver involvement, 82
Recruiting, 257–260
Refunds and rebates, 481–483
Refutational argument, 96. *See also* Message
    sidedness
Resonance strategy, 342–343. *See also* Creative
    strategy
Reverse direction price perception, 550. *See also*
    Pricing

Sales budgets
    line-item, 247
    program budget, 247
Sales force motivation, 263–266
Sales force quotas
    activity quotas, 252
    combination quotas, 252
    defined, 251
    expense quotas, 252
    profit quotas, 252
    sales volume quotas, 252
Sales management
    defined, 243
    directing, 261–267
    evaluation and control, 267
    functions of, 245–267
    organizing, 253–261
    planning, 245–253
    process, 244
    staffing, 256–260
Sales organizations, 253–256
Sales promotion
    defined, 4–5, 445–446
    overlays and groups promotions, 485–489
    planning, 452–454
    rapid growth of, 447–449
    role of, 449–451
    techniques, 454–458
    testing and evaluation of, 489–491
Sales promotion techniques
    delayed reward/franchise-holdings, 481–483
    delayed reward/trial impact, 467–479
    image reinforcement, 483–485
    immediate reward/franchise-holding, 479–481
    immediate reward/trial impact, 462–467
Sales representatives, 138–139
Sales training, 261–263
Sampling, 462–467

Selective demand, 299
Self-liquidating premiums, 483–484
Sender, 26
Shaping, 92. *See also* Preference
Sign, 29
Sign systems, 30–31
Signs and logos, 561–562
Simmons Market Research Bureau (SMRB),
    407–408
Situation analysis, 18
Sleeper effect, 136–137
Socialization, 147
Source
    attractiveness, 121–128
    attributes, 120–137
    credibility, 129–137
    defined, 119–120
    derogation, 133
    low-credibility, 132
    power, 120–121
Specialty advertising, 503–505
Starch Message Report Service, 408–410
Status-prestige, 131. *See also* Source
Stimulus
    distal, 33
    proximal, 33
Subliminal advertising, 349–351
Supportive argumentation, 133
Sweepstakes, 484–485

Target audience selection, 361
Telemarketing, 435–441
Television
    network, spot, local, and cable, 372–374
    programming segments, 371–372
    strengths and problems, 374–377
Theory of Reasoned Action, 87–91
Three modes of marketing, 8–16
Trace, 413
Transceivers, 27
Trustworthiness, 130–131. *See also* Source

Unique selling proposition (USP) strategy, 338. *See
    also* Creative strategy

VALS, 150–152
Values, 148–152
Verbal codes, 110–112
Vicarious learning, 93. *See also* Preference
Vicarious modeling, 300
Visual imagery, 113–116
Vocalizations, 113
Voice-path analysis, 415–416
Voice qualities, 113

Wheeler-Lea Amendment, 230–231
Word-of-mouth influence, 201–202